Student Solutions Manual

Kevin Bodden • Randy Gallaher

Lewis and Clark Community College

Statistics

SECOND EDITION

Informed Decisions Using Data

Michael Sullivan, III

PEARSON

Prentice
Hall

Upper Saddle River, NJ 07458

Editor-in-Chief: Sally Yagan
Executive Acquisitions Editor: Petra Recter
Supplements Editor: Joanne Wendelken
Executive Managing Editor: Kathleen Schiaparelli
Assistant Managing Editor: Karen Bosch
Production Editor: Jenelle J. Woodrup
Supplement Cover Manager: Paul Gourhan
Supplement Cover Designer: Joanne Alexandris
Manufacturing Buyer: Ilene Kahn
Manufacturing Manager: Alexis Heydt-Long

© 2007 Pearson Education, Inc.
Pearson Prentice Hall
Pearson Education, Inc.
Upper Saddle River, NJ 07458

Pearson Prentice Hall™ is a trademark of Pearson Education, Inc.

The author and publisher of this book have used their best efforts in preparing this book. These efforts include the development, research, and testing of the theories and programs to determine their effectiveness. The author and publisher make no warranty of any kind, expressed or implied, with regard to these programs or the documentation contained in this book. The author and publisher shall not be liable in any event for incidental or consequential damages in connection with, or arising out of, the furnishing, performance, or use of these programs.

Printed in the United States of America

10   9   8   7   6   5   4   3   2

ISBN 0-13-227558-9

Pearson Education Ltd., *London*
Pearson Education Australia Pty. Ltd., *Sydney*
Pearson Education Singapore, Pte. Ltd.
Pearson Education North Asia Ltd., *Hong Kong*
Pearson Education Canada, Inc., *Toronto*
Pearson Educación de Mexico, S.A. de C.V.
Pearson Education—Japan, *Tokyo*
Pearson Education Malaysia, Pte. Ltd.

Table of Contents

Chapter 1

Data Collection

1.1 Introduction to the Practice of Statistics

1. Statistics is the science of collecting, organizing, summarizing and analyzing information in order to answer questions or draw conclusions. The process of statistics is:
   (1) Identify the research objective.
   (2) Collect the information needed to answer the questions posed in part (1).
   (3) Organize and summarize the information.
   (4) Draw conclusions form the information.

3. information

5. Descriptive; inferential

7. An experimental group usually receives some sort of experimental drug or treatment, while the control group receives a placebo or a treatment whose effect on the response variable is known.

9. Variables

11. A discrete variable is a quantitative variable that has a finite or countable number of possible values. Continuous variables are also quantitative variables, but there are an infinite number of possible values that are not countable.

13. The process of statistic is to (1) identify the research objective, (2) collect the information needed to answer the questions posed in (1), (3) organize and summarize the information, and (4) draw conclusions from the information.

15. Qualitative
17. Qualitative
19. Quantitative

21. Quantitative
23. Quantitative
25. Qualitative

27. Discrete
29. Continuous
31. Discrete

33. Continuous
35. Discrete
37. Discrete

39. The population consists of all teenagers 13 to 17 years old who live in the United States. The sample consists of the 1,028 teenagers 13 to 17 years old who were contacted by the Gallup Organization.

41. The population consists of all of the soybeans plants in this farmer's crop. The sample consists of the 100 soybean plants that were selected by the farmer.

43. The population consists of all women 27 to 44 years of age with hypertension. The sample consists of the 7,373 women 27 to 44 years of age with hypertension who were included in the study.

1

45. (a) The research objective was to determine if the application of duct tape is as effective as cryotherapy in the treatment of common warts.

(b) The sample consisted of 51 patients with warts.

(c) Descriptive statistics: 85% of patients in group 1 and 60% of patients in group 2 had complete resolution of their warts.

(d) The conclusion was that duct tape is significantly more effective in treating warts that cryotherapy.

47. (a) The research objective was to determine whether music cognition and cognitions pertaining to abstract operations such as mathematical or spatial reasoning were related.

(b) The sample consisted of 36 college students.

(c) Descriptive statistics: The mean test scores after listening to Mozart were 119, while the mean test scores following silence were 110.

(d) The conclusion was that subjects perform better on abstract/spatial reasoning tests after listening to Mozart.

49. (a) The research objective was to determine the number of movies American adults aged 18 years or older have attended in a movie theater in the past 12 months.

(b) The sample consisted of 1,003 American adults aged 18 years or older.

(c) Descriptive statistics: 65% of the 1,003 adults surveyed said that they attended at least one movie in a movie theater in the past 12 months.

(d) The conclusion was that approximately 65% of all American adults 18 years or older have attended at least one movie in a movie theater in the past 12 months.

51. Individuals: Sanyo #PDP42H2W, Panasonic #PT-47WX54, Tatung #P50BSAT, RCA #HD50LPW42, RCA #D52W19, JVC #HD52Z575, Sony #KDF-60XS955. Variables: Size, Screen Type, Price. Data for "size": 42, 47, 50, 50, 52, 52, 60; data for "screen type": plasma, projection, plasma, projection, projection, projection, projection; data for "price": $2,994, $1,072, $4,248, $2,696, $1,194, $2,850, $4,100. The variable "size" is continuous; the variable "screen type" is qualitative; the variable "price" is discrete.

53. Individuals: Colorado, Missouri, Montana, New York, Texas. Variables: Minimum age for Driver's License (unrestricted); blood-alcohol concentration limit, mandatory belt-use law seating positions, maximum allowable speed limit, 2003. Data for "minimum age for driver's license": 17, 18, 15, 17, 16.5; data for "blood-alcohol concentration limit": 0.10, 0.08, 0.08, 0.08, 0.08; data for "mandatory belt-use law seating positions": front, front, all, all, front; data for "maximum allowable speed limit, 2003": 75, 70, 75, 65, 75. The variable "minimum age for driver's license" is continuous; the variable "blood-alcohol concentration limit" is continuous, the variable "mandatory belt-use law seating positions" is qualitative; the variable "maximum allowable speed limit, 2003" is continuous.

55. (a) Research question: Are levels of the substance BNP associated with heart trouble?

(b) The population consists of all people (presumably adults).

(c) The sample consists of the 1,034 patients who were actually included in the study.

(d) Descriptive statistics: People with the highest protein levels were 2.5 times more likely to die than those with the lowest protein levels.

(e) Inferences: Higher levels of BNP are associated with worse outcomes.

57. (a) Nominal   (b) Ordinal   (c) Nominal   (d) Ordinal   (e) Nominal

1.2 Observational Studies, Experiments, and Simple Random Sampling

1. An observational study uses data obtained by studying individuals in a sample without trying to manipulate or influence the variable(s) of interest. In a designed experiment, a treatment is applied to the individuals in a sample in order to isolate the effects of the treatment on a response variable. Observational studies are appropriate where the control of certain variables is either impossible or unethical. Designed experiments are appropriate when it is possible to control certain variables and this is necessary for the study (for example to establish causation).

3. Sampling is used in statistics because it can be prohibitively expensive or impossible to study each individual in the population.

5. frame

7. True

9. Observational study

11. Experiment

13. Observational study

15. Experiment

17. Observational study

19. Answers will vary.

21. (a) Answers will vary.   (b) Answers will vary.

23. (a) Starting at row 5, column 22, using two-digit numbers, and proceeding downward, we obtain the following values: 83, 94, 67, 84, 38, 22, 96, 24, 36, 36, 58, 34,.... We must disregard 94 and 96 because there are only 87 faculty members in the population. We must also disregard the second 36 because we are sampling without replacement. Thus, the 9 faculty members included in the sample are those numbered 83, 67, 84, 38, 22, 24, 36, 58, and 34.

(b) Answers may vary depending on the type of graphing calculator used. If using a TI-84, the sample will be: 4, 20, 52, 5, 24, 87, 67, 86, and 39.

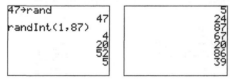

Note: We must disregard the second 20 because we are sampling without replacement.

3

25. (a) Number each student in the list of registered students, from 1 to 19,935. Generate 25 random numbers, without repetition, between 1 and 19,935 using a random number generator or table. Select the 25 students with these numbers.

(b) Answers will vary.

1.3 Other Effective Types of Sampling

1. Stratified random sampling may be appropriate if the population of interest can be divided into groups (or strata) that are homogeneous and non-overlapping.

3. Convenience samples are typically selected in a nonrandom manner. This means the results are not likely to represent the population. Convenience samples may also be self-selected, which will frequently result in sample bias.

5. stratified sample

7. False. In many cases, other sampling techniques may provide equivalent or more information about the population with less "cost" than simple random sampling.

9. Systematic

11. Cluster

13. Simple random

15. Cluster

17. Convenience

19. Systematic

21. Systematic

23. Answers will vary.

25. Answers will vary.

27. (a) $N = 4502, n = 50, 4502 / 50 = 90.04$; Thus, $k = 90$.

(b) Randomly select a number between 1 and 90. Suppose that we select 15. Then the individuals to be surveyed will be the 15th, 105th, 195th, 285th, and so on up to the 4425th employee on the company list.

29. Answers will vary. One design would be a stratified random sample, with two strata being commuters and noncommuters, as these two groups each might be fairly homogeneous in their reactions to the proposal.

31. Answers will vary. One design would be a cluster sample, with the clusters being city blocks. Randomly select city blocks and survey every household in the selected blocks.

33. Answers will vary. Since the company already has a list (frame) of 6,600 individuals with high cholesterol, a simple random sample would be an appropriate design.

35. The researcher should make a return visit or phone call. Allowing the spouse to answer is a form of convenience sampling and could lead to incorrect results.

37. Answers will vary.

1.4 Sources of Errors in Sampling

1. It is rare for frames to be completely accurate because the population may change frequently (for example the voter roll), making it difficult to keep the frame up to date. Also, the population may be very large (for example the population of the United States), making it difficult to obtain a complete frame.

3. A closed question is one in which the respondent must choose from a list of prescribed responses. An open question is one in which the respondent is free to choose his or her own response. Closed questions are easier to analyze, but limit the responses. Open questions allow respondents to state exactly how they feel, but are harder to analyze due to the variety of answers and possible misinterpretation of answers.

5. Trained interviewers generally obtain better survey results. For example, a talented interviewer will be able to elicit truthful responses even to sensitive questions.

7. A pro is that the interviewer is more likely to find the individual at home at this time. A con is that many individuals will be irritated at having their dinner interrupted and will refuse to respond.

9. Changing the order of questions helps prevent bias due to previous question answers or situations where respondents are more likely to pick earlier choices.

11. (a) Flawed sampling method. Only the first 50 students who enter the building have a chance of being surveyed.

    (b) A simple random sample would be a good choice of sampling method as the vice president would have access to a list of all students.

13. (a) Flawed survey. The question is poorly worded.

    (b) The survey should inform the respondent of the current penalty for selling a gun illegally and the question should be worded as: "Do you approve or disapprove of harsher penalties for individuals who sell guns illegally?" The order of "approve" and "disapprove" should be switched from one individual to the next.

15. (a) Flawed sampling method. Assuming the survey is written in English, non-English speaking homes will be unable to read the survey. This is likely the reason for the very low response rate.

    (b) The survey can be improved by using face-to-face or phone interviews.

17. (a) Flawed sampling method. The sample of weekday shoppers may not represent the eating habits of all shoppers at the mall. For example, individuals who shop in the evening or on weekends may have different tastes.

    (b) A stratified sample would better. Possible strata would be weekday, weeknight, and weekend.

19. (a) Flawed survey. The question is poorly worded.

    (b) The question should be reworded in a more neutral manner. One possible phrasing might be: "Do you believe that a marriage can be maintained after an extramarital relation?"

5

21. (a) Flawed survey. Students are unlikely to give honest answers if their teacher is administering the survey.

(b) An impartial party should administer the survey in order to increase the rate of truthful responses.

23. It is very likely that the order of these two questions will affect the survey results. To alleviate the response bias, either question B could be asked first, or the order of the two questions could be rotated randomly.

25. The two choices need to be rotate so that any response bias due to the ordering of the questions is minimized.

27. Some non-sampling errors presented in the article as leading to incorrect exit polls were poorly trained interviewers, interviewer bias, and over representation of female voters.

29. Answers will vary.   **31.** Answers will vary.

1.5 The Design of Experiments

1. (a) An experimental unit is a person, object, or some other well-defined item upon which a treatment is applied.

(b) A treatment is a condition applied to an experimental unit. It can be any combination of the explanatory variables.

(c) A response variable is a quantitative or qualitative variable that measures a response of interest to the experimenter.

(d) An explanatory variable measures a factor that might affect a response variable.

(e) An experiment is double-blind if neither the subject nor the experimenter knows what treatment is being administered to the experimental unit.

(f) A placebo is an innocuous treatment, such as a sugar pill, administered to a subject in a manner indistinguishable from an actual treatment.

(g) Confounding occurs when the effect of two explanatory variables on a response variable cannot be distinguished.

3. completely randomized; matched-pair

5. (a) The response variable is the achievement test scores.

(b) Some explanatory variables are teaching methods, grade level, intelligence, school district, and teacher. Controlled: grade level, school district, teacher. Manipulated: teaching method.

(c) The treatments are the new teaching method and the traditional method. There are 2 levels of treatment.

(d) The explanatory variables that are not controlled or manipulated are dealt with by random assignment into the two groups.

(e) This experiment has a completely randomized design.

(f) The subjects are the 500 students.

6

(g)

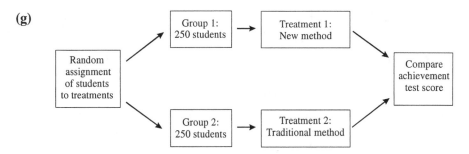

7. **(a)** This experiment has a matched-pair design.
   (b) The response variable is the difference in test scores.
   (c) The treatment is the mathematics course.

9. **(a)** This experiment has a completely randomized design.
   (b) The population being studied is adults with insomnia.
   (c) The response variable is the terminal wake time after sleep onset (WASO).
   (d) The explanatory variable is the type of intervention. The treatments are cognitive behavioral therapy (CBT), muscle relaxation training (RT), and the placebo.
   (e) The experimental units are the 75 adults with insomnia.
   (f)

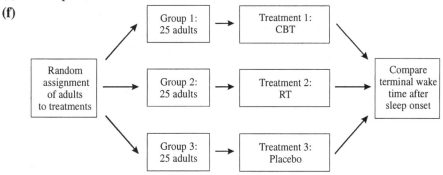

11. **(a)** This experiment has a completely randomized design.
    (b) The population being studied is adults over 60 years old and in good health.
    (c) The response variable is the standardized test of learning and memory.
    (d) The explanatory variable is the drug. The treatments are 40 milligrams of ginkgo 3 times per day and the matching placebo.
    (e) The experimental units are 98 men and 132 women over 60 years old in good health.
    (f)

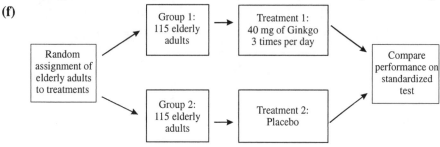

7

13. (a) This experiment has a matched-pair design.

(b) The response variable is the distance the yard stick falls.

(c) The explanatory variable is hand dominance. The treatment is dominant versus non-dominant hand.

(d) The experimental units are the 15 students.

(e) Professor Neil used a coin flip to eliminate bias due to starting on the dominant or non-dominant hand first on each trial.

(f)

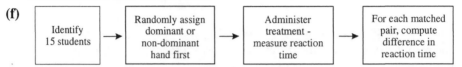

15. (a) This experiment has a randomized block design.

(b) The response variable is the score on the recall exam.

(c) The explanatory variable that is manipulated is the type of advertising. The treatment has 3 levels.

(d) Region of country is the variable that serves as the block.

(e)

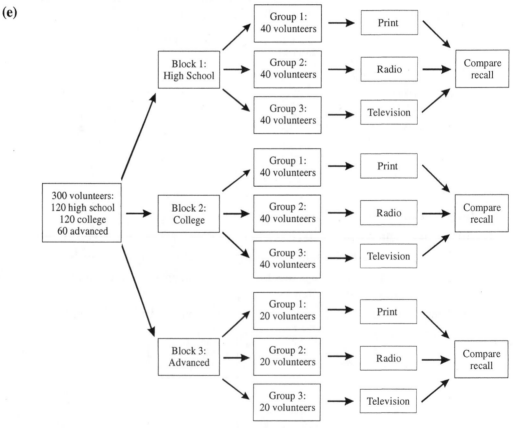

17. Answers will vary

19. Answers will vary. A completely randomized design is likely the best.

21. Answers will vary. A matched-pair design matched by type of exterior finish is likely the best.

23. Answers will vary. A randomized block design blocked by type of car is likely the best.

25. **(a)** The response variable is blood pressure.

    (b) The three explanatory variables are daily consumption of salt, daily consumption of fruits and vegetables, and the body's ability to process salt.

    (c) The daily consumption of salt should be manipulated. The daily consumption of fruits and vegetables can be controlled. The body's ability to process salt cannot be controlled. To deal with variability of the body's ability to process salt, randomize experimental units to each treatment group.

    (d) Answers will vary. Three levels of treatment might be a good choice – one level below the recommended daily allowance, one equal to the recommended daily allowance, and one above the recommended daily allowance.

27. Answers will vary.

Chapter 1 Review Exercises

1. Statistics is the science of collecting, organizing, summarizing and analyzing information in order to draw conclusions.

3. A sample is a subset of the population.

5. In a designed experiment, a treatment is applied to the individuals in a sample in order to isolate the effects of the treatment on the response variable.

7. Errors in sampling consist of sampling error (the error resulting from using sample data to estimate a characteristic of an entire population) and non-sampling error (from poor sampling design). Sampling error can be quantified by using the theory of probability. Some common non-sampling errors are non-response, which can be ameliorated by callback or incentives, and poorly worded questions, which can be avoided by careful survey design.

9. Quantitative; discrete   11. Quantitative; continuous   13. Qualitative

15. Observational study   17. Experiment   19. Convenience sample

21. Cluster sample

23. **(a)** Undercoverage or non-representative sample due to a poor sampling frame.

    (b) Interviewer error.

    (c) Data checks

25. Answers will vary.   27. Answers will vary.   29. Answers will vary.

31. (a) This experiment has a completely randomized design.

  (b) The response variable is the energy required to light the bulb.

  (c) The explanatory variable is the integrated circuit. The treatments are the old circuit and the new circuit.

  (d) The experimental units are the 200 fluorescent bulbs.

  (e)

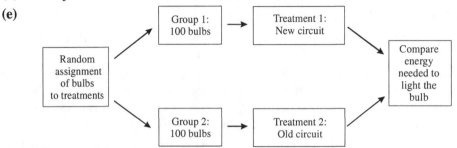

33. (a) This experiment has a randomized block design.

  (b) The response variable is the exam grade.

  (c) The explanatory variable is the notecard use. The treatments are notecard and no notecard.

  (d) The experimental units are the instructor's statistics students.

  (e)

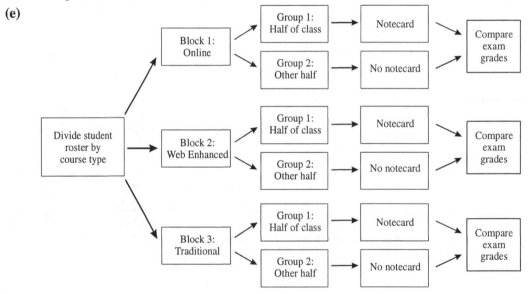

35. Answers will vary.

37. (a) Answers will vary. **(b)** Answers will vary.

39. In a completely randomized design, the experimental units are randomly assigned to one of the treatments. The value of the response variable is compared for each treatment. In a matched-pairs design, experimental units are "matched up" on the basis of some common characteristic (such as husband/wife, pre-post, or twins). The difference in the paired experimental units is analyzed.

Chapter 2

Organizing and Summarizing Data

2.1 Organizing Qualitative Data

1. Raw data are the data as originally collected, before they have been organized or coded.

3. It is a good idea to add up the frequencies in a frequency distribution as a check to see if you missed data or possibly counted the same data more than once. If the total of the frequencies does not equal the total number of data values, the distribution should be done again.

5. A Pareto chart is a bar chart with bars drawn in order of decreasing frequency or relative frequency.

7. Pareto charts emphasize those observations with the higher frequencies or relative frequencies. In a quality control situation, a Pareto chart helps identify the most frequently occurring problems.

9. **(a)** Large; 52%   **(b)** X-Large; 9%   **(c)** 23%

11. **(a)** United States   **(b)** ≈ 20 million   **(c)** Roughly $94 - 69 = 25$ million

13. **(a)** 397,157 votes

   (b) $62,041,268 + 59,028,548 + 463,635 + 397,157 + 144,451 + 223,249 = 122,298,308$

   Bush: $\dfrac{62,041,268}{122,298,308} \approx 0.507$ or 50.7%

   Kerry: $\dfrac{59,028,548}{122,298,308} \approx 0.483$ or 48.3%

   (c) $\dfrac{463,635}{122,298,308} \approx 0.0038$ or 0.38%; No, Ralph Nader will not receive presidential election funds since he received less than 5% of the votes.

15. **(a)** 0.16; 0.30   **(b)** Natural gas was the most popular source.

   (c) About $(107)(0.05) = 5.35$ million households used LPG.

   (d) Answers will vary; one possibility is the price of oil

   (e) Fuel Oil or Kerosene; oil prices

   (f) Both natural gas and liquid petroleum gas have remained rather steady.

17. **(a)** Total income = 793.7 + 131.8 + 713.0 + 143.8 = \$1782.3 billion.

Relative frequency of Individual Income Taxes = $\dfrac{793.7}{1782.3} \approx 0.4453$ and so on.

Source of Income	Relative Frequency
Individual Income Taxes	0.4453
Corporate Income Taxes	0.0739
Social Insurance Taxes	0.4000
Excise, Estate and Gift Taxes, Customs, and Miscellaneous Receipts	0.0807

(b) 44.53% of the government's income is attributed to individual income taxes.

(c)

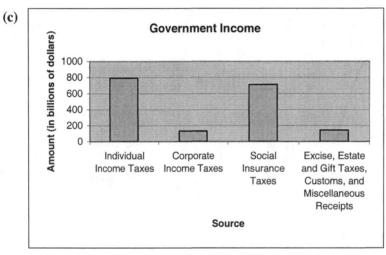

(d)

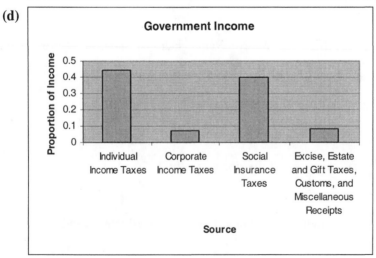

12

(e)

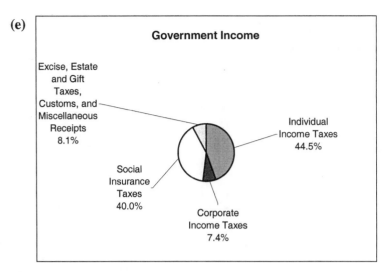

(f) Answers will vary.

19. (a) Total students surveyed = 125 + 324 + 552 + 1257 + 2518 = 4776
Relative frequency of "Never" = 125 / 4776 ≈ 0.0262 and so on.

Response	Relative Frequency
Never	0.0262
Rarely	0.0678
Sometimes	0.1156
Most of the time	0.2632
Always	0.5272

(b) 52.72%   **(c)** $0.0262 + 0.0678 = 0.0940$ or 9.40%

(d)

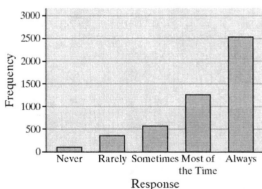

(e)

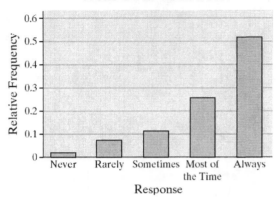

"How Often Do You Wear Your Seat Belt?"

(f)

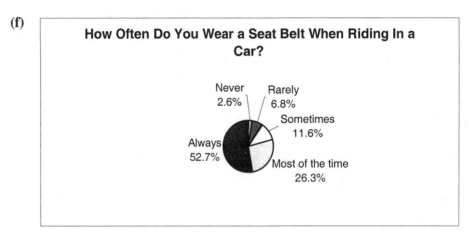

(g) The statement is inferential since it is inferring something about the entire population based on the results of a sample survey.

21. (a) Total foreign-born residents = 3384 + 12,362 + 2111 + 8375 + 4590 + 2680 = 33,502 (thousand).

Relative frequency for "Caribbean" = $\dfrac{3384}{33,502} \approx 0.1010$ and so on.

Region	Relative Frequency
Caribbean	0.1010
Central America	0.3690
South America	0.0630
Asia	0.2500
Europe	0.1370
Other Regions	0.0800

(b) 25.00% of foreign-born residents of the United States were born in Asia.

(c)

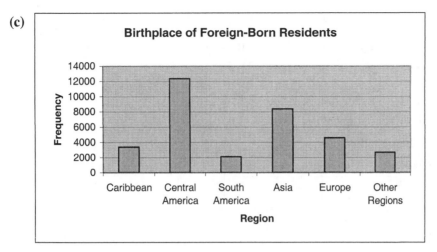

(d)

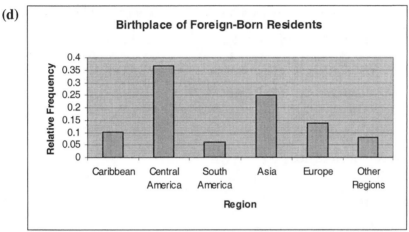

(e)

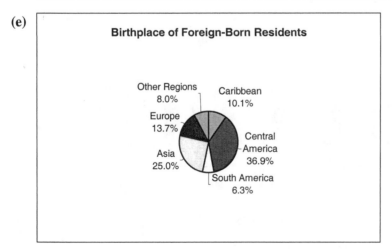

15

23. (a) Total males = 14.1 + 27.4 + 15.2 + 6.4 + 16.4 + 9.2 = 88.7 (million)

Relative frequency for "Not HS graduate" = $\dfrac{14.1}{88.7} \approx 0.159$ and so on.

	Males
Educational Attainment	Rel. Freq.
Not a high school graduate	0.159
High school graduate	0.309
Some college, but no degree	0.171
Associate's degree	0.072
Bachelor's degree	0.185
Advanced degree	0.104

(b) Total females = 14.5 + 31.9 + 16.6 + 8.8 + 16.9 + 7.9 = 96.6 (million)

Relative frequency for "Not HS graduate" = $\dfrac{14.5}{96.6} \approx 0.150$ and so on.

	Females
Educational Attainment	Rel. Freq.
Not a high school graduate	0.150
High school graduate	0.330
Some college, but no degree	0.172
Associate's degree	0.091
Bachelor's degree	0.175
Advanced degree	0.082

(c)

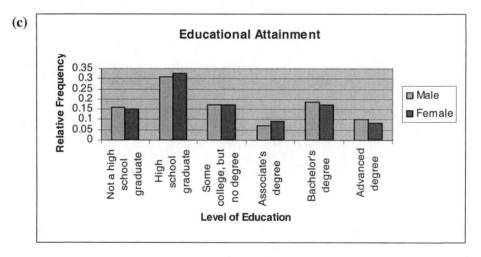

(d) Answers will vary.

25. (a), (b)   Total male victims = 650 + 3435 + 2990 + 2859 + 787 = 10,721

Relative frequency for "Less than 17" = $\dfrac{650}{10,721} \approx 0.0606$

Total female victims = 444 + 704 + 704 + 1085 + 442 = 3379

Relative frequency for "Less than 17" = $\dfrac{444}{3379} \approx 0.1314$

Relative Frequencies		
Age	Males	Females
Less than 17	0.0606	0.1314
17-24	0.3204	0.2083
25-34	0.2789	0.2083
35-54	0.2667	0.3211
55 or older	0.0734	0.1308

(c)

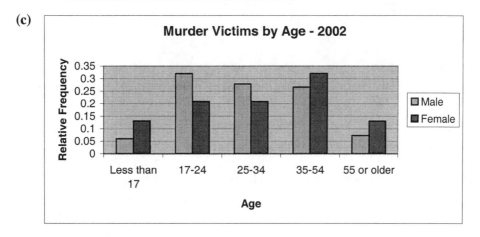

(d) Answers will vary.

27. (a), (b)   Total number of voters polled = 21 + 17 + 1 + 1 = 40

Relative frequency for Bush voters = $\dfrac{21}{40} = 0.525$ and so on.

Candidate	Frequency	Relative Frequency
Bush	21	0.525
Kerry	17	0.425
Nader	1	0.025
Badnarik	1	0.025

17

(c)

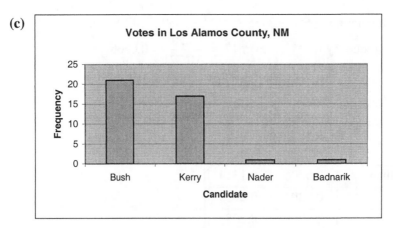

(d)

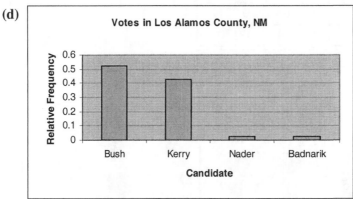

(e)

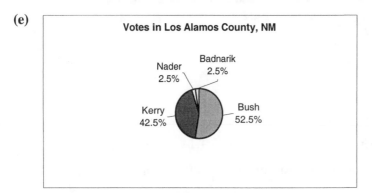

(f) Answers will vary. The conjecture would be inferential since a conclusion about the entire county is being made from sample data. Your confidence would increase with a larger sample since you have a larger portion of the voters in the county.

29. (a), (b)   Total number of players surveyed = 24

Relative frequency for "First Base" = $\dfrac{3}{24} = 0.1250$ and so on.

Position	Frequency	Relative Frequency
First Base	3	0.1250
Second Base	0	0.0000
Third Base	2	0.0833
Shortstop	1	0.0417
Pitcher	7	0.2917
Catcher	1	0.0417
Right Field	6	0.2500
Center Field	2	0.0833
Left Field	2	0.0833

(c) Pitchers appear to more lucrative since they make up the highest percent of the top 24 highest paid players.

(d) Second Base might be one to avoid since none of the top 24 highest paid players play second base.

(e)

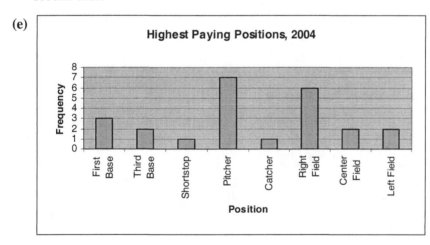

19

(f)

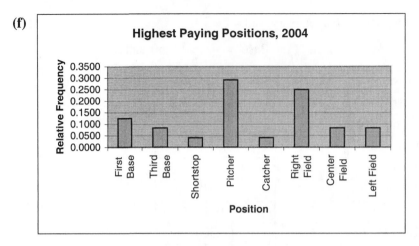

(g)

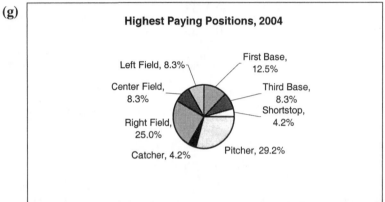

31. (a), (b)   Total number of students = 30

Relative frequency for "Spanish" = $\dfrac{14}{30} \approx 0.4667$ and so on.

Language	Frequency	Relative Frequency
Spanish	14	0.467
Chinese	3	0.100
German	3	0.100
Italian	2	0.067
Japanese	2	0.067
Russian	1	0.033
Latin	2	0.067
French	3	0.100

20

(c)

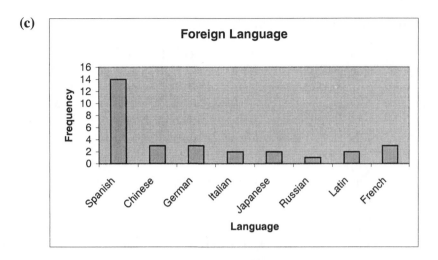

(d)

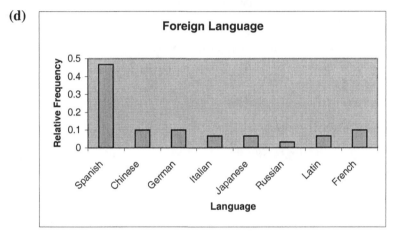

(e)

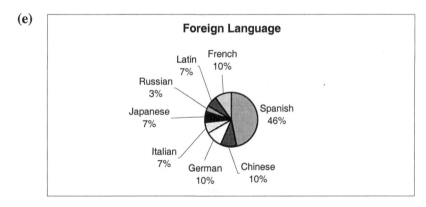

21

2.2 Organizing Quantitative Data – The Popular Displays

1. Answers will vary. We have already seen that the pattern of a distribution is the same, whether we look at frequencies or relative frequencies. However, in statistics we will often use data from a sample to guide us to conclusions about the larger population from which the sample is drawn. (This is called inferential statistics.) The actual frequencies for a sample do not, by themselves, give much useful information about the population, but the relative frequencies for the sample data will usually be similar to the relative frequencies for the population.

3. Not all the class widths are the same and the bars in a histogram should touch (unless there is a 0 frequency between two classes).

5. Answers will vary. Some possibilities follow: Histograms represent quantitative data, while bar graphs represent qualitative data. The bars in a histogram touch, but the bars in a bar graph do not touch. The width of the bars of a histogram has meaning, but the width of the bars in a bar graph is meaningless.

7. False. The distribution shape shown has a longer tail to the right so it is skewed right.

9. **(a)** 8   **(b)** 2   **(c)** 15   **(d)** $\dfrac{15}{100} = 0.15$ or 15%

   (e) The distribution is roughly symmetric.

11. **(a)** Total frequency $= 2+3+13+42+58+40+31+8+2+1 = 200$.

    (b) 10 (e.g. $70 - 60 = 10$)

    (c)

IQ Score (class)	Frequency
60–69	2
70–79	3
80–89	13
90–99	42
100–109	58
110–119	40
120–129	31
130–139	8
140–149	2
150–159	1

    (d) $100 - 109$ **(e)** $150 - 159$

    (f) $\dfrac{31}{200} = 0.155$ **(g)** Roughly bell-shaped.

13. (a) Total frequency $= 16 + 18 + 12 + 3 + 1 = 50$.

Relative frequency of 0 children $= 16/50 = 0.32$ and so on.

Number of Children Under Five	Relative Frequency
0	0.32
1	0.36
2	0.24
3	0.06
4	0.02

(b) $\dfrac{12}{50} = 0.24$ or 24%   **(c)** $\dfrac{18+12}{50} = \dfrac{30}{50} = 0.6$ or 60%

15. 10, 11, 14, 21, 24, 24, 27, 29, 33, 35, 35, 35, 37, 37, 38, 40, 40, 41, 42, 46, 46, 48, 49, 49, 53, 53, 55, 58, 61, 62

17. 1.2, 1.4, 1.6, 2.1, 2.4, 2.7, 2.7, 2.9, 3.3, 3.3, 3.3, 3.5, 3.7, 3.7, 3.8, 4.0, 4.1, 4.1, 4.3, 4.6, 4.6, 4.8, 4.8, 4.9, 5.3, 5.4, 5.5, 5.8, 6.2, 6.4

19. (a) 4   **(b)** Lower class limits: 25, 35, 45, 55; Upper class limits: 34, 44, 54, 64

(c) The class width is 10 years; e.g. $35 - 25 = 10$

21. (a) 4   **(b)** Lower class limits: 100, 200, 300, 400; Upper class limits: 199, 299, 399, 499

(c) The class width is 100 beds; e.g. $200 - 100 = 100$

23. (a) Total frequency = 28.9 + 35.7 + 35.1 + 24.7 = 124.4

Relative frequency for 25-34 = 28.9/124.4 = 0.2323 and so on.

Age	Relative Frequency
25-34	0.2323
35-44	0.2870
45-54	0.2822
55-64	0.1986

(b) **Number Covered by Health Insurance**

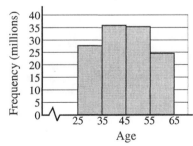

23

(c)   Number Covered by Health Insurance

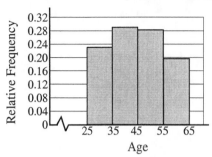

Total covered by health insurance $= 28.9 + 35.7 + 35.1 + 24.7 = 124.4$ (million).

Of the people covered by health insurance, $\dfrac{28.9}{124.4} \cdot 100 = 23.23\%$ were 25-34 years of

age, and $\dfrac{28.9 + 35.7}{124.4} \cdot 100 = \dfrac{64.6}{124.4} \cdot 100 = 51.93\%$ are 44 years of age or younger.

25. (a) Total admissions $= 6826 + 6800 + 5607 + 3593 = 22{,}826$

Relative frequency for 100-199 $= 6826/22{,}826 = 0.2990$ and so on.

Number of Beds	Relative Frequency
100-199	0.2990
200-299	0.2979
300-399	0.2456
400-499	0.1574

(b)

Hospital Admissions

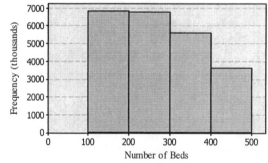

24

(c)

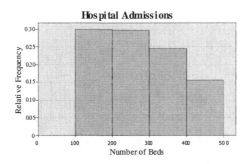

$\dfrac{5607}{22,826} \cdot 100 = 24.56\%$ of admissions were in hospitals with 300-399 beds, and

$\dfrac{5607 + 3593}{22,826} \cdot 100 = \dfrac{9200}{22,826} \cdot 100 = 40.30\%$ of admissions were in hospitals with 300 or more beds.

27. (a) and **(b)**

Relative frequency of 3 customers waiting $= 2/40 = 0.050$ and so on.

Number of Customers	Frequency	Relative Frequency
3	2	0.050
4	3	0.075
5	3	0.075
6	5	0.125
7	4	0.100
8	8	0.200
9	4	0.100
10	4	0.100
11	4	0.100
12	0	0.000
13	2	0.050
14	1	0.025

(c) $10.0 + 10.0 + 0.0 + 5.0 + 2.5 = 27.5\%.$

(d) $5.0 + 7.5 + 7.5 = 20.0\%.$

25

(e)

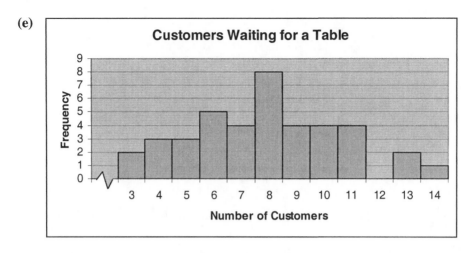

(f)

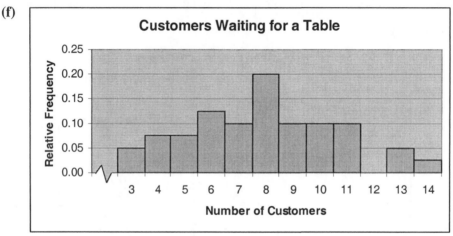

(g) The distribution is more or less symmetric.

29. (a) and **(b)**

Relative frequency for 20,000-22,499 = 3/51 = 0.0588 and so on.

Disposable Income ($)	Frequency	Relative Frequency
20,000 – 22,499	3	0.0588
22,500 – 24,999	10	0.1961
25,000 – 27,499	14	0.2745
27,500 – 29,999	12	0.2353
30,000 – 32,499	7	0.1373
32,500 – 34,999	2	0.0392
35,000 – 37,499	2	0.0392
37,500 – 39,999	0	0.0000
40,000 – 42,499	1	0.0196

(c)

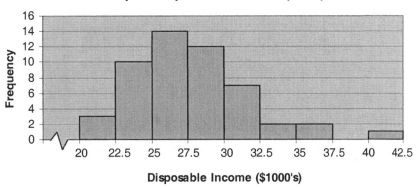

(d)

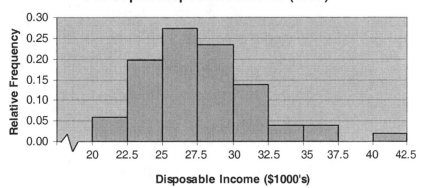

(e) The distribution appears to be slightly skewed right.

(f) Relative frequency for 20,000-23,999 = 10/51 = 0.1961 and so on.

Disposable Income ($)	Frequency	Relative Frequency
20,000 – 23,999	10	0.1961
24,000 – 27,999	22	0.4314
28,000 – 31,999	14	0.2745
32,000 – 35,999	3	0.0588
36,000 – 39,999	1	0.0196
40,000 – 43,999	1	0.0196

27

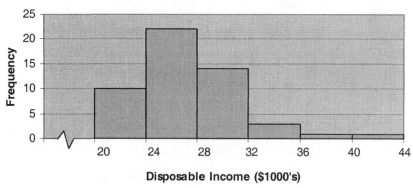

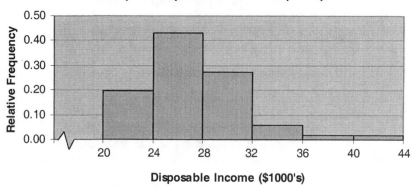

The distribution appears to be skewed right. While both distributions indicate the data are skewed right, the first distribution provides a more detailed look at the data. The second distribution is a bit coarser.

(g) Answers will vary.

31. (a) and **(b)**

Total number of data points $= 40$.

Relative frequency of 20–29 $= 1/40 = 0.025$ and so on.

HDL Cholesterol	Frequency	Relative Frequency
20–29	1	0.025
30–39	6	0.150
40–49	10	0.250
50–59	14	0.350
60–69	6	0.150
70–79	3	0.075

28

(c)

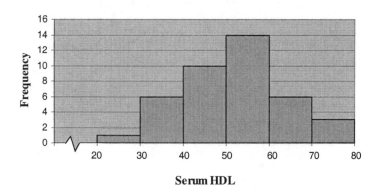

(d)

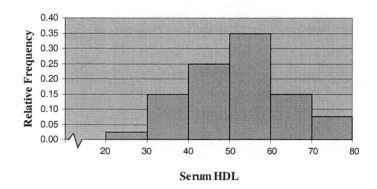

(e) The distribution appears to be roughly bell-shaped.

(f)

HDL Cholesterol	Frequency	Relative Frequency
20–24	0	0.000
25–29	1	0.025
30–34	2	0.050
35–39	4	0.100
40–44	2	0.050
45–49	8	0.200
50–54	9	0.225
55–59	5	0.125
60–64	4	0.100
65–69	2	0.050
70–74	3	0.075
Total	**40**	**1.000**

Serum HDL of 20-29 Year Olds

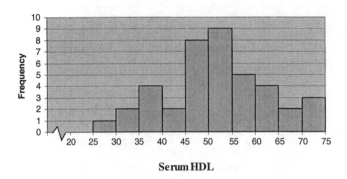

Serum HDL of 20-29 Year Olds

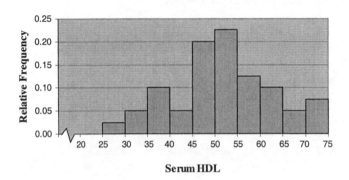

The distribution is roughly bell-shaped.

(g) The first distribution gives a smoother pattern. The additional detail in the second case does not provide much more information.

33. (a) and **(b)**

Relative frequency for 0.00-0.39 = 7/28 = 0.2500 and so on.

Dividend	Frequency	Relative Frequency
0.00 − 0.39	7	0.2500
0.40 − 0.79	4	0.1429
0.80 − 1.19	5	0.1786
1.20 − 1.59	2	0.0714
1.60 − 1.99	3	0.1071
2.00 − 2.39	4	0.1429
2.40 − 2.79	2	0.0714
2.80 − 3.19	1	0.0357

30

(c)

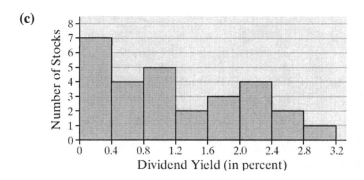

(d)

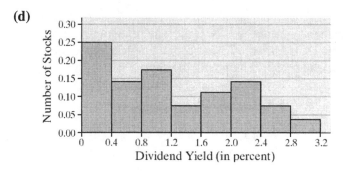

(e) The distribution is skewed right.

(f) Relative frequency for 0.00-0.79 = 11/28 = 0.3929 and so on.

Dividend	Frequency	Relative Frequency
0.00 – 0.79	11	0.3929
0.80 – 1.59	7	0.2500
1.60 – 2.39	7	0.2500
2.40 – 3.19	3	0.1071

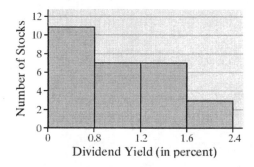

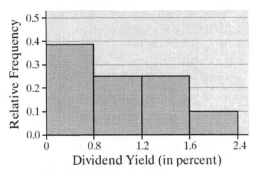

The distribution is skewed right.

(g) Both distributions indicate the data are skewed right. The first graph is preferred because it gives more detailed information. The second graph is a little too compressed to get a complete view of what is happening with the data.

35. 5 | 7 represents 57 years

```
4 | 23
4 | 667899
5 | 0011112244444
5 | 555566677778
6 | 0111244
6 | 589
```

37. 0 | 1 represents 1 gram

```
0 | 1288
1 | 1125667
2 | 333388
3 | 1335
4 | 0
```

39. (a) Rounded data:

```
54   0   75  64  16   8   94   9   32  90  35  88  56   0
41  62  23  83  17   0   51  49  13   3   60  60  38   8
 1   1  60  63  95  42  98  78  46  27  51  90  62  68
10  94  57  23  61  37  96  58  83
```

5 | 4 represents 54 percent

```
0 | 000113889
1 | 0367
2 | 337
3 | 2578
4 | 1269
5 | 114678
6 | 000122348
7 | 58
8 | 338
9 | 0044568
```

(b) The distribution does not really exhibit a clearly defined pattern. Of our four choices (uniform, symmetric, skewed left, skewed right), it appears that the distribution is more uniform than the others.

(c) Answers will vary. West Virginia is most likely represented by the data value 98.1. In 2004, roughly 99 percent of all energy generated in West Virginia was derived from coal.

41. (a) Number of problems per 100 vehicles, rounded to the nearest tens:

160   170   180   190   200   200   210   210   220   240

260   260   270   270   270   270   270   280   290   290

300   300   300   310   320   320   320   330   340   340

340   370   390   400   420   440   510

(b) │1│6 represents 160 problems per 100 vehicles│

1	6789
2	00112456677777899
3	000122234479
4	024
5	1

Answers will vary. This is not a terrible summary, but the data are heavily concentrated on two stems. There may be some features that are hidden because the data are too compressed.

(c) │1│6 represents 160 problems per 100 vehicles│

1	6789
2	001124
2	56677777899
3	0001222344
3	79
4	024
4	
5	1

Answers will vary. This is a better display of the data. Here we can see that the data, while still a little skewed right, is much more symmetric than the first display suggested. In addition, we can identify a potential outlier in the second display (509, rounded to 510) that was not evident in the first display.

43. (a) | 9 | 2 | 1 represents 29 years for best actor and 21 years for best actress |

Best Actor Age		Best Actress Age
9	2	145588
98877765210	3	01133334555589
7555332200	4	1112599
4221	5	
100	6	1
6	7	4
	8	0

(b) Answers will vary. One possibility: Academy Award winners for best actor tend to be older on the whole than winners for best actress.

45.

Dotplot of Customers Waiting at 6:00 pm

Number of Customers

2.3 Additional Displays of Quantitative Data

1. Answers will vary. A stem-and-leaf plot is generally preferred for small data sets since the original data is retained, otherwise a histogram is preferred. A frequency polygon may be preferred if comparing more than one data set.

3. An ogive is a line graph of cumulative frequencies or cumulative relative frequencies against upper class limits.

5. True

7. **(a)** 5; The class width is the difference between successive class midpoints. e.g. $27.5 - 22.5 = 5$

   (b) 35; the lower class limit of the fourth class is halfway between the midpoint of the third class (32.5) and the midpoint of the fourth class (37.5).

   (c) 39; the upper class limit of the fourth class is halfway between the midpoint of the fourth class (37.5) and the midpoint of the fifth class (42.5).

   (d) The highest frequency occurs for the fifth class. This corresponds to the age group 40-44 years of age.

   (e) The lowest frequency occurs for the twelfth class. This corresponds to the age group 75-79 years of age.

9. (a) 3; The class width is the difference between successive class upper limits. e.g.
$15 - 12 = 3$

(b) 16; since the upper class limit for the second class is 15, the lower class limit for the third class must be one unit higher.

(c) From the graph, it appears that about 90% of students had an ACT composite score of 27 or below.

(d) $(0.9)(1,171,460) = 1,054,314$ students had ACT composite scores of 27 or below.

11. (a) and **(b)**

Second class cumulative frequency = 28.9 + 35.7 = 64.6 and so on.
Total people not covered = $28.9 + 35.7 + 35.1 + 24.7 = 124.4$.

Second class cumulative relative frequency = $\dfrac{64.6}{124.4} = 0.5193$ and so on.

Age	Cumulative Frequency (millions)	Cumulative Relative Frequency
25 – 34	28.9	0.2323
35 – 44	64.6	0.5193
45 – 54	99.7	0.8104
55 – 64	124.4	1.0000

(c)

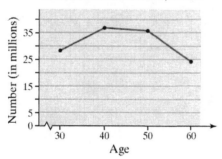

(d)

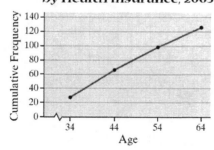

35

(e)

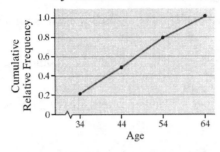

Number of People Covered by Health Insurance, 2003

13. **(a)** and **(b)**

Second class cumulative frequency = 6826 + 6800 = 13,626 and so on.
Total admissions = 22,286.

Second class cumulative relative frequency = $\dfrac{13,626}{22,826} = 0.5970$ and so on.

Number of Beds	Cumulative Frequency (thousands)	Cumulative Relative Frequency
100 – 199	6826	0.2990
200 – 299	13,626	0.5970
300 – 399	19,233	0.8426
400 – 499	22,826	1.0000

(c)

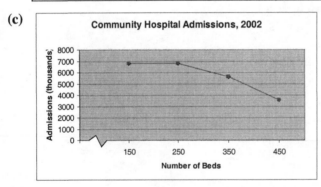

Community Hospital Admissions, 2002

(d)

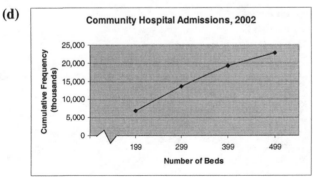

Community Hospital Admissions, 2002

36

(e)

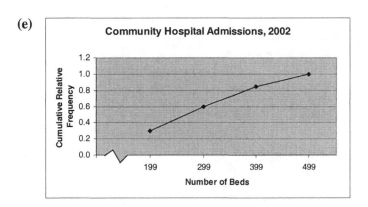

15. (a) and **(b)**

Second class cumulative frequency = 3 + 10 = 13 and so on.
Total states (and DC) = 51.

Second class cumulative relative frequency = $\dfrac{13}{51} = 0.2549$ and so on.

Disposable Income ($)	Cumulative Frequency	Cumulative Relative Frequency
$20,000 - 22,499$	3	0.0588
$22,500 - 24,999$	13	0.2549
$25,000 - 27,499$	27	0.5294
$27,500 - 29,999$	39	0.7647
$30,000 - 32,499$	46	0.9020
$32,500 - 34,999$	48	0.9412
$35,000 - 37,499$	50	0.9804
$37,500 - 39,999$	50	0.9804
$40,000 - 42,499$	51	1.0000

(c)

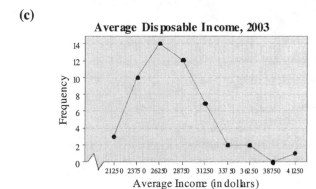

37

(d)

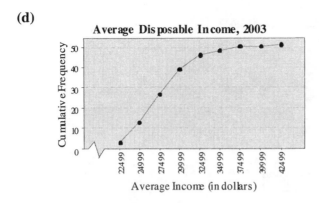

(e)

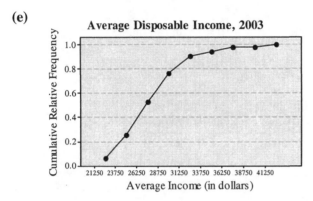

17. (a) The stock price remained stead for the first half of 2004. There were large jumps in price during August and November.

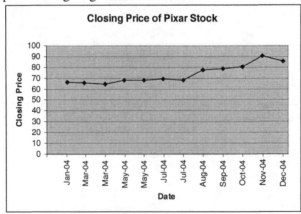

(b) The stock price increased the most during November. This could be explained by the release of 'The Incredibles'. Favorable reviews and large ticket sales could have boosted the value of the stock.

19. The percent of recent high school graduates enrolling in college seems to have increased slightly over the given time period. There seems to have been a larger increase in the mid-to-late 1990s, but overall the rate of increase seems to be fairly steady.

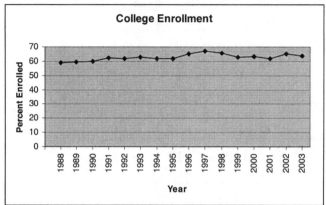

21. (a) Total frequency for financial stocks = 32.

Total frequency for energy stocks = 32.

Rate of Return	Frequency (Financial)	Frequency (Energy)
0.00 – 4.99	1	0
5.00 – 9.99	7	6
10.00 – 14.99	7	2
15.00 – 19.99	8	9
20.00 – 24.99	4	4
25.00 – 29.99	4	4
30.00 – 34.99	1	1
35.00 – 39.99	0	1
40.00 – 44.99	0	3
45.00 – 49.99	0	1
50.00 – 54.99	0	1

39

(b) Relative frequency of $0 - 4.99$ return (financial stocks) $= 1/32 = 0.0313$ and so on.
Relative frequency of $5.00 - 5.99$ return (energy stocks) $= 6/32 = 0.1875$ and so on.

Rate of Return	Relative Frequency (Financial)	Relative Frequency (Energy)
0.00 – 4.99	0.0313	0
5.00 – 9.99	0.2188	0.1875
10.00 – 14.99	0.2188	0.0625
15.00 – 19.99	0.2500	0.2813
20.00 – 24.99	0.1250	0.1250
25.00 – 29.99	0.1250	0.1250
30.00 – 34.99	0.0313	0.0313
35.00 – 39.99	0	0.0313
40.00 – 44.99	0	0.0938
45.00 – 49.99	0	0.0313
50.00 – 54.99	0	0.0313

(c)

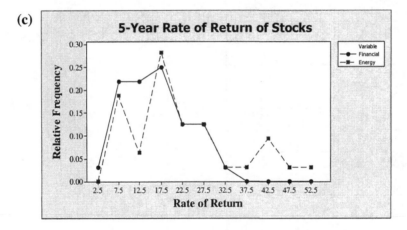

40

(d)

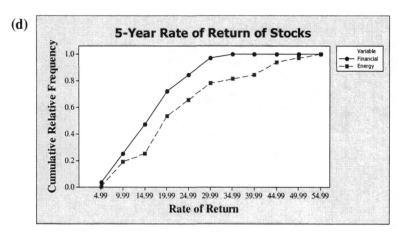

(e) Energy stocks gave a better return overall with a greater percentage of them giving higher returns than in the financial sector.

2.4 Graphical Misrepresentations of Data

1. The lengths of the bars are not proportional. The bar for Clinton should be slightly more than 9 times as long as for Carter. In addition, the relative difference in bar heights is not consistent. The difference between Carter and Reagan represents about 13 units while the difference between Reagan and Bush represents about 12 units. However, the difference in bar lengths between Reagan and Bush is about twice the difference between Carter and Reagan.

3. (a) The vertical axis starts at 28 instead of 0. This tends to indicate that the median earnings for females increased at a faster rate than actually occurred.

(b) This graph indicates that the median earnings for females has increased slightly over the given 5-year period.

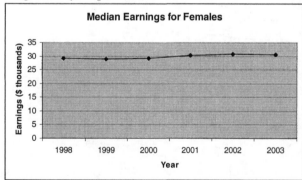

5. (a) The vertical axis starts at 0.1 instead of 0. This might cause the reader to conclude, for example, that the proportion of people aged 25-34 years old who are not covered by any type of health insurance is more than 4 times the proportion for those aged 55-64 years old.

(b)

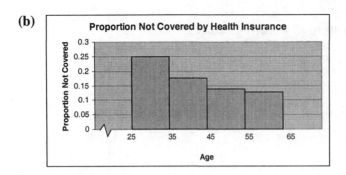

7. (a) The vertical axis starts at 35 without including a gap.

(b) The median household income is increasing rapidly.

9. (a) The bars do not have lengths that are in proportion to the percentages that they represent. For example, the housing bar should be slightly more than twice as long as the transportation bar.

(b) Adjust the lengths of the bars to be proportional.

11. (a)

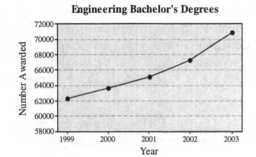

(b)

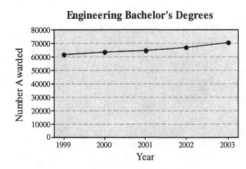

13. **(a)** From the politician's view:

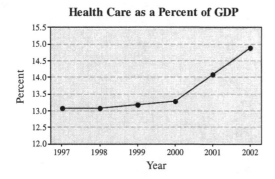

(b) From the health care industry view:

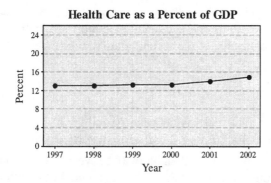

(c) An unbiased view:

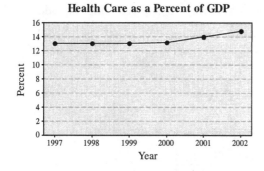

15. (a) Because the second graphic must be two times as large as the first graphic, the height and width of the second graph must increase by a factor of $\sqrt{2}$. So, if the first graphic is 1 inch by 1 inch, the second graphic should be $\sqrt{2}$ inches by $\sqrt{2}$ inches. An example of a graph that is not misleading:

Enrollment in Distance Learning

(b) Any graphic that is misleading will not have the dimensions mentioned in part (a). Typically, the second graphic would have a width and length that are both increased by a factor of 2. This would make the area of the second graphic four times as large as the area of the first graphic.

Chapter 2 Review Exercises

1. (a) The bar for natural gas appears to be halfway between 20 and 25, so it appears that the U.S. consumed about 22.5 quadrillion Btu in energy from natural gas during 2003.

(b) The corresponding bar in the graph is more than halfway between 0 and 5, but not quite to 5. Therefore, we might estimate that the U.S. consumed about 3 quadrillion Btu in energy from biomass during 2003.

(c) $39 + 22.5 + 22.5 + 7.5 + 3 + 3 + 0.5 = 98$
Total energy consumption in the U.S. during 2003 was about 98 quadrillion Btu.

(d) "Other" (including geothermal, wind, and solar) has the lowest frequency.

(e) No; the data are qualitative so order (and thus skewness) is irrelevant.

3. (a) Total homicides = 14,158

Relative frequency for Firearms = $\dfrac{9369}{14,158} \approx 0.6617$ and so on.

Type of Weapon	Relative Frequency
Firearms	0.6617
Knives or cutting intstruments	0.1248
Blunt objects (clubs, hammers, etc.)	0.0470
Personal weapons (hands, fists, etc.)	0.0659
Strangulation	0.0101
Fire	0.0073
Other weapon or not stated	0.0831

44

(b) The relative frequency is 0.0470, so 4.7% of the homicides were due to blunt objects.

(c)

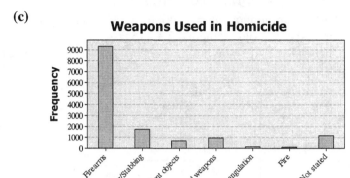

(d)

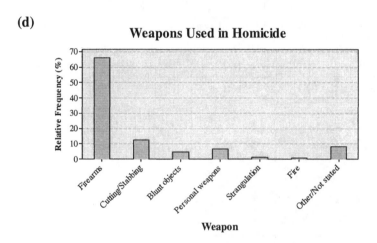

(e)

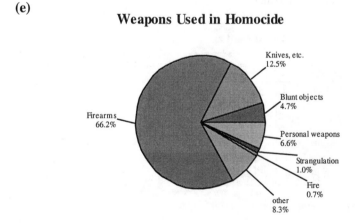

5. (a), **(b)**, and **(c)**

Total births = 7 + 415 + 1032 + 1087 + 976 + 468 + 101 = 4086

Relative frequency for 10-14 year old mothers = $7/4086 \approx 0.0017$ and so on.

Cumulative frequency for 15-19 year old mothers = 7 + 415 = 422 and so on.

Cumulative relative frequency for 15-19 year old mothers = $422/4086 \approx 0.1033$ and so on.

Age of Mother	Relative Frequency	Cumulative Frequency	Cumulative Relative Frequency
10 – 14	0.0017	7	0.0017
15 – 19	0.1016	422	0.1033
20 – 24	0.2526	1454	0.3558
25 – 29	0.2660	2541	0.6219
30 – 34	0.2389	3517	0.8607
35 – 39	0.1145	3985	0.9753
40 – 44	0.0247	4086	1.0000

(d) The distribution is roughly symmetric.

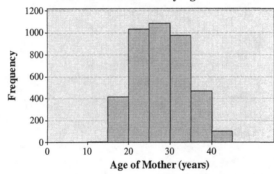

Live Births in the US by Age of Mother

(e)

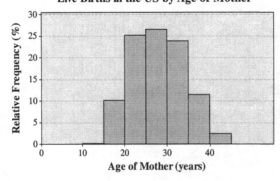

Live Births in the US by Age of Mother

(f)

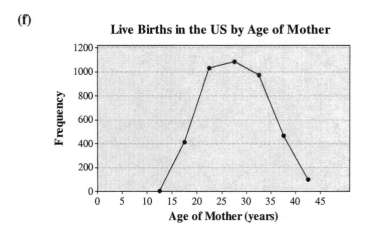

Live Births in the US by Age of Mother

(g)

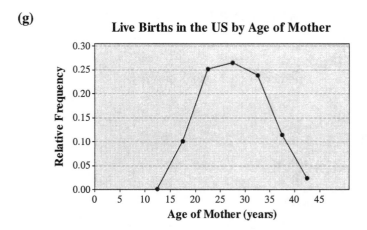

Live Births in the US by Age of Mother

(h)

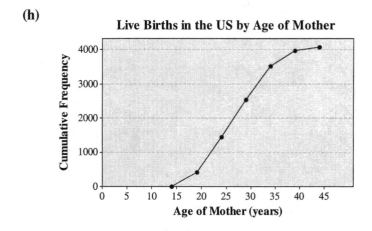

Live Births in the US by Age of Mother

(i)

Live Births in the US by Age of Mother

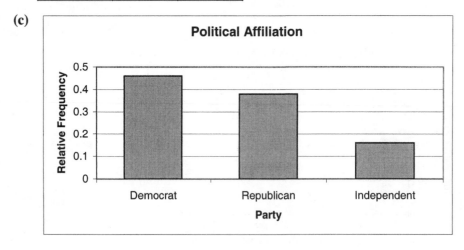

(j) From the relative frequency table, the relative frequency of 20-24 is 0.2526 and so the percentage is 25.26%.

(k) $0.2389 + 0.1145 + 0.0247 = 0.3781$
37.81% of live births were to mothers aged 30 years or older.

7. (a) and **(b)**

Affiliation	Frequency	Relative Frequency
Democrat	46	0.46
Republican	38	0.38
Independent	16	0.16

(c)

Political Affiliation

(d)

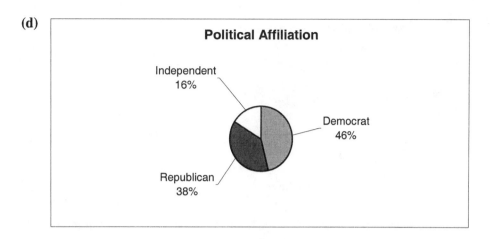

Political Affiliation

Independent 16%

Democrat 46%

Republican 38%

(e) Democrat appears to be the most common affiliation.

9. (a), (b), (c), and **(d)**

Family Size	Frequency	Relative Frequency	Cumulative Frequency	Cumulative Relative Frequency
0	7	0.1167	7	0.1167
1	7	0.1167	14	0.2333
2	18	0.3000	32	0.5333
3	20	0.3333	52	0.8667
4	7	0.1167	59	0.9833
5	1	0.0167	60	1.0000

(e) The distribution is more or less symmetric.

Number of Children for Couples Married 7 Years

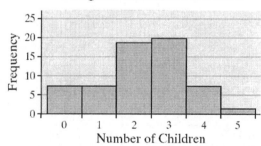

49

(f)

**Number of Children for
Couples Married 7 Years**

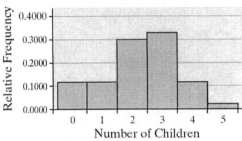

(g) From the relative frequency table, the relative frequency of two children is 0.3000 so 30% of the couples have two children.

(h) From the relative frequency table, the relative frequency of at least two children (i.e. two or more) is $0.3000 + 0.3333 + 0.1167 + 0.0167 = 0.7667$ or 76.67%. So, 76.67% of the couples have at least two children.

(i)

**Number of Children for
Couples Married 7 Years**

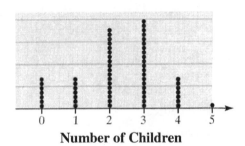

11. (a), **(b)**, **(c)**, and **(d)**

Class	Frequency	Relative Frequency	Cumulative Frequency	Cumulative Relative Frequency
2000 – 2399	2	0.0392	2	0.0392
2400 – 2799	4	0.0784	6	0.1176
2800 – 3199	8	0.1569	14	0.2745
3200 – 3599	6	0.1176	20	0.3922
3600 – 3999	4	0.0784	24	0.4706
4000 – 4399	8	0.1569	32	0.6275
4400 – 4799	8	0.1569	40	0.7843
4800 – 5199	6	0.1176	46	0.9020
5200 – 5599	2	0.0392	48	0.9412

50

(table continued)

Class	Frequency	Relative Frequency	Cumulative Frequency	Cumulative Relative Frequency
5600 – 5999	0	0.0000	48	0.9412
6000 – 6399	2	0.0392	50	0.9804
6400 – 6799	0	0.0000	50	0.9804
6800 – 7199	0	0.0000	50	0.9804
7200 – 7599	0	0.0000	50	0.9804
7600 – 7999	0	0.0000	50	0.9804
8000 – 8399	1	0.0196	51	1.0000

(e)

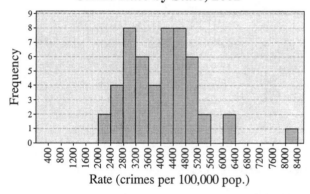

Crime Rate by State, 2002

The distribution is skewed right.

(f)

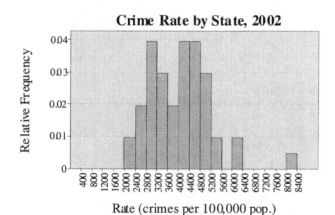

Crime Rate by State, 2002

(g)

Class	Frequency	Relative Frequency	Cumulative Frequency	Cumulative Relative Frequency
2000 – 2999	10	0.1961	10	0.1961
3000 – 3999	14	0.2745	24	0.4706
4000 – 4999	17	0.3333	41	0.8039
5000 – 5999	7	0.1373	48	0.9412
6000 – 6999	2	0.0392	50	0.9804
7000 – 7999	0	0.0000	50	0.9804
8000 – 8999	1	0.0196	51	1.0000

Crime Rate by State, 2002

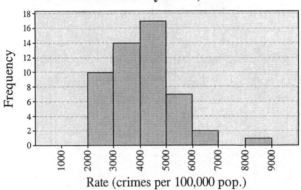

The distribution is skewed right.

Crime Rate by State, 2002

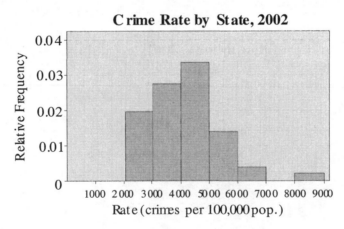

Answers will vary. Both class widths give a good overall picture of the distribution. The first class width provides a little more detail to the graph, but not necessarily enough to be worth the trouble.

13. (a), **(b)**, **(c)**, and **(d)**

Class	Frequency	Relative Frequency	Cumulative Frequency	Cumulative Relative Frequency
2.2000 – 2.2199	2	0.0588	2	0.0588
2.2200 – 2.2399	3	0.0882	5	0.1470
2.2400 – 2.2599	5	0.1471	10	0.2941
2.2600 – 2.2799	6	0.1765	16	0.4706
2.2800 – 2.2999	4	0.1176	20	0.5882
2.3000 – 2.3199	7	0.2059	27	0.7941
2.3200 – 2.3399	5	0.1471	32	0.9412
2.3400 – 2.3599	1	0.0294	33	0.9706
2.3600 – 2.3799	1	0.0294	34	1.0000

(e)

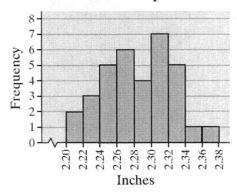

Diameter of Chocolate Chip Cookies

The distribution is roughly symmetric.

(f)

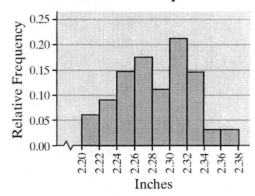

Diameter of Chocolate Chip Cookies

(g)

Class	Frequency	Relative Frequency	Cumulative Frequency	Cumulative Relative Frequency
2.2000 – 2.2399	5	0.1471	5	0.1471
2.2400 – 2.2799	11	0.3235	16	0.4706
2.2800 – 2.3199	11	0.3235	27	0.7941
2.3200 – 2.3599	6	0.1765	33	0.9706
2.3600 – 2.3999	1	0.0204	34	1.0000

The distribution is roughly symmetric.

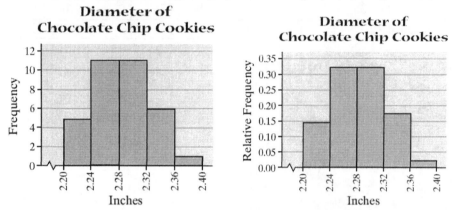

Answers will vary. Both class widths give a good overall picture of the distribution. The first class width provides a little more detail to the graph, but not necessarily enough to be worth the trouble. The second class width is preferred.

15. 1|7 represents 1.7 servings

```
 0 | 234456778
 1 | 47
 2 | 1334467
 3 | 2355589
 4 | 199
 5 | 13889
 6 | 017
 7 | 6
 8 | 3
 9 |
10 | 2
11 | 1
```

The distribution appears to be skewed right.

17. (a) and **(b)**

The minimum wage seems to stay constant for several years and then increase in small jumps. Overall, the minimum wage shows a slowly increasing trend with a stepwise pattern.

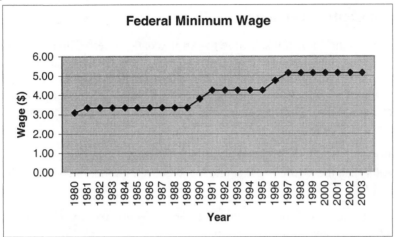

19. The graph cannot be interpreted because it lacks a vertical scale.

21. (a) A bar chart that would be misleading by exaggerating the difference would make the college graduate bar 88% wider **and** 88% taller than the high school graduate bar. This would make the area of the college graduate bar about 250% more than the area of the high school graduate bar.

(b) A bar chart that would not be misleading would have both bars the same width, but the college graduate bar would be 88% taller. This would make the total area of the college graduate bar 88% more than the area of the high school graduate bar. One example:

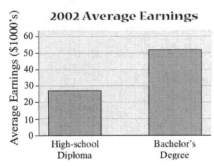

Chapter 3

Numerically Describing Data from One Variable

3.1 Measures of Central Tendency

1. A statistic is resistant if it is not sensitive to extreme data values. The median is resistant because it is a positional measure of central tendency and increasing the largest value or decreasing the smallest value does not affect the position of the center. The mean is not resistant because it is a function of the sum of the data values. Changing the magnitude of one value changes the sum of the values, and thus affects the mean. The mode is a resistant measure of center.

3. Since the distribution of household incomes in the United States is skewed to the right, the mean is greater than the median. Thus, the mean household income is $55,263 and the median is $41,349.

5. The mean will be larger because it will be influenced by the extreme data values that are to the right end (or high end) of the distribution.

7. The mode is used with qualitative data because the computations involved with the mean and median make no sense for qualitative data.

9. False. A data set may have multiple modes, or it may have no mode at all.

11. $\bar{x} = \dfrac{20+13+4+8+10}{5} = \dfrac{55}{5} = 11$

13. $\mu = \dfrac{3+6+10+12+14}{5} = \dfrac{45}{5} = 9$

15. $\dfrac{142}{59} \approx 2.4$. The mean price per ad slot is approximately $2.4 million.

17. Mean $= \dfrac{420+462+409+236}{4} = \dfrac{1527}{4} = \$381.75$

    Data in order: 236, 409, 420, 462

    Median $= \dfrac{409+420}{2} = \dfrac{829}{2} = \$414.50$

    No data value occurs more than once so there is no mode.

19. Mean $= \dfrac{3960+4090+3200+3100+2940+3830+4090+4040+3780}{9} = \dfrac{33,030}{9} = 3670$ psi

    Data in order: 2940, 3100, 3200, 3780, 3830, 3960, 4040, 4090, 4090

    Median = the 5th ordered data value = 3830 psi

    Mode = 4090 psi (because it is the only data value to occur twice)

56

21. (a) The histogram is skewed to the right, suggesting that the mean is greater than the median. That is, $\bar{x} > M$.

    (b) The histogram is symmetric, suggesting that the mean is approximately equal to the median. That is, $\bar{x} = M$.

    (c) The histogram is skewed to the left, suggesting that the mean is less than the median. That is, $\bar{x} < M$.

23. Los Angeles ATM fees:

$$\text{Mean} = \frac{2.00+1.50+1.50+1.00+1.50+2.00+0.00+2.00}{8} = \frac{11.50}{8} \approx \$1.44$$

Data in order: 0.00, 1.00, 1.50, 1.50, 1.50, 2.00, 2.00, 2.00

$$\text{Median} = \frac{1.50+1.50}{2} = \frac{3.00}{2} = \$1.50$$

Mode = \$1.50 and \$2.00 (because both values occur three times each)

New York City ATM fees:

$$\text{Mean} = \frac{1.50+1.00+1.00+1.25+1.25+1.50+1.00+0.00}{8} = \frac{8.50}{8} \approx \$1.06$$

Data in order: 0.00, 1.00, 1.00, 1.00, 1.25, 1.25, 1.50, 1.50

$$\text{Median} = \frac{1.00+1.25}{2} = \frac{2.25}{2} \approx \$1.13$$

Mode = \$1.00 (because it occurs the more than the other values)

The ATM fees in Los Angeles appear to be higher in general than those in New York City. All three measures of center were higher for Los Angeles than for New York. Explanations will vary. Possibilities for the difference may be the number of ATMs available or the amount of ATM usage in each city.

25. (a) $\mu = \dfrac{76+60+60+81+72+80+80+68+73}{9} = \dfrac{650}{9} \approx 72.2$ beats per minute

    (b) Samples and sample means will vary.

    (c) Answers will vary.

27. (a) $\mu = \dfrac{0+0+0+4+10+1+10+10+19+9+18+20+13+13+2+7+8+13}{18} = \dfrac{157}{18}$

    ≈ 8.7 goals per year

    (b) Samples and sample means will vary.

    (c) Answers will vary.

29. The distribution is relatively symmetric as is evidenced by both the histogram and the fact that the mean and median are approximately equal. Therefore, the mean is the better measure of central tendency.

31. (a) $\bar{x} \approx 51.1$; $M = 51$.

    (b) The mean is approximately equal to the median suggesting that the distribution is symmetric, and this is confirmed by the histogram.

33.

Weight of Plain M&Ms

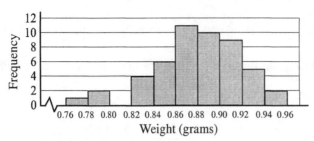

$\bar{x} \approx 0.874$ grams; $M = 0.88$ grams. The mean is approximately equal to the median suggesting that the distribution is symmetric. This is confirmed by the histogram (though is does appear to be slightly skewed left). The mean is the better measure of central tendency.

35.

Hours Worked per Week

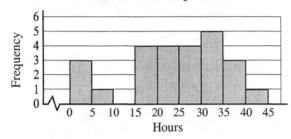

$\bar{x} = 22$ hour; $M = 25$ hours. The mean is smaller than the median suggesting that the distribution is skewed left. This is confirmed by the histogram. The median is the better measure of central tendency.

37. The highest frequency is 12,362, and so the mode region of birth is Central America.

39. The vote counts are: Bush = 21, Kerry = 17, Nader = 1, and Badnarik = 1. The mode candidate is Bush.

41. Sample size of 5:
    All data recorded correctly: $\bar{x} = 99.8$; $M = 100$.
    106 recorded at 160: $\bar{x} = 110.6$; $M = 100$.
Sample size of 12:
    All data recorded correctly: $\bar{x} \approx 100.4$; $M = 101$.
    106 recorded at 160: $\bar{x} \approx 104.9$; $M = 101$.
Sample size of 30:
    All data recorded correctly: $\bar{x} = 100.6$; $M = 99$.
    106 recorded at 160: $\bar{x} = 102.4$; $M = 99$.
For each sample size, the mean becomes larger while the median remains the same. As the sample size increases, the impact of the misrecorded data value on the mean decreases.

43. Samples and sample means will vary.

45. The amount of money lost per visitor is likely skewed to the right. Therefore, the median loss would be less than the mean because the mean amount would be inflated by those few visitors who lost very large amounts of money

47. The sum of the six number will be $6 \cdot 34 = 204$.

49. (a) Mean: $\dfrac{30+30+45+50+50+50+55+55+60+75}{10} = \dfrac{500}{10} = 50$. The mean is \$50,000.

Median: The ten data values are in order, so we average the two middle values.

$\dfrac{50+50}{2} = \dfrac{100}{2} = 50$. The median is \$50,000.

Mode: The mode is \$50,000 (the most frequent salary).

(b) Add \$2500 (\$2.5 thousand) to each salary to form the new data set.

New data set: 32.5, 32.5, 47.5, 52.5, 52.5, 52.5, 57.5, 57.5, 62.5, 77.5

Mean: $\dfrac{32.5+32.5+47.5+52.5+52.5+52.5+57.5+57.5+62.5+77.5}{10} = \dfrac{525}{10} = 52.5$

The new mean is \$52,500.

Median: The ten data values are in order, so we average the two middle values.

$\dfrac{52.5+52.5}{2} = \dfrac{105}{2} = 52.5$. The new median is \$52,500.

Mode: The new mode is \$52,500 (the most frequent new salary).

All three measures of central tendency increased by \$2500, which was the amount of the raises.

(c) Multiply each original data value by 1.05 to generate the new data set.

New data set: 31.5, 31.5, 47.25, 52.5, 52.5, 52.5, 57.75, 57.75, 63, 78.75

Mean: $\dfrac{31.5+31.5+47.25+52.5+52.5+52.5+57.75+57.75+63+78.75}{10} = \dfrac{525}{10} = 52.5$.

The new mean is \$52,500.

Median: The ten data values are in order, so we average the two middle values.

$\dfrac{52.5+52.5}{2} = \dfrac{105}{2} = 52.5$. The new median is \$52,500.

Mode: The new mode is \$52,500 (the most frequent new salary).

All three measures of central tendency increased by 5%, which was the amount of the raises.

(d) Add \$25 thousand to the largest data value to form the new data set.

New data set: 30, 30, 45, 50, 50, 50, 55, 55, 60, 100

Mean: $\dfrac{30+30+45+50+50+50+55+55+60+100}{10} = \dfrac{525}{10} = 52.5$. The new mean is \$52,500.

Median: The ten data values are in order, so we average the two middle values.

$\dfrac{50+50}{2} = \dfrac{100}{2} = 50$. The mew median is \$50,000.

Mode: The new mode is \$50,000 (the most frequent salary).

The mean was increased by \$2500, but the median and mode remained unchanged.

51. The largest data value is 0.94 and the smallest is 0.76. The mean after deleting those two data values is 0.875 grams. (Note: The value 0.94 occurs twice, but we only remove one.) The trimmed mean is more resistant than the regular mean. Note in this case that the trimmed mean 0.875 grams is approximately equal to the median 0.88 grams.

3.2 Measures of Dispersion

1. No. In comparing two populations, the larger the standard deviation, the more dispersed the distribution, provided that the variable of interest in both populations has the same unit of measurement. Since $5 \text{ inches} \approx 5 \times 2.54 = 12.7 \text{ centimeters}$, the distribution with a standard deviation of 5 inches is in fact more dispersed.

3. All data values are used in computing the standard deviation, including extreme values. Since a statistic is resistant only if it is not influenced by extreme data values, the standard deviation is not resistant.

5. A statistic is biased whenever that statistic consistently overestimates or underestimates a parameter.

7. The standard deviation is the square root of the variance.

9. True

11. From Section 3.1, Exercise 11, we know $\bar{x} = 11$.

Data, x_i	Sample Mean, $\bar{x}$	Deviations, $x_i - \bar{x}$	Squared Deviations, $(x_i - \bar{x})^2$
20	11	$20 - 11 = 9$	$9^2 = 81$
13	11	$13 - 11 = 2$	$2^2 = 4$
4	11	$4 - 11 = -7$	$(-7)^2 = 49$
8	11	$8 - 11 = -3$	$(-3)^2 = 9$
10	11	$10 - 11 = -1$	$(-1)^2 = 1$
		$\sum (x_i - \bar{x}) = 0$	$\sum (x_i - \bar{x})^2 = 144$

$$s^2 = \frac{\sum (x_i - \bar{x})^2}{n-1} = \frac{144}{5-1} = 36; \quad s = \sqrt{\frac{\sum (x_i - \bar{x})^2}{n-1}} = \sqrt{\frac{144}{5-1}} = \sqrt{36} = 6.$$

13. From Section 3.1, Exercise 13, we know $\mu = 9$.

Data, x_i	Population Mean, μ	Deviations, $x_i - \mu$	Squared Deviations, $(x_i - \mu)^2$
3	9	$3 - 9 = -6$	$(-6)^2 = 36$
6	9	$6 - 9 = -3$	$(-3)^2 = 9$
10	9	$10 - 9 = 1$	$1^2 = 1$
12	9	$12 - 9 = 3$	$3^2 = 9$
14	9	$14 - 9 = 5$	$5^2 = 25$
		$\sum (x_i - \mu) = 0$	$\sum (x_i - \mu)^2 = 80$

$$\sigma^2 = \frac{\sum (x_i - \mu)^2}{N} = \frac{80}{5} = 16; \quad \sigma = \sqrt{\frac{\sum (x_i - \mu)^2}{N}} = \sqrt{\frac{80}{5}} = \sqrt{16} = 4.$$

15. $\bar{x} = \dfrac{6 + 52 + 13 + 49 + 35 + 25 + 31 + 29 + 31 + 29}{10} = \dfrac{300}{10} = 30.$

Data, x_i	Sample Mean, $\bar{x}$	Deviations, $x_i - \bar{x}$	Squared Deviations, $(x_i - \bar{x})^2$
6	30	$6 - 30 = -24$	$(-24)^2 = 576$
52	30	$52 - 30 = 22$	$22^2 = 484$
13	30	$13 - 30 = -17$	$(-17)^2 = 289$
49	30	$49 - 30 = 19$	$19^2 = 361$
35	30	$35 - 30 = 5$	$5^2 = 25$
25	30	$25 - 30 = -5$	$(-5)^2 = 25$
31	30	$31 - 30 = 1$	$1^2 = 1$
29	30	$29 - 30 = -1$	$(-1)^2 = 1$
31	30	$31 - 30 = 1$	$1^2 = 1$
29	30	$29 - 30 = -1$	$(-1)^2 = 1$
		$\sum (x_i - \bar{x}) = 0$	$\sum (x_i - \bar{x})^2 = 1764$

$$s^2 = \frac{\sum (x_i - \bar{x})^2}{n - 1} = \frac{1764}{10 - 1} = 196; \quad s = \sqrt{\frac{\sum (x_i - \bar{x})^2}{N}} = \sqrt{\frac{1764}{9}} = \sqrt{196} = 14.$$

17. Range = Largest Data Value – Smallest Data Value = $462 - 236 = \$226$.
From Section 3.1, Exercise 17, we know $\bar{x} = \$381.75$.

Data, x_i	Sample Mean, $\bar{x}$	Deviations, $x_i - \bar{x}$	Squared Deviations, $(x_i - \bar{x})^2$
420	381.75	38.25	1463.0625
462	381.75	80.25	6440.0625
409	381.75	27.25	742.5625
236	381.75	−145.75	21,243.0625
		$\sum (x_i - \bar{x}) = 0$	$\sum (x_i - \bar{x})^2 = 29,888.75$

$$s^2 = \frac{\sum (x_i - \bar{x})^2}{n - 1} \approx \frac{29,888.75}{4 - 1} = 9,962.9 \ \$^2; \quad s = \sqrt{\frac{\sum (x_i - \bar{x})^2}{n - 1}} = \sqrt{\frac{29,888.75}{4 - 1}} \approx \$99.81$$

19. Range = Largest Data Value – Smallest Data Value $= 4090 - 2940 = 1150$ psi
To calculate the sample variance and the sample standard deviation, we use the computational formula:

Data value, x_i	Data value squared, x_i^2
3960	15,681,600
4090	16,728,100
3200	10,240,000
3100	9,610,000
2940	8,643,600
3830	14,668,900
4090	16,728,100
4040	16,321,600
3780	14,288,400
$\sum x_i = 33,020$	$\sum x_i^2 = 122,828,600$

$$s^2 = \frac{\sum x_i^2 - \frac{\left(\sum x_i\right)^2}{n}}{n-1}$$

$$= \frac{122,910,300 - \frac{(33,030)^2}{9}}{9-1} \approx 211,275 \text{ psi}^2;$$

$$s = \sqrt{\frac{122,910,300 - \frac{(33,030)^2}{9}}{9-1}} \approx 459.6 \text{ psi}$$

21. Histogram (b) depicts a higher standard deviation because the data is more dispersed, with data values ranging from 30 to 75. Histogram (a)'s data values only range from 40 to 60.

23. Los Angeles ATM fees:
Range = Largest Data Value – Smallest Data Value = 2.00 – 0.00 = $2.00.

Data value, x_i	Data value squared, x_i^2
2.00	4
1.50	2.25
1.50	2.25
1.00	1
1.50	2.25
2.00	4
0.00	0
2.00	4
$\sum x_i = 11.5$	$\sum x_i^2 = 19.75$

$$s = \sqrt{\frac{\sum x_i^2 - \frac{\left(\sum x_i\right)^2}{n}}{n-1}}$$

$$= \sqrt{\frac{19.75 - \frac{(11.5)^2}{8}}{8-1}}$$

$$\approx \$0.68$$

New York City ATM fees:
Range = Largest Data Value – Smallest Data Value = 1.50 – 0.00 = $1.50.

Data value, x_i	Data value squared, x_i^2
1.50	2.25
1.00	1
1.00	1
1.25	1.5625
1.25	1.5625
1.50	2.25
1.00	1
0.00	0
$\sum x_i = 8.5$	$\sum x_i^2 = 10.625$

$$s = \sqrt{\frac{\sum x_i^2 - \frac{\left(\sum x_i\right)^2}{n}}{n-1}}$$

$$= \sqrt{\frac{10.625 - \frac{(8.5)^2}{8}}{8-1}}$$

$$\approx \$0.48$$

Based on both the range and the standard deviation, ATM fees in Los Angeles have more dispersion than ATM fees in New York. Both the range and the standard deviation for Los Angeles are larger.

25. (a) We use the computational formula: $\sum x_i = 650$; $\sum x_i^2 = 47,474$; $N = 9$;

$$\sigma^2 = \frac{\sum x_i^2 - \frac{\left(\sum x_i\right)^2}{N}}{N} = \frac{47,474 - \frac{(650)^2}{9}}{9} \approx 58.8 \ (\text{beats/min.})^2;$$

$$\sigma = \sqrt{\frac{\sum x_i^2 - \frac{\left(\sum x_i\right)^2}{N}}{N}} = \sqrt{\frac{47,474 - \frac{(650)^2}{9}}{9}} \approx 7.7 \text{ beats/min.}$$

(b) Samples, sample variances, and sample standard deviations will vary.

(c) Answers will vary.

27. (a) We use the computational formula: $\sum x_i = 157$; $\sum x_i^2 = 2107$; $N = 18$;

$$\sigma^2 = \frac{\sum x_i^2 - \frac{\left(\sum x_i\right)^2}{N}}{N} = \frac{2107 - \frac{(157)^2}{18}}{18} \approx 41.0 \text{ goals}^2;$$

$$\sigma = \sqrt{\frac{\sum x_i^2 - \frac{\left(\sum x_i\right)^2}{N}}{N}} = \sqrt{\frac{2107 - \frac{(157)^2}{18}}{18}} \approx 6.4 \text{ goals}$$

(b) Samples, sample variances, and sample standard deviations will vary.

(c) Answers will vary.

29. (a) Ethan: $\mu = \dfrac{\sum x_i}{N} = \dfrac{9 + 24 + 8 + 9 + 5 + 8 + 9 + 10 + 8 + 10}{10} = \dfrac{100}{10} = 10 \text{ fish}$;

Range = Largest Data Value – Smallest Data Value = 24 – 5 = 19 fish

Drew: $\mu = \dfrac{\sum x_i}{N} = \dfrac{15 + 2 + 3 + 18 + 20 + 1 + 17 + 2 + 19 + 3}{10} = \dfrac{100}{10} = 10 \text{ fish}$;

Range = Largest Data Value – Smallest Data Value = 20 – 1 = 19 fish

Both fishermen have the same mean and range, so these values do not indicate any differences between their catches per day.

(b) Ethan: $\sum x_i = 100$; $\sum x_i^2 = 1236$; $N = 10$

$$\sigma = \sqrt{\frac{\sum x_i^2 - \frac{\left(\sum x_i\right)^2}{N}}{N}} = \sqrt{\frac{1236 - \frac{(100)^2}{10}}{10}} \approx 4.9 \text{ fish}$$

Drew: $\sum x_i = 100$; $\sum x_i^2 = 1626$; $N = 10$

$$\sigma = \sqrt{\dfrac{\sum x_i^2 - \dfrac{\left(\sum x_i\right)^2}{N}}{N}} = \sqrt{\dfrac{1626 - \dfrac{(100)^2}{10}}{10}} \approx 7.9 \text{ fish}$$

Yes, now there appears to be a difference in the two fishermen's records. Ethan had a more consistent fishing record, which is indicated by the smaller standard deviation.

(c) Answers will vary. One possibility follows: The range is limited as a measure of dispersion because it does not take all of the data values into account. It is obtained by using only the two most extreme data values. Since the standard deviation utilizes all of the data values, it provides a better overall representation of dispersion.

31. Range = Largest Data Value – Smallest Data Value = 73 – 28 = 45.
For the sample variance and sample standard deviation, we use the computational formula:
$\sum x_i = 2045$; $\sum x_i^2 = 109{,}151$; $n = 40$;

$$s^2 = \dfrac{\sum x_i^2 - \dfrac{\left(\sum x_i\right)^2}{n}}{n-1} = \dfrac{109{,}151 - \dfrac{(2045)^2}{40}}{40-1} \approx 118.0;\ s = \sqrt{\dfrac{109{,}151 - \dfrac{(2045)^2}{40}}{40-1}} \approx 10.9$$

33. (a) We use the computational formula: $\sum x_i = 43.71$; $\sum x_i^2 = 38.2887$; $n = 50$;

$$s = \sqrt{\dfrac{\sum x_i^2 - \dfrac{\left(\sum x_i\right)^2}{n}}{n-1}} = \sqrt{\dfrac{38.2887 - \dfrac{(43.71)^2}{50}}{50-1}} \approx 0.04 \text{ g}$$

(b) The histogram is approximately symmetric, so the Empirical Rule is applicable.

(c) Since 0.79 is exactly 2 standard deviations below the mean [0.79 = 0.87 – 2(0.04)] and 0.95 is exactly 2 standard deviations above the mean [0.95 = 0.87 + 2(0.04)], the Empirical Rule predicts that approximately 95% of the M&Ms will weigh between 0.79 and 0.95 grams.

(d) All except 1 of the M&Ms weigh between 0.79 and 0.95 grams. Thus, the actual percentage is 49/50 = 98%.

(e) Since 0.91 is exactly 1 standard deviation above the mean [0.91 = 0.87 + 0.04], the Empirical Rule predicts that 13.5% + 2.35% + 0.15% = 16% of the M&Ms will weigh more than 0.91 grams.

(f) Seven of the M&Ms weigh more than 0.91 grams (not including the ones that weigh exactly 0.91 grams). Thus, the actual percentage is 7/50 = 14%.

35. Car 1: $\sum x_i = 3352$; $\sum x_i^2 = 755{,}712$; $n = 15$

Measures of Center:

$$\overline{x} = \dfrac{\sum x_i}{n} = \dfrac{3352}{15} \approx 223.5 \text{ miles};\quad \text{Mode: none;}$$

$M = 223$ miles (the 8th value in the ordered data)

Measures of Dispersion:

Range = Largest Data Value – Smallest Data Value = 271 – 178 = 93 miles;

$$s^2 = \frac{\sum x_i^2 - \frac{\left(\sum x_i\right)^2}{n}}{n-1} = \frac{755{,}712 - \frac{(3352)^2}{15}}{15-1} \approx 475.1 \text{ miles}^2 ;$$

$$s = \sqrt{\frac{755{,}712 - \frac{(3352)^2}{15}}{15-1}} \approx 21.8 \text{ miles}$$

Car 2: $\sum x_i = 3558$; $\sum x_i^2 = 877{,}654$; $n = 15$

Measures of Center:

$$\bar{x} = \frac{\sum x_i}{n} = \frac{3558}{15} = 237.2 \text{ miles} ; \quad \text{Mode: none;}$$

$M = 230$ miles (the 8th value in the ordered data)

Measures of Dispersion:

Range = Largest Data Value – Smallest Data Value = 326 – 160 = 166 miles;

$$s^2 = \frac{\sum x_i^2 - \frac{\left(\sum x_i\right)^2}{n}}{n-1} = \frac{877{,}654 - \frac{(3558)^2}{15}}{15-1} \approx 2406.9 \text{ miles}^2 ;$$

$$s = \sqrt{\frac{877{,}654 - \frac{(3558)^2}{15}}{15-1}} \approx 49.1 \text{ miles}$$

The distribution for Car 1 is symmetric since the mean and median are approximately equal. The distribution for Car 2 is skewed right slightly since the mean is larger than the median. Both distributions have similar measures of center, but Car 2 has more dispersion which can be seen by its larger range, variance, and standard deviation. This means that the distance Car 1 can be driven on 10 gallons of gas is more consistent. Thus, Car 1 is probably the better car to buy.

37. (a) Financial Stocks: $\sum x_i = 502.9$; $\sum x_i^2 = 9591.0556$; $n = 32$

$$\bar{x} = \frac{\sum x_i}{n} = \frac{502.9}{32} \approx 15.716 ; \quad M = \frac{15.92 + 16.26}{2} = 16.09$$

Energy Stocks: $\sum x_i = 719.4$; $\sum x_i^2 = 21{,}213.3104$; $n = 32$

$$\bar{x} = \frac{\sum x_i}{n} = \frac{719.4}{32} \approx 22.481 ; \quad M = \frac{19.50 + 19.67}{2} = 19.585$$

Energy Stocks have higher mean and median rates of return.

(b) Financial Stocks: $s = \sqrt{\dfrac{\sum x_i^2 - \dfrac{\left(\sum x_i\right)^2}{n}}{n-1}} = \sqrt{\dfrac{9591.0556 - \dfrac{(502.9)^2}{32}}{32-1}} \approx 7.378$

Energy Stocks: $s = \sqrt{\dfrac{\sum x_i^2 - \dfrac{\left(\sum x_i\right)^2}{n}}{n-1}} = \sqrt{\dfrac{21{,}213.3104 - \dfrac{(719.4)^2}{32}}{32-1}} \approx 12.751$

Energy Stocks are riskier since they have a larger standard deviation.

39. (a) Since 70 is exactly 2 standard deviations below the mean [70 = 100 − 2(15)] and 130 is exactly 2 standard deviations above the mean [130 = 100 + 2(15)], the Empirical Rule predicts that approximately 95% of people has an IQ score between 70 and 130.

(b) Since about 95% of people has an IQ score between 70 and 30, then approximately 5% of people has an IQ score either less than 70 or greater than 130.

(c) Approximately 5% / 2 = 2.5% of people has an IQ score greater than 130.

41. (a) Approximately 95% of the data will be within 2 standard deviations of the mean. Now, 325 − 2(30) = 265 and 325 + 2(30) = 385. Thus, about 95% of pairs of kidneys will be between 265 and 385 grams.

(b) Since 235 is exactly 3 standard deviations below the mean [235 = 325 − 3(30)] and 415 is exactly 3 standard deviations above the mean [415 = 325 + 3(30)], the Empirical Rule predicts that about 99.7% of pairs of kidneys weighs between 235 and 415 grams.

(c) Since about 99.7% of pairs of kidneys weighs between 235 and 415 grams, then about 0.3% of pairs of kidneys weighs either less than 235 or more than 415 grams.

(d) Since 295 is exactly 1 standard deviations below the mean [295 = 325 − 30] and 385 is exactly 2 standard deviations above the mean [385 = 325 + 2(30)], the Empirical Rule predicts that approximately 34% + 34% + 13.5% = 81.5% of pairs of kidneys weighs between 295 and 385 grams.

43. (a) By Chebyshev's inequality, at least $\left(1-\dfrac{1}{k^2}\right)\cdot 100\% = \left(1-\dfrac{1}{3^2}\right)\cdot 100\% \approx 88.9\%$ of gasoline prices has prices within 3 standard deviations of the mean.

(b) By Chebyshev's inequality, at least $\left(1-\dfrac{1}{k^2}\right)\cdot 100\% = \left(1-\dfrac{1}{2.5^2}\right)\cdot 100\% = 84\%$ of gasoline prices has prices within $k = 2.5$ standard deviations of the mean. Now, 1.37 − 2.5(0.05) = 1.245 and 1.37 + 2.5(0.05) = 1.495. Thus, the gasoline prices that are within 2.5 standard deviations of the mean are from $1.245 to $1.495.

(c) Since 1.27 is exactly $k = 2$ standard deviations below the mean [1.27 = 1.37 − 2(0.05)] and 1.47 is exactly $k = 2$ standard deviations above the mean [1.47 = 1.37 + 2(0.05)], Chebyshev's theorem predicts that at least $\left(1-\dfrac{1}{k^2}\right)\cdot 100\% = \left(1-\dfrac{1}{2^2}\right)\cdot 100\% = 75\%$ of gas stations has prices between $1.27 and $1.47 per gallon.

66

45. When calculating the variability in team batting averages, we are finding the variability of means. When calculating the variability of all players, we are finding the variability of individuals. Since there is more variability among individuals than among means, the teams will have less variability.

47. Sample size of 5:
   All data recorded correctly: $s \approx 5.3$.
   106 recorded incorrectly as 160: $s \approx 27.9$.
   Sample size of 12:
   All data recorded correctly: $s \approx 14.7$.
   106 recorded incorrectly as 160: $s \approx 22.7$.
   Sample size of 30:
   All data recorded correctly: $s \approx 15.9$.
   106 recorded incorrectly as 160: $s \approx 19.2$.
   As the sample size increases, the impact of the misrecorded data value on the standard deviation decreases.

49. (a) The coefficient of variation for blood pressure before exercise is $\dfrac{14.1}{121} \cdot 100\% = 11.65\%$, while the coefficient of variation for blood pressure after exercise is $\dfrac{18.1}{135.9} \cdot 100\% = 13.32\%$. There is more variability in systolic blood pressure after exercise.

(b) The coefficient of variation for free calcium concentration in the group of people with normal blood pressure is $\dfrac{16.1}{107.9} \cdot 100\% = 14.92\%$, while the coefficient of variation for free calcium concentration in the group of people with high blood pressure is $\dfrac{31.7}{168.2} \cdot 100\% = 18.85\%$. There is more variability in free calcium concentration in the high blood pressure group.

51. (a) Skewness $= \dfrac{3(50-40)}{10} = 3$. The distribution is skewed to the right.

(b) Skewness $= \dfrac{3(100-100)}{15} = 0$. The distribution is perfectly symmetric.

(c) Skewness $= \dfrac{3(400-500)}{120} = -2.5$. The distribution is skewed to the left.

(d) Skewness $= \dfrac{3(0.8742-0.88)}{0.0397} \approx -0.44$. The distribution is slightly skewed to the left.

(e) Skewness $= \dfrac{3(104.136-104)}{6.249} \approx 0.07$. The distribution is symmetric.

3.3 Measures of Central Tendency and Dispersion from Grouped Data

1. When we approximate the mean and standard deviation from grouped data, we assume that all of the data points within each group can be approximated by the midpoint of that group.

3.

Class	Midpoint, x_i	Frequency, f_i	$x_i f_i$	$\overline{x}$	$x_i - \overline{x}$	$(x_i - \overline{x})^2 f_i$
$10-19$	$\dfrac{10+20}{2}=15$	8	120	32.8333	-17.8333	2544.2127
$20-29$	$\dfrac{20+30}{2}=25$	16	400	32.8333	-7.8333	981.7694
$30-39$	35	21	735	32.8333	2.1667	98.5864
$40-49$	45	11	495	32.8333	12.1667	1628.3145
$50-59$	55	4	220	32.8333	22.1667	1965.4504
		$\sum f_i = 60$	$\sum x_i f_i = 1970$			$\sum (x_i - \overline{x})^2 f = 7218.3334$

$$\overline{x} = \frac{\sum x_i f_i}{\sum f_i} = \frac{1970}{60} \approx 32.8333 \approx \$32.83 \;;\;\; s = \sqrt{\frac{\sum (x_i - \overline{x})^2 f}{(\sum f_i) - 1}} = \sqrt{\frac{7218.3334}{60-1}} \approx \$11.06$$

5.

Class	Midpoint, x_i	Frequency, f_i	$x_i f_i$	μ	$x_i - \mu$	$(x_i - \mu)^2 f_i$
$0-9$	$\dfrac{0+10}{2}=5$	31	155	17.3	-12.3	4689.99
$10-19$	$\dfrac{10+20}{2}=15$	39	585	17.3	-2.3	206.31
$20-29$	25	17	425	17.3	7.7	1007.93
$30-39$	35	6	210	17.3	17.7	1879.74
$40-49$	45	4	180	17.3	27.7	3069.16
$50-59$	55	2	110	17.3	37.7	2842.58
$60-69$	65	1	65	17.3	47.7	2275.29
		$\sum f_i = 100$	$\sum x_i f_i = 1730$			$\sum (x_i - \mu)^2 f = 15,971$

$$\mu = \frac{\sum x_i f_i}{\sum f_i} = \frac{1730}{100} = 17.3 \text{ days} \;;\;\; \sigma = \sqrt{\frac{\sum (x_i - \mu)^2 f}{\sum f_i}} = \sqrt{\frac{15,971}{100}} \approx 12.6 \text{ days}$$

7.

Class	Midpoint, x_i	Frequency, f_i (in millions)	$x_i f_i$	μ	$x_i - \mu$	$(x_i - \mu)^2 f_i$
25 – 34	$\dfrac{25+35}{2} = 30$	28.9	867	44.4695	−14.4695	6050.6898
35 – 44	$\dfrac{35+45}{2} = 40$	35.7	1428	44.4695	−4.4695	713.1586
45 – 54	50	35.1	1755	44.4695	5.5305	1073.5837
55 – 64	60	24.7	1482	44.4695	15.5305	5957.5518
		$\sum f_i = 124.4$	$\sum x_i f_i = 5532$			$\sum (x_i - \mu)^2 f = 13,794.9839$

$$\mu = \frac{\sum x_i f_i}{\sum f_i} = \frac{5532}{124.4} \approx 44.4695 \approx 44.5 \text{ yrs} \; ; \; \sigma = \sqrt{\frac{\sum (x_i - \mu)^2 f}{\sum f_i}} = \sqrt{\frac{13,794.9839}{124.4}} \approx 10.5 \text{ yrs}$$

9. (a)

Class	Midpt, x_i	f_i	$x_i f_i$	μ	$x_i - \mu$	$(x_i - \mu)^2 f_i$
50–59	$\dfrac{50+60}{2} = 55$	1	55	80.9350	−25.9350	672.6242
60–69	$\dfrac{60+70}{2} = 65$	308	20,020	80.9350	−15.9350	78,208.6613
70–79	75	1519	113,925	80.9350	5.9350	53,505.5977
80–89	85	1626	138,210	80.9350	4.0650	26,868.3900
90–99	95	503	47,785	80.9350	14.0650	99,505.5851
100–109	105	11	1155	80.9350	24.0650	6370.3665
		$\sum f_i = 3968$	$\sum x_i f_i = 321,150$			$\sum (x_i - \mu)^2 f = 265,131.2248$

$$\mu = \frac{\sum x_i f_i}{\sum f_i} = \frac{321,150}{3968} \approx 80.9350 \approx 80.9°F \; ; \; \sigma = \sqrt{\frac{\sum (x_i - \mu)^2 f}{\sum f_i}} = \sqrt{\frac{265,131.2248}{3968}} \approx 8.2°F$$

(b)

High Temperatures in August in Chicago

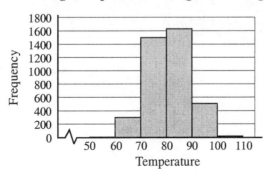

69

(c) By the Empirical Rule, 95% of the observations will be within 2 standard deviations of the mean. Now, $\mu - 2\sigma = 80.9 - 2(8.2) = 64.5$ and $\mu + 2\sigma = 80.9 + 2(8.2) = 97.3$, so 95% of the of days in August will have temperatures between $64.5°F$ and $97.3°F$.

11. (a)

Class	Midpoint, x_i	Freq, f_i	$x_i f_i$	μ	$x_i - \mu$	$(x_i - \mu)^2 f_i$
15 – 19	$\dfrac{15+20}{2} = 17.5$	93	1627.5	32.2721	−14.7721	20,293.99
20 – 24	$\dfrac{20+25}{2} = 22.5$	511	11,497.5	32.2721	−9.7721	48,787.40
25 – 29	27.5	1628	44,770	32.2721	−4.7721	37,074.34
30 – 34	32.5	2832	92,040	32.2721	0.2279	147.09
35 – 39	37.5	1843	69,112.5	32.2721	5.2279	50,370.92
40 – 44	42.5	377	16,022.5	32.2721	10.2279	39,437.95
		$\sum f_i = 7284$	$\sum x_i f_i = 235,070$			$\sum (x_i - \mu)^2 f = 196,111.69$

$$\mu = \frac{\sum x_i f_i}{\sum f_i} = \frac{235,070}{7284} \approx 32.2721 \approx 32.3 \text{ yr}; \quad \sigma = \sqrt{\frac{\sum (x_i - \mu)^2 f}{\sum f_i}} = \sqrt{\frac{196,111.69}{7284}} \approx 5.2 \text{ yr}$$

(b)

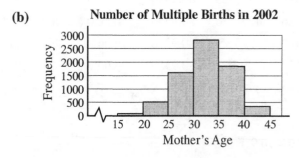

Number of Multiple Births in 2002

(c) By the Empirical Rule, 95% of the observations will be within 2 standard deviations of the mean. Now, $\mu - 2\sigma = 32.3 - 2(5.2) = 21.9$ and $\mu + 2\sigma = 32.3 + 2(5.2) = 42.7$, so 95% of mothers of multiple births will be between 21.9 and 42.7 years of age.

13.

Class	Midpt, x_i	Freq, f_i	$x_i f_i$	$\bar{x}$	$x_i - \bar{x}$	$(x_i - \bar{x})^2 f_i$
20 – 29	$\dfrac{20+30}{2} = 25$	1	25	51.75	−26.75	715.5625
30 – 39	$\dfrac{30+40}{2} = 35$	6	210	51.75	−16.75	1683.375
40 – 49	45	10	450	51.75	−6.75	455.625
50 – 59	55	14	770	51.75	3.25	147.875
60 – 69	65	6	390	51.75	13.25	1053.375
70 – 79	75	3	225	51.75	23.25	1621.6875
		$\sum f_i = 40$	$\sum x_i f_i = 2070$			$\sum (x_i - \bar{x})^2 f = 5677.5$

$$\bar{x} = \frac{\sum x_i f_i}{\sum f_i} = \frac{2070}{40} = 51.75 \approx 51.8 \quad \text{(compared to 51.1 using the raw data.);}$$

$$s = \sqrt{\frac{\sum (x_i - \bar{x})^2 f}{\left(\sum f_i\right) - 1}} = \sqrt{\frac{5677.5}{40 - 1}} \approx 12.1 \quad \text{(compared to 10.9 using the raw data.)}$$

15. $\text{GPA} = \bar{x}_w = \dfrac{\sum w_i x_i}{\sum w_i x_i} = \dfrac{5(3) + 3(4) + 4(4) + 3(2)}{5 + 3 + 4 + 3} = \dfrac{49}{15} \approx 3.27$

17. Cost per pound $= \bar{x}_w = \dfrac{\sum w_i x_i}{\sum w_i x_i} = \dfrac{4(\$3.50) + 3(\$2.75) + 2(\$2.25)}{4 + 3 + 2} \approx \$2.97 / \text{lb}$

19. (a)

Class	Midpt, x_i	Freq, f_i	$x_i f_i$	μ	$x_i - \mu$	$(x_i - \mu)^2 f_i$
0 – 9	5	20,225	101,125	35.6058	−30.6058	18,945,060.7
10 – 19	15	21,375	320,625	35.6058	−20.6058	9,075,803.5
20 – 29	25	20,437	510,925	35.6058	−10.6058	2,298,814.9
30 – 39	35	21,176	741,160	35.6058	−0.6058	7,771.5
40 – 49	45	22,138	996,210	35.6058	9.3942	1,953,700.5
50 – 59	55	16,974	933,570	35.6058	19.3942	6,384,515.4
60 – 69	65	10,289	668,785	35.6058	29.3942	8,889,891.4
70 – 79	75	6,923	519,225	35.6058	39.3942	10,743,824.4
80 – 89	85	3,053	259,505	35.6058	49.3942	7,448,669.7
90 – 99	95	436	41,420	35.6058	59.3942	1,538,064.6
		$\sum f_i = 143,026$	$\sum x_i f_i = 5,092,550$			$\sum (x_i - \mu)^2 f = 67,286,116.6$

$$\mu = \frac{\sum x_i f_i}{\sum f_i} = \frac{5,092,550}{143,026} \approx 35.6058 \approx 35.6 \text{ yr}; \quad \sigma = \sqrt{\frac{\sum (x_i - \mu)^2 f}{\sum f_i}} = \sqrt{\frac{67,286,116.6}{143,026}} \approx 21.7 \text{ yr}$$

(b)

Class	Midpt, x_i	Freq, f_i	$x_i f_i$	μ	$x_i - \mu$	$(x_i - \mu)^2 f_i$
0 – 9	5	19,319	96,595	38.0872	−33.0872	21,149,722.6
10 – 19	15	20,295	304,425	38.0872	−23.0872	10,817,616.6
20 – 29	25	19,459	486,475	38.0872	−13.0872	3,332,836.4
30 – 39	35	20,936	732,760	38.0872	−3.0872	199,536.9
40 – 49	45	22,586	1,016,370	38.0872	6.9128	1,079,312.8
50 – 59	55	17,864	982,520	38.0872	16.9128	5,109,868.6
60 – 69	65	11,563	751,595	38.0872	26.9128	8,375,067.1
70 – 79	75	9,121	684,075	38.0872	36.9128	12,427,862.3
80 – 89	85	5,367	456,195	38.0872	46.9128	11,811,751.5
90 – 99	95	1,215	115,425	38.0872	56.9128	3,935,466.2
		$\sum f_i = 147,725$	$\sum x_i f_i = 5,626,435$			$\sum (x_i - \mu)^2 f = 78,239,041.0$

$$\mu = \frac{\sum x_i f_i}{\sum f_i} = \frac{5,626,435}{147,725} \approx 38.0872 \approx 38.1 \text{ yr}; \quad \sigma = \sqrt{\frac{\sum (x_i - \mu)^2 f}{\sum f_i}} = \sqrt{\frac{78,239,041}{147,725}} \approx 23.0 \text{ yr}$$

(c) & (d) Females have both a higher mean age and more dispersion in age.

21.

Class	Frequency, f	Cumulative Frequency, CF
0 – 9	31	31
10 – 19	39	70
20 – 29	17	87
30 – 39	6	93
40 – 49	4	97
50 – 59	2	99
60 – 69	1	100

The total frequency is 100, so the position of the median is $\dfrac{n}{2} = \dfrac{100}{2} = 50$, which is in the

second class, 10 – 19. Then $M = L + \dfrac{\dfrac{n}{2} - CF}{f} \cdot i = 10 + \dfrac{50 - 31}{39}(20 - 10) \approx 14.9$ days .

23.

Class	Frequency, f (millions)	Cumulative Frequency, CF (millions)
25 – 34	28.9	28.9
35 – 44	35.7	64.6
45 – 54	35.1	99.7
55 – 64	24.7	124.4

The total frequency is 124.4 (million), so the position of the median is

$\dfrac{n}{2} = \dfrac{124.4}{2} = 62.2$, which is in the second class, 35 – 44. Then

$$M = L + \frac{\dfrac{n}{2} - CF}{f} \cdot i = 35 + \frac{62.2 - 28.9}{35.7}(45 - 35) \approx 44.3 \text{ years}.$$

25. From the table in Problem 5, the modal class (highest frequency class) is 10 – 19 days.

27. From the table in Problem 7, the modal class (highest frequency class) is 25 – 44 years.

29. **(a)** Answers will vary. One possibility follows: Many colleges do not permit students under age 16 to enroll in courses, so a reasonable midpoint to use would be 17.

(b) Answers will vary. One possibility follows: Since it is not likely that many students would be over 70 years old, a reasonable midpoint would be 60.

(c) Answers will vary depending on choices for midpoints in parts (a) and (b). Using the choices midpoints from above:

Class	Midpoint, x_i	Freq, f_i	$x_i f_i$
Less than 18	17	139	2363
18 – 19	$\dfrac{18+20}{2} = 19$	4089	77,691
20 – 21	$\dfrac{20+22}{2} = 21$	3357	70,497
22 – 24	$\dfrac{22+25}{2} = 23.5$	1661	39,033.5
25 – 29	$\dfrac{25+30}{2} = 27.5$	470	12,925
30 – 34	$\dfrac{30+35}{2} = 32.5$	145	4712.5
35 – 39	$\dfrac{35+40}{2} = 37.5$	95	3562.5
40 – 49	$\dfrac{40+50}{2} = 45$	117	5265
50 and above	60	21	1260
		$\sum f_i = 10,094$	$\sum x_i f_i = 217,309.5$

$$\mu = \frac{\sum x_i f_i}{\sum f_i} = \frac{217,309.5}{10,094} \approx 21.5 \text{ years}.$$ This estimate is a little higher than the actual mean age of 20.9 years.

3.4 Measures of Position

1. Answers will vary. The kth percentile of a set of data is the value which divides the bottom $k\%$ of the data from the top $(100-k)\%$ of the data. For example, if a data value lies at the 60th percentile, then approximately 60% of the data is below it and approximately 40% is above this value.

3. A four-star mutual fund is in the top 40% but not in the top 20% of its investment class. That is, it is above the bottom 60% but below the top 20% of the ranked funds.

5. To qualify for Mensa, one needs to have an IQ that is in the top 2% of people.

7. z-score for the 34-week gestation baby: $z = \dfrac{x-\mu}{\sigma} = \dfrac{2400-2600}{670} \approx -0.30$

   z-score for the 40-week gestation baby: $z = \dfrac{x-\mu}{\sigma} = \dfrac{3300-3500}{475} \approx -0.42$

   The weight of a 34-week gestation baby is 0.30 standard deviations below the mean, while the weight of a 40-week gestation baby is 0.42 standard deviations below the mean. Thus, the 40-week gestation baby weighs less relative to the gestation period.

9. z-score for the 75-inch man: $z = \dfrac{x-\mu}{\sigma} = \dfrac{75-69.6}{2.7} = 2$

   z-score for the 70-inch woman: $z = \dfrac{x-\mu}{\sigma} = \dfrac{70-64.1}{2.7} \approx 2.27$

   The height of the 75-inch man is 2 standard deviations above the mean, while the height of a 70-inch woman is 2.27 standard deviations above the mean. Thus, the 70-inch woman is relatively taller than the 75-inch man.

11. z-score for Jake Peavy: $z = \dfrac{x-\mu}{\sigma} = \dfrac{2.27-4.198}{0.772} \approx -2.50$

    z-score for Johann Santana: $z = \dfrac{x-\mu}{\sigma} = \dfrac{2.61-4.338}{0.785} \approx -2.20$

    Jake Peavy's 2004 ERA was 2.50 standard deviations below the mean, while Johann Santana's 2004 ERA was 2.20 standard deviations below the mean. Thus, Peavy had the better year relative to his peers.

13. The data provided in Table 17 are already listed in ascending order.

(a) $i = \left(\dfrac{k}{100}\right)(n+1) = \left(\dfrac{40}{100}\right)(51+1) = 20.8$. Since $i = 20.8$ is not an integer, we average

the 20th and 21st data values: $P_{40} = \dfrac{325.5 + 333.2}{2} = 329.35$. This means that

approximately 40% of the states have violent crime rates less than 329.35 crimes per 100,000 population, and approximately 60% of the states have violent crime rates more than this.

(b) $i = \left(\dfrac{k}{100}\right)(n+1) = \left(\dfrac{95}{100}\right)(51+1) = 49.4$. Since $i = 49.4$ is not an integer, we average

the 49th and 50th data values: $P_{95} = \dfrac{730.2 + 793.5}{2} = 761.85$. This means that

approximately 95% of the states have violent crime rates less than 761.85 crimes per 100,000 population, and approximately 5% of the states have violent crime rates more than this.

(c) $i = \left(\dfrac{k}{100}\right)(n+1) = \left(\dfrac{10}{100}\right)(51+1) = 5.2$. Since $i = 5.2$ is not an integer, we average the

5th and 6th data values: $P_{10} = \dfrac{173.4 + 221.0}{2} = 197.2$. This means that approximately

10% of the states have violent crime rates less than 197.2 crimes per 100,000 population, and approximately 90% of the states have violent crime rates more than this.

(d) Of the 51 states, 48 have a violent crime rate less than Florida's violent crime rate.

Percentile rank of Florida $= \left(\dfrac{48}{51}\right) \cdot 100 \approx 94$. Florida's violent crime rate is at the 94th

percentile. This means that approximately 94% of the states have violent crime rates that are less than that of Florida, and approximately 6% of the states have violent crime rates that are larger than that of Florida.

(e) Of the 51 states, 40 have a violent crime rate less than California's violent crime rate.

Percentile rank of California $= \left(\dfrac{40}{51}\right) \cdot 100 \approx 78$. California's violent crime rate is at the

78th percentile. This means that approximately 78% of the states have violent crime rates that are less than that of California, and approximately 22% of the states have violent crime rates that are larger than that of California.

15. (a) Computing the sample mean ($\bar{x}$) and sample standard deviation (s) for the data yields $\bar{x} = 3.9935$ inches and $s \approx 1.7790$ inches. Using these values as approximations for

the μ and σ, the z-score for $x = 0.97$ inches $z = \dfrac{x - \mu}{\sigma} \approx \dfrac{0.97 - 3.9935}{1.7790} \approx -1.70$. The

rainfall in 1971 (0.97 inches) is 1.70 standard deviations below the mean.

(b) The data provided are already listed in ascending order. There are $n = 20$ data points.

The index for the first quartile is $i = \left(\dfrac{25}{100}\right)(20+1) = 5.25$. Since $i = 5.2$ is not an

integer, we average the 5th and 6th data values: $Q_1 = \dfrac{2.47+2.78}{2} = 2.625$ inches. The

index for the second quartile is $i = \left(\dfrac{50}{100}\right)(20+1) = 10.5$. Since $i = 10.5$ is not an

integer, we average the 10th and 11th data values: $Q_2 = \dfrac{3.97+4.0}{2} = 3.985$ inches. The

index for the third quartile is $i = \left(\dfrac{75}{100}\right)(20+1) = 15.75$. Since $i = 15.75$ is not an

integer, we average the 15th and 16th data values: $Q_3 = \dfrac{5.22+5.50}{2} = 5.36$ inches.

(c) $\text{IQR} = Q_3 - Q_1 = 5.36 - 2.625 = 2.735$ inches

(d) Lower fence $= Q_1 - 1.5(\text{IQR}) = 2.625 - 1.5(2.735) = -1.478$ inches.

Upper fence $= Q_3 + 1.5(\text{IQR}) = 5.36 + 1.5(2.735) = 9.463$ inches.

According to this criterion, there are no outliers.

17. (a) Computing the sample mean ($\bar{x}$) and sample standard deviation (s) for the data yields $\bar{x} \approx 15.9227$ mg/L and $s \approx 7.3837$ mg/L. Using these values as approximations for the

μ and σ, the z-score for $x = 20.46$ mg/L is $z = \dfrac{x-\mu}{\sigma} \approx \dfrac{20.46-15.9227}{7.3837} \approx 0.61$. The

organic concentration of 20.46 mg/L is 0.61 standard deviations above the mean.

(b) There are $n = 33$ data points, and we must put them in ascending order:

5.2, 5.29, 5.3, 6.51, 7.4, 8.09, 8.81, 9.72, 10.3, 11.4, 11.9, 14, 14.86, 14.86, 14.9, 15.35, 15.42, 15.72, 15.91, 16.51, 16.87, 17.5, 17.9, 18.3, 19.8, 20.46, 20.46, 22.49, 22.74, 27.1, 29.8, 30.91, 33.67

The index for the first quartile is $i = \left(\dfrac{25}{100}\right)(33+1) = 8.5$. Since $i = 8.5$ is not an

integer, we average the 8th and 9th data values: $Q_1 = \dfrac{9.72+10.3}{2} = 10.01$ mg/L. The

index for the second quartile is $i = \left(\dfrac{50}{100}\right)(33+1) = 17$. Since $i = 17$ is an integer, the

17th data value is the second quartile: $Q_2 = 15.42$ mg/L. The index for the third

quartile is $i = \left(\dfrac{75}{100}\right)(33+1) = 25.5$. Since $i = 25.5$ is not an integer, we average the

25th and 26th data values: $Q_3 = \dfrac{19.8+20.46}{2} = 20.13$ mg/L.

(c) $\text{IQR} = Q_3 - Q_1 = 20.13 - 10.1 = 10.12$ mg/L

(d) Lower fence $= Q_1 - 1.5(\text{IQR}) = 10.01 - 1.5(10.12) = -5.17$ mg/L.

Upper fence $= Q_3 + 1.5(\text{IQR}) = 20.13 + 1.5(10.12) = 35.31$ mg/L.

According to this criterion, there are no outliers.

19. The first and third quartiles are $Q_1 = 433$ minutes and $Q_3 = 489.5$ minutes.

Upper fence $= Q_3 + 1.5(\text{IQR}) = 489.5 + 1.5(489.5 - 433) = 574.25$ minutes.

The cutoff point is 574 minutes. If more minutes are used, the customer is contacted.

21. (a) The first and third quartiles are $Q_1 = \$67$ and $Q_3 = \$479$.

Lower fence $= Q_1 - 1.5(\text{IQR}) = 67 - 1.5(479 - 67) = -\$551$

Upper fence $= Q_3 + 1.5(\text{IQR}) = 479 + 1.5(479 - 67) = \$1097$.

Therefore, $12,777 is an outlier because it is greater than the upper fence.

(b)

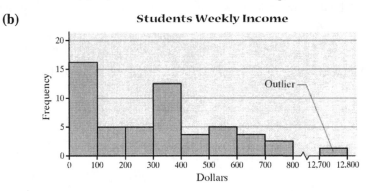

Students Weekly Income

(c) Answers will vary. One possibility is that a student may have provided his or her annual income instead of his or her weekly income.

23.

Pulse	z-score	
76	0.49	
60	− 1.59	
60	− 1.59	
81	1.14	
72	− 0.03	
80	1.01	
80	1.01	
68	− 0.55	
73	0.10	
μ 72.2	0.0	= mean of the z-scores
σ 7.671	1.00	= standard deviation of the z-scores

3.5 The Five-Number Summary and Boxplots

1. The median and interquartile range are better measures of central tendency and dispersion if the data are skewed or if the data contain outliers.

3. **(a)** The median is to the left of the center of the box and the right line is substantially longer than the left line, so the distribution is skewed right.

   (b) Reading the boxplot, the five-number summary is approximately: 0, 1, 3, 6, 16.

5. The data in ascending order are as follows:
   42, 43, 46, 46, 47, 48, 49, 49, 50, 50, $\boxed{51}$, 51, 51, 51, 52, 52, 54, 54, 54, 54, 54, $\boxed{55}$, 55, 55, 55, 56, 56, 56, 57, 57, 57, 57, $\boxed{58}$, 60, 61, 61, 61, 62, 64, 64, 65, 68, 69
   The smallest number (youngest president) in the data set is 42. The largest number in the data set is 69. The first quartile is $Q_1 = 51$ (the 11th data point). The median is $M = 55$ (the 22nd data point). The third quartile is $Q_3 = 58$ (the 33rd data point). The five-number summary is 42, 51, 55, 58, 69.
   The upper and lower fences are: Lower fence $= Q_1 - 1.5(\text{IQR}) = 51 - 1.5(58 - 51) = 40.5$;
   Upper fence $= Q_3 + 1.5(\text{IQR}) = 58 + 1.5(58 - 51) = 68.5$. Thus, 69 is an outlier.

   Age of Presidents at Inauguration

   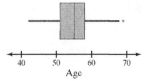

   The median is near the center of the box and the horizontal lines are approximately the same in length, so the distribution is symmetric.

7. The data is ascending order are as follows:
   1, 3, 3, 3, 3, 4, 4, 4, 5, $\boxed{7}$, 7, 7, 9, 10, 10, 10, 12, 13, 14, $\boxed{15}$, 16, 17, 17, 17, 17, 18, 19, 19, 21, $\boxed{22}$, 23, 25, 27, 27, 29, 32, 35, 36, 45
   The smallest number in the data set is 1. The largest number in the data set is 45. The first quartile is $Q_1 = 7$ (the 10th data point). The median is $M = 15$ (the 20th data point). The third quartile is $Q_3 = 22$ (the 30th data point). The five-number summary is 1, 7, 15, 22, 45. The upper and lower fences are:
   Lower fence $= Q_1 - 1.5(\text{IQR}) = 7 - 1.5(22 - 7) = -15.5$;
   Upper fence $= Q_3 + 1.5(\text{IQR}) = 22 + 1.5(22 - 7) = 44.5$. Thus, 45 is an outlier.

   Super Bowl Point Spreads

   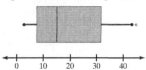

   The median is to the left of the center of the box and the right line is substantially longer than the left line, so the distribution is skewed right.

78

9. The data is ascending order are as follows:

0.598, 0.600, 0.600, 0.601, 0.602, 0.603, 0.605, 0.605, 0.605, 0.606, 0.607, 0.607, 0.608,
0.608, 0.608, 0.608, 0.608, 0.609, 0.610, 0.610, 0.610, 0.610, 0.611, 0.611, 0.612

The smallest number in the data set is 0.598. The largest is 0.612. The first quartile is

$Q_1 = \dfrac{0.603 + 0.605}{2} = 0.604$ (the mean of the 6th and 7th data points). The median is

$M = 0.608$ (the 13th data point). The third quartile is $Q_3 = \dfrac{0.610 + 0.610}{2} = 0.610$ (the mean

of the 19th and 20th data points). The five-number summary is 0.598, 0.604, 0.608, 0.610,
0.612. The upper and lower fences are:

Lower fence $= Q_1 - 1.5(IQR) = 0.604 - 1.5(0.610 - 0.604) = 0.595$;

Upper fence $= Q_3 + 1.5(IQR) = 0.610 + 1.5(0.610 - 0.604) = 0.619$.

Thus, there are no outliers.

Weight (in grams) of Tylenol Tablets

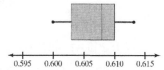

The median is to the right of the center of the box, so the distribution is skewed left.
Answers will vary concerning the source of variability in weight.

11. (a) The data is ascending order are as follows:

28, 32, 33, 35, 36, 38, 39, 44, 44, 45, 45, 46, 46, 48, 48, 48, 49, 50, 51, 51, 51, 52, 52,
53, 53, 54, 55, 56, 56, 58, 59, 60, 60, 62, 63, 66, 69, 70, 70, 73

The smallest number in the data set is 28. The largest number in the data set is 73. The

first quartile is $Q_1 = \dfrac{45 + 45}{2} = 45$ (the mean of the 10th and 11th data points). The

median is $M = \dfrac{51 + 51}{2} = 51$ (the mean of the 20th and 21st data points). The third

quartile is $Q_3 = \dfrac{58 + 59}{2} = 58.5$ (the 30th and 31st data points). The five-number

summary is 28, 45, 51, 58.5, 73.

(b) Lower fence $= Q_1 - 1.5(IQR) = 45 - 1.5(58.5 - 45) = 24.75$;

Upper fence $= Q_3 + 1.5(IQR) = 58.5 + 1.5(58.5 - 45) = 78.75$. There are no outliers.

Serum HDL Cholesterol Level

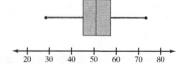

(c) The median is near the center of the box and the horizontal lines are approximately equal in length, so the distribution is symmetric. This is confirmed by the histogram.

(d) Since the distribution is symmetric and contains no outliers, the mean and standard deviation should be reported as the measures of central tendency and dispersion.

13. (a) The data is ascending order are as follows:

0, 0, 0, 0, 0, 0, 0, 0.41, 0.62, 0.64, 0.67, 0.89, 0.94, 1.05, 1.06, 1.15, 1.22, 1.35, 1.68, 1.7, 1.7, 2.04, 2.07, 2.16, 2.38, 2.45, 2.59, 2.83

The smallest number in the data set is 0. The largest number in the data set is 2.83.

The first quartile is $Q_1 = \dfrac{0 + 0.41}{2} = 0.205$ (the mean of the 7th and 8th data points). The

median is $M = \dfrac{1.05 + 1.06}{2} = 1.055$ (the mean of the 14th and 15th data points). The third

quartile is $Q_3 = \dfrac{1.7 + 2.04}{2} = 1.87$ (the 21st and 22nd data points). The five-number

summary is 0, 0.205, 1.055, 1.87, 2.83.

(b) Lower fence $= Q_1 - 1.5(IQR) = 0.205 - 1.5(1.87 - 0.205) = -2.2925$;

Upper fence $= Q_3 + 1.5(IQR) = 1.87 + 1.5(1.87 - 0.205) = 4.3675$.

Thus, there are no outliers.

Dividend Yield

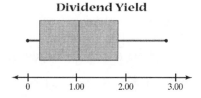

(c) The right line is substantially longer than the left line, so the distribution is skewed right. This is confirmed by the histogram.

(d) Since the distribution is skewed, the median and interquartile range should be reported as the measures of central tendency and dispersion.

15. The data in ascending order are:

Keebler: 20, 20, 21, 21, 21, 22, 23, 24, 24, 24, 25, 25, 26, 28, 28, 28, 28, 29, 31, 32, 33

Store Brand: 16, 17, 18, 21, 21, 21, 23, 23, 24, 24, 24, 25, 26, 26, 27, 27, 28, 29, 30, 31, 33

Since both sets of data contain $n = 21$ data points, the quartiles are in the same positions for both sets. Namely, the first quartile is the mean of the 5th and 6th data points, the median is the 11th data point, and the third quartile is the mean of the 16th and 17th data points.

The five-number summaries are:

Keebler: 20, 21.5, 25, 28, 33

Store Brand: 16, 21, 24, 27.5, 33

The fences for Keebler Chips Deluxe Chocolate Chip Cookies are:

Lower fence $= 21.5 - 1.5(28 - 21.5) = 11.75$; Upper fence $= 28 + 1.5(28 - 21.5) = 37.75$

80

The fences for the store brand chocolate chip cookies are:

Lower fence $= 21 - 1.5(27.5 - 21) = 11.25$;   Upper fence $= 27.5 + 1.5(27.5 - 21) = 37.25$

So, neither data set has any outliers.

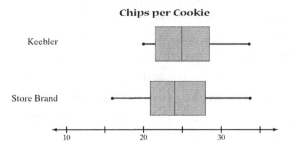

Chips per Cookie

Keebler appears to have both a higher number of chocolate chips per cookie and the more consistent number of chips per cookie.

17. The data in ascending order are:

McGwire: 340, 341, 350, 350, 360, 360, 360, 369, 370, 370, 370, 370, 377, 380, 380, 380, 380, 380, 385, 385, 388, 390, 390, 390, 390, 398, 400, 400, 409, 410, 410, 410, 410, 410, 420, 420, 420, 420, 420, 423, 425, 430, 430, 430, 430, 430, 430, 430, 440, 440, 440, 450, 450, 450, 450, 452, 458, 460, 460, 461, 470, 470, 470, 478, 480, 500, 510, 510, 527, 550

The smallest number in the data set is 340. The largest number is 550. The first quartile is $Q_1 = 380$ (the mean of the 17th and 18th data points). The median is $M = 420$ (the mean of the 35th and 36th data points). The third quartile is $Q_3 = 450$ (the mean of the 53rd and 54th data points). The five-number summary for Mark McGwire is 340, 380, 420, 450, 550. Lower fence $= 380 - 1.5(450 - 380) = 275$; Upper fence $= 450 + 1.5(450 - 380) = 555$. Thus, there are no outliers.

Sosa: 340, 344, 350, 350, 350, 360, 364, 364, 365, 366, 368, 370, 370, 370, 370, 370, 371, 380, 380, 380, 380, 380, 380, 388, 390, 390, 400, 400, 400, 400, 400, 405, 410, 410, 410, 410, 410, 414, 415, 420, 420, 420, 420, 420, 420, 420, 420, 430, 430, 430, 430, 430, 430, 433, 433, 434, 434, 440, 440, 440, 450, 460, 480, 480, 482, 500,

The smallest number in the data set is 340. The largest number is 500. The first quartile is $Q_1 = 370.5$ (the mean of the 16th and 17th data points). The median is $M = 410$ (the mean of the 33rd and 34th data points). The third quartile is $Q_3 = 430$ (the mean of the 50th and 51st data points). The five-number summary for Sammy Sosa is 340, 370.5, 410, 430, 500. Lower fence $= 370.5 - 1.5(430 - 370.5) = 281.25$;

Upper fence $= 430 + 1.5(430 - 370.5) = 519.25$. Thus, there are no outliers.

(**Note:** The TI-84 gives $Q_1 = 371$ because the calculator uses a different, but acceptable, procedure for determining the quartiles. In most cases, the different procedures produce the same results, but in this case, they differ slightly.)

Bonds: 320, 320, 347, 350, 360, 360, 360, 361, 365, 370, 370, 375, 375, 375, 375, 380, 380, 380, 380, 380, 385, 390, 390, 391, 394, 396, 400, 400, 400, 400, 404, 405, 410, 410, 410, 410, 410, 410, 410, 410, 410, 410, 411, 415, 415, 416, 417, 417, 420, 420, 420, 420, 420, 420, 420, 420, 429, 430, 430, 430, 430, 430, 435, 435, 436, 440, 440, 440, 440, 442, 450, 454, 488

The smallest number in the data set is 320. The largest number is 488. The first quartile is $Q_1 = 380$ (the mean of the 18th and 19th data points). The median is $M = 410$ (the 37th data point). The third quartile is $Q_3 = 420$ (the mean of the 55th and 56th data points). The five-number summary for Barry Bonds is 320, 380, 410, 420, 488.

Lower fence $= 380 - 1.5(420 - 380) = 320$; Upper fence $= 420 + 1.5(420 - 380) = 480$.

Thus, 488 is an outlier.

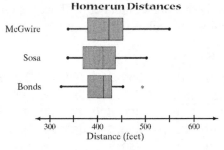

Homerun Distances

Mark McGwire appears to have longer distances. Barry Bonds appears to have the most consistent distances.

Chapter 3 Review Exercises

1. **(a)** $\bar{x} = \dfrac{\sum x}{n} = \dfrac{7925.1}{10} = 792.51$ m/s; $M = \dfrac{792.4 + 792.4}{2} = 792.4$ m/s

   Data in order: 789.6, 791.4, 791.7, 792.3, 792.4, 792.4, 793.1, 793.8, 794.0, 794.4

   (b) Range = Largest Data Value – Smallest Data Value = $974.4 - 789.6 = 4.8$ m/s.

Data, x_i	Sample Mean, $\bar{x}$	Deviations, $x_i - \bar{x}$	Squared Deviations, $(x_i - \bar{x})^2$
793.8	792.51	$793.8 - 792.51 = 1.29$	$1.29^2 = 1.6641$
793.1	792.51	$793.1 - 792.51 = 0.59$	$0.59^2 = 0.3481$
792.4	792.51	$792.4 - 792.51 = -0.11$	$(-0.11)^2 = 0.0121$
794.0	792.51	$7934.0792.51 = 1.49$	$1.49^2 = 2.2201$
791.4	792.51	$791.4 - 792.51 = -1.11$	$(-1.11)^2 = 1.2321$
792.4	792.51	$792.4 - 792.51 = -0.11$	$(-0.11)^2 = 0.0121$
791.7	792.51	$791.7 - 792.51 = -0.81$	$(-0.81)^2 = 0.6561$
792.3	792.51	$792.3 - 792.51 = -0.21$	$(-0.21)^2 = 0.0441$
789.6	792.51	$789.6 - 792.51 = -2.91$	$(-2.91)^2 = 8.4681$
794.4	792.51	$794.4 - 792.51 = 1.89$	$1.89^2 = 3.5721$
$\sum x = 7925.1$		$\sum(x_i - \bar{x}) = 0$	$\sum(x_i - \bar{x})^2 = 18.2290$

$$s^2 = \frac{\sum (x_i - \bar{x})^2}{n-1} = \frac{18.22904}{10-1} \approx 2.03 \ (m/s)^2 ; \quad s = \sqrt{\frac{\sum (x_i - \bar{x})^2}{n-1}} = \sqrt{\frac{18.22904}{10-1}} \approx 1.42 \ m/s .$$

3. (a) $\bar{x} = \frac{\sum x}{n} = \frac{91,610}{9} \approx 10,178.8889 \approx \$10,178.89 ; \quad M = \$9,980$

Data in order: 5500, 7200, 7889, 8998, $\boxed{9980}$, 10995, 12999, 13999, 14050

(b) Range = Largest Data Value – Smallest Data Value $= 14,050 - 5,500 = \$8,550$.

Data, x_i	Sample Mean, $\bar{x}$	Deviations, $x_i - \bar{x}$	Squared Deviations, $(x_i - \bar{x})^2$
14,050	10,178.8889	3871.1111	14,985,501.1
13,999	10,178.8889	3820.1111	14,593,248.8
12,999	10,178.8889	2820.1111	7,953,026.6
10,995	10,178.8889	816.1111	666,037.3
9,980	10,178.8889	−198.8889	39,556.8
8,998	10,178.8889	−1180.8889	1,394,498.6
7,889	10,178.8889	−2289.8889	5,243,591.2
7,200	10,178.8889	−2978.8889	8,873,779.1
5,550	10,178.8889	−4678.8889	21,892,001.3
$\sum x = 91,610$		$\sum (x_i - \bar{x}) = 0$	$\sum (x_i - \bar{x})^2 = 75,641,240.9$

$$s = \sqrt{\frac{\sum (x_i - \bar{x})^2}{n-1}} = \sqrt{\frac{75,641,240.9}{9-1}} \approx \$3,074.92 .$$

(c) $\bar{x} = \frac{\sum x}{n} = \frac{118,610}{9} \approx 13,178.8889 \approx \$13,178.89$

Data in order: 5500, 7200, 7889, 8998, $\boxed{9980}$, 10995, 12999, 13999, 41050
$M = \$9,980$; Range $= 41,050 - 5,500 = \$35,550$.

Data, x_i	Sample Mean, $\bar{x}$	Deviations, $x_i - \bar{x}$	Squared Deviations, $(x_i - \bar{x})^2$
41,050	13,178.8889	27,871.1111	776,798,833.9
13,999	13,178.8889	820.1111	672,582.2
12,999	13,178.8889	−179.8889	32,360.0
10,995	13,178.8889	−2183.8889	4,769,370.7
9,980	13,178.8889	−3198.8889	10,232,890.1
8,998	13,178.8889	−4180.8889	17,479,831.9
7,889	13,178.8889	−5289.8889	27,982,924.5
7,200	13,178.8889	−5978.8889	35,747,112.4
5,550	13,178.8889	−7678.8889	58,965,334.7
$\sum x = 118,610$		$\sum (x_i - \bar{x}) = 0$	$\sum (x_i - \bar{x})^2 = 932,681,240.9$

$$s = \sqrt{\frac{\sum (x_i - \bar{x})^2}{n-1}} = \sqrt{\frac{932,681,240.9}{9-1}} \approx \$10,797.46 .$$

The mean, range, and standard deviation are all changed considerably by the incorrectly entered data value. The median does not change. The median is resistant.

5. (a) $\mu = \dfrac{\sum x}{N} = \dfrac{933}{16} \approx 58.3$ years

Data in order: 44, 46, 51, 55, 56, 56, 56, 58, 59, 62, 62, 62, 64, 65, 68, 69

$M = \dfrac{58+59}{2} = 58.5$ years

The data is bimodal: 56 years and 62 years. Both have frequencies of 3.

(b) Range = 69 − 44 = 25 years
To calculate the population standard deviation, we use the computational formula:

$$\sigma = \sqrt{\dfrac{\sum x_i^2 - \dfrac{\left(\sum x_i\right)^2}{N}}{N}} = \sqrt{\dfrac{55{,}169 - \dfrac{(933)^2}{16}}{16}}$$

≈ 6.9 years

(c) Answers will vary depending on samples selected.

Data value, x_i	Data value squared, x_i^2
44	1936
56	3136
51	2601
46	2116
59	3481
56	3136
58	3364
55	3025
65	4225
64	4096
68	4624
69	4761
56	3136
62	3844
62	3844
62	3844
$\sum x_i = 933$	$\sum x_i^2 = 55{,}169$

7. (a) To find the mean, we determine $\sum x_i = 78$ and $n = 36$, so $\bar{x} = \dfrac{78}{36} \approx 2.2$ children .

To find the median, we put the data in order and find the mean of the 18th and 19th data values: $M = \dfrac{2+3}{2} = 2.5$ children .

(b) Range = 4 − 0 = 4 children. To find the standard deviation, we determine $\sum x_i^2 = 224$.

$$s = \sqrt{\dfrac{\sum x_i^2 - \dfrac{\left(\sum x_i\right)^2}{n}}{n-1}} = \sqrt{\dfrac{224 - \dfrac{(78)^2}{36}}{36-1}} \approx 1.3 \text{ children} .$$

9. (a) By the Empirical Rule, approximately 99.7% of the data will be within 3 standard deviations of the mean. Now, 600 − 3(53) = 441 and 600 + 3(53) = 759. Thus, about 99.7% of light bulbs have lifetimes between __441__ and __759__ hours.

(b) Since 494 is exactly 2 standard deviations below the mean [494 = 600 − 2(53)] and 706 is exactly 2 standard deviations above the mean [706 = 600 + 2(53)], the Empirical Rule predicts that approximately 95% of the light bulbs will have lifetimes between 494 and 706 hours.

(c) Since 547 is exactly 1 standard deviations below the mean [547 = 600 − 1(53)] and 706 is exactly 2 standard deviations above the mean [706 = 600 + 2(53)], the Empirical Rule predicts that approximately 34 + 47.5 = 81.5% of the light bulbs will have lifetimes between 547 and 706 hours.

84

(d) Since 441 hours is 3 standard deviations below the mean [441 = 600 − 3(53)], the Empirical Rule predicts that 0.15% of light bulbs will last less than 441 hours. Thus, the company should expect to replace about 0.15% of the light bulbs.

(e) By Chebyshev's theorem, at least $\left(1-\dfrac{1}{k^2}\right)\cdot 100\% = \left(1-\dfrac{1}{2.5^2}\right)\cdot 100\% = 84\%$ of all the light bulbs are within $k = 2.5$ standard deviations of the mean.

(f) Since 494 is exactly $k = 2$ standard deviations below the mean [494 = 600 − 2(53)] and 706 is exactly 2 standard deviations above the mean [706 = 600 + 2(53)], Chebyshev's inequality indicates that at least $\left(1-\dfrac{1}{k^2}\right)\cdot 100\% = \left(1-\dfrac{1}{2^2}\right)\cdot 100\% = 75\%$ of the light bulbs will have lifetimes between 494 and 706 hours.

11.

Class	Midpt, x_i	Freq, f_i	$x_i f_i$	μ	$x_i - \mu$	$(x_i - \mu)^2 f_i$
20 – 24	22.5	6035	135,787.5	42.2826	−19.7826	2,361,804.87
25 – 29	27.5	4352	119,680	42.2826	−14.7826	951,021.94
30 – 34	32.5	4083	132,697.5	42.2826	−9.7826	390,740.09
35 – 39	37.5	3933	147,487.5	42.2826	−4.7826	89,960.54
40 – 44	42.5	4194	178,245	42.2826	0.2174	198.22
45 – 49	47.5	3716	176,510	42.2826	5.2174	101,154.21
50 – 54	52.5	3005	157,762.5	42.2826	10.2174	313,707.76
55 – 59	57.5	2355	135,412.5	42.2826	15.2174	545,345.61
60 – 64	62.5	1664	104,000	42.2826	20.2174	680,148.79
65 – 69	67.5	1173	79,177.5	42.2826	25.2174	745,930.95
70 – 74	72.5	1025	74,312.5	42.2826	30.2174	935,918.54
75 – 79	77.5	895	69,362.5	42.2826	35.2174	1,110,037.41
80 – 84	82.5	744	61,380	42.2826	40.2174	1,203,374.81
		$\sum f_i = 37{,}174$	$\sum x_i f_i = 1{,}571{,}815$			$\sum (x_i - \mu)^2 f = 9{,}429{,}343.76$

(a) $\mu = \dfrac{\sum x_i f_i}{\sum f_i} = \dfrac{1{,}571{,}815}{37{,}174} \approx 42.2826 \approx 42.28$ years

(b) $\sigma = \sqrt{\dfrac{\sum (x_i - \mu)^2 f}{\sum f_i}} = \sqrt{\dfrac{9{,}429{,}343.76}{37{,}174}} \approx 15.93$ years

13. $\text{GPA} = \bar{x}_w = \dfrac{\sum w_i x_i}{\sum w_i x_i} = \dfrac{5(4)+4(3)+3(4)+3(2)}{5+4+3+3} = \dfrac{50}{15} \approx 3.33$

15. (a) Yankees: $\sum x_i = 184,193,950$ and $n = 29$, so $\mu_{\text{Yankees}} = \dfrac{184,193,950}{29} \approx \$6,351,516$.

Mets: $\sum x_i = 96,660,970$ and $n = 28$, so $\mu_{\text{Mets}} = \dfrac{96,660,970}{28} \approx \$3,452,177$.

(b) Yankees: $M_{\text{Yankees}} = \$3,100,000$ (the 15th data value)

Mets: $M_{\text{Mets}} = \dfrac{800,000 + 1,000,000}{2} = \$900,000$ (the mean of the 14th and 15th values)

(c) In both cases, the mean is substantially larger than the median, so both distributions are skewed right.

(d) Yankees: $\sum x_i^2 \approx 2.3001 \times 10^{15}$, so

$$\sigma_{\text{Yankees}} = \sqrt{\dfrac{\sum x_i^2 - \dfrac{\left(\sum x_i\right)^2}{N}}{N}} = \sqrt{\dfrac{2.3001 \times 10^{15} - \dfrac{(184,193,950)^2}{29}}{19}} \approx \$6,242,767.0$$

Mets: $\sum x_i^2 \approx 9.37457 \times 10^{14}$, so

$$\sigma_{\text{Mets}} = \sqrt{\dfrac{\sum x_i^2 - \dfrac{\left(\sum x_i\right)^2}{N}}{N}} = \sqrt{\dfrac{9.37457 \times 10^{14} - \dfrac{(96,660,970)^2}{28}}{28}} \approx \$4,643,606.1$$

(e) Yankees: $301,400; \$837,500; \$3,100,000; \$11,623,571.50; \$22,000,000$
Mets: \$300,000; \$318,750; \$900,000; \$4,666,666.50; \$17,166,667

(f) Fences for the Yankees:
Lower fence $= 837,500 - 1.5(11,623,571.50 - 837,500) = -\$15,341,607.25$
Upper fence $= 11,623,571.50 + 1.5(11,623,571.50 - 837,500) = \$27,802,678.75$
The Yankees have no outliers.
Fences for the Mets:
Lower fence $= 318,750 - 1.5(4,666,666.50 - 318,750) = -\$6,203,124.75$
Upper fence $= 4,666,666.50 + 1.5(4,666,666.50 - 318,750) = \$11,188,541.25$
The data values \$16,071,429 (Vaughn) and \$17,166,667 (Piazza) are outliers.

Salaries

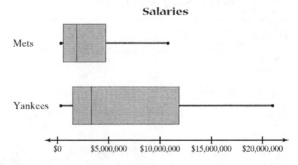

Annotations will vary. One possibility is that the Mets' salaries are clearly lower and less dispersed than the Yankees' salaries.

(g) In both boxplots, the median is to the left of the center of the box and the right line is substantially longer than the left line, so both distributions are skewed right.

(h) For both distributions, the median is the better measure of central tendency since the distributions are skewed.

17. The data provided are already listed in ascending order.

(a) $i = \left(\dfrac{k}{100}\right)(n+1) = \left(\dfrac{40}{100}\right)(88+1) = 35.6$. Since $i = 35.6$ is not an integer, we average

the 35th and 36th data values: $P_{40} = \dfrac{366,155+371,479}{2} = \$368,817$. This means that

approximately 40% of drivers in the 2004 Nextel Cup Series earned less than $368,817, and approximately 60% of drivers in the 2004 Nextel Cup Series earned more than $368,817.

(b) $i = \left(\dfrac{k}{100}\right)(n+1) = \left(\dfrac{95}{100}\right)(88+1) = 84.55$. Since $i = 84.55$ is not an integer, we average

the 84th and 85th data values: $P_{95} = \dfrac{5,692,620+6,221,710}{2} = \$5,957,165$. This means

that approximately 95% of drivers in the 2004 Nextel Cup Series earned less than $5,957,165, and approximately 5% of drivers in the 2004 Nextel Cup Series earned more than $5,957,165.

(c) $i = \left(\dfrac{k}{100}\right)(n+1) = \left(\dfrac{10}{100}\right)(88+1) = 8.9$. Since $i = 8.9$ is not an integer, we average the

8th and 9th data values: $P_{10} = \dfrac{65,175+70,550}{2} = \$67862.50$. This means that

approximately 10% of drivers in the 2004 Nextel Cup Series earned less than $67,862.50, and approximately 90% of drivers in the 2004 Nextel Cup Series earned more than $67,862.50.

(d) Of the 88 drivers in the 2004 Nextel Cup Series, 73 earned less than $4,117,750.

Percentile rank of $4,117,750 $= \left(\dfrac{73}{88}\right) \cdot 100 \approx 83$. Thus, $4,117,750 was at the 83rd

percentile. This means that approximately 83% of drivers in the 2004 Nextel Cup Series earned less than $4,117,750, and approximately 17% of drivers in the 2004 Nextel Cup Series earned more than $4,117,750.

(e) Of the 88 drivers in the 2004 Nextel Cup Series, 13 earned less than $116,359.

Percentile rank of $116,359 $= \left(\dfrac{13}{88}\right) \cdot 100 \approx 15$. Thus, $116,359 was at the 15th

percentile. This means that approximately 15% of drivers in the 2004 Nextel Cup Series earned less than $116,359, and approximately 85% of drivers in the 2004 Nextel Cup Series earned more than $116,359.

19. z-score for the female: $z = \dfrac{x-\mu}{\sigma} = \dfrac{160-156.5}{51.2} \approx 0.07$

z-score for the male: $z = \dfrac{x-\mu}{\sigma} = \dfrac{185-183.4}{40} = 0.04$

The weight of the 160-pound female is 0.07 standard deviations above the mean, while the weight of the 185-pound male is 0.04 standard deviations above the mean. Thus, the 160-pound female is relatively heavier.

Chapter 4

Describing the Relation between Two Variables

4.1 Scatter Diagrams and Correlation

1. Univariate data measures the value of a single variable for each individual in the study. Bivariate data measures values of two variables for each individual.

3. Two variables are positively associated if increases in the value of the explanatory variable tend to correspond to increases in the value of the response variable.

5. Since r measures only the strength and direction of *linear relationships*, obtaining $r = 0$ only means that there is no *linear* relation between the explanatory and response variable.

7. The linear correlation coefficient can only be calculated from bivariate *quantitative* data. The gender of a driver is a qualitative variable.

9. This statement makes no sense because the linear correlation coefficient is unitless; it cannot be 0.93 *bushel*.

11. Nonlinear   13. Linear; positive

15. (a) III   (b) IV   (c) II   (d) I

17. (a) There appears to be a positive, linear association between level of education and median income.

    (b) The point with rough coordinates $(24, 55{,}000)$ appears to stick out.

    Reasons may vary. One possibility: Cost of living may be higher due to harsher living conditions (e.g. additional shipping costs). In addition, it is not clear whether the median income includes income from the Permanent Fund Dividend that every resident receives.

19. (a)

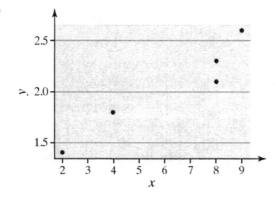

(b)

x_i	y_i	$\dfrac{x_i - \bar{x}}{s_x}$	$\dfrac{y_i - \bar{y}}{s_y}$	$\left(\dfrac{x_i - \bar{x}}{s_x}\right)\left(\dfrac{y_i - \bar{y}}{s_y}\right)$
2	1.4	−1.3847	−1.3867	1.9202
4	1.8	−0.7253	−0.5200	0.3772
6	2.1	0.5934	0.1300	0.0772
8	2.3	0.5934	0.5634	0.3343
9	2.6	0.9231	1.2134	1.1201

Mean 6.2 2.04   Total = 3.8290
S.D. 3.033 0.462   r = 0.9572

(c) There appears to be a positive linear association between x and y.

21. (a)

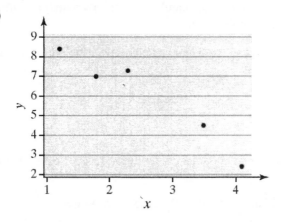

(b)

x_i	y_i	$\dfrac{x_i - \bar{x}}{s_x}$	$\dfrac{y_i - \bar{y}}{s_y}$	$\left(\dfrac{x_i - \bar{x}}{s_x}\right)\left(\dfrac{y_i - \bar{y}}{s_y}\right)$
1.2	8.4	−1.15120	1.02039	−1.17467
1.8	7	−0.65068	0.44437	−0.28914
2.3	7.3	−0.23358	0.56780	−0.13263
3.5	4.5	0.76747	−0.58426	−0.44840
4.1	2.4	1.26799	−1.44830	−1.83643

Mean 2.58 5.92   Total = −3.88127
S.D. 1.199 2.430   r = −0.9703

(c) There appears to be a negative linear association between x and y.

23. (a) Explanatory variable: Height; Response variable: Head Circumference

(b)

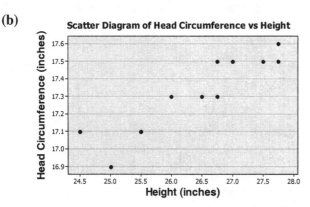

(c) $\sum x = 291$; $\sum y = 190.6$; $\sum x^2 = 7710.25$; $\sum y^2 = 3303.06$; $\sum xy = 5044.425$

$$r = \frac{\sum xy - \frac{1}{n}\sum x \cdot \sum y}{\sqrt{\left(\sum x^2 - \frac{1}{n}(\sum x)^2\right)\left(\sum y^2 - \frac{1}{n}(y)^2\right)}} \approx 0.9111$$

(d) There appears to be a fairly strong positive linear association between the height and head circumference of a child.

25. (a) We tend to be interested in the gas mileage of a car, so we will choose the weight to be the explanatory variable and the gas mileage to be the response variable.

(b)

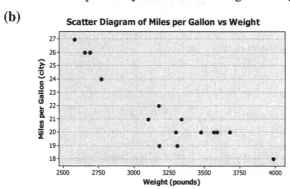

(c) $\sum x = 51,570$; $\sum y = 345$; $\sum x^2 = 168,595,350$; $\sum y^2 = 7553$; $\sum xy = 1,097,290$

$$r = \frac{\sum xy - \frac{1}{n}\sum x \cdot \sum y}{\sqrt{\left(\sum x^2 - \frac{1}{n}(\sum x)^2\right)\left(\sum y^2 - \frac{1}{n}(y)^2\right)}} \approx -0.8922$$

(d) There is a negative linear association between the weight of a car and its gas mileage.

27. (a) Since the researcher wants to predict the final grade, the explanatory variable is the number of days absent and the response variable is the final grade.

(b)

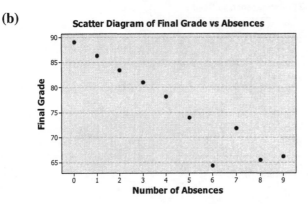

Scatter Diagram of Final Grade vs Absences

(c) $\sum x = 45$; $\sum y = 760.1$; $\sum x^2 = 285$; $\sum y^2 = 58,509.93$; $\sum xy = 3187.2$

$$r = \frac{\sum xy - \frac{1}{n}\sum x \cdot \sum y}{\sqrt{\left(\sum x^2 - \frac{1}{n}(\sum x)^2\right)\left(\sum y^2 - \frac{1}{n}(y)^2\right)}} \approx -0.9474$$

(d) There appears to be a strong negative linear association between final grade and number of absences.

(e) Going to class every day does not guarantee a passing grade. Factors will vary but may include time studying, hours working, number of credit hours, etc..

29. (a)

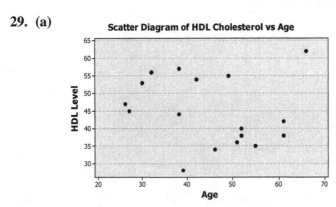

Scatter Diagram of HDL Cholesterol vs Age

Based on the scatter diagram, there appears to be no clear association between age and HDL level.

(b) $\sum x = 765$; $\sum y = 764$; $\sum x^2 = 36,851$; $\sum y^2 = 35,862$; $\sum xy = 34,065$

$$r = \frac{\sum xy - \frac{1}{n}\sum x \cdot \sum y}{\sqrt{\left(\sum x^2 - \frac{1}{n}(\sum x)^2\right)\left(\sum y^2 - \frac{1}{n}(y)^2\right)}} \approx -0.1637$$

(c) Based on the scatter diagram and the linear correlation coefficient, there appears to be little, if any, linear association between age and HDL level.

31. (a)   **Scatter Diagram of IQ vs MRI Count**

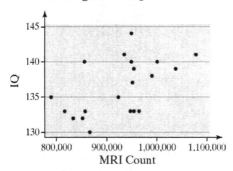

(b) $\sum x = 18,518,961$; $\sum y = 2728$; $\sum x^2 \approx 1.72565 \times 10^{13}$; $\sum y^2 = 372,396$;
$\sum xy = 2,529,103,155$

$$r = \frac{\sum xy - \frac{1}{n}\sum x \cdot \sum y}{\sqrt{\left(\sum x^2 - \frac{1}{n}(\sum x)^2\right)\left(\sum y^2 - \frac{1}{n}(y)^2\right)}} \approx 0.5482$$

This indicates that there is a weak positive linear association between MRI count and IQ.

(c)   **Scatter Diagram of IQ vs MRI Count**

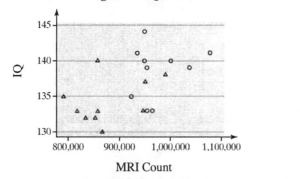

Looking at the scatter diagram, we can see that females tend to have lower MRI counts. When separating the two groups, even the weak linear relationship seems to disappear. Neither group presents any clear relationship between IQ and MRI counts.

93

(d) <u>Females:</u>

$\sum x = 8,765,495$; $\sum y = 1343$; $\sum x^2 \approx 7.7215 \times 10^{12}$; $\sum y^2 = 180,453$; $\sum xy = 1,177,863,984$

$$r = \frac{\sum xy - \frac{1}{n}\sum x \cdot \sum y}{\sqrt{\left(\sum x^2 - \frac{1}{n}\left(\sum x\right)^2\right)\left(\sum y^2 - \frac{1}{n}(y)^2\right)}} \approx 0.3591$$

<u>Males:</u>

$\sum x = 9,753,466$; $\sum y = 1385$; $\sum x^2 \approx 9.53498 \times 10^{12}$; $\sum y^2 = 191,943$; $\sum xy = 1,351,239,171$

$$r = \frac{\sum xy - \frac{1}{n}\sum x \cdot \sum y}{\sqrt{\left(\sum x^2 - \frac{1}{n}\left(\sum x\right)^2\right)\left(\sum y^2 - \frac{1}{n}(y)^2\right)}} \approx 0.2361$$

There appears to no linear relation between brain size (MRI count) and IQ. The moral of the story is to beware of lurking variables. Mixing distinct populations can produce misleading results that result in incorrect conclusions.

33. (a)

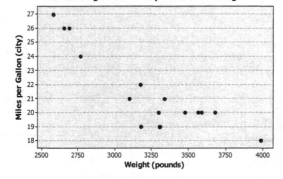

Scatter Diagram of Miles per Gallon vs Weight

(b) $\sum x = 54,876$; $\sum y = 376$; $\sum x^2 = 179,525,326$; $\sum y^2 = 7914$; $\sum xy = 1,160,105$

$$r = \frac{\sum xy - \frac{1}{n}\sum x \cdot \sum y}{\sqrt{\left(\sum x^2 - \frac{1}{n}\left(\sum x\right)^2\right)\left(\sum y^2 - \frac{1}{n}(y)^2\right)}} \approx -0.879 \text{ (with Taurus)}$$

(c) The linear correlation coefficient changed slightly, but not a tremendous amount. The Taurus is a heavier car and does not get very good gas mileage. The results are reasonable because the Ford Taurus falls pretty close to the general pattern of the other domestic cars studied.

94

(d)

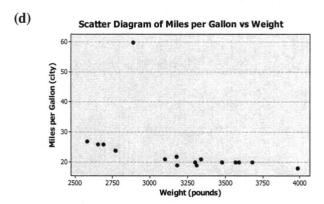

(e) $\sum x = 54,461$; $\sum y = 405$; $\sum x^2 = 176,954,401$; $\sum y^2 = 11,153$; $\sum xy = 1,270,710$

$$r = \frac{\sum xy - \frac{1}{n}\sum x \cdot \sum y}{\sqrt{\left(\sum x^2 - \frac{1}{n}(\sum x)^2\right)\left(\sum y^2 - \frac{1}{n}(y)^2\right)}} \approx -0.437 \text{ (with Prius, but not Taurus)}$$

This new value dramatically altered the value of the linear correlation coefficient. The Prius is an outlier which greatly affects the value of the correlation coefficient. The correlation dropped from -0.892 (moderately strong negative linear association) to -0.437 (relatively weak negative linear association)

(f) The Prius does not fit the general pattern because it is a hybrid car that runs on gas and electricity. The remaining cars are traditional domestic cars with gasoline engines.

35. (a) Data Set 1:

$\sum x = 99$; $\sum y = 82.52$; $\sum x^2 = 1001$; $\sum y^2 = 660.3244$; $\sum xy = 797.73$
$r \approx 0.82$

Data Set 2:

$\sum x = 99$; $\sum y = 82.24$; $\sum x^2 = 1001$; $\sum y^2 = 657.6896$; $\sum xy = 796.24$
$r \approx 0.82$

Data Set 3:

$\sum x = 99$; $\sum y = 82.5$; $\sum x^2 = 1001$; $\sum y^2 = 659.9762$; $\sum xy = 797.47$
$r \approx 0.82$

Data Set 4:

$\sum x = 99$; $\sum y = 82.51$; $\sum x^2 = 1001$; $\sum y^2 = 660.1325$; $\sum xy = 797.58$
$r \approx 0.82$

All four data sets yield roughly the same correlation coefficient, $r \approx 0.82$.

(b)

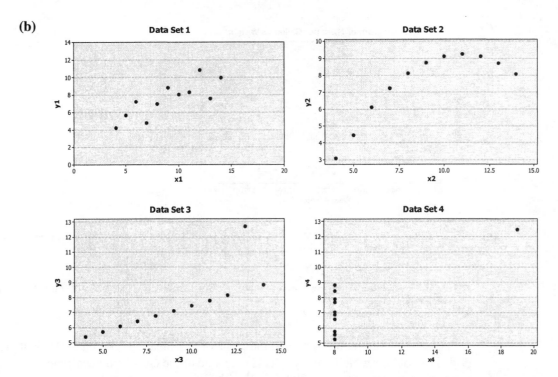

Although each data set yields about the same value for r, it is clear from the scatter diagrams that the relationships between x and y are different in each case. Therefore, it is necessary to look at the linear correlation coefficient along with a scatter diagram when analyzing bivariate data.

37. Begin by finding the linear correlation coefficient between each pair of variables. The following correlation matrix summarizes the correlation coefficients.

	Cisco Systems	Walt Disney	General Electric	Exxon Mobil
Walt Disney	0.264			
General Electric	0.770	0.622		
Exxon Mobil	0.499	0.757	0.855	
TECO Energy	−0.235	0.274	0.017	0.311

If your goal is to have the lowest correlation between two stocks (i.e. correlation close to 0), invest in General Electric and TECO Energy.

If your goal is to have one stock go up when the other goes down (i.e. negative association), invest in Cisco Systems and TECO Energy.

39. $r = 0.599$ implies that there is a positive linear relation between the number of television stations and life expectancy. But this is correlation, not causation. The more television stations a country has, the more affluent it tends to be. The more affluent, the better the healthcare which in turn helps increase the life expectancy.

41. (a) $\sum x = 28.2$; $\sum y = 25.4$; $\sum x^2 = 104.62$; $\sum y^2 = 91.2$; $\sum xy = 91.22$

$$r = \frac{\sum xy - \frac{1}{n}\sum x \cdot \sum y}{\sqrt{\left(\sum x^2 - \frac{1}{n}(\sum x)^2\right)\left(\sum y^2 - \frac{1}{n}(y)^2\right)}} \approx 0.2280$$

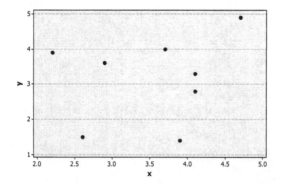

(b) $\sum x = 38.6$; $\sum y = 34.7$; $\sum x^2 = 212.78$; $\sum y^2 = 177.61$; $\sum xy = 187.94$

$$r = \frac{\sum xy - \frac{1}{n}\sum x \cdot \sum y}{\sqrt{\left(\sum x^2 - \frac{1}{n}(\sum x)^2\right)\left(\sum y^2 - \frac{1}{n}(y)^2\right)}} \approx 0.8598$$

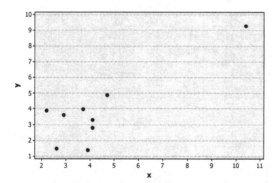

The additional data point increases r from a value that suggests no linear association to one that suggests a fairly strong linear association. However, the second scatter diagram shows that the new data point is very far from the rest of the data and so has a big influence on the value of r, even though there is no apparent association between the variables. Correlations should always be reported with scatter diagrams in order to check for potentially influential observations.

43. (a) Positive correlation because the more infants the more diapers will be needed.

(b) Negative correlation, because the lower the interest rates the more people can afford to buy a car.

(c) Negative correlation, because more exercise can lower cholesterol.

(d) Negative correlation, because the higher the price of a Big Mac, the fewer Big Macs and french fries will be sold.

(e) No correlation.

45. (a)

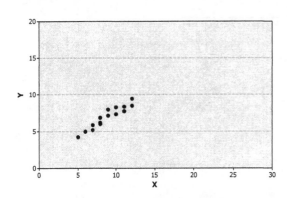

(b) $\sum x = 141$; $\sum y = 110.6$; $\sum x^2 = 1307$; $\sum y^2 = 797.14$; $\sum xy = 1018.3$

$$r = \frac{\sum xy - \frac{1}{n}\sum x \cdot \sum y}{\sqrt{\left(\sum x^2 - \frac{1}{n}(\sum x)^2\right)\left(\sum y^2 - \frac{1}{n}(y)^2\right)}} \approx 0.9518$$

(c)

x	10	12	14	14	16	16	16	16
y	8.4	10	10.4	11.8	12	12.4	12.2	13.8
x	18	18	20	20	22	22	24	24
y	14.4	16	16.6	14.8	16.8	15.6	17	19

(d)

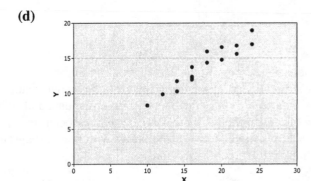

The values are larger for both x and y, and the data points are spread out a bit more, but the overall pattern of the data remains the same.

(e) $\sum x = 282$; $\sum y = 221.2$; $\sum x^2 = 5228$; $\sum y^2 = 3188.56$; $\sum xy = 4073.2$

$$r = \frac{\sum xy - \frac{1}{n}\sum x \cdot \sum y}{\sqrt{\left(\sum x^2 - \frac{1}{n}(\sum x)^2\right)\left(\sum y^2 - \frac{1}{n}(y)^2\right)}} \approx 0.9518$$

(f) Both correlation coefficients are 0.9518. Doubling the data values also doubles both the standard deviation and the mean. Therefore, the z-scores for each point, and hence the correlation coefficient, remain unchanged.

47. (a) It appears that SAT score combined with high school GPA is the best predictor of college GPA since they have the highest value for the correlation coefficient. A scatter diagram should also be examined to see if this is the case.

(b) Based on the correlation coefficient, it appears that SAT verbal score alone is the worst predictor of college GPA since it has the lowest value for the correlation coefficient. A scatter diagram should also be examined to see if this is the case.

4.2 Least Squares Regression

1. The least-squares regression line is the line that minimizes the sum of the squared vertical deviations from the line. That is, it minimizes the sum of the squared errors (residuals).

3. Values of the explanatory (or predictor) variable that are much larger or much smaller than those observed are considered to be "outside the scope of the model". That is, they lie outside the data values used to construct the model. It is dangerous to make such predictions because we cannot be certain of the behavior of the data for which we have no observations.

5. Answers will vary.

7. Each point on the least-squares regression line represents the mean value of the response variable for the corresponding value of the explanatory variable.

9. (a)

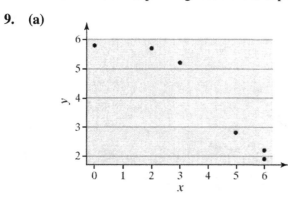

There appears to be a negative linear relationship between the x and y.

(b) $b_1 = r \cdot \dfrac{s_y}{s_x} = -0.9476938 \left(\dfrac{1.8239152}{2.42212} \right) \approx -0.7136$

$b_0 = \bar{y} - b_1 \bar{x} = 3.933 - (-0.7136)(3.667) \approx 6.5498$

$\hat{y} = -0.7136x + 6.5498$

(c)

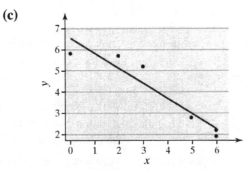

11. (a)

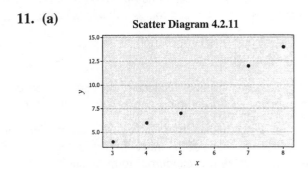

Scatter Diagram 4.2.11

(b) Using the points $(3,4)$ and $(8,14)$:

$m = \dfrac{14-4}{8-3} = 2$

$y - y_1 = m(x - x_1)$

$y - 4 = 2(x - 3)$

$y - 4 = 2x - 6$

$y = 2x - 2$

(c)

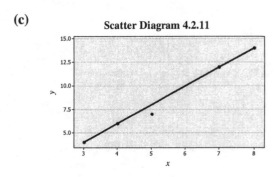

Scatter Diagram 4.2.11

100

(d) $\bar{x} = 5.4$; $\bar{y} = 8.6$; $s_x \approx 2.07364$; $s_y \approx 4.21901$; $r \approx 0.99443$

$$b_1 = r \cdot \frac{s_y}{s_x} = 0.99443 \left(\frac{4.21901}{2.07364} \right) \approx 2.0233$$

$$b_0 = \bar{y} - b_1 \bar{x} \approx -2.3256$$

$$\hat{y} = 2.0233x - 2.3256$$

(e)

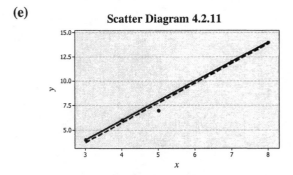

Scatter Diagram 4.2.11

(f)

x	y	$\hat{y} = 2x - 2$	$y - \hat{y}$	$(y - \hat{y})^2$
3	4	4	0	0
4	6	6	0	0
5	7	8	−1	1
7	12	12	0	0
8	14	14	0	0

Total =   1

Sum of squared residuals (computed line) = 1.0

(g)

x	y	$\hat{y}$	$y - \hat{y}$	$(y - \hat{y})^2$
3	4	3.7443	0.2557	0.0654
4	6	5.7676	0.2324	0.0540
5	7	7.7909	−0.7909	0.6255
7	12	11.8375	0.1625	0.0264
8	14	13.8608	0.1392	0.0194

Total =   0.7907

Sum of squared residuals (regression line) = 0.7907

(h) Answers will vary. The regression line gives a smaller sum of squared residuals and so is a better fit.

13. (a)

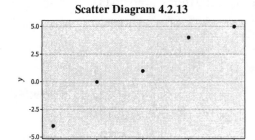

Scatter Diagram 4.2.13

(b) Using the points $(-2,-4)$ and $(2,5)$:

$$m = \frac{5-(-4)}{2-(-2)} = \frac{9}{4}$$

$$y - y_1 = m(x - x_1)$$

$$y - 5 = \frac{9}{4}(x-2)$$

$$y - 5 = \frac{9}{4}x - \frac{9}{2}$$

$$y = \frac{9}{4}x + \frac{1}{2} \quad \text{or} \quad y = 2.25x + 0.50$$

(c)

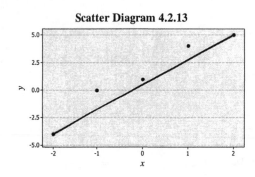

Scatter Diagram 4.2.13

(d) $\bar{x} = 0$; $\bar{y} = 1.2$; $s_x \approx 1.58114$; $s_y \approx 3.56371$; $r \approx 0.97609$

$$b_1 = r \cdot \frac{s_y}{s_x} = 0.97609\left(\frac{3.56371}{1.58114}\right) \approx 2.2000$$

$$b_0 = \bar{y} - b_1\bar{x} = 1.2$$

$$\hat{y} = 2.2x + 1.2$$

(e)

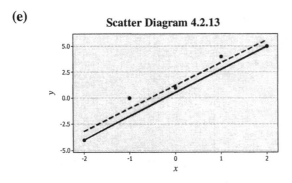

Scatter Diagram 4.2.13

(f)

x	y	$\hat{y} = 2.25x + 0.50$	$y - \hat{y}$	$(y - \hat{y})^2$
-2	-4	-4.00	0.00	0.0000
-1	0	-1.75	1.75	3.0625
0	1	0.50	0.50	0.2500
1	4	2.75	1.25	1.5625
2	5	5.00	0.00	0.0000

Total =   4.875

Sum of squared residuals (calculated line) = 4.875

(g)

x	y	$\hat{y}$	$y - \hat{y}$	$(y - \hat{y})^2$
-2	-4	-3.2	-0.8	0.64
-1	0	-1.0	1.0	1.00
0	1	1.2	-0.2	0.04
1	4	3.4	0.6	0.36
2	5	5.6	-0.6	0.36

Total =   2.40

Sum of squared residuals (regression line) = 2.4

(h) Answers will vary. The regression line gives a smaller sum of squared residuals and so is a better fit.

103

15. (a)

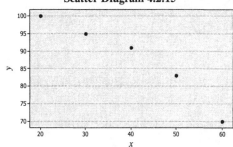

Scatter Diagram 4.2.15

(b) Using the points $(30,95)$ and $(60,70)$:

$$m = \frac{70-95}{60-30} = \frac{-25}{30} = -\frac{5}{6}$$

$$y - y_1 = m(x - x_1)$$

$$y - 95 = -\frac{5}{6}(x - 30)$$

$$y - 95 = -\frac{5}{6}x + 25$$

$$y = -\frac{5}{6}x + 120$$

(c)

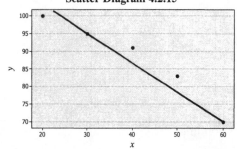

Scatter Diagram 4.2.15

(d) $\bar{x} = 40$; $\bar{y} = 87.8$; $s_x \approx 15.81139$; $s_y \approx 11.73456$; $r \approx -0.97014$

$$b_1 = r \cdot \frac{s_y}{s_x} = -0.97014\left(\frac{11.73456}{15.81139}\right) \approx -0.7200$$

$$b_0 = \bar{y} - b_1\bar{x} \approx 116.6$$

$$\hat{y} = -0.72x + 116.6$$

(e)

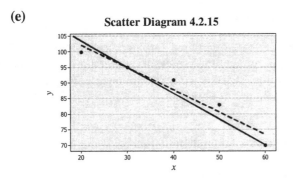

Scatter Diagram 4.2.15

(f)

x	y	$\hat{y} = -\frac{5}{6}x + 120$	$y - \hat{y}$	$(y - \hat{y})^2$
20	100	103.333	−3.333	11.1111
30	95	95.000	0.000	0.0000
40	91	86.667	4.333	18.7778
50	83	78.330	4.667	21.7778
60	70	70.000	0.000	0.0000

Total =   51.6667

Sum of squared residuals (calculated line) = 51.6667.

(g)

x	y	$\hat{y}$	$y - \hat{y}$	$(y - \hat{y})^2$
20	100	102.2	−2.2	4.84
30	95	95.0	0.0	0.00
40	91	87.8	3.2	10.24
50	83	80.6	2.4	5.76
60	70	73.4	−3.4	11.56

Total =   32.40

Sum of squared residuals (regression line) = 32.4

(h) Answers will vary. The regression line gives a smaller sum of squared residuals and so is a better fit.

Note: For the remaining problems, technology will be used to obtain the least-squares regression line.

105

17. (a) $\hat{y} = 0.1827x + 12.4932$ (using Minitab)

(b)   If height increases by 1 inch, head circumference will increase by about 0.1827 inches, on average. It is not appropriate to interpret the y-intercept since it is outside the scope of the model. In addition, it makes no sense to consider the head circumference of a child with a height of 0 inches.

(c) $x = 25$

$\hat{y} = 0.1827(25) + 12.4932 = 17.0607$ or about 17.06 inches.

(d)   residual $= y - \hat{y} = 16.9 - 17.06 = -0.16$ inches

This indicates that this head circumference is below average.

(e)

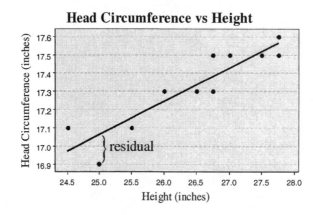

(f)   This is due to the natural variation in the head circumference of children who are 26.75 inches tall.

(g)   No, a height of 32 inches is well outside the scope of the model.

19. (a) $\hat{y} = -0.0062x + 41.4640$ (using Minitab)

(b)   For every 1 pound increase in weight, gas mileage in the city will decrease by about 0.0062 miles per gallon, on average. It is not appropriate to interpret the y-intercept. It is well beyond the scope of the model.

(c) $\hat{y} = -0.0062(3300) + 41.4640 = 21.004$ or about 21.0 miles per gallon.

residual $= y - \hat{y} = 20 - 21.004 = -1.004$ or about -1.0 miles per gallon

This indicates that the gas mileage for this Ford Mustang is below average.

(d)

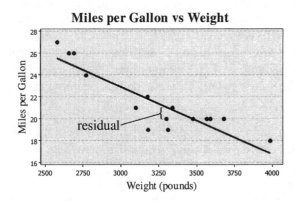

Miles per Gallon vs Weight

(e)   No; it would not be reasonable to use this least-squares regression line to predict the miles per gallon of a Toyota Prius. The data given are for domestic cars with gasoline engines. The Toyota Prius is a foreign-made hybrid car.

21. (a) $\hat{y} = -2.8273x + 88.7327$ (using a TI-84 Plus)

(b)   For every additional absence, the student's final grade decreases by about 2.8273 percentage points, on average. The final grade of students who miss no classes is 88.7327.

(c) $\hat{y} = -2.8273(5) + 88.7327 = 74.5962$ or about 74.60
residual $= y - \hat{y} = 73.9 - 74.60 = -0.70$
This indicates that the final grade for this number of absences is below average.

(d)

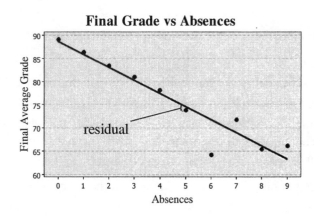

Final Grade vs Absences

(e)   No; 15 absences is out of the scope of the model.

23. (a) $\hat{y} = 0.00003x + 109.8940$ (using Minitab)

(b) The slope is close to 0. While this may partially be due to the weak linear relationship that is present, it could also be due to the magnitude of the values for the explanatory variable. The values for MRI counts are in the hundreds of thousands. If we coded our data so that x was the MRI count in hundreds of thousands, then the slope would be around 3. Even if the data were all in a straight line, the slope would be very small because of the size of the values for x. Therefore, before assuming the slope is 0, first check the magnitude of the data.

(c) We previously found that there was no apparent relation between the MRI count and IQ. Therefore, in both cases we would use $\overline{y}$ as our estimate. That is, for both cases, our estimate is $\hat{y} = \overline{y} \approx 136$.

25. Answers will vary. Mark Twain was poking fun at those who carelessly go beyond the scope of their data (model) by providing an extreme example of what can happen.

4.3 Diagnostics on the Least-Squares Regression Line

1. 75% of the total variation in the response variable is explained by the regression.

3. This indicates that the explanatory and response variables may not be linearly related.

5. An influential observation is one that significantly affects either the slope or the y-intercept of the least-squares regression line. If an influential observation is observed, it should be removed only if there is justification to do so. If the observation cannot be removed, one can collect more data so that additional point near the influential observation are obtained, or apply other techniques (beyond the scope of this text) that reduce the influence of the observation.

7. An influential observation can change either the slope or y-intercept (or both) of the least-squares regression line.

9. Knowing R^2 alone is not sufficient to determine the value of r. In this case, if $R^2 = 0.81$, then we have either $r = 0.9$ or $r = -0.9$ since both $(0.9)^2 = 0.81$ and $(-0.9)^2 = 0.81$. To determine which is the correct value for r, we need to know whether the relation has positive or negative association. We can determine this by looking at a scatter diagram or the slope of the regression line.

11. The constant variance assumption is violated; the variance of the residuals increases as the value of x increases.

13. There appears to be an outlier in the residual plot (a residual of 4).

15. (a) III   **(b)** II   **(c)** IV   **(d)** I

17. Yes; the point is influential because the two lines have substantially different slopes.

19. No; the point is not influential because there is very little change in either the slope or the y-intercept. The lines are almost identical.

21. (a)

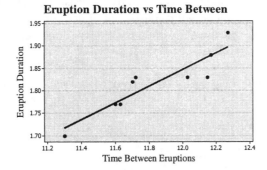

$\hat{y} = 0.1854x - 0.3779$ (using Minitab)

(b)

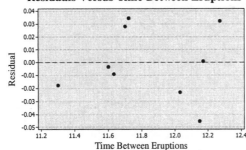

Yes, time between eruptions and length of eruption appear to be linearly related. None of the model conditions appear to have been violated.

(c)   83.0% of the variation in length of eruption is explained by the regression equation.

23. (a)   Looking at the scatter diagram, the data points do not appear to have a linear pattern. There does not appear to be a linear relation between calories and sugar content.

(b)   6.8% of the variability in sugar content is explained by the least-squares regression equation. This value is very low so it supports the conclusion from part (a).

(c)

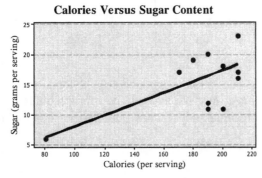

Yes, All-Bran is influential. There was a substantial change in the y-intercept of the least-squares regression line.

109

(d)   42.1% of the variability in sugar content is explained by the least squares regression equation. Influential data values can cause the coefficient of determination to increase substantially, thereby increasing the apparent strength of the relation between two variables.

25. (a)   From 4.1.23, we have $r = 0.9111$. Therefore, $R^2 = (0.9111)^2 \approx 0.830 = 83.0\%$.

(b)

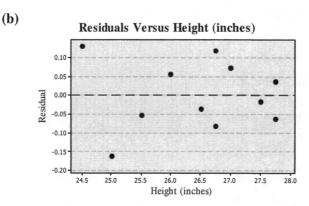

(c)   83.0% of the variation in head circumference is explained by the least-squares regression equation. The residual plot does not reveal any problems, so the linear model appears to be appropriate.

27. (a)   From 4.1.25, we have $r = -0.8922$. Therefore, $R^2 = (-0.8922)^2 \approx 0.796 = 79.6\%$.

(b)

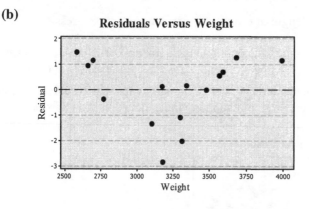

(c)   79.6% of the variation in miles per gallon is explained by the least-squares regression equation. For the most part a linear model appears to be appropriate. However, there may be some curvature in the residual plot which would indicate that the linear model is not appropriate.

29. (a)

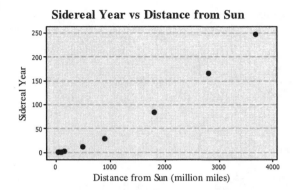

Sidereal Year vs Distance from Sun

(b) $\hat{y} = 0.0657x - 12.4967$ (using a TI-84 Plus)

(c)

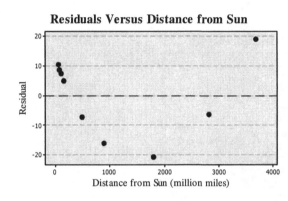

Residuals Versus Distance from Sun

(d) No; the U-shaped pattern in the residual plot indicates that a linear model is not appropriate.

31. (a) R^2 changes from $R^2 = 79.6\%$ to $R^2 = 52.7\%$. Adding the Viper substantially reduces the amount of variability in gas mileage explained by the least-squares regression equation.

(b)

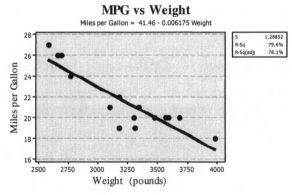

MPG vs Weight

(without Viper)

111

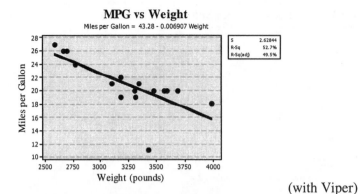

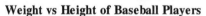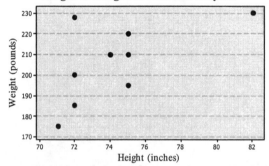

(with Viper)

The Viper is not influential since neither the slope nor the y-intercept are substantially altered. However, the Viper is an outlier since it lies well outside the overall pattern of the data.

33. (a)

Weight vs Height of Baseball Players

(b) With Randy Johnson:

$\hat{y} = 3.4631x - 51.091$ (using a TI-84 Plus)

$r = 0.6076$

(c) Without Randy Johnson:

$\hat{y} = 4.605x - 134.545$ (using a TI-84 Plus)

$r = 0.4589$

Removing Randy Johnson substantially changes the regression equation, particularly the y-intercept. The correlation coefficient substantially decreased.

(d) Yes, Randy Johnson is an influential observation because the y-intercept of the least-squares regression line changes substantially when he is removed.

35. (a)

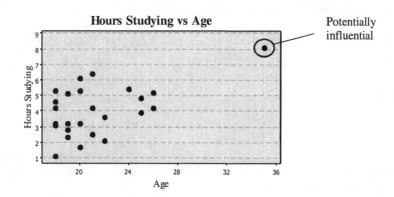

Potentially influential

(b) With all data:

$\hat{y} = 0.232x - 0.920$ (using Minitab)

(c) Without the point $(35, 8.1)$:

$\hat{y} = 0.1549x + 0.635$ (using Minitab)

(d)

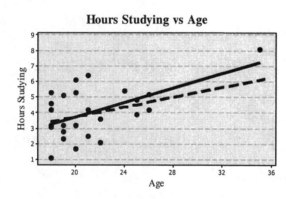

(e) The point $(35, 8.1)$ substantially increases both the slope and the y-intercept of the least-squares regression line. Therefore, it would be considered and influential observation.

113

4.4 Nonlinear Regression: Transformations (on CD)

1. The logarithm to the base a, where $a > 0$, $a \neq 1$, is $y = \log_a(x)$ if and only if $x = a^y$, where $x > 0$.

3. $\log y = \log\left(ab^x\right)$

$\qquad = \log a + \log b^x$

$\qquad = \log a + x \log b$

The linear form of $y = ab^x$ is $\log y = \log a + x \log b$. If we let $Y = \log y$, $B = \log b$ and $A = \log a$, then the linear form is $Y = A + Bx$.

For Problems 5-11, we use the fact that if $x = a^y$, then $y = \log_a x$.

5. $4^2 = 16 \quad \Leftrightarrow \quad 2 = \log_4 16$

7. $x^5 = 18 \quad \Leftrightarrow \quad 5 = \log_x 18$

9. $7^x = 15 \quad \Leftrightarrow \quad x = \log_7 15$

11. $5^3 = y \quad \Leftrightarrow \quad 3 = \log_5 y$

For Problems 13-19, we use the fact that if $y = \log_a x$, then $x = a^y$.

13. $\log_3 81 = 4 \quad \Leftrightarrow \quad 3^4 = 81$

15. $\log_a 14 = 3 \quad \Leftrightarrow \quad a^3 = 14$

17. $\log_4 c = 3 \quad \Leftrightarrow \quad 4^3 = c$

19. $\log_2 5 = k \quad \Leftrightarrow \quad 2^k = 5$

21. $\log_3(uv) = \log_3 u + \log_3 v$ (Property 1)

23. $\log_5 x^4 = 4\log_5 x$ (Property 2)

25. $\log_a\left(uv^2\right) = \log_a u + \log_a v^2$ (Property 1)

$\qquad = \log_a u + 2\log_a v$ (Property 2)

27. $\log\left(x^4 y^3\right) = \log x^4 + \log y^3$ (Property 1)

$\qquad = 4\log x + 3\log y$ (Property 2)

29. $\log 34 \approx 1.531$

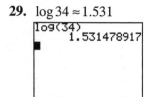

31. $\log 13.2 \approx 1.121$

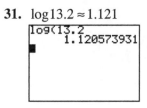

114

33. $10^{1.6} \approx 39.811$

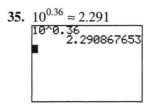

35. $10^{0.36} \approx 2.291$

```
10^0.36
         2.290867653
```

37. (a)

E-coli Population vs Time

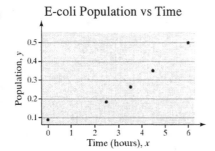

(b)

x	$Y = \log y$
0	−1.0458
2.5	−0.7447
3.5	−0.5850
4.5	−0.4559
6	−0.3010

Log(E-coli Population) vs Time

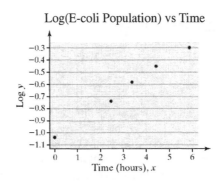

(c) Using technology: $\hat{Y} = 0.1266x - 1.0443$

(d) $\hat{y} = 10^{\hat{Y}} = 10^{0.1266x - 1.0443} = 10^{-1.0443} \cdot (10^{0.1266})^x = 0.0903(1.3384)^x$

(e) $y = 0.0903(1.3384)^7 = 0.69$

The predicted population after 7 hours is 0.69.

39. (a)

U.S. Population vs Time

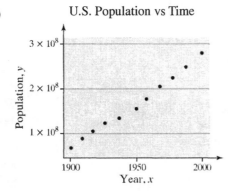

115

(b)

x	$Y = \log y$
1900	7.8220
1910	7.9649
1920	8.0254
1930	8.0906
1940	8.1211
1950	8.1799
1960	8.2536
1970	8.3081
1980	8.3551
1990	8.3957
2000	8.4494

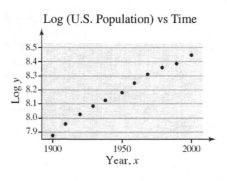

Log (U.S. Population) vs Time

(c) Using technology: $\hat{Y} = 0.0056x - 2.6593$

(d) $\hat{y} = 10^{\hat{Y}} = 10^{0.0056x - 2.6593} = 10^{-2.6593} \cdot (10^{0.0056})^x = 0.0022(1.013)^x$

(e) $\hat{y} = 0.0022(1.013)^{2010} = 414,388,653.$

The predicted population for the U.S. in 2010 is 414,388,653, or about 414 million.

(f) Adding the regression line to the scatter diagram in part (b), it appears that the regression line overestimates the population in 1990 and 2000. Therefore, it seems reasonable to believe it will also overestimate the population in 2010.

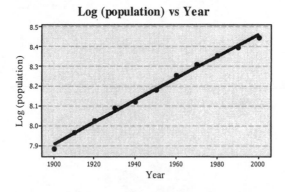

Log (population) vs Year

(g) Using the U.S. Census Bureau website (http://www.census.gov/ipc/www/usinterimproj/natprojtab01a.pdf) the predicted U.S. population in 2010 (as of March 2004 data) was 308,936,000. This is substantially lower than the prediction from our regression equation.

116

41. (a)   Sidereal Year vs Distance from Sun

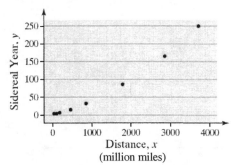

(b)

$X = \log x$	$Y = \log y$
1.5563	−0.6198
1.8261	−0.2076
1.9685	0
2.1523	0.2742
2.6839	1.0755
2.9479	1.4698
3.2516	1.9243
3.4467	2.2175
3.5653	2.3945

Sidereal Year vs Distance from Sun
(log-log Graph)

(c) Using technology: $\hat{Y} = 1.4994X - 2.9506$

(d) $\hat{y} = 10^{\hat{Y}} = 10^{1.4994X - 2.9506}$

$= 10^{-2.9506} \cdot 10^{1.4994\log(x)}$

$= 10^{-2.9506} \cdot \left(10^{\log(x)}\right)^{1.4994}$

$= 0.0011 x^{1.4994}$

43. (a)   Light Intensity vs Distance

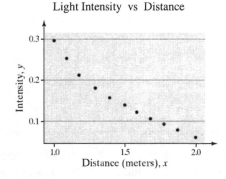

117

(b)

$X = \log x$	$Y = \log y$
0	−0.5280
0.0414	−0.5983
0.0792	−0.6873
0.1139	−0.7579
0.1461	−0.8141
0.1761	−0.8690
0.2041	−0.9412
0.2304	−0.9896
0.2553	−1.0348
0.2788	−1.0798
0.3010	−1.1342

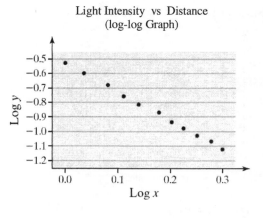

Light Intensity vs Distance
(log-log Graph)

(c) Using technology: $\hat{Y} = -2.012X - 0.5236$

(d) $\hat{y} = 10^{\hat{Y}} = 10^{-2.012X - 0.5236} = 10^{-0.5236} \cdot 10^{-2.012 \log(x)} = 10^{-0.5236} \cdot \left(10^{\log(x)}\right)^{-2.012} = 0.2995 x^{-2.012}$

(e) $\hat{y} = 0.2995(2.3)^{-2.012} = 0.05605$

The predicted intensity of a 100-watt light bulb that is 2.3 meters away is 0.05605.

Chapter 4 Review Exercises

1. (a)

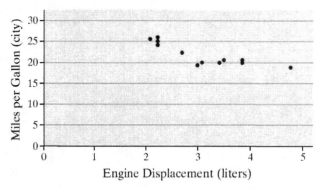

Engine Displacement vs Fuel Economy

(b) Using technology: $r = -0.8954$

(c) Based on the scatter diagram and the linear correlation coefficient, there appears to be a fairly strong negative linear association between engine displacement and fuel economy.

3. (a)

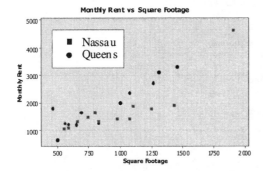

(b) Using technology:
Queens: $r = 0.909$
Nassau County: $r = 0.867$

(c) For both cases, there is a positive linear association between square footage and monthly rent.

(d) Yes; while smaller sized apartments (those less than 1000 square feet in area) seemed to have similar rents, the rents in Queens tended to be higher for larger apartments (those with 1000 square feet or more)..

5. (a) Using technology: $\hat{y} = -2.7977x + 30.3848$

(b)

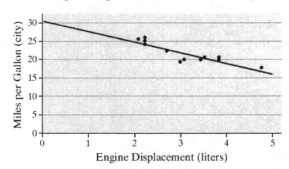

(c) The slope indicates that if the engine size is increased by 1 liter, the city fuel efficiency will be reduced by about 2.8 miles per gallon, on average. The y-intercept does not have a sensible interpretation because it would be making a prediction for a car with 0 engine displacement.

(d) $\hat{y} = -2.7977(3.8) + 30.4 \approx 19.8$ miles per gallon

(e) Residual: $y - \hat{y} = 20 - 19.8 = 0.2$ mpg

(f) The positive residual indicates that miles per gallon for the Ford Mustang is above normal.

119

7.   (a) Using technology: $\hat{y} = 2.2091x - 34.3148$

(b)

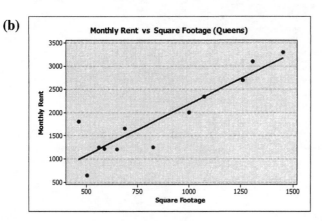

(c) The slope indicates that each additional square foot of space in the apartment will increase the monthly rent by $2.21. The y-intercept, being negative, does not have a sensible interpretation in this case (e.g. rent will not be negative).

(d)   Rent $= 2.2091x - 34.3148$

$$= 2.2091(825) - 34.3148$$

$$\approx 1788.2$$

or about $1788 per month.

(e) Residual: $y - \hat{y} = 1250 - 1788.2 = -538.2$

(f) The negative residual indicates that the apartment's rent is below average for apartments of that size.

9.   (a)

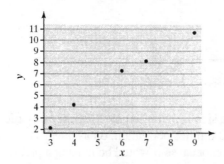

(b) Using the two points (3, 2.1) and (7, 8.1) gives:

$$m = \frac{8.1 - 2.1}{7 - 3} = \frac{3}{2} = 1.5$$

$$y - 2.1 = 1.5(x - 3)$$

$$y - 2.1 = 1.5x - 4.5$$

$$y = 1.5x - 2.4$$

120

(c)

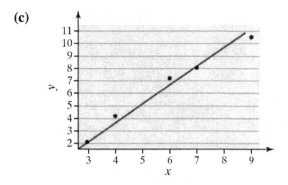

(d) Using technology, we get: $\hat{y} = 1.3877x - 1.6088$

(e)

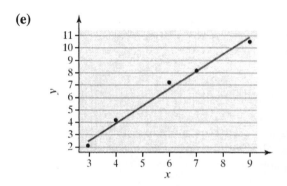

(f)

x	y	$\hat{y} = 1.5x - 2.4$	$y - \hat{y}$	$(y - \hat{y})^2$
3	2.1	2.1	0	0
4	4.2	3.6	0.6	0.36
6	7.2	6.6	0.6	0.36
7	8.1	8.1	0	0
9	10.6	11.1	−0.5	0.25

Total = 0.97

(g)

x	y	$\hat{y}$	$y - \hat{y}$	$(y - \hat{y})^2$
3	2.1	2.5543	−0.4543	0.20639
4	4.2	3.9420	0.2580	0.06656
6	7.2	6.7174	−0.4826	0.23290
7	8.1	8.1051	−0.0051	0.00003
9	10.6	10.8805	−0.2805	0.07868

Total = 0.58456

(h) The regression line gives a smaller sum of squared residuals and so is a better fit.

121

11. A linear model is appropriate: there is no pattern to the residuals and the variability stays the same.

13. A linear model is not appropriate because the amount of scatter in the residuals is clearly decreasing, indicating that the error variance is not constant.

15. (a) In Problem 1 we found that $r = -0.8954$. Therefore, $R^2 = (-0.8954)^2 \approx 0.8017$. We would say that 80.17% (or about 80.2%) of the variation in miles per gallon is explained by the least-squares regression equation.

(b)

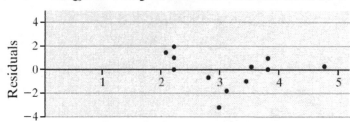

(c) The residuals seem to be forming a discernable pattern, possibly even getting smaller as engine displacement increases. The constant error variance assumption might be violated, so a linear model is not appropriate.

(d) The Ford Crown Victoria is potentially an outlier.

(e) 1a, 5b

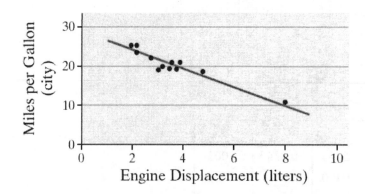

1b. Using technology: $r = -0.9421$

1c. Based on the scatter diagram and the correlation coefficient, there appears to be a strong negative linear relation between engine displacement and fuel economy.

5a. $\hat{y} = -2.3834x + 29.1454$

122

5c. The slope of the least-squares regression line indicates that, for each additional liter of engine displacement, fuel economy is lessened by about 2.4 miles per gallon in city driving. It is not appropriate to interpret the y-intercept because it is not possible to have zero engine displacement.

5d. $\hat{y} = -2.3834(3.8) + 29.1454 \approx 20.0885$ or about 20.09 miles per gallon.

A Ford Mustang with a 3.8 liter engine is predicted to get about 20.09 miles per gallon in the city.

5e. residual $= y - \hat{y} = 20 - 20.09 = -0.09$ miles per gallon

5f. The negative residual indicates that the miles per gallon are below average for a Ford Mustang.

15a. $R^2 = (-0.9421)^2 \approx 0.8876$

We would say that 88.76% (or about 88.8%) of the variation in miles per gallon is explained by the least-squares regression equation.

15b.

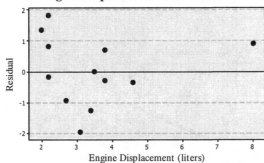

Engine Displacement Residual Plot

15c. The residuals are forming a discernable V-shaped pattern. The linear model may not be appropriate.

15d., e.

The Viper appears to fall in line with the general pattern, but the slope of the regression line does change some (from about -2.80 to about -2.38) with the addition of the Viper. Therefore, the Viper is not considered an outlier but it may be an influential observation. Note that the R^2 value increased substantially with the addition of the Viper.

The Mercury Sable is potentially an outlier. Removing the observation does not greatly change the regression line so it does not appear to be influential.

17. (a) From Problem 3, we have $r = 0.9093$ (Queens). Therefore,

$R^2 = (0.9093)^2 \approx 0.827 = 82.7\%$.

82.7% of the variation in monthly rent is explained by the least-squares regression equation.

(b)

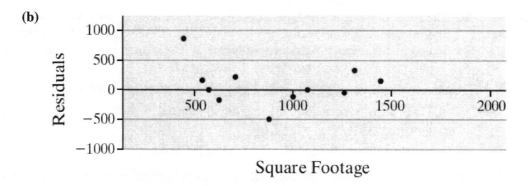

(c) The plot of the residuals shows no discernable pattern. Therefore, a linear model appears to be appropriate.

(d) The observation $(460, 1805)$ is both an outlier and an influential point. If we omit this point, the least-squares regression equation becomes $\hat{y} = 2.5315x - 399.25$. There is a substantial difference in the y-intercept of the equation.

19. (a) $\hat{y} = 2.0995x - 347.364$

(b)

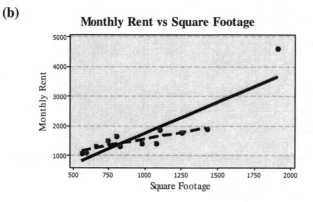

The 1906-square-foot apartment is clearly an outlier. Removing the observation dramatically changes the regression line, so it is also an influential observation. If this data point is removed, the least-squares regression line becomes $\hat{y} = 0.0779x + 675.295$. With that value removed, the rest of the data appears to be fit well by a linear model.

21. (a)

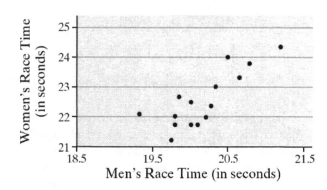

(b) Using technology: $r = 0.8352$

(c) The relation between men's and women's times seems to be positively associated. A strong correlation does not imply causation. While there appears to be a strong relationship between the two sets of data, men's times do not cause women's times.

23. While a relation may exist between wine consumption and heart-rate variability, we cannot say that increased wine consumption *causes* an increase in heart-rate variability. Correlation does not imply causation.

25. (a) Answers will vary.

(b) The slope can be interpreted as "the increase in the length of the school day decreases by about 0.01 hours for every 1 percent increase in the percentage of the district with low income", on average. The y-intercept can be interpreted as the length of the school day for a district with no low income families.

(c) $\hat{y} = -0.0102(20) + 7.11 = 6.906$

The school day is predicted to be about 6.9 hours long if 20% of the district is low income.

(d) Answers will vary. Because so many of the data values are clumped together, it is difficult to see any patterns. As shown, it does not appear that any of the model requirements are badly violated.

(e) Answers will vary. The likely candidates will be the three points with the highest percentage of low income population.

(f) Answers will vary.

(g) Answers will vary. There is some indication that there is a positive association between length of school day and PSAE score.

(h) Answers will vary. The scatter diagram indicates that there is some negative association between PSAE score and percentage of population as low income. However, it is likely not as strong as the correlation coefficient indicates. A few influential observations could be inflating the correlation coefficient.

(i) Answers will vary.

Chapter 5

Probability

5.1 Probability Rules

1. Empirical probability is based on the outcome of a probability experiment and is approximately equal to the relative frequency of the event. Classical probability is based on counting techniques and is equal to the ratio of the number of ways an event can occur to the number of possible outcomes in the experiment.

3. Outcomes are equally likely when each outcome has the same probability of occurring.

5. True

7. experiment

9. Rule 1 is satisfied since all of the probabilities in the model are greater than or equal to zero and less than or equal to one. Rule 2 is satisfied since the sum of the probabilities in the model is one: $0.3 + 0.15 + 0 + 0.15 + 0.2 + 0.2 = 1$. In this model, the outcome "blue" is an impossible event.

11. This cannot be a probability model because $P(\text{green}) < 0$.

13. Probabilities must be between 0 and 1, inclusive, so the only values which could be probabilities are: 0, 0.01, 0.35, and 1.

15. The probability of 0.42 means that approximately 42 out of every 100 hands will contain two cards of the same value and three cards of different value. No. Just because 42 of the 100 hands are likely to contain a pair, this does not mean it will definitely happen.

17. The probability that the next flip would result in a head is approximately $\dfrac{95}{100} = 0.95$.

19. $P(2) \neq \dfrac{1}{11}$ because the 11 possible outcomes are not equally likely.

21. The sample space is $S = \{1H, 2H, 3H, 4H, 5H, 6H, 1T, 2T, 3T, 4T, 5T, 6T\}$

23. The probability that a randomly selected three-year-old is enrolled in daycare is $P = 0.44$.

25. Event E contains 3 of the 10 equally likely outcomes, so $P(E) = \dfrac{3}{10} = 0.3$.

27. There are 10 equally likely outcomes and 5 are even numbers, so $P(E) = \dfrac{5}{10} = \dfrac{1}{2} = 0.5$.

29. $P(\text{plays organized sports}) = \dfrac{288}{500} = 0.576$

31. (a) Since 40 of the 100 equally likely tulip bulbs are red, $P(\text{red}) = \dfrac{40}{100} = 0.4$.

(b) Since 25 of the 100 equally likely tulip bulbs are purple, $P(\text{purple}) = \dfrac{25}{100} = 0.25$.

33. (a) The sample space is $S = \{0, 00, 1, 2, 3, 4,\ldots, 36\}$.

(b) Since the slot marked 8 is one of the 38 equally likely outcomes, $P(8) = \dfrac{1}{38} \approx 0.0263$. This means that, in many spins of such a roulette wheel, the long-run relative frequency of the ball landing on "8" will be close to $\dfrac{1}{38} \approx 0.0263 = 2.63\%$.

(c) Since there are 18 odd slots (1, 3, 5, 7, 9, 11, 13, 15, 17, 19, 21, 23, 25, 27, 29, 31, 33, 35) of the 38 equally likely outcomes, $\dfrac{18}{38} = \dfrac{9}{19} \approx 0.4737$. This means that, in many spins of such a roulette wheel, the long-run relative frequency of the ball landing in an odd slot will be close to $\dfrac{9}{19} \approx 0.4737 = 4.737\%$.

35. (a) The sample space of possible genotypes is $\{SS, Ss, sS, ss\}$.

(b) Only one of the four equally likely genotypes gives rise to sickle cell anemia, namely ss. Thus, the probability is $P(ss) = \dfrac{1}{4} = 0.25$. This means that of the many children who are offspring of two Ss parents, approximately $\dfrac{1}{4}$ will have sickle cell anemia.

(c) Two of the four equally likely genotypes result in a carrier, namely Ss and sS. Thus, the probability of this is $P(Ss \text{ or } sS) = \dfrac{2}{4} = \dfrac{1}{2} = 0.5$. This means that of the many children who are offspring of two Ss parents, approximately $\dfrac{1}{2}$ will not themselves have sickle cell anemia but will be carriers of sickle cell anemia.

37. (a) There are $125 + 324 + 552 + 1257 + 2518 = 4776$ college students in the survey. The individuals can be thought of as the trials of the probability experiment. The relative frequency of "Never" is $\dfrac{125}{4776} \approx 0.026$. We compute the relative frequencies of the other outcomes similarly and obtain the probability model below.

Response	Probability
Never	0.026
Rarely	0.068
Sometimes	0.116
Most of the time	0.263
Always	0.527

(b) Yes, it is unusual to find a college student who never wears a seatbelt. The approximate probability of this is only 0.026.

39. (a) There are $5 + 5 + 118 + 197 + 77 + 43 + 105 + 45 = 595$ police records included in the survey. The individuals can be thought of as the trials of the probability experiment. The relative frequency of "Pocket picking" is $\dfrac{5}{595} \approx 0.008$. We compute the relative frequencies of the other outcomes similarly and obtain the probability model below.

Type of Larceny Theft	Probability
Pocket picking	0.008
Purse snatching	0.008
Shoplifting	0.198
From motor vehicles	0.331
Motor vehicle accessories	0.129
Bicycles	0.072
From buildings	0.176
From coin-operated machines	0.076

(b) Yes, purse-snatching larcenies are unusual since the probability is only 0.008.

(c) No, larcenies from coin-operated machines are not unusual since the probability is 0.072.

41. Assignments A, B, C, and F are consistent with the definition of a probability model. Assignment D cannot be a probability model because it contains a negative probability, and Assignment E cannot be a probability model because is does not add up to 1.

43. Assignment B should be used if the coin is known to always come up tails.

45. (a) The sample space is $S = \{$John-Roberto; John-Clarice; John-Dominique; John-Marco, Roberto-Clarice; Roberto-Dominique; Roberto-Marco; Clarice-Dominique; Clarice-Marco; Dominique-Marco$\}$.

(b) Clarice-Dominique is one of the ten possible samples from part (a). Thus,
$$P(\text{Clarice and Dominique}) = \frac{1}{10} = 0.1.$$

(c) Four of the ten samples from part (a) include Clarice. Thus,
$$P(\text{Clarice attends}) = \frac{4}{10} = \frac{2}{5} = 0.4.$$

(d) Six of the ten samples from part (a) do not include John. Thus,
$$P(\text{John stays home}) = \frac{6}{10} = \frac{3}{5} = 0.6.$$

47. (a) Since 24 of the 73 homeruns went to right field, $P(\text{right field}) = \dfrac{24}{73} \approx 0.329$.

(b) Since 2 of the 73 homeruns went to left field, $P(\text{right field}) = \dfrac{2}{73} \approx 0.027$.

(c) Yes, it was unusual for Barry Bonds to his a homerun to left field. The probability is below 0.05.

49. Answers will vary depending on the results from the simulation.

51. If the dice were fair, then each outcome should occur approximately $\dfrac{400}{6} \approx 67$ times.

Since 1 and 6 occurred with considerably higher frequency, the dice appear to be loaded.

53. Half of all families are above the median and half are below, so

$P(\text{Income greater than } \$57{,}500) = \dfrac{1}{2}$.

5.2 The Addition Rule and Complements

1. Two events are disjoint if they have no outcomes in common.

3. $P(E) + P(F) - P(E \text{ and } F)$

5. E and $F = \{5, 6, 7\}$. No, E and F are not mutually exclusive because they have simple events in common.

7. F or $G = \{5, 6, 7, 8, 9, 10, 11, 12\}$. $P(F \text{ or } G) = P(F) + P(G) - P(F \text{ and } G) =$
$\dfrac{5}{12} + \dfrac{4}{12} - \dfrac{1}{12} = \dfrac{2}{3}$.

9. E and $G = \{\ \}$. Yes, E and G are mutually exclusive because they have no simple events in common.

11. $E^c = \{1, 8, 9, 10, 11, 12\}$. $P(E^c) = 1 - P(E) = 1 - \dfrac{6}{12} = \dfrac{1}{2}$.

13. $P(E \text{ or } F) = P(E) + P(F) - P(E \text{ and } F) = 0.25 + 0.45 - 0.15 = 0.55$

15. $P(E \text{ or } F) = P(E) + P(F) = 0.25 + 0.45 = 0.7$.

17. $P(E^c) = 1 - P(E) = 1 - 0.25 = 0.75$

19. $P(A \text{ or } B) = P(A) + P(B) - P(A \text{ and } B)$
$0.85 = 0.60 + P(B) - 0.05$
$P(B) = 0.85 - 0.60 + 0.05 = 0.30$

129

21. P(Titleist or Maxfli) = $\dfrac{9+8}{20} = \dfrac{17}{20}$.

23. $P\left(\text{Not Titleist}\right) = 1 - P\left(\text{Titleist}\right) = 1 - \dfrac{9}{20} = \dfrac{11}{20}$

25. **(a)** Rule 1 is satisfied since all of the probabilities in the model are between 0 and 1. Rule 2 is satisfied since the sum of the probabilities in the model is one: $0.668 + 0.125 + 0.048 + 0.067 + 0.017 + 0.007 + 0.068 = 1$.

    (b) $P\left(\text{gun or knife}\right) = 0.668 + 0.125 = 0.793$. This means that there is a 79.3% probability of randomly selecting a murder committed with a gun or a knife.

    (c) $P\left(\text{knife, blunt object, or strangulation}\right) = 0.125 + 0.048 + 0.017 = 0.190$. This means that there is a 19.0% probability of randomly selecting a murder committed with a knife, with a blunt object, or by strangulation.

    (d) $P\left(\text{not a gun or knife}\right) = 1 - 0.668 = 0.332$. This means that there is a 33.2% probability of randomly selecting a murder that was not committed with a gun.

    (e) Yes, murders by are unusual since the probability is only 0.017.

27. The total number of multiple births was $93 + 511 + 1628 + 2832 + 1843 + 377 + 117 = 7401$.

    (a) $P(30-39) = P(30-34) + P(35-39) = \dfrac{2832 + 1843}{7401} \approx 0.632$. This means that there is a 63.2% probability that a mother involved in a multiple birth was between 30 and 39 years old.

    (b) $P(\text{not } 30-39) = 1 - P(30-39) \approx 1 - 0.632 = 0.368$. This means that there is a 36.2% probability that a mother involved in a multiple birth was not between 30 and 39.

    (c) $P(\text{younger than } 45) = 1 - \dfrac{117}{7401} \approx 0.984$. This means that there is a 98.4% probability that a randomly selected mother involved in a multiple birth was younger than 45.

    (d) $P(\text{at least } 20) = 1 - \dfrac{93}{7401} \approx 0.987$. This means that there is a 98.4% probability that a randomly selected mother involved in a multiple birth was at least 20 years old.

29. **(a)** P(Heart or Club) = P(Heart) + P(Club) = $\dfrac{13}{52} + \dfrac{13}{52} = \dfrac{1}{2} = 0.5$.

    (b) P(Heart, Club, or Diamond) = P(Heart) + P(Club) + P(Diamond)
$$= \dfrac{13}{52} + \dfrac{13}{52} + \dfrac{13}{52} = \dfrac{3}{4} = 0.75\,.$$

    (c) P(Ace or Heart) = P(Ace) + P(Heart) − P(Ace of Hearts) = $\dfrac{4}{52} + \dfrac{13}{52} - \dfrac{1}{52} = \dfrac{4}{13} \approx 0.3077$.

130

31. (a) $P(\text{Not on Nov. 8}) = 1 - P(\text{On Nov. 8}) = 1 - \dfrac{1}{365} = \dfrac{364}{365} \approx 0.9973$

(b) $P(\text{Birthday not on the } 1^{st}) = 1 - P(\text{Birthday on the } 1^{st}) = 1 - \dfrac{12}{365} = \dfrac{353}{365} \approx 0.9671$

(c) $P(\text{Birthday on the } 31^{st}) = 1 - (\text{Birthday not on the } 31^{st}) = 1 - \dfrac{7}{365} = \dfrac{358}{365} \approx 0.9808$

(d) $P(\text{Birthday in Dec.}) = 1 - P(\text{Birthday not in Dec.}) = 1 - \dfrac{31}{365} = \dfrac{334}{365} \approx 0.9151$.

33. No, we cannot compute the probability of randomly selecting a citizen of the U.S. who has hearing problems or vision problems by adding the given probabilities because the events "hearing problems" and "vision problems" are not disjoint. That is, some people have both vision and hearing problems, but we do not know what the proportion is.

35. (a) $P(\text{only English or only Spanish}) = P(\text{only English}) + P(\text{only Spanish})$
$$= 0.82 + 0.11 = 0.93.$$

(b) $P(\text{not only English or only Spanish}) = 1 - P(\text{only English or only Spanish})$
$$= 1 - 0.93 = 0.07.$$

(c) $P(\text{not only English}) = 1 - P(\text{only English}) = 1 - 0.82 = 0.18.$

(d) No, the probability that a randomly selected household speaks Polish at home cannot equal 0.08 because the sum of the probabilities would be more than 1 and there would be no probability model.

37. (a) Of the 137,243 men included in the study, $782 + 91 + 141 = 1014$ died from cancer.
Thus, $P(\text{died from cancer}) = \dfrac{1014}{137,243} \approx 0.007$.

(b) Of the 137,243 men included in the study, $141 + 7725 = 7866$ were current cigar smokers. Thus, $P(\text{current cigar smoker}) = \dfrac{7866}{137,243} \approx 0.057$.

(c) Of the 137,243 men included in the study, 141 were current cigar smokers who died from cancer. Thus, $P(\text{died from cancer and current cigar smoker}) = \dfrac{141}{137,243} \approx 0.001$.

(d) Of the 137,243 men included in the study, 1014 died from cancer, 7866 were current cigar smokers, and 141 were current cigar smoker who died from cancer. Thus,
$$P(\text{died from cancer or current cigar smoker}) = \dfrac{1014}{137,243} + \dfrac{7866}{137,243} - \dfrac{141}{137,243} = \dfrac{8739}{137,243}$$
$$\approx 0.064.$$

39. (a) Of the 375 students surveyed, 231 were satisfied with student government. Thus,

$$P(\text{satisfied}) = \frac{231}{375} = \frac{77}{125} = 0.616.$$

(b) Of the 375 students surveyed, 94 were juniors. Thus, $P(\text{junior}) = \frac{94}{375} \approx 0.251.$

(c) Of the 375 students surveyed, 64 were juniors who were satisfied with student government. Thus, $P(\text{satisfied and junior}) = \frac{64}{375} \approx 0.171.$

(d) Of the 375 students surveyed, 231 were satisfied with student government, 94 were juniors, and 64 were juniors who were satisfied with student government. Thus,

$$P(\text{satisfied or junior}) = \frac{231}{375} + \frac{94}{375} - \frac{64}{375} = \frac{261}{375} = \frac{87}{125} = 0.696.$$

41. (a) Of the 1,392,301 military personnel, 226,232 are officers. Thus,

$$P(\text{officer}) = \frac{226,232}{1,392,301} \approx 0.162.$$

(b) Of the 1,392,301 military personnel, 363,595 are in the Navy. Thus,

$$P(\text{Navy}) = \frac{363,595}{1,392,301} \approx 0.261.$$

(c) Of the 1,392,301 military personnel, 53,428 are in the Navy officers. Thus,

$$P(\text{Navy officer}) = \frac{53,428}{1,392,301} \approx 0.038.$$

(d) Of the 1,392,301 military personnel, 226,232 are officers, 363,595 are in the Navy, and 53,428 are in the Navy officers. Thus,

$$P(\text{officer or Navy}) = \frac{226,232}{1,392,301} + \frac{363,595}{1,392,301} - \frac{53,428}{1,392,301} = \frac{536,399}{1,392,301} \approx 0.385.$$

5.3 Independence and the Multiplication Rule

1. independent **3.** Addition **5.** $P(E) \cdot P(F)$

7. (a) Dependent. Being cloudy affects the probability of rain.

(b) Independent. Having a flat tire would not affect the probability of an increase in the price of gasoline, and vice versa.

(c) Dependent. Smoking affects the probability of living at least 80 years.

9. $P(E \text{ and } F) = P(E) \cdot P(F) = (0.3)(0.6) = 0.18$ since E and F are independent.

11. $P(5 \text{ heads in a row}) = \left(\frac{1}{2}\right)\left(\frac{1}{2}\right)\left(\frac{1}{2}\right)\left(\frac{1}{2}\right)\left(\frac{1}{2}\right) = \left(\frac{1}{2}\right)^5 = \frac{1}{32} = 0.03125.$ This means that if a coin is flipped 5 times, the result would be 5 heads 3.125% of the time.

13. $P(2\text{ left-handed people}) = (0.13)(0.13) = 0.0169$.

   $P(\text{At least 1 is right-handed}) = 1 - P(2\text{ left-handed people}) = 1 - 0.0169 = 0.9831$.

15. **(a)** $P(\text{all 5 negative}) = (0.995)(0.995)(0.995)(0.995)(0.995) = (0.995)^5 \approx 0.9752$

   (b) $P(\text{at least one positive}) = 1 - P(\text{all 5 negative}) = 1 - 0.9752 = 0.0248$

17. **(a)** $P(\text{Both live to be 41}) = (0.99718)(0.99718) \approx 0.99437$

   (b) $P(\text{All 5 live to be 41}) = (0.99718)^5 \approx 0.98598$

   (c) This is the complement of the event in (b), so the probability is $1 - 0.98598 = 0.01402$ which is unusual.

19. **(a)** $P(\text{Both have Rh}^+ \text{ blood}) = (0.99)(0.99) = 0.9801$

   (b) $P(\text{All 6 have Rh}^+ \text{ blood}) = (0.99)^6 \approx 0.9415$

   (c) This is the complement of the event in (b), so the probability is $1 - 0.9415 = 0.0585$ which is not unusual.

21. **(a)** $P(\text{batter makes 10 consecutive outs}) = (0.70)^{10} \approx 0.0282$

   (b) Yes, cold streaks are unusual since the probability is 0.0282.

23. The probability that an individual satellite will not detect a missile is $1 - 0.9 = 0.1$, so
   $P(\text{none of the 4 will detect the missile}) = (0.1)^4 = 0.0001$. Thus,
   $P(\text{at least one of the 4 satellites will detect the missile}) = 1 - 0.0001 = 0.9999$.
   Answer will vary. Generally, one would probably feel safe since only 1 in 10,000 missiles should go undetected.

25. **(a)** $P(\text{two strikes in a row}) = (0.3)(0.3) = 0.09$

   (b) $P(\text{turkey}) = (0.3)^3 = 0.027$

   (c) $P(\text{strike followed by a non-strike}) = P(\text{strike}) \cdot P(\text{non-strike}) = (0.3)(0.7) = 0.21$

27. **(a)** $P(\text{all 3 have driven under the influence of alcohol}) = (0.29)^3 \approx 0.0244$

   (b) $P(\text{at least one has not driven under the influence of alcohol}) = 1 - 0.0244 = 0.9756$

   (c) The probability that an individual 21- to 25-year-old has not driven while under the influence of alcohol is $1 - 0.29 = 0.71$, so
   $P(\text{none of the 3 have driven under the influence of alcohol}) = (0.71)^3 \approx 0.3579$

   (d) $P(\text{at least one of the 3 has driven under the influence of alcohol}) = 1 - 0.3579 = 0.6421$

5.4 Conditional Probability and the General Multiplication Rule

1. $F; E$

3. $P(F \mid E) = \dfrac{P(E \text{ and } F)}{P(E)} = \dfrac{0.6}{0.8} = 0.75$

5. $P(F \mid E) = \dfrac{N(E \text{ and } F)}{N(E)} = \dfrac{420}{740} = 0.5676$

7. $P(E \text{ and } F) = P(E) \cdot P(F \mid E) = (0.8)(0.4) = 0.32$

9. No, the events "earn more than \$75,000 per year" and "earned a bachelor's degree" are not independent because P("earn more than \$75,000 per year" | "earned a bachelor's degree") $\neq P$("earn more than \$75,000 per year").

11. $P(\text{club}) = \dfrac{13}{52} = \dfrac{1}{4}$; $P(\text{club} \mid \text{black card}) = \dfrac{13}{26} = \dfrac{1}{2}$

13. $P(\text{rainy day} \mid \text{cloudy day}) = \dfrac{P(\text{rainy day and cloudy day})}{P(\text{cloudy day})} = \dfrac{0.21}{0.37} \approx 0.568$

15. $P(\text{white} \mid \text{16-17 year-old dropout}) = \dfrac{P(\text{white and 16-17 year-old dropout})}{P(\text{16-17 year-old dropout})} = \dfrac{0.058}{0.091} \approx 0.637$

17. (a) $P(\text{no health insurance} \mid \text{under 18}) = \dfrac{N(\text{no health insurance and under 18})}{N(\text{under 18})}$

$= \dfrac{8,531}{49,473 + 19,662 + 8,531} = \dfrac{8,531}{77,666} \approx 0.110$

(b) $P(\text{under 18} \mid \text{no health insurance}) = \dfrac{N(\text{under 18 and no health insurance})}{N(\text{no health insurance})}$

$= \dfrac{8,531}{8,531 + 25,678 + 9,106 + 258} = \dfrac{8,531}{43,573} \approx 0.196$

19. (a) $P(\text{16-20 years old} \mid \text{male}) = \dfrac{N(\text{16-20 year old and male})}{N(\text{male})}$

$= \dfrac{5,696}{228 + 5,696 + 13,553 + 14,395 + 4,947 + 3,159} = \dfrac{5,696}{41,978} \approx 0.136$

(b) $P(\text{male} \mid \text{16-20 years old}) = \dfrac{N(\text{male and 16-20 year old})}{N(\text{16-20 year old})} = \dfrac{5696}{5696 + 2386} = \dfrac{5696}{8082} \approx 0.705$

(c) The victim is probably male. There is a 70.5% probability that a driver fatality who is 16 – 20 years old will be male.

21. $P(\text{both televisions work}) = P(\text{1st works}) \cdot P(\text{2nd works}\,|\,\text{1st works}) = \dfrac{4}{6} \cdot \dfrac{3}{5} = 0.4$

$P(\text{at least one television does not work}) = 1 - P(\text{both televisions work}) = 1 - 0.4 = 0.6$

23. $P(\text{Dave 1st and Neta 2nd}) = P(\text{Dave 1st}) \cdot P(\text{Neta 2nd}\,|\,\text{Dave 1st}) = \dfrac{1}{5} \cdot \dfrac{1}{4} = \dfrac{1}{20} = 0.05$

25. (a) $P(\text{like both songs}) = P(\text{like 1st song}) \cdot P(\text{like 2nd song}\,|\,\text{like 1st song})$

$= \dfrac{5}{13} \cdot \dfrac{4}{12} = \dfrac{5}{39} \approx 0.128$

This is not a small enough probability to be considered unusual.

(b) $P(\text{dislike both songs}) = P(\text{dislike 1st song}) \cdot P(\text{dislike 2nd song}\,|\,\text{dislike 1st song})$

$= \dfrac{8}{13} \cdot \dfrac{7}{12} = \dfrac{14}{39} \approx 0.359$

(c) Since you either like both or neither or exactly one (and these are disjoint) then the probability that you like exactly one is given by

$P(\text{like exactly one song}) = 1 - \left(\dfrac{5}{39} + \dfrac{14}{39} \right) = \dfrac{20}{39} \approx 0.513$

(d) $P(\text{like both songs}) = P(\text{like 1st song}) \cdot P(\text{like 2nd song}) = \dfrac{5}{13} \cdot \dfrac{5}{13} = \dfrac{25}{169} \approx 0.148$

$P(\text{dislike both songs}) = P(\text{dislike 1st song}) \cdot P(\text{dislike 2nd song})$

$= \dfrac{8}{13} \cdot \dfrac{8}{13} = \dfrac{64}{169} \approx 0.379$

$P(\text{like exactly one song}) = 1 - \left(\dfrac{25}{169} + \dfrac{64}{169} \right) = \dfrac{80}{169} \approx 0.473$

27. (a) $P(\text{both red}) = \dfrac{12}{30} \cdot \dfrac{11}{29} = \dfrac{22}{145} = 0.152$

(b) $P(\text{1st red and 2nd yellow}) = \dfrac{12}{30} \cdot \dfrac{10}{29} = \dfrac{4}{29} \approx 0.138$

(c) $P(\text{1st yellow and 2nd red}) = \dfrac{10}{30} \cdot \dfrac{12}{29} = \dfrac{4}{29} \approx 0.138$

(d) Since one each of red and yellow must be either 1st red, 2nd yellow or vice versa, by the addition rule this probability is $P(\text{one red and one yellow}) = \dfrac{4}{29} + \dfrac{4}{29} = \dfrac{8}{29} \approx 0.276$.

29. $P(\text{female and smoker}) = P(\text{female}\,|\,\text{smoker}) \cdot P(\text{smoker}) = (0.217)(0.234) \approx 0.051$

It is not unusual to select a female who smokes.

31. (a) $P(10 \text{ different birthdays}) = \dfrac{365}{365} \cdot \dfrac{364}{365} \cdot \dfrac{363}{365} \cdot \dfrac{362}{365} \cdot \dfrac{361}{365} \cdot \dfrac{360}{365} \cdot \dfrac{359}{365} \cdot \dfrac{358}{365} \cdot \dfrac{357}{365} \cdot \dfrac{356}{365} \approx 0.883$

(b) $P(\text{At least 2 of the 10 share a common birthday}) = 1 - 0.883 = 0.117$

33. (a) $P(\text{being dealt 5 clubs}) = \dfrac{13}{52} \cdot \dfrac{12}{51} \cdot \dfrac{11}{50} \cdot \dfrac{10}{49} \cdot \dfrac{9}{48} = \dfrac{33}{66,640} \approx 0.000495$

(b) $P(\text{bing dealt a flush}) = 4\left(\dfrac{33}{66,640}\right) = \dfrac{33}{16,660} \approx 0.002$

35. (a) $P(\text{selecting two defective chips}) = \dfrac{50}{10,000} \cdot \dfrac{49}{9,999} \approx 0.0000245$

(b) Assuming independence, $P(\text{selecting two defective chips}) \approx (0.005)^2 = 0.000025$.

The difference in the results of parts (a) and (b) is only 0.0000005, so the assumption of independence did not significantly affect the probability.

37. $P(<18 \text{ years old}) = \dfrac{49,473 + 19,662 + 8,531}{316,169} = \dfrac{77,666}{316,169} \approx 0.246$

$P(\text{under 18} \mid \text{no health insurance}) = \dfrac{8,531}{8,531 + 25,678 + 9,106 + 258} = \dfrac{8,531}{43,573} \approx 0.196$

No, the events "<18 years old" and "no health insurance" are not independent since the preceding probabilities are not equal.

39. $P(\text{female}) = \dfrac{108 + 2386 + 4148 + 5017 + 1708 + 1529}{56,864} = \dfrac{14,896}{56,864} \approx 0.262$

$P(\text{female} \mid \text{16-20}) = \dfrac{2386}{5696 + 2386} = \dfrac{2386}{8082} \approx 0.295$

No, the events "female" and "16-20" are not independent since the preceding probabilities are not equal.

5.5 Counting Techniques

1. permutation

3. True

5. $5! = 5 \cdot 4 \cdot 3 \cdot 2 \cdot 1 = 120$

7. $10! = 10 \cdot 9 \cdot 8 \cdot 7 \cdot 6 \cdot 5 \cdot 4 \cdot 3 \cdot 2 \cdot 1 = 3,628,800$

9. $0! = 1$

11. $_6P_2 = \dfrac{6!}{(6-2)!} = \dfrac{6!}{4!} = 6 \cdot 5 = 30$

13. $_4P_4 = \dfrac{4!}{(4-4)!} = \dfrac{4!}{0!} = \dfrac{24}{1} = 24$

15. $_5P_0 = \dfrac{5!}{(5-0)!} = \dfrac{5!}{5!} = 1$

17. $_8P_3 = \dfrac{8!}{(8-3)!} = \dfrac{8!}{5!} = 8 \cdot 7 \cdot 6 = 336$

19. $_8C_3 = \dfrac{8!}{3!(8-3)!} = \dfrac{8!}{3!5!} = \dfrac{8 \cdot 7 \cdot 6}{3 \cdot 2 \cdot 1} = 56$

21. $_{10}C_2 = \dfrac{10!}{2!(10-2)!} = \dfrac{10!}{2!8!} = \dfrac{10 \cdot 9}{2 \cdot 1} = 45$

23. $_{52}C_1 = \dfrac{52!}{1!(52-1)!} = \dfrac{52!}{1!51!} = \dfrac{52}{1} = 52$

25. $_{48}C_3 = \dfrac{48!}{3!(48-3)!} = \dfrac{48!}{3!45!} = \dfrac{48 \cdot 47 \cdot 46}{3 \cdot 2 \cdot 1} = 17,296$

27. $ab,\ ac,\ ad,\ ae,\ ba,\ bc,\ bd,\ be,\ ca,\ cb,\ cd,\ ce,\ da,\ db,\ dc,\ de,\ ea,\ eb,\ ec,\ ed$
Since there are 20 permutations, $_5P_2 = 20$.

29. $ab,\ ac,\ ad,\ ae,\ bc,\ bd,\ be,\ cd,\ ce,\ de$
Since there are 10 permutations, $_5C_2 = 10$.

31. $6 \cdot 4 = 24$

33. $12! = 479,001,600$

35. $8! = 40,320$

37. $26 \text{ (one letter)} + 26^2 \text{ (two letters)} + 26^3 \text{ (three letters)} = 18,278$

39. (a) $10^4 = 10,000$

(b) $P(\text{guessing the correct code}) = \dfrac{1}{10,000} = 0.0001$

41. $26^8 \approx 2.08827 \times 10^{11}$

43. (a) $50^3 = 125,000$

(b) $P(\text{guessing the combination}) = \dfrac{1}{50^3} = \dfrac{1}{125,000} = 0.000008$

45. $_{40}P_3 = 40 \cdot 39 \cdot 38 = 59,280$

47. $_{20}P_4 = 20 \cdot 19 \cdot 18 \cdot 17 = 116,280$

49. $_{25}P_4 = 25 \cdot 24 \cdot 23 \cdot 22 = 303,600$

51. $_{50}C_5 = \dfrac{50 \cdot 49 \cdot 48 \cdot 47 \cdot 46}{5 \cdot 4 \cdot 3 \cdot 2 \cdot 1} = 2,118,760$

53. $_6C_2 = \dfrac{6 \cdot 5}{2 \cdot 1} = 15$

55. Since there are three S's, three T's and two I's amongst these ten letters, we can make
$\dfrac{10!}{3!3!2!1!1!} = 50,400$ distinguishable words.

57. $\dfrac{11!}{4!5!2!} = 6930$

59. There are $_{30}C_5 = 142,506$ possible choices (without regard to order), so the probability of
winning is $\dfrac{1}{142,506}$.

61. (a) $P(\text{all students}) = \dfrac{_8C_5}{_{18}C_5} = \dfrac{8\cdot7\cdot6\cdot5\cdot4}{5\cdot4\cdot3\cdot2\cdot1}\cdot\dfrac{5\cdot4\cdot3\cdot2\cdot1}{18\cdot17\cdot16\cdot15\cdot14} = \dfrac{1}{153} \approx 0.0065$

(b) $P(\text{all faculty}) = \dfrac{_{10}C_5}{_{18}C_5} = \dfrac{10\cdot9\cdot8\cdot7\cdot6}{5\cdot4\cdot3\cdot2\cdot1}\cdot\dfrac{5\cdot4\cdot3\cdot2\cdot1}{18\cdot17\cdot16\cdot15\cdot14} = \dfrac{1}{34} \approx 0.0294$

(c) $P(\text{2 students, 3 faculty}) = \dfrac{_8C_2\cdot{}_{10}C_3}{_{18}C_5} = \dfrac{8\cdot7}{2\cdot1}\cdot\dfrac{10\cdot9\cdot8}{3\cdot2\cdot1}\cdot\dfrac{5\cdot4\cdot3\cdot2\cdot1}{18\cdot17\cdot16\cdot15\cdot14} = \dfrac{20}{51} \approx 0.3922$

63. $P(\text{one or more defective}) = 1 - P(\text{none defective}) = 1 - \dfrac{116}{120}\cdot\dfrac{115}{119}\cdot\dfrac{114}{118}\cdot\dfrac{113}{117} \approx 0.1283$

65. (a) $P(\text{you like 2 of the 4 songs}) = \dfrac{_5C_2\cdot{}_8C_2}{_{13}C_4} \approx 0.3916$

(b) $P(\text{you like 3 of the 4 songs}) = \dfrac{_5C_3\cdot{}_8C_1}{_{13}C_4} \approx 0.1119$

(c) $P(\text{you like all 4 songs}) = \dfrac{_5C_4\cdot{}_8C_0}{_{13}C_4} \approx 0.0070$

67. (a) Five cards can be selected from a deck in $_{52}C_5 = 2{,}598{,}960$ ways.

(b) There are $_4C_3 = 4$ ways of choosing 3 two's, and so on for each denomination. Hence, there are $13\cdot4 = 52$ ways of choosing three of a kind.

(c) There are $_{12}C_2 = 66$ choices of two additional denominations (different from that of the three of a kind) and 4 choices of suit for the first remaining card and then, for each choice of suit for the first remaining card, there are 4 choices of suit for the last card. This gives a total of $66\cdot4\cdot4 = 1056$ ways of choosing the last two cards.

(d) $P(\text{three of a kind}) = \dfrac{52\cdot1056}{2{,}598{,}960} \approx 0.0211$

69. $P(\text{all 4 modems work}) = \dfrac{17}{20}\cdot\dfrac{16}{19}\cdot\dfrac{15}{18}\cdot\dfrac{14}{17} \approx 0.4912$

5.6 Bayes's Rule (on CD)

1.

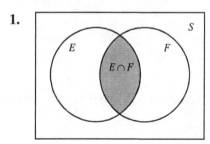

138

3. To partition a sample space S into three subsets A_1, A_2, and A_3 means that S is separated into three nonempty subsets where the subsets are all pairwise disjoint $A_1 \cup A_2 \cup A_3 = S$.

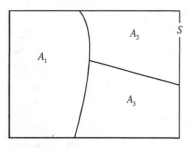

5. Answers will vary.

7. From the figure, $P(E \mid A) = 0.6$.

9. From the figure, $P(E^c \mid A) = 0.4$.

11. From the figure, $P(E \mid C) = 0.4$.

13. $P(E) = P(A) \cdot P(E \mid A) + P(B) \cdot P(E \mid B) + P(B) \cdot P(E \mid B)$
$= 0.2(0.6) + 0.55(0.7) + 0.25(0.4) = 0.12 + 0.385 + 0.1 = 0.605$

15. $P(A \mid E) = \dfrac{P(A) \cdot P(E \mid A)}{P(E)} = \dfrac{0.2(0.6)}{0.2(0.6) + 0.55(0.7) + 0.25(0.4)} = \dfrac{0.12}{0.605} \approx 0.198$

17. $P(C \mid E) = \dfrac{P(C) \cdot P(E \mid C)}{P(E)} = \dfrac{0.25(0.4)}{0.2(0.6) + 0.55(0.7) + 0.25(0.4)} = \dfrac{0.1}{0.605} \approx 0.165$

19. $P(B \mid E) = \dfrac{P(B) \cdot P(E \mid B)}{P(E)} = \dfrac{0.55(0.7)}{0.2(0.6) + 0.55(0.7) + 0.25(0.4)} = \dfrac{0.385}{0.605} \approx 0.636$

21. $P(E) = P(A_1) \cdot P(E \mid A_1) + P(A_2) \cdot P(E \mid A_2) = 0.55(0.06) + 0.45(0.08) = 0.069$

23. $P(E) = P(A_1) \cdot P(E \mid A_1) + P(A_2) \cdot P(E \mid A_2) + P(A_3) \cdot P(E \mid A_3)$
$= 0.35(0.25) + 0.45(0.18) + 0.2(0.14) = 0.1965$

25. (a) $P(A_1 \mid E) = \dfrac{P(A_1) \cdot P(E \mid A_1)}{P(E)} = \dfrac{0.55(0.06)}{0.069} \approx 0.4783$

(b) $P(A_2 \mid E) = \dfrac{P(A_2) \cdot P(E \mid A_2)}{P(E)} = \dfrac{0.45(0.08)}{0.069} \approx 0.5217$

27. (a) $P(A_1 \mid E) = \dfrac{P(A_1) \cdot P(E \mid A_1)}{P(E)} = \dfrac{0.35(0.25)}{0.1965} \approx 0.4453$

(b) $P(A_2 \mid E) = \dfrac{P(A_2) \cdot P(E \mid A_2)}{P(E)} = \dfrac{0.45(0.18)}{0.1965} \approx 0.4122$

(c) $P(A_3 \mid E) = \dfrac{P(A_3) \cdot P(E \mid A_3)}{P(E)} = \dfrac{0.2(0.14)}{0.1965} \approx 0.1425$

139

29. (a)

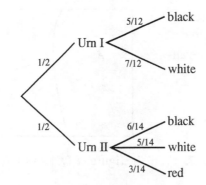

$$P(B) = B \cap U_1 + B \cap U_2$$

$$= \frac{1}{2}\left(\frac{5}{12}\right) + \frac{1}{2}\left(\frac{6}{14}\right)$$

$$= \frac{71}{168} \approx 0.4226$$

(b) $P(B) = P(U_1) \cdot P(B \mid U_1) + P(U_2) \cdot P(B \mid U_2) = \frac{1}{2}\left(\frac{5}{12}\right) + \frac{1}{2}\left(\frac{6}{14}\right) = \frac{71}{168} \approx 0.4226$

(c) $P(U_1 \mid B) = \dfrac{P(U_1) \cdot P(B \mid U_1)}{P(B)} = \dfrac{(1/2)(5/12)}{71/168} = \dfrac{35}{71} \approx 0.4930$

(d) $P(U_1 \mid R) = 0$ since there are no red balls in urn I.

$P(U_2 \mid R) = 1$ since the only red balls are in urn II.

31. (a)

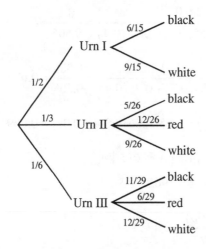

$$P(B) = B \cap U_1 + B \cap U_2 + B \cap U_3$$

$$= \frac{1}{2}\left(\frac{6}{15}\right) + \frac{1}{3}\left(\frac{5}{26}\right) + \frac{1}{6}\left(\frac{11}{29}\right)$$

$$= \frac{617}{1885} \approx 0.3273$$

(b) $P(B) = P(U_1) \cdot P(B \mid U_1) + P(U_2) \cdot P(B \mid U_2) + P(U_3) \cdot P(B \mid U_3)$

$$= \frac{1}{2}\left(\frac{6}{15}\right) + \frac{1}{3}\left(\frac{5}{26}\right) + \frac{1}{6}\left(\frac{11}{29}\right) = \frac{617}{1885} \approx 0.3273$$

(c) $P(U_1 \mid B) = \dfrac{P(U_1) \cdot P(B \mid U_1)}{P(B)} = \dfrac{(1/2)(6/15)}{617/1885} = \dfrac{377}{617} \approx 0.6110$

(d) $P(R) = P(U_1) \cdot P(R \mid U_1) + P(U_2) \cdot P(R \mid U_2) + P(U_3) \cdot P(R \mid U_3)$

$$= \frac{1}{2}(0) + \frac{1}{3}\left(\frac{9}{26}\right) + \frac{1}{6}\left(\frac{12}{29}\right) = \frac{139}{754} \approx 0.1844;$$

$$P(U_1 | R) = \frac{P(U_1) \cdot P(R|U_1)}{P(R)} = \frac{(1/2)(0)}{139/754} = 0 \quad \text{(note that no red balls are in urn I)};$$

$$P(U_2 | R) = \frac{P(U_2) \cdot P(R|U_2)}{P(R)} = \frac{(1/3)(9/26)}{139/754} = \frac{87}{139} \approx 0.6259;$$

$$P(U_3 | R) = \frac{P(U_3) \cdot P(R|U_3)}{P(R)} = \frac{(1/6)(12/29)}{139/754} = \frac{52}{139} \approx 0.3741.$$

33. **(a)** $P(\text{colorblind}) = P(\text{male}) \cdot P(\text{colorblind} | \text{male}) + P(\text{female}) \cdot P(\text{colorblind} | \text{female})$

$$= 0.491(0.08) + 0.509(0.0064) = 0.0425376 \approx 0.0425$$

(b) $P(\text{female} | \text{colorblind}) = \dfrac{P(\text{female}) \cdot P(\text{colorblind} | \text{female})}{P(\text{colorblind})} = \dfrac{0.509(0.0064)}{0.0425376} \approx 0.0766$

35. **(a)** $P(M) = P(A_1) \cdot P(M | A_1) + P(A_2) \cdot P(M | A_2) + P(A_3) \cdot P(M | A_3)$

$$+ P(A_4) \cdot P(M | A_4) + P(A_5) \cdot P(M | A_5) + P(A_6) \cdot P(M | A_6)$$

$$= 0.154(0.477) + 0.320(0.460) + 0.172(0.472)$$

$$+ 0.082(0.434) + 0.179(0.500) + 0.093(0.555)$$

$$= 0.478545 \approx 0.4785$$

(b) $P(A_6 | M) = \dfrac{P(A_6) \cdot P(M | A_6)}{P(M)} = \dfrac{0.093(0.555)}{0.478545} \approx 0.1079$

(c) $P(A_1 | M) = \dfrac{P(A_1) \cdot P(M | A_1)}{P(M)} = \dfrac{0.154(0.477)}{0.478545} \approx 0.1535$

37. **(a)** $P(D) = P(A_1) \cdot P(D | A_1) + P(A_2) \cdot P(D | A_2) + P(A_3) \cdot P(D | A_3)$

$$= 0.163(0.74) + 0.600(0.540) + 0.237(0.500) = 0.56312 \approx 0.5631$$

(b) $P(A_3 | D) = \dfrac{P(A_3) \cdot P(D | A_3)}{P(D)} = \dfrac{0.237(0.500)}{0.56312} \approx 0.2104$

(c) $P(A_1 | D) = \dfrac{P(A_1) \cdot P(D | A_1)}{P(D)} = \dfrac{0.163(0.74)}{0.56312} \approx 0.2142$

39. $P(\text{found } G) = P(G) \cdot P(\text{found } G | G) + P(I) \cdot P(\text{found } G | I)$

$$= 0.95(0.90) + 0.05(0.01) = 0.8555$$

$$P(I | \text{found } G) = \frac{P(I) \cdot P(\text{found } G | I)}{P(\text{found } G)} = \frac{0.05(0.01)}{0.8555} \approx 0.00058$$

Chapter 5 Review Exercises

1. **(a)** Probabilities must be between 0 and 1, so the possible probabilities are: 0, 0.75, 0.41.

   (b) Probabilities must be between 0 and 1, so the possible probabilities are: $\dfrac{2}{5}, \dfrac{1}{3}, \dfrac{6}{7}$.

3. Event E contains 2 of the 5 equally likely outcomes, so $P(E) = \dfrac{2}{5} = 0.4$.

5. Since $P(E) = \dfrac{1}{5} = 0.2$, we have $P(E^c) = 1 - \dfrac{1}{5} = \dfrac{4}{5} = 0.8$.

7. Since events E and F are mutually exclusive, $P(E \text{ or } F) = P(E) + P(F) = 0.36 + 0.12 = 0.48$.

9. No, events E and F are not independent because $P(E) \cdot P(F) = 0.8 \cdot 0.5 = 0.40 \neq P(E \text{ and } F)$.

11. $P(E \mid F) = \dfrac{P(E \text{ and } F)}{P(F)} = \dfrac{0.35}{0.7} = 0.5$.

13. **(a)** $P(\text{green}) = \dfrac{2}{38} = \dfrac{1}{19} \approx 0.0526$. This means that, in many games of roulette, the metal ball lands on green approximately 5.26% of the time.

    (b) $P(\text{green or red}) = \dfrac{2 + 18}{38} = \dfrac{20}{38} = \dfrac{10}{19} \approx 0.5263$. This means that, in many games of roulette, the metal ball lands on green or red approximately 52.63% of the time.

    (c) $P(00 \text{ or red}) = \dfrac{1 + 18}{38} = \dfrac{19}{38} = \dfrac{1}{2} = 0.5$. This means that, in many games of roulette, the metal ball lands on 00 or red approximately 50% of the time.

    (d) Since 31 is an odd number and the odd slots are colored red, $P(31 \text{ and black}) = 0$. This is called an impossible event.

15. **(a)** Of the 575 accidents, 301 were alcohol related, so $P(\text{alcohol related}) = \dfrac{301}{575} \approx 0.5235$.

    (b) Of the 575 accidents, $575 - 301 = 275$ were not alcohol related, so
    $P(\text{not alcohol related}) = \dfrac{274}{575} \approx 0.4765$.

    (c) $P(\text{both were alcohol related}) = \dfrac{301}{575} \cdot \dfrac{300}{574} = \dfrac{258}{943} \approx 0.2736$

    (d) $P(\text{neither was alcohol related}) = \dfrac{274}{575} \cdot \dfrac{273}{574} \approx 0.2266$

    (e) $P(\text{at least one of the two was alcohol related}) \approx 1 - 0.2266 = 0.7734$

17. (a) There are $5+99,402+14,580+3,790+164=117,936$ workers included in the table. The individuals can be thought of as the trials of the probability experiment. The relative frequency of "Private wage and salary worker" is $\dfrac{99,402}{117,936} \approx 0.8428$. We compute the relative frequencies of the other outcomes similarly and obtain the probability model below.

Type of Worker	Probability
Private wage and salary worker	0.8428
Government worker	0.1236
Self-employed worker	0.0321
Unpaid family worker	0.0014

(b) Yes, it is unusual for a Louisville worker to be an unpaid family worker since the probability is only 0.0014.

(c) Yes, it is unusual for a Louisville worker to be self-employed since the probability is only 0.0321.

19. (a) Of the 3,978,668 births included in the table, 268,005 are postterm. Thus,
$$P(\text{posterm}) = \frac{268,005}{3,978,668} \approx 0.0674.$$

(b) Of the 3,978,668 births included in the table, 2,622,283 weighed 3000 to 3999 grams. Thus, $P(3000 \text{ to } 3999 \text{ grams}) = \dfrac{2,622,005}{3,978,668} \approx 0.6591$.

(c) Of the 3,978,668 births included in the table, 192,566 both weighed 3000 to 3999 grams and were postterm. Thus, $P(3000 \text{ to } 3999 \text{ grams and postterm}) = \dfrac{192,566}{3,978,668} \approx 0.0484$.

(d) $P(3000 \text{ to } 3999 \text{ grams or postterm})$
$= P(3000 \text{ to } 3999 \text{ grams}) + P(\text{postterm}) - P(3000 \text{ to } 3999 \text{ grams and postterm})$
$= 0.6591 + 0.0674 - 0.0484 = 0.6781.$

(e) Of the 3,978,668 births included in the table, 32 both weighed less than 1000 grams and were postterm. Thus, $P(\text{less than } 1000 \text{ grams and postterm}) = \dfrac{32}{3,978,668} \approx 0.000008$.

This event is highly unlikely, but not impossible.

(f) $P(3000 \text{ to } 3999 \text{ grams} \mid \text{postterm}) = \dfrac{N(3000 \text{ to } 3999 \text{ grams and postterm})}{N(\text{postterm})}$

$= \dfrac{192,566}{268,005} \approx 0.7185$

(g) No, the events "postterm baby" and "weighs 3000 to 3999 grams" are not independent since $P(3000 \text{ to } 3999 \text{ grams}) \cdot P(\text{postterm}) = 0.6591(0.0674) = 0.0444 \neq P(3000 \text{ to } 3999 \text{ grams and postterm}) = 0.0484.$

21. **(a)** P(complaint filed online) $= 0.63$.

(b) P(complaint not filed online) $= 1 - 0.63 = 0.37$.

(c) P(all 5 complaints filed online) $= (0.63)^5 \approx 0.099$.

(d) P(at least one of the five complaints not filed online) $= 1 - 0.099 = 0.901$.

(e) P(none of the 5 complaints filed online) $= (0.37)^5 \approx 0.007$.

(f) P(at least one of the five complaints filed online) $= 1 - 0.007 = 0.993$.

23. $P\left(\text{matching the winning PICK 3 numbers}\right) = \dfrac{1}{10} \cdot \dfrac{1}{10} \cdot \dfrac{1}{10} = \dfrac{1}{1000} = 0.001$.

25. $P\left(\text{accept shipment}\right) = \dfrac{9}{10} \cdot \dfrac{8}{9} = 0.8$

27. $26 \cdot 26 \cdot 10^4 = 6{,}760{,}000$ license plates

29. $6! = 720$ different arrangements

31. $_{55}C_8 = 1{,}217{,}566{,}350$ samples possible

33. $P\left(\text{winning Arizona's Fantasy 5}\right) = \dfrac{1}{_{35}C_5} = \dfrac{1}{324{,}632} \approx 0.000003$

35. **(a)** $P\left(\text{all three are Merlot}\right) = \dfrac{5}{12} \cdot \dfrac{4}{11} \cdot \dfrac{3}{10} = \dfrac{1}{22} \approx 0.0455$

(b) $P\left(\text{exactly two are Merlot}\right) = \dfrac{_5C_2 \cdot _7C_1}{_{12}C_3} = \dfrac{5 \cdot 4}{2 \cdot 1} \cdot \dfrac{7}{1} \cdot \dfrac{3 \cdot 2 \cdot 1}{12 \cdot 11 \cdot 10} = \dfrac{7}{22} \approx 0.3182$

(c) $P\left(\text{none are Merlot}\right) = \dfrac{7}{12} \cdot \dfrac{6}{11} \cdot \dfrac{5}{10} = \dfrac{7}{44} \approx 0.1591$

37. Subjective probabilities are probabilities based on educated guesses. Examples will vary.

39. **(a)** Since 20 of the 70 homeruns went to left field, $P\left(\text{left field}\right) = \dfrac{34}{70} = \dfrac{17}{35} \approx 0.4857$. Mark McGwire hit 48.57% of his home runs to left field that year.

(b) Since none of the 70 homeruns went to right field, $P\left(\text{right field}\right) = \dfrac{0}{70} = 0$.

(c) No. While Mark McGwire did not hit any home runs to right field in 1998, this does not imply that it is impossible for him to hit a right-field homerun.

Chapter 6

Discrete Probability Distributions

6.1 Probability Distributions

1. A random variable is a numerical measure of the outcome of a probability experiment, so its value is determined by chance.

3. For a discrete probability distribution, each probability must be between 0 and 1 (inclusive) and the sum of the probabilities must equal one.

5. The historical average is based on long-term results. Short-term results can vary dramatically. A batting average of 0.300 means the batter averages 3 hits out of 10 at-bats *in the long run*. It does not mean that he will get 3 hits out of *every* 10 at-bats. A batter in a dry spell is not "due for a hit" nor is a batter with a hitting streak "due for an out". These dry spells and streaks will get washed out in the long run.

7. (a) The number of light bulbs that burn out, X, is a discrete random variable because the value of the random variable results from counting.
Possible values: $x = 0, 1, 2, 3, \ldots, 20$

(b) The time it takes to fly from New York City to Los Angeles is a continuous random variable because time is measured. If we let the random variable T represent the time it takes to fly from New York City to Los Angeles, the possible values for T are all positive real numbers; that is $t > 0$.

(c) The number of hits to a web site in a day is a discrete random variable because the value of the random variable results from counting. If we let the random variable X represent the number of hits, then the possible values of X are $x = 0, 1, 2, \ldots$.

(d) The amount of snow in Toronto during the winter is a continuous random variable because the amount of snow is measured. If we let the random variable S represent the amount of snow in Toronto during the winter, the possible values for S are all nonnegative real numbers; that is $s \geq 0$.

9. (a) The amount of rain in Seattle during April is a continuous random variable because the amount of rain is measured. If we let the random variable R represent the amount of rain, the possible values for R are all nonnegative real numbers; that is, $r \geq 0$.

(b) The number of fish caught during a fishing tournament is a discrete random variable because the value of the random variable results from counting. If we let the random variable X represent the number of fish caught, the possible values of X are $x = 0, 1, 2, \ldots$.

(c) The number of customers arriving at a bank between noon and 1:00 P.M. is a discrete random variable because the value of the random variable results from counting. If we let the random variable X represent the number of customers arriving at the bank between noon and 1:00 P.M., the possible values of X are $x = 0, 1, 2, ...$

(d) The time required to download a file from the Internet is a continuous random variable because time is measured. If we let the random variable T represent the time required to download a file, the possible values of T are all positive real numbers; that is, $t > 0$.

11. Yes, because $\sum P(x) = 1$ and $0 \le P(x) \le 1$ for all x.

13. No, because $P(50) < 0$.

15. No, because $\sum P(x) = 0.95 \ne 1$.

17. We need the sum of all the probabilities to equal 1. For the given probabilities, we have $0.4 + 0.1 + 0.2 = 0.7$. For the sum of the probabilities to equal 1, the missing probability must be $1 - 0.7 = 0.3$. That is, $P(4) = 0.3$.

19. (a) This is a discrete probability distribution because all the probabilities are between 0 and 1 (inclusive) and the sum of the probabilities is 1.

(b)

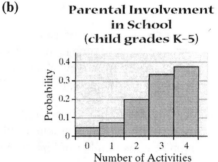

Parental Involvement in School (child grades K-5)

(c) $\mu_X = \sum [x \cdot P(x)] = 0(0.035) + 1(0.074) + ... + 4(0.374) = 2.924 \approx 2.9$

On average, the number of activities that at least one parent of a K-5th grader is involved in is expected to be about 2.9.

(d) $\sigma_X^2 = \sum [(x - \mu_X)^2 \cdot P(x)]$

$= (0 - 2.924)^2 (0.035) + (1 - 2.924)^2 (0.074) + ... + (4 - 2.924)^2 (0.374)$

≈ 1.176 or about 1.2

(e) $\sigma_X = \sqrt{\sigma_X^2} = \sqrt{1.176} \approx 1.085$ or about 1.1.

(f) $P(3) = 0.320$

(g) $P(3 \text{ or } 4) = P(3) + P(4) = 0.320 + 0.374 = 0.694$

146

21. (a) This is a discrete probability distribution because all the probabilities are between 0 and 1 (inclusive) and the sum of the probabilities is 1.

(b)

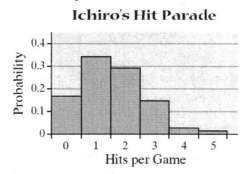

Ichiro's Hit Parade

(c) $\mu_X = \sum\left[x \cdot P(x)\right] = 0(0.1677) + 1(0.3354) + \ldots + 5(0.0248) = 1.6273 \approx 1.6$

Over many games, Ichiro is expected to average about 1.6 hits per game.

(d) $\sigma_X^2 = \sum\left[(x - \mu_X)^2 \cdot P(x)\right]$

$= (0 - 1.6273)^2(0.1677) + (1 - 1.6273)^2(0.3354) + \ldots + (5 - 1.6273)^2(0.0248)$

≈ 1.389

$\sigma_X = \sqrt{\sigma^2{}_X} \approx \sqrt{1.389} \approx 1.179$ or about 1.2

(e) $P(2) = 0.2857$

(f) $P(X > 1) = 1 - P(X \le 1) = 1 - P(0 \text{ or } 1)$

$= 1 - (0.1677 + 0.3354) = 1 - 0.5031 = 0.4969$

23. (a) Total number of World Series $= 15 + 15 + 18 + 33 = 81.$

x (games played)	$P(x)$
4	$\dfrac{15}{81} \approx 0.1852$
5	$\dfrac{15}{81} \approx 0.1852$
6	$\dfrac{18}{81} \approx 0.2222$
7	$\dfrac{33}{81} \approx 0.4074$

(b) **Distribution of Games Played (World Series 1923-2004)**

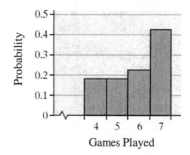

(c) $\mu_X = \sum\left[x \cdot P(x)\right]$

$\approx 4 \cdot (0.1852) + 5 \cdot (0.1852) + 6 \cdot (0.2222) + 7 \cdot (0.4074)$

≈ 5.852 or about 5.9 games

The World Series, if played many times, would be expected to last about 5.9 games on average.

(d) $\sigma_X^2 = \sum(x - \mu_x)^2 \cdot P(x)$

$\approx (4 - 5.852)^2 \cdot 0.1852 + (5 - 5.852)^2 \cdot 0.1852$

$+ (6 - 5.852)^2 \cdot 0.2222 + (7 - 5.852)^2 \cdot 0.4074$

≈ 1.311

$\sigma_X = \sqrt{\sigma_X^2} \approx \sqrt{1.311} \approx 1.145$ or about 1.1 games

25. (a) Total number students (in thousands) = 3635 + 3633 + 3673 + ... + 3532 = 29,164.

x (grade level)	$P(x)$
1	$\dfrac{3635}{29,164} \approx 0.1246$
2	$\dfrac{3633}{29,164} \approx 0.1246$
3	$\dfrac{3673}{29,164} \approx 0.1259$
4	$\dfrac{3708}{29,164} \approx 0.1271$
5	$\dfrac{3701}{29,164} \approx 0.1269$
6	$\dfrac{3658}{29,164} \approx 0.1254$
7	$\dfrac{3624}{29,164} \approx 0.1243$
8	$\dfrac{3532}{29,164} \approx 0.1211$

(b)

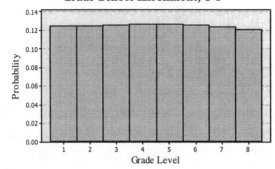

Grade School Enrollment, 1-8

(c) $\mu_X = \sum \left[x \cdot P(x) \right]$

$\approx 1(0.1246) + 2(0.1246) + 3(0.1259) + \ldots + 8(0.1211) \approx 4.486$ or   about 4.5

The average grade level for all students enrolled in grades 1-8 in the US in 2000 was about 4.5.

(d) $\sigma_X^2 = \sum (x - \mu_x)^2 \cdot P(x)$

$\approx (1 - 4.486)^2 \cdot 0.1246 + (2 - 4.486)^2 \cdot 0.1246 + \ldots + (8 - 4.486)^2 \cdot 0.1211 \approx 5.195$

$\sigma_X = \sqrt{\sigma_X^2} \approx \sqrt{5.195} \approx 2.279$ or about 2.3

27. (a) $P(4) = 0.119$

(b) $P(4 \text{ or } 5) = P(4) + P(5) = 0.119 + 0.103 = 0.222$

(c) $P(X \geq 6) = P(6) + P(7) + P(8) = 0.027 + 0.031 + 0.050 = 0.108$

(d) $E(X) = \sum x \cdot P(x)$

$= 1(0.241) + 2(0.257) + 3(0.172) + \ldots + 8(0.050)$

$= 3.041$ or about 3.0

We would expect the mother to have had 3 live births.

29. $E(X) = \sum x \cdot P(x)$

$= (200)(0.999546) + (200 - 250,000)(0.000454) = \$86.50$

If the company sells many of these policies to 20-year old females, then they will make an average of \$86.50 per policy.

31. Let X = the profit from the investment

Profit, x ($)	50,000	10,000	−50,000
Probability	0.2	0.7	0.1

$E(X) = (50,000)(0.2) + (10,000)(0.7) + (-50,000)(0.1) = 12,000$

The expected profit for the investment is \$12,000.

33. Let X = player winnings for \$5 bet on a single number.

Winnings, x (\$)	175	−5
Probability	$\dfrac{1}{38}$	$\dfrac{37}{38}$

$$E(X) = (175)\left(\frac{1}{38}\right) + (-5)\left(\frac{37}{38}\right) = -\$0.26$$

The expected value of the game to the player is a loss of \$0.26. If you played the game 1000 times, you would expect to lose $1000 \cdot (\$0.26) = \$260$.

35. (a) $E(X) = \sum x \cdot P(x)$

$= (15,000,000)(0.00000000684) + (200,000)(0.00000028)$

$+ (10,000)(0.000001711) + (100)(0.000153996) + (7)(0.004778961)$

$+ (4)(0.007881463) + (3)(0.01450116) + (0)(0.9726824222)$

≈ 0.30

After many \$1 plays, you would expect to win an average of \$0.30 per play. That is, you would lose an average of \$0.70 per \$1 play for a net profit of -\$0.70. (Note: the given probabilities reflect changes made in April 2005 to create larger jackpots that are built up more quickly. It is interesting to note that prior to the change, the expected cash prize was still \$0.30)

(b)   We need to find the break-even point. That is, the point where we expect to win the same amount that we pay to play. Let x be the grand prize. Set the expected value equation equal to 1 (the cost for one play) and then solve for x.

$$E(X) = \sum x \cdot P(x)$$

$1 = (x)(0.00000000684) + (200,000)(0.00000028)$

$+ (10,000)(0.000001711) + (100)(0.000153996) + (7)(0.004778961)$

$+ (4)(0.007881463) + (3)(0.01450116) + (0)(0.9726824222)$

$1 = 0.196991659 + 0.00000000684x$

$0.803008341 = 0.00000000684x$

$117,398,880.3 = x$

$118,000,000 \approx x$

The grand prize should be at least \$118,000,000 to expect a profit after many \$1 plays. (Note: prior to the changes mentioned in part (a), the grand prize only needed to be about \$100 million to expect a profit after many \$1 plays)

(c)   No, the size of the grand prize does not affect your chance of winning. Your chance of winning the grand prize is determined by the number of balls that are drawn and the number of balls that are picked from. The size of the grand prize will impact your expected winnings.

37. Answers will vary. The simulations illustrate the Law of Large Numbers.

6.2 The Binomial Probability Distributions

1. A probability experiment is said to be a binomial probability experiment provided:
   a) The experiment consists of a fixed number, n, of trials.
   b) The trials are all independent.
   c) For each trial there are two mutually exclusive (disjoint) outcomes, success or failure.
   d) The probability of success, p, is the same for each trial.

3. If the binomial probability distribution is roughly bell-shaped, then the Empirical Rule can be used to check for unusual observations. As a rule of thumb, the probability distribution for a binomial random variable will be approximately bell-shaped if $np(1-p) \geq 10$.

   In a bell-shaped distribution, about 95% of all observations lie within two standard deviations of the mean. That is, about 95% of the observations lie between $\mu - 2\sigma$ and $\mu + 2\sigma$. An observation would be considered unusual if it is more than two standard deviations above or below the mean because this will occur less than 5% of the time.

5. For a small, fixed value of n, the shape of the binomial probability histogram will be determined by the value of p. The histogram will be skewed right for $p < 0.5$, skewed left for $p > 0.5$, and symmetric (and approximately bell-shaped) for $p = 0.5$. The skewness becomes stronger as p approaches either 0 or 1.

7. This is not a binomial experiment because there are more than two possible values for the random variable 'age'.

9. This is a binomial experiment. There is a fixed number of trials ($n = 100$ where each trial corresponds to administering the drug to one of the 100 individuals), the trials are independent (due to random selection), there are two outcomes (favorable or unfavorable response), and the probability of a favorable response is assumed to be constant for each individual.

11. This is not a binomial experiment because the trials (cards) are not independent and probability of getting an ace changes for each trial (card). Because the cards are not replaced, the probability of getting an ace on the second card depends on what was drawn first.

13. This is not a binomial experiment because the number of trials is not fixed.

15. This is a binomial experiment. There is a fixed number of trials ($n = 10$ where each trial corresponds to selecting one of the 10 stocks), the trials are independent (due to random selection), there are two outcomes (stock rises or does not rise in value), and there is a fixed probability of each stock rising in any one year (48%).

17. Using $P(x) = {}_nC_x p^x (1-p)^{n-x}$ with $x = 3$, $n = 10$ and $p = 0.4$:

$$P(3) = {}_{10}C_3 \cdot (0.4)^3 \cdot (1-0.4)^{10-3} = \frac{10!}{3!(10-3)!} \cdot (0.4)^3 \cdot (0.6)^7$$

$$= 120 \cdot (0.064) \cdot (0.0279936) \approx 0.2150$$

19. Using $P(x) = {}_nC_x p^x (1-p)^{n-x}$ with $x = 38$, $n = 40$ and $p = 0.99$:

$$P(38) = {}_{40}C_{38} \cdot (0.99)^{38} \cdot (1-0.99)^{40-38} = \frac{40!}{38!(40-38)!} \cdot (0.99)^{38} \cdot (0.01)^2$$

$$= 780 \cdot (0.6825...) \cdot (0.0001) \approx 0.0532$$

21. Using $P(x) = {}_nC_x p^x (1-p)^{n-x}$ with $x = 3$, $n = 8$ and $p = 0.35$:

$$P(3) = {}_8C_3 \cdot (0.35)^3 \cdot (1-0.35)^{8-3} = \frac{8!}{3!(8-3)!} \cdot (0.35)^3 \cdot (0.65)^5$$

$$= 56 \cdot (0.42875)(0.116029...) \approx 0.2786$$

23. Using $n = 9$ and $p = 0.2$:

$$P(X \le 3) = P(0) + P(1) + P(2) + P(3)$$

$$= {}_9C_0 \cdot (0.2)^0 (0.8)^9 + {}_9C_1 \cdot (0.2)^1 (0.8)^8 + {}_9C_2 \cdot (0.2)^2 (0.8)^7 + {}_9C_3 \cdot (0.2)^3 (0.8)^6$$

$$\approx 0.134218 + 0.301990 + 0.301990 + 0.176161 \approx 0.9144$$

25. Using $n = 7$ and $p = 0.5$:

$$P(X > 3) = P(X \ge 4)$$

$$= P(4) + P(5) + P(6) + P(7)$$

$$= {}_7C_4 \cdot (0.5)^4 (0.5)^3 + {}_7C_5 \cdot (0.5)^5 (0.5)^2 + {}_7C_6 \cdot (0.5)^6 (0.5)^1 + {}_7C_7 \cdot (0.5)^7 (0.5)^0$$

$$= 0.2734375 + 0.1640625 + 0.0546875 + 0.0078125 = 0.5$$

27. Using $n = 12$ and $p = 0.35$:

$$P(X \le 4) = P(0) + P(1) + P(2) + P(3) + P(4)$$

$$= {}_{12}C_0 \cdot (0.35)^0 (0.65)^{12} + {}_{12}C_1 \cdot (0.35)^1 (0.65)^{11} + {}_{12}C_2 \cdot (0.35)^2 (0.65)^{10}$$

$$+ {}_{12}C_3 \cdot (0.35)^3 (0.65)^9 + {}_{12}C_4 \cdot (0.35)^4 (0.65)^8$$

$$\approx 0.005688 + 0.036753 + 0.108846 + 0.195365 + 0.236692 \approx 0.5833$$

29. (a)

Distribution		$x \cdot P(x)$	$(x-\mu_x)^2 \cdot P(x)$
x	$P(x)$	0.0000	0.3812
0	0.1176	0.3025	0.1936
1	0.3025	0.6483	0.0130
2	0.3241	0.5557	0.2667
3	0.1852	0.2381	0.2881
4	0.0595	0.0510	0.1045
5	0.0102	0.0044	0.0129
6	0.0007	Σ 1.8000	1.2600

(b) $\mu_X = 1.8$ (from first column in table above and to the right)

$\sigma_X = \sqrt{\sigma_X^2} = \sqrt{1.26} \approx 1.1$ (from second column in table above and to the right)

(c) $\mu_X = n \cdot p = 6 \cdot (0.3) = 1.8$ and $\sigma_X = \sqrt{n \cdot p \cdot (1 - p)} = \sqrt{(1.8) \cdot (0.7)} \approx 1.1$

(d)

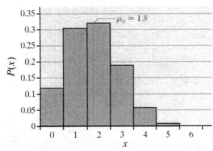

Probability Histogram

The distribution is skewed right.

31. (a)

Distribution		$x \cdot P(x)$	$(x - \mu_x)^2 \cdot P(x)$
x	$P(x)$		
0	0.0000	0.0000	0.0002
1	0.0001	0.0001	0.0033
2	0.0012	0.0024	0.0271
3	0.0087	0.0261	0.1224
4	0.0389	0.1556	0.2942
5	0.1168	0.5840	0.3578
6	0.2336	1.4016	0.1315
7	0.3003	2.1021	0.0187
8	0.2253	1.8024	0.3519
9	0.0751	0.6759	0.3801
Σ		6.7502	1.6872

(b) $\mu_X = 6.75$ (from first column in table above and to the right)

$\sigma_X = \sqrt{\sigma_X^2} = \sqrt{1.6872} \approx 1.3$ (from second column in table above and to the right)

(c) $\mu_X = n \cdot p = 9 \cdot (0.75) = 6.75$ and $\sigma_X = \sqrt{n \cdot p \cdot (1 - p)} = \sqrt{(6.75) \cdot (0.25)} \approx 1.3$

(d)

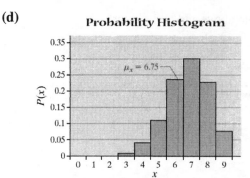

Probability Histogram

The distribution is skewed left.

33. (a)

Distribution			$x \cdot P(x)$	$(x - \mu_x)^2 \cdot P(x)$
x	$P(x)$			
0	0.0010		0.0000	0.0250
1	0.0098		0.0098	0.1568
2	0.0439		0.0878	0.3952
3	0.1172		0.3516	0.4690
4	0.2051		0.8204	0.2053
5	0.2461		1.2305	0.0000
6	0.2051		1.2306	0.2049
7	0.1172		0.8204	0.4686
8	0.0439		0.3512	0.3950
9	0.0098		0.0882	0.1568
10	0.0010		0.0100	0.0250
		Σ	5.0005	2.5016

(b) $\mu_X = 5.0$ (from first column in table above and to the right)

$\sigma_X = \sqrt{\sigma_X^2} = \sqrt{2.5016} \approx 1.6$ (from second column in table above and to the right)

(c) $\mu_X = n \cdot p = 10 \cdot (0.5) = 5$ and $\sigma_X = \sqrt{n \cdot p \cdot (1-p)} = \sqrt{5 \cdot (0.5)} = 1.6$

(d)   **Probability Histogram**

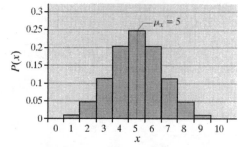

The distribution is symmetric.

154

35. (a)   This is a binomial experiment because it satisfies each of the four requirements:
1) There are a fixed number of trials ($n = 15$).
2) The trials are all independent (randomly selected).
3) For each trial, there are only two possible outcomes ('on time' and 'not on time').
4) The probability of "success" (i.e. on time) is the same for all trials ($p = 0.9$).

(b)   We have $n = 15$, $p = 0.9$, and $x = 14$. In the binomial table, we go to the section for $n = 15$ and the column that contains $p = 0.9$. Within the $n = 15$ section, we look for the row $x = 14$.

$P(14) = 0.3432$

There is a 0.3432 probability that in a random sample of 15 such flights, exactly 14 will be on time.

(c)   Here we wish to find $P(X \geq 14)$. Using the compliment rule we can write:

$$P(X \geq 14) = 1 - P(X < 14) = 1 - P(X \leq 13)$$

Now using the cumulative binomial table, we go to the section for $n = 15$ and the column that contains $p = 0.9$. Within the $n = 15$ section, we look for the row $x = 13$.

$P(X \leq 13) = 0.4510$

Therefore, $P(X \geq 14) = 1 - 0.4510 = 0.5490$.

In a random sample of 15 such flights, there is a 0.5490 probability that at least 14 flights will be on time.

(d) $P(X < 14) = P(X \leq 13) = 0.4510$ [from part (c)].

In a random sample of 15 such flights, there is a 0.4510 probability that less than 14 flights will be on time.

(e)   Using the binomial probability table we get:

$$P(12 \leq X \leq 14) = P(12) + P(13) + P(14) = 0.1285 + 0.2669 + 0.3432 = 0.7386$$

Using the cumulative binomial probability table we get:

$$P(12 \leq X \leq 14) = P(X \leq 14) - P(X \leq 11) = 0.7941 - 0.0556 = 0.7385$$

In a random sample of 15 such flights, there is a 0.7385 probability that between 12 and 14 flights, inclusive, will be on time.

37. (a)   We have $n = 20$, $p = 0.2$, and $x = 5$. In the binomial table, we go to the section for $n = 20$ and the column that contains $p = 0.2$. Within the $n = 20$ section, we look for the row $x = 5$.

$P(5) = 0.1746$

There is a 0.1746 probability that in a random sample of 20 U.S. households, exactly 5 will have some type of high-speed internet access.

(b)   Here we wish to find $P(X \geq 10)$. Using the compliment rule we can write:

$$P(X \geq 10) = 1 - P(X < 10) = 1 - P(X \leq 9)$$

Now using the cumulative binomial table, we go to the section for $n = 20$ and the column that contains $p = 0.2$. Within the $n = 20$ section, we look for the row $x = 9$. $P(X \leq 9) = 0.9974$. Therefore, $P(X \geq 10) = 1 - 0.9974 = 0.0026$.

There is a 0.0026 probability that in a random sample of 20 U.S. households, at least 10 will have some type of high-speed internet access. This result is considered unusual since the probability is less than 0.05.

(c)   Here we wish to find $P(X < 4)$. Using the cumulative binomial table, we get:

$$P(X < 4) = P(X \leq 3) = 0.4114$$

There is a 0.4114 probability that in a random sample of 20 U.S. households, less than 4 will have some type of high-speed internet access.

(d)   Using the binomial probability table we get:

$$P(2 \leq X \leq 5) = P(2) + P(3) + P(4) + P(5)$$
$$= 0.1369 + 0.2054 + 0.2182 + 0.1746 = 0.7351$$

Using the cumulative binomial probability table we get:

$$P(2 \leq X \leq 5) = P(X \leq 5) - P(X \leq 1) = 0.8042 - 0.0692 = 0.7350$$

There is a 0.7350 probability that in a random sample of 20 U.S. households, between 2 and 5 households, inclusive, will have some type of high-speed internet access.

39. (a)   We have $n = 25$, $p = 0.669$, and $x = 22$.

$$P(22) = {}_{25}C_{22} \cdot (0.669)^{22} (0.331)^{3} \approx 0.0120$$

There is a 0.0120 probability that in a random sample of 25 murders, exactly 22 were committed with a firearm.

(b)   The numbers between 14 and 16, inclusive, are 14, 15, and 16. Therefore,

$$P(14 \leq X \leq 16) = P(14,\ 15,\ \text{or } 16) = P(14) + P(15) + P(16)$$

$$= {}_{25}C_{14} \cdot (0.669)^{14} (0.331)^{11} + {}_{25}C_{15} \cdot (0.669)^{15} (0.331)^{10} + {}_{25}C_{16} \cdot (0.669)^{16} (0.331)^{9}$$
$$\approx 0.08378 + 0.12418 + 0.15687 \approx 0.3648$$

There is a 0.3648 probability that in a random sample of 25 murders, between 14 and 16, inclusive, were committed with a firearm.

(c)   The numbers that are 22 or more are 22, 23, 24, and 25. Therefore,

$$P(X \geq 22) = P(22) + P(23) + P(24) + P(25)$$

$$= {}_{25}C_{22} \cdot (0.669)^{22} (0.331)^{3} + {}_{25}C_{23} \cdot (0.669)^{23} (0.331)^{2}$$
$$+ {}_{25}C_{24} \cdot (0.669)^{24} (0.331)^{1} + {}_{25}C_{25} \cdot (0.669)^{25} (0.331)^{0}$$
$$\approx 0.01204 + 0.00317 + 0.00053 + 0.00004 \approx 0.0158$$

It would be considered unusual for 22 or more murders in a random sample of 25 murders to have been committed with a firearm since the probability of this happening is less than 0.05.

41. (a)   We have $n = 10$, $p = 0.75$, and $x = 6$. Using the binomial probability table, we get:
$P(6) = 0.1460$

There is a 0.1460 probability that in a random sample of 10 adult Americans, exactly 6 would be satisfied with the job the nation's airlines are doing.

(b)   Using the cumulative binomial probability table, we get:
$P(X < 7) = P(X \le 6) = 0.2241$

There is a 0.2241 probability that in a random sample of 10 adult Americans, fewer than 7 would be satisfied with the job the nation's airlines are doing.

(c)   Using the complement rule and the cumulative binomial probability table, we get:
$P(X \ge 5) = 1 - P(X < 5) = 1 - P(X \le 4) = 1 - 0.0197 = 0.9803$

There is a 0.9803 probability that in a random sample of 10 adult Americans, 5 or more would be satisfied with the job the nation's airlines are doing.

(d)   Using the binomial probability table, we get:
$P(5 \le X \le 8) = P(5) + P(6) + P(7) + P(8)$
$$= 0.0584 + 0.1460 + 0.2503 + 0.2818$$
$$= 0.7365$$

Using the cumulative binomial probability table, we get:
$P(5 \le X \le 8) = P(X \le 8) - P(X \le 4) = 0.7560 - 0.0197 = 0.7363$

There is a 0.7363 probability that in a random sample of 10 adult Americans, between 5 and 8, inclusive, would be satisfied with the job the nation's airlines are doing.

43. (a)   We have $n = 100$ and $p = 0.9$.
$$\mu_X = n \cdot p = 100(0.9) = 90; \quad \sigma_X = \sqrt{np(1-p)} = \sqrt{90(0.1)} = \sqrt{9} = 3$$

(b)   In a random sample of 100 such flights, we expect 90 to be on time.

(c) $P(80) = {}_{100}C_{80} \cdot (0.9)^{80} (0.1)^{20} \approx 0.0012 < 0.05$

Since the probability is less than 0.05, it would be unusual if 80 or fewer flights in a random sample of 100 flights were on time.

45. (a)   We have $n = 100$ and $p = 0.20$.
$$\mu_X = n \cdot p = 100(0.2) = 20; \quad \sigma = \sqrt{np(1-p)} = \sqrt{20(0.8)} = \sqrt{16} = 4$$

(b)   In a random sample of 100 U.S. households, we expect 20 to have some type of high-speed internet access.

(c)   Since $np(1-p) = 16 > 10$, we can use the Empirical Rule to check for unusual observations.

18 is below the mean, and we have $\mu_X - 2\sigma_X = 20 - 2(4) = 12$.

This indicates that 18 is within two standard deviations of the mean. It would not be unusual to observe 18 U.S. households with some type of high-speed internet access.

Note: $P(18) = {}_{100}C_{18} \cdot (0.2)^{18} (0.8)^{82} \approx 0.0909 > 0.05$

47. (a)   We have $n = 100$ and $p = 0.669$.

$E(X) = n \cdot p = 100(0.669) = 66.9$ murders by firearm.

(b)   Since $np(1-p) = 100(0.669)(0.331) \approx 22.1 > 10$, we can use the Empirical Rule to check for unusual observations.

$\sigma_X = \sqrt{np(1-p)} = \sqrt{66.9(0.331)} \approx 4.7$

75 is above the mean, and we have $\mu_X + 2\sigma_X = 66.9 + 2(4.7) = 76.3$.

This indicates that 75 is within two standard deviations of the mean. Therefore, it would not be considered unusual to find that 75 murders, from a sample of 100, were committed using a firearm.

49.   Since $np(1-p) > 10$, we can use the Empirical rule to check for unusual observations.

$\mu_X = n \cdot p = 400(0.184) = 73.6$; $\sigma_X = \sqrt{np(1-p)} = \sqrt{73.6(0.816)} \approx 7.7$

86 is above the mean and we have $\mu_X + 2\sigma_X = 73.6 + 2(7.7) = 89$. Since 86 is within two standard deviations of the mean, it would not be considered unusual if 86 patients from a sample of 400 experienced headaches as a side effect.

51. (a), (b), (d)   Answers will vary.

(c)   We have $n = 10$, $p = 0.8$, and $x = 10$.

$P(10) = {}_{10}C_{10} \cdot (0.8)^{10}(0.2)^0 \approx 0.1074$

(e) $P(X \geq 8) = P(8) + P(9) + P(10)$

$$= {}_{10}C_8 \cdot (0.8)^8(0.2)^2 + {}_{10}C_9 \cdot (0.8)^9(0.2)^1 + {}_{10}C_{10} \cdot (0.8)^{10}(0.2)^0$$
$$\approx 0.30199 + 0.26844 + 0.10737$$
$$= 0.6778$$

(f) $E(X) = n \cdot p = 10(0.8) = 8$ free throws; simulated means will vary.

53. (a)   If 27% of residents of the United States 25 years old or older have earned at least a bachelor's degree, then we would expect to randomly select $10 \div (0.27) \approx 37.04$. Since we cannot sample a fractional number, we must sample 38 residents 25 years or older.

(note: if we had rounded down to 37, the expected number would have been less than 10, which is not what we required)

(b)   We would like the probability, $P(X \geq 10)$, to be 0.99 or greater, with $p = 0.27$ and n to be determined. $P(X \geq 10) = 1 - P(X \leq 9) = 1 - (P(0) + \ldots + P(9))$ and using technology we find that:

when $n = 64$, $P(X \geq 10) = 1 - P(X \leq 9) = 1 - 0.0107 = 0.9893$;

when $n = 65$, $P(X \geq 10) = 1 - P(X \leq 9) = 1 - 0.0089 = 0.9911$.

Thus the minimum number we would need in our sample is 65 residents 25 years and older.

55. The table gives both the hypergeometric probabilities (column 2) and the binomial probabilities (column 3), using parameters $N = 500, n = 20$, and $p = 0.75$.

x	$P(x) = \dfrac{(_{N \cdot p}C_x) \cdot (_{N \cdot (1-p)}C_{n-x})}{_N C_n}$	$P(x) = {_n}C_x p^x (1-p)^{n-x}$
15	0.2065	0.2023
16	0.1920	0.1897
17	0.1329	0.1339
	0.5314	0.5259

(a) $P(15) = 0.2065$

(b) $P(15 \text{ or } 16 \text{ or } 17) = 0.2065 + 0.1920 + 0.1329 = 0.5314$.

(c) $\dfrac{n}{N} = \dfrac{20}{500} = 0.04$, i.e. the sample is only 4% of the population. From column 3, the binomial probabilities are $P(15) = 0.2023$ and $P(15 \text{ or } 16 \text{ or } 17) = 0.5259$, both of which are very close to the hypergeometric probabilities.

6.3 The Poisson Probability Distribution

1. A random variable X, measuring the number of successes in a fixed interval, follows a Poisson process provided that following conditions are met:
   (1)   the probability of two or more successes in any sufficiently small subinterval is 0;
   (2)   the probability of success is the same for any two intervals of equal length;
   (3)   the number of successes in any interval is independent of the number of successes in any other non-overlapping (disjoint) interval.

3. $\lambda = 10$ hits per minute, $t = 5$ minutes (from 7:30 P.M. to 7:35 P.M.).

5. $\lambda = 0.07$ flaws per linear foot, $t = 20$ linear feet of timber.

7. Use $P(x) = \dfrac{\mu^x}{x!} \cdot e^{-\mu}$ to find the following, assuming $\mu = 5$:

(a) $P(6) = \dfrac{5^6}{6!} \cdot e^{-5} = 0.1462$

(b) $P(X < 6) = P(X \le 5) = P(0) + P(1) + P(2) + P(3) + P(4) + P(5)$

$$= \frac{5^0}{0!} \cdot e^{-5} + \frac{5^1}{1!} \cdot e^{-5} + \frac{5^2}{2!} \cdot e^{-5} + \frac{5^3}{3!} \cdot e^{-5} + \frac{5^4}{4!} \cdot e^{-5} + \frac{5^5}{5!} \cdot e^{-5} = 0.6160$$

(c) $P(X \ge 6) = 1 - P(X < 6) = 1 - 0.6160 = 0.3840$

159

(d) $P(2 \le X \le 4) = P(2) + P(3) + P(4) = \dfrac{5^2}{2!} \cdot e^{-5} + \dfrac{5^3}{3!} \cdot e^{-5} + \dfrac{5^4}{4!} \cdot e^{-5} = 0.4001$

9. Use $P(x) = \dfrac{(\lambda t)^x}{x!} \cdot e^{-\lambda t}$ to find the following, given $\lambda = 0.07$, $t = 10$, and $\lambda t = 0.7$:

(a) $P(4) = \dfrac{0.7^4}{4!} \cdot e^{-0.7} = 0.0050$

(b) $P(X < 4) = P(X \le 3) = P(X = 0) + P(1) + P(2) + P(3)$

$= \dfrac{0.7^0}{0!} \cdot e^{-0.7} + \dfrac{0.7^1}{1!} \cdot e^{-0.7} + \dfrac{0.7^2}{2!} \cdot e^{-0.7} + \dfrac{0.7^3}{3!} \cdot e^{-0.7} = 0.9942$

(c) $P(X \ge 4) = 1 - P(X < 4) = 1 - 0.9942 = 0.0058$

(d) $P(4 \le X \le 6) = P(4) + P(5) + P(6) = \dfrac{0.7^4}{4!} \cdot e^{-0.7} + \dfrac{0.7^5}{5!} \cdot e^{-0.7} + \dfrac{0.7^6}{6!} \cdot e^{-0.7} = 0.0057$

(e) $\mu_x = \lambda t = (0.07)(10) = 0.7$ and $\sigma_x = \sqrt{\lambda t} = \sqrt{0.7} \approx 0.8$

11. We are given that the hits occur at a rate of 1.4 per minute, so $\lambda = 1.4$; and the interval of time we are interested in is 5 minutes (from 7:30 P.M. to 7:35 P.M.), so $t = 5$. Therefore, $\lambda t = (1.4)(5) = 7$.

(a) $P(7) = \dfrac{7^7}{7!} e^{-7} \approx 0.1490$

On about 15 out of every 100 days, exactly 7 hits will occur between 7:30 P.M. and 7:35 P.M.

(b) $P(X < 7) = P(X \le 6) = P(0) + ... + P(6)$

$= \dfrac{7^0}{0!} e^{-7} + \dfrac{7^1}{1!} e^{-7} + \dfrac{7^2}{2!} e^{-7} + \dfrac{7^3}{3!} e^{-7} + \dfrac{7^4}{4!} e^{-7} + \dfrac{7^5}{5!} e^{-7} + \dfrac{7^6}{6!} e^{-7}$

$\approx 0.00091 + 0.00638 + 0.02234 + 0.05213 + 0.09123 + 0.12772 + 0.14900$

≈ 0.4497

On about 45 out of every 100 days, fewer than 7 hits will occur between 7:30 P.M. and 7:35 P.M.

(c)   Use the Complement Rule: $P(X \ge 7) = 1 - P(X < 7) = 1 - 0.4497 = 0.5503$.

On about 55 out of every 100 days, at least 7 hits will occur between 7:30 P.M. and 7:35 P.M.

13. We are given that FDAL level for insect filth in peanut butter is 0.3 insect fragments per gram, so $\lambda = 0.3$; and the interval we are interested in is 5 grams (the 5-gram sample), so $t = 5$. Therefore, $\lambda t = (0.3)(5) = 1.5$.

(a) $P(2) = \dfrac{(1.5)^2}{2!} e^{-1.5} \approx 0.2510$

In about 25 out of every hundred 5-gram samples of peanut butter, exactly 2 insect fragments will be found.

(b) $P(X < 2) = P(X \le 1) = P(0) + P(1) \approx 0.22313 + 0.33470 \approx 0.5578$

In about 56 out of every hundred 5-gram samples of peanut butter, fewer than 2 insect fragments will be found.

(c) Use the Complement Rule: $P(X \ge 2) = 1 - P(X < 2) = 1 - 0.5578 = 0.4422$.

In about 44 out of every hundred 5-gram samples of peanut butter, at least 2 insect fragments will be found.

(d) Use the Complement Rule: $P(X \ge 1) = 1 - P(X < 1) = 1 - P(0) = 1 - 0.2231 = 0.7769$

In about 78 out of every hundred 5-gram samples of peanut butter, at least 1 insect fragment will be found.

(e) $P(X \ge 4) = 1 - P(X < 4) = 1 - P(X \le 3)$

$= 1 - \left[P(0) + P(1) + P(2) + P(3) \right]$

$\approx 1 - \left[0.22313 + 0.33470 + 0.25102 + 0.12551 \right]$

$= 1 - 0.93436 \approx 0.0656$

Since $P(X \ge 4) > 0.05$, it would not be unusual for a 5-gram sample of peanut butter to contain four or more insect fragments.

15. (a) We are given that fatalities occur at the rate of 0.04 per 100 million miles. If we think in terms of 100 million mile units, we have $\lambda = 0.04$. The interval we are interested in is 100 million miles, so $t = 1$ (that is, 1 one hundred million mile unit). Therefore, $\lambda t = (0.04)(1) = 0.04$.

$P(0) = \dfrac{(0.04)^0}{0!} e^{-0.04} = e^{-0.04} \approx 0.9608$

In about 96 out of every 100 one hundred million-mile samples, no deaths will occur.

(b) $P(X \ge 1) = 1 - P(X < 1) = 1 - P(0) = 1 - 0.9608 = 0.0392$

In about 4 out of every 100 one hundred million-mile samples, at least one death will occur.

(c) $P(X > 1) = 1 - P(X \le 1) = 1 - \left[P(0) + P(1) \right]$

$= 1 - \left[\dfrac{(0.04)^0}{0!} e^{-0.04} + \dfrac{(0.04)^1}{1!} e^{-0.04} \right] \approx 1 - 0.9992 = 0.0008$

In about 8 out of every 10,000 one hundred million-mile samples, more than one death will occur.

17. We are given that major hurricanes strike Florida at a rate of 24 per 104 year interval. That is, $\lambda = \dfrac{24}{104} \approx 0.231$ major hurricanes per year. The time interval we are interested in is one year, so $t = 1$.

$$P(X \geq 3) = 1 - P(X < 3) = 1 - P(X \leq 2)$$
$$= 1 - [P(0) + P(1) + P(2)]$$
$$= 1 - \left[\frac{(0.231)^0}{0!} \cdot e^{-0.231} + \frac{(0.231)^1}{1!} \cdot e^{-0.231} + \frac{(0.231)^2}{2!} \cdot e^{-0.231} \right]$$
$$\approx 1 - [0.9983] = 0.0017$$

Since this probability is less than 0.05, the 2004 hurricane season in Florida does appear to be unusual.

19. (a) and **(b)**

Use technology and the given parameters $\lambda = 0.2$ and $t = 30$ to construct a table:

x	$P(x) = \dfrac{(\lambda t)^x}{x!} \cdot e^{-\lambda t}$	Expected # of restaurants having x arrivals $= 200 \cdot P(x)$	Observed number of restaurants having x arrivals
0	0.0025	0.50	0
1	0.0149	2.97	4
2	0.0446	8.92	5
3	0.0892	17.85	13
4	0.1339	26.77	23
5	0.1606	32.12	25
6	0.1606	32.12	28
7	0.1377	27.54	25
8	0.1033	20.65	27
9	0.0688	13.77	21
10	0.0413	8.26	15
11	0.0225	4.51	5
12	0.0113	2.25	3
13	0.0052	1.04	2
14	0.0022	0.45	2
15	0.0009	0.18	0
16	0.0003	0.07	2

(c)   The observed frequencies are lower for fewer cars and higher for more cars, so the advertising campaign appears to be effective.

21. (a) and **(c)**

Use technology to construct a table:

x	Observed Frequency	Proportion of years = Frequency ÷ 200	$x \cdot$ proportion of years	$P(x) = \dfrac{(0.61)^x}{x!} \cdot e^{-0.61}$
0	109	0.545	0.000	0.5434
1	65	0.325	0.325	0.3314
2	22	0.110	0.220	0.1011
3	3	0.015	0.045	0.0206
4	1	0.005	0.020	0.0031
		Total =	0.610	

(b) From the data in the table, the mean number of deaths per year is 0.610.

(c) Using $\mu = 0.61$ we calculate the Poisson probabilities as shown in the last column.

(d) Answers will vary. These probabilities are very close to the relative frequencies, so the random variable X appears to follow a Poisson distribution.

23. (a) $E(X) = \lambda t = \dfrac{23.8}{100} \cdot (500) = 119$ colds.

(b) – (g) Answers will vary.

6.4 The Hypergeometric Probability Distribution (On CD)

1. In both cases, the random variable X represents the number of successes in n trials of an experiment, where each trial results in one of two mutually exclusive (disjoint) outcomes classified as "success" or "failure". The binomial probability distribution requires that each trial be independent of the others and that the probability of success remain the same for each trial. This is not the case for the hypergeometric probability distribution. For the hypergeometric probability distribution, the population size is finite and there are a fixed number of successes in the population. The sample is obtained without replacement, so the trials are not independent and the probability of success does not remain constant. If the population size is infinite, there is no difference between the hypergeometric distribution and the binomial distribution.

3. n is the sample size an there cannot be more successes than trials. Therefore, we must have $x \le n$. In turn, the population only contains k successes. Therefore, we must also have $x \le k$. If the sample size n is larger than the number of successes in the population (that is, $n > k$), we are still restricted by the fact that there are only k successes in the population. Therefore, the possible values of the random variable must be less than or equal to the smaller of the sample size (n) and the total number of successes in the population (k).

5. This is a hypergeometric probability experiment because:
   1) The population is finite ($N = 49$ numbers).
   2) There are only two possible outcomes (number matches or does not match).
   3) The sample size is $n = 6$ and is drawn without replacement.
   There are only 6 matching numbers so $k = 6$. The possible values for X are $x = 0, 1, 2, ..., 6$.

7. This is a hypergeometric probability experiment because:
   1) The population is finite ($N = 250$ numbers).
   2) There are only two possible outcomes (chip is defective or chip is not defective).
   3) The sample size is $n = 20$ and is drawn without replacement.
   There are only 12 chips that are defective so $k = 12$. The possible values for X are $x = 0, 1, 2, ..., 12$.

9. Given $N = 150$, $n = 20$, $k = 30$, and $X = 5$:
$$P(5) = \frac{\left(_{30}C_5\right)\left(_{150-30}C_{20-5}\right)}{_{150}C_{20}} = \frac{\left(_{30}C_5\right)\left(_{120}C_{15}\right)}{_{150}C_{20}} = 0.1856$$

11. Given $N = 230$, $n = 15$, $k = 200$, and $X = 12$:
$$P(12) = \frac{\left(_{200}C_{12}\right)\left(_{230-200}C_{15-12}\right)}{_{230}C_{15}} = \frac{\left(_{200}C_{12}\right)\left(_{30}C_3\right)}{_{230}C_{15}} = 0.1939$$

13. Given $N = 150$, $n = 20$, and $k = 30$:
$$\mu_X = n \cdot \frac{k}{N} = 20 \cdot \frac{30}{150} = 4 \, ;$$
$$\sigma_X = \sqrt{\left(\frac{N-n}{N-1}\right) \cdot n \cdot \frac{k}{N} \cdot \frac{N-k}{N}} = \sqrt{\left(\frac{150-20}{150-1}\right) \cdot 20 \cdot \frac{30}{150} \cdot \frac{150-30}{150}} \approx 1.67$$

15. Given $N = 230$, $n = 15$, and $k = 200$:
$$\mu_X = n \cdot \frac{k}{N} = 15 \cdot \frac{200}{230} \approx 13.0 \, ;$$
$$\sigma_X = \sqrt{\left(\frac{N-n}{N-1}\right) \cdot n \cdot \frac{k}{N} \cdot \frac{N-k}{N}} = \sqrt{\left(\frac{230-15}{230-1}\right) \cdot 15 \cdot \frac{200}{230} \cdot \frac{230-200}{230}} \approx 1.26$$

17. We are given $N = 49$, $n = 6$, and $k = 6$:

   (a) $P(3) = \dfrac{\left(_6C_3\right)\left(_{49-6}C_{6-3}\right)}{_{49}C_6} = \dfrac{\left(_6C_3\right)\left(_{43}C_3\right)}{_{49}C_6} = 0.0177$

   There is a 0.0177 probability of matching 3 numbers.

   (b) $P(4) = \dfrac{\left(_6C_4\right)\left(_{49-6}C_{6-4}\right)}{_{49}C_6} = \dfrac{\left(_6C_4\right)\left(_{43}C_2\right)}{_{49}C_6} = 0.0010$

   There is a 0.0010 probability of matching 4 numbers.

(c) $P(5) = \dfrac{\left(_6C_5\right)\left(_{49-6}C_{6-5}\right)}{_{49}C_6} = \dfrac{\left(_6C_5\right)\left(_{43}C_1\right)}{_{49}C_6} = 0.0000184$

There is a 0.0000184 probability of matching 5 numbers.

(d) $P(6) = \dfrac{\left(_6C_6\right)\left(_{49-6}C_{6-6}\right)}{_{49}C_6} = \dfrac{\left(_6C_6\right)\left(_{43}C_0\right)}{_{49}C_6} = 0.0000001$

There is a 0.0000001 probability of matching 6 numbers.

(e) $P(\text{win}) = P(3) + P(4) + P(5) + P(6)$

$\qquad = 0.0177 + 0.0010 + 0.0000184 + 0.0000001$

$\qquad = 0.0187185$

There is a 0.0187185 probability of purchasing a winning ticket. This probability is less than 0.05, so it would be considered unusual to purchase a winning ticket.

(f) $\mu_X = n \cdot \dfrac{k}{N} = 6 \cdot \dfrac{6}{49} \approx 0.7$;

$\sigma_X = \sqrt{\left(\dfrac{N-n}{N-1}\right) \cdot n \cdot \dfrac{k}{N} \cdot \dfrac{N-k}{N}} = \sqrt{\left(\dfrac{49-6}{49-1}\right) \cdot 6 \cdot \dfrac{6}{49} \cdot \dfrac{49-6}{49}} \approx 0.76$

For a randomly selected ticket, we expect to match 0.7 numbers.

19. We are given $N = 250$, $n = 20$, and $k = 12$:

(a) $P(4) = \dfrac{\left(_{12}C_4\right)\left(_{250-12}C_{20-4}\right)}{_{250}C_{20}} = \dfrac{\left(_{12}C_4\right)\left(_{238}C_{16}\right)}{_{250}C_{20}} = 0.0087$

There is a 0.0087 probability of obtaining 4 defective chips.

(b) $P(3) = \dfrac{\left(_{12}C_3\right)\left(_{250-12}C_{20-3}\right)}{_{250}C_{20}} = \dfrac{\left(_{12}C_3\right)\left(_{238}C_{17}\right)}{_{250}C_{20}} = 0.0507$

There is a 0.0507 probability of obtaining 3 defective chips.

(c) $P(0) = \dfrac{\left(_{12}C_0\right)\left(_{250-12}C_{20-0}\right)}{_{250}C_{20}} = \dfrac{\left(_{12}C_0\right)\left(_{238}C_{20}\right)}{_{250}C_{20}} = 0.3590$

There is a 0.3590 probability of obtaining no defective chips.

(d) $P(14) = 0$ because the random variable cannot take on the value 14. The minimum of n and k is 12. Therefore, the possible values for the random variable are $x = 0, 1, 2, ..., 12$.

(e) $E(X) = \mu_X = n \cdot \dfrac{k}{N} = 20 \cdot \dfrac{12}{250} = 0.96$

In a random sample of 20 chips, we expect to obtain 0.96 defective chips on average.

21. Let the random variable X represent the number of jurors on the jury who will never convict. From the problem statement, we get $N = 30$, $n = 12$, and $k = 2$.
Here it will take less work if we find the probability of avoiding a hung jury and subtracting from 1. To avoid a hung jury, we need $X = 0$.

$$P(0) = \frac{\left(_2C_0\right)\left(_{30-2}C_{12-0}\right)}{_{30}C_{12}} = \frac{\left(_2C_0\right)\left(_{28}C_{12}\right)}{_{30}C_{12}} = 0.3517$$

Since, $1 - 0.3517 = 0.6483$, there is a 0.6483 probability of having a hung jury.(Note: Here we are assuming that there will never be a hung jury unless one of the two potential jurors who will never convict is on the jury.)

23. Let the random variable X represent the number of cylinders that pass inspection. From the problem statement we have $N = 200$ and $n = 4$. To accept the shipment, we must obtain 0 defective cylinders. That is, we want $X = 0$.

(a)   If 10% are defective, we have $k = (0.1)(200) = 20$.

$$P(0) = \frac{\left(_{20}C_0\right)\left(_{200-20}C_{4-0}\right)}{_{200}C_4} = \frac{\left(_{20}C_0\right)\left(_{180}C_4\right)}{_{200}C_4} = 0.6539$$

If 10% are defective, there is a 0.6539 probability that the shipment is accepted.

(b)   If 20% are defective, we have $k = (0.2)(200) = 40$.

$$P(0) = \frac{\left(_{40}C_0\right)\left(_{200-40}C_{4-0}\right)}{_{200}C_4} = \frac{\left(_{40}C_0\right)\left(_{160}C_4\right)}{_{200}C_4} = 0.4065$$

If 20% are defective, there is a 0.4065 probability that the shipment is accepted.

(c)   If 40% are defective, we have $k = (0.4)(200) = 80$.

$$P(0) = \frac{\left(_{80}C_0\right)\left(_{200-80}C_{4-0}\right)}{_{200}C_4} = \frac{\left(_{80}C_0\right)\left(_{120}C_4\right)}{_{200}C_4} = 0.1270$$

If 40% are defective, there is a 0.1270 probability that the shipment is accepted.

(d)   If 60% are defective, we have $k = (0.6)(200) = 120$.

$$P(0) = \frac{\left(_{120}C_0\right)\left(_{200-120}C_{4-0}\right)}{_{200}C_4} = \frac{\left(_{120}C_0\right)\left(_{80}C_4\right)}{_{200}C_4} = 0.0245$$

If 60% are defective, there is a 0.0245 probability that the shipment is accepted.

(e)   If 80% are defective, we have $k = (0.8)(200) = 160$.

$$P(0) = \frac{\left(_{160}C_0\right)\left(_{200-160}C_{4-0}\right)}{_{200}C_4} = \frac{\left(_{160}C_0\right)\left(_{40}C_4\right)}{_{200}C_4} = 0.0014$$

If 80% are defective, there is a 0.0014 probability that the shipment is accepted.

(f)

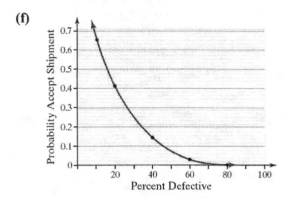

Chapter 6 Review Exercises

1. (a) The number of inches of snow that falls in Buffalo during the winter season is a continuous random variable because its value results from a measurement. If we let the random variable S represent the number of inches of snow, the possible values for S are all nonnegative real numbers. That is, $s \geq 0$.

(b) The number of days snow accumulates in Buffalo during the winter season is a discrete random variable because its value results from counting. If we let the random variable X represent the number of days for which snow accumulates, the possible values for X are integers between 0 and 91, inclusive (assuming the winter season lasts for 91 days). That is, $x = 0, 1, 2, \ldots 91$.

(c) The number of golf balls hit into the ocean on the famous 18th hole at Pebble Beach is a discrete random variable because its value results from a count. If we let the random variable X represent the number of golf balls hit into the ocean, the possible values for X are nonnegative integers. That is, $x = 0, 1, 2, \ldots$

3. This is not a valid probability distribution because the sum of the probabilities does not equal 1.

5. (a) Total number of Stanley Cups
$= 20 + 16 + 17 + 13 = 66$.

x (games played)	$P(x)$
4	$\dfrac{20}{66} \approx 0.3030$
5	$\dfrac{16}{66} \approx 0.2424$
6	$\dfrac{17}{66} \approx 0.2576$
7	$\dfrac{13}{66} \approx 0.1970$

(b)

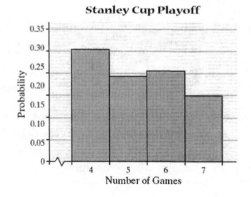

167

(c) $\mu_X = \sum [x \cdot P(x)]$

$\approx 4 \cdot (0.3030) + 5 \cdot (0.2424) + 6 \cdot (0.2576) + 7 \cdot (0.1970)$

≈ 5.349 or about 5.3 games

The Stanley Cup, if played many times, would be expected to last about 5.3 games.

(d) $\sigma_X^2 = \sum (x - \mu_x)^2 \cdot P(x)$

$\approx (4 - 5.349)^2 \cdot 0.3030 + (5 - 5.349)^2 \cdot 0.2424$

$\qquad + (6 - 5.349)^2 \cdot 0.2576 + (7 - 5.349)^2 \cdot 0.1970$

≈ 1.227

$\sigma_X = \sqrt{\sigma_X^2} \approx \sqrt{1.227} \approx 1.108$ or about 1.1 games

7. $E(X) = \sum x \cdot P(x) = \$200 \cdot (0.998592) + (-\$99,800) \cdot (0.001408) = \$59.20$.

If the company insures many 35-year-old males, then they will make an average profit of $59.20 per male.

9. This is a binomial experiment. There are a fixed number of trials ($n = 10$) where each trial corresponding to a randomly chosen freshman, the trials are independent, there are only two possible outcomes (graduated or did not graduate within six years), and the probability of a graduation within six years is fixed for all trials ($p = 0.54$).

11. (a)   We have $n = 10$, $p = 0.08$, and $x = 0$.

$P(0) = {}_{10}C_0 \cdot (0.08)^0 (0.92)^{10} \approx 0.4344$

In about 43% of random samples of 10 females 20–34 years old, there will be 0 females with high serum cholesterol.

(b) $P(2) = {}_{10}C_2 \cdot (0.08)^2 (0.92)^8 \approx 0.1478$

In about 15% of random samples of 10 females 20–34 years old, there will be 2 females with high serum cholesterol.

(c) $P(X \geq 2) = 1 - P(X < 1) = 1 - P(X \leq 1) = 1 - [P(0) - P(1)]$

$= 1 - [0.4344 + 0.3777] = 1 - 0.8121 = 0.1879$

In about 19% of random samples of 10 females 20–34 years old, there will be at least 2 females with high serum cholesterol.

(d)   The probability that 9 will **not** have high cholesterol is the same as the probability that 1 **will** have high cholesterol, which is $P(1) = 0.3777$.

In about 38% of random samples of 10 females 20–34 years old, there will be 9 females who *do not* have high serum cholesterol.

168

(e) $E(X) = n \cdot p = 250(0.08) = 20$; $\sigma_X = \sqrt{np(1-p)} = \sqrt{20(0.92)} \approx 4.3$

(f) No. Since $np \cdot (1-p) = 18.4 > 10$, we can use the Empirical Rule to check for unusual observations. We have that 12 is below the mean and $\mu - 2\sigma = 20 - 2 \cdot 4.3 = 11.4$. This indicates that 12 is within two standard deviations of the mean, so observing 12 females with high serum cholesterol in a random sample of 250 females 20–34 years old would not be unusual.

13. (a) We have $n = 20$ and $p = 0.15$.

Using the binomial probability table, we get: $P(6) = 0.0454$

(b) Using the cumulative binomial probability table, we get:
$$P(X < 4) = P(X \le 3) = 0.6477$$

(c) Using the complement rule and the cumulative binomial probability table, we get:
$$P(X \ge 2) = 1 - P(X < 2)$$
$$= 1 - P(X \le 1)$$
$$= 1 - 0.1756 = 0.8244$$

(d) Obtaining 17 households that **were not** tuned into the 2005 NCAA championship is the same as obtaining 3 households that **were** tuned in. That is,
$$P(17 \text{ were not}) = P(3 \text{ were}) = P(3) = 0.2428$$

(e) $E(X) = \mu_X = n \cdot p = 500(0.15) = 75$

(f) Yes; since $np(1-p) = 63.75 > 10$, we can use the Empirical Rule to check for unusual observations.
$\sigma_X = \sqrt{np(1-p)} = \sqrt{75(0.85)} = \sqrt{63.75} \approx 7.984$ or about 8.0
$\mu - 2\sigma \approx 75 - 16 = 59$ and $\mu + 2\sigma \approx 75 + 16 = 91$
Since 95 is outside this range of values, it would be considered an unusual observation.

15. (a)

Distribution		$x \cdot P(x)$	$(x - \mu_x)^2 \cdot P(x)$
x	$P(x)$	0	0.3277
0	0.3277	0.4096	0.0000
1	0.4096	0.4096	0.2048
2	0.2048	0.1536	0.2048
3	0.0512	0.0256	0.0576
4	0.0064	0.0016	0.0051
5	0.0003	Σ 1.0000	0.8000

(b) $\mu_X = 1$ (from first column in table above and to the right)

$\sigma_X = \sqrt{\sigma_X^2} = \sqrt{0.8} \approx 0.9$ (from second column in table above and to the right)

(c) $\mu_X = np = 5(0.2) = 1$ and $\sigma_X = \sqrt{np \cdot (1-p)} = \sqrt{5(0.2)(0.8)} \approx 0.9$.

(d)

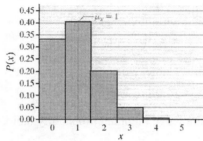

**Binomial
Probability Distribution**

The distribution is skewed right.

17. Use $P(x) = \dfrac{(\lambda t)^x}{x!} \cdot e^{-\lambda t}$ with $\lambda = 0.05$ and $t = 8$ so that $\lambda t = 0.4$:

(a) $P(3) = \dfrac{0.4^3}{3!} \cdot e^{-0.4} = 0.0072$

(b) $P(X < 3) = P(0) + P(1) + P(2) = 0.67032 + 0.26813 + 0.05363 \approx 0.9921$

(c) $P(X \geq 3) = 1 - P(X < 3) = 1 - 0.9921 = 0.0079$

(d) $P(3 \leq X \leq 5) = P(3) + P(4) + P(5) = 0.00715 + 0.00072 + 0.00006 \approx 0.0079$

(e) $\mu_X = \lambda t = (0.05) \cdot 8 = 0.4$; $\sigma_X = \sqrt{\lambda t} = \sqrt{0.4} \approx 0.6$

19. We are given that cars arrive at the rate of 0.41 cars per minute, so $\lambda = 0.41$. The time interval of interest is 10 minutes (4:00 P.M. and 4:10 P.M), so $t = 10$. Therefore, $\lambda t = 0.41(10) = 4.1$

(a) $P(4) = \dfrac{4.1^4}{4!} \cdot e^{-4.1} \approx 0.1951$

On about 20% of days, exactly 4 cars will arrive at the bank's drive-through window between 4:00 P.M. and 4:10 P.M.

170

(b) $P(X < 4) = P(X \le 3) = P(0) + P(1) + P(2) + P(3)$

$$= \frac{4.1^0}{0!} \cdot e^{-4.1} + \frac{4.1^1}{1!} \cdot e^{-4.1} + \frac{4.1^2}{2!} \cdot e^{-4.1} + \frac{4.1^3}{3!} \cdot e^{-4.1}$$

$$\approx 0.01657 + 0.06795 + 0.13929 + 0.19037$$

$$\approx 0.4142$$

On about 41% of days, fewer than 4 cars will arrive at the bank's drive-through window between 4:00 P.M. and 4:10 P.M.

(c) Using the complement rule, we get: $P(X \ge 4) = 1 - P(X < 4) = 1 - 0.4142 = 0.5858$

On about 59% of days, at least 4 cars will arrive at the bank's drive-through window between 4:00 P.M. and 4:10 P.M.

21. We have that maintenance calls occur at the rate of two per month, so $\lambda = 2$. The time interval of interest is one month, so $t = 1$. Therefore, $\lambda t = (2)(1) = 2$.

$$P(X > 4) = 1 - P(X \le 4)$$

$$= 1 - \left[\frac{2^0}{0!} \cdot e^{-2} + \frac{2^1}{1!} \cdot e^{-2} + \frac{2^2}{2!} \cdot e^{-2} + \frac{2^3}{3!} \cdot e^{-2} + \frac{2^4}{4!} \cdot e^{-2} \right]$$

$$= 1 - 0.9473 = 0.0527$$

Since $P(X > 4) > 0.05$, it would not be unusual for the copy machine to require more than 4 maintenance calls in a given month.

23. If $np \cdot (1 - p) \ge 10$, then the Empirical Rule can be used to check for unusual observations.

25. In sampling from large populations without replacement, the trials may be assumed to be independent provided that the sample size is small in relation to the size of the population. As a general rule of thumb, this condition is satisfied if the sample size is less than 5% of the population size.

Chapter 7

The Normal Probability Distribution

7.1 Properties of the Normal Distribution

1. For the graph to be that of a probability density function,
   (1) The area under the graph over all possible values of the random variable must equal 1;
   (2) The graph must be greater than or equal to 0 for all possible values of the random variable. That is, the graph of the equation must lie on or above the horizontal axis for all possible values of the random variable.

3. The area under the graph of a probability density function can be interpreted as either:
   (1) The proportion of the population with the characteristic described by the interval; or
   (2) The probability that a randomly selected individual from the population has the characteristic described by the interval.

5. $\mu - \sigma$; $\mu + \sigma$

7. No, the graph cannot represent a normal density function because it is not symmetric.

9. No, the graph cannot represent a normal density function because it crosses below the horizontal axis. That is, it is not always greater than or equal to 0.

11. Yes, the graph can represent a normal density function.

13. The figure presents the graph of the density function with the area we wish to find shaded. The width of the rectangle is $10 - 5 = 5$ and the height is $\frac{1}{30}$. Thus, the area between 5 and 10 is $5\left(\frac{1}{30}\right) = \frac{1}{6}$. The probability that the friend is between 5 and 10 minutes late is $\frac{1}{6}$.

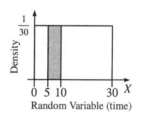

15. The figure presents the graph of the density function with the area we wish to find shaded. The width of the rectangle is $30 - 20 = 10$ and the height is $\frac{1}{30}$. Thus, the area between 20 and 30 is $10\left(\frac{1}{30}\right) = \frac{1}{3}$. The probability that the friend is at least 20 minutes late is $\frac{1}{3}$.

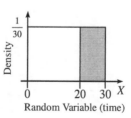

172

17. (a)

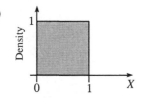

(b) $P(0 \le X \le 0.2) = 1(0.2 - 0) = 0.2$

(c) $P(0.25 \le X \le 0.6) = 1(0.6 - 0.25) = 0.35$

(d) $P(X \ge 0.95) = 1(1 - 0.95) = 0.05$

(e) Answers will vary.

19. The histogram is symmetrical and bell-shaped, so a normal distribution can be used as a model for the variable.

21. The histogram is skewed to the right, so normal distribution cannot be used as a model for the variable.

23. Graph A matches $\mu = 10$ and $\sigma = 2$, and graph B matches $\mu = 10$ and $\sigma = 3$. We can tell because a higher standard deviation makes the graph shorter and more spread out.

25. The center is at 2, so $\mu = 2$. The distance to the inflection points is ± 3, so $\sigma = 3$.

27. The center is at 100, so $\mu = 100$. The distance to the inflection points is ± 15, so $\sigma = 15$.

29. (a)

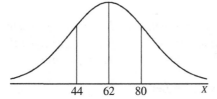

(b)

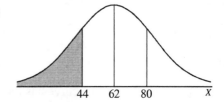

(c) Interpretation 1: 15.87% of the cell phone plans in the United States is less than $44.00 per month. Interpretation 2: The probability is 0.1587 that a randomly selected cell phone plan in the United States is less than $44.00 per month.

31. (a)

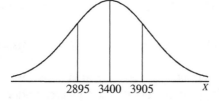

(b)

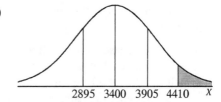

(c) Interpretation 1: 2.28% of all full-term babies has a birth weight of at least 4410 grams. Interpretation 2: The probability is 0.0228 that the birth weight of a randomly chosen full-term baby is at least 4410 grams.

33. (a) Interpretation 1: The proportion of human pregnancies that last more than 280 days is 0.1908. Interpretation 2: The probability is 0.1908 that a randomly selected human pregnancy lasts more than 280 days.

(b) Interpretation 1: The proportion of human pregnancies that last between 230 and 260 days is 0.3416. Interpretation 2: The probability is 0.3416 that a randomly selected human pregnancy lasts between 230 and 260 days.

35. (a) $Z_1 = \dfrac{X_1 - \mu}{\sigma} = \dfrac{8-10}{3} = -\dfrac{2}{3} \approx -0.67$

(b) $Z_2 = \dfrac{X_2 - \mu}{\sigma} = \dfrac{12-10}{3} = \dfrac{2}{3} \approx 0.67$

(c) The area between Z_1 and Z_2 is also 0.495.

37. (a), (b)

Histogram of Driving Distance

(c) The normal density function appears to describe the distance Michael hits a pitching wedge fairly accurately. Looking at the graph, the normal curve is a fairly good approximation to the histogram.

7.2 The Standard Normal Distribution

Note: The answers provided in this section have been calculated using the Standard Normal Table provided in the textbook. Answers found using technology may differ from those shown since answers computed using technology do not involve rounding of z-scores.

1. The standard normal curve has the following properties:
   (1) It is symmetric about its mean $\mu = 0$ and has standard deviation $\sigma = 1$.
   (2) Its highest point occurs at $\mu = 0$.
   (3) It has inflection points at -1 and 1.
   (4) The area under the curve is 1.
   (5) The area under the curve to the right of $\mu = 0$ equals the area under the curve to the left of $\mu = 0$, which equals 0.5.
   (6) As z increases, the graph approaches, but never equals, zero. As z decreases, the graph approaches, but never equals, zero.
   (7) It satisfies the Empirical Rule: Approximately 68% of the area under the standard normal curve is between -1 and 1. Approximately 95% of the area under the standard normal curve is between -2 and 2. Approximately 99.7% of the area under the standard normal curve is between -3 and 3.

3. False. Although the area is very close to 1 (and for all practical purposes we may assume it is approximately 1), it is not exactly 1 because the normal curve continues indefinitely to the right.

5. The standard normal tables give the areas to the left of any Z-value. Thus we just need to look up each Z and read off the corresponding area from the tables. The areas are:

(a) The area to the left of $Z = -2.45$ is 0.0071.

(b) The area to the left of $Z = -0.43$ is 0.3336.

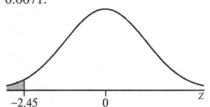

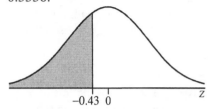

(c) The area to the left of $Z = 1.35$ is 0.9115.

(d) The area to the left of $Z = 3.49$ is 0.9998.

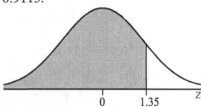

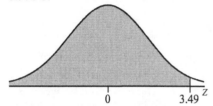

7. The standard normal tables give the areas to the left of any Z-value. Thus we first need to look up each Z–value and read off the corresponding area from the tables. Then the area to the right is 1 – the area to the left. This gives:

(a) The area to the right of $Z = -3.01$ is $1 - 0.0013 = 0.9987$

(b) The area to the right of $Z = -1.59$ is $1 - 0.0559 = 0.9441$.

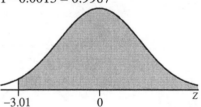

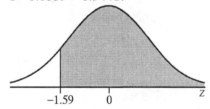

(c) The area to the right of $Z = 1.78$ is $1 - 0.9625 = 0.0375$.

(d) The area to the right of $Z = 3.11$ is $1 - 0.9991 = 0.0009$.

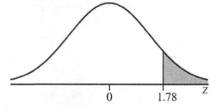

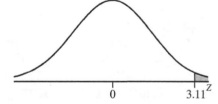

175

9. To find the area between two Z-values we first look up the area to the left of each Z-value in the standard normal tables, and then we find the difference between these areas.

(a) The area to the left of $Z = -2.04$ is 0.0207, and the area to the left of $Z = 2.04$ is 0.9793. Thus, the area between is $0.9793 - 0.0207 = 0.9586$.

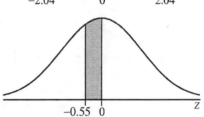

(b) The area to the left of $Z = -0.55$ is 0.2912, and the area to the left of $Z = 0$ is 0.5000. Thus, the area between is $0.5000 - 0.2912 = 0.2088$.

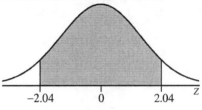

(c) The area to the left of $Z = -1.04$ is 0.1492, and the area to the left of $Z = 2.76$ is 0.9971. Thus, the area between is $0.9971 - 0.1492 = 0.8479$.

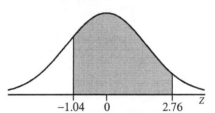

11. (a) The area to the left of $Z = -2$ is 0.0228, and the area to the right of $Z = 2$ is $1 - 0.9772 = 0.0228$. Thus, the total area is $0.0228 + 0.0228 = 0.0456$.

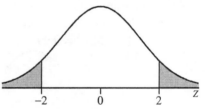

(b) The area to the left of $Z = -1.56$ is 0.0594, and the area to the right of $Z = 2.56$ is $1 - 0.9948 = 0.0052$. Thus, the total area is $0.0594 + 0.0052 = 0.0646$.

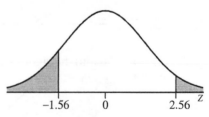

(c) The area to the left of $Z = -0.24$ is 0.4052, and the area to the right of $Z = 1.20$ is $1 - 0.8849 = 0.1151$. Thus, the total area is $0.4052 + 0.1151 = 0.5203$.

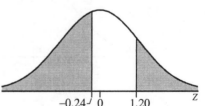

13. (a) The area to the left of $Z = -1.34$ is 0.0901, and the area to the left of $Z = 2.01$ is 0.9778. Thus, the area between is $0.9778 - 0.0901 = 0.8877$.

(b) The area to the left of $Z = -1.96$ is 0.0250, and the area to the right of $Z = 1.96$ is $1 - 0.9750 = 0.0250\ 0.9750$. Thus, the total area is $0.0250 + 0.0250 = 0.0500$.

176

(c) The area to the left of $Z = -2.33$ is 0.0099, and the area to the left of $Z = 2.33$ is 0.9901 and so the area between $Z = -2.33$ and $Z = 2.33$ is $0.9901 - 0.0099 = 0.9802$.

15. The area in the interior of the standard normal table that is closest to 0.1000 is 0.1003, corresponding to $Z = -1.28$.

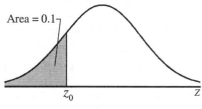

17. The area in the interior of the standard normal table that is closest to 0.9800 is 0.9798, corresponding to $Z = 2.05$.

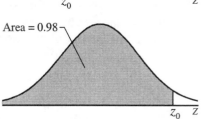

19. The area to the left of the unknown Z-score is $1 - 0.25 = 0.75$. The area in the interior of the standard normal table that is closest to 0.7500 is 0.7486, corresponding to $Z = 0.67$.

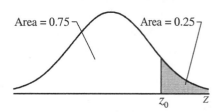

21. The area to the left of the unknown Z-score is $1 - 0.89 = 0.11$. The area in the interior of the standard normal table that is closest to 0.1100 is 0.1093, corresponding to $Z = -1.23$.

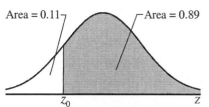

23. The Z-scores for the middle 80% are the Z-scores for the top and bottom 10%. The area in the interior of the standard normal table that is closest to 0.1000 is 0.1003, corresponding to $Z = -1.28$. By symmetry, the Z-score for the top 10% is $Z = 1.28$.

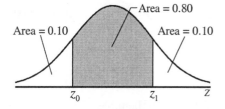

25. The Z-scores for the middle 99% are the Z-scores for the top and bottom 0.5%. The area in the interior of the standard normal table that are closest to 0.0050 are 0.0049 and 0.0051 and so we use the average of their corresponding Z-scores: -2.58 and -2.57, respectively. This gives $Z = -2.575$. By symmetry, the Z-score for the top 0.5% is $Z = 2.575$.

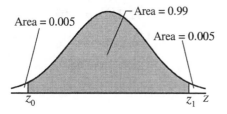

27. The area to the right of the unknown Z-value is 0.05, o the area to the left is $1 - 0.05 = 0.9500$. From the interior of the normal tables we find that the Z-scores 1.64 and 1.65 have corresponding areas of 0.9495 and 0.9505, respectively, which are equally close to 0.95. Therefore, we take the average of the two Z-scores, giving $z_{0.05} = 1.645$.

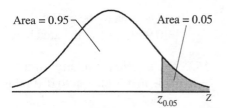

29. The area to the right of the unknown Z-value is 0.01, so the area to the left is $1 - 0.01 = 0.99$. The area in the interior of the normal tables that is closest to 0.9900 is 0.9901, so $z_{0.01} = 2.33$.

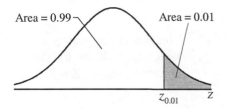

31. The area to the right of the unknown Z-value is 0.20, so the area to the left is $1 - 0.20 = 0.80$. The area in the interior of the normal tables that is closest to 0.8000 is 0.7995, so $z_{0.20} = 0.84$.

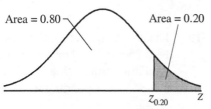

33. From the table, $P(Z < 1.93) = 0.9732$.

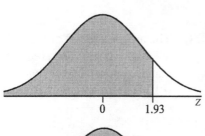

35. From the table, $P(Z < -2.98) = 0.0014$, so $P(Z > -2.98) = 1 - 0.0014 = 0.9986$.

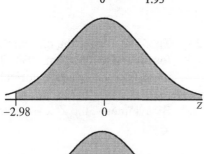

37. From the table, $P(Z < -1.20) = 0.1151$ and $P(Z < 2.34) = 0.9904$. Thus, $P(-1.20 \le Z < 2.34) = 0.9904 - 0.1151 = 0.8753$.

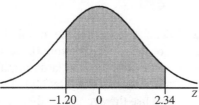

39. From the table, $P(Z < 1.84) = 0.9671$, so
$P(Z \geq 1.84) = 1 - 0.9671 = 0.0329$.

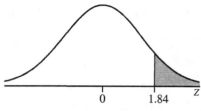

41. From the table, $P(Z \leq 0.72) = 0.7642$

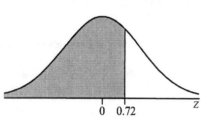

43. From the table, $P(Z < -2.56) = 0.0052$.
Also, $P(Z \leq 1.39) = 0.9177$, so
$P(Z > 1.39) = 1 - 0.9177 = 0.0823$. Thus,
$P(Z < -2.56 \text{ or } Z > 1.39) = 0.0052 + 0.0823$
$= 0.0875$

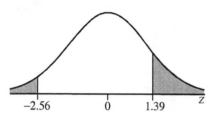

45. From the table, $P(Z < -1.00) = 0.1587$ and $P(Z < 1.00) = 0.8413$, so $P(-1 < Z < 1) = 0.8413 - 0.1587 = 0.6826$. Thus, approximately 68% of the data lies within 1 standard deviation of the mean. Similarly, $P(Z < -2.00) = 0.0228$ and $P(Z < 2.00) = 0.9772$, so $P(-2 < Z < 2) = 0.9772 - 0.0228 = 0.9544$. Thus, approximately 95% of the data lies within 2 standard deviations of the mean. Likewise, $P(Z < -3.00) = 0.0013$ and $P(Z < 3.00) = 0.9987$, so and $P(-3 < Z < 3) = 0.9987 - 0.0013 = 0.9974$. Thus, approximately 99.7% of the data lies within 3 standard deviations of the mean.

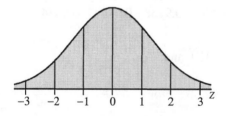

47. By symmetry, the area to the right of $Z = 2.55$ is also 0.0054.

49. By symmetry, the area between $Z = 0.53$ and $Z = 1.24$ is also 0.1906.

7.3 Applications of the Normal Distribution

Note: The answers provided in this section have been calculated using the Standard Normal Table provided in the textbook. Answers found using technology may differ from those shown since answers computed using technology do not involve rounding of z-scores.

1. To find the area under any normal curve:
   (1) Draw the curve and shade the relevant area.

   (2) Convert the values of X to Z-scores using the formula $Z = \dfrac{X - \mu}{\sigma}$.

   (3) Draw a standard normal curve and shade the relevant area.
   (4) Find the area under the standard normal curve.

3. $Z = \dfrac{X - \mu}{\sigma} = \dfrac{35 - 50}{7} \approx -2.14$. From

   the table, the area to the left is 0.0162,
   so $P(X > 35) = 1 - 0.0162 = 0.9838$.

   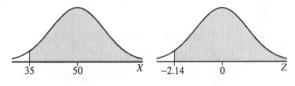

5. $Z = \dfrac{X - \mu}{\sigma} = \dfrac{45 - 50}{7} \approx -0.71$. From

   the table, the area to the left is 0.2389,
   so $P(X \le 45) = 0.2389$.

   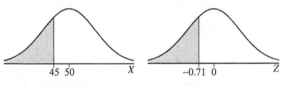

7. $Z_1 = \dfrac{X - \mu}{\sigma} = \dfrac{40 - 50}{7} \approx -1.43$ and

   $Z_2 = \dfrac{X - \mu}{\sigma} = \dfrac{65 - 50}{7} \approx 2.14$. From

   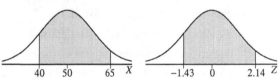

   the table, the area to the left of $Z_1 = -1.43$ is 0.0764 and the area to the left of $Z_2 = 2.14$ is
   0.9838, so $P(40 < X < 65) = 0.9838 - 0.0764 = 0.9074$.

9. $Z_1 = \dfrac{X - \mu}{\sigma} = \dfrac{55 - 50}{7} \approx 0.71$ and

   $Z_2 = \dfrac{X - \mu}{\sigma} = \dfrac{70 - 50}{7} \approx 2.86$. From

   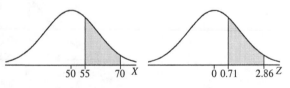

   the table, the area to the left of $Z_1 = 0.71$ is 0.7611 and the area to the left of $Z_2 = 2.86$ is
   0.9979, so $P(55 \le X \le 70) = 0.9979 - 0.7611 = 0.2368$.

11. $Z_1 = \dfrac{X - \mu}{\sigma} = \dfrac{38 - 50}{7} \approx -1.71$ and

    $Z_2 = \dfrac{X - \mu}{\sigma} = \dfrac{55 - 50}{7} \approx 0.71$.

    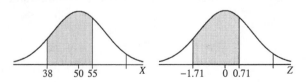

    From the table, the area to the left of $Z_1 = -1.71$ is 0.0436 and the area to the left of
    $Z_2 = 0.71$ is 0.7611, so $P(38 < X \le 55) = 0.7611 - 0.0436 = 0.7175$.

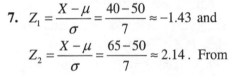
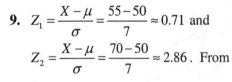
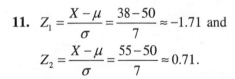

13. The figure to the right shows the normal curve with the unknown value of X separating the bottom 9% of the distribution from the top 91% of the distribution. From the table, the area closest to 0.09 is 0.0901, which corresponds to the Z-value -1.34. Thus, the 9th percentile for X is $X = \mu + Z\sigma = 50 + (-1.34)(7) = 40.62$.

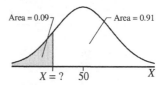

15. The figure to the right shows the normal curve with the unknown value of X separating the bottom 81% of the distribution from the top 19% of the distribution. From the table, the area closest to 0.81 is 0.8106, which corresponds to the Z-value 0.88. Thus, the 81st percentile for X is $X = \mu + Z\sigma = 50 + 0.88(7) = 56.16$.

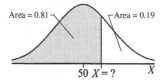

17. (a) $Z = \dfrac{X - \mu}{\sigma} = \dfrac{20 - 21}{1} = -1.00$.

From the table, the area to the left of $Z = -1.00$ is 0.1587, so $P(X < 20) = 0.1587$.

(b) $Z = \dfrac{X - \mu}{\sigma} = \dfrac{22 - 21}{1} = 1.00$.

From the table, the area to the left of $Z = 1.00$ is 0.8413, so $P(X > 22) = 1 - 0.8413 = 0.1587$.

(c) $Z_1 = \dfrac{X - \mu}{\sigma} = \dfrac{19 - 21}{1} = -2.00$

and $Z_2 = \dfrac{X - \mu}{\sigma} = \dfrac{21 - 21}{1} = 0$.

From the table, the area to the left of $Z_1 = -2.00$ is 0.0228 and the area to the left of $Z_2 = 0$ is 0.5000, so $P(19 \le X \le 21) = 0.5000 - 0.0228 = 0.4772$.

(d) $Z = \dfrac{X - \mu}{\sigma} = \dfrac{18 - 21}{1} = -3.00$.

From the table, the area to the left of $Z = -3.00$ is 0.0013, so $P(X < 18) = 0.0013$. Yes, it would be unusual for an egg to hatch in less than 18 days.

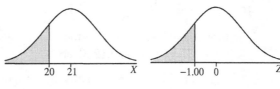

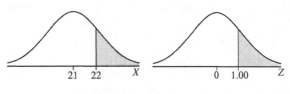

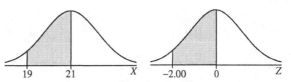

19. (a) $Z_1 = \dfrac{X - \mu}{\sigma} = \dfrac{1000 - 1262}{118} \approx -2.22$

and $Z_2 = \dfrac{1400 - 1262}{118} \approx 1.17$.

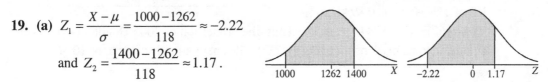

From the table, the area to the left of $Z_1 = -2.22$ is 0.0132 and the area to the left of $Z_2 = 1.17$ is 0.8790, so $P(1000 \le X \le 1400) = 0.8790 - 0.0132 = 0.8658$.

(b) $Z = \dfrac{X - \mu}{\sigma} = \dfrac{1000 - 1262}{118} \approx -2.22$.

From the table, the area to the
left of $Z = -2.22$ is 0.0132, so
$P(X < 1000) = 0.0132$.

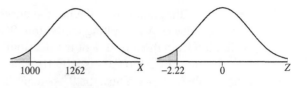

(c) $Z = \dfrac{X - \mu}{\sigma} = \dfrac{1200 - 1262}{118} \approx -0.53$.

From the table, the area to the
left of $Z = -0.53$ is 0.2981, so.

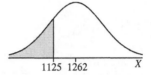

$P(X > 1200) = 1 - 0.2981 = 0.7019$. Thus, the proportion of 18-ounce bags of Chip
Ahoy! cookies that contains more than 1200 chocolate chips is 0.7019, or 70.19%.

(d) $Z = \dfrac{X - \mu}{\sigma} = \dfrac{1125 - 1262}{118} \approx -1.16$.

From the table, the area to the
left of $Z = -1.16$ is 0.1230, so

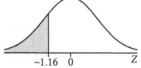

$P(X < 1125) = 0.1230$. Thus, the proportion of 18-ounce bags of Chip Ahoy! cookies
that contains less than 1125 chocolate chips is 0.1230, or 12.30%.

(e) $Z = \dfrac{X - \mu}{\sigma} = \dfrac{1475 - 1262}{118} \approx 1.81$.

From the table, the area to the
left of $Z = 1.81$ is 0.9649, so

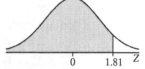

$P(X < 1475) = 0.9649$. Thus, an 18-ounce bag of Chip Ahoy! cookies containing 1475
chocolate chips is at the 96th percentile.

(f) $Z = \dfrac{X - \mu}{\sigma} = \dfrac{1050 - 1262}{118} \approx -1.80$.

From the table, the area to the
left of $Z = -1.80$ is 0.0359, so

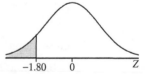

$P(X < 1050) = 0.0359$. Thus, an 18-ounce bag of Chip Ahoy! cookies that containing
1050 chocolate chips is at the 4th percentile.

21. (a) $Z = \dfrac{X - \mu}{\sigma} = \dfrac{60 - 56}{3.2} = 1.25$.

From the table, the area to the
left of $Z = -0.40$ is 0.8944, so

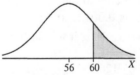
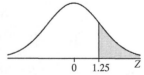

$P(X > 60) = 1 - 0.8944 = 0.1056$. Thus, the proportion of 2005 Honda Insights with
automatic transmissions that gets over 60 miles per gallon is 0.1056, or 10.56%.

(b) $Z = \dfrac{X-\mu}{\sigma} = \dfrac{50-56}{3.2} \approx -1.88$.

From the table, the area to the
left of $Z = -1.88$ is 0.0301, so

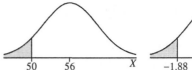

$P(X \le 50) = 0.0301$. Thus, the proportion of 2005 Honda Insights with automatic transmissions that gets 50 miles per gallon or less is 0.0301, or 3.01%.

(c) $Z_1 = \dfrac{X-\mu}{\sigma} = \dfrac{58-56}{3.2} \approx 0.63$ and

$Z_2 = \dfrac{62-56}{3.2} \approx 1.88$. From the

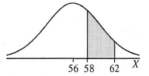
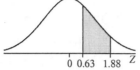

table, the area to the left of $Z_1 = 0.63$ is 0.7357 and the area to the left of $Z_2 = 1.88$ is 0.9699, so $P(58 \le X \le 60) = 0.9699 - 0.7357 = 0.2342$.

(d) $Z = \dfrac{X-\mu}{\sigma} = \dfrac{45-56}{3.2} \approx -3.44$.

From the table, the area to the
left of $Z = -3.44$ is 0.0003, so

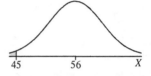
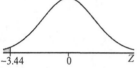

$P(X < 45) = 0.0003$. Thus, the proportion of 2005 Honda Insights with automatic transmissions that gets less than 45 miles per gallon or less is 0.0003, or 0.03%.

23. (a) $Z = \dfrac{X-\mu}{\sigma} = \dfrac{60-64.1}{2.8} \approx -1.46$.

From the table, the area to the left
of $Z = -1.46$ is 0.0721, so

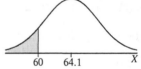
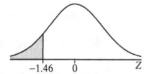

$P(X \le 60) = 0.0721$. Thus, a 20- to 29-year-old female who is 60 inches tall is at the 7th percentile.

(b) $Z = \dfrac{X-\mu}{\sigma} = \dfrac{70-64.1}{2.8} \approx 2.11$.

From the table, the area to the left
of $Z = 2.11$ is 0.9826, so

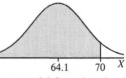
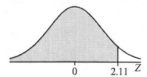

$P(X \le 70) = 0.9826$. Thus, a 20- to 29-year-old female who is 70 inches tall is at the 98th percentile.

(c) $Z_1 = \dfrac{X-\mu}{\sigma} = \dfrac{60-64.1}{2.8} \approx -1.46$

and $Z_2 = \dfrac{70-64.1}{2.8} \approx 2.11$. From

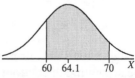
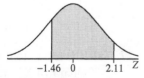

the table, the area to the left of $Z_1 = -1.46$ is 0.0721 and the area to the left of $Z_2 = 2.11$ is 0.9826 so $P(60 < X < 70) = 0.9826 - 0.0721 = 0.9105$. Thus, the proportion of 20- to 29-year-old females between 60 and 70 inches is 0.9105, or 91.05%.

(d) $Z = \dfrac{X-\mu}{\sigma} = \dfrac{70-64.1}{2.8} \approx 2.11$.

From the table, the area to the
left of $Z = -2.63$ is 0.9826, so

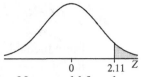

$P(X > 70) = 1 - 0.9826 = 0.0174$. Yes, it is unusual for a 20- to 29-year-old female to
be taller than 70 inches.

25. (a) $Z = \dfrac{X-\mu}{\sigma} = \dfrac{24.9-25}{0.07} \approx -1.43$.

From the table, the area to the
left of $Z = -1.43$ is 0.0764, so

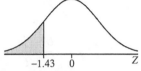

$P(X < 24.9) = 0.0764$. Thus, the proportion of rods that has a length less than 24.9 cm
is 0.0764, or 7.64%.

(b) $Z_1 = \dfrac{X-\mu}{\sigma} = \dfrac{24.85-25}{0.07} \approx -2.14$

and $Z_2 = \dfrac{25.15-25}{0.07} \approx 2.14$.

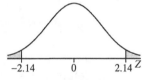

From the table, the area to the left of $Z_1 = -2.14$ is 0.0162, so $P(X < 24.85) = 0.0162$.
The area to the left of $Z_2 = 2.14$ is 0.9838, so $P(X > 25.15) = 1 - 0.9838 = 0.0162$.
Thus, $P(X < 24.85 \text{ or } X > 25.15) = 2(0.0162) = 0.0324$. The proportion of rods that
will be discarded is 0.0324, or 3.24%.

(c) The manager should expect to discard $5000(0.0324) = 162$ of the 5000 steel rods.

(d) $Z_1 = \dfrac{X-\mu}{\sigma} = \dfrac{24.9-25}{0.07} \approx -1.43$

and $Z_2 = \dfrac{25.1-25}{0.07} \approx 1.43$. From

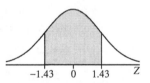

the table, the area to the left of $Z_1 = -1.43$ is 0.0764 and the area to the left of
$Z_2 = 1.43$ is 0.9236, so $P(24.9 \le X \le 25.1) = 0.9236 - 0.0764 = 0.8472$. Thus, 0.8472,
or 84.72%, of the rods manufactured will be between 24.9 and 25.1 cm. Let n
represent the number of rods that must be manufactured. Then $0.8472n = 10{,}000$, so
$n = \dfrac{10{,}000}{0.8472} \approx 11{,}803.59$. Increase this to the next whole number: 11,804. To meet the
order, the manager should manufacture 11,804 rods.

27. (a) The figure to the right shows the normal curve with the
unknown X-value separating the bottom 17% of the
distribution from the top 83%. From the table, the area
closest to 0.17 is 0.1711, which corresponds to the Z-
value -0.95. Thus, the 17th percentile for incubation
times of fertilized chicken eggs is $X = \mu + Z\sigma = 21 + (-0.95)(1) \approx 20$ days.

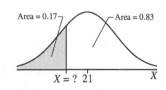

(b) The figure to the right shows the normal curve with the unknown X-values separating the middle 95% of the distribution from the bottom 2.5% and the top 2.5%. From the table, the area 0.0250 corresponds to the Z-value -1.96. Likewise, the area $0.0250 + .095 = 0.975$

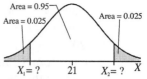

corresponds to the Z-value 1.96. Now, $X_1 = \mu + Z_1\sigma = 21 + (-1.96)(1) \approx 19$ and

$X_2 = \mu + Z_2\sigma = 21 + 1.96(1) \approx 23$. Thus, the incubation times that make up the middle 95% of fertilized chicken eggs is between 19 and 23 days.

29. (a) The figure to the right shows the normal curve with the unknown X-value separating the bottom 30% of the distribution from the top 70%. From the table, the area closest to 0.30 is 0.3015, which corresponds to the Z-

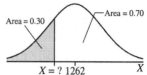

value -0.52. Thus, the 30th percentile for the number of chocolate chips in an 18-ounce bag of Chip Ahoy! cookies is $X = \mu + Z\sigma = 1262 + (-0.52)(118) \approx 1201$ chocolate chips.

(b) The figure to the right shows the normal curve with the unknown X-values separating the middle 99% of the distribution from the bottom 0.5% and the top 0.5%. From the table, the areas 0.0049 and 0.0051 are equally close to 0.005. We average the corresponding Z-values

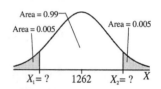

-2.58 and -2.57 to obtain $Z_1 = -2.575$. Likewise, the area $0.005 + 0.99 = 0.995$ is equally close 0.9949 and 0.9951. We average the corresponding Z-values 2.57 and 2.58 to obtain $Z_2 = 2.575$. Now, $X_1 = \mu + Z_1\sigma = 1262 + (-2.575)(118) \approx 958$ and

$X_2 = \mu + Z_2\sigma = 1262 + 2.575(118) \approx 1566$. Thus, the number of chocolate chips makes up the middle 99% of 18-ounce bags of Chip Ahoy! cookies is 958 to 1566 chips.

31. (a) The figure to the right shows the normal curve with the unknown X-value separating the bottom 97% of the distribution from the top 3%. From the table, the area closest to 0.97 is 0.9699, which corresponds to the Z-

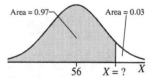

value 1.88. Thus, the 97th percentile gasoline mileage for the model year 2005 Insight with an automatic transmission is $X = \mu + Z\sigma = 56 + 1.88(3.2) \approx 62.0$ miles per gallon.

(b) The figure to the right shows the normal curve with the unknown X-values separating the middle 86% of the distribution from the bottom 7% and the top 7%. From the table, the area closest to 0.07 is 0.0694, which corresponds to the Z-value -1.48. Likewise, the area

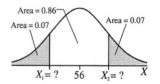

closest to $0.07 + 0.86 = 0.93$ is 0.9306 which corresponds to the Z-value 1.48. Now, $X_1 = \mu + Z_1\sigma = 56 + (-1.48)(3.2) \approx 51.3$ and $X_2 = \mu + Z_2\sigma = 56 + 1.48(3.2) \approx 60.7$. Thus, the mileage that makes up the middle 86% gasoline mileage of the model year 2005 Insight is between 51.3 and 60.7 miles per gallon.

33. (a) Note: Since normal distributions are continuous, we use the intervals $15 \leq X < 20$, $20 \leq X < 25$, ..., $40 \leq X < 45$ for the ages instead of the discrete intervals $15 \leq X \leq 19$, $20 \leq X \leq 24$, ..., $40 \leq X \leq 44$ that are provided. We find the Z-score for each lower limit from the relative frequency distribution and look up the area to the left of each Z-score in the standard normal table:

$$X_1 = 15: \ Z_1 = \frac{X - \mu}{\sigma} = \frac{15 - 31.77}{5.19} \approx -3.23 \text{, which corresponds area } 0.0006;$$

$$X_2 = 20: \ Z_2 = \frac{20 - 31.77}{5.19} \approx -2.27 \text{, which corresponds with area } 0.0116;$$

$$X_3 = 25: \ Z_3 = \frac{25 - 31.77}{5.19} \approx -1.30 \text{, which corresponds with area } 0.0968;$$

$$X_4 = 30: \ Z_4 = \frac{30 - 31.77}{5.19} \approx -0.34 \text{, which corresponds with area } 0.3669;$$

$$X_5 = 35: \ Z_5 = \frac{35 - 31.77}{5.19} \approx 0.62 \text{, which corresponds with area } 0.7324;$$

$$X_6 = 40: \ Z_6 = \frac{40 - 31.77}{5.19} \approx 1.59 \text{, which corresponds with area } 0.9441;$$

$$X_7 = 45: \ Z_7 = \frac{45 - 31.77}{5.19} \approx 2.55 \text{, which corresponds with area } 0.9946.$$

Thus, $P(15 \leq X < 20) = P(-3.23 \leq Z < -2.27) = 0.0116 - 0.0006 = 0.0110$;

$P(20 \leq X < 25) = P(-2.27 \leq Z < -1.30) = 0.0968 - 0.0116 = 0.0852$;

$P(25 \leq X < 30) = P(-1.30 \leq Z < -0.34) = 0.3669 - 0.0968 = 0.2701$;

$P(30 \leq X < 35) = P(-0.34 \leq Z < 0.62) = 0.7324 - 0.3669 = 0.3655$;

$P(35 \leq X < 40) = P(0.62 \leq Z < 1.59) = 0.9441 - 0.7324 = 0.2117$;

$P(40 \leq X < 45) = P(1.59 \leq Z < 2.55) = 0.9946 - 0.9441 = 0.0505$.

Summarizing the results, we have:

Age	Proportion
$15 \leq X < 20$	0.0110
$20 \leq X < 25$	0.0852
$25 \leq X < 30$	0.2701
$30 \leq X < 35$	0.3655
$35 \leq X < 40$	0.2117
$40 \leq X < 45$	0.0505

(b) Answers will vary. One possibility follows: The results from part (a) agree well with the actual relative frequencies. Therefore, it appears that the ages of multiple-birth mothers are approximately normally distributed.

7.4 Assessing Normality

1. Explanations will vary. One possibility follows: Normal random variables are linearly related to their Z-scores (by the formula $X = \mu + \sigma Z$), so the plot of X-values against their expected Z-values should be linear.

3. The plotted points do not lie within the provided bounds, so the data are not from a population that is normally distributed.

5. The plotted points do not lie within the provided bounds, so the data are not from a population that is normally distributed.

7. The normal probability plot is roughly linear, and all the data lie within the provided bounds, so the sample data should come from a population that is normally distributed.

9. (a) The normal probability plot is roughly linear, and all the data lie within the provided bounds, so the sample data should come from a population that is normally distributed.

   (b) $\sum x = 48,815$, $\sum x^2 = 61,211,861$, and $n = 40$. Thus, $\bar{x} = \dfrac{\sum x}{n} = \dfrac{49,895}{40} \approx 1247.4$ chips

   and $s = \sqrt{\dfrac{\sum x^2 - \dfrac{(\sum x)^2}{n}}{n-1}} = \sqrt{\dfrac{62,635,301 - \dfrac{(49,895)^2}{40}}{40-1}} \approx 101.0$ chips.

   (c) $\mu - \sigma \approx \bar{x} - s = 1247.1 - 101.0 = 1146.1$ and
   $\mu + \sigma \approx \bar{x} + s = 1247.1 + 101.0 = 1348.1$.

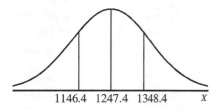

1146.4 1247.4 1348.4   X

   (d) $Z = \dfrac{X - \mu}{\sigma} = \dfrac{1000 - 1247.4}{101.0} \approx -2.45$.
   From the table, the area to the left of $Z = -2.45$ is 0.0071, so
   $P(X > 1000) = 1 - 0.0071 = 0.9929$.

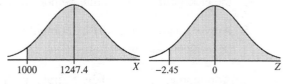

   (e) $Z_1 = \dfrac{X_1 - \mu}{\sigma} = \dfrac{1200 - 1247.4}{101.0} \approx -0.47$;

   $Z_2 = \dfrac{X_2 - \mu}{\sigma} = \dfrac{1400 - 1247.4}{101.0} \approx 1.51$.

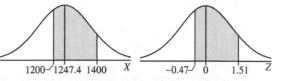

   From the table, the area to the left of $Z_1 = -0.47$ is 0.3192 and the area to the left of $Z_2 = 1.51$ is 0.9345. Thus, $P(1200 \le X \le 1400) = 0.9345 - 0.3192 = 0.6153$. The proportion of 18-ounce bags of Chips Ahoy! that contains between 1200 and 1400 chips is 0.6153, or 61.53%.

11. The normal probability plot is roughly linear, so the sample data should come from a population that is normally distributed.

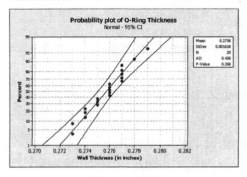

13. The plotted points are not linear and do not lie within the provided bounds, so the data are not from a population that is normally distributed.

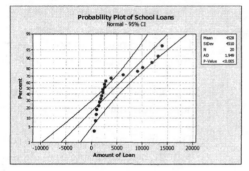

7.5 The Normal Approximation to the Binomial Probability Distribution

Note: The answers provided in this section have been calculated using the Standard Normal Table provided in the textbook. Answers found using technology may differ from those shown since answers computed using technology do not involve rounding of z-scores.

1. A probability experiment is a binomial experiment if all the following are true:
(1) The experiment is performed n independent times.
(2) For each trial there are two mutually exclusive outcomes - success or failure.
(3) The probability of success, p, is the same for each trial of the experiment.

3. We must use a correction for continuity when using the normal distribution to approximate binomial probabilities because we are using a continuous density function to approximate the probability of a discrete random variable.

5. Approximate $P(X \geq 40)$ by computing the area under the normal curve to the right of $X = 39.5$.

7. Approximate $P(X = 8)$ by computing the area under the normal curve between $X = 7.5$ and $X = 8.5$.

9. Approximate $P(18 \leq X \leq 24)$ by computing the area under the normal curve between $X = 17.5$ and $X = 24.5$.

11. Approximate $P(X > 20) = P(X \geq 21)$ by computing the area under the normal curve to the right of $X = 20.5$.

13. Approximate $P(X > 500) = P(X \geq 501)$ by computing the area under the normal curve to the right of $X = 500.5$.

15. Using $P(x) = {}_nC_x p^x (1-p)^{n-x}$, with the parameters $n = 60$ and
$p = 0.4$, we get $P(20) = {}_{60}C_{20}(0.4)^{20}(0.6)^{40} \approx 0.0616$. Now
$np(1-p) = 60 \cdot 0.4 \cdot (1-0.4) = 14.4 \geq 10$, so the normal
approximation can be used, with $\mu_X = np = 60(0.4) = 24$ and

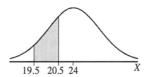

$\sigma_X = \sqrt{np(1-p)} = \sqrt{14.4} \approx 3.795$. With continuity correction we calculate:

$$P(20) \approx P(19.5 < X < 20.5) = P\left(\frac{19.5 - 24}{3.795} < Z < \frac{20.5 - 24}{3.795}\right) = P(-1.19 < Z < -0.92)$$

$$= 0.1788 - 0.1170 = 0.0618.$$

17. Using $P(x) = {}_nC_x p^x (1-p)^{n-x}$, with the parameters $n = 40$ and $p = 0.25$, we get
$P(30) = {}_{40}C_{30}(0.25)^{30}(0.75)^{70} \approx 4.1 \times 10^{-11}$. Now $np(1-p) = 40 \cdot 0.25 \cdot (1-0.25) = 7.5$,
which is below 10, so the normal approximation cannot be used.

19. Using $P(x) = {}_nC_x p^x (1-p)^{n-x}$, with the parameters $n = 75$ and
$p = 0.75$, we get $P(60) = {}_{75}C_{60}(0.75)^{60}(0.25)^{15} \approx 0.0677$. Now
$np(1-p) = 75 \cdot 0.75 \cdot (1-0.75) = 14.0625 \geq 10$, so the normal
approximation can be used, with $\mu_X = 75(0.75) = 56.25$ and

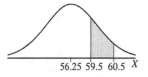

$\sigma_X = \sqrt{np(1-p)} = \sqrt{14.0625} = 3.75$. With continuity correction we calculate:

$$P(60) \approx P(59.5 < X < 60.5) = P\left(\frac{59.5 - 56.25}{3.75} < Z < \frac{60.5 - 56.25}{3.75}\right) = P(0.87 < Z < 1.13)$$

$$= 0.8707 - 0.8078 = 0.0630.$$

21. From the parameters $n = 150$ and $p = 0.9$, we get $\mu_X = np = 150 \cdot 0.9 = 135$ and
$\sigma_X = \sqrt{np \cdot (1-p)} = \sqrt{150 \cdot 0.9 \cdot (1-0.9)} = \sqrt{13.5} \approx 3.674$. Note that $np(1-p) = 13.5 \geq 10$,
so the normal approximation to the binomial can be used.

(a) $P(130) \approx P(129.5 < X < 130.5) = P\left(\frac{129.5 - 135}{3.674} < Z < \frac{130.5 - 135}{3.674}\right)$

$= P(-1.50 < Z < -1.22) = 0.1112 - 0.0668 = 0.0444$

(b) $P(X \geq 130) \approx P(X \geq 129.5) = P\left(Z \geq \frac{129.5 - 135}{3.674}\right) = P(Z \geq -1.55) = 1 - 0.0668 = 0.9332$

(c) $P(X < 125) = P(X \leq 124) \approx P(X \leq 124.5) = P\left(Z \leq \frac{124.5 - 135}{3.674}\right) = P(Z \leq -2.86) = 0.0021$

(d) $P(125 \leq X \leq 135) \approx P(124.5 \leq X \leq 135.5) = P\left(\frac{124.5 - 135}{3.674} < Z < \frac{135.5 - 135}{3.674}\right)$

$= P(-2.86 < Z < 0.14) = 0.5557 - 0.0021 = 0.5536$

23. From the parameters $n = 600$ and $p = 0.02$ we get $\mu_x = np = 600 \cdot 0.02 = 12$ and
$\sigma_X = \sqrt{np \cdot (1-p)} = \sqrt{600 \cdot 0.02 \cdot (1-0.02)} = \sqrt{11.76} \approx 3.429$. Note that
$np(1-p) = 11.76 \geq 10$, so the normal approximation to the binomial can be used.

(a) $P(20) \approx P(19.5 \leq X \leq 20.5) = P\left(\dfrac{19.5-12}{3.429} \leq Z \leq \dfrac{20.5-12}{3.429}\right) = P(2.19 \leq Z \leq 2.48)$

$= 0.9934 - 0.9857 = 0.0077$

(b) $P(X \leq 20) \approx P(X \leq 20.5) = P\left(Z \leq \dfrac{20.5-12}{3.429}\right) = P(Z \leq 2.48) = 0.9934$

(c) $P(X \geq 22) \approx P(X \geq 21.5) = P\left(Z \geq \dfrac{21.5-12}{3.429}\right) = P(Z \geq 2.77) = 1 - 0.9972 = 0.0028$

(d) $P(20 \leq X \leq 30) \approx P(19.5 \leq X \leq 30.5) = P\left(\dfrac{19.5-12}{3.429} \leq Z \leq \dfrac{30.5-12}{3.429}\right)$

$= P(2.19 \leq Z \leq 5.39) = 1.0000 - 0.9857 = 0.0143$

25. From the parameters $n = 400$ and $p = 0.05$ we get $\mu_x = np = 400 \cdot 0.05 = 20$ and
$\sigma_X = \sqrt{np \cdot (1-p)} = \sqrt{400 \cdot 0.05 \cdot (1-0.05)} = \sqrt{19} \approx 4.359$. Note that $np(1-p) = 19 \geq 10$, so
the normal approximation to the binomial can be used.

(a) $P(20) \approx P(19.5 \leq X \leq 20.5) = P\left(\dfrac{19.5-20}{4.359} \leq Z \leq \dfrac{20.5-20}{4.359}\right) = P(-0.11 \leq Z \leq 0.11)$

$= 0.5438 - 0.4562 = 0.0876$

(b) $P(X \leq 15) \approx P(X \leq 15.5) = P\left(Z \leq \dfrac{15.5-20}{4.359}\right) = P(Z \leq -1.03) = 0.1515$

(c) $P(X \geq 30) \approx P(X \geq 29.5) = P\left(Z \geq \dfrac{29.5-20}{4.359}\right) = P(Z \geq 2.18) = 1 - 0.9854 = 0.0146$

(d) $P(10 \leq X \leq 32) \approx P(9.5 \leq X \leq 32.5) = P\left(\dfrac{9.5-20}{4.359} \leq Z \leq \dfrac{32.5-20}{4.359}\right)$

$= P(-2.41 \leq Z \leq 2.87) = 0.9979 - 0.0080 = 0.9899$

27. From the parameters $n = 200$ and $p = 0.55$, we get $\mu_x = np = 200 \cdot 0.55 = 110$ and
$\sigma_X = \sqrt{np \cdot (1-p)} = \sqrt{200 \cdot 0.55 \cdot (1-0.55)} = \sqrt{49.5} \approx 7.036$. Note that $np(1-p) = 49.5 \geq 10$,
so the normal approximation to the binomial can be used.

(a) $P(X \geq 130) \approx P(X \geq 129.5) = P\left(Z \geq \dfrac{129.5-110}{7.036}\right) = P(Z \geq 2.77) = 1 - 0.9972 = 0.0028$

(b) Since the result is very unusual, it contradicts the results of the *Current Population Survey*. Explanations will vary. One possibility follows: It is likely that this is a sample is from a population with higher than 55% of the male students living at home.

29. From the parameters $n = 150$ and $p = 0.42$, we get $\mu_x = np = 150 \cdot 0.42 = 63$ and
$\sigma_X = \sqrt{np \cdot (1-p)} = \sqrt{150 \cdot 0.42 \cdot (1-0.42)} = \sqrt{36.54} \approx 6.045$. Note that
$np(1-p) = 36.54 \geq 10$, so the normal approximation to the binomial can be used.

(a) $P(X \geq 80) \approx P(X \geq 79.5) = P\left(Z \geq \dfrac{79.5 - 63}{6.045}\right) = P(Z \geq 2.73) = 1 - 0.9968 = 0.0032$

(b) Since the result is very unusual, it contradicts the results of the Gallup poll. Explanations will vary. One possibility follows: The result suggests that the preference for boys is higher among the students of this college than among the population sampled by the Gallup poll.

Chapter 7 Review Exercises

Note: The answers provided in this section have been calculated using the Standard Normal Table provided in the textbook. Answers found using technology may differ from those shown since answers computed using technology do not involve rounding of z-scores.

1. (a) μ is the center (and peak) of the normal distribution and so $\mu = 60$.

(b) σ is the distance from the center to the points of inflection, so $\sigma = 70 - 60 = 10$.

(c) Interpretation 1: The proportion of the population with X-values above 75 is 0.0668. Interpretation 2: The probability of a randomly selected individual having an X-value above 75 is 0.0668.

(d) Interpretation 1: The proportion of the population with X-values between 50 and 75 is 0.7745. Interpretation 2: The probability of a randomly selected individual having an X-value between 50 and 75 is 0.7745.

3. (a) $Z_1 = \dfrac{X_1 - \mu}{\sigma} = \dfrac{18 - 20}{4} = -0.50$ **(b)** $Z_2 = \dfrac{X_2 - \mu}{\sigma} = \dfrac{21 - 20}{4} = 0.25$

(c) The area between Z_1 and Z_2 is also 0.2912.

5. Using the standard normal table, the area to the left of $Z = -1.04$ is 0.1492.

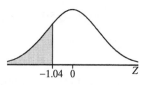

7. Using the standard normal table, the area between $Z = -0.34$ and $Z = 1.03$ is $0.8485 - 0.3669 = 0.4816$.

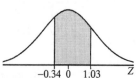

9. $P(Z < 1.19) = 0.8830$

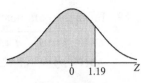

11. $P(-1.21 \le Z \le 2.28) = 0.9887 - 0.1131 = 0.8756$

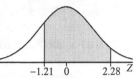

13. We look for 0.8400 in the interior of the tables and find that 0.8389 is closest, corresponding to $Z = 0.99$.

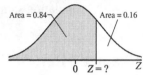

15. The Z-scores for the middle 92% are the Z-scores for the top and bottom 4%. From the interior of the tables, the area closest to 0.0400 is 0.0401, corresponding to $Z_1 = -1.75$. By symmetry the other Z-score is $Z_2 = 1.75$.

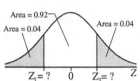

17. $z_{0.20}$ is the Z-score that cuts off an area of 0.20 in the top tail and so has an area of $1 - 0.20 = 0.80$ below it. The area in the interior of the tables that is closest to 0.8000 is 0.7995, corresponding to $Z = 0.84$. Hence $z_{0.20} = 0.84$.

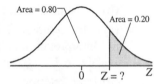

19.
$$P(X > 55) = P\left(Z > \frac{55 - 50}{6}\right) \approx P(Z > 0.83)$$
$$= 1 - 0.7967 = 0.2033 \, .$$

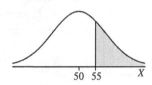

21.
$$P(65 < X < 85) = P\left(\frac{65 - 70}{10} < Z < \frac{85 - 70}{10}\right)$$
$$= P(-0.50 < Z < 1.50) = 0.9332 - 0.3085 = 0.6247$$

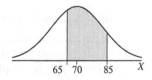

23. (a) $P(X \ge 75,000) = P\left(Z \ge \dfrac{75,000 - 70,000}{4,400}\right)$

$\approx P(Z \ge 1.14) = 1 - 0.8729 = 0.1271$ or 12.71%.

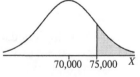

(b) $P(X \le 60,000) = P\left(Z \le \dfrac{60,000 - 70,000}{4,400}\right)$

$\approx P(Z \le -2.27) = 0.0116$ or 1.16%.

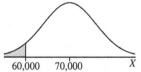

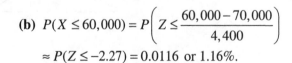

192

(c) $P(65,000 \le X \le 80,000)$

$$= P\left(\frac{65,000-70,000}{4,400} \le Z \le \frac{80,000-70,000}{4,400}\right)$$

$$\approx P(-1.14 \le Z \le 2.27) = 0.9884 - 0.1271 = 0.8613$$

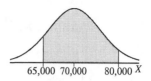

(d) We need the cut-off for the bottom 2%. The area closest to 0.0200 in the interior of the tables is 0.0202, corresponding to $Z = -2.05$. Then $X = \mu + Z\sigma =$ $70,000 + (-2.05)(4,400) = 60,980$ miles.

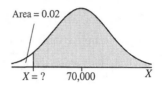

25. (a) $P(X > 180) = P\left(Z > \dfrac{180-171}{39.8}\right) \approx P(Z > 0.23)$

$\quad\quad = 1 - 0.5910 = 0.4090$ or 40.9%.

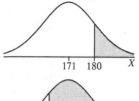

(b) $P(150 < X < 200) = P\left(\dfrac{150-171}{39.8} < Z < \dfrac{200-171}{39.8}\right)$

$\quad\quad \approx P(-0.53 < Z < 0.73) = 0.7673 - 0.2981 = 0.4692$ or 46.92%.

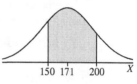

(c) $P(X < 140) = P\left(Z < \dfrac{140-171}{39.8}\right)$

$\quad\quad \approx P(Z < -0.78) = 0.2177$

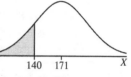

(d) The area in the interior of the normal tables that is closest to 0.1000 is 0.1003, corresponding to $Z = -1.28$. Then $X = \mu + Z\sigma = 171 - 1.28(39.8) = 120.056$ or 120.

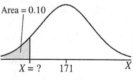

(e) The area in the interior of the normal tables that is closest to 0.2500 is 0.2514, corresponding to $Z = -0.67$. Then $X = \mu + Z\sigma = 171 - 0.67(39.8) = 144$ which is close to the reported value of 145.

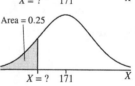

27. (a) $P(X > 5.25) = P\left(Z > \dfrac{5.25-5.11}{0.062}\right) \approx P(Z > 2.26)$

$\quad\quad = 1 - 0.9881 = 0.0119$ or 1.19%.

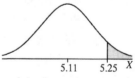

(b) $P(X < 5) = P\left(Z < \dfrac{5-5.11}{0.062}\right) \approx -1.77 = 0.0384$ or 3.84%.

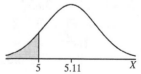

(c) $P(5 \le X \le 5.25) = P\left(\dfrac{5-5.11}{0.062} \le Z \ge \dfrac{5.25-5.11}{0.062}\right)$

$= P(-1.77 < Z < 2.26) = 0.9881 - 0.0384 = 0.9497$ or 94.97%.

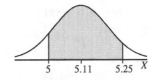

29. (a) $np(1-p) = 200 \cdot 0.08 \cdot (1-0.08) = 14.72 \ge 10$, so the normal distribution can be used to approximate the binomial distribution. The parameters are $\mu_X = np = 200(0.08) = 16$ and $\sigma_X = \sqrt{np(1-p)} = \sqrt{200 \cdot 0.08 \cdot (1-0.08)} \approx 3.837$.

(b) $P(15) \approx P(14.5 \le X \le 15.5)$

$= P\left(\dfrac{14.5-16}{3.837} \le Z \le \dfrac{15.5-16}{3.837}\right)$

$\approx P(-.39 \le Z \le -0.13) = 0.4483 - 0.3483 = 0.1000$.

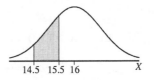

There is about a 10% chance that 15 out of a random sample of 200 20–34-year-old females will have high serum cholesterol.

(c) $P(X > 20) = P(X \ge 21) \approx P(X > 20.5)$

$= P\left(Z > \dfrac{20.5-16}{3.837}\right) = P(Z > 1.17)$

$= 1 - 0.8790 = 0.1210$.

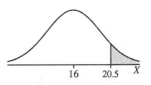

There is about a 12.1% chance that more than 20 out of a random sample of 200 20–34-year-old females will have high serum cholesterol.

(d) $P(X \ge 15) \approx P(X > 14.5) = P\left(Z > \dfrac{14.5-16}{3.837}\right)$

$= P(Z > -0.39) = 1 - 0.3483 = 0.6517$. There is about a 65.17% chance that at least 15 out of a random sample of 200 20–34-year-old females will have high serum cholesterol.

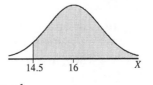

(e) $P(X < 25) = P(X \le 24) \approx P(X < 24.5)$

$= P\left(Z < \dfrac{24.5-16}{3.837}\right) = P(Z < 2.22) = 0.9868$. There is about a 98.68% chance that fewer than 25 out of a random sample of 200 20–34-year-old females will have high serum cholesterol.

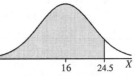

(f) $P(15 \le X \le 25) \approx P(14.5 < X < 25.5)$

$= P\left(\dfrac{14.5-16}{3.837} < Z < \dfrac{25.5-16}{3.837}\right)$

$= P(-0.39 < Z < 2.48) = 0.9934 - 0.3483 = 0.6451$.

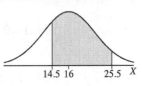

There is about a 64.51% chance that between 15 and 25 out of a random sample of 200 20–34-year-old females will have high serum cholesterol.

31. The normal probability plot is roughly linear, and all the data lie within the provided bounds, so the sample data should come from a population that is normally distributed.

33. The normal probability plot is roughly linear, so the sample data should come from a population that is normally distributed.

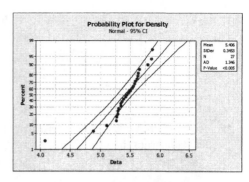

35. (a) $P(X > 25) = P\left(Z > \dfrac{25-29}{2}\right) = P(Z > -2)$

$= 1 - 0.0228 = 0.9772$. Thus, 0.9772, or 97.72%, of automatic four-wheel-drive 2005 Ford Escape HEVs gets more than 25 miles per gallon.

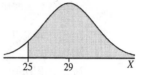

(b) $P(X < 30) = P\left(Z < \dfrac{30-29}{2}\right) = P(Z < 0.5) = 0.6915$

Thus, 0.6915, or 0.69.15%, of automatic four-wheel-drive 2005 Ford Escape HEVs gets less than 30 miles per gallon.

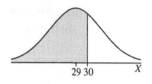

(c) $P(26 \le X \le 34) = P\left(\dfrac{26-29}{2} \le Z \le \dfrac{34-29}{2}\right)$

$= P(-1.5 \le Z \le 2.5) = 0.9938 - 0.0668 = 0.9270$

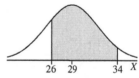

(d) $P(X > 35) = P\left(Z > \dfrac{35-29}{2}\right) = P(Z > 3)$

$= 1 - 0.9987 = 0.0013$

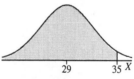

(e) $P(X \le 32) = P\left(Z \le \dfrac{32-29}{2}\right) = P(Z \le 1.5) = 0.9332$

So, an automatic four-wheel-drive 2005 Ford Escape HEV that gets 32 miles per gallons is at the 93rd percentile rank.

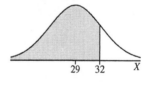

(f) $P(X \le 25) = P\left(Z \le \dfrac{25-29}{2}\right) = P(Z \le -2) = 0.0228$

So, an automatic four-wheel-drive 2005 Ford Escape HEV that gets 25 miles per gallons is at the 2nd percentile rank.

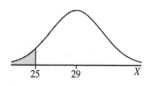

37. (a)

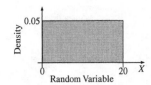

(b) Probability = area under the uniform density curve
= height × width = $0.05 \cdot (5-0) = 0.25$.

(c) Probability = area under the uniform density curve
= height × width = $0.05 \cdot (18-10) = 0.40$.

39. Answers may vary. One possibility follows:

(1) Construct the probability plot either by using technology or by the following steps:

Step 1: Arrange the data in ascending order.

Step 2: Compute $f_i = \dfrac{i-0.375}{n+.025}$, where i is the index (i.e., the position of the data value in order) and n is the number of observations.

Step 3: Find the Z-score corresponding to f_i from the standard normal table.

Step 4: Plot the observed values on the horizontal axis and the corresponding expected Z-scores on the vertical axis.

(2) If the normal probability plot is roughly linear, conclude that the data come from a population that is approximately normal.

Chapter 8

Sampling Distributions

8.1 Distribution of the Sample Mean

1. The sampling distribution of a statistic (such as the sample mean) is the probability distribution for all possible values of the statistic computed from samples of fixed size, n.

3. standard error of the mean

5. The mean of the sampling distribution of $\bar{x}$ is given by $\mu_{\bar{x}} = \mu$ and the standard deviation is given by $\sigma_{\bar{x}} = \dfrac{\sigma}{\sqrt{n}}$.

7. four; To see this, note that $\sigma_{\bar{x}} = \dfrac{\sigma}{\sqrt{4n}} = \dfrac{1}{2} \cdot \dfrac{\sigma}{\sqrt{n}}$.

9. The sampling distribution would be exactly normal. The mean and standard deviation would be $\mu_{\bar{x}} = \mu = 30$ and $\sigma_{\bar{x}} = \dfrac{\sigma}{\sqrt{n}} = \dfrac{8}{\sqrt{10}} \approx 2.53$.

Note: The answers to the exercises in this section are based on values from the standard normal table. Since answers computed using technology do not involve rounding of Z-scores, they will often differ from the answers given below in the third and fourth decimal places.

11. $\mu_{\bar{x}} = \mu = 80$; $\sigma_{\bar{x}} = \dfrac{\sigma}{\sqrt{n}} = \dfrac{14}{\sqrt{49}} = \dfrac{14}{7} = 2$

13. $\mu_{\bar{x}} = \mu = 52$; $\sigma_{\bar{x}} = \dfrac{\sigma}{\sqrt{n}} = \dfrac{10}{\sqrt{21}} \approx 2.182$

15. (a) Since $\mu = 80$ and $\sigma = 14$, the mean and standard deviation of the sampling distribution of $\bar{x}$ are given by:

$\mu_{\bar{x}} = \mu = 80$; $\sigma_{\bar{x}} = \dfrac{\sigma}{\sqrt{n}} = \dfrac{14}{\sqrt{49}} = \dfrac{14}{7} = 2$

We are not told that the population is normally distributed, but we do have a large sample size ($n \geq 30$). Therefore, we can use the Central Limit Theorem to say that the sampling distribution of $\bar{x}$ is approximately normal.

(b) $P(\bar{x} > 83) = P\left(Z > \dfrac{83 - 80}{2}\right) = P(Z > 1.50) = 1 - P(Z \leq 1.50) = 1 - 0.9332 = 0.0668$

(c) $P(\bar{x} \le 75.8) = P\left(Z \le \dfrac{75.8 - 80}{2}\right) = P(Z \le -2.10) = 0.0179$

(d) $P(78.3 < \bar{x} < 85.1) = P\left(\dfrac{78.3 - 80}{2} < Z < \dfrac{85.1 - 80}{2}\right) = P(-0.85 < Z < 2.55)$

$$= 0.9946 - 0.1977 = 0.7969$$

17. (a) The population must be normally distributed. If this is the case, then the sampling distribution of $\bar{x}$ is exactly normal. The mean and standard deviation of the sampling distribution are $\mu_{\bar{x}} = \mu = 64$ and $\sigma_{\bar{x}} = \dfrac{\sigma}{\sqrt{n}} = \dfrac{17}{\sqrt{12}} \approx 4.907$.

(b) $P(\bar{x} < 67.3) = P\left(Z < \dfrac{67.3 - 64}{17/\sqrt{12}}\right) = P(Z < 0.67) = 0.7486$

(c) $P(\bar{x} \ge 65.2) = P\left(Z \ge \dfrac{65.2 - 64}{17/\sqrt{12}}\right) = P(Z \ge 0.24) = 1 - P(Z < 0.24)$

$$= 1 - 0.5948 = 0.4052$$

19. (a) $P(X < 260) = P\left(Z < \dfrac{260 - 266}{16}\right) = P(Z < -0.38) = 0.3520$

(b) $\mu_{\bar{x}} = \mu = 266$; $\sigma_{\bar{x}} = \dfrac{\sigma}{\sqrt{n}} = \dfrac{16}{\sqrt{20}}$

$P(\bar{x} < 160) = P\left(Z < \dfrac{260 - 266}{16/\sqrt{20}}\right) = P(Z < -1.68) = 0.0465$

(c) $\mu_{\bar{x}} = \mu = 266$; $\sigma_{\bar{x}} = \dfrac{\sigma}{\sqrt{n}} = \dfrac{16}{\sqrt{50}}$

$P(\bar{x} < 160) = P\left(Z < \dfrac{260 - 266}{16/\sqrt{50}}\right) = P(Z < -2.65) = 0.0040$

(d) Answers will vary. Part (c) indicates that this would be an unusual observation. Therefore, we would conclude that the sample came from a population whose mean gestation period is less than 266 days.

(e) $\mu_{\bar{x}} = \mu = 266$; $\sigma_{\bar{x}} = \dfrac{\sigma}{\sqrt{n}} = \dfrac{16}{\sqrt{15}}$

$P(256 \le \bar{x} \le 276) = P\left(\dfrac{256 - 266}{16/\sqrt{15}} \le Z \le \dfrac{276 - 266}{16/\sqrt{15}}\right)$

$$= P(-2.42 \le Z \le 2.42)$$

$$= 0.9922 - 0.0078 = 0.9844$$

21. (a) $P(X > 95) = P\left(Z > \dfrac{95 - 85}{21.25}\right) = P(Z > 0.47) = 1 - P(Z \le 0.47) = 1 - 0.6808 = 0.3192$

(b) $\mu_{\bar{x}} = \mu = 85$; $\sigma_{\bar{x}} = \dfrac{\sigma}{\sqrt{n}} = \dfrac{21.25}{\sqrt{20}}$

$$P(\bar{x} > 95) = P\left(Z > \dfrac{95 - 85}{21.25/\sqrt{20}}\right) = P(Z > 2.10) = 1 - P(Z \le 2.10)$$
$$= 1 - 0.9821 = 0.0179$$

(c) $\mu_{\bar{x}} = \mu = 85$; $\sigma_{\bar{x}} = \dfrac{\sigma}{\sqrt{n}} = \dfrac{21.25}{\sqrt{30}}$

$$P(\bar{x} > 95) = P\left(Z > \dfrac{95 - 85}{21.25/\sqrt{30}}\right) = P(Z > 2.58) = 1 - P(Z \le 2.58)$$
$$= 1 - 0.9951 = 0.0049$$

(d) Increasing the sample size in this case caused the probability to decrease. Since 95 is larger than the mean and we are looking for $P(\bar{x} > 95)$, we are essentially computing a probability of being in the upper tail of the distribution. Increasing the sample size makes the sampling distribution of $\bar{x}$ less variable, reducing the probability that we would get an observation far out in either tail.

(e) Answers will vary. From part (c) we see that this is an unusual observation. Therefore, we would conclude that the mean time between eruptions of Old Faithful is longer than 85 minutes.

23. (a) $P(X > 0) = P\left(Z > \dfrac{0 - 0.007233}{0.04135}\right) = P(Z > -0.17) = 1 - P(Z \le -0.17)$
$$= 1 - 0.4325 = 0.5675$$

(b) $\mu_{\bar{x}} = \mu = 0.007233$; $\sigma_{\bar{x}} = \dfrac{\sigma}{\sqrt{n}} = \dfrac{0.04135}{\sqrt{12}}$

$$P(\bar{x} > 0) = P\left(Z > \dfrac{0 - 0.007233}{0.04135/\sqrt{12}}\right) = P(Z > -0.61) = 1 - P(Z \le -0.61)$$
$$= 1 - 0.2709 = 0.7291$$

(c) $\mu_{\bar{x}} = \mu = 0.007233$; $\sigma_{\bar{x}} = \dfrac{\sigma}{\sqrt{n}} = \dfrac{0.04135}{\sqrt{24}}$

$$P(\bar{x} > 0) = P\left(Z > \dfrac{0 - 0.007233}{0.04135/\sqrt{24}}\right) = P(Z > -0.86) = 1 - P(Z \le -0.86)$$
$$= 1 - 0.1949 = 0.8051$$

(d) $\mu_{\bar{x}} = \mu = 0.007233$; $\sigma_{\bar{x}} = \dfrac{\sigma}{\sqrt{n}} = \dfrac{0.04135}{\sqrt{36}}$

$$P(\bar{x} > 0) = P\left(Z > \dfrac{0 - 0.007233}{0.04135/\sqrt{36}}\right) = P(Z > -1.05) = 1 - P(Z \le -1.05)$$
$$= 1 - 0.1469 = 0.8531$$

(e)   Answers will vary. Based on these results, it appears that the likelihood of having a positive rate of return increases as the length of time of the investment increases.

25. (a)   Without knowing the shape of the distribution, we would need a sample size of at least 30 so we could apply the Central Limit Theorem.

(b) $P(\bar{x} < 10) = P\left(Z < \dfrac{10 - 11.4}{3.2/\sqrt{40}}\right) = P(Z < -2.77) = 0.0028$

27. (a)   The sampling distribution of $\bar{x}$ is approximately normal because this is a large sample, $n = 50 > 30$. From the Central Limit Theorem, as the sample size increased, the sampling distribution of the mean becomes more normal.

(b) $\mu_{\bar{x}} = \mu = 3$, assuming that we are sampling from a population that is exactly at the

FDAL, and $\sigma_{\bar{x}} = \dfrac{\sigma}{\sqrt{n}} = \dfrac{\sqrt{3}}{\sqrt{50}} = \sqrt{\dfrac{3}{50}} \approx 0.245$.

(c) $P(\bar{x} \ge 3.6) = P\left(Z \ge \dfrac{3.6 - 3}{\sqrt{3}/\sqrt{50}}\right) = P(Z \ge 2.45) = 1 - 0.9929 = 0.0071$

This probability indicates that this is an unusual outcome. It appears that this sample comes from a population with a higher mean than 3 insect fragments per ten-gram portion.

29. We have a large sample, $n = 60$, so we can use the Central Limit Theorem to say that the sampling distribution of $\bar{x}$ is approximately normal.

$\mu_{\bar{x}} = \mu = 50$; $\sigma_{\bar{x}} = \dfrac{\sigma}{\sqrt{n}} = \dfrac{16}{\sqrt{60}}$

$P(\bar{x} \le 45) = P\left(Z \le \dfrac{45 - 50}{16/\sqrt{60}}\right) = P(Z \le -2.42) = 0.0078$

This probability is very small. Since it is less than 0.05, it would be unusual for a random sample of 60 college football players from the given population to average 45 or fewer strong blows to the head.

31. (a) $\mu = \dfrac{\sum x}{N} = \dfrac{232}{6} \approx 38.7$

The population mean age is 38.7 years.

(b) 37, 43;   37, 29;   37, 47;   37, 36;   37, 40;   43, 29;   43, 47;   43, 36;   43, 40;
29, 47;   29, 36;   29, 40;   47, 36;   47, 40;   36, 40

(c) Obtain each sample mean by adding the two ages in a sample and dividing by two.

$$\overline{x} = \frac{37+43}{2} = 40 \text{ yr} ; \ \overline{x} = \frac{37+29}{2} = 33 \text{ yr} ; \ \overline{x} = \frac{37+47}{2} = 41 \text{ yr} ; \ \overline{x} = \frac{37+36}{2} = 36.5 \text{ yr} ,$$

etc.

$\overline{x}$	32.5	33	34.5	36	36.5	38	38.5	39.5	40	41.5	42	43.5	45
$P(\overline{x})$	$\frac{1}{15}$	$\frac{1}{15}$	$\frac{1}{15}$	$\frac{1}{15}$	$\frac{1}{15}$	$\frac{2}{15}$	$\frac{1}{15}$	$\frac{1}{15}$	$\frac{1}{15}$	$\frac{2}{15}$	$\frac{1}{15}$	$\frac{1}{15}$	$\frac{1}{15}$

(d) $\mu_{\overline{x}} = (32.5)\left(\frac{1}{15}\right) + (33)\left(\frac{1}{15}\right) + ... + (45)\left(\frac{1}{15}\right) \approx 38.7$ years

Notice that this is the same value we obtained in part (a) for the population mean.

(e) $P(35.7 \leq \overline{x} \leq 41.7) = \frac{1}{15} + \frac{1}{15} + \frac{2}{15} + \frac{1}{15} + \frac{1}{15} + \frac{1}{15} + \frac{2}{15} = \frac{9}{15} = 0.6$

(f) for part (b):
37, 43, 29;   37, 43, 47;   37, 43, 36;   37, 43, 40;   37, 29, 47;   37, 29, 36;
37, 29, 40;   37, 47, 36;   37, 47, 40;   37, 36, 40;   43, 29, 47;   43, 29, 36;
43, 29, 40;   43, 47, 36;   43, 47, 40;   43, 36, 40;   29, 47, 36;   29, 47, 40;
29, 36, 40;   47, 36, 40

for part (c):
Obtain each sample mean by adding the three ages in a sample and dividing by three.

$$\overline{x} = \frac{37+43+29}{3} \approx 36.3 \text{ yr} ; \ \overline{x} = \frac{37+43+47}{3} \approx 42.3 \text{ yr} ; \ \overline{x} = \frac{37+43+36}{3} = 38.7 \text{ yr} ; \text{ etc.}$$

$\overline{x}$	34	35	35.3	36	36.3	37.3	37.7	38.7	39.7	40	41	41.3	42	42.3	43.3
$P(\overline{x})$	$\frac{1}{20}$	$\frac{1}{20}$	$\frac{1}{20}$	$\frac{1}{20}$	$\frac{1}{20}$	$\frac{1}{10}$	$\frac{1}{10}$	$\frac{1}{10}$	$\frac{1}{10}$	$\frac{1}{10}$	$\frac{1}{20}$	$\frac{1}{20}$	$\frac{1}{20}$	$\frac{1}{20}$	$\frac{1}{20}$

for part (d):

$$\mu_{\overline{x}} = (34)\left(\frac{1}{20}\right) + (35)\left(\frac{1}{20}\right) + ... + (43.3)\left(\frac{1}{20}\right) \approx 38.7 \text{ years}$$

Notice that this is the same value we obtained previously.

for part (e):

$$P(35.7 \leq \overline{x} \leq 41.7) = \frac{14}{20} = \frac{7}{10}$$

With the larger sample size, the probability of obtaining a sample mean within 3 years of the population mean has increased.

33. (a) – (c) Answers will vary.

(d) $\mu_{\bar{x}} = \mu = 100$; $\sigma_{\bar{x}} = \dfrac{\sigma}{\sqrt{n}} = \dfrac{16}{\sqrt{20}} = \dfrac{8}{\sqrt{5}} \approx 3.6$

(e)   Answers will vary.

(f) $P(\bar{x} > 108) = P\left(Z > \dfrac{108 - 100}{16/\sqrt{20}}\right) = P(Z > 2.24) = 1 - P(Z \le 2.24) = 1 - 0.9875 = 0.0125$

(g)   Answers will vary.

35. (a) – (b)   Answers will vary. Using $\mu = 50$ and $\sigma = 10$, we get:

For (a): $\mu_{\bar{x}} = \mu = 50$; $\sigma_{\bar{x}} = \dfrac{\sigma}{\sqrt{n}} = \dfrac{10}{\sqrt{5}}$

For (b): $\mu_{\bar{x}} = \mu = 50$; $\sigma_{\bar{x}} = \dfrac{\sigma}{\sqrt{n}} = \dfrac{10}{\sqrt{10}}$

(c)   We can use the Central Limit Theorem to say that the sampling distribution is approximately normal since we have a large sample (that is, $n \ge 30$).

$\mu_{\bar{x}} = \mu = 50$; $\sigma_{\bar{x}} = \dfrac{\sigma}{\sqrt{n}} = \dfrac{10}{\sqrt{50}} = \dfrac{2}{\sqrt{2}}$

(d)   Answers will vary. As the sample size increases, we should see the sampling distribution become more normally distributed.

8.2 Distribution of the Sample Proportion

1. 0.44; $p = \dfrac{220}{500} = 0.44$

3. False; while it is possible for the sample proportion to have the same value as the population proportion, it will not always have the same value.

5. The sampling distribution of $\hat{p}$ is approximately normal if $np(1 - p) \ge 10$ (assuming that $n \le 0.05N$).

7. $25,000(0.05) = 1250$

The sample size, $n = 500$, is less than 5% of the population size and $np(1 - p) = 500(0.4)(0.6) = 120 > 10$.

The distribution of $\hat{p}$ is approximately normal, with mean $\mu_{\hat{p}} = p = 0.4$ and standard

deviation $\sigma_{\hat{p}} = \sqrt{\dfrac{p(1 - p)}{n}} = \sqrt{\dfrac{0.4(1 - 0.4)}{500}} \approx 0.022$.

9. $25,000(0.05) = 1250$

The sample size, $n = 1000$, is less than 5% of the population size and
$np(1-p) = 1000(0.103)(0.897) = 92.391 > 10$.

The distribution of $\hat{p}$ is approximately normal, with mean $\mu_{\hat{p}} = p = 0.103$ and standard

deviation $\sigma_{\hat{p}} = \sqrt{\dfrac{p(1-p)}{n}} = \sqrt{\dfrac{0.103(1-0.103)}{1000}} \approx 0.010$.

11. (a) $10,000(0.05) = 500$

The sample size, $n = 75$, is less than 5% of the population size and
$np(1-p) = 75(0.8)(0.2) = 12 > 10$.

The distribution of $\hat{p}$ is approximately normal, with mean $\mu_{\hat{p}} = p = 0.8$ and standard

deviation $\sigma_{\hat{p}} = \sqrt{\dfrac{p(1-p)}{n}} = \sqrt{\dfrac{0.8(1-0.8)}{75}} \approx 0.046$.

(b) $P(\hat{p} \geq 0.84) = P\left(Z \geq \dfrac{0.84 - 0.8}{\sqrt{0.8(0.2)/75}} \right) = P(Z \geq 0.87) = 1 - P(Z < 0.87)$

$= 1 - 0.8078 = 0.1922$

(c) $P(\hat{p} \leq 0.68) = P\left(Z \leq \dfrac{0.68 - 0.8}{\sqrt{0.8(0.2)/75}} \right) = P(Z \leq -2.60) = 0.0047$

13. (a) $1,000,000(0.05) = 50,000$

The sample size, $n = 1000$, is less than 5% of the population size and
$np(1-p) = 1000(0.35)(0.65) = 227.5 > 10$.

The distribution of $\hat{p}$ is approximately normal, with mean $\mu_{\hat{p}} = p = 0.35$ and

standard deviation $\sigma_{\hat{p}} = \sqrt{\dfrac{p(1-p)}{n}} = \sqrt{\dfrac{0.35(1-0.35)}{1000}} \approx 0.015$.

(b) $\hat{p} = \dfrac{x}{n} = \dfrac{390}{1000} = 0.39$

$P(X \geq 390) = P(\hat{p} \geq 0.39) = P\left(Z \geq \dfrac{0.39 - 0.35}{\sqrt{0.53(0.65)/1000}} \right) = P(Z \geq 2.65)$

$= 1 - P(Z < 2.65) = 1 - 0.9960 = 0.0040$

(c) $\hat{p} = \dfrac{x}{n} = \dfrac{320}{1000} = 0.32$

$$P(X \le 320) = P(\hat{p} \le 0.32) = P\left(Z \ge \dfrac{0.32 - 0.35}{\sqrt{0.53(0.65)/1000}}\right) = P(Z \le -1.99) = 0.0233$$

15. (a) $5000(0.05) = 250$

The sample size, $n = 100$, is less than 5% of the population size and
$np(1-p) = 100(0.3)(0.7) = 21 > 10$.

The distribution of $\hat{p}$ is approximately normal, with mean $\mu_{\hat{p}} = p = 0.3$ and standard

deviation $\sigma_{\hat{p}} = \sqrt{\dfrac{p(1-p)}{n}} = \sqrt{\dfrac{0.3(1-0.3)}{100}} \approx 0.046$.

(b) $\hat{p} = \dfrac{x}{n} = \dfrac{37}{100} = 0.37$

$$P(X > 37) = P(\hat{p} > 0.37) = P\left(Z > \dfrac{0.37 - 0.3}{\sqrt{0.3(0.7)/100}}\right) = P(Z > 1.53)$$

$$= 1 - P(Z \le 1.53) = 1 - 0.9370 = 0.0630$$

We have a result that occurs about 6 times in 100. While this probability is low, it is larger than 0.05 so we would not consider this unusual.

(c) $\hat{p} = \dfrac{x}{n} = \dfrac{18}{100} = 0.18$

$$P(X \le 18) = P(\hat{p} \le 0.18) = P\left(Z \ge \dfrac{0.18 - 0.3}{\sqrt{0.3(0.7)/100}}\right) = P(Z \le -2.62) = 0.0044$$

This probability is less than 0.05 so the result would be considered unusual. We obtained a result that would occur about 4 times in 1000.

17. (a)   Our sample size, $n = 500$, is less than 5% of the population size and
$np(1-p) = 500(0.26)(0.74) = 96.2 > 10$.

The distribution of $\hat{p}$ is approximately normal, with mean $\mu_{\hat{p}} = p = 0.26$ and

standard deviation $\sigma_{\hat{p}} = \sqrt{\dfrac{p(1-p)}{n}} = \sqrt{\dfrac{0.26(1-0.26)}{500}} \approx 0.020$.

(b) $P(\hat{p} < 0.24) = P\left(Z < \dfrac{0.24 - 0.26}{\sqrt{0.26(0.74)/500}}\right) = P(Z < -1.02) = 0.1539$

(c) $\hat{p} = \dfrac{x}{n} = \dfrac{150}{500} = 0.3$

$$P(X \geq 150) = P(\hat{p} \geq 0.3) = P\left(Z \geq \dfrac{0.3 - 0.26}{\sqrt{0.26(0.74)/500}}\right) = P(Z \geq 2.04)$$

$$= 1 - P(Z < 2.04) = 1 - 0.9793 = 0.0207$$

This probability is less than 0.05 so the result would be considered unusual. We obtained a result that would occur about 2 times in 100.

19. (a) $np(1-p) = 800(0.43)(0.57) = 196.08 > 10$.

$$\mu_{\hat{p}} = p = 0.43; \quad \sigma_{\hat{p}} = \sqrt{\dfrac{p(1-p)}{n}} = \sqrt{\dfrac{0.43(1-0.43)}{800}} \approx 0.018$$

$$P(\hat{p} \leq 0.40) = P\left(Z \leq \dfrac{0.40 - 0.43}{\sqrt{0.43(0.57)/800}}\right) = P(Z \leq -1.71) = 0.0436$$

(b) $P(\hat{p} \geq 0.45) = P\left(Z \geq \dfrac{0.45 - 0.43}{\sqrt{0.43(0.57)/800}}\right) = P(Z \geq 1.14) = 1 - P(Z < 1.14)$

$$= 1 - 0.8729 = 0.1271$$

We have a result that occurs about 13 times in 100. This probability is larger than 0.05 so we would not consider the result to be unusual.

21. (a) To say the sampling distribution of $\hat{p}$ is approximately normal, we need $np(1-p) \geq 10$ and $n \leq 0.05N$.

With $p = 0.1$, we need

$n(0.1)(1-0.1) \geq 10$

$n(0.1)(0.9) \geq 10$

$n(0.09) \geq 10$

$n \geq 111.11$

Therefore, we need a sample size of 112, or 62 more.

(b) With $p = 0.2$, we need

$n(0.2)(1-0.2) \geq 10$

$n(0.2)(0.8) \geq 10$

$n(0.16) \geq 10$

$n \geq 62.5$

Therefore, we need a sample size of 63, or 13 more.

23. (a) – (d) Answers will depend on simulation results.

(e) $\mu_{\hat{p}} = p = 0.3$; $\sigma_{\hat{p}} = \sqrt{\dfrac{p(1-p)}{n}} = \sqrt{\dfrac{0.3(1-0.3)}{765}} \approx 0.017$

25. (a) $\hat{p} = \dfrac{x}{n} = \dfrac{410}{500} = 0.82$

(b) $N = 6502$; $n = 500$; $\hat{p} = 0.82$

$$\sigma_{\hat{p}} = \sqrt{\dfrac{\hat{p}(1-\hat{p})}{n-1} \cdot \left(\dfrac{N-n}{N}\right)} = \sqrt{\dfrac{0.82(1-0.82)}{500-1} \cdot \left(\dfrac{6502-500}{6502}\right)} \approx 0.017$$

Chapter 8 Review Exercises

1. Answers will vary. A sampling distribution of a statistic is a probability distribution for all possible values of the statistic computed from a sample of size n.

3. The sampling distribution of $\hat{p}$ is approximately normal if $np(1-p) \geq 10$ and $n \leq 0.05N$.

5. (a) $P(X > 2625) = P\left(Z > \dfrac{2625-2600}{50}\right) = P(Z > 0.5) = 1 - P(Z \leq 0.5)$

$= 1 - 0.6915 = 0.3085$

This result is not unusual since $P(X > 2625) = 0.3085 > 0.05$.

(b) Since the population is normally distributed, the sampling distribution of $\bar{x}$ will be normal, regardless of the sample size. The mean of the distribution is $\mu_{\bar{x}} = \mu = 2600$ kcal, and the standard deviation is $\sigma_{\bar{x}} = \dfrac{\sigma}{\sqrt{n}} = \dfrac{50}{\sqrt{20}}$ kcal.

(c) $P(\bar{x} > 2625) = P\left(Z > \dfrac{2625-2600}{50/\sqrt{20}}\right) = P(Z > 2.24) = 1 - P(Z \leq 2.24)$

$= 1 - 0.9875 = 0.0125$

This result is unusual since $P(\bar{x} > 2625) = 0.0125 < 0.05$.

7. (a) We are not told that the population distribution is normally distributed, but we have a large sample ($n = 30$) so we can use the Central Limit Theorem to say that the sampling distribution of $\bar{x}$ is approximately normal.

The mean of the sampling distribution is $\mu_{\bar{x}} = \mu = 0.75$ inch and the standard deviation is $\sigma_{\bar{x}} = \dfrac{\sigma}{\sqrt{n}} = \dfrac{0.004}{\sqrt{30}} \approx 0.00073$ inch.

(b) The inspector will determine the machine needs an adjustment if the sample mean is either less than 0.748 inch or more than 0.752 inch.

$$P(\text{needs adjustment}) = P(\bar{x} < 0.748) + P(\bar{x} > 0.752)$$

$$= P\left(Z < \frac{0.748 - 0.75}{0.004 / \sqrt{30}}\right) + P\left(Z > \frac{0.752 - 0.75}{0.004 / \sqrt{30}}\right)$$

$$= P(Z < -2.74) + P(Z > 2.74)$$

$$= P(Z < -2.74) + 1 - P(Z \le 2.74)$$

$$= 0.0031 + 1 - 0.9969 = 0.0062$$

There is a 0.0062 probability that the inspector will determine the machine needs an adjustment.

9. (a) Our sample size, $n = 600$, is less than 5% of the population size and
$$np(1 - p) = 600(0.72)(0.28) = 120.96 > 10.$$

The distribution of $\hat{p}$ is approximately normal, with mean $\mu_{\hat{p}} = p = 0.72$ and

standard deviation $\sigma_{\hat{p}} = \sqrt{\dfrac{p(1-p)}{n}} = \sqrt{\dfrac{0.72(1-0.72)}{600}} \approx 0.018$.

(b) $P(\hat{p} \le 0.70) = P\left(Z \le \dfrac{0.70 - 0.72}{\sqrt{0.72(0.28)/600}}\right) = P(Z \le -1.09) = 0.1379$

(c) $\hat{p} = \dfrac{x}{n} = \dfrac{450}{600} = 0.75$

$$P(X \ge 450) = P(\hat{p} \ge 0.75) = P\left(Z \ge \dfrac{0.75 - 0.72}{\sqrt{0.72(0.28)/600}}\right) = P(Z \ge 1.64)$$

$$= 1 - P(Z < 1.64) = 1 - 0.9495 = 0.0505$$

This probability is more than 0.05 so the result would not be considered unusual. We obtained a result that would occur about 5 times in 100.

11. (a) Our sample size, $n = 200$, is less than 5% of the population size and
$$np(1 - p) = 200(0.09)(0.91) = 16.38 > 10.$$

The distribution of $\hat{p}$ is approximately normal, with mean $\mu_{\hat{p}} = p = 0.09$ and

standard deviation $\sigma_{\hat{p}} = \sqrt{\dfrac{p(1-p)}{n}} = \sqrt{\dfrac{0.09(1-0.91)}{200}} \approx 0.020$.

(b) $P(\hat{p} \le 0.06) = P\left(Z \le \dfrac{0.06 - 0.09}{\sqrt{0.09(0.91)/200}}\right) = P(Z \le -1.48) = 0.0694$

(c) $\hat{p} = \dfrac{x}{n} = \dfrac{25}{200} = 0.125$

$$P(X \geq 25) = P(\hat{p} > 0.125) = P\left(Z > \dfrac{0.125 - 0.09}{\sqrt{0.09(0.91)/200}}\right) = P(Z > 1.73)$$

$$= 1 - P(Z \leq 1.73) = 1 - 0.9582 = 0.0418$$

This probability is less than 0.05 so the result would be considered unusual. We obtained a result that would occur about 4 times in 100.

13. $\mu = \$71,401$; $\sigma = \$26,145$; $n = 100$

$$P(\overline{x} < 65,000) = P\left(Z < \dfrac{65,000 - 71,401}{26,145/\sqrt{100}}\right) = P(Z < -2.45) = 0.0071$$

There is a 0.0071 probability that a random sample of 100 public high school principals has an average salary under $65,000.

Chapter 9

Estimating the Value of a Parameter Using Confidence Intervals

9.1 The Logic in Constructing Confidence Intervals about a Population Mean Where the Population Standard Deviation is Known

1. The margin of error of a confidence interval of a parameter depends on the level of confidence, the sample size, and the standard deviation of the population.

3. The margin of error decreases as the sample size increases because the Law of Large Numbers states that as the sample size increases the sample mean approaches the value of the population mean.

5. The mean age of the population is a fixed value (i.e., constant), so it is not probabilistic. The 95% level of confidence refers to confidence in the method by which the interval is obtained, not the specific interval. A better interpretation would be: "We are confident that the interval 21.4 years to 28.8 years, obtained by using our method, is one of the 95% of confidence intervals that contains the mean."

7. No, a Z-interval should not be constructed because the data are not normal since a point is outside the bounds of the normal probability plot. Also, the data and contain outliers which can be seen in the boxplot.

9. No, a Z-interval should not be constructed because the data are not normal since points are outside the bounds of the normal probability plot. From the boxplot, the data are skewed right.

11. Yes, a Z-interval can be constructed. The plotted points are all within the bounds of the normal probability plot, which also has a generally linear pattern. The boxplot shows that there are no outliers.

13. For a 98% confidence interval, we use $\alpha = 1 - 0.98 = 0.02$, so $z_{\alpha/2} = z_{0.01}$ which is the z-score with area 0.99 below it. The closest area in the tables to 0.9900 is 0.9901 corresponding to $z_{0.01} = 2.33$

15. For a 85% confidence interval we use $\alpha = 1 - 0.85 = 0.15$, so $z_{\alpha/2} = z_{0.075}$ which is the z-score with area 0.9250 below it. The closest area in the tables to 0.9250 is 0.9251 corresponding to $z_{0.075} = 1.44$.

17. (a) For 95% confidence the critical value is $z_{0.025} = 1.96$. Then:

$$\text{Lower bound} = \overline{x} - z_{0.025} \cdot \frac{\sigma}{\sqrt{n}} = 34.2 - 1.96 \cdot \frac{5.3}{\sqrt{35}} \approx 34.2 - 1.76 = 32.44$$

$$\text{Upper bound} = \overline{x} + z_{0.025} \cdot \frac{\sigma}{\sqrt{n}} = 34.2 + 1.96 \cdot \frac{5.3}{\sqrt{35}} \approx 34.2 + 1.76 = 35.96.$$

(b) Lower bound $= \bar{x} - z_{0.025} \cdot \dfrac{\sigma}{\sqrt{n}} = 34.2 - 1.96 \cdot \dfrac{5.3}{\sqrt{50}} \approx 34.2 - 1.47 = 32.73$

Upper bound $= \bar{x} + z_{0.025} \cdot \dfrac{\sigma}{\sqrt{n}} = 34.2 + 1.96 \cdot \dfrac{5.3}{\sqrt{50}} \approx 34.2 + 1.47 = 35.67$.

Increasing the sample size decreases the margin of error.

(c) For 99% confidence the critical value is $z_{0.005} = 2.575$. Then:

Lower bound $= \bar{x} - z_{0.005} \cdot \dfrac{\sigma}{\sqrt{n}} = 34.2 - 2.575 \cdot \dfrac{5.3}{\sqrt{35}} \approx 34.2 - 2.31 = 31.89$

Upper bound $= \bar{x} + z_{0.005} \cdot \dfrac{\sigma}{\sqrt{n}} = 34.2 + 2.575 \cdot \dfrac{5.3}{\sqrt{35}} \approx 34.2 + 2.31 = 36.51$.

Increasing the level of confidence increases the margin of error.

(d) Since a sample size of $n = 15$ is less than 30, we can only compute a confidence interval in this way if the population from which we are sampling is normal.

19. (a) For 96% confidence the critical value is $z_{0.02} = 2.05$. Then:

Lower bound $= \bar{x} - z_{0.02} \cdot \dfrac{\sigma}{\sqrt{n}} = 108 - 2.05 \cdot \dfrac{13}{\sqrt{25}} \approx 108 - 5.33 = 102.67$

Upper bound $= \bar{x} + z_{0.02} \cdot \dfrac{\sigma}{\sqrt{n}} = 108 + 2.05 \cdot \dfrac{13}{\sqrt{25}} \approx 108 + 5.33 = 113.33$.

(b) Lower bound $= \bar{x} - z_{0.02} \cdot \dfrac{\sigma}{\sqrt{n}} = 108 - 2.05 \cdot \dfrac{13}{\sqrt{10}} \approx 108 - 8.43 = 99.57$

Upper bound $= \bar{x} + z_{0.02} \cdot \dfrac{\sigma}{\sqrt{n}} = 108 + 2.05 \cdot \dfrac{13}{\sqrt{10}} \approx 108 + 8.43 = 116.43$.

Decreasing the sample size increases the margin of error.

(c) For 88% confidence the critical value is $z_{0.06} = 1.555$. Then:

Lower bound $= \bar{x} - z_{0.06} \cdot \dfrac{\sigma}{\sqrt{n}} = 108 - 1.555 \cdot \dfrac{13}{\sqrt{25}} \approx 108 - 4.04 = 103.96$

Upper bound $= \bar{x} + z_{0.06} \cdot \dfrac{\sigma}{\sqrt{n}} = 108 + 1.555 \cdot \dfrac{13}{\sqrt{25}} \approx 108 + 4.04 = 112.04$.

Decreasing the level of confidence decreases the margin of error.

(d) No. Each sample size is too small to insure the $\bar{x}$ sampling distribution is normal.

(e) The outliers would have increased the mean, shifting the confidence interval to the right. If there are outliers then we should not use this approach to compute a confidence interval.

21. For 95% confidence the critical value is $z_{0.025} = 1.96$. Then:

$$\text{Lower bound} = \bar{x} - z_{0.025} \cdot \frac{\sigma}{\sqrt{n}} = 8.17 - 1.96 \cdot \frac{1.2}{\sqrt{1120}} \approx 8.17 - 0.07 = 8.10 \text{ hours}$$

$$\text{Upper bound} = \bar{x} + z_{0.025} \cdot \frac{\sigma}{\sqrt{n}} = 8.17 + 1.96 \cdot \frac{1.2}{\sqrt{1120}} \approx 8.17 + 0.07 = 8.24 \text{ hours}$$

We are 95% confident that the population mean amount of sleep each night between 8.10 and 8.24 hours.

23. For 90% confidence the critical value is $z_{0.05} = 1.645$. Then:

$$\text{Lower bound} = \bar{x} - z_{0.05} \cdot \frac{\sigma}{\sqrt{n}} = 9.2 - 1.645 \cdot \frac{6.7}{\sqrt{1175}} \approx 9.2 - 0.32 = 8.88 \text{ hours}$$

$$\text{Upper bound} = \bar{x} + z_{0.05} \cdot \frac{\sigma}{\sqrt{n}} = 9.2 + 1.645 \cdot \frac{6.7}{\sqrt{1175}} \approx 9.2 + 0.32 = 9.52 \text{ hours}$$

We are 90% confident that the population mean amount of time spent with friends each week is between 8.88 and 9.52 hours.

25. (a) $\bar{x} = \dfrac{225 + 462 + 729 + 753}{4} = \dfrac{2169}{4} = \$542.25$

(b) Yes. All the data values lie within the bounds on the normal probability plot, indicating that the data should come from a population that is normal. The boxplot does not show any outliers.

(c) For 95% confidence the critical value is $z_{0.025} = 1.96$. Then:

$$\text{Lower bound} = \bar{x} - z_{0.025} \cdot \frac{\sigma}{\sqrt{n}} = 542.25 - 1.96 \cdot \frac{220}{\sqrt{4}} = 542.25 - 215.6 = \$326.65$$

$$\text{Upper bound} = \bar{x} + z_{0.025} \cdot \frac{\sigma}{\sqrt{n}} = 542.25 + 1.96 \cdot \frac{220}{\sqrt{4}} = 542.25 + 215.6 = \$757.85$$

We are 95% confident that the population mean cost of repairs is between \$326.65 and \$757.85.

(d) For 90% confidence the critical value is $z_{0.05} = 1.645$. Then:

$$\text{Lower bound} = \bar{x} - z_{0.05} \cdot \frac{\sigma}{\sqrt{n}} = 542.25 - 1.645 \cdot \frac{220}{\sqrt{4}} = 542.25 - 180.95 = \$361.30$$

$$\text{Upper bound} = \bar{x} + z_{0.05} \cdot \frac{\sigma}{\sqrt{n}} = 542.25 + 1.645 \cdot \frac{220}{\sqrt{4}} = 542.25 + 180.95 = \$723.20$$

We are 90% confident that the population mean cost of repairs is between \$361.30 and \$723.20.

(e) When the level of confidence is decreased, the width of the confidence interval is also decreased. This result is reasonable because, if we are less confident that the interval will contain the population mean, then the interval does not need to be as wide.

27. (a) $\bar{x} = \dfrac{\Sigma x}{15} = \dfrac{677}{15} \approx 45.1$ years

(b) Yes. All the data values lie within the bounds on the normal probability plot, indicating that the data should come from a population that is normal. The boxplot does not show any outliers.

(c) For 95% confidence the critical value is $z_{0.025} = 1.96$. Then:

$$\text{Lower bound} = \bar{x} - z_{0.025} \cdot \frac{\sigma}{\sqrt{n}} = 45.1 - 1.96 \cdot \frac{7.9}{\sqrt{15}} \approx 45.1 - 4.0 = 41.1 \text{ years}$$

$$\text{Upper bound} = \bar{x} + z_{0.025} \cdot \frac{\sigma}{\sqrt{n}} = 45.1 + 1.96 \cdot \frac{7.9}{\sqrt{15}} \approx 45.1 + 4.0 = 49.1 \text{ years}$$

We are 95% confident that the population mean age of the clients who purchase investment property from this agent is between 41.13 and 49.13 years.

(d) No, the real estate agent's clients do not appear to differ in age from the general population since the mean age, 47, reported by the National Association of Realtors is contained within our confidence interval.

29. (a) $\bar{x} = \dfrac{\Sigma x}{15} = \dfrac{725}{15} \approx 48.3$

(b) For 95% confidence the critical value is $z_{0.025} = 1.96$. Then:

$$\text{Lower bound} = \bar{x} - z_{0.025} \cdot \frac{\sigma}{\sqrt{n}} = 48.3 - 1.96 \cdot \frac{12.5}{\sqrt{15}} = 48.3 - 6.3 = 42.0$$

$$\text{Upper bound} = \bar{x} + z_{0.025} \cdot \frac{\sigma}{\sqrt{n}} = 48.3 + 1.96 \cdot \frac{12.5}{\sqrt{15}} = 48.3 + 6.3 = 54.6$$

Dr. Oswiecmiski is 95% confident that the population mean serum HDL level of his 20- to 29-year old male patients is between 42.0 and 54.6.

(c) No, Dr. Oswiecmiski's patients do not appear to have a serum HDL different from the general population since the mean serum HDL, 47, reported by U.S. National Center for Health Statistics is contained within our confidence interval.

(d) To obtain a more precise (i.e., smaller) interval, Dr. Oswiecmiski should either increase his sample size or decrease his confidence level.

31. (a) $\bar{x} = \dfrac{\Sigma x}{40} = \dfrac{65.61}{40} \approx 1.64$ million shares

(b) For 90% confidence the critical value is $z_{0.05} = 1.645$. Then:

$$\text{Lower bound} = \bar{x} - z_{0.05} \cdot \frac{\sigma}{\sqrt{n}} = 1.64 - 1.645 \cdot \frac{1.00}{\sqrt{40}} \approx 1.64 - 0.26 = 1.38 \text{ million shares}$$

$$\text{Upper bound} = \bar{x} + z_{0.05} \cdot \frac{\sigma}{\sqrt{n}} = 1.64 + 1.645 \cdot \frac{1.00}{\sqrt{40}} \approx 1.64 + 0.26 = 1.90 \text{ million shares}$$

We are 90% confident that the population mean number of shares of Harley Davidson stock traded in 2004 is between 1.38 and 1.90 million shares per day.

(c) The point estimate is $\bar{x} = \dfrac{\sum x}{40} = \dfrac{69.7}{40} \approx 1.74$ million shares

$$\text{Lower bound} = \bar{x} - z_{0.05} \cdot \frac{\sigma}{\sqrt{n}} = 1.74 - 1.645 \cdot \frac{1.00}{\sqrt{40}} \approx 1.74 - 0.26 = 1.48 \text{ million shares}$$

$$\text{Upper bound} = \bar{x} + z_{0.05} \cdot \frac{\sigma}{\sqrt{n}} = 1.74 + 1.645 \cdot \frac{1.00}{\sqrt{40}} \approx 1.74 + 0.26 = 2.00 \text{ million shares}$$

We are 90% confident that the population mean number of shares of Harley Davidson stock traded in 2004 is between 1.48 and 2.00 million shares per day.

(d) The intervals obtained in parts (a) and (c) are different because the different samples resulted in different sample means. In this case, the sample mean from part (c) is 100,000 shares larger than the sample mean from part (a).

33. (a) Since the length of dramas (i.e., the population) is not normally distributed, the sample must be large so that the $\bar{x}$ distribution will be approximately normally distributed.

(b) For 99% confidence the critical value is $z_{0.005} = 2.575$. Then:

$$\text{Lower bound} = \bar{x} - z_{0.05} \cdot \frac{\sigma}{\sqrt{n}} = 138.3 - 2.575 \cdot \frac{27.3}{\sqrt{30}} \approx 138.3 - 12.8 = 125.5 \text{ minutes}$$

$$\text{Upper bound} = \bar{x} + z_{0.05} \cdot \frac{\sigma}{\sqrt{n}} = 138.3 + 2.575 \cdot \frac{27.3}{\sqrt{30}} \approx 138.3 + 12.8 = 151.1 \text{ minutes}$$

The student is 99% confident that the population mean length of a drama is between 125.5 and 151.1 minutes.

35. (a) $\bar{x} = \dfrac{\sum x}{n} = \dfrac{1,632,765}{33} \approx 49,477.7$ miles.

(b) For a 99% confidence interval we use $z_{.005} = 2.575$.

$$\text{Lower bound} = \bar{x} - z_{0.005} \cdot \frac{\sigma}{\sqrt{n}}$$

$$= 49,477.7 - 2.575 \cdot \frac{19,700}{\sqrt{33}} \approx 49,477.7 - 8,830.5 = 40,647.2 \text{ miles}$$

$$\text{Upper bound} = \bar{x} + z_{0.005} \cdot \frac{\sigma}{\sqrt{n}}$$

$$= 49,477.7 + 2.575 \cdot \frac{19,700}{\sqrt{33}} \approx 49,477.7 + 8,830.5 = 58,308.2 \text{ miles}$$

The researcher is 99% confident that the population mean number of miles on a four-year-old Saturn SC1 in the Chicago area is between 40,647.2 and 58,308.2 miles.

(c) For a 95% confidence interval we use $z_{0.025} = 1.96$.

$$\text{Lower bound} = \bar{x} - z_{0.025} \cdot \frac{\sigma}{\sqrt{n}}$$

$$= 49,477.7 - 1.96 \cdot \frac{19,700}{\sqrt{33}} \approx 49,477.7 - 6,721.5 = 42,756.2 \text{ miles}$$

Upper bound $= \bar{x} + z_{0.025} \cdot \dfrac{\sigma}{\sqrt{n}}$

$= 49,477.7 + 1.96 \cdot \dfrac{19,700}{\sqrt{33}} \approx 49,477.7 + 6,721.5 = 56,199.2$ miles

The researcher is 95% confident that the population mean number of miles on a four-year-old Saturn SC1 in the Chicago area is between 42,756.2 and 56,199.2 miles.

(d) Decreasing the level of confidence decreases the width of the confidence interval.

(e) No. This sample was obtained only from Saturns in the Chicago area, so the results cannot be generalized to the entire United States.

37. For 99% confidence, we use $z_{0.005} = 2.575$. So, $n = \left(\dfrac{z_{\alpha/2} \cdot \sigma}{E} \right)^2 = \left(\dfrac{2.575 \cdot 13.4}{2} \right)^2 \approx 297.65$, which we must increase to 298 subjects.

For 95% confidence we use $z_{0.025} = 1.96$. So, $n = \left(\dfrac{1.96 \cdot 13.4}{2} \right)^2 \approx 172.45$, which we must increase to 173 subjects.

Decreasing the level of confidence decreases the required sample size.

39. For 95% confidence, we use $z_{0.025} = 1.96$. So, $n = \left(\dfrac{z_{\alpha/2} \cdot \sigma}{E} \right)^2 = \left(\dfrac{1.96 \cdot 16.6}{1} \right)^2 \approx 1058.59$, which we must increase to 1059 subjects.

41. (a) For 90% confidence, we use $z_{0.05} = 1.645$. So,

$n = \left(\dfrac{z_{\alpha/2} \cdot \sigma}{E} \right)^2 = \left(\dfrac{1.645 \cdot 19,700}{1000} \right)^2 \approx 1050.18$, which we must increase to 1051 cars.

(b) $n = \left(\dfrac{z_{\alpha/2} \cdot \sigma}{E} \right)^2 = \left(\dfrac{1.645 \cdot 19,700}{500} \right)^2 \approx 4200.72$, which we must increase to 4201 cars.

(c) Doubling the required accuracy (that is, cutting the margin of error in half) will approximately quadruple the require sample size. This increase is expected because the sample size is inversely proportional to the square of the error. To half the error we must increase the sample size by a factor of $\left(\dfrac{1}{1/2} \right)^2 = 4$.

43. (a), (b) Answers will vary.

(c) 95% of 20 is $0.95(20) = 19$. We would expect about 19 of the 20 samples to generate confidence intervals that include the population mean. The actual results will vary.

45. (a), (b) Answers will vary.

(c) If these were truly "95% confidence intervals," then we would expect approximately 95% of the 100 samples, or 95 samples, to generate confidence intervals that include the population mean. Actual results will vary.

(d) Since the sample size, $n = 6$, is small and since we are sampling from a non-normal population, the sampling distribution of the sample mean is not normal, so our method for computing a 95% confidence interval is not valid. In other words, it is not true that close to 95% of our intervals contain the population mean.

47. The sample size must be increased by a factor of 4. This is because the sample size, n, is inversely proportional to the square of the error, E. To decrease the error by a factor of $\frac{1}{2}$

we must increase the sample size by a factor of $\left(\dfrac{1}{1/2}\right)^2 = 4$.

49. (a) Data Set I: $\bar{x} = \dfrac{\Sigma x}{n} = \dfrac{793}{8} = 99.125$; Data Set II: $\bar{x} = \dfrac{\Sigma x}{n} = \dfrac{1982}{20} = 99.1$;

Data Set III: $\bar{x} = \dfrac{\Sigma x}{n} = \dfrac{2971}{30} \approx 99.033$

(b) For 95% confidence the critical value is $z_{0.025} = 1.96$.

Set I: Lower bound $= \bar{x} - z_{0.025} \cdot \dfrac{\sigma}{\sqrt{n}} = 99.125 - 1.96 \cdot \dfrac{15}{\sqrt{8}} \approx 99.125 - 10.394 = 88.731$

Upper bound $= \bar{x} + z_{0.025} \cdot \dfrac{\sigma}{\sqrt{n}} = 99.125 + 1.96 \cdot \dfrac{15}{\sqrt{8}} \approx 99.125 + 10.394 = 109.519$

Set II: Lower bound $= \bar{x} - z_{0.025} \cdot \dfrac{\sigma}{\sqrt{n}} = 99.1 - 1.96 \cdot \dfrac{15}{\sqrt{20}} \approx 99.1 - 6.574 = 92.526$

Upper bound $= \bar{x} + z_{0.025} \cdot \dfrac{\sigma}{\sqrt{n}} = 99.1 + 1.96 \cdot \dfrac{15}{\sqrt{20}} \approx 99.1 + 6.574 = 105.674$

Set III: Lower bound $= \bar{x} - z_{0.025} \cdot \dfrac{\sigma}{\sqrt{n}} = 99.033 - 1.96 \cdot \dfrac{15}{\sqrt{30}} \approx 99.033 - 5.368 = 93.665$

Upper bound $= \bar{x} + z_{0.025} \cdot \dfrac{\sigma}{\sqrt{n}} = 99.033 + 1.96 \cdot \dfrac{15}{\sqrt{30}} \approx 99.033 + 5.368 = 104.401$

(c) As the size of the sample increases, the width of the confidence interval decreases.

(d) Set I: $\bar{x} = \dfrac{\Sigma x}{n} = \dfrac{703}{8} = 87.875$;

Lower bound $= \bar{x} - z_{0.025} \cdot \dfrac{\sigma}{\sqrt{n}} = 87.875 - 1.96 \cdot \dfrac{15}{\sqrt{8}} \approx 87.875 - 10.394 = 77.481$

Upper bound $= \bar{x} + z_{0.025} \cdot \dfrac{\sigma}{\sqrt{n}} = 87.875 + 1.96 \cdot \dfrac{15}{\sqrt{8}} \approx 87.875 + 10.394 = 98.269$

Set II: $\bar{x} = \dfrac{\Sigma x}{n} = \dfrac{1892}{20} = 94.6$;

215

$$\text{Lower bound} = \bar{x} - z_{0.025} \cdot \frac{\sigma}{\sqrt{n}} = 94.6 - 1.96 \cdot \frac{15}{\sqrt{20}} \approx 94.6 - 6.574 = 88.026$$

$$\text{Upper bound} = \bar{x} + z_{0.025} \cdot \frac{\sigma}{\sqrt{n}} = 94.6 + 1.96 \cdot \frac{15}{\sqrt{20}} \approx 94.6 + 6.574 = 101.174$$

Set III: $\bar{x} = \dfrac{\sum x}{n} = \dfrac{2881}{30} \approx 96.033$

$$\text{Lower bound} = \bar{x} - z_{0.025} \cdot \frac{\sigma}{\sqrt{n}} = 96.033 - 1.96 \cdot \frac{15}{\sqrt{30}} \approx 96.033 - 5.368 = 90.665$$

$$\text{Upper bound} = \bar{x} + z_{0.025} \cdot \frac{\sigma}{\sqrt{n}} = 96.033 + 1.96 \cdot \frac{15}{\sqrt{30}} \approx 96.033 + 5.368 = 101.401$$

(e) The confidence intervals for both Data Set II and Data Set III still capture the population mean, 100, with the incorrect entry. The interval from Data Set I does not capture the population mean when the incorrect entry is made. The concept of robustness is illustrated. As the sample size increases the distribution of $\bar{x}$ becomes more normal, making the confidence interval more robust against the effect of the incorrect entry.

51. (a) Answers will vary depending on the results from the applet. You should expect 95% of the intervals to contain the population mean.

(b) Answers will vary depending on the results from the applet.

(c) Answers will vary depending on the results from the applet. You should expect 95% of the intervals to contain the population mean.

(d) Confidence intervals for the samples of size $n = 10$ should be wider than the confidence intervals for the samples of size $n = 50$.

9.2 Confidence Intervals about a Population Mean in Practice Where the Population Standard Deviation is Unknown.

1. We can construct a Z-interval if the sample is random, the population from which the sample is drawn is normal or the sample size is large $(n \geq 30)$, and the population standard deviation, σ, is known. A t-interval should be constructed if the sample is random, the population from which the sample is drawn is normal, but the population standard deviation, σ, is unknown. Neither interval can be constructed if the sample is not random, the population is not normal and the sample size small, or when there are outliers.

3. Robust means that the procedure is accurate when there are moderate departures from normality in the distribution of the population.

5. Similarities: Both the standard normal distribution and the t-distribution are probability density functions; both have mean $\mu = 0$, and both are symmetric about their means. Differences: t-distributions vary for different sample sizes while there is only one standard normal distribution. t-distributions have longer and thicker tails than the standard normal distribution which has most of its area between -3 and 3.

7. **(a)** From the row with df = 25 and the column headed 0.10, we read $t = 1.316$.

   (b) From the row with df = 30 and the column headed 0.05, we read $t = 1.697$.

   (c) From the row with df = 18 and the column headed 0.01, we read $t = 2.552$. By symmetry, the t-value with an area to the *left* of 0.01 is $t = -2.552$.

   (d) For a 90% confidence interval, we want the t-value with an area in the right tail of 0.05. With df = 20, we read from the tables that $t = 1.725$.

9. **(a)** For 96% confidence, $\alpha/2 = 0.02$. Since $n = 25$, then df = 24. The critical value is $t_{0.02} = 2.172$. Then:

   $$\text{Lower bound} = \bar{x} - t_{0.02} \cdot \frac{s}{\sqrt{n}} = 108 - 2.172 \cdot \frac{10}{\sqrt{25}} \approx 108 - 4.3 = 103.7$$

   $$\text{Upper bound} = \bar{x} + t_{0.02} \cdot \frac{s}{\sqrt{n}} = 108 + 2.172 \cdot \frac{10}{\sqrt{25}} \approx 108 + 4.3 = 112.3$$

   (b) Since $n = 10$, then df = 9. The critical value is $t_{0.02} = 2.398$. Then:

   $$\text{Lower bound} = \bar{x} - t_{0.02} \cdot \frac{s}{\sqrt{n}} = 108 - 2.398 \cdot \frac{10}{\sqrt{10}} \approx 108 - 7.6 = 100.4$$

   $$\text{Upper bound} = \bar{x} + t_{0.02} \cdot \frac{s}{\sqrt{n}} = 108 + 2.398 \cdot \frac{10}{\sqrt{10}} \approx 108 + 7.6 = 115.6$$

   Decreasing the sample size increases the margin of error.

   (c) For 90% confidence, $\alpha/2 = 0.05$. With 24 degrees of freedom, $t_{0.02} = 1.711$. Then:

   $$\text{Lower bound} = \bar{x} - t_{0.02} \cdot \frac{s}{\sqrt{n}} = 108 - 1.711 \cdot \frac{10}{\sqrt{25}} \approx 108 - 3.4 = 104.6$$

   $$\text{Upper bound} = \bar{x} + t_{0.02} \cdot \frac{s}{\sqrt{n}} = 108 + 1.711 \cdot \frac{10}{\sqrt{25}} \approx 108 + 3.42 = 111.4$$

   Decreasing the level of confidence decreases the margin of error.

   (d) No, because in all cases the sample was small ($n < 30$), so the population must be normally distributed.

11. **(a)** For 95% confidence, $\alpha/2 = 0.025$. Since $n = 35$, then df = 34. The critical value is $t_{0.025} = 2.032$. Then:

   $$\text{Lower bound} = \bar{x} - t_{0.025} \cdot \frac{s}{\sqrt{n}} = 18.4 - 2.032 \cdot \frac{4.5}{\sqrt{35}} \approx 18.4 - 1.55 = 16.85$$

   $$\text{Upper bound} = \bar{x} + t_{0.025} \cdot \frac{s}{\sqrt{n}} = 18.4 + 2.032 \cdot \frac{4.5}{\sqrt{35}} \approx 18.4 + 1.55 = 19.95$$

   (b) Since $n = 50$, then df = 49, but since there is no row in the tables for 49 degrees of freedom we use df = 50 instead. The critical value is $t_{0.025} = 2.009$. Then:

   $$\text{Lower bound} = \bar{x} - t_{0.025} \cdot \frac{s}{\sqrt{n}} = 18.4 - 2.009 \cdot \frac{4.5}{\sqrt{50}} \approx 18.4 - 1.28 = 17.12$$

$$\text{Upper bound} = \overline{x} + t_{0.025} \cdot \frac{s}{\sqrt{n}} = 18.4 + 2.009 \cdot \frac{4.5}{\sqrt{50}} \approx 18.4 + 1.28 = 19.68$$

Increasing the sample size decreases the margin of error.

(c) For 99% confidence, $\alpha/2 = 0.005$. With 34 degrees of freedom, $t_{0.005} = 2.728$. Then:

$$\text{Lower bound} = \overline{x} - t_{0.005} \cdot \frac{s}{\sqrt{n}} = 18.4 - 2.728 \cdot \frac{4.5}{\sqrt{35}} \approx 18.4 - 2.08 = 16.32$$

$$\text{Upper bound} = \overline{x} + t_{0.005} \cdot \frac{s}{\sqrt{n}} = 18.4 + 2.728 \cdot \frac{4.5}{\sqrt{35}} \approx 18.4 + 2.08 = 20.48$$

Increasing the level of confidence increases the margin of error.

(d) For a small sample ($n = 15$), the population must be normally distributed.

13. For 99% confidence, $\alpha/2 = 0.005$. Since $n = 1006$, then df = 1005. There is no row in the table for 1005 degrees of freedom, so we use df = 1000 instead. The critical value is $t_{0.005} = 2.581$. Then:

$$\text{Lower bound} = \overline{x} - t_{0.005} \cdot \frac{s}{\sqrt{n}} = 13.4 - 2.581 \cdot \frac{16.6}{\sqrt{1006}} \approx 13.4 - 1.35 = 12.05 \text{ books.}$$

$$\text{Upper bound} = \overline{x} - t_{0.005} \cdot \frac{s}{\sqrt{n}} = 13.4 + 2.581 \cdot \frac{16.6}{\sqrt{1006}} \approx 13.4 + 1.35 = 14.75 \text{ books.}$$

We are 99% confident that the population mean number of books read by Americans during 2005 was between 12.05 and 14.75 books.

15. For 95% confidence, $\alpha/2 = 0.025$. Since $n = 81$, then df = 80 and $t_{0.025} = 1.990$. Then:

$$\text{Lower bound} = \overline{x} - t_{0.025} \cdot \frac{s}{\sqrt{n}} = 4.6 - 1.990 \cdot \frac{15.9}{\sqrt{81}} \approx 4.6 - 3.52 = 1.08 \text{ days.}$$

$$\text{Upper bound} = \overline{x} + t_{0.025} \cdot \frac{s}{\sqrt{n}} = 4.6 + 1.990 \cdot \frac{15.9}{\sqrt{81}} \approx 4.6 + 3.52 = 8.12 \text{ days.}$$

We are 95% confident that the population mean incubation period of patients with SARS is between 1.08 and 8.12 days.

17. For 95% confidence, $\alpha/2 = 0.025$. Since $n = 1028$, then df = 1027. There is no row in the table for 1027 degrees of freedom, so we use df = 1000 instead. The critical value is $t_{0.025} = 1.962$. Then:

$$\text{Lower bound} = \overline{x} - t_{0.025} \cdot \frac{s}{\sqrt{n}} = 13 - 1.962 \cdot \frac{2.3}{\sqrt{1028}} \approx 13 - 0.14 = 12.86 \text{ hours.}$$

$$\text{Upper bound} = \overline{x} + t_{0.025} \cdot \frac{s}{\sqrt{n}} = 13 + 1.962 \cdot \frac{2.3}{\sqrt{1028}} \approx 13 + 0.14 = 13.14 \text{ hours.}$$

The pollster is 95% confident that the population mean number of hours that teenagers what TV each week is between 12.86 and 13.14 hours.

19. Using technology, we find $\overline{x} \approx 1.315\%$ and $s \approx 1.010\%$.

For 90% confidence, $\alpha/2 = 0.05$. Since $n = 11$, then df = 10 and $t_{0.05} = 1.812$. Then:

218

$$\text{Lower bound} = \bar{x} - t_{0.05} \cdot \frac{s}{\sqrt{n}} = 1.315 - 1.812 \cdot \frac{1.010}{\sqrt{11}} \approx 1.315 - 0.552 = 0.763\,\%.$$

$$\text{Upper bound} = \bar{x} + t_{0.05} \cdot \frac{s}{\sqrt{n}} = 1.315 + 1.812 \cdot \frac{1.010}{\sqrt{11}} \approx 1.315 + 0.552 = 1.867\,\%.$$

The stock analyst is 90% confident that the population mean dividend yield for financial stock is between 0.763% and 1.867%.

21. Using technology, we find $\bar{x} \approx 15.92$ mg/L and $s \approx 7.38$ mg/L.

For 99% confidence, $\alpha / 2 = 0.005$. Since $n = 33$, then df = 32 and $t_{0.005} = 2.738$. Then:

$$\text{Lower bound} = \bar{x} - t_{0.005} \cdot \frac{s}{\sqrt{n}} = 15.92 - 2.738 \cdot \frac{7.38}{\sqrt{33}} \approx 15.92 - 3.52 = 12.40 \text{ mg/L.}$$

$$\text{Upper bound} = \bar{x} + t_{0.005} \cdot \frac{s}{\sqrt{n}} = 15.92 + 2.738 \cdot \frac{7.38}{\sqrt{33}} \approx 15.92 + 3.52 = 19.44 \text{ mg/L.}$$

We are 99% confident that the population mean concentration of dissolved organic carbon in organic soil is between 12.40 and 19.44 mg/L.

23. (a) Yes. The normal probability plot indicates that the data come from a population that is approximately normal, and the box plot indicates that there are no outliers.

(b) Using technology, $\bar{x} \approx 38.3$ weeks and $s \approx 10.0$ weeks.

For 95% confidence, $\alpha / 2 = 0.025$. Since $n = 12$, then df = 11 and $t_{0.025} = 2.201$.

$$\text{Lower bound} = \bar{x} - t_{0.025} \cdot \frac{s}{\sqrt{n}} = 38.3 - 2.201 \cdot \frac{10.0}{\sqrt{12}} \approx 38.3 - 6.4 = 31.9 \text{ weeks.}$$

$$\text{Upper bound} = \bar{x} + t_{0.025} \cdot \frac{s}{\sqrt{n}} = 38.3 + 2.201 \cdot \frac{10.0}{\sqrt{12}} \approx 38.3 + 6.4 = 44.7 \text{ weeks.}$$

We are 95% confident that the population mean age at which a baby first crawls is between 31.9 and 44.6 weeks.

(c) The sample size could be increased in order to increase the accuracy of the interval without changing the confidence level.

25. (a) Yes. The normal probability plot indicates that the data come from a population that is approximately normal, and the box plot indicates that there are no outliers.

(b) Using technology, $\bar{x} = 167.5$ days and $s \approx 21.9$ days.

For 95% confidence, $\alpha / 2 = 0.025$. Since $n = 10$, then df = 9 and $t_{0.025} = 2.262$.

$$\text{Lower bound} = \bar{x} - t_{0.025} \cdot \frac{s}{\sqrt{n}} = 167.5 - 2.262 \cdot \frac{21.9}{\sqrt{10}} \approx 167.5 - 15.7 = 151.8 \text{ days.}$$

$$\text{Upper bound} = \bar{x} + t_{0.025} \cdot \frac{s}{\sqrt{n}} = 167.5 + 2.262 \cdot \frac{21.9}{\sqrt{10}} \approx 167.5 + 15.7 = 183.2 \text{ days.}$$

We are 95% confident that the population mean length of the growing season in the Chicago area is between 151.85 and 183.15 days.

(c) The sample size could be increased in order to increase the accuracy of the interval without change the confidence level.

27. (a)

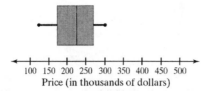

100 150 200 250 300 350 400 450 500
Price (in thousands of dollars)

(b) Using technology with the outlier $459,900 included, $\bar{x} \approx \$236,358.3$ and $s \approx \$86,759.4$. For 99% confidence, $\alpha/2 = 0.005$. Since $n = 12$, then df = 11 and $t_{0.005} = 3.106$.

$$\text{Lower bound} = 236,358.3 - 3.106 \cdot \frac{86,759.4}{\sqrt{12}} \approx 236,358.3 - 77,790.6 = \$158,567.7$$

$$\text{Upper bound} = 236,358.3 + 3.106 \cdot \frac{86,759.4}{\sqrt{12}} \approx 236,358.3 + 77,790.6 = \$314,148.9$$

With the outlier included, the 99% confidence interval is from $158,567.7 to $314,148.9.

(c) Using technology with the outlier $459,900 removed, $\bar{x} \approx \$216,036.4$ and $s \approx \$53,184.0$. Since the outlier was removed, $n = 11$, df = 10, and $t_{0.005} = 3.169$.

$$\text{Lower bound} = 216,036.4 - 3.169 \cdot \frac{53,184.0}{\sqrt{11}} \approx 216,036.4 - 50,816.8 = \$165,219.6$$

$$\text{Upper bound} = 216,036.4 + 3.169 \cdot \frac{53,184.0}{\sqrt{11}} \approx 216,036.4 + 50,816.8 = \$266,853.2$$

With the outlier removed, the 99% confidence interval is from $165,219.6 to $266,853.2.

(d) The inclusion of the outlier makes the confidence interval wider.

29. (a), (b), (c) Answers will vary.

(d) 95% of 20 is $0.95(20) = 19$. We would expect about 19 of the 20 samples to generate confidence intervals that include the population mean. The actual results will vary.

31. Answers will vary.

9.3 Confidence Intervals about a Population Proportion

1. The best point estimate of the population proportion is the sample proportion $\hat{p}$.

3. Answers will vary. One possibility follows: By using a prior estimate of p the researcher will get a better estimate of the required sample size, which will be smaller than the "worst-case" sample size given by using no prior estimate of p.

5. $\hat{p} = \dfrac{x}{n} = \dfrac{30}{150} = 0.20$. For 90% confidence, $z_{\alpha/2} = z_{0.05} = 1.645$.

$$\text{Lower bound} = \hat{p} - z_{0.05} \cdot \sqrt{\frac{\hat{p}(1-\hat{p})}{n}} = 0.20 - 1.645 \cdot \sqrt{\frac{0.2(1-0.2)}{150}} \approx 0.20 - 0.054 = 0.146$$

$$\text{Upper bound} = \hat{p} + z_{0.05} \cdot \sqrt{\frac{\hat{p}(1-\hat{p})}{n}} = 0.20 + 1.645 \cdot \sqrt{\frac{0.2(1-0.2)}{150}} \approx 0.20 + 0.054 = 0.254$$

220

7. $\hat{p} = \dfrac{x}{n} = \dfrac{120}{500} = 0.24$. For 99% confidence, $z_{\alpha/2} = z_{0.005} = 2.575$.

Lower bound $= \hat{p} - z_{0.005} \cdot \sqrt{\dfrac{\hat{p}(1-\hat{p})}{n}} = 0.24 - 2.575 \cdot \sqrt{\dfrac{0.24(1-0.24)}{500}} \approx 0.24 - 0.049 = 0.191$

Upper bound $= \hat{p} + z_{0.005} \cdot \sqrt{\dfrac{\hat{p}(1-\hat{p})}{n}} = 0.24 + 2.575 \cdot \sqrt{\dfrac{0.24(1-0.24)}{500}} \approx 0.24 + 0.049 = 0.289$

9. $\hat{p} = \dfrac{x}{n} = \dfrac{860}{1100} \approx 0.7818$. For 94% confidence, $z_{\alpha/2} = z_{.03} = 1.88$.

Lower bound

$= \hat{p} - z_{0.03} \cdot \sqrt{\dfrac{\hat{p}(1-\hat{p})}{n}} = 0.7818 - 1.88 \cdot \sqrt{\dfrac{0.7818(1-0.7818)}{1100}} \approx 0.7818 - 0.0234 \approx 0.758$

Upper bound

$= \hat{p} + z_{0.03} \cdot \sqrt{\dfrac{\hat{p}(1-\hat{p})}{n}} = 0.7818 + 1.88 \cdot \sqrt{\dfrac{0.7818(1-0.7818)}{1100}} \approx 0.7818 + 0.0234 \approx 0.805$

11. (a) $\hat{p} = \dfrac{x}{n} = \dfrac{47}{863} \approx 0.054$

(b) The sample size $n = 843$ is less than 5% of the population, and
$n\hat{p}(1-\hat{p}) \approx 863 \cdot 0.054 \cdot (1-0.054) \approx 44 \geq 10$.

(c) For 90% confidence, $z_{\alpha/2} = z_{0.05} = 1.645$.
Lower bound

$= \hat{p} - z_{0.05} \cdot \sqrt{\dfrac{\hat{p}(1-\hat{p})}{n}} = 0.054 - 1.645 \cdot \sqrt{\dfrac{0.054(1-0.054)}{863}} \approx 0.054 - 0.013 = 0.041$

Upper bound

$= \hat{p} + z_{0.05} \cdot \sqrt{\dfrac{\hat{p}(1-\hat{p})}{n}} = 0.054 + 1.645 \cdot \sqrt{\dfrac{0.054(1-0.054)}{863}} \approx 0.054 + 0.013 = 0.067$

(d) We are 90% confident that the population proportion of Lipitor users who will have a headache as a side effect is between 0.041 and 0.067 (i.e., between 4.1% and 6.7%).

13. (a) $\hat{p} = \dfrac{x}{n} = \dfrac{302}{1008} \approx 0.300$

(b) The sample size $n = 1008$ is less than 5% of the population, and
$n\hat{p}(1-\hat{p}) \approx 1008 \cdot 0.300 \cdot (1-0.300) = 211.68 \geq 10$.

(c) For 98% confidence, $z_{\alpha/2} = z_{0.01} = 2.33$.
Lower bound

$= \hat{p} - z_{0.01} \cdot \sqrt{\dfrac{\hat{p}(1-\hat{p})}{n}} = 0.300 - 2.33 \cdot \sqrt{\dfrac{0.300(1-0.300)}{1008}} \approx 0.300 - 0.034 = 0.266$

Upper bound

$$= \hat{p} + z_{0.01} \cdot \sqrt{\frac{\hat{p}(1-\hat{p})}{n}} = 0.300 + 2.33 \cdot \sqrt{\frac{0.300(1-0.300)}{1008}} \approx 0.300 + 0.034 = 0.334$$

The Gallup Organization is 98% confident that the population proportion of adults 18 or older who believe the United States is spending too little on national defense and military purposes is between 0.266 and 0.334 (i.e., between 26.6% and 33.4%).

15. (a) $\hat{p} = \dfrac{x}{n} = \dfrac{381}{2114} \approx 0.180$. The sample size $n = 2114$ is less than 5% of the population, and $n\hat{p}(1-\hat{p}) \approx 2114 \cdot 0.180 \cdot (1-0.180) \approx 312.03 \geq 10$.

(b) For 90% confidence, $z_{\alpha/2} = z_{0.05} = 1.645$.

Lower bound

$$= \hat{p} - z_{0.05} \cdot \sqrt{\frac{\hat{p}(1-\hat{p})}{n}} = 0.180 - 1.645 \cdot \sqrt{\frac{0.180(1-0.180)}{2114}} \approx 0.180 - 0.014 = 0.166$$

Upper bound

$$= \hat{p} + z_{0.05} \cdot \sqrt{\frac{\hat{p}(1-\hat{p})}{n}} = 0.180 + 1.645 \cdot \sqrt{\frac{0.180(1-0.180)}{2114}} \approx 0.180 + 0.014 = 0.194$$

The Harris Organization is 90% confident that the proportion of adults who follow professional football whose favorite team is the Green Bay Packers is between 0.166 and 0.194 (i.e., between 16.6% and 19.4%).

(c) For 99% confidence, $z_{\alpha/2} = z_{0.005} = 2.575$.

Lower bound

$$= \hat{p} - z_{0.005} \cdot \sqrt{\frac{\hat{p}(1-\hat{p})}{n}} = 0.180 - 2.575 \cdot \sqrt{\frac{0.180(1-0.180)}{2114}} \approx 0.180 - 0.022 = 0.158$$

Upper bound

$$= \hat{p} + z_{0.005} \cdot \sqrt{\frac{\hat{p}(1-\hat{p})}{n}} = 0.180 + 2.575 \cdot \sqrt{\frac{0.180(1-0.180)}{2114}} \approx 0.180 + 0.022 = 0.202$$

The Harris Organization is 99% confident that the proportion of adults who follow professional football whose favorite team is the Green Bay Packers is between 0.158 and 0.202 (i.e., 15.8% and 20.2%).

(d) Increasing the level of confidence causes the confidence interval to widen.

17. For 99% confidence, $z_{\alpha/2} = z_{0.005} = 2.575$.

(a) Using $\hat{p} = 0.44$, $n = \hat{p}(1-\hat{p})\left(\dfrac{z_{\alpha/2}}{E}\right)^2 = 0.44(1-0.44)\left(\dfrac{2.575}{0.03}\right)^2 \approx 1815.3$, which we must increase to 1816 subjects.

(b) $n = 0.25\left(\dfrac{z_{\alpha/2}}{E}\right)^2 = 0.25\left(\dfrac{2.575}{0.03}\right)^2 \approx 1841.8$, which we must increase to 1842 subjects.

19. For 90% confidence, $z_{\alpha/2} = z_{0.05} = 1.645$.

(a) Using $\hat{p} = 0.55$, $n = \hat{p}(1-\hat{p})\left(\dfrac{z_{\alpha/2}}{E}\right)^2 = 0.55(1-0.55)\left(\dfrac{1.645}{0.04}\right)^2 \approx 418.6$, which we must

increase to 419 subjects.

(b) $n = 0.25\left(\dfrac{z_{\alpha/2}}{E}\right)^2 = 0.25\left(\dfrac{1.645}{0.04}\right)^2 \approx 422.8$, which must increase to 423 subjects.

21. For 98% confidence, $z_{\alpha/2} = z_{0.01} = 2.33$.

(a) Using $\hat{p} = 0.23$, $n = \hat{p}(1-\hat{p})\left(\dfrac{z_{\alpha/2}}{E}\right)^2 = 0.23(1-0.23)\left(\dfrac{2.33}{0.02}\right)^2 \approx 2403.6$, which we

must increase to 2404 subjects.

(b) $n = 0.25\left(\dfrac{z_{\alpha/2}}{E}\right)^2 = 0.25\left(\dfrac{2.33}{0.02}\right)^2 \approx 3393.1$, which must increase to 3394 subjects.

23. For 95% confidence, $z_{\alpha/2} = z_{0.025} = 1.96$.

$n = \hat{p}(1-\hat{p})\left(\dfrac{z_{\alpha/2}}{E}\right)^2 = 0.64(1-0.64)\left(\dfrac{1.96}{0.03}\right)^2 \approx 983.4$. So, 984 people were surveyed.

25. Answers may vary. One possibility follows: The confidence interval for the percentage intending to vote for George Bush was $(49-3,\ 49+3) = (46\%,\ 52\%)$. Likewise, the percentage intending to vote for John Kerry was $(47-3,\ 47+3) = (44\%,\ 50\%)$. Since these intervals overlap, it is possible that the true percentage intending to vote for John Kerry could have been greater than the true percentage intending to vote for George Bush, or vice versa. Hence, the result was too close to call.

27. (a), (b), (c) Answers will vary.

(d) As the sample size n increases, the proportion of intervals that capture p gets closer and closer to the level of confidence.

9.4 Confidence Intervals about a Population Standard Deviation

1. (1) The chi-squared distribution is not symmetric but is skewed to the right.
(2) The actual shape of the chi-squared distribution depends on the degrees of freedom
(3) As the number of degrees of freedom increases, the chi-squared distribution become more nearly symmetric.
(3) The values of χ^2 are nonnegative.

3. After the population is shown to be normal, a confidence interval for the standard deviation is obtained by as follows:
Step 1: Compute the sample variance.
Step 2: Determine the critical values using the desired confidence level, the correct degrees of freedom, and the χ^2 distribution table.

Step 3: Construct the confidence interval for the population variance by using the formulas

$$\text{Lower bound} = \frac{(n-1)s^2}{\chi^2_{\alpha/2}} \quad \text{and Upper bound} = \frac{(n-1)s^2}{\chi^2_{1-\alpha/2}}$$

Step 4: Compute the square root of the lower bound and the upper bound to find the confidence interval for the population standard deviations.

5. $df = n-1 = 19$ and, for 90% confidence, $\alpha/2 = 0.05$. From the table, $\chi^2_{0.05} = 30.144$ and $\chi^2_{1-0.05} = \chi^2_{0.95} = 10.117$.

7. $df = n-1 = 22$ and, for 98% confidence, $\alpha/2 = 0.01$. From the table, $\chi^2_{0.01} = 40.289$ and $\chi^2_{1-0.01} = \chi^2_{0.99} = 9.542$.

9. **(a)** $df = n-1 = 19$ and, for 90% confidence, $\alpha/2 = 0.05$.
   From the table, $\chi^2_{0.05} = 30.144$ and $\chi^2_{1-0.05} = \chi^2_{0.95} = 10.117$.

   $$\text{Lower bound} = \frac{(n-1)s^2}{\chi^2_{\alpha/2}} = \frac{19 \cdot 12.6}{30.144} \approx 7.94; \quad \text{Upper bound} = \frac{(n-1)s^2}{\chi^2_{1-\alpha/2}} = \frac{19 \cdot 12.6}{10.117} \approx 23.66$$

   (b) $df = n-1 = 29$ and, for 90% confidence, $\alpha/2 = 0.05$.
   From the table, $\chi^2_{0.05} = 42.557$ and $\chi^2_{1-0.05} = \chi^2_{0.95} = 17.708$.

   $$\text{Lower bound} = \frac{(n-1)s^2}{\chi^2_{\alpha/2}} = \frac{29 \cdot 12.6}{42.557} \approx 8.59; \quad \text{Upper bound} = \frac{(n-1)s^2}{\chi^2_{1-\alpha/2}} = \frac{29 \cdot 12.6}{17.708} \approx 20.63.$$

   Increasing the sample size decreases the width of the confidence interval.

   (c) $df = n-1 = 19$ and, for 98% confidence, $\alpha/2 = 0.01$.
   From the table, $\chi^2_{0.05} = 36.191$ and $\chi^2_{1-0.01} = \chi^2_{0.99} = 7.633$.

   $$\text{Lower bound} = \frac{(n-1)s^2}{\chi^2_{\alpha/2}} = \frac{19 \cdot 12.6}{36.191} \approx 6.61; \quad \text{Upper bound} = \frac{(n-1)s^2}{\chi^2_{1-\alpha/2}} = \frac{19 \cdot 12.6}{7.633} \approx 31.36.$$

   Increasing the level of confidence increases the width of the confidence interval.

11. $df = n-1 = 12-1 = 11$ and, for 95% confidence, $\alpha/2 = 0.025$.
    From the table, $\chi^2_{0.025} = 21.920$ and $\chi^2_{1-0.025} = \chi^2_{0.975} = 3.816$.

    $$\text{Lower bound} = \sqrt{\frac{(n-1)s^2}{\chi^2_{\alpha/2}}} = \sqrt{\frac{11 \cdot (10.00)^2}{21.920}} \approx 7.08 \text{ weeks};$$

    $$\text{Upper bound} = \sqrt{\frac{(n-1)s^2}{\chi^2_{1-\alpha/2}}} = \sqrt{\frac{11 \cdot (10.00)^2}{3.816}} \approx 16.98 \text{ weeks}.$$

    Essential Baby can be 95% confident that the population standard deviation of the time at which babies first crawl is between 7.08 and 16.98 weeks.

13. $df = n-1 = 10-1 = 9$ and, for 99% confidence, $\alpha/2 = 0.005$.
    From the table, $\chi^2_{0.005} = 23.589$ and $\chi^2_{1-0.005} = \chi^2_{0.995} = 1.735$.

$$\text{Lower bound } = \sqrt{\frac{(n-1)s^2}{\chi^2_{\alpha/2}}} = \sqrt{\frac{9 \cdot (21.88)^2}{23.589}} \approx 13.51 \text{ days;}$$

$$\text{Upper bound } = \sqrt{\frac{(n-1)s^2}{\chi^2_{1-\alpha/2}}} = \sqrt{\frac{9 \cdot (21.88)^2}{1.735}} \approx 49.83 \text{ days.}$$

The agricultural researcher can be 99% confident that the population standard deviation of the growing season in Chicago is between 13.51 and 49.83 days.

15. **(a)** From the probability plot shown to the right, the data appear to be from a population that is normally distributed.

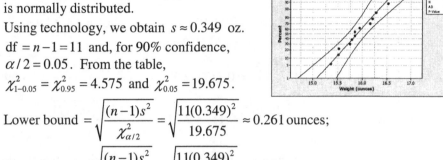

   (b) Using technology, we obtain $s \approx 0.349$ oz.

   (c) df $= n - 1 = 11$ and, for 90% confidence, $\alpha/2 = 0.05$. From the table, $\chi^2_{1-0.05} = \chi^2_{0.95} = 4.575$ and $\chi^2_{0.05} = 19.675$.

$$\text{Lower bound } = \sqrt{\frac{(n-1)s^2}{\chi^2_{\alpha/2}}} = \sqrt{\frac{11(0.349)^2}{19.675}} \approx 0.261 \text{ ounces;}$$

$$\text{Upper bound } = \sqrt{\frac{(n-1)s^2}{\chi^2_{1-\alpha/2}}} = \sqrt{\frac{11(0.349)^2}{4.575}} \approx 0.541 \text{ ounces}$$

   (d) No. In fact we can be 90% confident that the population standard deviation is between 0.261 and 0.541 ounces, and so above 0.20 ounces.

17. From the normal tables, we get $z_{0.975} = -1.96$ and $z_{0.025} = 1.96$. With $v = 100$, we get

$$\chi^2_{0.975} \approx \frac{\left(z_{0.975} + \sqrt{2v-1}\right)^2}{2} = \frac{\left(-1.96 + \sqrt{2 \cdot 100 - 1}\right)^2}{2} = 73.772 \text{ (compared to the tables' value}$$

of 74.222) and $\chi^2_{0.025} \approx \dfrac{\left(z_{0.025} + \sqrt{2v-1}\right)^2}{2} = \dfrac{\left(1.96 + \sqrt{2 \cdot 100 - 1}\right)^2}{2} = 129.070$ (compared to the tables' value of 129.561).

9.5 Putting It All Together: Which Procedure Do I Use?

1. We construct a t-interval when we are estimating the population mean, we do not know the population standard deviation, and the underlying population is normally distributed. If the underlying population is not normally distributed, we can construct a t-interval to estimate the population mean provide the sample size is large ($n \geq 30$).
We construct a Z-interval when we are estimating the population mean, we know the population standard deviation, and the underlying population is normally distributed. If the underlying population is not normally distributed, we can construct a Z-interval to estimate the population mean provided the sample size is large ($n \geq 30$). We also construct a Z-interval when we are estimating the population proportion, provided the sample is smaller than 5% of the population and $np(1-p) \geq 10$.

3. We construct a Z-interval because we are estimating a population mean, we know the population standard deviation, and the underlying population is normally distributed. For 95% confidence the critical value is $z_{0.025} = 1.96$. Then:

$$\text{Lower bound} = \bar{x} - z_{0.025} \cdot \frac{\sigma}{\sqrt{n}} = 60 - 1.96 \cdot \frac{20}{\sqrt{14}} \approx 49.52$$

$$\text{Upper bound} = \bar{x} + z_{0.025} \cdot \frac{\sigma}{\sqrt{n}} = 60 + 1.96 \cdot \frac{20}{\sqrt{14}} \approx 70.48.$$

5. $\hat{p} = \dfrac{35}{300} \approx 0.117$. The sample size $n = 300$ is less than 5% of the population, and $n\hat{p}(1 - \hat{p}) \approx 300 \cdot 0.117 \cdot (1 - 0.883) \approx 31.0 \geq 10$, so we can construct a Z-interval. For 99% confidence the critical value is $z_{0.005} = 2.575$. Then:

$$\text{Lower bound} = \hat{p} - z_{0.005} \cdot \sqrt{\frac{\hat{p}(1 - \hat{p})}{n}} = 0.117 - 2.575 \cdot \sqrt{\frac{0.117(1 - 0.117)}{300}} \approx 0.069$$

$$\text{Upper bound} = \hat{p} + z_{0.005} \cdot \sqrt{\frac{\hat{p}(1 - \hat{p})}{n}} = 0.117 + 2.575 \cdot \sqrt{\frac{0.117(1 - 0.117)}{300}} \approx 0.165$$

7. We construct a t-interval because we are estimating the population mean, we do not know the population standard deviation, and the underlying population is normally distributed. For 90% confidence, $\alpha / 2 = 0.05$. Since $n = 12$, then df = 11 and $t_{0.05} = 1.796$. Then:

$$\text{Lower bound} = \bar{x} - t_{0.05} \cdot \frac{s}{\sqrt{n}} = 45 - 1.796 \cdot \frac{14}{\sqrt{12}} \approx 37.74$$

$$\text{Upper bound} = \bar{x} + t_{0.05} \cdot \frac{s}{\sqrt{n}} = 45 + 1.796 \cdot \frac{14}{\sqrt{12}} \approx 52.26$$

9. We construct a t-interval because we are estimating the population mean, we do not know the population standard deviation, and the underlying population is normally distributed. For 99% confidence, $\alpha / 2 = 0.005$. Since $n = 40$, then df = 39 and $t_{0.050} = 2.708$. Then:

$$\text{Lower bound} = \bar{x} - t_{0.005} \cdot \frac{s}{\sqrt{n}} = 120.5 - 2.708 \cdot \frac{12.9}{\sqrt{40}} \approx 114.98$$

$$\text{Upper bound} = \bar{x} + t_{0.005} \cdot \frac{s}{\sqrt{n}} = 120.5 + 2.708 \cdot \frac{12.9}{\sqrt{40}} \approx 126.02$$

11. df $= n - 1 = 12 - 1 = 11$ and, for 90% confidence, $\alpha / 2 = 0.05$.
From the table, $\chi^2_{0.05} = 19.675$ and $\chi^2_{1-0.05} = \chi^2_{0.95} = 4.575$.

$$\text{Lower bound} = \frac{(n-1)s^2}{\chi^2_{\alpha/2}} = \frac{11 \cdot 23.7}{19.675} \approx 13.25 \text{; Upper bound} = \frac{(n-1)s^2}{\chi^2_{1-\alpha/2}} = \frac{11 \cdot 23.7}{4.575} \approx 56.98$$

13. We construct a t-interval because we are estimating the population mean, we do not know the population standard deviation, and the underlying population is normally distributed. For 95% confidence, $\alpha / 2 = 0.025$. Since $n = 40$, then df = 39 and $t_{0.025} = 2.023$. Then:

Lower bound $= \bar{x} - t_{0.025} \cdot \dfrac{s}{\sqrt{n}} = 54 - 2.023 \cdot \dfrac{8}{\sqrt{40}} \approx 51.4$ months;

Upper bound $= \bar{x} + t_{0.025} \cdot \dfrac{s}{\sqrt{n}} = 54 + 2.023 \cdot \dfrac{8}{\sqrt{40}} \approx 56.6$ months.

We can be 95% confident that the population of felons convicted of aggravated assault serve a mean sentence between 51.4 and 56.6 months.

15. We construct a Z-interval because we are estimating a population mean, we know the population standard deviation, and the underlying population is normally distributed. For 90% confidence the critical value is $z_{0.05} = 1.645$. Then:

Lower bound $= \bar{x} - z_{0.05} \cdot \dfrac{\sigma}{\sqrt{n}} = 3137 - 1.645 \cdot \dfrac{2694}{\sqrt{100}} \approx \$2693.84$

Upper bound $= \bar{x} + z_{0.05} \cdot \dfrac{\sigma}{\sqrt{n}} = 3137 + 1.645 \cdot \dfrac{2694}{\sqrt{100}} \approx \$3580.16$.

The Internal Revenue Service can be 90% confident that the population mean additional tax owed is between \$2693.84 and \$3580.16.

17. $\hat{p} = \dfrac{606}{1010} = 0.6$. The sample size $n = 1010$ is less than 5% of the population, and $n\hat{p}(1-\hat{p}) = 1010 \cdot 0.6 \cdot (1-0.6) = 242.4 \geq 10$, so we can construct a Z-interval:
For 90% confidence the critical value is $z_{0.05} = 1.645$. Then:

Lower bound $= \hat{p} - z_{0.05} \cdot \sqrt{\dfrac{\hat{p}(1-\hat{p})}{n}} = 0.6 - 1.645 \cdot \sqrt{\dfrac{0.6(1-0.6)}{1010}} \approx 0.575$

Upper bound $= \hat{p} + z_{0.05} \cdot \sqrt{\dfrac{\hat{p}(1-\hat{p})}{n}} = 0.6 + 1.645 \cdot \sqrt{\dfrac{0.6(1-0.6)}{1010}} \approx 0.625$

The Gallup Organization can be 90% confident that the population proportion of adult Americans who are worried about having enough money for retirement is between 0.575 and 0.625 (i.e., between 57.5% and 62.5%).

19. The normal probability plot and boxplot show that the data are normal with no outliers. We construct a Z-interval because we are estimating a population mean, and we know the population standard deviation. For 95% confidence the critical value is $z_{0.025} = 1.96$. The data give $n = 15$ and $\bar{x} = 69.85$ inches. Then:

Lower bound $= \bar{x} - z_{0.025} \cdot \dfrac{\sigma}{\sqrt{n}} = 69.85 - 1.96 \cdot \dfrac{2.9}{\sqrt{15}} \approx 68.38$ inches;

Upper bound $= \bar{x} + z_{0.025} \cdot \dfrac{\sigma}{\sqrt{n}} = 69.85 + 1.96 \cdot \dfrac{2.9}{\sqrt{15}} \approx 71.32$ inches.

We are 95% confident that the population mean height of 20- to 29-year-old males is between 69.38 and 71.32 inches.

21. The box plot indicates an outlier in the data, so we cannot compute a confidence interval.

23. The normal probability plot and boxplot show that the data are normal with no outliers. We construct a t-interval because we are estimating the population mean and we do not know the population standard deviation. The data give $n = 15$, $\bar{x} \approx 109.33$ and $s \approx 14.38$. With df = 14, we use $t_{0.025} = 2.145$. Then:

$$\text{Lower bound} = \bar{x} - t_{0.025} \cdot \frac{s}{\sqrt{n}} = 109.33 - 2.145 \cdot \frac{14.38}{\sqrt{15}} \approx 101.4 \text{ beats per minute;}$$

$$\text{Upper bound} = \bar{x} + t_{0.025} \cdot \frac{s}{\sqrt{n}} = 109.33 + 2.145 \cdot \frac{14.38}{\sqrt{15}} \approx 117.3 \text{ beats per minute.}$$

We can be 95% confident that the population mean pulse rate for women after 3 minutes of exercise is between 101.4 and 117.3 beats per minute.

Chapter 9 Review Exercises

1. For a 99% confidence interval we want the t-value with an area in the right tail of 0.005. With df = 17, we read from the table that $t_{0.005} = 2.898$.

3. df $= n - 1 = 21$ and for 95% confidence, $\alpha / 2 = 0.025$. From the table, $\chi^2_{1-0.025} = \chi^2_{0.975} = 10.283$ and $\chi^2_{0.025} = 35.479$.

5. (a) For 90% confidence the critical value is $z_{0.05} = 1.645$. Then:

$$\text{Lower bound} = \bar{x} - z_{0.05} \cdot \frac{\sigma}{\sqrt{n}} = 54.8 - 1.645 \cdot \frac{10.5}{\sqrt{20}} \approx 54.8 - 3.86 = 50.94$$

$$\text{Upper bound} = \bar{x} + z_{0.05} \cdot \frac{\sigma}{\sqrt{n}} = 54.8 + 1.645 \cdot \frac{10.5}{\sqrt{20}} \approx 54.8 + 3.86 = 58.66.$$

(b) $$\text{Lower bound} = \bar{x} - z_{0.05} \cdot \frac{\sigma}{\sqrt{n}} = 54.8 - 1.645 \cdot \frac{10.5}{\sqrt{30}} \approx 54.8 - 3.15 = 51.65$$

$$\text{Upper bound} = \bar{x} + z_{0.05} \cdot \frac{\sigma}{\sqrt{n}} = 54.8 + 1.645 \cdot \frac{10.5}{\sqrt{30}} \approx 54.8 + 3.15 = 57.95.$$

Increasing the sample size decreases the width of the confidence interval.

(c) For 99% confidence the critical value is $z_{0.005} = 2.575$. Then:

$$\text{Lower bound} = \bar{x} - z_{0.05} \cdot \frac{\sigma}{\sqrt{n}} = 54.8 - 2.575 \cdot \frac{10.5}{\sqrt{20}} \approx 54.8 - 6.05 = 48.75$$

$$\text{Upper bound} = \bar{x} + z_{0.05} \cdot \frac{\sigma}{\sqrt{n}} = 54.8 + 2.575 \cdot \frac{10.5}{\sqrt{20}} \approx 54.8 + 6.05 = 60.85.$$

Increasing the level of confidence increases the width of the confidence interval.

7. (a) The size of the sample ($n = 40$) is sufficiently large to apply the Central Limit Theorem and conclude that the sampling distribution of $\bar{x}$ is approximately normal.

(b) We construct a Z-interval because we are estimating a population mean and we know the population standard deviation. For 90% confidence the critical value is $z_{0.05} = 1.645$.

Lower bound $= \bar{x} - z_{0.05} \cdot \dfrac{\sigma}{\sqrt{n}} = 100,294 - 1.645 \cdot \dfrac{4600}{\sqrt{40}} \approx 99,098$ miles;

Upper bound $= \bar{x} + z_{0.05} \cdot \dfrac{\sigma}{\sqrt{n}} = 100,294 + 1.645 \cdot \dfrac{4600}{\sqrt{40}} \approx 101,490$ miles.

Michelin can be 90% confident that the mean mileage for its HydroEdge tire is between 99,098 and 101,490 miles.

(c) For 95% confidence the critical value is $z_{0.05} = 1.96$.

Lower bound $= \bar{x} - z_{0.05} \cdot \dfrac{\sigma}{\sqrt{n}} = 100,294 - 1.96 \cdot \dfrac{4600}{\sqrt{40}} \approx 98,868$ miles;

Upper bound $= \bar{x} + z_{0.05} \cdot \dfrac{\sigma}{\sqrt{n}} = 100,294 + 1.96 \cdot \dfrac{4600}{\sqrt{40}} \approx 101,720$ miles.

Michelin can be 95% confident that the mean mileage for its HydroEdge tire is between 99,868 and 101,720 miles.

(d) For 99% confidence, we use $z_{0.005} = 2.575$. So, $n = \left(\dfrac{z_{\alpha/2} \cdot \sigma}{E} \right)^2 = \left(\dfrac{2.575 \cdot 4600}{1500} \right)^2 \approx 62.4$,

which we must increase to 63 tires.

9. (a) Since the mean is larger than the median, the distribution of the population is skewed right. Therefore, since the population is not normally distributed, a large sample is necessary in order to apply Central Limit Theorem and construct a confidence interval about the mean.

(b) We construct a t-interval because we are estimating a population mean and we do not know the population standard deviation. For 90% confidence, $\alpha/2 = 0.05$. Since $n = 1028$, then df = 1027. There is no row in the table for 1027 degrees of freedom, so we use df = 1000 instead. The critical value is $t_{0.05} = 1.646$.

Lower bound $= \bar{x} - t_{0.05} \cdot \dfrac{s}{\sqrt{n}} = 13 - 1.646 \cdot \dfrac{5.8}{\sqrt{1028}} \approx 12.70$ hours per week;

Upper bound $= \bar{x} + t_{0.05} \cdot \dfrac{s}{\sqrt{n}} = 13 + 1.646 \cdot \dfrac{5.8}{\sqrt{1028}} \approx 13.30$ hours per week.

The Gallup Organization can be 90% confident that the mean number of hours that 13- to 17-year-olds watch television is between 12.70 and 13.30 hours per week.

11. (a) USA: $\bar{x} \approx 42.3$ hours per week.   Canada: $\bar{x} = 40.8$ hours per week.

(b) We construct a Z-interval because we are estimating a population mean and we know the population standard deviation. For 99% confidence the critical value is $z_{0.005} = 2.575$.

Lower bound $= \bar{x} - z_{0.005} \cdot \dfrac{\sigma}{\sqrt{n}} = 42.3 - 2.575 \cdot \dfrac{12.8}{\sqrt{15}} \approx 33.8$ hours per week;

Upper bound $= \bar{x} + z_{0.005} \cdot \dfrac{\sigma}{\sqrt{n}} = 42.3 + 2.575 \cdot \dfrac{12.8}{\sqrt{15}} \approx 50.8$ hours per week.

The Gallup Organization can be 99% confident that the population mean number of hours worked per week by adults in the U.S. is between 33.82 and 50.84 hours per week.

(c) Lower bound $= \bar{x} - z_{0.005} \cdot \dfrac{\sigma}{\sqrt{n}} = 40.8 - 2.575 \cdot \dfrac{10.8}{\sqrt{15}} \approx 33.6$ hours per week;

Upper bound $= \bar{x} + z_{0.005} \cdot \dfrac{\sigma}{\sqrt{n}} = 40.8 + 2.575 \cdot \dfrac{10.8}{\sqrt{15}} \approx 48.0$ hours per week.

The Gallup Organization can be 99% confident that the population mean number of hours worked per week by adults in the Canada is between 33.6 and 48.0 hours per week.

(d) No. It does not appear that Americans work more than Canadians since the confidence intervals overlap.

13. (a) Since the sample size is large ($n \geq 30$), $\bar{x}$ has an approximately normal distribution.

(b) We construct a t-interval because we are estimating a population mean and we do not know the population standard deviation. For 95% confidence, $\alpha/2 = 0.025$. Since $n = 60$, then df = 59. There is no row in the table for 59 degrees of freedom, so we use df = 60 instead. The critical value is $t_{0.025} = 2.000$. Then:

Lower bound $= \bar{x} - t_{0.025} \cdot \dfrac{s}{\sqrt{n}} = 2.27 - 2.000 \cdot \dfrac{1.22}{\sqrt{60}} \approx 1.95$ children;

Upper bound $= \bar{x} + t_{0.025} \cdot \dfrac{s}{\sqrt{n}} = 2.27 + 2.000 \cdot \dfrac{1.22}{\sqrt{60}} \approx 2.59$ children.

We are 95% confident that couples who have been married for 7 years have a population mean number of children between 1.95 and 2.59.

(c) For 99% confidence, $\alpha/2 = 0.005$. The critical value is $t_{0.005} = 2.660$. Then:

Lower bound $= \bar{x} - t_{0.025} \cdot \dfrac{s}{\sqrt{n}} = 2.27 - 2.660 \cdot \dfrac{1.22}{\sqrt{60}} \approx 1.85$ children;

Upper bound $= \bar{x} + t_{0.025} \cdot \dfrac{s}{\sqrt{n}} = 2.27 + 2.660 \cdot \dfrac{1.22}{\sqrt{60}} \approx 2.69$ children.

We are 95% confident that couples who have been married for 7 years have a population mean number of children between 1.85 and 2.69.

15. (a) Using technology, we obtain $\bar{x} \approx 3.243$ liters and $s \approx 0.487$ liters.

(b) Yes. The plotted points are generally linear and stay within the bounds of the normal probability plot. The boxplot shows that there are no outliers.

(c) We construct a t-interval because we are estimating a population mean and we do not know the population standard deviation. For 95% confidence, $\alpha/2 = 0.025$. Since $n = 12$, then df = 11 and $t_{0.025} = 2.201$. Then:

Lower bound $= \bar{x} - t_{0.025} \cdot \dfrac{s}{\sqrt{n}} = 3.243 - 2.201 \cdot \dfrac{0.487}{\sqrt{12}} \approx 2.934$ liters;

Upper bound $= \bar{x} + t_{0.025} \cdot \dfrac{s}{\sqrt{n}} = 3.243 + 2.201 \cdot \dfrac{0.487}{\sqrt{12}} \approx 3.552$ liters.

The researchers can be 95% confident that the true population mean blood plasma volume is between 2.934 and 3.552 liters.

(d) For 99% confidence, $\alpha/2 = 0.005$. For df = 11, $t_{0.005} = 3.106$. Then:

$$\text{Lower bound} = \bar{x} - t_{0.005} \cdot \frac{s}{\sqrt{n}} = 3.243 - 3.106 \cdot \frac{0.487}{\sqrt{12}} \approx 2.806 \text{ liters.}$$

$$\text{Upper bound} = \bar{x} + t_{0.005} \cdot \frac{s}{\sqrt{n}} = 3.243 + 3.106 \cdot \frac{0.487}{\sqrt{12}} \approx 3.680 \text{ liters.}$$

The researchers can be 99% confident that the true population mean blood plasma volume is between 2.806 and 3.680 liters

(e) From the table, with df = 11 and $\alpha/2 = 0.005$, we find $\chi^2_{1-0.005} = \chi^2_{0.995} = 2.603$ and $\chi^2_{0.005} = 26.757$. Then:

$$\text{Lower bound} = \sqrt{\frac{(n-1)s^2}{\chi^2_{\alpha/2}}} = \sqrt{\frac{11(0.487)^2}{26.757}} \approx 0.312 \text{ liters;}$$

$$\text{Upper bound} = \sqrt{\frac{(n-1)s^2}{\chi^2_{\alpha/2}}} = \sqrt{\frac{11(0.487)^2}{2.603}} \approx 1.001 \text{ liters.}$$

The researchers can be 99% confident that the true population standard deviation of blood plasma volume is between 0.312 and 1.001 liters.

17. From the data sets, we have the following information: USA: $\bar{x} \approx 42.3$ hours per week, $s \approx 14.2$ hours per week, and $n = 15$; Canada: $\bar{x} = 40.8$ hours per week, $s \approx 12.7$ hours per week, and $n = 15$. We construct t-intervals because we are estimating population means and we do not know the population standard deviation. For 99% confidence, $\alpha/2 = 0.005$. For df = 14, $t_{0.005} = 2.977$. Then:

For the USA: Lower bound $= \bar{x} - t_{0.005} \cdot \dfrac{s}{\sqrt{n}} = 42.3 - 2.977 \cdot \dfrac{14.2}{\sqrt{15}} \approx 31.4$ hours per week;

Upper bound $= \bar{x} + t_{0.005} \cdot \dfrac{s}{\sqrt{n}} = 42.3 + 2.977 \cdot \dfrac{14.2}{\sqrt{15}} \approx 53.2$ hours per week.

The Gallup Organization can be 99% confident that the population mean number of hours worked per week by adults in the U.S. is between 31.4 and 53.2 hours per week.

For Canada: Lower bound $= \bar{x} - t_{0.005} \cdot \dfrac{s}{\sqrt{n}} = 42.3 - 2.977 \cdot \dfrac{14.2}{\sqrt{15}} \approx 31.4$ hours per week;

Upper bound $= \bar{x} + t_{0.005} \cdot \dfrac{s}{\sqrt{n}} = 40.8 + 2.977 \cdot \dfrac{12.7}{\sqrt{15}} \approx 50.6$ hours per week.

The Gallup Organization can be 99% confident that the population mean number of hours worked per week by adults in the Canada is between 31.0 and 50.6 hours. Since the confidence intervals overlap, it does not appear that Americans work more than Canadians.

19. (a) $\hat{p} = \dfrac{x}{n} = \dfrac{58}{678} \approx 0.086$

(b) For 95% confidence, $z_{\alpha/2} = z_{.025} = 1.96$.

$$\text{Lower bound} = \hat{p} - z_{.025} \cdot \sqrt{\frac{\hat{p}(1-\hat{p})}{n}} = 0.086 - 1.96 \cdot \sqrt{\frac{0.086(1-0.086)}{678}} \approx 0.065$$

Upper bound $= \hat{p} + z_{.025} \cdot \sqrt{\dfrac{\hat{p}(1-\hat{p})}{n}} = 0.086 + 1.96 \cdot \sqrt{\dfrac{0.086(1-0.086)}{678}} \approx 0.107$

The Centers for Disease Control can be 95% confident that the population proportion of adult males aged 20–34 years who have hypertension is between 0.065 and 0.107 (i.e. between 6.5% and 10.7%).

(c) $n = \hat{p}(1-\hat{p})\left(\dfrac{z_{\alpha/2}}{E}\right)^2 = 0.086(1-0.086)\left(\dfrac{1.96}{.03}\right)^2 \approx 335.5$, which we must increase to 336 subjects.

(d) $n = 0.25\left(\dfrac{z_{\alpha/2}}{E}\right)^2 = 0.25\left(\dfrac{1.96}{.03}\right)^2 \approx 1067.1$, which we must increase to 1068 subjects.

21. From the data sets, we have the following information: USA: $s \approx 14.2$ hours per week and $n = 15$; Canada: $s \approx 12.7$ hours per week and $n = 15$. With df $= n - 1 = 14$ and for 95% confidence, $\alpha/2 = 0.025$. From the table, $\chi^2_{1-0.025} = \chi^2_{0.975} = 5.629$ and $\chi^2_{0.025} = 26.119$.

(a) For the U.S.: Lower bound $= \sqrt{\dfrac{(n-1)s^2}{\chi^2_{\alpha/2}}} = \sqrt{\dfrac{14(14.2)^2}{26.119}} \approx 10.4$ hours per week;

Upper bound $= \sqrt{\dfrac{(n-1)s^2}{\chi^2_{1-\alpha/2}}} = \sqrt{\dfrac{14(14.2)^2}{5.629}} = 22.4$ hours per week

(b) For Canada: Lower bound $= \sqrt{\dfrac{(n-1)s^2}{\chi^2_{\alpha/2}}} = \sqrt{\dfrac{14(12.7)^2}{26.119}} = 9.3$ hours per week;

Upper bound $= \sqrt{\dfrac{(n-1)s^2}{\chi^2_{1-\alpha/2}}} = \sqrt{\dfrac{14(12.7)^2}{5.629}} = 20.0$ hours per week

(c) Since the intervals overlap, we cannot conclude that the hours worked per week by Canadians are less dispersed than those worked by Americans.

23. The area to the left of $t = -1.56$ is also 0.0681, because the t-distribution is symmetric.

25. The properties of the Student's t-distribution follow:
1. It is symmetric around $t = 0$.
2. It is different for different sample sizes.
3. The area under the curve is 1; half the area is to the right of 0 and half the area is to the left of 0.
4. As t gets extremely large, the graph approaches, but never equals, zero. Similarly, as t gets extremely small (negative), the graph approaches, but never equals, zero.
5. The area in the tails of the t-distribution is greater than the area in the tails of the standard normal distribution.
6. As the sample size n increases, the distribution (and the density curve) of the t-distribution becomes more like those of the standard normal distribution.

Chapter 10

Testing Claims Regarding a Parameter

10.1 The Language of Hypothesis Testing

1. A Type I error is the error of rejecting H_0 when in fact H_0 is true. A Type II error is the error of **not** rejecting H_0 when in fact H_1 is true.

3. As we decrease α (the probability of rejecting a true H_0), we are effectively making it less likely that we will reject H_0 since we require stronger evidence against H_0 as α decreases. This means that it is also more likely that we will fail to reject H_0 when H_1 is really true, so β increases. Thus, β increases as α decreases.

5. In a hypothesis test we make a judgement about the validity of a hypothesis based on the available data. If the data contradicts H_0 then we reject H_0. However, if the available data do not contradict H_0, this does not guarantee that H_0 is true. Consider the court system in the U.S., where suspects are assumed to be innocent until proven guilty. An acquittal does not mean the suspect is innocent, merely that there was not enough evidence to reject the assumption of innocence.

7. False; sample evidence will never prove a null hypothesis is true. We assume the null is true and try to gather enough evidence to say that the null is not true. Failing to reject a null hypothesis does not imply that the hypothesis is actually true, just that there was not enough evidence to reject the assumption that it is true.

9. Parameter $= \mu$. Right-tailed since $H_1 : \mu > 5$

11. Parameter $= \sigma$. Two-tailed since $H_1 : \sigma \neq 4.2$

13. Parameter $= \mu$. Left-tailed since $H_1 : \mu < 120$

15. **(a)** $H_0 : p = 0.118$, $H_1 : p < 0.118$
    The alternative hypothesis is $<$ because the sociologist believes the percent has decreased.

    (b) We make a Type I error if the sample evidence leads us to reject H_0 and believe that the percentage of registered births to teenage mothers is less than 11.8% when, in fact, it is not less than 11.8%.

    (c) We make a Type II error if we fail to reject the null hypothesis that the percentage of registered births to teenage mothers is equal to 11.8% when, in fact, the percentage of registered births to teenage mothers is less than 11.8%.

17. (a) $H_0 : \mu = \$243,756$; $H_1 : \mu > \$243,756$

The alternative hypothesis is > because the real estate broker believes the mean price has increased.

(b) We make a Type I error if the sample evidence leads us to reject H_0 and believe that the mean price of a single-family home is more than \$243,756 when, in fact, it is \$243,756.

(c) We make a Type II error if we fail to reject the null hypothesis that the mean price of a single-family home is \$243,756, when, in fact, it is more than \$243,756.

19. (a) $H_0 : \sigma = 0.7$ p.s.i.; $H_1 : \sigma < 0.7$ p.s.i.

The alternative hypothesis is < because the quality control manager believes the standard deviation of the required pressure has been reduced.

(b) We make a Type I error if the sample evidence leads us to reject H_0 and believe that the standard deviation in the pressure required is less than 0.7 p.s.i when, in fact, it is 0.7 p.s.i.

(c) We make a Type II error if we fail to reject the null hypothesis that the standard deviation in the pressure required is 0.7 p.s.i when, in fact, it is less than 0.7 p.s.i.

21. (a) $H_0 : \mu = \$49.91$; $H_1 : \mu \neq \$49.91$

The alternative hypothesis is $\neq$ because no direction of change is given. The researcher feels the mean monthly bill has changed but this could mean an increase or a decrease.

(b) We make a Type I error if the sample evidence leads us to reject H_0 and believe that the mean monthly cell phone bill is not \$49.91 when, in fact, it is \$49.91.

(c) We make a Type II error if we fail to reject the null hypothesis that the mean monthly cell phone bill is \$49.91 when, in fact, it is different than \$49.91.

23. There is sufficient evidence to support the claim that the percentage of registered births in the U.S. to teenage mothers is less than 11.8%.

25. There is not sufficient evidence to support the agent's claim that the mean price of a single-family home has increased from \$243,756.

27. There is not sufficient evidence to support the manager's claim that the standard deviation in the pressure required has been reduced from 0.7 p.s.i.

29. There is sufficient evidence to support the researcher's claim that the average monthly cell phone bill is different from \$49.91.

31. There is not sufficient evidence to support the sociologist's claim that the percentage of registered births to teenage mothers is less than 11.8%.

33. There is sufficient evidence to support the agent's claim that the mean price of a single-family home has increased from \$243,756.

35. (a) $H_0 : \mu = 98.4$ pounds ; $H_1 : \mu > 98.4$ pounds

   (b) There is sufficient evidence to support the dietician's claim that the per capita consumption of fruits has risen from 98.4 pounds.

   (c) Since we rejected a true null, this would be a Type I error. The level of significance, α, is the probability of making a Type I error. Therefore, the probability is 0.05.

37. (a) $H_0 : p = 0.102$; $H_1 : p < 0.102$

   (b) There is not sufficient evidence to support the officer's claim that the percentage of high school students who have tried marijuana for the first time before the age of 13 has decreased.

   (c) Since we failed to reject a false null, this would be a Type II error.

39. Let $\mu =$ the mean increase in gas mileage for cars using the Platinum Gasaver. Then the hypotheses would be $H_0 : \mu = 0$ versus $H_1 : \mu > 0$.

41. Answers will vary.

10.2   Testing Claims about a Population Mean Assuming the Population Standard Deviation is Known

1. The sample must have been obtained using simple random sampling and either the population from which the sample is selected is normally distributed, or the sample size is large ($n \geq 30$).

3. For $\alpha = 0.05$ in a two-tailed test, the critical values are $\pm z_{\alpha/2} = \pm z_{0.025} = \pm 1.96$.

5. The P-value is the probability of obtaining sample data at least as extreme as that observed, assuming that the null hypothesis is true. A small P-value indicates that the observed data are very unlikely to result from chance variation in samples, and so is evidence that the null hypothesis is not true. More specifically, we will reject the null hypothesis if P-value $< \alpha$.

7. This indicates that 2% of random samples from the same population will give a sample mean as extreme or more extreme than our observed sample mean, assuming that $\mu = \mu_0$. Since this is an unlikely occurrence, we would probably conclude that our sample data provide strong enough evidence to reject H_0, although this depends on the level of significance that we are using.

9. Answers will vary. Statistical significance typically refers to absolute differences; that is, whether the observed difference is due to chance. Practical significance typically refers to relative differences; that is, whether the observed difference is large enough to cause concern.

11. (a) $z_0 = \dfrac{\bar{x} - \mu_0}{\sigma / \sqrt{n}} = \dfrac{47.1 - 50}{12 / \sqrt{24}} = -1.18$

(b) This is a left-tailed test so the critical value is $-z_{0.05} = -1.645$.

(c)

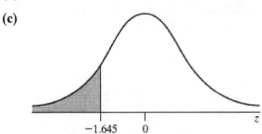

(d) Since $-1.18 > -1.645$, the test statistic is not in the critical region. The researcher will not reject the null hypothesis.

13. (a) $z_0 = \dfrac{\bar{x} - \mu_0}{\sigma / \sqrt{n}} = \dfrac{104.8 - 100}{7 / \sqrt{23}} = 3.29$

(b) This is a two-tailed test so the critical values are $\pm z_{0.005} = \pm 2.575$.

(c)

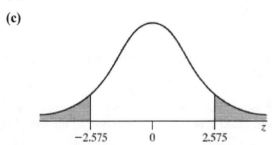

(d) Since $3.29 > 2.575$, the test statistic is in the critical region. The researcher will reject the null hypothesis.

15. (a) The test statistic is $z_0 = \dfrac{\bar{x} - \mu_0}{\sigma / \sqrt{n}} = \dfrac{18.3 - 20}{3 / \sqrt{18}} = -2.40$.

This is a left-tailed test so we get $P-\text{value} = P(Z < -2.40) = 0.0082$

About 0.82% of samples will have a sample mean that is at least this low, if the population mean is $\mu = 20$

(b) Since $P\text{-value} = 0.0082 < 0.0500 = \alpha$, the researcher will reject the null hypothesis.

17. (a) No, because this sample is large ($n \geq 30$).

(b) The test statistic is $z_0 = \dfrac{\bar{x} - \mu_0}{\sigma / \sqrt{n}} = \dfrac{101.2 - 105}{12 / \sqrt{35}} = -1.87$.

This is a two-tailed test so we have $P\text{-value} = 2 \cdot P(Z < -1.87) = 2 \cdot 0.0307 = 0.0614$.

About 6.14% of samples will result in a sample mean that is at least this extreme, if the population mean is 105.

(c) Since $P\text{-value} = 0.0614 > 0.0200 = \alpha$, the researcher will not reject the null hypothesis.

19. Hypotheses: $H_0 : \mu = 63.7$ inches ; $H_1 : \mu > 63.7$ inches

Significance level: $\alpha = 0.05$

Test Statistic: $z_0 = \dfrac{\overline{x} - \mu_0}{\sigma / \sqrt{n}} = \dfrac{63.9 - 63.7}{3.5 / \sqrt{45}} = 0.38$

Classical approach:

This is a right-tailed test so our critical value is $z_\alpha = z_{0.05} = 1.645$ and the critical region lies to the right of our critical value. Since $z_0 = 0.38 < 1.645 = z_{0.05}$, the test statistic does not fall in the critical region. Therefore, the null hypothesis is not rejected.

P-value approach:

$P\text{-value} = P(Z > 0.38) = 1 - P(Z \le 0.38) = 1 - 0.6480 = 0.3520$

Since we have $P\text{-value} = 0.3520 > 0.05 = \alpha$, the null hypothesis is not rejected.

Conclusion:

There is not sufficient evidence for the researcher to claim that the mean height of women aged 20 years or older has increased since 1994.

21. (a) It is necessary for SAT verbal scores to be normally distributed because there is a small sample ($n < 30$).

(b) Hypotheses: $H_0 : \mu = 515$; $H_1 : \mu < 515$

Significance level: $\alpha = 0.10$

Test Statistic: $z_0 = \dfrac{\overline{x} - \mu_0}{\sigma / \sqrt{n}} = \dfrac{458 - 515}{112 / \sqrt{20}} = -2.28$

Classical approach:

This is a left-tailed test so our critical value is $-z_\alpha = -z_{0.10} = -1.28$ and the critical region lies to the left of our critical value.

Since $z_0 = -2.28 < -1.28 = -z_{0.10}$, the test statistic falls in the critical region. Therefore, the null hypothesis is rejected.

P-value approach:

$P\text{-value} = P(Z < -2.28) = 0.0113$

Since we have $P\text{-value} = 0.0113 < 0.10 = \alpha$, the null hypothesis is rejected.

Conclusion:

There is sufficient evidence for the researcher to claim that the mean SAT verbal score is lower for students whose first language is not English.

23. (a) The plotted points are all within the bounds of the normal probability plot, which also has a generally linear pattern. The boxplot shows that there are no outliers. The conditions for a hypothesis test are satisfied.

(b) Hypotheses: $H_0 : \mu = 5.03$, $H_1 : \mu < 5.03$

Significance level: $\alpha = 0.01$

Using technology, $\bar{x} = 4.811$

Test Statistic: $z_0 = \dfrac{\bar{x} - \mu_0}{\sigma / \sqrt{n}} = \dfrac{4.811 - 5.03}{0.2 / \sqrt{19}} = -4.77$

Classical approach:

This is a left-tailed test so the critical value is $-z_{0.01} = -2.33$. Since the test statistic is in the critical region, we reject the null hypothesis.

P-value approach:

$P\text{-value} = P(Z < -4.77) < 0.0001$

Since we have $P\text{-value} < 0.0001 < 0.01 = \alpha$, the null hypothesis is rejected.

Conclusion:

There is enough evidence to support the claim that the acidity of the rain has increased (its pH is less than 5.03).

25. (a) The plotted points are all within the bounds of the normal probability plot, which also has a generally linear pattern. The boxplot shows that there are no outliers. The conditions for a hypothesis test are satisfied.

(b) Hypotheses: $H_0 : \mu = 64.05$ ounces, $H_1 : \mu \neq 64.05$ ounces

Significance level: $\alpha = 0.01$

Using technology, $\bar{x} = 64.007$

Test Statistic: $z_0 = \dfrac{\bar{x} - \mu_0}{\sigma / \sqrt{n}} = \dfrac{64.007 - 64.05}{0.06 / \sqrt{22}} = -3.36$

Classical approach:

This is a two-tailed test so our critical values are $\pm z_{\alpha/2} = \pm z_{0.005} = \pm 2.575$.

Since $-3.36 < -2.575$, the test statistic falls in the critical region and the null hypothesis is rejected.

P-value approach:

$$P\text{-value} = 2 \cdot P(Z > |-3.36|) = 2 \cdot P(Z > 3.36)$$
$$= 2(1 - P(Z < 3.36)) = 2(1 - 0.9996)$$
$$= 2(0.0004) = 0.0008$$

Since we have $P\text{-value} < 0.01 = \alpha$, the null hypothesis is rejected.

Conclusion:

There is enough evidence to indicate that the mean amount of juice in each bottle is not 64.05 ounces.

(c) Since the null hypothesis has been rejected, the process should be stopped so the machine can be recalibrated.

(d) Answers will vary. Using $\alpha = 0.1$ means that we will reject a true null 10% of the time. Stopping the machine process to recalibrate, when unnecessary, delays production which can lead to increased costs, lost revenue, and lower profits.

27. **(a)** The plotted points are all within the bounds of the normal probability plot and the boxplot shows that there are no outliers. The conditions for a hypothesis test are satisfied.

    (b) Hypotheses: $H_0 : \mu = 8.33$ years , $H_1 : \mu < 8.33$ years

    Significance level: $\alpha = 0.1$

    Using technology, $\bar{x} \approx 7.6$ years

    Test Statistic: $z_0 = \dfrac{\bar{x} - \mu_0}{\sigma / \sqrt{n}} = \dfrac{7.6 - 8.33}{3.8 / \sqrt{18}} = -0.82$

    Classical approach:

    This is a left-tailed test so our critical value is $-z_\alpha = -z_{0.1} = -1.28$.

    Since $-0.82 > -1.28$, the test statistic does not fall in the critical region and the null hypothesis is not rejected.

    P-value approach:

    P-value $= P(Z < -0.82) = 0.2061$

    Since we have P-value $> 0.1 = \alpha$, the null hypothesis is not rejected.

    Conclusion:

    There is not sufficient evidence to indicate that cars are younger today than in 1995.

29. Hypotheses: $H_0 : \mu = 694$ acres ; $H_1 : \mu > 694$ acres

    Significance level: $\alpha = 0.05$

    Test Statistic: $z_0 = \dfrac{\bar{x} - \mu_0}{\sigma / \sqrt{n}} = \dfrac{731 - 694}{212 / \sqrt{40}} = 1.10$

    Classical approach:

    This is a right-tailed test so our critical value is $z_\alpha = z_{0.05} = 1.645$.

    Since $z_0 = 1.10 < 1.645 = z_{0.05}$, the test statistic does not fall in the critical region and the null hypothesis is not rejected.

    P-value approach:

    P-value $= P(Z > 1.10) = 1 - P(Z \le 1.10) = 1 - 0.8643 = 0.1357$

    Since we have P-value $= 0.1357 > 0.05 = \alpha$, the null hypothesis is not rejected.

    Conclusion:

    There is not sufficient evidence for the researcher to claim that the mean number of acres per farm has increased since 1990.

31. Hypotheses: $H_0 : \mu = 31.8$ (million shares); $H_1 : \mu \ne 31.8$ (million shares)
Significance level: $\alpha = 0.05$
Test Statistic: $z_0 = \dfrac{\overline{x} - \mu_0}{\sigma / \sqrt{n}} = \dfrac{23.5 - 31.8}{14.8 / \sqrt{35}} = -3.32$

Classical approach:
This is a two-tailed test so our critical values are $\pm z_{\alpha/2} = \pm z_{0.025} = \pm 1.96$.
Since $z_0 = -3.32 < -1.96 = -z_{0.025}$, the test statistic falls in the critical region and the null hypothesis is rejected.
P-value approach:
$P\text{-value} = 2 \cdot P\left(Z > \left|-3.32\right|\right) = 2 \cdot P\left(Z > 3.32\right) = 2\left(0.0005\right) = 0.001$
Since we have $P\text{-value} = 0.001 < 0.05 = \alpha$, the null hypothesis is rejected.
Conclusion:
There is sufficient evidence for the analyst to claim the stock volume is different in 2004.

33. From Problem 25, $\overline{x} = 64.007$ oz, $\sigma = 0.06$ oz, $n = 22$. Using $\alpha = 0.01$, we have $z_{\alpha/2} = 2.575$.

Lower bound $= \overline{x} - z_{0.005} \cdot \dfrac{\sigma}{\sqrt{n}} = 64.007 - 2.575 \cdot \dfrac{0.06}{\sqrt{22}} = 64.007 - 0.033 = 63.974$ oz

Upper bound $= \overline{x} + z_{0.005} \cdot \dfrac{\sigma}{\sqrt{n}} = 64.007 + 2.575 \cdot \dfrac{0.06}{\sqrt{22}} = 64.007 + 0.033 = 64.040$ oz

The 99% confidence interval for this data is $\left(63.974, 64.040\right)$. Since $\mu_0 = 64.05$ is not in this interval, we conclude that the true mean amount in the bottles differs from 64.05 oz (i.e we are rejecting the null hypothesis).

35. From Problem 31, $\overline{x} = 23.5$ (million shares), $\sigma = 14.8$ (million shares), $n = 35$. Using $\alpha = 0.05$, we have $z_{\alpha/2} = 1.96$.

Lower bound $= \overline{x} - z_{0.025} \cdot \dfrac{\sigma}{\sqrt{n}} = 23.5 - 1.96 \cdot \dfrac{14.8}{\sqrt{35}} = 23.5 - 4.90 = 18.60$ (million shares)

Upper bound $= \overline{x} + z_{0.025} \cdot \dfrac{\sigma}{\sqrt{n}} = 23.5 + 1.96 \cdot \dfrac{14.8}{\sqrt{35}} = 23.5 + 4.90 = 28.40$ (million shares)

The 95% confidence interval for this data is $\left(18.60, 28.40\right)$. Since $\mu_0 = 31.8$ (million shares) is not in this interval, we reject the null and we conclude that there is sufficient evidence to indicate that the mean stock volume is different in 2004.

37. (a) $H_0 : \mu = 514$; $H_1 : \mu > 514$

(b) The test statistic is $z_0 = \dfrac{\overline{x} - \mu_0}{\sigma/\sqrt{n}} = \dfrac{518 - 514}{113/\sqrt{1800}} = 1.50$

Classical approach:

This is a right-tailed test so our critical value is $z_\alpha = z_{0.1} = 1.28$.

Since $1.50 > 1.28$, the test statistic falls in the critical region and the null hypothesis is rejected.

P-value approach:

$P\text{-value} = P(Z > 1.50) = 1 - P(Z \le 1.50) = 1 - 0.9332 = 0.0668$

Since we have $P\text{-value} = 0.0668 < 0.1 = \alpha$, the null hypothesis is rejected.

Conclusion:

There is sufficient evidence to support the claim that the mean score of students taking this review is greater than 514.

(c) Answers will vary. In some states this would be regarded as a highly significant increase, although in most states it is not likely to be thought of as an increase that has any practical significance.

(d) The test statistic is now $z_0 = \dfrac{\overline{x} - \mu_0}{\sigma/\sqrt{n}} = \dfrac{518 - 514}{113/\sqrt{400}} = 0.71$.

Classical approach:

This is a right-tailed test so our critical value is $z_\alpha = z_{0.1} = 1.28$.

Since $0.71 < 1.28$, the test statistic does not fall in the critical region and the null hypothesis is not rejected.

P-value approach:

$P\text{-value} = P(Z > 0.71) = 1 - P(Z \le 0.71) = 1 - 0.7611 = 0.2389$

Since we have $P\text{-value} = 0.2389 > 0.1000 = \alpha$, the null hypothesis is not rejected.

Conclusion:

There is not sufficient evidence to support the claim that the mean score of students taking this review is greater than 514.

39. **(a)** Answers will vary.

(b) Since the samples all come from a population that has mean equal to 80, approximately 10% of them (or 5 out of the 50 samples) should give a sample mean that is in the critical region at a 10% level of significance.

(c) Answers will vary.

(d) Answers will vary. The true mean is in fact 80, and the null hypothesis is correct. Therefore, to reject it would be to commit a Type I error.

41. **(a)** $H_0 : \mu = 150$ sec; $H_1 : \mu < 150$ sec

(b) Answers will vary. If the catalyst has no effect, then there is only a 2% probability of observing as short a mean reaction time as the researchers got from their experiment. Since this is a rather unlikely outcome, the researchers have fairly strong evidence for concluding that the catalyst does reduce the reaction time.

10.3 Testing Claims About a Population Mean in Practice

1. The sample must have been obtained using simple random sampling, and the sample has no outliers and the population from which the sample is selected is normally distributed or the sample size is large ($n \geq 30$).

3. For $\alpha = 0.05$ in a two-tailed test with 12 df, the critical values are $\pm t_{\alpha/2} = \pm t_{0.025} = \pm 2.179$.

5. (a) $t_0 = \dfrac{\overline{x} - \mu_0}{s/\sqrt{n}} = \dfrac{47.1 - 50}{10.3/\sqrt{24}} = -1.379$

   (b) This is a left-tailed test with $24 - 1 = 23$ df so the critical value is $-t_{0.05} = -1.714$.

   (c) The critical region is shaded.

   (d) Since the test statistic is not in the critical region, we do not reject the null hypothesis.

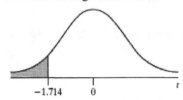

7. (a) $t_0 = \dfrac{\overline{x} - \mu_0}{s/\sqrt{n}} = \dfrac{104.8 - 100}{9.2/\sqrt{23}} = 2.502$

   (b) This is a two-tailed test with $23 - 1 = 22$ df so the critical values are $\pm t_{0.005} = \pm 2.819$

   (c) The critical region is shaded.

   (d) Since the test statistic is not in the critical region, we do not reject the null hypothesis.

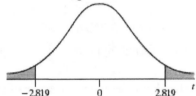

9. (a) $t_0 = \dfrac{\overline{x} - \mu_0}{s/\sqrt{n}} = \dfrac{18.3 - 20}{4.3/\sqrt{18}} = -1.677$.

   (b) The P-value region is shaded.

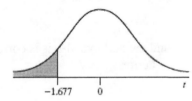

242

(c) This is a left-tailed test with $18 - 1 = 17$ df. The P-value is the area under the t-distribution to the left of the test statistic, $t_0 = -1.677$. Because of symmetry, the area under the distribution to the left of -1.677 equals the area under the distribution to the right of 1.677. Since $t = 1.677$ is between 1.333 and 1.740, we conclude that $0.05 < P\text{-value} < 0.10$ (reading from the top of the table). Between 5% and 10% of samples will have a sample mean at least this low, if the population mean is 20.
[Note: technology gives the P-value more accurately as 0.055884]

(d) Since $P\text{-value} > 0.05 = \alpha$, we do not reject the null hypothesis.

11. (a) No, because this sample is large ($n \geq 30$).

(b) $t_0 = \dfrac{\overline{x} - \mu_0}{s / \sqrt{n}} = \dfrac{101.9 - 105}{5.9 / \sqrt{35}} = -3.108$.

(c) The P-value region is shaded.

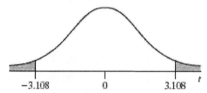

(d) This is a two-tailed test with $35 - 1 = 34$ df. Because this is a two-tailed test, the P-value is the sum of the area under the t-distribution to the left of $t_0 = -3.108$ and to the right of 3.108. Since 3.108 is between 3.002 and 3.348, we conclude that $0.001 < \frac{1}{2} P\text{-value} < 0.0025$ (reading from the top of the table). Note that for a two-tailed test we must double the values that we read from the top of the table (using symmetry and the fact that the table only gives the area in **one** tail). Thus, $0.002 < P\text{-value} < 0.005$. Between 0.2% and 0.5% of samples will have a sample mean this far from 105, if the population mean is 105.
[Note: technology gives the P-value more accurately as 0.003788]

(e) Since $P\text{-value} < 0.005 < 0.010 = \alpha$, we reject the null hypothesis.

13. $H_0 : \mu = 9.02 \text{ cm}^3$; $H_1 : \mu < 9.02 \text{ cm}^3$

$t_0 = \dfrac{\overline{x} - \mu_0}{s / \sqrt{n}} = \dfrac{8.10 - 9.02}{0.7 / \sqrt{12}} = -4.553$

$\alpha = 0.01$

d.f. $= n - 1 = 12 - 1 = 11$

Classical approach:
Because this is a left-tailed test with 11 degrees of freedom, the critical value is $-t_{0.01} = -2.718$.

Since $-4.553 < -2.718$, the test statistic falls within the critical region. The null hypothesis is rejected.

P-value approach:

This is a left-tailed test with 11 degrees of freedom. The *P*-value is the area under the *t*-distribution to the left of the test statistic, $t_0 = -4.553$. Because of symmetry, the area under the distribution to the left of -4.553 equals the area under the distribution to the right of 4.553. Since $t = 4.553$ is greater than 4.437, we conclude that *P*-value < 0.0005 (reading from the top of the table). Since *P*-value $< 0.0005 < \alpha = 0.01$, we reject the null hypothesis. [Note: technology gives the *P*-value more accurately as 0.000413]

Conclusion:

There is sufficient evidence to support the claim that the mean hippocampal volume in alcoholic adolescents is less than the normal volume of 9.02 cm^3.

15. $H_0 : \mu = 1000 \text{ mg} ; \; H_1 : \mu > 1000 \text{ mg}$

$$t_0 = \frac{\bar{x} - \mu_0}{s / \sqrt{n}} = \frac{1081 - 1000}{426 / \sqrt{50}} = 1.344$$

$\alpha = 0.05; \quad \text{d.f.} = n - 1 = 50 - 1 = 49$

Classical approach:

Because this is a right-tailed test with 49 degrees of freedom, the critical value is $t_{0.05} = 1.676$ (using the row for 50 d.f.; the closest value to our d.f.). Since $1.344 < 1.676$, the test statistic does not fall within the critical region. The null hypothesis is not rejected.

P-value approach:

This is a right-tailed test with 49 degrees of freedom. The *P*-value is the area under the *t*-distribution to the right of the test statistic, $t_0 = 1.344$. Using the row for 50 d.f. (the closest value to our d.f.), we find that $t = 1.344$ is between 1.299 and 1.676. We conclude that $0.05 < $ *P*-value < 0.1 (reading from the top of the table). Since *P*-value $> 0.05 = \alpha$, we do not reject the null hypothesis. [Note: technology gives the *P*-value more accurately as 0.092489]

Conclusion:

There is not sufficient evidence to support the IDFA's claim that male teenagers consume more than the recommended daily amount of 1000 mg of calcium.

17. (a) The hypotheses are $H_0 : \mu = 98.6°\text{F}$, $H_1 : \mu < 98.6°\text{F}$. The test statistic is

$$t_0 = \frac{\bar{x} - \mu_0}{s / \sqrt{n}} = \frac{98.2 - 98.6}{0.7 / \sqrt{700}} = -15.119. \text{ This is a left-tailed test with 699 df.}$$

We use 1000 df (the closest value to our d.f.) so the critical value is $-t_{0.01} = -2.330$. Since $-15.119 < -2.330$, the test statistic is in the critical region and we reject the null hypothesis. There is enough evidence to support the claim that the mean temperature of humans is less than $98.6°$ F.

(b) From the 1000 df. row, $t = 15.119 > 3.300$. We conclude that P-value $< .0005 < \alpha$ and reject the null hypothesis. Less than 0.05% of random samples will have a sample mean temperature this low, if the population mean temperature is 98.6° F. There is enough evidence to support the claim that the mean temperature of humans is less than 98.6° F.

19. (a) $H_0 : \mu = 40.7$ years, $H_1 : \mu \neq 40.7$ years

$$t_0 = \frac{\overline{x} - \mu_0}{s / \sqrt{n}} = \frac{38.9 - 40.7}{9.6 / \sqrt{32}} = -1.061$$

$\alpha = 0.05$;   df $= 32 - 1 = 31$

<u>Classical approach:</u>
This is a two-tailed test with 31 df so the critical values are $\pm t_{0.025} = \pm 2.040$. Since $-2.040 < -1.061 < 2.040$, the test statistic is **not** in the critical region and we do not reject the null hypothesis.

<u>P-value approach:</u>
Because this is a two-tailed test, the P-value is the sum of the area under the t-distribution to the left of -1.061 and to the right of 1.061. Since 1.061 is between 1.054 and 1.309, we conclude that $0.1 < \frac{1}{2} P$-value < 0.15 (reading from the top of the table). Note that for a two-tailed test we must double the values that we read from the top of the table (using symmetry and the fact that the table only gives the area in **one** tail). Thus, $0.2 < P$-value < 0.3. Between 20% and 30% of random samples will have a sample mean age this far from 40.7 years if the population mean age is 40.7 years. Since P-value $> \alpha$, we do not reject the null hypothesis.
[Note: technology gives the P-value more accurately as 0.297039]

<u>Conclusion:</u>
There is not enough evidence to support the sociologist's claim that the mean age of death-row inmates is different from 40.7 years.

(b) $\overline{x} = 38.9$ years, $s = 9.6$ years, $n = 32$. Using $\alpha = 0.05$, we have $t_{\alpha/2} = t_{0.025} = 2.037$.

$$\text{Lower bound} = \overline{x} - t_{0.025} \cdot \frac{s}{\sqrt{n}} = 38.9 - 2.037 \cdot \frac{9.6}{\sqrt{32}} = 35.44 \text{ years}$$

$$\text{Upper bound} = \overline{x} + t_{0.025} \cdot \frac{s}{\sqrt{n}} = 38.9 + 2.037 \cdot \frac{9.6}{\sqrt{32}} = 42.36 \text{ years}$$

The 95% confidence interval for this data is $(35.44, 42.36)$. Since $\mu_0 = 40.7$ years is in this interval, we do not reject the null hypothesis. We conclude that there is not sufficient evidence to support the sociologist's claim that the mean age of death-row inmates is different from 40.7 years.

21. (a) The plotted points are all within the bounds of the normal probability plot, which also has a generally linear pattern. The boxplot shows that there are no outliers. The conditions for a hypothesis test are satisfied.

(b) $H_0 : \mu = 1.68$ inches, $H_1 : \mu \neq 1.68$ inches.

Using technology, $\bar{x} = 1.681$ inches and $s = 0.0045$ inches. The test statistic is
$$t_0 = \frac{\bar{x} - \mu_0}{s/\sqrt{n}} = \frac{1.681 - 1.68}{0.0045/\sqrt{12}} = 0.770 .$$ This is a two-tailed test with 11 df so the critical

values are $\pm t_{0.025} = \pm 2.201$. Since $-2.201 < 0.770 < 2.201$, the test statistic is not in the critical region, we do not reject the null hypothesis. There is not enough evidence to support the claim that the mean diameter of Maxfli XS golf balls is different from 1.68 inches.

(c) From the 11 df row, we see $t = 0.770$ is between 0.697 and 0.876. We conclude that $0.20 < \frac{1}{2} P\text{-value} < 0.25$, so $0.40 < P\text{-value} < 0.50$. Between 40% and 50% of random samples will have a sample mean diameter at least this far from 1.68 inches if the population mean diameter is 1.68 inches. Since $P\text{-value} > \alpha$, we do reject the null hypothesis. There is not enough evidence to support the claim that the mean diameter of Maxfli XS golf balls is different from 1.68 inches.
[Note: technology gives the P-value more accurately as 0.452898]

23. (a) The plotted points are all within the bounds of the normal probability plot and the boxplot shows that there are no outliers. The conditions for a hypothesis test are satisfied.

(b) $H_0 : \mu = 84.3$ seconds; $H_1 : \mu < 84.3$ seconds

Using technology, $\bar{x} = 78$ seconds and $s = 15.21$ seconds.
$$t_0 = \frac{\bar{x} - \mu_0}{s/\sqrt{n}} = \frac{78 - 84.3}{15.21/\sqrt{10}} = -1.310$$
$\alpha = 0.10$; df $= 10 - 1 = 9$

Classical approach:
This is a left-tailed test with 9 df so the critical value is $-t_{0.10} = -1.383$. Since $-1.310 > -1.383$, the test statistic is not in the critical region and we do not reject the null hypothesis.

P-value approach:
From the 9 df row, we see $t = 1.310$ is between 1.100 and 1.383. We conclude that $0.1 < P\text{-value} < 0.15$. Between 10% and 15% of random samples will have a sample mean waiting time of 78 seconds or less if the population mean wait time is 84.3 seconds. Since $P\text{-value} > \alpha$, we do not reject the null hypothesis.
[Note: technology gives the P-value more accurately as 0.111282]

Conclusion:
There is not enough evidence to support the claim that the new drive-thru system results in a mean wait time that is less than 84.3 seconds.

25. (a) Based on the graphs, the data appear to be normally distributed with no outliers.

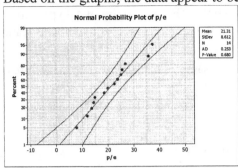
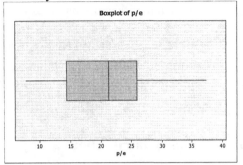

(b) <u>Classical approach:</u>

$H_0 : \mu = 22.0$; $H_1 : \mu < 22.0$

$\alpha = 0.05$

Using technology, $\bar{x} = 21.31$ and $s = 8.61$. The test statistic is

$t_0 = \dfrac{\bar{x} - \mu_0}{s/\sqrt{n}} = \dfrac{21.31 - 22.0}{8.61/\sqrt{14}} = -0.300$. This is a left-tailed test with 13 df so the critical

value is $-t_{0.05} = -1.771$. Since $-0.300 > -1.771$, the test statistic is not in the critical

region and we do not reject the null hypothesis. There is not enough evidence to support the claim that the P/E ratio is lower than the December 1, 2000, level of 22.0.

(c) <u>*P*-value approach:</u>

From the 13 df row, we see $t = 0.300$ is less than 0.694. We conclude that *P*-value > 0.25. More than 25% of random samples will have a sample mean P/E ratio this low or lower if the true mean is 22.0. Since *P*-value $> \alpha$, we do not reject the null hypothesis. There is not enough evidence to support the claim that the P/E ratio is lower than the December 1, 2000, level of 22.0.

[Note: technology gives the *P*-value more accurately as 0.385235]

27. (a) The plotted points are all within the bounds of the normal probability plot, which also has a generally linear pattern. The boxplot shows that there are no outliers. The conditions for a hypothesis test are satisfied.

(b) The hypotheses are $H_0 : \mu = 130$ mm Hg, $H_1 : \mu < 130$ mm Hg. The *P*-value is $0.088 > 0.05$ so the nursing student will not reject the null hypothesis. There is not enough evidence to support the claim that the mean systolic blood pressure of her male patients is less than 130 mm Hg.

29. The farmer's analysis may be correct, but his data come from only a small sample in a localized area. His farm may not be representative of the entire country. In addition, since he has a small sample, he should first test to see that the data are normal and that there are no outliers in the data.

31. (a) Answers will vary. We would expect 50 samples out of 1000 (i.e. 5%) to result in a rejection of the null hypothesis at $\alpha = 0.05$. The probability of a Type I error is $\alpha = 0.05$. Discrepancies might occur if the requirements for hypothesis testing of the mean (e.g. normality) are not met.

(b) Answers will vary. We would expect 50 samples out of 1000 (i.e. 5%) to result in a rejection of the null hypothesis at $\alpha = 0.05$.

10.4 Testing Claims About a Population Proportion

1. The sample must have been obtained using simple random sampling and $np_0(1-p_0) \geq 10$ with $n \leq 0.05N$.

3. (a) Note that $np_0(1-p_0) = 200 \cdot 0.3(1-0.3) = 12.6 \geq 10$ so the requirements of the hypothesis test are satisfied. Next we calculate $\hat{p} = \dfrac{75}{200} = 0.375$.

Then $z_0 = \dfrac{\hat{p} - p_0}{\sqrt{p_0(1-p_0)/n}} = \dfrac{0.375 - 0.3}{\sqrt{0.3(1-0.3)/200}} = 2.31$.

This is a right-tailed test so the critical value is $z_{0.05} = 1.645$. Since $2.31 > 1.645$, the test statistic is in the critical region and we reject the null hypothesis.

(b) From the normal table we get that the P-value is
$P\text{-value} = P(Z > 2.31) = 1 - P(Z \leq 2.31) = 1 - 0.9896 = 0.0104 < 0.05$
so we reject the null hypothesis.

5. (a) Note that $np_0(1-p_0) = 150 \cdot 0.55(1-0.55) = 37.125 \geq 10$ so the requirements of the hypothesis test are satisfied. Next we calculate $\hat{p} = \dfrac{78}{150} = 0.52$.

Then $z_0 = \dfrac{\hat{p} - p_0}{\sqrt{p_0(1-p_0)/n}} = \dfrac{0.52 - 0.55}{\sqrt{0.55(1-0.55)/150}} = -0.74$.

This is a left-tailed test so the critical value is $-z_{0.1} = -1.28$. Since $-0.74 > -1.28$, the test statistic is not in the critical region and we do not reject the null hypothesis.

(b) From the normal table we get that the P-value is
$P\text{-value} = P(Z < -0.74) = 0.2296 > 0.1$ so we do not reject the null hypothesis.

7. **(a)** Note that $np_0(1-p_0) = 500 \cdot 0.9(1-0.9) = 45 \geq 10$ so the requirements of the hypothesis test are satisfied. Next we calculate $\hat{p} = \dfrac{440}{500} = 0.88$.

Then $z_0 = \dfrac{\hat{p} - p_0}{\sqrt{p_0(1-p_0)/n}} = \dfrac{0.88 - 0.9}{\sqrt{0.9(1-0.9)/500}} = -1.49$.

This is a two-tailed test so the critical values are $\pm z_{0.025} = \pm 1.96$. Since $-1.96 < -1.49 < 1.96$, the test statistic is not in the critical region and we do not reject the null hypothesis.

   (b) From the normal table we get that the P-value is
$$P\text{-value} = 2 \cdot P(Z > |-1.49|) = 2 \cdot P(Z > 1.49) = 2(1 - P(Z \leq 1.49))$$
$$= 2(1 - 0.9319) = 2(0.0681) = 0.1362 > 0.05$$
so we do not reject the null hypothesis.

9. The hypotheses are $H_0 : p = 0.019$, $H_1 : p > 0.019$.

Note that $np_0(1-p_0) = 863 \cdot 0.019(1-0.019) = 16.1 \geq 10$ so the requirements of the hypothesis test are satisfied. From the survey, $\hat{p} = \dfrac{19}{863} = 0.022$.

$z_0 = \dfrac{\hat{p} - p_0}{\sqrt{p_0(1-p_0)/n}} = \dfrac{0.022 - 0.019}{\sqrt{0.019(1-0.019)/863}} = 0.65$

$\alpha = 0.01$

Classical approach:
This is a right-tailed test so the critical value is $z_{0.01} = 2.33$. Since $0.65 < 2.33$, the test statistic is not in the critical region and we do not reject the null hypothesis.

P-value approach:
From the normal table we get that the P-value is
$$P\text{-value} = P(Z > 0.65) = 1 - P(Z \leq 0.65) = 1 - 0.7422 = 0.2578 > 0.01$$
so we do not reject the null hypothesis.

Conclusion:
There is not enough evidence to support the claim that more than 1.9% of Lipitor users experience flu-like symptoms as a side effect.

11. The hypotheses are $H_0 : p = 0.81$, $H_1 : p \neq 0.81$.

Note that $np_0(1-p_0) = 1006(0.81)(1-0.81) \approx 154.8 \geq 10$ so the requirements of the hypothesis test are satisfied. From the survey, $\hat{p} = \dfrac{835}{1006} \approx 0.830$.

$z_0 = \dfrac{\hat{p} - p_0}{\sqrt{p_0(1-p_0)/n}} = \dfrac{0.830 - 0.81}{\sqrt{0.81(1-0.81)/1006}} = 1.62$

$\alpha = 0.05$

Classical approach:

This is a two-tailed test so the critical values are $\pm z_{\alpha/2} = \pm z_{0.025} = \pm 1.96$.

Since $-1.96 < 1.62 < 1.96$, the test statistic is not in the critical region and we do not reject the null hypothesis.

P-value approach:

From the normal table we get that the P-value is

$$P\text{-value} = 2 \cdot P(Z > 1.62) = 2 \cdot (1 - P(Z \le 1.62)) = 2(1 - 0.9474)$$

$$= 2(0.0526) = 0.1052 > 0.05$$

so we do not reject the null hypothesis.

Conclusion:

There is not enough evidence to support the claim that the percent of adults who have read at least one book in the last year is different from 1990.

13. The hypotheses are $H_0 : p = 0.38$, $H_1 : p < 0.38$.

Note that $np_0(1 - p_0) = 1122(0.38)(1 - 0.38) \approx 264.3 \ge 10$ so the requirements of the

hypothesis test are satisfied. From the survey, $\hat{p} = \dfrac{337}{1122} \approx 0.300$.

$$z_0 = \frac{\hat{p} - p_0}{\sqrt{p_0(1 - p_0)/n}} = \frac{0.300 - 0.38}{\sqrt{0.38(1 - 0.38)/1122}} = -5.52$$

$\alpha = 0.05$

Classical approach:

This is a left-tailed test so the critical value is $-z_{0.05} = -1.645$. Since $-5.52 < -1.645$, the test statistic is in the critical region and we reject the null hypothesis.

P-value approach:

From the normal table we get that the P-value is $P\text{-value} = P(Z < -5.52) < 0.0001 < 0.05$ so we reject the null hypothesis.

Conclusion:

There is enough evidence to support the claim that the proportion of families with children under the age of 18 who eat dinner together 7 nights a week has decreased from 2001.

15. The hypotheses are $H_0 : p = 0.30$, $H_1 : p \ne 0.30$.

Note that $np_0(1 - p_0) = 280(0.30)(1 - 0.30) = 58.8 \ge 10$ so the requirements of the

hypothesis test are satisfied. From the sample results, $\hat{p} = \dfrac{112}{280} = 0.40$.

$$z_0 = \frac{\hat{p} - p_0}{\sqrt{p_0(1 - p_0)/n}} = \frac{0.40 - 0.30}{\sqrt{0.30(1 - 0.30)/280}} = 3.65$$

$\alpha = 0.1$

Classical approach:
This is a two-tailed test so the critical values are $\pm z_{\alpha/2} = \pm z_{0.05} = \pm 1.645$. Since $3.65 > 1.645$, the test statistic is in the critical region and we reject the null hypothesis.

P-value approach:
From the normal table we get that the P-value is
$$P\text{-value} = 2 \cdot P(Z > 3.65) = 2 \cdot (1 - P(Z \le 3.65)) = 2(1 - 0.9999) = 2(0.0001) = 0.0002 < 0.1$$
so we reject the null hypothesis.

Conclusion:
There is enough evidence to support the claim that the percentage of employed adults satisfied with their chances for promotion is different from the percentage in 1998.

17. The hypotheses are $H_0 : p = 0.40$, $H_1 : p < 0.40$.

Note that $np_0(1-p_0) = 1004(0.40)(1-0.40) \approx 241 \ge 10$ so the requirements of the hypothesis test are satisfied. From the survey, $\hat{p} = \dfrac{372}{1004} \approx 0.371$.

$$z_0 = \frac{\hat{p} - p_0}{\sqrt{p_0(1-p_0)/n}} = \frac{0.371 - 0.40}{\sqrt{0.40(1-0.40)/1004}} = -1.88$$
$\alpha = 0.05$

Classical approach:
This is a left-tailed test so the critical value is $-z_{0.05} = -1.645$. Since $-1.88 < -1.645$, the test statistic is in the critical region and we reject the null hypothesis.

P-value approach:
From the normal table we get that the P-value is $P\text{-value} = P(Z < -1.88) = 0.0301 < 0.05$ so we reject the null hypothesis.

Conclusion:
There is enough evidence to support the claim that the proportion of 2005 adults aged 18 years or older having a "great deal" of confidence in the public schools is lower than in 1995.

19. The hypotheses are $H_0 : p = 0.37$, $H_1 : p < 0.37$.

Note that $np_0(1-p_0) = 150(0.37)(1-0.37) \approx 35 \ge 10$ so the requirements of the hypothesis test are satisfied. From the survey, $\hat{p} = \dfrac{54}{150} = 0.36$.

$$z_0 = \frac{\hat{p} - p_0}{\sqrt{p_0(1-p_0)/n}} = \frac{0.36 - 0.37}{\sqrt{0.37(1-0.37)/150}} = -0.25$$
$\alpha = 0.05$

Classical approach:
This is a left-tailed test so the critical value is $-z_{0.05} = -1.645$. Since $-0.25 > -1.645$, the test statistic is not in the critical region and we do not reject the null hypothesis.

P-value approach:

From the normal table we get that the *P*-value is $P\text{-value} = P(Z < -0.25) = 0.4013 > 0.05$ so we do not reject the null hypothesis.

Conclusion:

There is not enough evidence to support the veterinarian's claim that less than 37% of pet owners speak to their pets on the answering machine or telephone.

21. The hypotheses are $H_0 : p = 0.04$, $H_1 : p < 0.04$.

Note that $np_0(1 - p_0) = 120 \cdot 0.04(1 - 0.04) = 4.6 < 10$ so we must use small sample techniques. Since this is a left-tailed test we need to calculate the probability of 3 or fewer successes in 120 binomial trials with $p = 0.04$. Using technology we get:

$P = P(X \le 3) = P(X = 0) + \ldots + P(X = 3) = 0.0075 + \ldots + 0.1515 = 0.2887 > 0.05$ so we do not reject the null hypothesis. There is not enough evidence to support the claim that fewer than 4% of pregnant mothers smoke more than 21 cigarettes per day.

23. The hypotheses are $H_0 : p = 0.096$, $H_1 : p > 0.096$.

Note that $np_0(1 - p_0) = 80 \cdot 0.096(1 - 0.096) = 6.9 < 10$ so we must use small sample techniques. Since this is a right-tailed test we need to calculate the probability of 13 or more successes in 80 binomial trials with $p = 0.096$. Using technology we get:

$P = P(X \ge 13) = 1 - P(X < 12)) = 1 - (P(X = 0) + \ldots + P(X = 12)) = 1 - 0.9590 = 0.0410 < 0.1$ so we reject the null hypothesis. There is enough evidence to support the claim that more than 9.6% of Californians have to travel more than 60 minutes to work.

25. (a) Answers will vary. Some reasons include the economy, taxes, foreign policy, etc.

(b) The hypotheses are $H_0 : p = 0.48$, $H_1 : p < 0.48$.

Note that $np_0(1 - p_0) = 1100 \cdot 0.48(1 - 0.48) = 274.56 \ge 10$ so the requirements of the hypothesis test are satisfied. From the survey, $\hat{p} = \dfrac{506}{1100} = 0.46$.

The test statistic is $z_0 = \dfrac{\hat{p} - p_0}{\sqrt{p_0(1 - p_0)/n}} = \dfrac{0.46 - 0.48}{\sqrt{0.48(1 - 0.48)/1100}} = -1.33$.

From the normal table we get that the *P*-value is $P\text{-value} = P(Z < -1.33) = 0.0918$.

The final decision depends on the choice of α. If $\alpha > 0.0918$, we would reject the null hypothesis and conclude that the proportion of Americans who approve of the job Bush is doing is less than in April. Otherwise, we fail to reject the null.

10.5 Testing Claims About a Population Standard Deviation

1. The sample must have been obtained using simple random sampling and the population must be normally distributed.

3. **(a)** df $= 24 - 1 = 23$; $\chi_0^2 = \dfrac{(n-1)s^2}{\sigma_0^2} = \dfrac{23 \cdot (47.2)^2}{(50)^2} = 20.496$

   (b) This is a left-tailed test with 23 df and $\alpha = 0.05$, so the critical value is
   $\chi_{1-\alpha}^2 = \chi_{.95}^2 = 13.091$.

   (c) The critical region is shaded.

   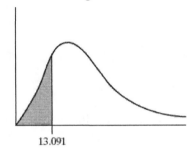

   13.091

   (d) No; the researcher will not reject the hull hypothesis because the test statistic is not in the critical region.

5. **(a)** df $= 18 - 1 = 17$; $\chi_0^2 = \dfrac{(n-1)s^2}{\sigma_0^2} = \dfrac{17 \cdot (2.4)^2}{(1.8)^2} = 30.222$

   (b) This is a right-tailed test with 17 df and $\alpha = 0.10$, so the critical value is $\chi_{.10}^2 = 24.769$.

   (c) The critical region is shaded.

   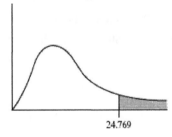

   24.769

   (d) Yes, because the test statistic is in the critical region. The researcher will reject H_0.

253

7. (a) $df = 12 - 1 = 11$; $\chi_0^2 = \frac{(n-1)s^2}{\sigma_0^2} = \frac{11 \cdot (4.8)^2}{(4.3)^2} = 13.707$

(b) This is a two-tailed test with 11 df and $\alpha = 0.05$, so the critical values are $\chi_{.975}^2 = 3.816$ and $\chi_{.025}^2 = 21.920$.

(c) The critical region is shaded.

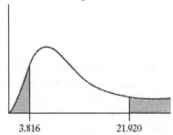

3.816   21.920

(d) No, because the test statistic is not in the critical region. The researcher will not reject H_0.

9. The hypotheses are $H_0 : \sigma = 4.0$, $H_1 : \sigma < 4.0$. The test statistic is

$$\chi_0^2 = \frac{(n-1)s^2}{\sigma_0^2} = \frac{24 \cdot (3.01)^2}{(4.0)^2} = 13.590.$$ This is a left-tailed test with 24 df and $\alpha = 0.05$, so

the critical value is $\chi_{1-\alpha}^2 = \chi_{.95}^2 = 13.848$. Since the test statistic is in the critical region, we reject the null hypothesis. There is enough evidence to support the claim that the fund has moderate risk.

11. The hypotheses are $H_0 : \sigma = 0.004$ inch, $H_1 : \sigma < 0.004$ inch. The test statistic is

$$\chi_0^2 = \frac{(n-1)s^2}{\sigma_0^2} = \frac{24 \cdot (0.0025)^2}{(0.004)^2} = 9.375.$$ This is a left-tailed test with 24 df and $\alpha = 0.01$,

so the critical value is $\chi_{1-\alpha}^2 = \chi_{.99}^2 = 10.856$. Since the test statistic is in the critical region, we reject the null hypothesis. There is enough evidence to support the claim that the standard deviation has decreased.

13. The hypotheses are $H_0 : \sigma = 0.2$, $H_1 : \sigma \neq 0.2$. The test statistic is

$$\chi_0^2 = \frac{(n-1)s^2}{\sigma_0^2} = \frac{18 \cdot (0.1708)^2}{(0.2)^2} = 13.128.$$ This is a two-tailed test with 18 df and $\alpha = 0.05$,

so the critical values are $\chi_{1-\alpha/2}^2 = \chi_{.975}^2 = 8.231$ and $\chi_{\alpha/2}^2 = \chi_{.025}^2 = 31.526$. Since the test statistic is not in the critical region, we do not reject the null hypothesis. There is not enough evidence to support the claim that the standard deviation is different from 0.2.

15. If we assume that we give the manufacturer of Maxfli golf balls the benefit of the doubt, then we will not reject the manufatrer's claim that the golf balls meet the specification unless there is strong evidence that the standard deviation of their diameters exceeds 0.004 inches. In that case, the hypotheses are $H_0 : \sigma = 0.004$ inch, $H_1 : \sigma > 0.004$ inch. The sample standard deviation is $s = 0.0045$ inch (using technology) so the test statistic is

$$\chi_0^2 = \frac{(n-1)s^2}{\sigma_0^2} = \frac{11 \cdot (0.0045)^2}{(0.004)^2} = 13.922.$$ This is a right-tailed test with 11 df and $\alpha = 0.01$,

so the critical value is $\chi_{.01}^2 = 24.725$. Since the test statistic is not in the critical region, we do not reject the null hypothesis. There is not enough evidence to support the claim that the standard deviation exceeds the specification.

17. The hypotheses are $H_0 : \sigma = 8.3$ points, $H_1 : \sigma < 8.3$ points. The test statistic is

$$\chi_0^2 = \frac{(n-1)s^2}{\sigma_0^2} = \frac{24 \cdot (6.7)^2}{(8.3)^2} = 15.639.$$ This is a left-tailed test with 24 df and $\alpha = 0.10$, so

the critical value is $\chi_{.90}^2 = 15.659$. Since the test statistic is in the critical region, we reject the null hypothesis. There is enough evidence to support the claim that Allen Iverson is more consistent than other shooting guards in the NBA.

19. (a) The points lie within the bounds of the normal plot and have a generally linear pattern.

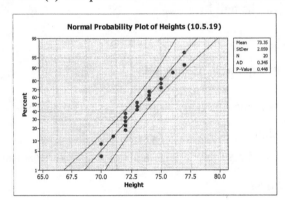 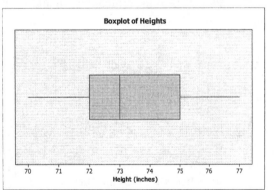

(b) Using technology we get $s = 2.059$ inches.

(c) The hypotheses are $H_0 : \sigma = 2.9$ inches, $H_1 : \sigma < 2.9$ inches. The test statistic is

$$\chi_0^2 = \frac{(n-1)s^2}{\sigma_0^2} = \frac{19 \cdot (2.059)^2}{(2.9)^2} = 9.578.$$ This is a left-tailed test with 19 df and $\alpha = 0.01$,

so the critical value is $\chi_{.99}^2 = 7.633$. Since the test statistic is not in the critical region, we do not reject the null hypothesis. There is not enough evidence to support the claim that the standard deviation of heights of major-league baseball players is less than 2.9 inches.

21. $\chi_0^2 = 13.590$ with 24 df. We scan across the 24 df row and find that the test statistic is between $12.401 = \chi_{.975}^2$ and $13.848 = \chi_{.95}^2$. It follows that P-value is between $1 - 0.975 = 0.025$ and $1 - 0.95 = 0.05$, since this is a left-tailed test. That is, $0.025 < P$-value < 0.05. If we use technology we can determine that P-value $= 0.0446$.

10.6 Putting It All Together: Which Method Do I Use?

1. To test a claim about a population mean, we must use a simple random sample that is either drawn from a normally distributed population, or the sample must have at least 30 subjects. Assuming the prerequisites are met, use a normal model to test a claim if the population standard deviation (or variance) is known and use a Student's t-distribution if the population standard deviation (or variance) is not known.

3. Hypotheses: $H_0 : \mu = 70$; $H_1 : \mu < 70$

$$z_0 = \frac{\bar{x} - \mu_0}{\sigma / \sqrt{n}} = \frac{60 - 70}{20 / \sqrt{14}} = -1.87; \quad \alpha = 0.1$$

Classical approach:
This is a left-tailed test so the critical value is $-z_{0.10} = -1.28$. Since $-1.87 < -1.28$, the test statistic is in the critical region and we reject the null hypothesis.

P-value approach:
P-value $= P(Z < -1.87) = 0.0307$

Since we have P-value $< 0.10 = \alpha$, the null hypothesis is rejected.

Conclusion:
There is enough evidence to support the claim that the population mean is less than 70.

5. The hypotheses are $H_0 : p = 0.5$, $H_1 : p > 0.5$.

Note that $np_0(1 - p_0) = 200 \cdot 0.5(1 - 0.5) = 50 \geq 10$ so the requirements of the hypothesis test are satisfied. From the survey, $\hat{p} = \frac{115}{200} = 0.575$.

$$z_0 = \frac{\hat{p} - p_0}{\sqrt{p_0(1 - p_0)/n}} = \frac{0.575 - 0.5}{\sqrt{0.5(1 - 0.5)/200}} = 2.12; \quad \alpha = 0.05$$

Classical approach:
This is a right-tailed test so the critical value is $z_{0.05} = 1.645$. The test statistic is in the critical region so we reject the null hypothesis.

P-value approach:
From the normal table we get that the P-value is P-value $= P(Z > 2.12) = 0.0170 < 0.05$ so we reject the null hypothesis.

Conclusion:
There is enough evidence to support the claim that more than 50% of those with a valid driver's license drive an American-made automobile.

7. $H_0 : \mu = 25$, $H_1 : \mu \neq 25$

$$t_0 = \frac{\overline{x} - \mu_0}{s / \sqrt{n}} = \frac{23.8 - 25}{6.3 / \sqrt{15}} = -0.738 \; ; \quad \alpha = 0.01 \; ; \quad df = 15 - 1 = 14$$

Classical approach:
This is a two-tailed test with 14 df so the critical values are $\pm t_{0.005} = \pm 2.977$. Since
$-2.977 < -0.738 < 2.977$, the test statistic is not in the critical region and we do not reject
the null hypothesis.

P-value approach:
Using the row for 14 degrees of freedom, we see that $0.692 < 0.738 < 0.868$. Therefore,
$0.2 < \frac{1}{2} P\text{-value} < 0.25$ and $0.4 < P\text{-value} < 0.5$. Since $P\text{-value} > \alpha$, we do not reject the
null hypothesis. [Note: technology gives the P-value more accurately as 0.472875]

Conclusion:
There is not enough evidence to support the claim that the population mean is different
from 25.

9. The hypotheses are $H_0 : \sigma^2 = 10$, $H_1 : \sigma^2 > 10$.

The test statistic is $\chi_0^2 = \dfrac{(n-1)s^2}{\sigma_0^2} = \dfrac{15 \cdot (13.7)}{10} = 20.55$. This is a right-tailed test with 15 df

and $\alpha = 0.05$, so the critical value is $\chi_{.05}^2 = 24.996$. Since the test statistic is not in the
critical region, we do not reject the null hypothesis. There is not enough evidence to
support the claim that the population variance is more than 10.
[Note: using technology, the P-value = 0.151833]

11. $H_0 : \mu = 100$, $H_1 : \mu > 100$.

$$t_0 = \frac{\overline{x} - \mu_0}{s / \sqrt{n}} = \frac{108.5 - 100}{17.9 / \sqrt{40}} = 3.003 \; ; \quad \alpha = 0.05 \; ; \quad df = 40 - 1 = 39$$

Classical approach:
This is a right-tailed test with 39 df so the critical value is $t_{0.05} = 1.685$. Since
$3.003 > 1.685$, the test statistic is in the critical region and we reject the null hypothesis.

P-value approach:
From the 39 df row, we see $t = 3.003$ is between 2.976 and 3.313. We conclude that
$0.001 < P\text{-value} < 0.0025$. Since $P\text{-value} < \alpha$, we reject the null hypothesis.
[Note: technology gives the P-value more accurately as 0.002323]

Conclusion:
There is enough evidence to support the claim that the population mean is more than 100.

13. (a) Hypotheses: $H_0 : \mu = 2.5$; $H_1 : \mu \neq 2.5$

Significance level: $\alpha = 0.1$

Test Statistic: $z_0 = \dfrac{\overline{x} - \mu_0}{\sigma / \sqrt{n}} = \dfrac{2.6 - 2.5}{1.2 / \sqrt{1006}} = 2.64$

Classical approach:
This is a two-tailed test so our critical values are $\pm z_{\alpha/2} = \pm z_{0.05} = \pm 1.645$. Since $2.64 > 1.645$, the test statistic falls in the critical region and the null hypothesis is rejected.

P-value approach:
$P\text{-value} = 2 \cdot P(Z > 2.64) = 2(1 - 0.9959) = 2(0.0041) = 0.0082$

Since we have $P\text{-value} < \alpha$, the null hypothesis is rejected.

Conclusion:
There is enough evidence to support the claim that the mean ideal number of children has changed since 1985.

(b) Answers will vary. The difference does not appear to be practically significant (a difference of only 0.1), but social and economic implications might need to be considered before drawing any conclusions (e.g. what is the impact of a 4% increase in the number of children on schools?).

15. The hypotheses are $H_0 : \sigma = 7000$ psi, $H_1 : \sigma > 7000$ psi.

The test statistic is $\chi_0^2 = \dfrac{(n-1)s^2}{\sigma_0^2} = \dfrac{19 \cdot (7500)^2}{(7000)^2} = 21.811$. This is a right-tailed test with 19 df and $\alpha = 0.01$, so the critical value is $\chi_{.01}^2 = 36.191$. Since the test statistic is not in the critical region, we do not reject the null hypothesis. There is not enough evidence to support the claim that the population standard deviation exceeds 7000 psi.
[Note: using technology, the $P\text{-value} = 0.293763$]

17. $H_0 : \mu = 6.3$, $H_1 : \mu < 6.3$

$t_0 = \dfrac{\overline{x} - \mu_0}{s / \sqrt{n}} = \dfrac{6.05 - 6.3}{1.75 / \sqrt{41}} = -0.915$; $\alpha = 0.05$; df $= 41 - 1 = 40$

Classical approach:
This is a left-tailed test with 40 df so the critical value is $-t_{0.05} = -1.684$. Since $-0.915 > -1.684$, the test statistic is not in the critical region and we do not reject the null hypothesis.

P-value approach:
From the 40 df row, we see $t = 0.915$ is between 0.851 and 1.050. We conclude that $0.15 < P\text{-value} < 0.20$. Since $P\text{-value} > \alpha$, we do not reject the null hypothesis.
[Note: technology gives the $P\text{-value}$ more accurately as 0.182907]

Conclusion:
There is not enough evidence to support the agent's claim that the interest rates are lower than in 2001.

19. $H_0 : \mu = \$774$, $H_1 : \mu \neq \$774$

$$t_0 = \frac{\bar{x} - \mu_0}{s/\sqrt{n}} = \frac{735 - 774}{48.31/\sqrt{35}} = -4.776; \quad \alpha = 0.01; \quad df = 35 - 1 = 34$$

Classical approach:
This is a two-tailed test with 34 df so the critical values are $\pm t_{0.005} = \pm 2.728$. Since $-4.776 < -2.728$, the test statistic is in the critical region and we reject the null hypothesis.

P-value approach:
From the 34 df row, we see $t = 4.776 > 3.591$. We conclude that $\frac{1}{2}$P-value < 0.0005 and P-value < 0.001. Since P-value $< \alpha$, we reject the null hypothesis.
[Note: technology gives the P-value more accurately as 0.000033]

Conclusion:
There is enough evidence to support the claim that the mean expenditure for auto insurance is different from the 2002 amount.

21. $H_0 : \mu = 8$ minutes, $H_1 : \mu < 8$ minutes

$$t_0 = \frac{\bar{x} - \mu_0}{s/\sqrt{n}} = \frac{7.34 - 8}{3.2/\sqrt{49}} = -1.444; \quad \alpha = 0.01; \quad df = 49 - 1 = 48 \text{ (use 50 in the table)}$$

Classical approach:
This is a left-tailed test with 48 df (use 50 in the table) so the critical value is $-t_{0.01} = -2.403$. Since $-1.444 > -2.403$, the test statistic is not in the critical region and we do not reject the null hypothesis.

P-value approach:
From the 50 df row, we see $t = 1.444$ is between 1.299 and 1.676. We conclude that $0.05 < $ P-value < 0.10. Since P-value $> \alpha$, we do not reject the null hypothesis.
[Note: technology gives the P-value more accurately as 0.077652]

Conclusion:
There is not enough evidence to support the claim that the mean wait time is less than 8 minutes.

10.7 The Probability of a Type II Error and the Power of the Test

1. A Type II error is the error of **not** rejecting H_0 when in fact H_1 is true.

3. As the true mean gets closer to the hypothesized value of the mean, the probability of making a Type II error increases so the power of the test decreases. This result is reasonable because sample results consistent with the hypothesized mean are likely to be very similar to sample results consistent with the true mean—it will be difficult to distinguish between the two means based on sample data.

5. **(a)** A Type II error would occur if the sample data led to a conclusion of not rejecting $H_0 : \mu = 50$ when in fact $\mu < 50$.

   (b) This is a left-sided test with $\alpha = 0.05$ and $-z_\alpha = -1.645$.
   We will not reject the null if we get a sample mean greater than
   $$\bar{x} = 50 - 1.645 \cdot \frac{12}{\sqrt{24}} = 45.97 . \text{ Therefore, if } \mu = 48 , \text{ then}$$
   $$P(\text{Type II error}) = P\left(Z > \frac{45.97 - 48}{12/\sqrt{24}} \right) = P(Z > -0.83) = 1 - 0.2033 = 0.7967 = \beta$$
   Power $= 1 - 0.7967 = 0.2033$

   (c) $P(\text{Type II error}) = P\left(Z > \frac{45.97 - 49.2}{12/\sqrt{24}} \right) = P(Z > -1.32) = 1 - 0.0934 = 0.9066 = \beta$
   Power $= 1 - 0.9066 = 0.0934$

7. **(a)** A Type II error would occur if the sample data led to a conclusion of not rejecting $H_0 : \mu = 100$ when in fact $\mu \neq 100$.

   (b) This is a two-sided test with $\alpha = 0.01$ and $\pm z_{\alpha/2} = \pm 2.575$.
   We will not reject the null if we get a sample mean between
   $$\bar{x}_L = 100 - 2.575 \cdot \frac{7}{\sqrt{23}} = 100 - 3.76 = 96.24 \text{ and } \bar{x}_U = 100 + 3.76 = 103.76 . \text{ Thus,}$$
   $$P(\text{Type II error}) = P\left(\frac{96.24 - 103}{7/\sqrt{23}} < Z < \frac{103.76 - 103}{7/\sqrt{23}} \right)$$
   $$= P(-4.63 < Z < 0.52) = 0.6985 - 0 = 0.6985 = \beta$$
   Power $= 1 - 0.6985 = 0.3015$

   (c) $P(\text{Type II error}) = P\left(\frac{96.24 - 101.4}{7/\sqrt{23}} < Z < \frac{103.76 - 101.4}{7/\sqrt{23}} \right)$
   $$= P(-3.54 < Z < 1.62) = 0.9474 - 0.0002 = 0.9472 = \beta$$
   Power $= 1 - 0.9472 = 0.0528$

9. **(a)** A Type II error would occur if the sample data led to a conclusion of not rejecting $H_0 : \mu = 20$ when in fact $\mu < 20$.

(b) This is a left-sided test with $\alpha = 0.05$ and $-z_\alpha = -1.645$.

We will not reject the null if we get a sample mean greater than

$\overline{x} = 20 - 1.645 \cdot \dfrac{3}{\sqrt{18}} = 18.84$. Thus,

$$P(\text{Type II error}) = P\left(Z > \frac{18.84 - 17.4}{3/\sqrt{18}}\right) = P(Z > 2.04) = 1 - 0.9793 = 0.0207 = \beta$$

Power $= 1 - 0.0207 = 0.9793$

(c) $P(\text{Type II error}) = P\left(Z > \dfrac{18.84 - 19.2}{3/\sqrt{18}}\right) = P(Z > -0.51) = 1 - 0.3050 = 0.6950 = \beta$

Power $= 1 - 0.6950 = 0.3050$

11. (a) A Type II error would occur if the sample data led to a conclusion of not rejecting $H_0 : \mu = 105$ when in fact $\mu \neq 105$.

(b) This is a two-sided test with $\alpha = 0.1$ and $\pm z_{\alpha/2} = \pm 1.645$.

We will not reject the null if we get a sample mean between

$\overline{x}_L = 105 - 1.645 \cdot \dfrac{12}{\sqrt{35}} = 105 - 3.34 = 101.66$ and $\overline{x}_U = 105 + 3.34 = 108.34$. Thus,

$$P(\text{Type II error}) = P\left(\frac{101.66 - 101.8}{12/\sqrt{35}} < Z < \frac{108.34 - 101.8}{12/\sqrt{35}}\right)$$
$$= P(-0.07 < Z < 3.22) = 0.9994 - 0.4721 = 0.5273 = \beta$$

Power $= 1 - 0.5273 = 0.4727$

(c) $P(\text{Type II error}) = P\left(\dfrac{101.66 - 103.1}{12/\sqrt{35}} < Z < \dfrac{108.34 - 103.1}{12/\sqrt{35}}\right)$
$$= P(-0.71 < Z < 2.58) = 0.9951 - 0.2389 = 0.7562 = \beta$$

Power $= 1 - 0.7562 = 0.2438$

13. (a) A Type II error would occur if the sample data led to a conclusion of not rejecting $H_0 : \mu = 63.7$ inches when in fact $\mu > 63.7$ inches .

(b) This is a right-sided test with $\alpha = 0.05$ and $z_\alpha = 1.645$.

We will not reject the null if we get a sample mean less than

$\overline{x} = 63.7 + 1.645 \cdot \dfrac{6.5}{\sqrt{45}} = 65.29$ inches . Thus,

$$P(\text{Type II error}) = P\left(Z < \frac{65.29 - 64}{6.5/\sqrt{45}}\right) = P(Z < 1.33) = 0.9082 = \beta$$

Power $= 1 - 0.9082 = 0.0918$

(c) $P(\text{Type II error}) = P\left(Z < \dfrac{65.29 - 66}{6.5/\sqrt{45}}\right) = P(Z < -0.73) = 0.2327 = \beta$

Power $= 1 - 0.2327 = 0.7673$

15. (a) A Type II error would occur if the sample data led to a conclusion of not rejecting $H_0 : \mu = 515$ when in fact $\mu < 515$.

(b) This is a left-sided test with $\alpha = 0.01$ and $-z_\alpha = -2.33$.

We will not reject the null if we get a sample mean greater than

$\bar{x} = 515 - 2.33 \cdot \dfrac{112}{\sqrt{20}} = 456.6$. Thus,

$P(\text{Type II error}) = P\left(Z > \dfrac{456.6 - 500}{112/\sqrt{20}}\right) = P(Z > -1.73) = 1 - 0.0418 = 0.9582 = \beta$

Power $= 1 - 0.9582 = 0.0418$

(c) $P(\text{Type II error}) = P\left(Z > \dfrac{456.6 - 480}{112/\sqrt{20}}\right) = P(Z > -0.93) = 1 - 0.1762 = 0.8238 = \beta$

Power $= 1 - 0.8238 = 0.1762$

17. $\bar{x} = 50 - 2.33 \cdot \dfrac{12}{\sqrt{24}} = 44.29$

$P(\text{Type II error}) = P\left(Z > \dfrac{44.29 - 48}{12/\sqrt{24}}\right) = P(Z > -1.51) = 1 - 0.0655 = 0.9345 = \beta$

Power $= 0.0655 < 0.2033$.

Lowering α has the effect of lowering the power of the test.

19. (a) We would reject H_0 if $Z_0 < -1.645$, i.e., if $Z_0 = \dfrac{\hat{p} - 0.75}{\sqrt{0.75(1 - 0.75)/500}} < -1.645$, and

hence if $\hat{p} < 0.75 - 1.645\sqrt{0.75(1 - 0.75)/500} = 0.718$.

$P(\text{Type II error}) = P\left(\hat{p} > 0.718 \text{ given that } p = 0.70\right)$

$$= P\left(Z > \dfrac{0.718 - 0.70}{\sqrt{0.70(1 - 0.70)/500}}\right)$$

$$= P(Z > 0.88) = 1 - 0.8106 = 0.1894$$

(b) Power $= 1 - 0.1894 = 0.8106$

Chapter 10 Review Exercises

1. **(a)** The hypotheses are $H_0 : \mu = \$4277$ versus $H_1 : \mu > \$4277$.

   (b) We make a Type I error if the sample evidence leads us to reject H_0 and believe that the mean outstanding credit card debt per cardholder is more than \$4277 when, in fact, it is \$4277 (i.e. reject H_0 when H_0 is true).

   (c) We make a Type II error if we fail to reject the null hypothesis that the mean outstanding credit card debt per cardholder is \$4277 when, in fact, it is more than \$4277 (i.e. do not reject H_0 when in fact H_0 is false).

   (d) If the null hypothesis is not rejected, this means there was not enough evidence to support the claim that the mean outstanding credit card debt per cardholder is more than \$4277.

   (e) If the null hypothesis is rejected, this means there was sufficient evidence to support the claim that the mean outstanding credit card debt per cardholder is more than \$4277.

3. $P(\text{Type I Error}) = \alpha = 0.05$

5. **(a)** $z_0 = \dfrac{\bar{x} - \mu_0}{\sigma / \sqrt{n}} = \dfrac{28.6 - 30}{4.5 / \sqrt{12}} = -1.08$.

   (b) This is a left-tailed test so the critical value is $-z_{0.05} = -1.645$.

   (c) The critical region is shaded.

   (d) Since the test statistic is not in the critical region, we do not reject the null hypothesis.

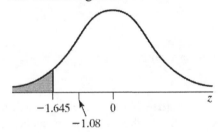

   (e) P-value $= P(Z < -1.08) = 0.1401$.

7. **(a)** Since σ is unknown, the test statistic is a t-statistic. $t_0 = \dfrac{\bar{x} - \mu_0}{s / \sqrt{n}} = \dfrac{7.3 - 8}{1.8 / \sqrt{15}} = -1.506$.

   (b) This is a two-tailed test with 14 df so the critical values are $\pm t_{0.01} = \pm 2.624$.

(c) The critical region is shaded.

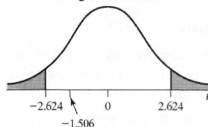

$$-2.624 \qquad 0 \qquad 2.624$$
$$-1.506$$

(d) Since the test statistic is not in the critical region, we do not reject the null hypothesis.

(e) In the 14 df row, $t = 1.506$ is between 1.345 and 1.761 so $0.05 < \frac{1}{2}P < 0.10$. Thus $0.10 < P < 0.20$. [Note: technology gives the P-value more accurately as 0.154253]

9. (a) $H_0 : p = 0.6$, $H_1 : p > 0.6$

Note that $np_0(1 - p_0) = 250 \cdot 0.6(1 - 0.6) = 60 \geq 10$ so the requirements of the hypothesis test are satisfied. Next we calculate $\hat{p} = \dfrac{165}{250} = 0.66$. Then

$$z_0 = \frac{\hat{p} - p_0}{\sqrt{p_0(1 - p_0)/n}} = \frac{0.66 - 0.6}{\sqrt{0.6(1 - 0.6)/250}} = 1.94 \;.$$ This is a right-tailed test so the critical value is $z_{0.05} = 1.645$. The test statistic is in the critical region so we reject the null hypothesis.

(b) From the normal table we get that the P-value is $P = 1 - 0.9738 = 0.0262 < 0.05$ so we reject the null hypothesis.

11. (a) $\chi_0^{\;2} = \dfrac{(n-1)s^2}{\sigma_0^2} = \dfrac{17 \cdot (4.9)^2}{(5.2)^2} = 15.095$

(b) This is a two-tailed test with 17 df so the critical values are $\chi_{1-\alpha/2}^2 = \chi_{.975}^2 = 7.564$ and $\chi_{\alpha/2}^2 = \chi_{.025}^2 = 30.191$.

(c) The critical region is shaded.

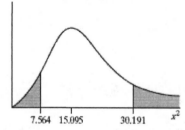

$$7.564 \quad 15.095 \qquad 30.191 \qquad x^2$$

(d) No, the researcher will not reject the null hypothesis because the test statistic is not in the critical region.

264

13. The hypotheses are $H_0 : \mu = 0.875$ inch , $H_1 : \mu > 0.875$ inch .

$\bar{x} = 0.876$ inch and $s = 0.005$ inch ; $df = 35$

The test statistic is $t_0 = \dfrac{\bar{x} - \mu_0}{s / \sqrt{n}} = \dfrac{0.876 - 0.875}{0.005 / \sqrt{36}} = 1.2$.

Classical approach:
This is a right-tailed test with 35 degrees of freedom so the critical value is $t_{0.05} = 1.690$.
Since the test statistic is not in the critical region, we do not reject the null hypothesis.

P-value approach:
Using the row for 35 degrees of freedom, we find $1.052 < 1.2 < 1.306$. Therefore, $0.10 < P$-value < 0.15 . Since P-value > 0.05 , we do not reject the null hypothesis. [Note: technology gives the P-value more accurately as 0.119100]

Conclusion:
There is not enough evidence to support the claim that the mean distance between the retaining rings is more than 0.875 inch.

15. The hypotheses are $H_0 : \mu = 474$, $H_1 : \mu > 474$.

Using technology, $\bar{x} = 539$. The test statistic is $z_0 = \dfrac{\bar{x} - \mu_0}{\sigma / \sqrt{n}} = \dfrac{539 - 474}{103 / \sqrt{50}} = 4.46$.

Classical approach:
This is a right-tailed test so the critical value is $z_{0.01} = 2.33$. Since the test statistic is in the critical region, we reject the null hypothesis.

P-value approach:
This is a right-tailed test so P-value $= P(Z > 4.46) < 0.0001$. Since $0.0001 < 0.01$, we reject the null hypothesis.

Conclusion:
There is enough evidence to support the claim that the mean SAT math score is higher for students who use a calculator "frequently".

17. (a) The hypotheses are $H_0 : \mu = 300$ mg , $H_1 : \mu > 300$ mg . The test statistic is

$t_0 = \dfrac{\bar{x} - \mu_0}{s / \sqrt{n}} = \dfrac{326 - 300}{342 / \sqrt{404}} = 1.528$. This is a right-tailed test with 403 df, which we

approximate by 100 df, so the critical value is $t_{0.05} = 1.660$. Since the test statistic is not in the critical region, we do not reject the null hypothesis. There is not enough evidence to support the claim that 20–39-year-old males consume too much cholesterol. [Note: technology gives the P-value as $0.063642 > \alpha$]

(b) If the nutritionist were to reject the null hypothesis, and the null hypothesis were true, then this would be a Type I error. In this test the nutritionist did not reject the null hypothesis. If in fact the alternative hypothesis is true, then a Type II error has been made.

(c) The probability of making a Type I error is $\alpha = 0.05$.

19. (a) The plotted points are all within the bounds of the normal probability plot, which also has a generally linear pattern. The boxplot shows that there are no outliers. The conditions for a hypothesis test are satisfied.

(b) The hypotheses are $H_0 : \mu = 4.61$, $H_1 : \mu < 4.61$.

Using technology, $\bar{x} = 4.4808$. The test statistic is

$$z_0 = \frac{\bar{x} - \mu_0}{\sigma / \sqrt{n}} = \frac{4.4808 - 4.61}{0.26 / \sqrt{25}} = -2.48.$$

Classical approach:

This is a left-tailed test so the critical value is $-z_{0.01} = -2.33$. Since the test statistic is in the critical region, we reject the null hypothesis.

P-value approach:

This is a left-tailed test so P-value $= P(Z < -2.48) = 0.0066 < \alpha$. About 0.66% of samples will have a sample mean pH this low, if the population mean pH is 4.61. Reject H_0.

Conclusion:

There is enough evidence to support the claim that the acidity of the rain has increased (its pH is less than 4.61).

21. The hypotheses are $H_0 : p = 0.56$, $H_1 : p > 0.56$.

Note that $np_0(1 - p_0) = 300 \cdot 0.56(1 - 0.56) = 73.92 \geq 10$ so the requirements of the

hypothesis test are satisfied. From the survey, $\hat{p} = \frac{170}{300} \approx 0.567$.

The test statistic is $z_0 = \frac{\hat{p} - p_0}{\sqrt{p_0(1 - p_0)/n}} = \frac{0.567 - 0.56}{\sqrt{0.56(1 - 0.56)/300}} = 0.24.$

Classical approach:

This is a right-tailed test so the critical value is $z_{0.01} = 2.33$. The test statistic is not in the critical region so we do not reject the null hypothesis.

P-value approach:

This is a right-tailed test so P-value $= P(Z > 0.24) = 0.4052$. Since $0.4052 > 0.01$, we do not reject the null hypothesis.

Conclusion:

There is not enough evidence to support the claim that the percentage of cases of tuberculosis that are among foreign-born residents has increased.

23. The hypotheses are $H_0 : \sigma = 104$, $H_1 : \sigma > 104$. The test statistic is

$$\chi_0^2 = \frac{(n-1)s^2}{\sigma_0^2} = \frac{22 \cdot (112)^2}{(104)^2} = 25.515.$$ This is a right-tailed test with 22 df so the critical

value is $\chi_{.10}^2 = 30.813$. Since the test statistic is not in the critical region, we do not reject the null hypothesis. There is not enough evidence to support the claim that students in low-income households have a higher standard deviation of SAT scores than students in high-income households.

25. (a) Since this is a right-tailed test with critical value $z_{0.01} = 2.33$, the sample mean that separates the rejection region from the non-rejection region is

$$\bar{x} = 474 + 2.33 \cdot \frac{103}{\sqrt{50}} = 507.94.$$

Then $P(\text{Type II error}) = P\left(Z < \frac{507.94 - 510}{103/\sqrt{50}}\right) = P(Z < -0.14) = 0.4443 = \beta$

(b) Power $= 1 - 0.4443 = 0.5557$

27. The hypotheses are $H_0 : p = 0.40$, $H_1 : p > 0.40$.

Note that $np_0(1 - p_0) = 40 \cdot 0.40(1 - 0.40) = 9.6 < 10$ so we must use small sample techniques. Since this is a right-tailed test we need to calculate the probability of 18 or more successes in 40 binomial trials with $p = 0.40$. Using technology we get:
$P\text{-value} = P(X \geq 18) = P(X = 18) + \ldots + P(X = 40) = 0.3115 > 0.05$ so we do not reject the null hypothesis. There is not enough evidence to support the claim that the proportion of adolescents who pray daily is more than 40%.

29. The hypotheses are $H_0 : \mu = 73.2$, $H_1 : \mu < 73.2$.

$\bar{x} = 72.8$ and $s = 12.3$; df $= 3850$

The test statistic is $t_0 = \frac{\bar{x} - \mu_0}{s/\sqrt{n}} = \frac{72.8 - 73.2}{12.3/\sqrt{3851}} = -2.018$.

Classical approach:
This is a left-tailed test with 3850 degrees of freedom (use ∞ in the t-table) so the critical value is $-t_{0.05} = -1.645$. The test statistic is in the critical region, so reject the null hypothesis.

P-value approach:
Using the row for 1000 degrees of freedom we have $1.960 < 2.018 < 2.054$. Therefore, $0.02 < P\text{-value} < 0.025$. Between 2% and 2.5% of samples of the same size from this population will have a sample mean as low or lower than observed. Since $P\text{-value} < 0.05$, we reject the null hypothesis. [Technology gives the P-value more accurately as 0.021825]

Conclusion:
There is enough evidence to support the claim, from a statistical viewpoint, that the scores on the final exam decreased under the new format. The data are statistically significant, but there is no real practical significance. A difference of 0.4 points (less than ½ of a percentage point) is practically insignificant when compared to the savings in resources by the university. For all practical purposes, the average scores would be considered the same.

Chapter 11

Inferences on Two Samples

11.1   Inferences about Two Means: Dependent Samples

1. independent

3. Since the researcher claims the mean of population 1, μ_1, is less than the mean of population 2, μ_2, in matched pair data, the difference $\mu_1 - \mu_2$ should be negative. Thus, define $H_1 : \mu_d < 0$ with $d_i = X_i - Y_i$.

5. Since the members of the two samples are married to each other, the sampling is dependent.

7. Because the 80 students are randomly allocated to one of two groups, the sampling is independent.

9. Because the two sets of twins are chosen at random, the sampling is independent.

11. (a)

Observation	1	2	3	4	5	6	7
X_i	7.6	7.6	7.4	5.7	8.3	6.6	5.6
Y_i	8.1	6.6	10.7	9.4	7.8	9.0	8.5
$d_i = X_i - Y_i$	−0.5	1.0	−3.3	−3.7	0.5	−2.4	−2.9

(b) Using technology, $\overline{d} \approx -1.614$ and $s_d \approx 1.915$.

(c) The hypotheses are $H_0 : \mu_d = 0$ versus $H_1 : \mu_d < 0$. The level of significance is $\alpha = 0.05$. The test statistic is $t_0 = \dfrac{\overline{d}}{s_d / \sqrt{n}} = \dfrac{-1.614}{1.915 / \sqrt{7}} \approx -2.230$.

Classical approach: Since this is a left-tailed test with 6 degrees of freedom, the critical value is $-t_{0.05} = -1.943$. Since the test statistic $t_0 \approx -2.230$ is less than the critical value $-t_{0.05} = -1.943$ (i.e., since the test statistic fall within the critical region), we reject H_0.

P-value approach: The P-value for this left-tailed test is the area under the t-distribution with 6 degrees of freedom to the left of the test statistic $t_0 = -2.230$, which by symmetry is equal to the area to the right of $t_0 = 2.230$. From the t-distribution table in the row corresponding to 6 degrees of freedom, 2.230 falls between 1.943 and 2.447 whose right-tail areas are 0.05 and 0.025, respectively. So, $0.025 < P\text{-value} < 0.05$. (Using technology, we find P-value = 0.0336.) Because the P-value is less than the level of significance $\alpha = 0.05$, we reject H_0.

Conclusion: There is sufficient evidence at the $\alpha = 0.05$ level of significance to support the claim that $\mu_d < 0$.

(d) For $\alpha = 0.05$ and df = 6, $t_{\alpha/2} = t_{0.025} = 2.447$. Then:

Lower bound: $\overline{d} - t_{0.025} \cdot \dfrac{s_d}{\sqrt{n}} = -1.614 - 2.447 \cdot \dfrac{1.915}{\sqrt{7}} \approx -3.385$;

Upper bound: $\overline{d} + t_{0.025} \cdot \dfrac{s_d}{\sqrt{n}} = -1.614 + 2.447 \cdot \dfrac{1.915}{\sqrt{7}} \approx 0.157$.

We can be 95% confident that the mean difference is between -3.385 and 0.157.

13. (a) These are matched-pair data because two measurements (A and B) are taken on the same round.

(b)

Obs	1	2	3	4	5	6	7	8	9	10	11	12
A	793.8	793.1	792.4	794.0	791.4	792.4	791.4	792.3	789.6	794.4	790.9	793.5
B	793.2	793.3	792.6	793.8	791.6	791.6	791.6	792.4	788.5	794.7	791.3	793.5
d_i	0.6	−0.2	−0.2	0.2	−0.2	0.8	0.1	−0.1	1.1	−0.3	−0.4	0

Using technology, $\overline{d} \approx 0.117$ feet per second and $s_d \approx 0.475$ feet per second, where we measure differences as $A - B$. The hypotheses are $H_0 : \mu_d = 0$ versus $H_1 : \mu_d \neq 0$. The level of significance is $\alpha = 0.01$. The test statistic is $t_0 = \dfrac{\overline{d}}{s_d / \sqrt{n}} = \dfrac{0.117}{0.475 / \sqrt{12}} \approx 0.853$.

<u>Classical approach</u>: Since this is a two-tailed test with 11 degrees of freedom, the critical values are $\pm t_{0.005} = \pm 3.106$. Since the test statistic $t_0 \approx 0.853$ falls between the critical values $\pm t_{0.005} = \pm 3.106$ (i.e., since the test statistic does not fall within the critical regions), we do not reject H_0.

<u>P-value approach</u>: The P-value for this two-tailed test is the area under the t-distribution with 11 degrees of freedom to the right of the test statistic $t_0 = 0.853$ plus the area to the left of $t_0 = -0.853$. From the t-distribution table in the row corresponding to 11 degrees of freedom, 0.853 falls between 0.697 and 0.876 whose right-tail areas are 0.25 and 0.20, respectively. We must double these values in order to get the total area in both tails: 0.50 and 0.40. So, $0.40 < P\text{-value} < 0.50$. (Using technology, we find P-value ≈ 0.413.) Because the P-value is greater than the level of significance $\alpha = 0.01$, we do not reject H_0.

<u>Conclusion</u>: There is not sufficient evidence at the $\alpha = 0.01$ level of significance to support the claim that there is a difference in the measurements of velocity between device A and device B.

(c) For $\alpha = 0.01$ and df = 11, $t_{\alpha/2} = t_{0.005} = 3.106$. Then:

Lower bound: $\overline{d} - t_{0.005} \cdot \dfrac{s_d}{\sqrt{n}} = 0.117 - 3.106 \cdot \dfrac{0.475}{\sqrt{12}} \approx -0.309$ feet per second;

Upper bound: $\overline{d} + t_{0.005} \cdot \dfrac{s_d}{\sqrt{n}} = 0.117 + 3.106 \cdot \dfrac{0.475}{\sqrt{12}} \approx 0.543$ feet per second.

We can be 99% confident that the population mean difference measurement is between -0.309 and 0.543 feet per second.

(d)

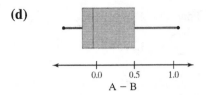

Since a difference of 0 is located in the middle 50%, the boxplot supports the conclusion found in part (b).

15. (a) Answer will vary. One possibility follows: It is important to take the measurements on the same date because the clarity of the water may be affected by the time of year.

(b)

Observation	1	2	3	4	5	6	7	8
Initial depth	38	58	65	74	56	36	56	52
Depth 5 years later	52	60	72	72	54	48	58	60
d_i = 5-year depth – Initial depth	14	2	7	–2	–2	12	2	8

Using technology, $\overline{d} = 5.125$ inches and $s_d \approx 6.081$ inches, where we measure differences as Depth 5 years later – Initial depth. The hypotheses are $H_0 : \mu_d = 0$ versus $H_1 : \mu_d > 0$. The level of significance is $\alpha = 0.05$. The test statistic is

$$t_0 = \frac{\overline{d}}{s_d / \sqrt{n}} = \frac{5.125}{6.081 / \sqrt{8}} \approx 2.384 \,.$$

Classical approach: Since this is a right-tailed test with 7 degrees of freedom, the critical value is $t_{0.05} = 1.895$. Since the test statistic $t_0 \approx 2.384$ falls to the right of the critical value $t_{0.05} = 1.895$ (i.e., since the test statistic falls within the critical region), we reject H_0.

P-value approach: The P-value for this right-tailed test is the area under the t-distribution with 7 degrees of freedom to the right of the test statistic $t_0 = 2.384$. From the t-distribution table in the row corresponding to 7 degrees of freedom, 2.384 falls between 2.365 and 2.517 whose right-tail areas are 0.025 and 0.02, respectively. So, $0.02 < P\text{-value} < 0.025$. (Using technology, we find $P\text{-value} \approx 0.024$.) Because the P-value is less than the level of significance $\alpha = 0.05$, we reject H_0.

Conclusion: There is sufficient evidence at the $\alpha = 0.05$ level of significance to support the claim that there has been improvement in the clarity of the water in the 5-year period.

(c) For $\alpha = 0.05$ and df = 7, $t_{\alpha/2} = t_{0.025} = 2.365$. Then:

Lower bound: $\overline{d} - t_{0.025} \cdot \dfrac{s_d}{\sqrt{n}} = 5.125 - 2.365 \cdot \dfrac{6.081}{\sqrt{8}} \approx 0.04$ inches;

Upper bound: $\overline{d} + t_{0.025} \cdot \dfrac{s_d}{\sqrt{n}} = 5.125 + 2.365 \cdot \dfrac{6.081}{\sqrt{8}} \approx 10.21$ inches.

We can be 95% confident that the population mean difference in clarity between the initial measurements and those taken 5 years later is between 0.04 inches and 10.21 inches.

(d)

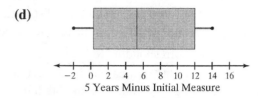

5 Years Minus Initial Measure

Since a difference of 0 does not fall in the middle 50%, the boxplot supports the conclusion found in part (b).

17.

Observation	1	2	3	4	5	6	7	8	9	10	11	12	13
Height of father	70.3	67.1	70.9	66.8	72.8	70.4	71.8	70.1	69.9	70.8	70.2	70.4	72.4
Height of son	74.1	69.2	66.9	69.2	68.9	70.2	70.4	69.3	75.8	72.3	69.2	68.6	73.9
d_i = son − father	3.8	2.1	−4.0	2.4	−3.9	−0.2	−1.4	−0.8	5.9	1.5	−1.0	−1.8	1.5

Using technology, $\bar{d} \approx 0.315$ inches and $s_d \approx 2.897$ inches, where we measure differences as son − father. The hypotheses are $H_0 : \mu_d = 0$ versus $H_1 : \mu_d > 0$. The level of

significance is $\alpha = 0.1$. The test statistic is $t_0 = \dfrac{\bar{d}}{s_d / \sqrt{n}} = \dfrac{0.315}{2.897 / \sqrt{13}} \approx 0.392$.

Classical approach: Since this is a right-tailed test with 12 degrees of freedom, the critical value is $t_{0.10} = 1.356$. Since the test statistic $t_0 \approx 0.392$ does not fall to the right of the critical value $t_{0.10} = 1.356$ (i.e., since the test statistic falls outside the critical region), we do not reject H_0.

P-value approach: The P-value for this right-tailed test is the area under the t-distribution with 12 degrees of freedom to the right of the test statistic $t_0 = 0.392$. From the t-distribution table in the row corresponding to 12 degrees of freedom, 0.392 falls to the left of 0.695, whose right-tail area is 0.25. So, P-value > 0.25. (Using technology, we find P-value ≈ 0.351.) Because the P-value is greater than the level of significance $\alpha = 0.10$, we do not reject H_0.

Conclusion: There is not sufficient evidence at the $\alpha = 0.10$ level of significance to support the researcher's claim that sons are taller than their fathers.

19.

Specimen	1	2	3	4	5	6	7	8	9
Steel ball	50	57	61	71	68	54	65	51	53
Diamond	52	56	61	74	69	55	68	51	56
d_i	2	−1	0	3	1	1	3	0	3

Using technology, $\bar{d} \approx 1.3$ and $s_d = 1.5$, where we measure differences as diamond − steel ball. The hypotheses are $H_0 : \mu_d = 0$ versus $H_1 : \mu_d \neq 0$. The level of

significance is $\alpha = 0.05$. The test statistic is $t_0 = \dfrac{\bar{d}}{s_d / \sqrt{n}} = \dfrac{1.3}{1.5 / \sqrt{9}} \approx 2.6$.

Classical approach: Since this is a two-tailed test with 8 degrees of freedom, the critical values are $\pm t_{0.025} = \pm 2.306$. Since the test statistic $t_0 \approx 2.6$ falls to the right of the critical value $t_{0.025} = 2.306$ (i.e., since the test statistic falls within the critical region), we reject H_0.

P-value approach: The *P*-value for this two-tailed test is the area under the *t*-distribution with 8 degrees of freedom to the right of the test statistic $t_0 = 2.6$ plus the area to the left of $t_0 = -2.6$. From the *t*-distribution table in the row corresponding to 8 degrees of freedom, 2.667 falls between 2.449 and 2.896 whose right-tail areas are 0.02 and 0.01, respectively. We must double these values in order to get the total area in both tails: 0.04 and 0.02. So, $0.02 < P\text{-value} < 0.04$. (Using technology, we find $P\text{-value} \approx 0.029$.) Because the *P*-value is less than the level of significance $\alpha = 0.05$, we reject H_0.

Conclusion: There sufficient evidence at the $\alpha = 0.05$ level of significance to support the manufacturer's claim that the two indenters result in different measurements.

21.

Subject	1	2	3	4	5	6	7	8	9
Normal	4.47	4.24	4.58	4.65	4.31	4.80	4.55	5.00	4.79
Impaired	5.77	5.67	5.51	5.32	5.83	5.49	5.23	5.61	5.63
d_i		1.30	1.43	0.93	0.67	1.52	0.69	0.68	0.61	0.84

Using technology, $\overline{d} \approx 0.963$ seconds and $s_d \approx 0.358$ seconds, where we measure differences as Impaired $-$ Normal. For $\alpha = 0.05$ and df $= 8$, $t_{\alpha/2} = t_{0.025} = 2.306$. Then:

Lower bound: $\overline{d} - t_{0.025} \cdot \dfrac{s_d}{\sqrt{n}} = 0.963 - 2.306 \cdot \dfrac{0.358}{\sqrt{9}} \approx 0.69$ seconds;

Upper bound: $\overline{d} + t_{0.025} \cdot \dfrac{s_d}{\sqrt{n}} = 0.963 + 2.306 \cdot \dfrac{0.358}{\sqrt{9}} \approx 1.24$ seconds.

We can be 95% confident that the population mean difference in reaction time when teenagers are driving impaired from when driving normally is between 0.69 and 1.24 seconds.

23. (a) Answers may vary. One possibility follows: Matching by both driver and car for the two different octane levels is important as a means of controlling the experiment, since both the car and the driver can potentially affect the overall mileage.

(b) Answers may vary. One possibility follows: Conducting the experiment on a closed track allows for control so that all cars and drivers can be put through the exact same conditions.

(c) No, neither variable is normally distributed. Both have at least one point outside the bounds of the normal probability plot.

(d) Yes, the differences in mileages appear to the approximately normally distributed since all of the points fall within the boundaries of the probability plot.

(e) From the MINITAB printout, $\overline{d} \approx 5.091$ miles and $s_d \approx 14.876$ miles, where the differences are 92 octane minus 87 octane. The hypotheses are $H_0 : \mu_d = 0$ versus $H_1 : \mu_d > 0$. The level of significance is $\alpha = 0.05$. The test statistic is $t_0 \approx 1.14$.

Classical approach: Since this is a right-tailed test with 10 degrees of freedom, the critical value is $t_{0.05} = 1.812$. Since the test statistic $t_0 \approx 1.14$ does not fall to the right of the critical value $t_{0.05} = 1.812$ (i.e., since the test statistic does not fall within the critical region), we fail to reject H_0.

272

P-value approach: From the MINITAB printout, we find that *P*-value ≈ 0.141. Because the *P*-value is greater than the level of significance $\alpha = 0.05$, we do not reject H_0.

Conclusion: Thus, there not sufficient evidence at the $\alpha = 0.05$ level of significance to support the claim that cars get better mileage when using 92-octain gasoline than when using 87-octane gasoline.

11.2   Inferences about Two Means: Independent Samples

1. To test a hypothesis regarding the difference of two means with unknown population standard deviations, (1) the samples must be obtained using simple random sampling, (2) the samples must be independent, and (3) the populations from which the samples are drawn must be normally distributed or the sample sizes must be large (i.e., $n_1 \geq 30$ and $n_2 \geq 30$).

3. **(a)** $H_0 : \mu_1 = \mu_2$ versus $H_1 : \mu_1 \neq \mu_2$. The level of significance is $\alpha = 0.05$. Since the sample size of both groups is 15, we use $n_1 - 1 = 14$ degrees of freedom. The test statistic is $t_0 = \dfrac{(\overline{x}_1 - \overline{x}_2) - (\mu_1 - \mu_2)}{\sqrt{\dfrac{s_1^2}{n_1} + \dfrac{s_2^2}{n_2}}} = \dfrac{(15.3 - 14.2) - 0}{\sqrt{\dfrac{3.2^2}{15} + \dfrac{3.5^2}{15}}} \approx 0.898$.

Classical approach: Since this is a two-tailed test with 14 degrees of freedom, the critical values are $\pm t_{0.025} = \pm 2.145$. Since the test statistic $t_0 \approx 0.898$ is between than the critical values $\pm t_{0.025} = \pm 2.145$ (i.e., since the test statistic does not fall within the critical region), we do not reject H_0 .

P-value approach: The *P*-value for this two-tailed test is the area under the *t*-distribution with 14 degrees of freedom to the right of $t_0 = 0.898$ plus the area to the left of -0.898. From the *t*-distribution table in the row corresponding to 14 degrees of freedom, 0.898 falls between 0.868 and 1.076 whose right-tail areas are 0.20 and 0.15, respectively. We must double these values in order to get the total area in both tails: 0.40 and 0.30. So, $0.30 < P\text{-value} < 0.40$. (Using technology, we find *P*-value = 0.3767.) Because the *P*-value is greater than the level of significance $\alpha = 0.05$, we do not reject H_0 .

Conclusion: There is not sufficient evidence at the $\alpha = 0.05$ level of significance to support the claim that the population means are different.

(b) For a 95% confidence interval with df = 14, we use $t_{\alpha/2} = t_{0.025} = 1.761$. Then:

Lower bound:

$$(\overline{x}_1 - \overline{x}_2) - t_{\alpha/2} \cdot \sqrt{\frac{s_1^2}{n_1} + \frac{s_2^2}{n_2}} = (15.3 - 14.2) - 2.145 \cdot \sqrt{\frac{3.2^2}{15} + \frac{3.5^2}{15}} \approx 1.1 - 2.63 = -1.53 ;$$

Upper bound:

$$(\overline{x}_1 - \overline{x}_2) + t_{\alpha/2} \cdot \sqrt{\frac{s_1^2}{n_1} + \frac{s_2^2}{n_2}} = (15.3 - 14.2) + 2.145 \cdot \sqrt{\frac{3.2^2}{15} + \frac{3.5^2}{15}} \approx 1.1 + 2.63 = 3.73 .$$

We can be 95% confident that the mean difference is between -1.53 and 3.73.

5. (a) $H_0 : \mu_1 = \mu_2$ versus $H_1 : \mu_1 > \mu_2$. The level of significance is $\alpha = 0.10$. Since the smaller sample size is $n_2 = 18$, we use $n_2 - 1 = 18 - 1 = 17$ degrees of freedom. The test statistic is $t_0 = \dfrac{(\bar{x}_1 - \bar{x}_2) - (\mu_1 - \mu_2)}{\sqrt{\dfrac{s_1^2}{n_1} + \dfrac{s_2^2}{n_2}}} = \dfrac{(50.2 - 42.0) - 0}{\sqrt{\dfrac{6.4^2}{25} + \dfrac{9.9^2}{18}}} \approx 3.081$.

Classical approach: Since this is a right-tailed test with 17 degrees of freedom, the critical value is $t_{0.10} = 1.333$. Since the test statistic $t_0 \approx 3.081$ is to the right of the critical value (i.e., since the test statistic falls within the critical region), we reject H_0.

P-value approach: The P-value for this right-tailed test is the area under the t-distribution with 17 degrees of freedom to the right of $t_0 = 3.081$. From the t-distribution table in the row corresponding to 17 degrees of freedom, 3.081 falls between 2.898 and 3.222 whose right-tail areas are 0.005 and 0.0025, respectively. Thus, $0.0025 < P$-value < 0.005. (Using technology, we find P-value = 0.0024.) Because the P-value is less than the level of significance $\alpha = 0.10$, we reject H_0.

Conclusion: There is sufficient evidence at the $\alpha = 0.01$ level of significance to support the claim that $\mu_1 > \mu_2$.

(b) For a 90% confidence interval with df = 17, we use $t_{\alpha/2} = t_{0.05} = 1.740$. Then:

Lower bound:

$$(\bar{x}_1 - \bar{x}_2) - t_{\alpha/2} \cdot \sqrt{\dfrac{s_1^2}{n_1} + \dfrac{s_2^2}{n_2}} = (50.2 - 42.0) - 1.740 \cdot \sqrt{\dfrac{6.4^2}{25} + \dfrac{9.9^2}{18}} \approx 8.2 - 4.63 = 3.57;$$

Upper bound:

$$(\bar{x}_1 - \bar{x}_2) + t_{\alpha/2} \cdot \sqrt{\dfrac{s_1^2}{n_1} + \dfrac{s_2^2}{n_2}} = (50.2 - 42.0) + 1.740 \cdot \sqrt{\dfrac{6.4^2}{25} + \dfrac{9.9^2}{18}} \approx 8.2 + 4.63 = 12.83.$$

We can be 90% confident that the mean difference is between 3.57 and 12.83.

7. (a) $H_0 : \mu_1 = \mu_2$ versus $H_1 : \mu_1 < \mu_2$. The level of significance is $\alpha = 0.02$. Since the smaller sample size is $n_2 = 25$, we use $n_2 - 1 = 25 - 1 = 24$ degrees of freedom. The test statistic is $t_0 = \dfrac{(\bar{x}_1 - \bar{x}_2) - (\mu_1 - \mu_2)}{\sqrt{\dfrac{s_1^2}{n_1} + \dfrac{s_2^2}{n_2}}} = \dfrac{(103.4 - 114.2) - 0}{\sqrt{\dfrac{12.3^2}{32} + \dfrac{13.2^2}{25}}} \approx -3.158$.

Classical approach: Since this is a left-tailed test with 24 degrees of freedom, the critical value is $-t_{0.02} = -2.172$. Since the test statistic $t_0 \approx -3.158$ is to the left of the critical value (i.e., since the test statistic falls within the critical region), we reject H_0.

P-value approach: The P-value for this left-tailed test is the area under the t-distribution with 24 degrees of freedom to the left of $t_0 \approx -3.158$, which is equivalent to the area to the right of $t_0 \approx 3.158$. From the t-distribution table in the row corresponding to 24 degrees of freedom, 3.158 falls between 3.091 and 3.467 whose right-tail area is are 0.0025 and 0.001 Thus, $0.001 < P\text{-value} < 0.0025$. (Using technology, we find $P\text{-value} = 0.0013$.) Because the P-value is less than the level of significance $\alpha = 0.02$, we reject H_0.

Conclusion: There is sufficient evidence at the $\alpha = 0.02$ level of significance to support the claim that $\mu_1 < \mu_2$.

(b) For a 90% confidence interval with df = 24, we use $t_{\alpha/2} = t_{0.05} = 1.711$. Then:

Lower bound: $(\bar{x}_1 - \bar{x}_2) - t_{\alpha/2} \cdot \sqrt{\dfrac{s_1^2}{n_1} + \dfrac{s_2^2}{n_2}} = (103.4 - 114.2) - 1.711 \cdot \sqrt{\dfrac{12.3^2}{32} + \dfrac{13.2^2}{25}}$

$$\approx -10.8 - 5.85 = -16.65;$$

Upper bound: $(\bar{x}_1 - \bar{x}_2) + t_{\alpha/2} \cdot \sqrt{\dfrac{s_1^2}{n_1} + \dfrac{s_2^2}{n_2}} = (103.4 - 114.2) + 1.711 \cdot \sqrt{\dfrac{12.3^2}{32} + \dfrac{13.2^2}{25}}$

$$\approx -10.8 + 5.85 = -4.95.$$

We can be 90% confident that the mean difference is between -16.65 and -4.95.

9. (a) $H_0 : \mu_1 = \mu_2$ versus $H_1 : \mu_1 > \mu_2$. The level of significance is $\alpha = 0.01$. Since the smaller sample size is $n_1 = 55$, we use $n_1 - 1 = 55 - 1 = 54$ degrees of freedom. The test statistic is $t_0 = \dfrac{(\bar{x}_1 - \bar{x}_2) - (\mu_1 - \mu_2)}{\sqrt{\dfrac{s_1^2}{n_1} + \dfrac{s_2^2}{n_2}}} = \dfrac{(14.8 - 8.1) - 0}{\sqrt{\dfrac{12.5^2}{55} + \dfrac{12.7^2}{60}}} \approx 2.849$.

Classical approach: This is a right-tailed test with 54 degrees of freedom. However, since our t-distribution table does not contain a row for 54, we use df = 50. Thus, the critical value is $t_{0.01} = 2.403$. Since the test statistic $t_0 \approx 2.849$ is to the right of the critical value (i.e., since the test statistic falls within the critical region), we reject H_0.

P-value approach: The P-value for this right-tailed test is the area under the t-distribution with 54 degrees of freedom to the right of $t_0 = 2.849$. From the t-distribution table in the row corresponding to 50 degrees of freedom (since the table does not contain a row for df = 54), 2.849 falls between 2.678 and 2.937 whose right-tail areas are 0.005 and 0.0025, respectively. Thus, $0.0025 < P\text{-value} < 0.005$. (Using technology, we find $P\text{-value} = 0.0026$.) Because the P-value is less than the level of significance $\alpha = 0.01$, we reject H_0.

Conclusion: There is sufficient evidence at the $\alpha = 0.01$ level of significance to support the claim that the mean improvement in the treatment group was greater than the mean improvement in the control group. The drug appears to be effective in improving the Young-Mania Rating Scale score.

(b) For a 95% confidence interval with df = 50 (since there is no row for 54), we use $t_{\alpha/2} = t_{0.025} = 2.009$. Then:

Lower bound: $(\bar{x}_1 - \bar{x}_2) - t_{\alpha/2} \cdot \sqrt{\dfrac{s_1^2}{n_1} + \dfrac{s_2^2}{n_2}} = (14.8 - 8.1) - 2.009 \cdot \sqrt{\dfrac{12.5^2}{55} + \dfrac{12.7^2}{60}}$

$$\approx 6.7 - 4.72 = 1.98 \text{ points};$$

Upper bound: $(\bar{x}_1 - \bar{x}_2) + t_{\alpha/2} \cdot \sqrt{\dfrac{s_1^2}{n_1} + \dfrac{s_2^2}{n_2}} = (14.8 - 8.1) + 2.009 \cdot \sqrt{\dfrac{12.5^2}{55} + \dfrac{12.7^2}{60}}$

$$\approx 6.7 + 4.72 = 11.42 \text{ points.}$$

Researchers are 95% confident that the mean Young-Mania Rating Scale score for the treatment group is between 1.98 and 11.42 points higher than that of the control group.

11. (a) This is an observational study, since no treatment is imposed.

   (b) Answer will vary. One possibility follows: Though we do not know if the population is normally distributed, the sample sizes are sufficiently large ($n_{\text{arrival}} = n_{\text{departure}} = 35$).

   (c) $H_0 : \mu_{\text{arrival}} = \mu_{\text{departure}}$ versus $H_1 : \mu_{\text{arrival}} \neq \mu_{\text{departure}}$. The level of significance is $\alpha = 0.05$. Since the sample size of both groups is 35, we use $n_{\text{arrival}} - 1 = 34$ degrees of freedom. The test statistic is $t_0 = \dfrac{(\bar{x}_{\text{arr}} - \bar{x}_{\text{dep}}) - (\mu_{\text{arr}} - \mu_{\text{dep}})}{\sqrt{\dfrac{s_{\text{arr}}^2}{n_{\text{arr}}} + \dfrac{s_{\text{dep}}^2}{n_{\text{dep}}}}} = \dfrac{(269 - 260) - 0}{\sqrt{\dfrac{53^2}{35} + \dfrac{34^2}{35}}} \approx 0.846$.

   Classical approach: Since this is a two-tailed test with 34 degrees of freedom, the critical values are $\pm t_{0.025} = \pm 2.032$. Since the test statistic $t_0 \approx 0.846$ is between the critical values (i.e., since the test statistic does not fall within the critical regions), we do not reject H_0.

   P-value approach: The P-value for this two-tailed test is the area under the t-distribution with 34 degrees of freedom to the right of $t_0 \approx 0.846$ plus the area to the left of $t_0 \approx -0.846$. From the t-distribution table in the row corresponding to 34 degrees of freedom, 0.846 falls between 0.682 and 0.852 whose right-tail areas are 0.25 and 0.20, respectively. We must double these values in order to get the total area in both tails: 0.50 and 0.40. So, $0.40 < P\text{-value} < 0.50$. (Using technology, we find P-value = 0.4013.) Since the P-value is greater than the level of significance $\alpha = 0.05$, we do not reject H_0.

   Conclusion: There is not sufficient evidence at the $\alpha = 0.05$ level of significance to support the researcher's claim that travelers walk at different speeds depending on whether they are arriving or departing an airport.

   (d) For a 95% confidence interval with df = 34, we use $t_{\alpha/2} = t_{0.025} = 2.032$. Then:

   Lower bound: $(\bar{x}_{\text{arr}} - \bar{x}_{\text{dep}}) - t_{\alpha/2} \cdot \sqrt{\dfrac{s_{\text{arr}}^2}{n_{\text{arr}}} + \dfrac{s_{\text{dep}}^2}{n_{\text{dep}}}} = (269 - 260) - 2.032 \cdot \sqrt{\dfrac{53^2}{35} + \dfrac{34^2}{35}}$

   $$\approx 9 - 21.63 = -12.63 \text{ ft/min;}$$

   Upper bound: $(\bar{x}_{\text{arr}} - \bar{x}_{\text{dep}}) + t_{\alpha/2} \cdot \sqrt{\dfrac{s_{\text{arr}}^2}{n_{\text{arr}}} + \dfrac{s_{\text{dep}}^2}{n_{\text{dep}}}} = (269 - 260) + 2.032 \cdot \sqrt{\dfrac{53^2}{35} + \dfrac{34^2}{35}}$

   $$\approx 9 + 21.63 = 30.63 \text{ ft/min.}$$

   We can be 95% confident that the mean difference in walking speed between passengers arriving and departing an airport is between -12.63 and 30.63 feet per minute.

13. (a) Yes, Welch's t-test can be used. We can treat each sample as a simple random sample of all mixtures of each type. The samples were obtained independently. We are told that a normal probability plot indicates that the data could come from a population that is normal, with no outliers.

(b) $H_0 : \mu_{67-0-301} = \mu_{67-0-400}$ versus $H_1 : \mu_{67-0-301} < \mu_{67-0-400}$. The level of significance is $\alpha = 0.05$. Using technology, the summary statistics are $\overline{x}_{67-0-301} \approx 3669$, $s_{67-0-301} \approx 459$, and $n_{67-0-301} = 9$, and $\overline{x}_{67-0-400} = 4483$, $s_{67-0-400} \approx 474$, and $n_{67-0-400} = 10$. Since the smaller sample size is $n_{67-0-301} = 9$, we use $n_{67-0-301} - 1 = 8$ degrees of freedom. The critical t-value is $t_{0.05} = 1.860$. The test statistic is

$$t_0 = \frac{(\overline{x}_{67-0-301} - \overline{x}_{67-0-400}) - (\mu_{67-0-301} - \mu_{67-0-400})}{\sqrt{\dfrac{s_{67-0-301}^2}{n_{67-0-301}} + \dfrac{s_{67-0-400}^2}{n_{67-0-400}}}} = \frac{(3669 - 4483) - 0}{\sqrt{\dfrac{459^2}{9} + \dfrac{474^2}{10}}} \approx -3.800.$$

Classical approach: Since this is a left-tailed test with 8 degrees of freedom, the critical value is $-t_{0.05} = -1.860$. Since the test statistic $t_0 \approx -3.800$ is to the left of the critical value (i.e., since the test statistic falls within the critical region), we reject H_0.

P-value approach: The P-value for this left-tailed test is the area under the t-distribution with 8 degrees of freedom to the left of $-t_0 = -3.800$, which is equivalent to the area to the right of $t_0 = 3.800$. From the t-distribution table in the row corresponding to 8 degrees of freedom, 3.800 falls between 3.355 and 3.833 whose right-tail areas are 0.005 and 0.0025, respectively. Thus, $0.0025 < P\text{-value} < 0.005$. (Using technology, we find P-value $= 0.0007$.) Because the P-value is less than the level of significance $\alpha = 0.05$, we reject H_0.

Conclusion: There is sufficient evidence at the $\alpha = 0.05$ level of significance to support the engineer's claim that mixture 67-0-400 is stronger than mixture 67-0-301.

(c) For a 90% confidence interval with df = 8, we use $t_{\alpha/2} = t_{0.05} = 1.860$. Then:

Lower bound:

$$(\overline{x}_{67-0-301} - \overline{x}_{67-0-400}) - t_{\alpha/2} \cdot \sqrt{\frac{s_{67-0-301}^2}{n_{67-0-301}} + \frac{s_{67-0-400}^2}{n_{67-0-400}}} = (3669 - 4483) - 1.860 \cdot \sqrt{\frac{459^2}{9} + \frac{474^2}{10}}$$

$$\approx -814 - 398 = -1212 \text{ psi};$$

Upper bound:

$$(\overline{x}_{67-0-301} - \overline{x}_{67-0-400}) + t_{\alpha/2} \cdot \sqrt{\frac{s_{67-0-301}^2}{n_{67-0-301}} + \frac{s_{67-0-400}^2}{n_{67-0-400}}} = (3669 - 4483) + 1.860 \cdot \sqrt{\frac{459^2}{9} + \frac{474^2}{10}}$$

$$\approx -814 + 398 = -416 \text{ psi.}$$

We can be 90% confident that the mean strength of mixture 67-0-301 is between 416 and 1212 pounds per square inch weaker than the mean strength of mixture 67-0-400. Equivalently, we can be 90% confident that the mean strength of mixture 67-0-400 is between 416 and 1212 pounds per square inch stronger than the mean strength of mixture 67-0-301.

(d)   Yes, the boxplots support the results from part (b). From the boxplot, mixture 67-0-400 clearly appears to be stronger than mixture 67-0-301.

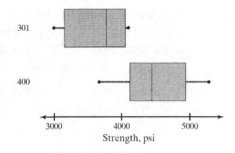

15. (a) $H_0 : \mu_{\text{carpeted}} = \mu_{\text{uncarpeted}}$ versus $H_1 : \mu_{\text{carpeted}} > \mu_{\text{uncarpeted}}$. The level of significance is $\alpha = 0.05$. Using technology, the summary statistics are $\bar{x}_1 = 11.2$, $s_1 \approx 2.68$, and $n_1 = 8$ and $\bar{x}_2 \approx 9.79$, $s_2 \approx 3.21$, and $n_2 = 8$. Since the sample size of both groups is 8, we use $n_{\text{carpeted}} - 1 = 7$ degrees of freedom. The test statistic is

$$t_0 = \frac{(\bar{x}_{\text{carpeted}} - \bar{x}_{\text{uncarpeted}}) - (\mu_{\text{carpeted}} - \mu_{\text{uncarpeted}})}{\sqrt{\dfrac{s_{\text{carpeted}}^2}{n_{\text{carpeted}}} + \dfrac{s_{\text{uncarpeted}}^2}{n_{\text{uncarpeted}}}}} = \frac{(11.2 - 9.79) - 0}{\sqrt{\dfrac{2.68^2}{8} + \dfrac{3.21^2}{8}}} \approx 0.954 .$$

Classical approach: Since this is a right-tailed test with 7 degrees of freedom, the critical value is $t_{0.05} = 1.895$. Since the test statistic $t_0 \approx 0.954$ is not to the right of the critical value (i.e., since the test statistic does not fall within the critical region), we do not reject H_0.

P-value approach: The P-value for this right-tailed test is the area under the t-distribution with 7 degrees of freedom to the right of $t_0 \approx 0.954$. From the t-distribution table in the row corresponding to 7 degrees of freedom, 0.954 falls between 0.896 and 1.119 whose right-tail areas are 0.20 and 0.15, respectively. So, $0.15 < P\text{-value} < 0.20$. (Using technology, we find P-value = 0.1780.) Since the P-value is greater than the level of significance $\alpha = 0.05$, we do not reject H_0.

Conclusion: There is not sufficient evidence at the $\alpha = 0.05$ level of significance to support the claim that carpeted rooms have more bacteria than uncarpeted rooms.

(b) For a 95% confidence interval with df = 7, we use $t_{\alpha/2} = t_{0.025} = 2.365$. Then: Lower bound:

$$(\bar{x}_{\text{carpeted}} - \bar{x}_{\text{uncarpeted}}) - t_{\alpha/2} \cdot \sqrt{\dfrac{s_{\text{carpeted}}^2}{n_{\text{carpeted}}} + \dfrac{s_{\text{uncarpeted}}^2}{n_{\text{uncarpeted}}}} = (11.2 - 9.79) - 2.365 \cdot \sqrt{\dfrac{2.68^2}{8} + \dfrac{3.21^2}{8}}$$

$$\approx 1.41 - 3.50 = -2.09 \text{ bacteria/cubic foot;}$$

Upper bound:

$$(\bar{x}_{\text{carpeted}} - \bar{x}_{\text{uncarpeted}}) + t_{\alpha/2} \cdot \sqrt{\dfrac{s_{\text{carpeted}}^2}{n_{\text{carpeted}}} + \dfrac{s_{\text{uncarpeted}}^2}{n_{\text{uncarpeted}}}} = (11.2 - 9.79) + 2.365 \cdot \sqrt{\dfrac{2.68^2}{8} + \dfrac{3.21^2}{8}}$$

$$\approx 1.41 + 3.50 = 4.91 \text{ bacteria/cubic foot.}$$

We are 95% confident that the true mean difference in the number of bacteria in per cubic foot is between –2.08 and 4.90.

17. Since both sample sizes are sufficiently large ($n_{AL} = n_{NL} = 30$), so we can use Welch's t-test. The hypotheses are $H_0: \mu_{AL} = \mu_{NL}$ versus $H_1: \mu_{AL} > \mu_{NL}$. The level of significance is $\alpha = 0.05$. We are given the summary statistics $\bar{x}_{AL} = 6.0$ and $s_{AL} = 3.5$, $\bar{x}_{NL} = 4.3$, and $s_{NL} = 2.6$. Since the sample size of both groups is 30, we use $n_{AL} - 1 = 29$ degrees of

freedom. The test statistic is $t_0 = \dfrac{(\bar{x}_{AL} - \bar{x}_{NL}) - (\mu_{AL} - \mu_{NL})}{\sqrt{\dfrac{s_{AL}^2}{n_{AL}} + \dfrac{s_{NL}^2}{n_{NL}}}} = \dfrac{(6.0 - 4.3) - 0}{\sqrt{\dfrac{3.5^2}{30} + \dfrac{2.6^2}{30}}} \approx 2.136$.

Classical approach: Since this is a right-tailed test with 29 degrees of freedom, the critical value is $t_{0.025} = 2.045$. Since the test statistic $t_0 \approx 2.136$ falls to the right of the critical value 2.045 (i.e., since the test statistic falls within the critical region), we reject H_0.

P-value approach: The P-value for this right-tailed test is the area under the t-distribution with 29 degrees of freedom to the right of $t_0 \approx 2.136$. From the t-distribution table in the row corresponding to 29 degrees of freedom, 2.136 falls between 2.045 and 2.150 whose right-tail areas are 0.025 and 0.02, respectively. So, $0.02 < P\text{-value} < 0.025$. (Using technology, we find $P\text{-value} = 0.0187$.) Since the P-value is less than the level of significance $\alpha = 0.05$, we reject H_0.

Conclusion: There is sufficient evidence at the $\alpha = 0.05$ level of significance to support the claim that games played with a designated hitter result in more runs.

19. For this 90% confidence level with $df = 40 - 1 = 39$, we use $t_{\alpha/2} = t_{0.05} = 1.685$. Then:
Lower bound:

$$(\bar{x}_{\text{no children}} - \bar{x}_{\text{children}}) - t_{\alpha/2} \cdot \sqrt{\dfrac{s_{\text{no children}}^2}{n_{\text{no children}}} + \dfrac{s_{\text{children}}^2}{n_{\text{children}}}} = (5.62 - 4.10) - 1.685 \cdot \sqrt{\dfrac{2.43^2}{40} + \dfrac{1.82^2}{40}}$$

$$\approx 1.52 - 0.81 = 0.71 \text{ hour;}$$

Upper bound:

$$(\bar{x}_{\text{no children}} - \bar{x}_{\text{children}}) + t_{\alpha/2} \cdot \sqrt{\dfrac{s_{\text{no children}}^2}{n_{\text{no children}}} + \dfrac{s_{\text{children}}^2}{n_{\text{children}}}} = (5.62 - 4.10) + 1.685 \cdot \sqrt{\dfrac{2.43^2}{40} + \dfrac{1.82^2}{40}}$$

$$\approx 1.52 + 0.81 = 2.33 \text{ hours.}$$

We can be 90% confident that the mean difference in daily leisure time between adults without children and those with children is between 0.71 and 2.33 hours. Since the confidence interval does not include zero, we can conclude that there is a significance difference in the leisure time of adults without children and those with children.

21. **(a)** The hypotheses are $H_0: \mu_{\text{men}} = \mu_{\text{women}}$ versus $H_1: \mu_{\text{men}} < \mu_{\text{women}}$.

(b) From the MINITAB printout, $P\text{-value} = 0.0051$. Because the P-value is less than the level of significance $\alpha = 0.01$, the researcher will reject H_0. Thus, there is sufficient evidence at the $\alpha = 0.01$ level of significance to support the claim that the mean step pulse of men is lower than the mean step pulse of women.

(c) From the MINITAB printout, the 95% confidence interval is $(-10.7, -1.5)$. We can be 95% confident that the mean step pulse of men is between 1.5 and 10.7 beats per minute lower than the mean step pulse of women

11.3 Inference about Two Population Proportions

1. Under the null hypothesis, $p_1 = p_2$ and we should use the best estimate of this common value, which is obtained by pooling the data from both samples. However, when finding a confidence interval, the sample proportions are not pooled because no assumption about their equality is made.

3. (a) The hypotheses are $H_0 : p_1 = p_2$ versus $H_1 : p_1 > p_2$.

(b) The two sample estimates are $\hat{p}_1 = \dfrac{x_1}{n_1} = \dfrac{368}{541} \approx 0.680$ and $\hat{p}_2 = \dfrac{x_2}{n_2} = \dfrac{351}{593} \approx 0.592$. The

pooled estimate is $\hat{p} = \dfrac{x_1 + x_2}{n_1 + n_2} = \dfrac{368 + 351}{541 + 593} \approx 0.634$. The test statistic is

$$z_0 = \frac{\hat{p}_1 - \hat{p}_2}{\sqrt{\hat{p}(1-\hat{p})}\sqrt{1/n_1 + 1/n_2}} = \frac{0.680 - 0.592}{\sqrt{0.634(1-0.634)}\sqrt{1/541 + 1/593}} \approx 3.07 \,.$$

(c) This is a right-tailed test, so the critical value is $z_\alpha = z_{0.05} = 1.645$. Since the test statistic is in the critical region, we reject H_0. There is sufficient evidence to support the claim that $p_1 > p_2$.

(d) P-value $= P(z_0 \geq 3.07) = 1 - 0.9989 = 0.0011$. Since the P-value is less than $\alpha = 0.05$, we reject H_0. There is sufficient evidence to support the claim that $p_1 > p_2$.

5. (a) The hypotheses are $H_0 : p_1 = p_2$ versus $H_1 : p_1 \neq p_2$.

(b) The two sample estimates are $\hat{p}_1 = \dfrac{x_1}{n_1} = \dfrac{28}{254} \approx 0.110$ and $\hat{p}_2 = \dfrac{x_2}{n_2} = \dfrac{36}{301} \approx 0.120$. The

pooled estimate is $\hat{p} = \dfrac{x_1 + x_2}{n_1 + n_2} = \dfrac{28 + 36}{254 + 301} \approx 0.115$. The test statistic is

$$z_0 = \frac{\hat{p}_1 - \hat{p}_2}{\sqrt{\hat{p}(1-\hat{p})}\sqrt{1/n_1 + 1/n_2}} = \frac{0.110 - 0.120}{\sqrt{0.115(1-0.115)}\sqrt{1/254 + 1/301}} \approx -0.37 \,.$$

(c) This is a two-tailed test, so the critical values are $\pm z_{0.025} = \pm 1.96$. Since the test statistic is not in the critical region, we do not reject H_0. There is not sufficient evidence to support the claim that $p_1 \neq p_2$.

(d) P-value $= 2 \cdot P(z_0 \leq -0.37) = 2 \cdot 0.3557 = 0.7114$. Since the P-value is larger than $\alpha = 0.05$, we do not reject H_0. There is not sufficient evidence to support the claim that $p_1 \neq p_2$.

7. We have $\hat{p}_1 = \dfrac{x_1}{n_1} = \dfrac{368}{541} \approx 0.680$ and $\hat{p}_2 = \dfrac{x_2}{n_2} = \dfrac{421}{593} \approx 0.710$. For a 90% confidence level, we

use $\pm z_{0.05} = \pm 1.645$. Then:

Lower Bound: $(\hat{p}_1 - \hat{p}_2) - z_{\alpha/2} \cdot \sqrt{\dfrac{\hat{p}_1(1-\hat{p}_1)}{n_1} + \dfrac{\hat{p}_2(1-\hat{p}_2)}{n_2}}$

$$= (0.680 - 0.710) - 1.645 \cdot \sqrt{\dfrac{0.680(1-0.680)}{541} + \dfrac{0.710(1-0.710)}{593}}$$

$$\approx -0.030 - 0.045 = -0.075$$

Upper Bound: $(\hat{p}_1 - \hat{p}_2) + z_{\alpha/2} \cdot \sqrt{\dfrac{\hat{p}_1(1-\hat{p}_1)}{n_1} + \dfrac{\hat{p}_2(1-\hat{p}_2)}{n_2}}$

$$= (0.680 - 0.710) + 1.645 \cdot \sqrt{\dfrac{0.680(1-0.680)}{541} + \dfrac{0.710(1-0.710)}{593}}$$

$$\approx -0.030 + 0.045 = 0.015$$

9. We have $\hat{p}_1 = \dfrac{x_1}{n_1} = \dfrac{28}{254} \approx 0.110$ and $\hat{p}_2 = \dfrac{x_2}{n_2} = \dfrac{36}{301} \approx 0.120$. For a 95% confidence interval

we use $\pm z_{0.025} = \pm 1.96$. Then:

Lower Bound: $(\hat{p}_1 - \hat{p}_2) - z_{\alpha/2} \cdot \sqrt{\dfrac{\hat{p}_1(1-\hat{p}_1)}{n_1} + \dfrac{\hat{p}_2(1-\hat{p}_2)}{n_2}}$

$$= (0.110 - 0.120) - 1.96 \cdot \sqrt{\dfrac{0.110(1-0.110)}{254} + \dfrac{0.120(1-0.120)}{301}}$$

$$\approx -0.010 - 0.053 = -0.063$$

Upper Bound: $(\hat{p}_1 - \hat{p}_2) + z_{\alpha/2} \cdot \sqrt{\dfrac{\hat{p}_1(1-\hat{p}_1)}{n_1} + \dfrac{\hat{p}_2(1-\hat{p}_2)}{n_2}}$

$$= (0.110 - 0.120) + 1.96 \cdot \sqrt{\dfrac{0.110(1-0.110)}{254} + \dfrac{0.120(1-0.120)}{301}}$$

$$\approx -0.010 + 0.053 = 0.043$$

11. (a) We first verify the requirements to perform the hypothesis test: (1) Each sample can be thought of as a simple random sample; (2) We have $x_1 = 107$, $n_1 = 710$, $x_2 = 67$, and

$n_2 = 611$, so $\hat{p}_1 = \dfrac{x_1}{n_1} = \dfrac{107}{710} \approx 0.151$ and $\hat{p}_2 = \dfrac{x_2}{n_2} = \dfrac{67}{611} \approx 0.110$. Thus, $n_1 \hat{p}_1(1-\hat{p}_1) =$

$710(0.151)(1-0.151) \approx 91.0 \geq 10$ and $n_2 \hat{p}_2(1-\hat{p}_2) = 611(0.110)(1-0.110) \approx 59.8 \geq 10$;

and (3) Each sample is less than 5% of the population. Thus, the requirements are met, and we can conduct the test. The hypotheses are $H_0 : p_1 = p_2$ versus $H_1 : p_1 > p_2$. From before, the two sample estimates are $\hat{p}_1 \approx 0.151$ and $\hat{p}_2 \approx 0.110$. The pooled estimate is

$$\hat{p} = \frac{x_1 + x_2}{n_1 + n_2} = \frac{107 + 67}{710 + 611} \approx 0.132. \text{ The test statistic is}$$

$$z_0 = \frac{\hat{p}_1 - \hat{p}_2}{\sqrt{\hat{p}(1-\hat{p})}\sqrt{1/n_1 + 1/n_2}} = \frac{0.151 - 0.110}{\sqrt{0.132(1-0.132)}\sqrt{1/710 + 1/611}} \approx 2.20.$$

Classical approach: This is a right-tailed test, so the critical value is $z_\alpha = z_{0.05} = 1.645$. Since the test statistic falls in the critical region, we reject H_0.

P-value approach: P-value $= P(z_0 \geq 2.20) = 1 - 0.9861 = 0.0139$. Since this P-value is less than the $\alpha = 0.05$ level of significance, we reject H_0.

Conclusion: There is sufficient evidence at the $\alpha = 0.05$ level of significance to support the claim that a higher percentage of subjects in the treatment group (taking Prevnar) experienced fever as a side effect than in the control group.

(b) For a 90% confidence interval we use $\pm z_{0.05} = \pm 1.645$. Then:

Lower bound: $(\hat{p}_1 - \hat{p}_2) - z_{\alpha/2} \cdot \sqrt{\dfrac{\hat{p}_1(1-\hat{p}_1)}{n_1} + \dfrac{\hat{p}_2(1-\hat{p}_2)}{n_2}}$

$$= (0.151 - 0.110) - 1.645 \cdot \sqrt{\frac{0.151(1-0.151)}{710} + \frac{0.110(1-0.110)}{611}}$$

$$\approx 0.041 - 0.030 = 0.011$$

Upper bound: $(\hat{p}_1 - \hat{p}_2) + z_{\alpha/2} \cdot \sqrt{\dfrac{\hat{p}_1(1-\hat{p}_1)}{n_1} + \dfrac{\hat{p}_2(1-\hat{p}_2)}{n_2}}$

$$= (0.151 - 0.110) + 1.645 \cdot \sqrt{\frac{0.151(1-0.151)}{710} + \frac{0.110(1-0.110)}{611}}$$

$$\approx 0.041 + 0.030 = 0.071$$

We can be 90% confident that the difference in the proportion of subjects who experience a fever as a side effect between the experimental and control groups is between 0.011 and 0.071.

13. (a) We first verify the requirements to perform the hypothesis test: (1) Each sample can be thought of as a simple random sample; (2) we have $x_8 = 114$, $n_8 = 320$, $x_c = 112$, and $n_c = 350$, so $\hat{p}_8 = \dfrac{x_8}{n_8} = \dfrac{114}{320} \approx 0.356$ and $\hat{p}_c = \dfrac{x_c}{n_c} = \dfrac{112}{350} = 0.320$. Thus, $n_8 \hat{p}_8 (1 - \hat{p}_8) = 320(0.356)(1-0.356) \approx 73.4 \geq 10$ and $n_c \hat{p}_c (1 - \hat{p}_c) = 350(0.32)(1-0.32) \approx 76.2 \geq 10$; and (3) each sample is less than 5% of the population. Thus, the requirements are met, so we can conduct the test. The hypotheses are $H_0: p_8 = p_c$ versus $H_1: p_8 > p_c$. From before, the two sample estimates are $\hat{p}_8 \approx 0.356$ and $\hat{p}_c = 0.320$. The pooled estimate is $\hat{p} = \dfrac{x_8 + x_c}{n_8 + n_c} = \dfrac{114 + 112}{320 + 350} \approx 0.337$. The test statistic is

$$z_0 = \frac{\hat{p}_8 - \hat{p}_c}{\sqrt{\hat{p}(1-\hat{p})}\sqrt{1/n_8 + 1/n_c}} = \frac{0.356 - 0.320}{\sqrt{0.337(1-0.337)}\sqrt{1/320 + 1/350}} \approx 0.98.$$

Classical approach: This is a right-tailed test, so the critical value is $z_\alpha = z_{0.10} = 1.28$. Since the test statistic does not fall in the critical region, we do not reject H_0.

P-value approach: P-value $= P(z_0 \geq 0.98) = 1 - 0.8365 = 0.1635$. Since this P-value is greater than the $\alpha = 0.10$ level of significance, we do not reject H_0.

Conclusion: There is not sufficient evidence at the $\alpha = 0.10$ level of significance to support the claim that a higher proportion of individuals with at most an eighth-grade education consume too much cholesterol than of those with some college education.

(b) For a 95% confidence interval we use $\pm z_{0.025} = \pm 1.96$. Then:

Lower bound: $(\hat{p}_8 - \hat{p}_c) - z_{\alpha/2} \cdot \sqrt{\dfrac{\hat{p}_8(1-\hat{p}_8)}{n_8} + \dfrac{\hat{p}_c(1-\hat{p}_c)}{n_c}}$

$$= (0.356 - 0.320) - 1.96 \cdot \sqrt{\frac{0.356(1-0.356)}{320} + \frac{0.320(1-0.320)}{350}}$$

$$\approx 0.036 - 0.072 = -0.036$$

Upper bound: $(\hat{p}_8 - \hat{p}_c) + z_{\alpha/2} \cdot \sqrt{\dfrac{\hat{p}_8(1-\hat{p}_8)}{n_8} + \dfrac{\hat{p}_c(1-\hat{p}_c)}{n_c}}$

$$= (0.356 - 0.320) + 1.96 \cdot \sqrt{\frac{0.356(1-0.356)}{320} + \frac{0.320(1-0.320)}{350}}$$

$$\approx 0.036 + 0.072 = 0.108$$

We can be 95% confident that the difference in the proportion of individuals with at most an eighth-grade education and individuals with some college education who consume too much cholesterol is between −0.036 and 0.108.

15. Yes. Based on the following hypothesis test using a $\alpha = 0.01$ level of significance, we can say that the proportion of American adults who smoked at least one cigarette in the past week has decreased since 1990.

We first verify the requirements to perform the hypothesis test: (1) Each sample can be thought of as a simple random sample; (2) we have $x_{2005} = 226$, $n_{2005} = 1028$, $x_{1990} = 278$, and $n_{1990} = 278$, so $\hat{p}_{2005} = \dfrac{x_{2005}}{n_{2005}} = \dfrac{226}{1028} \approx 0.220$ and $\hat{p}_{1990} = \dfrac{x_{1990}}{n_{1990}} = \dfrac{278}{1028} \approx 0.270$. Thus,

$n_{2005}\hat{p}_{2005}(1-\hat{p}_{2005}) = 1028(0.220)(1-0.220) \approx 176.4 \geq 10$ and $n_{1990}\hat{p}_{1990}(1-\hat{p}_{1990}) = 1028(0.270)(1-0.270) \approx 202.6 \geq 10$; and (3) each sample is less than 5% of the population.

Thus, the requirements are met, so we can conduct the hypothesis test. The hypotheses are $H_0 : p_{2005} = p_{1990}$ versus $H_1 : p_{2005} < p_{1990}$. The two sample estimates are $\hat{p}_{2005} \approx 0.220$ and

$\hat{p}_{1990} \approx 0.270$. The pooled estimate is $\hat{p} = \dfrac{x_{2005} + x_{1990}}{n_{2005} + n_{1990}} = \dfrac{226 + 278}{1028 + 1028} \approx 0.245$. The test statistic is $z_0 = \dfrac{\hat{p}_{2005} - \hat{p}_{1990}}{\sqrt{\hat{p}(1-\hat{p})}\sqrt{1/n_{2005} + 1/n_{1990}}} = \dfrac{0.220 - 0.270}{\sqrt{0.245(1-0.245)}\sqrt{1/1028 + 1/1028}} \approx -2.64$.

<u>Classical approach</u>: This is a left-tailed test, so the critical value is $-z_\alpha = -z_{0.05} = -1.645$. Since the test statistic falls in the critical region, we reject H_0.

<u>P-value approach</u>: P-value $= P(z_0 \leq -2.64) = 0.0041$. Since this P-value is less than the $\alpha = 0.01$ level of significance, we reject H_0.

<u>Conclusion</u>: There is sufficient evidence to support the claim that the proportion of adults who smoked in the last week has decreased from 1990 to 2005.

17. (a) We first verify the requirements to perform the hypothesis test: (1) Each sample can be thought of as a simple random sample; (2) we have $x_1 = 33$, $n_1 = 200,000$, $x_2 = 115$, and $n_2 = 200,000$, so $\hat{p}_1 = \dfrac{x_1}{n_1} = \dfrac{33}{200,000} = 0.000165$ and $\hat{p}_2 = \dfrac{x_2}{n_2} = \dfrac{115}{200,000} \approx 0.000575$.

Therefore, $n_1\hat{p}_1(1-\hat{p}_1) = 200,000(0.000165)(1-0.000165) \approx 33.0 \geq 10$ and $n_2\hat{p}_2(1-\hat{p}_2) = 200,000(0.000575)(1-0.000575) \approx 114.9 \geq 10$; and (3) each sample is less than 5% of the population. Thus, the requirements are met, so we can conduct the test. The hypotheses are $H_0 : p_1 = p_2$ versus $H_1 : p_1 < p_2$. From before, the two sample estimates are $\hat{p}_1 \approx 0.000165$ and $\hat{p}_2 \approx 0.000575$. The pooled estimate is

$\hat{p} = \dfrac{x_1 + x_2}{n_1 + n_2} = \dfrac{33 + 115}{200,000 + 200,000} \approx 0.00037$. The test statistic is

$z_0 = \dfrac{\hat{p}_1 - \hat{p}_2}{\sqrt{\hat{p}(1-\hat{p})}\sqrt{1/n_1 + 1/n_2}} = \dfrac{0.000165 - 0.000575}{\sqrt{0.00037(1-0.00037)}\sqrt{1/200000 + 1/200000}} \approx -6.74$.

<u>Classical approach</u>: This is a left-tailed test, so the critical value is $-z_\alpha = -z_{0.01} = -2.33$. Since the test statistic falls in the critical region, we reject H_0.

<u>P-value approach</u>: P-value $= P(z_0 \leq -6.74) < 0.0001$. Since this P-value is less than the $\alpha = 0.01$ level of significance, we reject H_0.

<u>Conclusion</u>: There is sufficient evidence at the $\alpha = 0.01$ level of significance to support the claim that the proportion of children in the experimental group who contracted polio is less than the proportion of children in the control group who contracted polio.

(b) For a 90% confidence interval we use $\pm z_{0.05} = \pm 1.645$. Then:

Lower bound:

$(\hat{p}_1 - \hat{p}_2) - z_{\alpha/2} \cdot \sqrt{\dfrac{\hat{p}_1(1-\hat{p}_1)}{n_1} + \dfrac{\hat{p}_2(1-\hat{p}_2)}{n_2}}$

$= (0.000165 - 0.000575) - 1.645 \cdot \sqrt{\dfrac{0.000165(1-0.000165)}{200,000} + \dfrac{0.000575(1-0.000575)}{200,00}}$

$\approx -0.0004 - 0.0001 = -0.0005$

Upper bound:

$$(\hat{p}_1 - \hat{p}_2) + z_{\alpha/2} \cdot \sqrt{\frac{\hat{p}_1(1-\hat{p}_1)}{n_1} + \frac{\hat{p}_2(1-\hat{p}_2)}{n_2}}$$

$$= (0.000165 - 0.000575) + 1.645 \cdot \sqrt{\frac{0.000165(1-0.000165)}{200,000} + \frac{0.000575(1-0.000575)}{200,00}}$$

$$\approx -0.0004 + 0.0001 = -0.0003$$

We can be 90% confident that the difference in the proportion of children who contracted polio with the vaccine versus without the vaccine is between -0.0005 and -0.0003, and that a smaller proportion of children contracted polio in the experimental group.

19. (a) We first verify the requirements to perform the hypothesis test: (1) Each sample can be thought of as a simple random sample; (2) we have $x_{\text{Clarinex}} = 50$, $n_{\text{Clarinex}} = 1655$, $x_{\text{placebo}} = 31$, and $n_{\text{placebo}} = 1652$, so $\hat{p}_{\text{Clarinex}} = \frac{50}{1655} \approx 0.030$ and $\hat{p}_{\text{placebo}} = \frac{31}{1652} \approx 0.019$.

Therefore, $n_{\text{Clarinex}} \hat{p}_{\text{Clarinex}}(1 - \hat{p}_{\text{Clarinex}}) = 1655(0.030)(1-0.030) \approx 48.2 \geq 10$ and

$n_{\text{placebo}} \hat{p}_{\text{placebo}}(1 - \hat{p}_{\text{placebo}}) = 1652(0.019)(1-0.019) \approx 30.8 \geq 10$; and (3) each sample is less than 5% of the population. Thus, the requirements are met, so we can conduct the test. The hypotheses are $H_0 : p_{\text{Clarinex}} = p_{\text{placebo}}$ versus $H_1 : p_{\text{Clarinex}} > p_{\text{placebo}}$. From before, the two sample estimates are $\hat{p}_{\text{Clarinex}} \approx 0.030$ and $\hat{p}_{\text{placebo}} \approx 0.019$. The pooled estimate is

$\hat{p} = \dfrac{x_{\text{Clarinex}} + x_{\text{placebo}}}{n_{\text{Clarinex}} + n_{\text{placebo}}} = \dfrac{50+31}{1655+1652} \approx 0.024$. The test statistic is

$$z_0 = \frac{\hat{p}_{\text{Clarinex}} - \hat{p}_{\text{placebo}}}{\sqrt{\hat{p}(1-\hat{p})}\sqrt{1/n_{\text{Clarinex}} + 1/n_{\text{placebo}}}} = \frac{0.030 - 0.019}{\sqrt{0.024(1-0.024)}\sqrt{1/1655 + 1/1652}} \approx 2.07.$$

Classical approach: This is a right-tailed test, so the critical value is $z_\alpha = z_{0.05} = 1.645$. Since the test statistic falls in the critical region, we reject H_0.

P-value approach: P-value $= P(z_0 \geq 2.07) = 1 - 0.9808 = 0.0192$. Since this P-value is less than the $\alpha = 0.05$ level of significance, we reject H_0.

Conclusion: There is sufficient evidence at the $\alpha = 0.05$ level of significance to support the claim that the proportion of individuals taking Clarinex and experiencing dry mouth is greater than that of those taking the placebo.

(b) No, the difference between the experimental group and the control group is not practically significant. Both Clarinex and the placebo have fairly low proportions of individuals that experience dry mouth.

21. Answers may vary. One possibility follows: No. The headline is not accurate since there is not a statistically significant difference in the percentage of gun owners from the 1999 poll to the 2004 poll. This is shown in the following test:

We first verify the requirements to perform the hypothesis test: (1) Each sample can be thought of as a simple random sample; (2) we have $x_{2004} = 431$, $n_{2004} = 1134$, $x_{1999} = 408$, and $n_{1999} = 1134$, so $\hat{p}_{2004} = \dfrac{431}{1134} \approx 0.380$ and $\hat{p}_{1999} = \dfrac{408}{1134} \approx 0.360$. Therefore,

$n_{2004}\hat{p}_{2004}\left(1 - \hat{p}_{2004}\right) = 1134(0.380)(1 - 0.380) \approx 267 \geq 10$ and $n_{1999}\hat{p}_{1999}\left(1 - \hat{p}_{1999}\right) =$
$1134(0.360)(1 - 0.360) \approx 261 \geq 10$; and (3) each sample is less than 5% of the population. Thus, the requirements are met, so we can conduct the test. The hypotheses are $H_0 : p_{2004} = p_{1999}$ versus $H_1 : p_{2004} > p_{1999}$. From before, the two sample estimates are $\hat{p}_{2004} \approx 0.380$ and $\hat{p}_{1999} \approx 0.360$. The pooled estimate is

$\hat{p} = \dfrac{x_{2004} + x_{1999}}{n_{2004} + n_{1999}} = \dfrac{431 + 408}{1134 + 1134} \approx 0.370$. The test statistic is

$z_0 = \dfrac{\hat{p}_{2004} - \hat{p}_{1999}}{\sqrt{\hat{p}(1-\hat{p})}\sqrt{1/n_{2004} + 1/n_{1999}}} = \dfrac{0.380 - 0.360}{\sqrt{0.370(1-0.370)}\sqrt{1/1134 + 1/1134}} \approx 0.99$.

Classical approach: This is a right-tailed test, so the critical value for a $\alpha = 0.10$ level of significance is $z_\alpha = z_{0.10} = 1.28$. Since the test statistic does not fall in the critical region, we do not reject H_0.

P-value approach: P-value $= P(z_0 \geq 0.99) = 1 - 0.8389 = 0.1611$. Since this P-value is greater than the $\alpha = 0.10$ level of significance, we do not reject H_0.

Conclusion: There is not sufficient evidence at the $\alpha = 0.10$ level of significance to support the claim that the proportion of gun owners in 2004 is greater than that in 1999.

23. (a) $n = n_1 = n_2 = \left[\hat{p}_1(1 - \hat{p}_1) + \hat{p}_2(1 - \hat{p}_2)\right]\left(\dfrac{z_{\alpha/2}}{E}\right)^2$

$= \left[0.219(1 - 0.219) + 0.197(1 - 0.197)\right]\left(\dfrac{1.96}{0.03}\right)^2 \approx 1405.3$, which we increase to 1406.

(b) $n = n_1 = n_2 = 0.5\left(\dfrac{z_{\alpha/2}}{E}\right)^2 = 0.5\left(\dfrac{1.96}{0.03}\right)^2 = 2134.2$, which we increase to 2135.

25. Since the P-value is less than 0.05, there is sufficient evidence at the $\alpha = 0.05$ level of significance to support the claim that caffeine citrate is more effective than placebo in treating sleep apnea.

11.4 Inference about Two Population Standard Deviations

1. The test for comparing two population standard deviations is not robust, so even small departures from normality adversely affect the test, making it unreliable. Therefore, I the test for comparing two population standard deviations, the samples must come from populations that are normally distributed.

3. $F_{0.05,9,10} = 3.02$

5. $\alpha = 0.05$, so $\dfrac{\alpha}{2} = 0.025$. Thus, $F_{0.025,6,8} = 4.65$ and $F_{0.975,6,8} = \dfrac{1}{F_{0.025,8,6}} = \dfrac{1}{5.60} \approx 0.18$.

7. $F_{0.90,25,20} = \dfrac{1}{F_{0.10,20,25}} = \dfrac{1}{1.72} \approx 0.58$

9. $F_{0.05,45,15} = \dfrac{F_{0.05,40,15} + F_{0.05,50,15}}{2} = \dfrac{2.20 + 2.18}{2} = 2.19$

11. The hypotheses are $H_0 : \sigma_1 = \sigma_2$ versus $H_1 : \sigma_1 \neq \sigma_2$. The test statistic is

$$F_0 = \frac{s_1^2}{s_2^2} = \frac{3.2^2}{3.5^2} \approx 0.84.$$

Classical approach: This is a two-tailed test with $n_1 = n_2 = 16$ and $\alpha = 0.05$. So, $\dfrac{\alpha}{2} = 0.025$, and the critical values are $F_{0.025,15,15} = 2.86$ and $F_{0.975,15,15} = \dfrac{1}{F_{0.025,15,15}} = \dfrac{1}{2.86} \approx 0.35$. Since the test statistic does not fall in the critical regions, we do not reject H_0.

P-value approach: Using technology, we find P-value ≈ 0.7330. Since this P-value is greater than the $\alpha = 0.05$ level of significance, we do no reject H_0.

Conclusion: There is not sufficient evidence at the $\alpha = 0.05$ level of significance to support the claim that $\sigma_1 \neq \sigma_2$.

13. The hypotheses are $H_0 : \sigma_1 = \sigma_2$ versus $H_1 : \sigma_1 > \sigma_2$. The test statistic is

$$F_0 = \frac{s_1^2}{s_2^2} = \frac{9.9^2}{6.4^2} \approx 2.39.$$

Classical approach: This is a right-tailed test with $n_1 = 26$, $n_2 = 19$, and $\alpha = 0.01$. So, the critical value is $F_{0.01,25,18}$, which we approximate by $F_{0.01,25,20} = 2.84$. Since the test statistic does not fall in the critical region, we do not reject H_0.

P-value approach: Using technology, we find P-value ≈ 0.0303. Since this P-value is greater than the $\alpha = 0.01$ level of significance, we do no reject H_0.

Conclusion: There is not sufficient evidence at the $\alpha = 0.01$ level of significance to support the claim that $\sigma_1 > \sigma_2$.

15. The hypotheses are $H_0 : \sigma_1 = \sigma_2$ versus $H_1 : \sigma_1 < \sigma_2$. The test statistic is

$$F_0 = \frac{s_1^2}{s_2^2} = \frac{8.3^2}{13.2^2} \approx 0.40 \, .$$

Classical approach: This is a left-tailed test with $n_1 = 51$, $n_2 = 26$, and $\alpha = 0.1$. So, the

critical value is $F_{0.90,50,25} = \dfrac{1}{F_{0.10,25,50}} = \dfrac{1}{1.53} \approx 0.65$. Since the test statistic falls in the

critical region, we reject H_0.

P-value approach: Using technology, we find P-value ≈ 0.0026. Since this P-value is less than the $\alpha = 0.1$ level of significance, we reject H_0.

Conclusion: There is sufficient evidence at the $\alpha = 0.1$ level of significance to support the claim that $\sigma_1 < \sigma_2$.

17. The hypotheses are $H_0 : \sigma_1 = \sigma_2$ versus $H_1 : \sigma_1 \neq \sigma_2$. The test statistic is

$$F_0 = \frac{s_1^2}{s_2^2} = \frac{12.5^2}{12.7^2} \approx 0.97 \, .$$

Classical approach: This is a two-tailed test with $n_1 = 55$, $n_2 = 60$, and $\alpha = 0.05$. The

critical values are $F_{0.025,54,59}$ and $F_{0.975,54,59}$, which we approximate by $F_{0.025,50,50} = 1.75$ and

$F_{0.975,54,59} = \dfrac{1}{F_{0.025,59,54}} \approx \dfrac{1}{F_{0.025,60,50}} = \dfrac{1}{1.72} \approx 0.58$. Since the test statistic does not fall in the

critical region, we do not reject H_0.

P-value approach: Using technology, we find P-value ≈ 0.9087. Since this P-value is greater than the $\alpha = 0.05$ level of significance, we do not reject H_0.

Conclusion: There is not sufficient evidence at the $\alpha = 0.05$ level of significance to support the claim that the standard deviation in the treatment group is different from the standard deviation in the control group.

19. The hypotheses are $H_0 : \sigma_1 = \sigma_2$ versus $H_1 : \sigma_1 > \sigma_2$. The test statistic is

$$F_0 = \frac{s_1^2}{s_2^2} = \frac{17.07^2}{6.48^2} \approx 6.94 \, .$$

Classical approach: This is a right-tailed test with $n_1 = n_2 = 65$ and $\alpha = 0.01$. So, the critical value is $F_{0.01,64,64}$, which we approximate by $F_{0.01,60,50} = 1.91$. Since the test statistic falls in the critical region, we reject H_0.

P-value approach: Using technology, we find P-value $\approx 2.625 \times 10^{-13}$. Since this P-value is less than the $\alpha = 0.01$ level of significance, we reject H_0.

Conclusion: There is sufficient evidence than the $\alpha = 0.01$ level of significance to support the claim that the treatment group had a higher standard deviation for serum retinal concentration than did the control group.

21. (a) The hypotheses are $H_0 : \sigma_1 = \sigma_2$ versus $H_1 : \sigma_1 < \sigma_2$, where σ_1 = the standard deviation of waiting time for a single line. Using technology, we find the sample standard deviations are $s_1 \approx 0.574$ minutes and $s_2 \approx 1.012$ minutes. The test statistic is

$$F_0 = \frac{s_1^2}{s_2^2} = \frac{0.574^2}{1.012^2} \approx 0.32.$$

Classical approach: This is a left-tailed test with $n_1 = n_2 = 20$ and $\alpha = 0.05$. The critical value is $F_{0.95,19,19}$. We approximate this by $F_{0.95,20,20} = \dfrac{1}{F_{0.05,20,20}} = \dfrac{1}{2.12} \approx 0.47$.

Since the test statistic falls in the critical region, we reject H_0.

P-value approach: Using technology, we find P-value ≈ 0.0087. Since this P-value is less than the $\alpha = 0.05$ level of significance, we reject H_0.

Conclusion: There is sufficient evidence at the $\alpha = 0.05$ level of significance to support the claim that the standard deviation of waiting time in a single line is less than the standard deviation for wait time in the multiple lines.

(b) The boxplot indicates that there is much greater variability in the waiting times for multiple lines than for a single line.

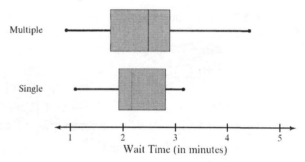

23. (a) The normal probability plots are roughly linear, so we conclude that the data come from normal distributions. Thus, this requirement of the F-test is satisfied.

(b) Since P-value $= 0.169$ is larger than the $\alpha = 0.05$ level of significance, she should not reject H_0. The test supports the previous decision.

(c) Using technology, we find that the sample standard deviations are $s_f \approx 10.35$ and $s_m \approx 14.60$. The test statistic is $F_0 = \dfrac{s_f^2}{s_m^2} = \dfrac{14.60^2}{10.35^2} \approx 1.99$. If we test the hypotheses

$H_0 : \sigma_m = \sigma_f$ versus $H_1 : \sigma_m > \sigma_f$, then this is a right-tailed test with df = 19 for the numerator and df = 16 for the denominator. We can only approximate these by 20 df and 15 df, respectively. Since $F_{0.10,20,15} = 1.92$ and $F_{0.05,20,15} = 2.33$, the P-value should be close to 0.10 which is consistent with the given P-value (0.0844).

289

Chapter 11 Review Exercises

1. Dependent, since the members of the two samples are matched by diagnosis.

3. Independent because the subjects are randomly selected from two distinct populations.

5. (a) $F_{0.05,8,9} = 3.23$

   (b) $\alpha = 0.05$, so $\dfrac{\alpha}{2} = 0.025$. Thus, $F_{0.025,10,5} = 6.62$ and $F_{0.975,10,5} = \dfrac{1}{F_{0.025,5,10}} = \dfrac{1}{4.24} \approx 0.24$.

7. (a)

Observation	1	2	3	4	5	6
X_i	34.2	32.1	39.5	41.8	45.1	38.4
Y_i	34.9	31.5	39.5	41.9	45.5	38.8
$d_i = X_i - Y_i$	−0.7	0.6	0	−0.1	−0.4	−0.4

   (b) Using technology, $\bar{d} \approx -0.167$ and $s_d \approx 0.450$.

   (c) The hypotheses are $H_0 : \mu_d = 0$ versus $H_1 : \mu_d < 0$. The level of significance is $\alpha = 0.05$. The test statistic is $t_0 = \dfrac{\bar{d}}{s_d / \sqrt{n}} = \dfrac{-0.167}{0.450 / \sqrt{6}} \approx -0.909$.

   Classical approach: Since this is a left-tailed test with 5 degrees of freedom, the critical value is $-t_{0.05} = -2.015$. Since the test statistic $t_0 \approx -0.909$ is greater than the critical value $-t_{0.05} = -1.943$ (i.e., since the test statistic does not fall within the critical region), we do not reject H_0.

   P-value approach: The P-value for this left-tailed test is the area under the t-distribution with 5 degrees of freedom to the left of the test statistic $t_0 \approx -0.909$, which by symmetry is equal to the area to the right of $t_0 \approx 0.909$. From the t-distribution table in the row corresponding to 5 degrees of freedom, 0.909 falls between 0.727 and 0.920 whose right-tail areas are 0.25 and 0.20, respectively. So, $0.20 < P\text{-value} < 0.25$. (Using technology, we find P-value = 0.2030.) Because the P-value is greater than the $\alpha = 0.05$ level of significance, we do not reject H_0.

   Conclusion: There is not sufficient evidence at the $\alpha = 0.05$ level of significance to support the claim that the population mean difference is less than zero.

   (d) For 98% confidence, we use $\alpha = 0.02$. With df = 5, we jave $t_{\alpha/2} = t_{0.01} = 3.365$. Then:

   Lower bound: $\bar{d} - t_{0.01} \cdot \dfrac{s_d}{\sqrt{n}} = -0.167 - 3.365 \cdot \dfrac{0.450}{\sqrt{6}} \approx -0.79$;

   Upper bound: $\bar{d} + t_{0.01} \cdot \dfrac{s_d}{\sqrt{n}} = -0.167 + 3.365 \cdot \dfrac{0.450}{\sqrt{6}} \approx 0.45$.

   We can be 98% confident that the mean difference is between −0.79 and 0.45.

9. (a) $H_0 : \mu_1 = \mu_2$ versus $H_1 : \mu_1 \neq \mu_2$. The level of significance is $\alpha = 0.1$. Since the smaller sample size is $n_2 = 8$, we use $n_2 - 1 = 7$ degrees of freedom. The test statistic is $t_0 = \dfrac{(\bar{x}_1 - \bar{x}_2) - (\mu_1 - \mu_2)}{\sqrt{\dfrac{s_1^2}{n_1} + \dfrac{s_2^2}{n_2}}} = \dfrac{(32.4 - 28.2) - 0}{\sqrt{\dfrac{4.5^2}{13} + \dfrac{3.8^2}{8}}} \approx 2.290$.

Classical approach: Since this is a two-tailed test with 7 degrees of freedom, the critical values are $\pm t_{0.05} = \pm 1.895$. Since the test statistic $t_0 \approx 2.290$ is to the right of the critical value 1.895 (i.e., since the test statistic falls within the critical regions), we reject H_0.

P-value approach: The P-value for this two-tailed test is the area under the t-distribution with 7 degrees of freedom to the right of $t_0 = 2.290$ plus the area to the left of $-t_0 = -2.290$. From the t-distribution table in the row corresponding to 7 degrees of freedom, 2.290 falls between 1.895 and 2.365 whose right-tail areas are 0.05 and 0.025, respectively. We must double these values in order to get the total area in both tails: 0.10 and 0.05. Thus, $0.05 < P\text{-value} < 0.10$. (Using technology, we find P-value $= 0.0351$.) Because the P-value is less than the $\alpha = 0.10$ level of significance, we reject H_0.

Conclusion: There is sufficient evidence at the $\alpha = 0.1$ level of significance to support the claim that $\mu_1 \neq \mu_2$.

(b) For a 90% confidence interval with df = 7, we use $t_{\alpha/2} = t_{0.05} = 1.895$. Then:

Lower bound: $(\bar{x}_1 - \bar{x}_2) - t_{\alpha/2} \cdot \sqrt{\dfrac{s_1^2}{n_1} + \dfrac{s_2^2}{n_2}} = (32.4 - 28.2) - 1.895 \cdot \sqrt{\dfrac{4.5^2}{13} + \dfrac{3.8^2}{8}}$

$$\approx 4.2 - 3.47 = 0.73;$$

Upper bound: $(\bar{x}_1 - \bar{x}_2) + t_{\alpha/2} \cdot \sqrt{\dfrac{s_1^2}{n_1} + \dfrac{s_2^2}{n_2}} = (32.4 - 28.2) + 1.895 \cdot \sqrt{\dfrac{4.5^2}{13} + \dfrac{3.8^2}{8}}$

$$\approx 4.2 + 3.47 = 7.67.$$

We are 90% confident that the population mean difference is between 0.73 and 7.67.

(c) The hypotheses are $H_0 : \sigma_1 = \sigma_2$ versus $H_1 : \sigma_1 \neq \sigma_2$. The test statistic is

$$F_0 = \frac{s_1^2}{s_2^2} = \frac{4.5^2}{3.8^2} \approx 1.40.$$

Classical approach: This is a two-tailed test with $n_1 = 13$, $n_2 = 8$, and $\alpha = 0.05$. The critical values are $F_{0.025,12,7}$, which we approximate by $F_{0.025,10,7} = 4.76$ and

$F_{0.975,12,7} = \dfrac{1}{F_{0.025,7,12}} = \dfrac{1}{3.61} \approx 0.28$. Since the test statistic does not fall in the critical

region, we do not reject H_0.

P-value approach: Using technology, we find P-value ≈ 0.6734. Since this P-value is greater than the $\alpha = 0.05$ level of significance, we do not reject H_0.

Conclusion: There is not sufficient evidence at the $\alpha = 0.05$ level of significance to support the claim that the standard deviation in population 1 is different from the standard deviation in population 2.

11. (a) $H_0 : \mu_1 = \mu_2$ versus $H_1 : \mu_1 > \mu_2$. The level of significance is $\alpha = 0.01$. Since the smaller sample size is $n_2 = 41$, we use $n_2 - 1 = 40$ degrees of freedom. The test

statistic is $t_0 = \dfrac{(\bar{x}_1 - \bar{x}_2) - (\mu_1 - \mu_2)}{\sqrt{\dfrac{s_1^2}{n_1} + \dfrac{s_2^2}{n_2}}} = \dfrac{(48.2 - 45.2) - 0}{\sqrt{\dfrac{8.4^2}{45} + \dfrac{10.3^2}{41}}} \approx 1.472$.

Classical approach: Since this is a right-tailed test with 40 degrees of freedom, the critical value is $t_{0.01} = 2.423$. Since the test statistic $t_0 \approx 1.472$ is to the left of the critical value (i.e., since the test statistic does not fall within the critical region), we do not reject H_0.

P-value approach: The P-value for this right-tailed test is the area under the t-distribution with 40 degrees of freedom to the right of $t_0 \approx 1.472$. From the t-distribution table in the row corresponding to 40 degrees of freedom, 1.472 falls between 1.303 and 1.684 whose right-tail areas are 0.10 and 0.05, respectively. Thus, $0.05 < P\text{-value} < 0.10$. (Using technology, we find P-value = 0.0726.) Because the P-value is greater than the $\alpha = 0.01$ level of significance, we do not reject H_0.

Conclusion: There is not sufficient evidence at the $\alpha = 0.01$ level of significance to support the claim that the mean of population 1 is larger than the mean of population 2.

(b) For a 90% confidence interval with df = 40, we use $t_{\alpha/2} = t_{0.05} = 1.684$. Then:

Lower bound: $(\bar{x}_1 - \bar{x}_2) - t_{\alpha/2} \cdot \sqrt{\dfrac{s_1^2}{n_1} + \dfrac{s_2^2}{n_2}} = (48.2 - 45.2) - 1.684 \cdot \sqrt{\dfrac{8.4^2}{45} + \dfrac{10.3^2}{41}}$

$$\approx 3.0 - 3.43 = -0.43;$$

Upper bound: $(\bar{x}_1 - \bar{x}_2) + t_{\alpha/2} \cdot \sqrt{\dfrac{s_1^2}{n_1} + \dfrac{s_2^2}{n_2}} = (48.2 - 45.2) + 1.684 \cdot \sqrt{\dfrac{8.4^2}{45} + \dfrac{10.3^2}{41}}$

$$\approx 3.0 + 3.43 = 6.43.$$

We are 90% confident that the population mean difference is between -0.43 and 6.43.

(c) The hypotheses are $H_0 : \sigma_1 = \sigma_2$ versus $H_1 : \sigma_1 < \sigma_2$. The test statistic is

$F_0 = \dfrac{s_1^2}{s_2^2} = \dfrac{8.4^2}{10.3^2} \approx 0.67$.

Classical approach: This is a left-tailed test with $n_1 = 45$, $n_2 = 41$, and $\alpha = 0.01$. The

critical values is $F_{0.99, 44, 40} = \dfrac{1}{F_{0.01, 40, 44}} \approx \dfrac{1}{F_{0.01, 40, 50}} \approx \dfrac{1}{2.01} \approx 0.50$. Since the test statistic

does not fall in the critical region, we do not reject H_0.

P-value approach: Using technology, we find P-value ≈ 0.0940. Since this P-value is greater than the $\alpha = 0.01$ level of significance, we do not reject H_0.

Conclusion: There is not sufficient evidence at the $\alpha = 0.01$ level of significance to support the claim that the standard deviation in population 1 is less than the standard deviation in population 2.

13. (a) The hypotheses are $H_0 : p_1 = p_2$ versus $H_1 : p_1 \neq p_2$.

(b) The two sample estimates are $\hat{p}_1 = \dfrac{x_1}{n_1} = \dfrac{451}{555} \approx 0.813$ and $\hat{p}_2 = \dfrac{x_2}{n_2} = \dfrac{510}{600} = 0.850$. The

pooled estimate is $\hat{p} = \dfrac{x_1 + x_2}{n_1 + n_2} = \dfrac{451 + 510}{555 + 600} \approx 0.832$. The test statistic is

$$z_0 = \frac{\hat{p}_1 - \hat{p}_2}{\sqrt{\hat{p}(1-\hat{p})}\sqrt{1/n_1 + 1/n_2}} = \frac{0.813 - 0.850}{\sqrt{0.832(1-0.832)}\sqrt{1/555 + 1/600}} \approx -1.68.$$

(c) This is a two-tailed test, so the critical values are $\pm z_{0.025} = \pm 1.96$. Since the test statistic does not fall in the critical region, we do not reject H_0. There is not sufficient evidence to support the claim that $p_1 \neq p_2$.

(d) P-value $= 2 \cdot P(z_0 \leq -1.68) = 2 \cdot 0.0465 = 0.0930$. Since the P-value is greater than $\alpha = 0.05$, we do not reject H_0. There is not sufficient evidence to support the claim that $p_1 \neq p_2$.

15. (a) Since the same individual is used for both measurements, the sampling method is dependent.

(b)

Student	1	2	3	4	5	6	7	8	9	10
Height (inches)	59.5	69	77	59.5	74.5	63	61.5	67.5	73	69
Arm span (inches)	62	65.5	76	63	74	66	61	69	70	71
d_i	-2.5	3.5	1	-3.5	0.5	-3	0.5	-1.5	3	-2

Using technology, $\bar{d} = -0.4$ inches and $s_d \approx 2.470$ inches, where we measure differences as Height minus Arm span. The hypotheses are $H_0 : \mu_d = 0$ versus $H_1 : \mu_d \neq 0$. The level of significance is $\alpha = 0.05$. The test statistic is

$$t_0 = \frac{\bar{d}}{s_d / \sqrt{n}} = \frac{-0.4}{2.470 / \sqrt{10}} \approx -0.512.$$

Classical approach: Since this is a two-tailed test with 9 degrees of freedom, the critical values are $\pm t_{0.025} = \pm 2.262$. Since the test statistic $t_0 \approx -0.512$ falls between the critical values $\pm t_{0.025} = \pm 2.262$ (i.e., since the test statistic does not fall within the critical regions), we do not reject H_0.

P-value approach: The P-value for this two-tailed test is the area under the t-distribution with 9 degrees of freedom to the left of the test statistic $t_0 = -0.512$ plus the area to the right of $t_0 = 0.512$. From the t-distribution table in the row corresponding to 9 degrees of freedom, 0.512 falls to the left of 0.703 whose right-tail area is 0.25. We must double this value in order to get the total area in both tails: 0.50. So, P-value > 0.50. (Using technology, we find P-value ≈ 0.6209.) Because the P-value is greater than the $\alpha = 0.05$ level of significance, we do not reject H_0.

Conclusion: There is not sufficient evidence at the $\alpha = 0.05$ level of significance to reject the student's claim that an individual's arm span equals the individual's height.

17. (a) Since the cars selected for the McDonald's sample had no bearing on the cars selected for the Wendy's sample, the testing method is independent.

(b) The hypotheses are $H_0 : \mu_{\text{McD}} = \mu_{\text{W}}$ versus $H_1 : \mu_{\text{McD}} \neq \mu_{\text{W}}$. Using technology, the summary statistics are $\bar{x}_{\text{McD}} \approx 133.60$ seconds, $s_{\text{McD}} \approx 39.61$ seconds, and $n_{\text{McD}} = 30$, and $\bar{x}_{\text{W}} \approx 219.14$, $s_{\text{W}} \approx 102.85$, and $n_{\text{W}} = 27$. Since the smaller sample size is $n_{\text{W}} = 27$, we use $n_{\text{W}} - 1 = 26$ degrees of freedom. The test statistic is

$$t_0 = \frac{(\bar{x}_{\text{McD}} - \bar{x}_{\text{W}}) - (\mu_{\text{McD}} - \mu_{\text{W}})}{\sqrt{\dfrac{s_{\text{McD}}^2}{n_{\text{McD}}} + \dfrac{s_{\text{W}}^2}{n_{\text{W}}}}} = \frac{(133.60 - 219.14) - 0}{\sqrt{\dfrac{39.61^2}{30} + \dfrac{102.85^2}{27}}} \approx -4.059$$

Classical approach: Since this is a two-tailed test with 26 degrees of freedom, the critical values are $\pm t_{0.05} = \pm 1.706$. Since the test statistic $t_0 \approx -4.059$ is to the left of -1.706 (i.e., since the test statistic falls within the critical regions), we reject H_0.

P-value approach: The P-value for this two-tailed test is the area under the t-distribution with 26 degrees of freedom to the left of $t_0 \approx -4.059$ plus the area to the left of $t_0 \approx 4.059$. From the t-distribution table in the row corresponding to 26 degrees of freedom, 4.059 falls to the right of 3.707 whose right-tail area is 0.0005. We must double this value in order to get the total area in both tails: 0.001. So, P-value < 0.001. (Using technology, we find P-value $= 0.0003$.) Since the P-value is less than $\alpha = 0.1$, we reject H_0.

Conclusion: There is sufficient evidence at the $\alpha = 0.1$ level of significance to support the claim that the population mean wait time is different for McDonald's and Wendy's drive-through windows.

(c) Yes, the boxplots support the results from part (b). From the boxplot, there appears to be a difference in the wait times for McDonald's and Wendy's drive-through windows.

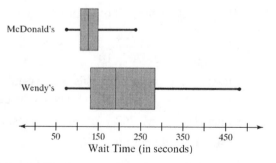

294

19. (a) We first verify the requirements to perform the hypothesis test: (1) Each sample can be thought of as a simple random sample; (2) We have $x_1 = 27$, $n_1 = 696$, $x_2 = 49$, and $n_2 = 678$, so $\hat{p}_1 = \dfrac{x_1}{n_1} = \dfrac{27}{696} \approx 0.039$ and $\hat{p}_2 = \dfrac{x_2}{n_2} = \dfrac{49}{678} \approx 0.072$. Thus, $n_1 \hat{p}_1 (1 - \hat{p}_1) = 696(0.039)(1 - 0.039) \approx 26 \geq 10$ and $n_2 \hat{p}_2 (1 - \hat{p}_2) = 678(0.072)(1 - 0.072) \approx 45 \geq 10$; and (3) Each sample is less than 5% of the population. Thus, the requirements are met, and we can conduct the test. The hypotheses are $H_0 : p_1 = p_2$ versus $H_1 : p_1 < p_2$. From before, the two sample estimates are $\hat{p}_1 \approx 0.039$ and $\hat{p}_2 \approx 0.072$. The pooled estimate is $\hat{p} = \dfrac{x_1 + x_2}{n_1 + n_2} = \dfrac{27 + 49}{696 + 678} \approx 0.055$. The test statistic is

$$z_0 = \frac{\hat{p}_1 - \hat{p}_2}{\sqrt{\hat{p}(1 - \hat{p})}\sqrt{1/n_1 + 1/n_2}} = \frac{0.039 - 0.072}{\sqrt{0.055(1 - 0.055)}\sqrt{1/696 + 1/678}} \approx -2.68 .$$

Classical approach: This is a left-tailed test, so the critical value is $-z_{0.01} = -2.33$. Since the test statistic falls in the critical region, we reject H_0.

P-value approach: P-value = $P(z_0 \leq -2.68) = 0.0037$. Since this P-value is less than the $\alpha = 0.01$ level of significance, we reject H_0.

Conclusion: There is sufficient evidence at the $\alpha = 0.01$ level of significance to support the claim that a lower proportion of women in the experimental group experienced a bone fracture than in the control group.

(b) For a 95% confidence interval we use $\pm z_{0.025} = \pm 1.96$. Then:

Lower bound: $(\hat{p}_1 - \hat{p}_2) - z_{\alpha/2} \cdot \sqrt{\dfrac{\hat{p}_1(1 - \hat{p}_1)}{n_1} + \dfrac{\hat{p}_2(1 - \hat{p}_2)}{n_2}}$

$$= (0.039 - 0.072) - 1.96 \cdot \sqrt{\frac{0.039(1 - 0.039)}{696} + \frac{0.072(1 - 0.072)}{678}}$$

$$\approx -0.033 - 0.024 = -0.057$$

Upper bound: $(\hat{p}_1 - \hat{p}_2) + z_{\alpha/2} \cdot \sqrt{\dfrac{\hat{p}_1(1 - \hat{p}_1)}{n_1} + \dfrac{\hat{p}_2(1 - \hat{p}_2)}{n_2}}$

$$= (0.039 - 0.072) + 1.96 \cdot \sqrt{\frac{0.039(1 - 0.039)}{696} + \frac{0.072(1 - 0.072)}{678}}$$

$$\approx -0.033 + 0.024 = -0.009$$

We can be 95% confident that the difference in the proportion of women who experience a bone fracture between the experimental and control group is between -0.057 and -0.009.

(c) This is a completely randomized design. The treatment is the drug. It has two levels: 5 mg of Actonel versus the placebo.

21. (a) $n = n_1 = n_2 = \left[\hat{p}_1(1-\hat{p}_1) + \hat{p}_2(1-\hat{p}_2) \right] \left(\dfrac{z_{\alpha/2}}{E} \right)^2$

$= \left[0.188(1-0.188) + 0.205(1-0.205) \right] \left(\dfrac{1.645}{0.02} \right)^2 \approx 2135.3$, which we must increase to 2136.

(b) $n = n_1 = n_2 = 0.5 \left(\dfrac{z_{\alpha/2}}{E} \right)^2 = 0.5 \left(\dfrac{1.645}{0.02} \right)^2 \approx 3382.5$, which we must increase to 3383.

23. The hypotheses are $H_0 : \sigma_{\text{McD}} = \sigma_{\text{W}}$ versus $H_1 : \sigma_{\text{McD}} < \sigma_{\text{W}}$. From problem 17, we know $s_{\text{McD}} \approx 39.61$ seconds and $s_{\text{W}} \approx 102.85$ seconds.   The test statistic is

$F_0 = \dfrac{s_{\text{McD}}^2}{s_{\text{W}}^2} = \dfrac{39.61^2}{102.85^2} \approx 0.15$.

<u>Classical approach</u>: This is a left-tailed test with $n_{\text{McD}} = 30$ and $n_{\text{W}} = 27$. The critical

values is $F_{0.95,29,26}$, which we approximate by $F_{0.95,25,25} = \dfrac{1}{F_{0.05,25,25}} = \dfrac{1}{2.23} \approx 0.45$. Since the

test statistic falls in the critical regions, we reject H_0.

<u>P-value approach</u>: Using technology, we find $P\text{-value} \approx 1.25 \times 10^{-7}$. Since this P-value is less than the $\alpha = 0.05$ level of significance, we reject H_0.

<u>Conclusion</u>: There is sufficient evidence at the $\alpha = 0.05$ level of significance to support the claim that the standard deviation in wait time at Wendy's is more than the standard deviation in wait time at McDonald's.

25. From problem 15, we have $\bar{d} = -0.4$ inches and $s_d \approx 2.470$ inches. For 95% confidence, we use $\alpha = 0.05$, so with df = 9 we have $t_{\alpha/2} = t_{0.025} = 2.262$. Then:

Lower bound: $\bar{d} - t_{0.025} \cdot \dfrac{s_d}{\sqrt{n}} = -0.4 - 2.262 \cdot \dfrac{2.470}{\sqrt{10}} \approx -2.17$;

Upper bound: $\bar{d} + t_{0.025} \cdot \dfrac{s_d}{\sqrt{n}} = -0.4 + 2.262 \cdot \dfrac{2.470}{\sqrt{10}} \approx 1.37$.

We can be 95% confident that the mean difference between height and arm span is between −2.17 and 1.37. The interval contains zero, which supports we conclude that there is not sufficient evidence at the $\alpha = 0.05$ level of significance to reject the claim that arm span and height are equal.

27. From problem 17, we have $\bar{x}_{\text{McD}} \approx 133.60$ seconds $s_{\text{McD}} \approx 39.61$ seconds, and $n_{\text{McD}} = 30$, and $\bar{x}_{\text{W}} \approx 219.14$, $s_{\text{W}} \approx 102.85$, and $n_{\text{W}} = 27$. For a 95% confidence interval with df = 26, we use $t_{\alpha/2} = t_{0.025} = 2.056$. Then:

Lower bound:

$$(\bar{x}_{\text{McD}} - \bar{x}_{\text{W}}) - t_{\alpha/2} \cdot \sqrt{\frac{s_{\text{McD}}^2}{n_{\text{McD}}} + \frac{s_{\text{W}}^2}{n_{\text{W}}}} = (133.60 - 219.14) - 2.056 \cdot \sqrt{\frac{39.61^2}{30} + \frac{102.85^2}{27}}$$

$$\approx -85.54 - 43.33 = -128.87 \text{ seconds};$$

Upper bound:

$$(\bar{x}_{\text{McD}} - \bar{x}_{\text{W}}) + t_{\alpha/2} \cdot \sqrt{\frac{s_{\text{McD}}^2}{n_{\text{McD}}} + \frac{s_{\text{W}}^2}{n_{\text{W}}}} = (133.60 - 219.14) + 2.056 \cdot \sqrt{\frac{39.61^2}{30} + \frac{102.85^2}{27}}$$

$$\approx -85.54 + 43.33 = -42.21 \text{ seconds.}$$

We can be 95% confident that the mean difference in wait times between McDonald's and Wendy's drive-through windows is between −128.87 and −42.21 seconds.

Answer will vary. One possibility is that McDonald's might advertise that customers have a shorter wait when using their drive-through window than when using Wendy's.

Chapter 12
Inference on Categorical Data

12.1 Goodness of Fit Test

1. These procedures are for testing whether sample data are a good fit with a hypothesized distribution.

3. The sample data must be obtained one by random sampling, all expected frequencies must be greater than or equal to 1, and no more than 20% of the expected frequencies should be less than 5.

5. Each expected count is $n \cdot p_i$ where $n = 500$. This gives expected counts of 100, 50, 225 and 125 respectively.

7. **(a)**

Observed (O_i)	Expected (E_i)	$(O_i - E_i)^2$	$(O_i - E_i)^2 / E_i$
30	25	25	1
20	25	25	1
28	25	9	0.36
22	25	9	0.36
		$\chi_0^2 =$	2.72

(b) df $= 4 - 1 = 3$

(c) $\chi_{0.05}^2 = 7.815$

(d) The test statistic is not in the (right-tailed) critical region so we do not reject H_0.

9. **(a)**

Observed (O_i)	Expected (E_i)	$(O_i - E_i)^2$	$(O_i - E_i)^2 / E_i$
1	1.6	0.36	0.225
38	25.6	153.76	6.006
132	153.6	466.56	3.038
440	409.6	924.16	2.256
389	409.6	424.36	1.0363
		$\chi_0^2 =$	12.561

(b) df $= 5 - 1 = 4$

(c) $\chi_{0.05}^2 = 9.488$

(d) The test statistic is in the (right-tailed) critical region so we reject H_0. There is sufficient evidence to reject the claim that the random variable X is binomial with $n = 4$ and $p = 0.8$.

11. We summarize the observed and expected counts in the following table:

	Observed (O_i)	Expected (E_i)	$(O_i - E_i)^2$	$(O_i - E_i)^2 / E_i$
Brown	61	52	81	1.558
Yellow	64	56	64	1.143
Red	54	52	4	0.077
Blue	61	96	1225	12.760
Orange	96	80	256	3.2
Green	64	64	0	0
			$\chi_0^2 =$	18.738

Since all the expected cell counts are greater than or equal to 5, the requirements for the goodness-of-fit test are satisfied.

Classical approach: The critical value, with df $= 6 - 1 = 5$, is $\chi_{0.05}^2 = 11.071$. Since the test statistic is in the critical region, we reject the null hypothesis.

P-value approach: Using the chi-square table, we find the row that corresponds to 5 degrees of freedom. The value of 18.738 is greater than 16.750, which has an area under the chi-square distribution of 0.005 to the right. Therefore, we have P-value < 0.005. Since P-value $< \alpha$, we reject the null hypothesis.
[Note: using technology, we find P-value $= 0.0022 < \alpha$ so the null hypothesis is rejected.]

Conclusion: There is enough evidence to support the claim that the distribution of colors of plain M&M's differs from that claimed by M&M/Mars.

13. **(a)** Answers will vary. Because of the seriousness of the situation, we would want to have strong evidence that there is fraudulent activity. Therefore, we would want to select a small value for α, such as $\alpha = 0.01$.

(b) We summarize the observed and expected counts in the following table:

	Observed (O_i)	Expected (E_i)	$(O_i - E_i)^2$	$(O_i - E_i)^2 / E_i$
1	36	60.2	585.64	9.728
2	32	35.2	10.24	0.291
3	28	25	9	0.360
4	26	19.4	43.56	2.245
5	23	15.8	51.84	3.281
6	17	13.4	12.96	0.967
7	15	11.6	11.56	0.997
8	16	10.2	33.64	3.298
9	7	9.2	4.84	0.526
			$\chi_0^2 =$	21.693

Since all the expected cell counts are greater than or equal to 5, the requirements for the goodness-of-fit test are satisfied. Our hypotheses are:

H_0 : the digits obey Benford's law

H_1 : the digits do not obey Benford's law

Classical approach: The critical value, with df $= 9 - 1 = 8$, is $\chi_{0.01}^2 = 20.090$. Since the test statistic is in the critical region, we reject the null hypothesis.

P-value approach: Using the chi-square table, we find the row that corresponds to 8 degrees of freedom. The value of 21.693 is greater than 20.090, which has an area under the chi-square distribution of 0.01 to the right, and less than 21.955, which has an area under the chi-square distribution of 0.005 to the right. Therefore, we have $0.005 < P$-value < 0.01. Since P-value $< \alpha$, we reject the null hypothesis. [Note: using technology, we find P-value $= 0.0055 < \alpha = 0.01$ and reject H_0]

Conclusion: There is enough evidence to reject the null hypothesis. The digits do not appear to obey Benford's law.

(c) Answers will vary. Based on the results from part (b), it appears that the employee is guilty of embezzlement at the $\alpha = 0.01$ level of significance.

15. We summarize the observed and expected counts in the following table:

	Observed Count (O_i)	Expected Count (E_i)	$(O_i - E_i)^2$	$(O_i - E_i)^2 / E_i$
Jan	40	$500/12 = 41.667$	2.778	0.067
Feb	38	41.667	13.444	0.323
Mar	41	41.667	0.444	0.011
Apr	40	41.667	2.778	0.067
May	42	41.667	0.111	0.003

Jun	41	41.667	0.444	0.011
Jul	45	41.667	11.111	0.267
Aug	44	41.667	5.444	0.131
Sep	44	41.667	5.444	0.131
Oct	43	41.667	1.778	0.043
Nov	39	41.667	7.111	0.171
Dec	43	41.667	1.778	0.043
			$\chi_0^2 =$	1.268

Since all the expected cell counts are greater than or equal to 5, the requirements for the goodness-of-fit test are satisfied. Our hypotheses are:

H_0 : distribution of birth months is uniform

H_1 : distribution of birth months is not uniform

Classical approach: The critical value, with df $= 12 - 1 = 11$, is $\chi_{0.05}^2 = 19.675$. Since the test statistic is not in the critical region, we do not reject the null hypothesis.

P-value approach: Using the chi-square table, we find the row that corresponds to 11 degrees of freedom. The value of 1.268 is less than 2.603, which has an area under the chi-square distribution of 0.995 to the right. Therefore, we have P-value > 0.995. Since P-value $> \alpha$, we do not reject the null hypothesis.
[Note: using technology, we find P-value $= 0.9998 > \alpha = 0.05$ so the null hypothesis is not rejected.]

Conclusion: There is not enough evidence to reject the null hypothesis. The birth months appear to occur with equal frequency.

17. We summarize the observed and expected counts in the following table:

	Observed Count (O_i)	Expected Count (E_i)	$(O_i - E_i)^2$	$(O_i - E_i)^2 / E_i$
Sunday	39	$300 / 7 = 42.857$	14.878	0.347
Monday	40	42.857	8.163	0.190
Tuesday	30	42.857	165.306	3.857
Wednesday	40	42.857	8.163	0.190
Thursday	41	42.857	3.449	0.080
Friday	49	42.857	37.735	0.880
Saturday	61	42.857	329.163	7.680
			$\chi_0^2 =$	13.227

Since all the expected cell counts are greater than or equal to 5, the requirements for the goodness-of-fit test are satisfied. Our hypotheses are:

H_0 : distribution of pedestrian fatalities is uniformly distributed during the week

H_1 : distribution of pedestrian fatalities is not uniformly distributed during the week

301

Classical approach: The critical value, with df $= 7 - 1 = 6$, is $\chi^2_{0.05} = 12.592$. Since the test statistic is in the critical region, we reject the null hypothesis.

P-value approach: Using the chi-square table, we find the row that corresponds to 6 degrees of freedom. The value of 13.227 is greater than 12.592, which has an area under the chi-square distribution of 0.05 to the right. Therefore, we have P-value < 0.05. Since P-value $< \alpha$, we reject the null hypothesis.
[Note: using technology, we find P-value $= 0.0396 < \alpha = 0.05$ so the null hypothesis is rejected.]

Conclusion: There is enough evidence to reject the null hypothesis. There is enough evidence to indicate that pedestrian deaths are not uniformly distributed over the days of the week.

19. (a)

	RelativeFrequency	Observed Frequency	Expected Frequency
K-3	0.329	15	8.225
4-8	0.393	7	9.825
9-12	0.278	3	6.95

(b) Since all the expected cell counts are greater than or equal to 5, the requirements for the goodness-of-fit test are satisfied. Our hypotheses are:

H_0 : grade distribution is the same as the national distribution

H_1 : grade distribution is not the same as the national distribution

$$\chi^2_0 = \frac{(15-8.225)^2}{8.225} + \frac{(7-9.825)^2}{9.825} + \frac{(3-6.95)^2}{6.95} = 8.638$$

Classical approach: The critical value, with df $= 3 - 1 = 2$, is $\chi^2_{0.05} = 5.991$. Since the test statistic is in the critical region, we reject the null hypothesis.

P-value approach: Using the chi-square table, we find the row that corresponds to 2 degrees of freedom. The value of 8.638 is greater than 7.378, which has an area under the chi-square distribution of 0.025 to the right. Therefore, we have P-value $< 0.025 < 0.05$. Since P-value $< \alpha$, we reject the null hypothesis.
[Note: using technology, we find P-value $= 0.0133 < \alpha = 0.05$ so the null hypothesis is rejected.]

Conclusion: There is enough evidence to reject the null hypothesis. There is enough evidence to indicate that the grade distribution in the social worker's district is different from the national proportions.

21. (a) Answers will vary.

(b) Each of the five numbers should be equally likely so the proportions should all be 20%.

(c) Answers will vary.

23. (a), (b)

	Observed Count (O_i)	Expected Rel. Freq.	Expected Count (E_i)	$(O_i - E_i)^2$	$(O_i - E_i)^2 / E_i$
Low	15	0.071	11.36	13.2496	1.166
Not Low	145	0.929	148.64	13.2496	0.089
	160			$\chi_0^2 =$	1.255

The critical value, with df $= 2 - 1 = 1$, is $\chi_{0.05}^2 = 3.841$. Since the test statistic is not in the critical region, we do not reject H_0. There is not enough evidence to support the claim that the percentage of low-birth-weight babies is higher for mothers 35–39 years old.

(c) Note that $n \cdot p_0 (1 - p_0) = 160(0.071)(1 - 0.071) \approx 10.6 \geq 10$ so the requirements of the hypothesis test are satisfied.

The hypotheses are $H_0 : p = 0.071$, $H_1 : p > 0.071$. From the sample data,

$\hat{p} = \dfrac{15}{160} \approx 0.094$. The test statistic is

$$z_0 = \frac{\hat{p} - p_0}{\sqrt{p_0(1 - p_0)/n}} = \frac{0.094 - 0.071}{\sqrt{0.071(1 - 0.071)/160}} = 1.13$$

This is a right-tailed test so the critical value is $z_{0.05} = 1.645$. The test statistic is not in the critical region so we do not reject the null hypothesis.

25. The sum is 0, as shown below. The observed frequencies and the expected frequencies must both sum to $n = 100$, in this example, so the sum of their differences must be 0.

Observed (O_i)	Expected (E_i)	$O_i - E_i$
30	25	5
20	25	−5
28	25	3
22	25	−3
	Total =	0

12.2 Contingency Tables and Association

1. A marginal distribution is a frequency or relative frequency distribution of either the row or column variable in a contingency table. A conditional distribution is the relative frequency of each category of one variable, given a specific value of the other variable in a contingency table.

3. The correlation coefficient is a numerical measure of association between quantitative variables. In this section we are considering the association between qualitative variables—variables which take non-numerical values—and it does not make sense to talk of correlation between such variables.

5. (a), (b) The column totals give the frequency marginal distribution of age. The row totals give the frequency marginal distribution of poverty level. To find the relative frequencies we divide each row or column total by the grand total = 32,986. For example, the relative frequency of Age < 18 is 17,2654/32,986 = 0.523.

Poverty Level	Age				Total	Relative Frequency
	< 18	18–44	45–64	≥65		
Below	7571	3693	1718	1025	14,007	0.425
Above	9694	4745	2282	2258	18,979	0.575
Total	17,265	8438	4000	3283	32,986	1
Relative Frequency	0.523	0.256	0.121	0.100	1	

(c) The percentage below the poverty level is the relative frequency of the row corresponding to below the poverty level = 42.5%.

(d) The percentage aged less than 18 years is the relative frequency of the column corresponding to age < 18, which =52.3%.

(e)

Poverty Level	Age			
	< 18	18–44	45–64	≥65
Below	7571/14,007 = 0.541	3393/14,007 = 0.264	1718/14,007 = 0.123	1025/14,007 = 0.073
Above	9694/18,979 = 0.511	4745/18,979 = 0.250	2282/18,979 = 0.120	2258/18,979 = 0.119

(f)

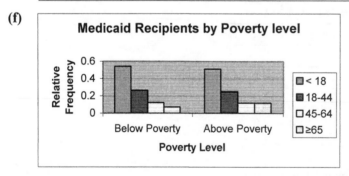

(g) Answers will vary. There does not seem to be much of an association between poverty level and age of Medicaid recipients. The percentage for each of the first three age groups is higher for the below the poverty line group than in the above the poverty line group. The percentage for those who are at least 65 years of age is higher for the above the poverty line group.

7. (a), (b) The column totals give the frequency marginal distribution of gender. The row totals give the frequency marginal distribution of age. To find the relative frequencies we divide each row or column total by the grand total = 26,438. For example, the relative frequency of Male is 19,701/26,438 = 0.745.

Age	Gender		Total	Relative Frequency
	Male	**Female**		
16–24	4,901	1,601	6,502	0.246
25–34	3,693	1,003	4,696	0.178
35–44	3,493	1,143	4,636	0.175
45–54	3,032	979	4,011	0.152
55–64	1,866	679	2,545	0.096
65–69	594	228	822	0.031
> 69	2,105	1,100	3,205	0.121
Unknown	17	4	21	0.001
Total	19,701	6,737	26,438	
Relative Frequency	0.745	0.255		

(c) 17.8% of drivers killed were between 25 and 34 (relative frequency of that row).

(d) 25.5% of drivers killed were female (relative frequency of that column).

(e)

Age	Gender	
	Male	**Female**
16–24	4901/19,701 = 0.249	1601/6,737 = 0.238
25–34	0.187	0.149
35–44	0.177	0.170
45–54	0.154	0.145
55–64	0.095	0.101
65–69	0.030	0.034
> 69	0.107	0.163
Unknown	0.001	0.001

(f)

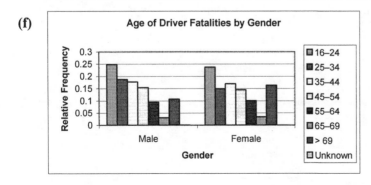

(g) Answers will vary. There is some association between age and gender as there is a somewhat higher percentage of younger fatalities among males than among females, and a higher percentage of unknown ages among females than among males.

9. (a), (b) The column totals give the frequency marginal distribution of cause of death. The row totals give the frequency marginal distribution of age.

Age	Cause of Death				Total	Relative Frequency
	Accidents	Malignant Neoplasms	Heart Disease	Cerebro-Vascular		
1–4 years	1679	383	186	59	2307	0.002
5–14 years	2561	1060	252	83	3956	0.003
15–24 years	14,966	1628	1083	204	17881	0.012
25–44 years	27,844	19,041	16,283	3004	66172	0.044
45–64 years	23,669	144,936	101,713	15,971	286,289	0.191
≥ 65 years	33,976	387,475	564,204	138,397	1,124,052	0.749
Total	104,695	554,523	683,721	157,718	1,500,657	
Relative Frequency	0.070	0.370	0.456	0.105		

(c) The percentage of deaths due to accidents is 7.0% (relative frequency of that column).

(d) The percentage of deaths of people aged 15–24 years is 1.2% (relative frequency of that row).

(e)

Age	Cause of Death			
	Accidents	Malignant Neoplasms	Heart Disease	Cerebro-Vascular
1–4 years	1679/104,695 = 0.0160	383/554,523 = 0.0007	186/683,721 = 0.0003	59/157,718 = 0.0004
5–14 years	0.025	0.002	0.0004	0.001
15–24 years	0.143	0.003	0.002	0.001
25–44 years	0.266	0.034	0.024	0.019
45–64 years	0.226	0.261	0.149	0.101
≥ 65 years	0.325	0.699	0.825	0.878

(f)

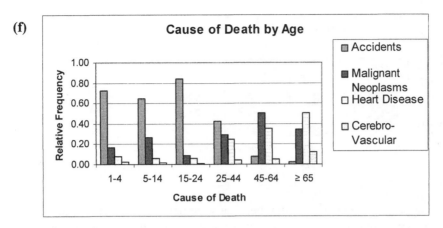

(g) Answers will vary. There is a strong association between age and cause of death. For example, the percent of deaths due to accidents is high for those aged 24 years or younger, but drops off rapidly as age increases. The percent of deaths due to heart disease increases as the percent due to accidents decreases.

11. (a), (b) The column totals give the frequency marginal distribution of year. The row totals give the frequency marginal distribution of age.

Age	Year			Total	Relative Frequency
	1990	**1995**	**2000**		
≤ 19 years	369	274	244	887	0.207
20–24 years	532	441	430	1403	0.327
≥ 25 years	713	645	640	1998	0.466
Total	1614	1360	1314	4288	
Relative Frequency	0.376	0.317	0.306		

(c) The percentage of abortions performed in 1990 is 37.6% (relative frequency of that column).

(d) The percentage of women 19 years or younger is 20.7% (relative frequency of that row).

(e)

Age	Year		
	1990	**1995**	**2000**
≤ 19 years	369/1614 = 0.229	274/1360 = 0.201	244/1314 = 0.186
20–24 years	0.330	0.324	0.327
≥ 25 years	0.442	0.474	0.487

307

(f)

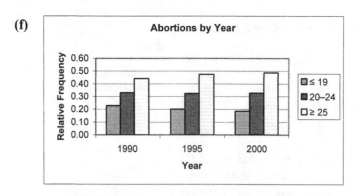

(g) There appears to be an association between year and age as the percentage of abortions by older women has risen over the years, and the percentage by younger women has declined.

13. (a)

	Accepted	Denied
Male	$\dfrac{98}{620} \approx 0.158$	$\dfrac{522}{620} \approx 0.842$
Female	$\dfrac{90}{290} \approx 0.310$	$\dfrac{200}{290} \approx 0.690$

(b) 0.158 of male applicants was accepted while 0.310 of female applicants was accepted.

(c) Based on the table we might conclude that a higher proportion of females was accepted.

(d)

Business School

	Accepted	Denied
Male	$\dfrac{90}{600} = 0.150$	$\dfrac{510}{600} = 0.850$
Female	$\dfrac{10}{70} \approx 0.143$	$\dfrac{60}{70} \approx 0.857$

Social Work School

	Accepted	Denied
Male	$\dfrac{8}{20} = 0.400$	$\dfrac{12}{20} = 0.600$
Female	$\dfrac{80}{220} \approx 0.364$	$\dfrac{140}{220} \approx 0.636$

0.15 of male applicants to the Business School was accepted while 0.143 of the female applicants was accepted.

(e) 0.40 of male applicants to the Social Work School was accepted while 0.364 of the female applicants was accepted.

(f) Answers will vary. Many programs are limited in the number of new enrollments. The Business School accepted about 15% of all applicants while the Social Work School accepted about 37% of all applicants. Many more males applied to the Business School where the likelihood of being denied is much greater. Many more females applied to the Social Work School where the likelihood of being accepted is much greater.

12.3 Tests for Independence and the Homogeneity of Proportions

1. The chi-square test for independence is a test of a single population and is to determine if there is an association between two characteristics of that population. The chi-square test for homogeneity is a test to determine if two distinct populations are the same with respect to a single characteristic, i.e. if that characteristic is exhibited by the same percentage of the two populations.

3. **(a)** $\chi^2 = \sum \dfrac{(O_i - E_i)^2}{E_i} = \dfrac{(34 - 36.26)^2}{36.26} + \cdots + \dfrac{(17 - 20.89)^2}{20.89} = 1.701$

   (b) df $= (2-1)(3-1) = 2$ so the critical value is $\chi^2_{0.05} = 5.991$. The test statistic is less than the critical value so we do not reject H_0. There is not enough evidence to support the claim that the two variables are dependent.

   (c) Using technology we get $P = 0.428$. (Answers may vary due to rounding.)

5. The hypotheses are $H_0 : p_1 = p_2 = p_3$ and $H_1 :$ at least one proportion differs from the others. df $= (2-1)(3-1) = 2$ so the critical value is $\chi^2_{0.01} = 9.210$. The expected counts are calculated as $\dfrac{\text{(row total)} \cdot \text{(column total)}}{\text{(table total)}} = \dfrac{229 \cdot 120}{363} = 75.70$ (for the first cell) so on. The observed and expected counts are shown in the table below. The test statistic is

   $\chi^2_0 = \sum \dfrac{(O_i - E_i)^2}{E_i} = \dfrac{(76 - 75.70)^2}{75.70} + \cdots + \dfrac{(49 - 43.56)^2}{43.56} = 1.988$ which is less than the

   critical value so we do not reject H_0. Using technology we get P-value $= 0.370$.

	Category 1	Category 2	Category 3	Total
Success	76	84	69	229
	(75.70)	(78.86)	(74.44)	
Failure	44	41	49	134
	(44.30)	(46.14)	(43.56)	
Total	120	125	118	363

7. (a) The expected counts are calculated as $\dfrac{(\text{row total}) \cdot (\text{column total})}{(\text{table total})} = \dfrac{199 \cdot 150}{380} = 78.55$

(for the first cell) and so on, giving the following table of observed and expected counts:

Sexual Activity	Family Structure				Total
	Both Parents	One Parent	Parent/ Stepparent	Nonparental Guardian	
Had intercourse	64	59	44	32	199
	(78.55)	(52.37)	(41.89)	(26.18)	
Did not have	86	41	36	18	181
	(71.45)	(47.63)	(38.11)	(23.82)	
Total	150	100	80	50	380

(b) All expected frequencies are greater than 5 so all requirements for a chi-square test are satisfied.

(c) $\chi_0^2 = \sum \dfrac{(O_i - E_i)^2}{E_i} = \dfrac{(64 - 78.55)^2}{78.55} + \cdots + \dfrac{(18 - 23.82)^2}{23.82} = 10.357$

(d) $df = (2-1)(4-1) = 3$ so the critical value is $\chi_{0.05}^2 = 7.815$. The test statistic is greater than the critical value so we reject H_0.

There is enough evidence to support the claim that family structure and sexual activity are dependent.

(e) The biggest difference between observed and expected occurs under the family structure in which both parents are present. Fewer females were sexually active than was expected when both parents were present. This means that having both parents present seems to have an impact on whether the child is sexually active.

(f) The conditional frequencies and bar chart show that sexual activity varies by family structure.

Sexual Activity	Both Parents	One Parent	Parent/Stepparent	Nonparent Guardian
Had Intercourse	$\dfrac{64}{150} \approx 0.427$	0.590	0.550	0.640
Did Not Have Intercourse	0.573	0.410	0.450	0.360

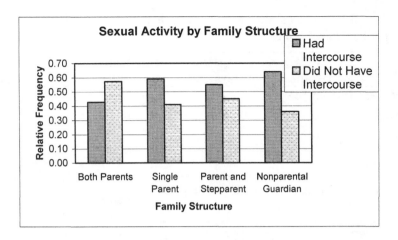

(g)   Using technology we get that P-value $= 0.0158 < \alpha$.

9. (a)   The expected counts and observed counts are shown in the table:

Area	Level of Education				Total
	Not HS Graduate	**HS Graduate**	**Some College**	**Graduated College**	
Northeast	52	123	70	94	339
	(66.90)	(108.80)	(80.99)	(82.31)	
Midwest	123	146	102	96	467
	(92.16)	(149.89)	(111.57)	(113.38)	
South	119	204	148	144	615
	(121.36)	(197.39)	(146.93)	(149.32)	
West	62	106	111	104	383
	(75.58)	(122.93)	(91.50)	(92.99)	
Total	356	579	431	438	1804

All expected frequencies are greater than 5 so the requirements for a chi-square test are satisfied. Using technology we calculate $\chi_0^2 = 32.926$. df $= (4-1)(4-1) = 9$ so the critical value is $\chi_{0.05}^2 = 16.919$. The test statistic is greater than the critical value so we reject H_0. [P-value $= 0.0001 < \alpha$]

There is enough evidence to support the claim that level of education and region of the United States are dependent.

(b)   From the calculations we find that the cell that contributed the most to the test statistic is the cell corresponding to "Midwest" and "Not a HS Graduate". The expected frequency was lower than the observed frequency suggesting that the Midwest has a higher proportion than other regions of people who are not high-school graduates.

311

(c)   The conditional frequencies and bar chart show that the amount of education varies by region of the United States.

Area	Not HS Graduate	HS Graduate	Some College	Graduated College
Northeast	0.146	0.212	0.162	0.215
Midwest	0.346	0.252	0.237	0.219
South	0.334	0.352	0.343	0.329
West	0.174	0.183	0.258	0.237

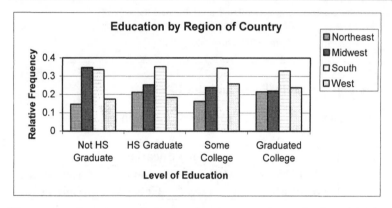

11. (a)   The expected counts and observed counts are shown in the table:

Opinion	Age Group			Total
	18–29 Years	**30–49 Years**	**> 49 Years**	
For	172	313	258	743
	(163.65)	(303.92)	(275.43)	
Against	52	103	119	274
	(60.35)	(112.08)	(101.57)	
Total	224	416	377	1017

All expected frequencies are greater than 5 so all requirements for a chi-square test are satisfied. Using technology we calculate $\chi_0^2 = 6.681$. df $= (2-1)(3-1) = 2$ so the critical value is $\chi_{0.05}^2 = 5.991$. The test statistic is greater than the critical value so we reject H_0. There is enough evidence to support the claim that opinion about the limited legalization of marijuana and age are dependent.

(b)   Using technology we get $P = 0.035$.

(c) The conditional frequencies and bar chart show that the percentage in favor of limited legalization of marijuana declines with age.

Opinion	18–29 Years	30–49 Years	> 49 Years
For	0.768	0.752	0.684
Against	0.232	0.248	0.316

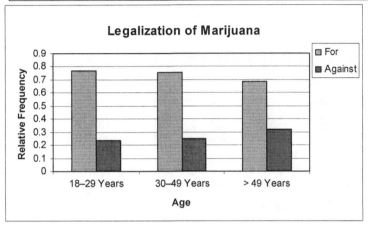

13. (a) The expected counts and observed counts are shown in the table:

Gender	Delinquency				Total
	Person	Property	Drugs	Public Order	
Female	24	85	7	28	144
	(23.23)	(86.78)	(8.83)	(25.15)	
Male	97	367	39	103	606
	(97.77)	(365.22)	(37.17)	(105.85)	
Total	121	452	46	131	750

All expected frequencies are greater than 5 so all requirements for a chi-square test are satisfied. Using technology we calculate $\chi_0^2 = 0.946$. $\text{df} = (2-1)(4-1) = 3$ so the critical value is $\chi_{0.05}^2 = 7.815$. The test statistic is less than the critical value so we do not reject H_0. There is not enough evidence to support the claim that type of delinquency and gender are dependent.

(b) Using technology we get P-value $= 0.814$.

(c)   The conditional frequencies and bar chart show that the distribution of genders is very similar for all offenses.

Gender	Person	Property	Drugs	Public Order
Female	0.198	0.188	0.152	0.214
Male	0.802	0.812	0.848	0.786

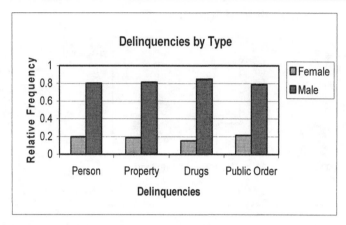

15. (a) $H_0 : p_{18-29} = p_{30-49} = p_{50-64} = p_{>64}$

H_1 : at least one of the proportions is different from the rest

The expected counts and observed counts are shown in the table:

Smoking Status	Age				Total
	18–29 Years	30–49 Years	50–64 Years	> 64 Years	
Smoked	24	21	23	12	80
	(20.00)	(20.00)	(20.00)	(20.00)	
Did not smoke	56	59	57	68	240
	(60.00)	(60.00)	(60.00)	(60.00)	
Total	80	80	80	80	320

All expected frequencies are greater than 5 so all requirements for a chi-square test are satisfied. Using technology we calculate $\chi_0^2 = 6.000$. df $= (2-1)(4-1) = 3$ so the critical value is $\chi_{0.05}^2 = 7.815$. The test statistic is less than the critical value so we do not reject H_0. There is not enough evidence to support the claim that the proportion of smokers differs by age group.

(b)   Using technology we get P-value $= 0.112$

(c) The conditional frequencies and bar chart show that the distribution of smokers is very similar for all age groups, except perhaps the over 64 years group.

Smoking Status	18–29 Years	30–49 Years	50–64 Years	> 64 Years
Smoked	0.300	0.263	0.288	0.150
Did not smoke	0.700	0.738	0.713	0.850

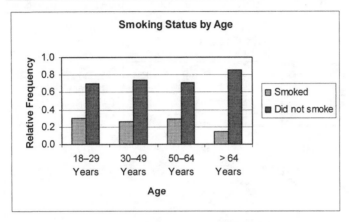

17. (a) $H_0 : p_{\text{placebo}} = p_{50\text{ mg}} = p_{100\text{ mg}} = p_{200\text{ mg}} = p_{\text{Naproxen}}$

H_1 : at least one of the proportions is not equal to the rest

The expected counts and observed counts are shown in the table:

Side Effect	Treatment					Total
	Placebo	Celebrex 50 mg	Celebrex 100 mg	Celebrex 200 mg	Naproxen 500 mg	
Ulcer	5	8	7	13	34	67
	(13.12)	(14.09)	(13.73)	(13.36)	(12.70)	
No Ulcer	212	225	220	208	176	1041
	(203.88)	(218.91)	(213.27)	(207.64)	(197.30)	
Total	217	233	227	221	210	1108

All expected frequencies are greater than 5 so all requirements for a chi-square test are satisfied. Using technology we calculate $\chi_0^2 = 49.703$. df $= (2-1)(5-1) = 4$ so the critical value is $\chi_{0.01}^2 = 13.277$. The test statistic is greater than the critical value so we reject H_0. There is enough evidence to support the claim that the incidence of ulcers varies by treatment.

(b) Using technology we get P-value < 0.001.

(c) The conditional frequencies and bar chart show that the percentage of subjects suffering ulcers varies by treatment.

Side Effect	Placebo	Celebrex 50 mg	Celebrex 100 mg	Celebrex 200 mg	Naproxen 500 mg
Ulcer	0.023	0.034	0.031	0.059	0.162
No Ulcer	0.977	0.966	0.969	0.941	0.838

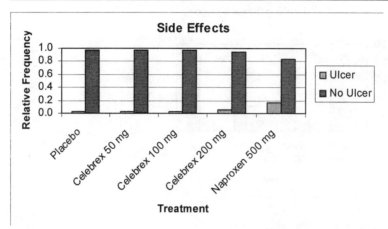

19. (a) The expected counts and observed counts are shown in the table. Since there were no individuals who gave "career" as a reason for dropping, we have omitted that category from the analysis.

Gender	Drop Reason			Total
	Personal	**Work**	**Course**	
Female	5	3	13	21
	(4.62)	(6.72)	(9.66)	
Male	6	13	10	29
	(6.38)	(9.28)	(13.34)	
Total	11	16	23	50

(b) All expected frequencies are greater than 1 and only one (out of six) expected frequency is less than 5. All requirements for a chi-square test are satisfied. Using technology we calculate $\chi_0^2 = 5.595$. df $= (2-1)(3-1) = 2$ so the critical value is $\chi_{0.10}^2 = 4.605$. The test statistic is greater than the critical value so we reject H_0. There is enough evidence to support the claim that reason for dropping and gender are dependent.

(c) Using technology we get P-value $= 0.061$.

(d) The conditional frequencies and bar chart show that the distribution of genders varies by reason for dropping.

	Personal	**Work**	**Course**
Female	0.455	0.188	0.565
Male	0.545	0.813	0.435

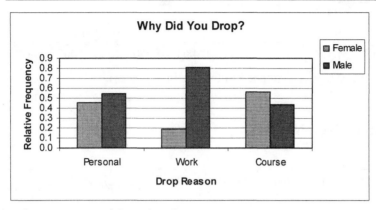

21. (a) The expected and observed counts are shown in the table.

Smoking Status	**Year**		**Total**
	1998	**2004**	
Smoked	282	222	504
	(252)	(252)	
Did not smoke	725	785	1510
	(755)	(755)	
Total	1007	1007	2014

(b) All expected frequencies are greater than 5 so the requirements for a chi-square test are satisfied. Using technology we calculate $\chi_0^2 = 9.527$.

(c) $H_0 : p_{1998} = p_{2004}$ versus $H_1 : p_{1998} \neq p_{2004}$

df $= (2-1)(2-1) = 1$ so the critical value is $\chi_{0.10}^2 = 3.841$. The test statistic is greater than the critical value so we reject H_0. There is enough evidence to support the claim that the percentage of Americans who have smoked at least one cigarette in the past week changed from 1998 to 2004.

317

(d)   The two sample estimates of percentage of smokers are $\hat{p}_1 = \dfrac{x_1}{n_1} = \dfrac{282}{1007} \approx 0.280040$,

$\hat{p}_2 = \dfrac{x_2}{n_2} = \dfrac{222}{1007} \approx 0.220457$. The pooled estimate is

$\hat{p} = \dfrac{x_1 + x_2}{n_1 + n_2} = \dfrac{282 + 222}{1007 + 1007} \approx 0.250248$. The test statistic is

$z_0 = \dfrac{\hat{p}_1 - \hat{p}_2}{\sqrt{\hat{p}(1-\hat{p})}\sqrt{1/n_1 + 1/n_2}} = \dfrac{0.280040 - 0.220457}{\sqrt{0.250248(1-0.250248)}\sqrt{1/1007 + 1/1007}} = 3.087$

and $z_0^2 = 9.530 \approx \chi_0^2$ (if rounded to two decimal places).

Chapter 12 Review Exercises

1.

Observed Count (O_i)	Expected Rel. Freq.	Expected Count (E_i)	$(O_i - E_i)^2$	$(O_i - E_i)^2 / E_i$
233	18/38	236.84	14.76	0.062
237	18/38	236.84	0.02	0.000
30	2/38	26.32	13.57	0.516
500		500	$\chi_0^2 =$	0.578

The critical value, with df $= 3 - 1 = 2$, is $\chi_{0.05}^2 = 5.991$. Since the test statistic is less than the critical value, we do not reject H_0. There is not enough evidence to support the claim that the roulette wheel is out of balance.

3.

Observed Count (O_i)	Expected Rel. Freq.	Expected Count (E_i)	$(O_i - E_i)^2$	$(O_i - E_i)^2 / E_i$
89	0.191	95.50	42.25	0.442
152	0.344	172.00	400.00	2.326
83	0.174	87.00	16.00	0.184
39	0.07	35.00	16.00	0.457
93	0.147	73.50	380.25	5.173
44	0.075	37.50	42.25	1.127
500		500	$\chi_0^2 =$	9.709

The critical value, with df $= 6 - 1 = 5$, is $\chi_{0.10}^2 = 9.236$. Since the test statistic is greater than the critical value, we reject H_0. There is enough evidence to support the claim that the distribution of educational attainment has changed since 1994.

5. (a), (b) The column totals give the frequency marginal distribution of region. The row totals give the frequency marginal distribution of firearm. To find the relative frequencies we divide each row or column total by the grand total = 517. For example, the relative frequency of Handgun is 390/517 = 0.754.

Firearm	Region				Total	Rel. Freq.
	Northeast	Midwest	South	West		
Handgun	43	79	182	86	390	0.754
Rifle	7	21	45	20	93	0.180
Shotgun	3	5	20	6	34	0.066
Total	53	105	247	112	517	
Relative Frequency	0.103	0.203	0.478	0.217		

(c) The percentage killed by a handgun is the relative frequency of the corresponding row, which = 75.4%.

(d) The percentage from the northeast is the relative frequency of the corresponding column, which = 10.3%.

(e)

Firearm	Region			
	Northeast	Midwest	South	West
Handgun	43/53 = 0.811	79/105 = 0.752	0.737	0.768
Rifle	0.132	0.200	0.182	0.179
Shotgun	0.057	0.048	0.081	0.054

(f)

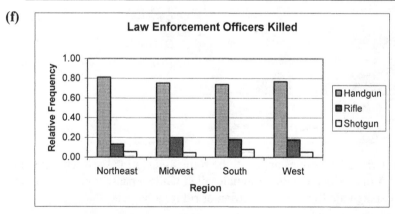

(g) Answers will vary. There does not appear to be much of an association between type of firearm and region. Handgun use is slightly more prevalent in the Northeast while shotgun use is less prevalent. However, the overall distribution is very similar for each region.

7. (a), (b) The column totals give the frequency marginal distribution of gender. The row totals give the frequency marginal distribution of type of fatality. To find the relative frequencies we divide each row or column total by the grand total = 1,578.

Type of Fatality	Gender		Total	Relative Frequency
	Male	Female		
Passenger in Vehicle	588	568	1156	0.733
Pedestrian	215	114	329	0.208
Bicycle	79	14	93	0.059
Total	882	696	1578	
Relative Frequency	0.559	0.441		

(c)   The percentage that were male is 55.9% (relative frequency of that column).

(d)   The percentage killed while riding a bicycle is 5.9% (relative frequency of that row).

(e)

Type of Fatality	Male	Female
Passenger in Vehicle	588/882 = 0.667	568/696 = 0.816
Pedestrian	0.244	0.164
Bicycle	0.090	0.020

(f)

(g)   Answers will vary. There does appear to be some association between type of fatality and gender. A higher percentage of females died while a passenger in a vehicle, while a lower percentage died while a pedestrian or riding a bicycle.

9. (a)   The expected counts are calculated as

$$\frac{(\text{row total})\cdot(\text{column total})}{(\text{table total})} = \frac{1{,}016 \cdot 732}{2{,}033} = 365.82 \text{ (for the first cell)}$$

and so on, giving the following table of observed and expected counts:

Date	Belief				Total
	God Guiding	**God had no Part**	**God Created**	**Other/No Opinion**	
February 2001	376	122	457	61	1,016
	(365.82)	(116.94)	(467.27)	(65.97)	
June 1993	356	112	478	71	1,017
	(366.18)	(117.06)	(467.73)	(66.03)	
Total	732	234	935	132	2,033

(b) All expected frequencies are greater than 5 so all requirements for a chi-square test are satisfied.

(c) $\chi_0^2 = \sum \dfrac{(O_i - E_i)^2}{E_i} = \dfrac{(376 - 365.82)^2}{365.82} + \cdots + \dfrac{(71 - 66.03)^2}{66.03} = 2.203$

(d) df $= (2-1)(4-1) = 3$ so the critical values is $\chi_{0.05}^2 = 7.815$. The test statistic is less than the critical value so we do not reject H_0. There is not enough evidence to support the claim that these beliefs are dependent on the date of the survey.

(e) From the calculations we find that 'Other/No Opinion' in 2001 contributed the most to the test statistic. The expected frequency was greater than the observed frequency.

(f) The conditional frequencies and bar chart show that beliefs appear not to have changed very much.

	God Guiding	**God had no Part**	**God Created**	**Other**
February 2001	0.370	0.120	0.450	0.060
June 1993	0.350	0.110	0.470	0.070

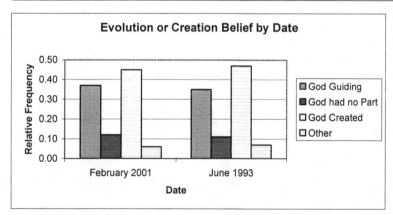

The distributions appear to be very similar. This supports the conclusion from part (d).

(g) Using technology we get that P-value $= 0.531$. Since P-value $< \alpha$, we would not reject the null hypothesis.

11. The expected counts and observed counts are shown in the table:

Race	Region				Total
	Not HS Graduate	HS Graduate	Some College	Graduated College	
White	421	520	656	400	1997
	(405.65)	(459.03)	(690.83)	(441.49)	
Black	56	57	158	28	299
	(60.74)	(68.73)	(103.43)	(66.10)	
American Indian etc	2	4	6	9	21
	(4.27)	(4.83)	(7.26)	(4.64)	
Asian	13	8	11	40	72
	(14.63)	(16.55)	(24.91)	(15.92)	
Hispanic	38	17	68	101	224
	(45.50)	(51.49)	(77.49)	(49.52)	
Other	17	8	24	50	99
	(20.11)	(22.76)	(34.25)	(21.89)	
Total	547	614	923	628	2712

All expected frequencies are greater than 1 and 3 out of 24 (which is less than 20%) of them are less than 5 so all requirements for a chi-square test are satisfied. Using technology we calculate $\chi_0^2 = 242.829$. df $= (6-1)(4-1) = 15$ so the critical value is $\chi_{0.01}^2 = 30.578$. The test statistic is greater than the critical value so we reject H_0. There is enough evidence to support the claim that race and region of the United States are dependent.

13. The expected counts and observed counts are shown in the table:

Symptoms	Region				Total
	Northeast	Midwest	South	West	
Within Last Year	26	31	23	35	115
	(28.75)	(28.75)	(28.75)	(28.75)	
Not Within Last Year	94	89	97	85	365
	(91.25)	(91.25)	(91.25)	(91.25)	
Total	120	120	120	120	480

All expected frequencies are greater than 5 so all requirements for a chi-square test are satisfied. Using technology we calculate $\chi_0^2 = 3.877$. df $= (2-1)(4-1) = 3$ so the critical value is $\chi_{0.05}^2 = 7.815$. The test statistic is less than the critical value so we do not reject H_0. There is not enough evidence to support the claim that the proportion of people who have had colds in the last year varies by region.

322

15. The expected counts and observed counts are shown in the table:

Response	Age				Total
	18–29	**30–49**	**50 – 64**	**65 or Older**	
Morning	97	177	210	210	694
	(179.60)	(175.81)	(172.01)	(166.58)	
Night	234	147	107	97	585
	(151.40)	(148.19)	(144.99)	(140.42)	
Total	331	324	317	307	1279

All expected frequencies are greater than 5 so all requirements for a chi-square test are satisfied. Using technology we calculate $\chi_0^2 = 126.168$. df $= (2-1)(4-1) = 3$ so the critical value is $\chi_{0.05}^2 = 7.815$. The test statistic is greater than the critical value so we reject H_0. There is enough evidence to support the claim that the proportion of Americans who are morning persons or night person varies by age group.

Chapter 13

Comparing Three or More Means

13.1 Comparing Three or More Means

1. analysis of variance.

3. The mean square due to treatment estimate of σ^2 is a weighted average of the squared deviations of each sample mean from the grand mean of all the samples. The mean square due to error estimate of σ^2 is the weighted average of the sample variances.

5.

Source of Variation	Sum of Squares	Degrees of Freedom	Mean Squares	F - Test Statistic
Treatment	387	2	$\dfrac{387}{2} = 193.5$	$\dfrac{193.5}{297.852} \approx 0.650$
Error	8042	27	$\dfrac{8042}{27} \approx 297.852$	
Total	8429	29		

7. $\bar{x} = \dfrac{10 \cdot 40 + 10 \cdot 42 + 10 \cdot 44}{10 + 10 + 10} = \dfrac{1260}{30} = 42$;

$\text{MST} = \dfrac{10(40-42)^2 + 10(42-42)^2 + 10(44-42)^2}{3-1} = \dfrac{80}{2} = 40$;

$\text{MSE} = \dfrac{(10-1) \cdot 48 + (10-1) \cdot 31 + (10-1) \cdot 25}{30-3} = \dfrac{936}{27} \approx 34.667$; $F = \dfrac{40}{34.667} \approx 1.154$

9. $\bar{x}_1 = \dfrac{28 + 23 + 30 + 27}{4} = \dfrac{108}{4} = 27$; $\bar{x}_2 = \dfrac{22 + 25 + 17 + 23}{4} = \dfrac{87}{4} = 21.75$;

$\bar{x}_3 = \dfrac{25 + 24 + 19 + 30}{4} = \dfrac{98}{4} = 24.5$; $\bar{x} = \dfrac{28 + 23 + 30 + ... + 19 + 30}{12} = \dfrac{293}{12} \approx 24.417$;

$s_1^2 = \dfrac{(28-27)^2 + (23-27)^2 + (30-27)^2 + (27-27)^2}{4-1} = \dfrac{26}{3} \approx 8.667$;

$s_2^2 = \dfrac{(22-21.75)^2 + (25-21.75)^2 + (17-21.75)^2 + (23-21.75)^2}{4-1} = \dfrac{34.75}{3} \approx 11.583$;

$s_3^2 = \dfrac{(25-24.5)^2 + (24-24.5)^2 + (19-24.5)^2 + (30-24.5)^2}{4-1} = \dfrac{61}{3} \approx 20.333$;

$\text{MST} = \dfrac{4(27-24.417)^2 + 4(21.75-24.417)^2 + 4(24.5-24.417)^2}{3-1} \approx \dfrac{55.167}{2} \approx 27.584$;

$\text{MSE} = \dfrac{(4-1) \cdot 8.667 + (4-1) \cdot 11.583 + (4-1) \cdot 20.333}{12-3} = \dfrac{121.749}{9} \approx 13.528$;

$F = \dfrac{27.584}{13.528} \approx 2.04$.

11. (a) The hypotheses are $H_0 : \mu_{\text{sludge plot}} = \mu_{\text{spring disk}} = \mu_{\text{no till}}$ versus H_1 : at least one mean differs from the others.

(b) (1) Each sample must be a simple random sample.
(2) The three samples must be independent of each other.
(3) The samples must come from normally distributed populations.
(4) The populations must have equal variances.

(c) Since P-value $= 0.007$ is smaller than the $\alpha = 0.05$ level of significance, we reject H_0. There is sufficient evidence to conclude that at least one plot type has a mean number of plants that differs from the other means.

(d) Yes, the boxplots support the results obtained in part (c). The boxplots indicate that significantly more plants are growing in the spring disk plot than in the other plot types.

(e) The needed summary statistics are: $\overline{x}_{\text{sludge plot}} \approx 28.333$, $\overline{x}_{\text{spring disk}} = 33$, $\overline{x}_{\text{no till}} = 28.5$, $\overline{x} \approx 29.944$, $s^2_{\text{sludge plot}} \approx 7.867$, $s^2_{\text{spring disk}} = 3.2$, $s^2_{\text{no till}} = 6.7$, $n_{\text{sludge plot}} = n_{\text{spring disk}} = n_{\text{no till}} = 6$, $n = 18$, and $k = 3$. Thus,

$$\text{MST} = \frac{6(28.333 - 29.994)^2 + 6(33 - 29.994)^2 + 6(28.5 - 29.994)^2}{3-1} \approx \frac{84.114}{2} \approx 42.057,$$

$$\text{MSE} = \frac{(6-1) \cdot 7.867 + (6-1) \cdot 3.2 + (6-1) \cdot 6.7}{18-3} = \frac{88.835}{15} \approx 5.922, \text{ and}$$

$$F = \frac{42.057}{5.922} \approx 7.10.$$

13. (a) The hypotheses are $H_0 : \mu_M = \mu_T = \mu_W = \mu_R = \mu_F$ versus H_1 : at least one mean differs from the others.

(b) (1) Each sample must be a simple random sample.
(2) The five samples must be independent of each other.
(3) The samples must come from normally distributed populations.
(4) The populations must have equal variances.

(c) Since P-value ≈ 0.000 is smaller than the $\alpha = 0.01$ level of significance, we reject H_0. There is sufficient evidence to conclude that at least one weekday has a mean number of births that differs from the other means.

(d) Yes, from the boxplots it appears that Monday has fewer births than other weekdays.

(e) The needed summary statistics are: $\overline{x}_M \approx 10,696.3$, $\overline{x}_T \approx 12,237.1$, $\overline{x}_W \approx 11,586.9$, $\overline{x}_R \approx 11,897.9$, $\overline{x}_F \approx 12,002.9$, $\overline{x} = 11,684.2$, $s^2_M = 279,042.5$, $s^2_T \approx 633,537.8$, $s^2_W \approx 136,085.3$, $s^2_R \approx 252,402.7$, $s^2_F \approx 166,186.1$ $n_M = n_T = n_W = n_R = n_F = 8$, $n = 40$, and $k = 5$. Thus,

$$\text{MST} = \frac{8(10,696.3 - 11,684.2)^2 + 8(12,237.1 - 11,684.2)^2 + ... + 8(12,002.9 - 11,684.2)^2}{5-1}$$

$$\approx \frac{11,506,795.9}{4} \approx 2,876,698.8,$$

$$MSE = \frac{(8-1)\cdot 279{,}042.5 + (8-1)\cdot 633{,}537.8 + \ldots + (8-1)\cdot 116{,}186.1}{40-5}$$

$$= \frac{10{,}270{,}780.8}{35} \approx 293{,}450.9, \text{ and}$$

$$F = \frac{2{,}876{,}698.8}{293{,}450.9} \approx 9.80.$$

(f) From the boxplots, Monday appears to have significantly fewer births than the other days.

15. (a) The hypotheses are $H_0 : \mu_{\text{Financial}} = \mu_{\text{Energy}} = \mu_{\text{Utilities}}$ versus H_1 : at least one mean differs from the others.

(b) (1) Each sample is a simple random sample.
(2) The three samples are independent of each other.
(3) The samples are from normally distributed populations.
(4) $s_{\text{Financial}} \approx 5.12$, $s_{\text{Energy}} \approx 4.87$, and $s_{\text{Utilities}} \approx 4.53$. The largest sample standard deviation is less than twice the smallest sample standard deviation, so the requirement that the populations have equal variances is satisfied.

(c) Using MINITAB, we obtain the following output:

One-way ANOVA: Financial, Energy, Utilities

Source	DF	SS	MS	F	P
Factor	2	97.6	48.8	2.08	0.150
Error	21	493.3	23.5		
Total	23	590.9			

Since P-value ≈ 0.150 is larger than the $\alpha = 0.05$ level of significance, we do not reject H_0. There is not sufficient evidence to conclude that at least one mean is different from the others.

(d)

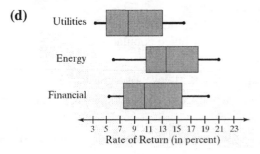

17. (a) The hypotheses are $H_0 : \mu_{\text{Large Fam. Car}} = \mu_{\text{Pass. Van}} = \mu_{\text{Mid. Util. Veh.}}$ versus H_1 : at least one mean differs from the others.

(b) (1) Each sample is a simple random sample.
(2) The three samples are independent of each other.
(3) The samples are from normally distributed populations.
(4) $s_{\text{Large Fam. Car}} \approx 3.26$, $s_{\text{Pass. Van}} \approx 3.73$, and $s_{\text{Mid. Util. Veh.}} \approx 3.39$. The largest sample standard deviation is less than twice the smallest sample standard deviation, so the requirement that the populations have equal variances is satisfied.

(c) Using MINITAB, we obtain the following output:

One-way ANOVA: Large Family Cars, Passenger Vans, Midsize Utility Vehicles
```
Source   DF     SS     MS     F      P
Factor    2   70.6   35.3   2.94  0.079
Error    18  216.0   12.0
Total    20  286.6
```

Since P-value ≈ 0.079 is larger than the $\alpha = 0.01$ level of significance, we do not reject H_0. There is not sufficient evidence to conclude that at least one mean is different from the others.

(d)

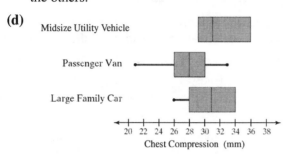

Chest Compression (mm)

19. (a) The hypotheses are $H_0 : \mu_{\text{Alaska}} = \mu_{\text{Florida}} = \mu_{\text{Texas}}$ versus $H_1 :$ at least one mean differs from the others.

(b) (1) Each sample is a simple random sample.
(2) The three samples are independent of each other.
(3) The samples are from normally distributed populations.
(4) $s_{\text{Alaska}} \approx 0.252$, $s_{\text{Florida}} \approx 0.283$, and $s_{\text{Texas}} \approx 0.397$. The largest sample standard deviation is less than twice the smallest sample standard deviation, so the requirement that the populations have equal variances is satisfied.

(c) Using MINITAB, we obtain the following output:

One-way ANOVA: Alaska, Florida, Texas
```
Source   DF     SS     MS     F      P
Factor    2  1.168  0.584  5.81  0.014
Error    15  1.507  0.100
Total    17  2.674
```

Since P-value ≈ 0.014 is less than $\alpha = 0.05$, we reject H_0. There is sufficient evidence to conclude that at least one mean is different from the others.

(d)

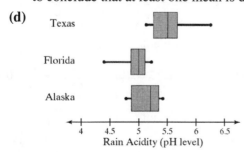

Rain Acidity (pH level)

21. **(a)** The hypotheses are $H_0 : \mu_{67-0-301} = \mu_{67-0-400} = \mu_{67-0-353}$ versus H_1 : at least one mean differs from the others.

   (b) $s_{67-0-301} \approx 107.8$, $s_{67-0-400} \approx 385.0$, and $s_{67-0-353} \approx 195.8$. Since the largest standard deviation is greater than twice the smallest standard deviation (i.e., since $385.0 > 2 \cdot 107.8$), the rule of thumb for meeting the ANOVA requirement of equal variances is violated, and so we cannot perform an ANOVA.

13.2   Post Hoc Tests on One-Way Analysis of Variance

1. The purpose of multiple comparison tests is to determine which means differ significantly. We use them when the results of a one-way ANOVA lead us to reject the null hypothesis, telling us that at least one of the means is different.

3. **(a)** We look in the table of critical values for Tukey's Test with $\alpha = 0.05$ and where the row corresponding to $v = 10$ intersects with the column corresponding to $k = 3$ to find the critical value $q_{0.05,10,3} = 3.877$.

   (b) We look in the table of critical values for Tukey's Test with $\alpha = 0.05$ and where the row corresponding to $v = 24$ intersects with the column corresponding to $k = 5$ to find the critical value $q_{0.05,24,5} = 4.166$.

   (c) We look in the table of critical values for Tukey's Test with $\alpha = 0.05$ and where the row corresponding to $v = 30$ (since there is no row in the table for $v = 32$) intersects with the column corresponding to $k = 8$ to find the critical value $q_{0.05,32,8} \approx q_{0.05,30,8} = 4.602$.

   (d) For this test, $k = 5$ and $v = n - k = 65 - 5 = 60$, so we look in the table with $\alpha = 0.05$ and where the row corresponding to $v = 60$ intersects with the column corresponding to $k = 5$ to find the critical value $q_{0.05,60,5} = 3.977$.

5. Arrange the sample means in ascending order: $\bar{x}_2 = 9.1$, $\bar{x}_1 = 9.5$, $\bar{x}_3 = 18.1$. Now $n = 5 \cdot 3 = 15$ and $k = 3$, so $v = n - k = 12$ and the critical value is $q_{0.05,12,3} = 3.773$.

   We first test $H_0 : \mu_3 = \mu_2$. The test statistic is $q = \dfrac{\bar{x}_3 - \bar{x}_2}{\sqrt{\frac{s^2}{2} \cdot \left(\frac{1}{n_3} + \frac{1}{n_2}\right)}} = \dfrac{18.1 - 9.1}{\sqrt{\frac{26.2}{2} \cdot \left(\frac{1}{5} + \frac{1}{5}\right)}} \approx 3.932$.

   Since this test statistic is greater than $q_{0.05,12,3} = 3.773$, we reject $H_0 : \mu_3 = \mu_2$.

   Next, we test $H_0 : \mu_3 = \mu_1$. The test statistic is $q = \dfrac{\bar{x}_3 - \bar{x}_1}{\sqrt{\frac{s^2}{2} \cdot \left(\frac{1}{n_3} + \frac{1}{n_1}\right)}} = \dfrac{18.1 - 9.5}{\sqrt{\frac{26.2}{2} \cdot \left(\frac{1}{5} + \frac{1}{5}\right)}} \approx 3.757$.

   Since this test statistic is less than $q_{0.05,12,3} = 3.773$, we do not reject $H_0 : \mu_3 = \mu_1$.

   Finally, we test $H_0 : \mu_1 = \mu_2$. The test statistic is $q = \dfrac{\bar{x}_1 - \bar{x}_2}{\sqrt{\frac{s^2}{2} \cdot \left(\frac{1}{n_1} + \frac{1}{n_2}\right)}} = \dfrac{9.5 - 9.1}{\sqrt{\frac{26.2}{2} \cdot \left(\frac{1}{5} + \frac{1}{5}\right)}} \approx 0.175$.

   Since this test statistic is less than $q_{0.05,12,3} = 3.773$, we do not reject $H_0 : \mu_1 = \mu_2$.

   The results of the test are ambiguous since we have that $\mu_1 = \mu_3$ and $\mu_1 = \mu_2$, but $\mu_2 \neq \mu_3$. That is, we have: $\underline{\mu_2 \quad \mu_1} \quad \mu_3$.

7. (a) The hypotheses are $H_0 : \mu_1 = \mu_2 = \mu_3$ versus H_1 : at least one mean differs from the others. Using MINITAB, we obtain the following output:

One-way ANOVA: Sample 1, Sample 2, Sample 3
```
Source  DF     SS     MS     F      P
Factor   2   641.3  320.7  9.27  0.002
Error   15   519.2   34.6
Total   17  1160.5
```

Since P-value ≈ 0.002 is less than the $\alpha = 0.05$ level of significance, we reject H_0. There is sufficient evidence to conclude that at least one mean differs from the others.

(b) Using MINITAB, we obtain the following output:

```
Tukey 95% Simultaneous Confidence Intervals
All Pairwise Comparisons

Individual confidence level = 97.97%

Sample 1 subtracted from:
```
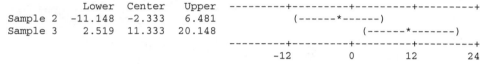
```
           Lower   Center  Upper
Sample 2  -11.148  -2.333  6.481
Sample 3    2.519  11.333  20.148
```

```
Sample 2 subtracted from:

           Lower   Center  Upper
Sample 3   4.852  13.667  22.481
```

From the output we have:

$-11.148 < \mu_2 - \mu_1 < 6.481$. This interval contains 0, so we do not reject $H_0 : \mu_1 = \mu_2$.

$2.519 < \mu_3 - \mu_1 < 20.148$. This interval does not contain 0, so we reject $H_0 : \mu_1 = \mu_3$.

$4.852 < \mu_3 - \mu_2 < 22.481$. This interval does not contain 0, so we reject $H_0 : \mu_2 = \mu_3$.

Thus, we have $\mu_1 = \mu_2 \neq \mu_3$. That is, we have: $\underline{\mu_1 \quad \mu_2} \quad \underline{\mu_3}$.

(c) The boxplots shown to the right support the result of parts (a) and (b).

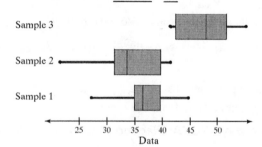

9. From the provided output, we have:

$1.021 < \mu_{\text{spring disk}} - \mu_{\text{sludge plot}} < 8.313$. This interval does not contain 0, so we reject

$H_0 : \mu_{\text{sludge plot}} = \mu_{\text{spring disk}}$.

$-3.479 < \mu_{\text{no till}} - \mu_{\text{sludge plot}} < 3.813$. This interval contains 0, so we do not reject

$H_0 : \mu_{\text{sludge plot}} = \mu_{\text{no till}}$.

$-8.146 < \mu_{\text{no till}} - \mu_{\text{spring disk}} < -0.854$. This interval does not contain 0, so we reject

$H_0 : \mu_{\text{spring disk}} = \mu_{\text{no till}}$.

Thus, we have $\mu_{\text{sludge plot}} = \mu_{\text{no till}} \neq \mu_{\text{spring disk}}$. That is, we have: $\underline{\mu_{\text{sludge plot}} \quad \mu_{\text{no till}} \quad \mu_{\text{spring disk}}}$.

From the pairwise comparisons, it appears that the spring disk method has a greater mean number of plants. Therefore, we should recommend spring disk method of planting.

11. We use MINITAB to obtain the following output:

```
Tukey 95% Simultaneous Confidence Intervals
All Pairwise Comparisons

Individual confidence level = 97.97%

Alaska subtracted from:

            Lower   Center   Upper  -------+---------+---------+---------+-
Florida   -0.7015  -0.2267  0.2482       (-------*-------)
Texas     -0.0849   0.3900  0.8649                 (------*-------)
                                        -------+---------+---------+---------+-
                                         -0.60      0.00      0.60      1.20

Florida subtracted from:

            Lower   Center   Upper  -------+---------+---------+---------+-
Texas      0.1418   0.6167  1.0915                   (-------*-------)
                                        -------+---------+---------+---------+-
                                         -0.60      0.00      0.60      1.20
```

From the output, we have:

$-0.7015 < \mu_{\text{Florida}} - \mu_{\text{Alaska}} < 0.2482$. This interval contains 0, so we do not reject

$H_0 : \mu_{\text{Alaska}} = \mu_{\text{Florida}}$.

$-0.0849 < \mu_{\text{Texas}} - \mu_{\text{Alaska}} < 0.8649$. This interval does not contain 0, so we reject

$H_0 : \mu_{\text{Alaska}} = \mu_{\text{Texas}}$.

$0.1418 < \mu_{\text{Texas}} - \mu_{\text{Florida}} < 1.0915$. This interval does not contain 0, so we do not reject

$H_0 : \mu_{\text{Florida}} = \mu_{\text{Texas}}$.

The results are ambiguous. We have that $\mu_{\text{Alaska}} = \mu_{\text{Florida}}$ and $\mu_{\text{Florida}} = \mu_{\text{Texas}}$, but

$\mu_{\text{Alaska}} \neq \mu_{\text{Texas}}$. That is, we have: $\underline{\mu_{\text{Florida}} \quad \mu_{\text{Alaska}} \quad \mu_{\text{Texas}}}$.

13. (a) The hypotheses are $H_0 : \mu_{\text{Placebo}} = \mu_{\text{Rit 10}} = \mu_{\text{Rit 17.5}} = \mu_{\text{Add 7.5}} = \mu_{\text{Add 12.5}}$ versus H_1 : at least one mean differs from the others. Using MINITAB, we obtain the following output:

One-way ANOVA: Placebo, Ritalin 10 m, Ritalin 17.5, Adderall 7.5, Adderall 12.

Source	DF	SS	MS	F	P
Factor	4	7297	1824	5.75	0.001
Error	30	9519	317		
Total	34	16816			

Since P-value $= 0.001$ is less than the $\alpha = 0.05$ level of significance, we reject H_0.

There is sufficient evidence to support the hypothesis that at least one of the mean abilities to follow rules is different from the others.

(b) Using MINITAB, we obtain the following output:

```
Tukey 95% Simultaneous Confidence Intervals
All Pairwise Comparisons

Individual confidence level = 99.31%

Placebo subtracted from:

          Lower   Center   Upper   -----+---------+---------+---------+----
Rit 10     0.25    27.86   55.46                    (--------*--------)
Rit 17.5   1.11    28.71   56.32                    (---------*--------)
Add 7.5    4.11    31.71   59.32                    (---------*--------)
Add 12.5  16.40    44.00   71.60                        (---------*--------)
                                   -----+---------+---------+---------+----
                                      -30        0        30        60


Rit 10 subtracted from:

          Lower   Center   Upper   -----+---------+---------+---------+----
Rit 17.5 -26.75     0.86   28.46              (--------*--------)
Add 7.5  -23.75     3.86   31.46              (---------*--------)
Add 12.5 -11.46    16.14   43.75                  (--------*---------)
                                   -----+---------+---------+---------+----
                                      -30        0        30        60


Rit 17.5 subtracted from:

          Lower   Center   Upper   -----+---------+---------+---------+----
Add 7.5  -24.60     3.00   30.60             (--------*--------)
Add 12.5 -12.32    15.29   42.89                 (--------*--------)
                                   -----+---------+---------+---------+----
                                      -30        0        30        60


Add 7.5 subtracted from:

          Lower   Center   Upper   -----+---------+---------+---------+----
Add 12.5 -15.32    12.29   39.89                (--------*--------)
                                   -----+---------+---------+---------+----
                                      -30        0        30        60
```

From the output, we have:

$0.25 < \mu_{\text{Rit 10}} - \mu_{\text{Placebo}} < 55.46$. This interval does not contain 0, so we reject

$H_0 : \mu_{\text{Placebo}} = \mu_{\text{Rit 10}}$.

$1.11 < \mu_{\text{Rit 17.5}} - \mu_{\text{Placebo}} < 56.32$. This interval does not contain 0, so we reject

$H_0 : \mu_{\text{Placebo}} = \mu_{\text{Rit 17.5}}$.

$4.11 < \mu_{\text{Add 7.5}} - \mu_{\text{Placebo}} < 59.32$. This interval does not contain 0, so we reject

$H_0 : \mu_{\text{Placebo}} = \mu_{\text{Add 7.5}}$.

$16.40 < \mu_{\text{Add 12.5}} - \mu_{\text{Placebo}} < 71.60$. This interval does not contain 0, so we reject

$H_0 : \mu_{\text{Placebo}} = \mu_{\text{Add 12.5}}$.

$-26.75 < \mu_{\text{Rit 17.5}} - \mu_{\text{Rit 10}} < 28.46$. This interval contains 0, so we do not reject

$H_0 : \mu_{\text{Rit 10}} = \mu_{\text{Rit 17.5}}$.

$-23.75 < \mu_{\text{Add 7.5}} - \mu_{\text{Rit 10}} < 31.46$. This interval contains 0, so we do not reject

$H_0 : \mu_{\text{Rit 10}} = \mu_{\text{Add 7.5}}$.

$-11.5 < \mu_{\text{Add 12.5}} - \mu_{\text{Rit 10}} < 43.75$. This interval contains 0, so we do not reject

$H_0 : \mu_{\text{Rit 10}} = \mu_{\text{Add 12.5}}$.

$-24.60 < \mu_{\text{Add 7.5}} - \mu_{\text{Rit 17.5}} < 30.60$. This interval contains 0, so we do not reject

331

$H_0 : \mu_{\text{Rit 17.5}} = \mu_{\text{Add 7.5}}$.

$-12.32 < \mu_{\text{Add 12.5}} - \mu_{\text{Rit 17.5}} < 42.89$. This interval contains 0, so we do not reject

$H_0 : \mu_{\text{Rit 17.5}} = \mu_{\text{Add 12.5}}$.

$-15.32 < \mu_{\text{Add 12.5}} - \mu_{\text{Add 7.5}} < 39.89$. This interval contains 0, so we do not reject

$H_0 : \mu_{\text{Add 7.5}} = \mu_{\text{Add 12.5}}$.

Thus, we have that $\mu_{\text{Placebo}} \neq \mu_{\text{Rit 10}} = \mu_{\text{Rit 17.5}} = \mu_{\text{Add 7.5}} = \mu_{\text{Add 12.5}}$. That is, we have:

$\underline{\mu_{\text{Placebo}}} \quad \mu_{\text{Rit 10}} \quad \mu_{\text{Rit 17.5}} \quad \mu_{\text{Add 7.5}} \quad \mu_{\text{Add 12.5}}$. The mean ability to follow rules of a child taking the placebo is less than the mean ability to follow rules of a child taking any of the four drug treatments.

(c) The boxplots shown to the right support the result of parts (a) and (b).

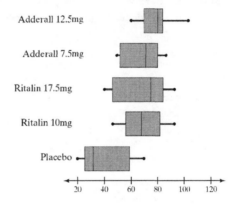

15. (a) The hypotheses are $H_0 : \mu_{\text{nonsmokers}} = \mu_{\text{light smokers}} = \mu_{\text{heavy smokers}}$ versus H_1 : at least one mean differs from the others. Using MINITAB, we obtain the following output:

One-way ANOVA: Nonsmokers, Light Smokers, Heavy Smokers

```
Source  DF     SS     MS      F      P
Factor   2  1437.4  718.7  17.09  0.000
Error   18   756.9   42.0
Total   20  2194.3
```

Since P-value ≈ 0.000 is less than the $\alpha = 0.05$ level of significance, we reject H_0.

There is sufficient evidence to support the hypothesis that at least one of the mean heart rates is different from the others.

(b) Using MINITAB, we obtain the following output:

```
Tukey 95% Simultaneous Confidence Intervals
All Pairwise Comparisons
Individual confidence level = 98.00%

Nonsmokers subtracted from:

                Lower   Center   Upper   ----+---------+---------+---------+-----
Light Smokers   3.152   12.000  20.848                        (------*------)
Heavy Smokers  11.295   20.143  28.991                             (-------*------)
                                         ----+---------+---------+---------+-----
                                          -12         0        12        24

Light Smokers subtracted from:

                Lower   Center   Upper   ----+---------+---------+---------+-----
Heavy Smokers  -0.705    8.143  16.991                   (-------*------)
                                         ----+---------+---------+---------+-----
                                          -12         0        12        24
```

From the output, we have:

$3.152 < \mu_{\text{light smokers}} - \mu_{\text{nonsmokers}} < 20.848$. This interval does not contain 0, so we reject

$H_0 : \mu_{\text{nonsmokers}} = \mu_{\text{light smokers}}$.

$11.295 < \mu_{\text{heavy smokers}} - \mu_{\text{nonsmokers}} < 28.991$. This interval does not contain 0, so we reject

$H_0 : \mu_{\text{nonsmokers}} = \mu_{\text{heavy smokers}}$.

$-0.705 < \mu_{\text{heavy smokers}} - \mu_{\text{light smokers}} < 16.991$. This interval contains 0, so we do not reject

$H_0 : \mu_{\text{light smokers}} = \mu_{\text{heavy smokers}}$.

Thus, we have that $\mu_{\text{nonsmokers}} \neq \mu_{\text{light smokers}} = \mu_{\text{heavy smokers}}$. That is, we have:

$\underline{\mu_{\text{nonsmokers}} \quad \mu_{\text{light smokers}} \quad \mu_{\text{heavy smokers}}}$. It appears that the mean heart rate of

nonsmokers is lower than the mean heart rate of smokers and that the mean heat rate of smokers is the same regardless if they are light smokers or heavy smokers.

(c) The boxplots shown to the right support the result of parts (a) and (b).

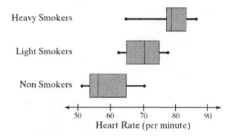

17. (a) The hypotheses are $H_0 : \mu_{\text{skim}} = \mu_{\text{mixed}} = \mu_{\text{whole}}$ versus H_1 : at least one mean differs from the others. Using MINITAB, we obtain the following output:

One-way ANOVA: Skim Milk, Mixed Milk, Whole Milk

```
Source  DF      SS     MS      F      P
Factor   2  117596  58798  70.51  0.000
Error   21   17511    834
Total   23  135107
```

Since P-value ≈ 0.000 is less than the $\alpha = 0.05$ level of significance, we reject H_0. There is sufficient evidence to support the hypothesis that at least one of the mean calcium intake levels is different from the others.

(b) Using MINITAB, we obtain the following output:

```
Tukey 95% Simultaneous Confidence Intervals
All Pairwise Comparisons

Individual confidence level = 98.00%

Skim Milk subtracted from:
```

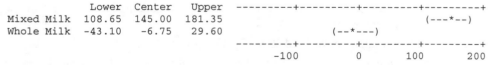

```
Mixed Milk subtracted from:
```

From the output, we have:

$108.65 < \mu_{mixed} - \mu_{skim} < 181.35$. This interval does not contain 0, so we reject

$H_0 : \mu_{skim} = \mu_{mixed}$.

$-43.10 < \mu_{whole} - \mu_{skim} < 29.60$. This interval contains 0, so we do not reject

$H_0 : \mu_{skim} = \mu_{whole}$.

$-188.10 < \mu_{whole} - \mu_{mixed} < -115.40$. This interval does not contain 0, so we reject

$H_0 : \mu_{mixed} = \mu_{whole}$.

Thus, we have that $\mu_{mixed} \neq \mu_{skim} = \mu_{whole}$. That is, we have: $\underline{\mu_{mixed}}\quad \underline{\mu_{skim}\quad \mu_{whole}}$.

It appears that the mean calcium intake of children who drank mixed milk is different from the mean calcium intakes of children who drank skim or whole milk.

(c) The boxplots shown to the right support the result of parts (a) and (b).

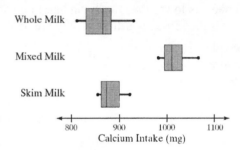

13.3 The Randomized Complete Block Design

1. In a completely randomized design, the researcher examines a single factor fixed at k levels and randomly distributes the experimental units among the levels. In a randomized complete block design, there is a factor whose level cannot be fixed. So the researcher partitions the experimental units according to this factor, forming blocks which may form homogeneous groups. Within each block, the experimental units are assigned to one of the treatments.

3. *Randomized* means that the order in which the treatment is applied within each block is random. *Complete* refers to the fact that each block gets every treatment.

5. A researcher can deal with explanatory variables by:
    (1) Controlling their levels so that they remain fixed throughout the experiment;
    (2) Manipulating or setting them at a fixed level; or
    (3) Randomizing so that any effects cannot be identified or controlled are minimized.

7. **(a)** The treatment P-value $= 0.013$ is sufficient evidence against the null hypothesis that the population means are equal. The researcher will conclude that at least one population mean is different from the others.

    (b) The mean square error is MSE $= 17.517$.

    (c) The P-values comparing treatment 3 with treatments 1 and 2 are small (less than 0.05) while the P-value comparing treatments 1 and 2 is large. Therefore, we conclude that means 1 and 2 are the same, but mean 3 is different. That is, we conclude $\mu_1 = \mu_2 \neq \mu_3$ or $\underline{\mu_1\quad \mu_2}\quad \underline{\mu_3}$.

334

9. (a) The treatment *P*-value = 0.108 is not sufficient evidence against the null hypothesis that the population means are equal. In other words, the researcher does not reject the null hypothesis that population means are equal.

(b) The mean square error is MSE = 0.944.

(c) We would only use Tukey's test if the null hypothesis from part (a) had been rejected.

11. (a) Using MINITAB, we obtain the following output:

Two-way ANOVA: Response versus Block, Treatment
```
Source      DF     SS     MS      F      P
Block        4   5.836  1.459  10.13  0.003
Treatment    2   4.468  2.234  15.51  0.002
Error        8   1.152  0.144
Total       14  11.456
```

Since the treatment *P*-value = 0.002, we reject the null hypothesis that the population means are equal. Thus, we conclude that at least one mean is different from the others.

(b) Using MINITAB, we obtain the following output:

```
Tukey 95.0% Simultaneous Confidence Intervals
Response Variable Response
All Pairwise Comparisons among Levels of Treatment

Treatment = 1  subtracted from:

Treatment   Lower   Center    Upper   --------+---------+---------+--------
2          -1.606  -0.920  -0.2344            (---------*---------)
3          -1.986  -1.300  -0.6144   (--------*---------)
                                     --------+---------+---------+--------
                                        -1.40     -0.70      0.00

Treatment = 2  subtracted from:

Treatment   Lower   Center    Upper   --------+---------+---------+--------
3          -1.066  -0.3800  0.3056                   (---------*--------)
                                     --------+---------+---------+--------
                                        -1.40     -0.70      0.00

Tukey Simultaneous Tests
Response Variable Response
All Pairwise Comparisons among Levels of Treatment

Treatment = 1  subtracted from:

            Difference    SE of             Adjusted
Treatment    of Means   Difference  T-Value  P-Value
2             -0.920      0.2400    -3.833    0.0123
3             -1.300      0.2400    -5.417    0.0016

Treatment = 2  subtracted from:

            Difference    SE of             Adjusted
Treatment    of Means   Difference  T-Value  P-Value
3             -0.3800     0.2400    -1.583    0.3066
```

The interval for Treatment 2 minus Treatment 1 does not include 0 and the *P*-value = 0.0123 for this comparison, which is small, so reject the null hypothesis that $\mu_1 = \mu_2$. Likewise, the interval for Treatment 3 minus Treatment 1 does not include 0 and the *P*-value = 0.0016, which is small, so we reject the null hypothesis that $\mu_1 = \mu_3$. Finally, the interval for Treatment 3 minus Treatment 2 does include 0 and the *P*-value = 0.3066, which is not small, so we do not reject the null hypothesis that $\mu_2 = \mu_3$. Thus, the Tukey's tests indicate that the means of Treatments 2 and 3 are equal, but the mean of Treatment 1 is different. That is, we conclude: $\mu_1 \neq \mu_2 = \mu_3$ or $\underline{\mu_1} \quad \underline{\mu_2 \quad \mu_3}$.

(c) The boxplots shown to the right
support the results found in parts (a)
and (b).

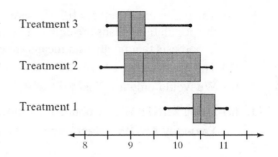

13. (a) The sample standard deviations for the provided data are $s_{87\text{ Octane}} \approx 1.240$, $s_{89\text{ Octane}} \approx 1.439$,
and $s_{92\text{ Octane}} \approx 1.225$. Since the largest standard deviation is less than twice the smallest,
$1.439 < 2(1.225)$, the requirement for equal population variances is satisfied.

(b) Using MINITAB, we obtain the following output:

Two-way ANOVA: Miles per Gallon versus Car and Driver, Octane level

```
Source          DF      SS       MS      F      P
Car and Driver   5  25.0161  5.00322  92.84  0.000
Octane level     2   1.1411  0.57056  10.59  0.003
Error           10   0.5389  0.05389
Total           17  26.6961
```

Since the treatment (octane level) P-value = 0.003, there is sufficient evidence that the
mean number of miles per gallon is different among the three octane levels at the
$\alpha = 0.05$ level of significance.

(c) Using MINITAB, we obtain the following output:

```
Tukey 95.0% Simultaneous Confidence Intervals
Response Variable Miles
All Pairwise Comparisons among Levels of Octane level

Octane level = 1  subtracted from:

Octane
level    Lower   Center   Upper
2      -0.3344  0.03333  0.4010
3       0.1823  0.55000  0.9177
```

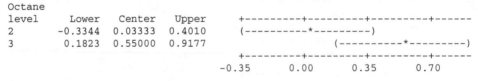

```
Octane level = 2  subtracted from:

Octane
level   Lower  Center   Upper
3      0.1490  0.5167  0.8844
```

```
Tukey Simultaneous Tests
Response Variable Miles per Gallon
All Pairwise Comparisons among Levels of Octane level

Octane level = 1  subtracted from:

Octane  Difference    SE of              Adjusted
level    of Means  Difference  T-Value   P-Value
2         0.03333    0.1340    0.2487    0.9666
3         0.55000    0.1340    4.1037    0.0055
```

```
Octane level = 2 subtracted from:

Octane  Difference     SE of                 Adjusted
level   of Means    Difference  T-Value     P-Value
3         0.5167       0.1340     3.855       0.0081
```

The interval for 89 octane minus 87 octane includes 0 and the P-value $= 0.9966$ for this comparison, which is not small, so we do not reject the null hypothesis that $\mu_{87} = \mu_{89}$. The interval for 92 octane minus 87 octane does not include 0 and the P-value $= 0.0055$, which is small, so we reject the null hypothesis that $\mu_{87} = \mu_{92}$. Finally, the interval for 92 octane minus 89 octane does not include 0 and the P-value $= 0.0081$, which is small, so we reject the null hypothesis that $\mu_{89} = \mu_{92}$. We conclude $\mu_{87} = \mu_{89} \neq \mu_{92}$ or

$$\underline{\mu_{87} \quad \mu_{89}} \quad \mu_{92}$$

(d) The Tukey's tests indicate that the mean gasoline mileages for 87 octane and 89 octane are equal, but the mean gasoline mileage for 92 octane is different. In fact, since the confidence intervals for 92 octane minus 87 octane and 92 octane minus 87 octane contain all positive values, we can conclude that the mean gasoline mileage for 92 octane is higher than for 87 octane and 89 octane.

15. (a) The sample standard deviations for the provided data are $s_{\text{Jeep}} \approx 448$, $s_{\text{Saturn}} \approx 453$, $s_{\text{Toyota}} \approx 830$, and $s_{\text{Hyundai}} \approx 614$. Since the largest standard deviation is less than twice the smallest, $830 < 2(448)$, the requirement for equal population variances is satisfied.

(b) Using MINITAB, we obtain the following output:

Two-way ANOVA: Cost versus Location, Brand

```
Source     DF     SS       MS       F       P
Location    3  3404468  1134823  10.09   0.003
Model       3   926488   308829   2.75   0.105
Error       9  1012007   112445
Total      15  5342964
```

Since the treatment (model) P-value $= 0.105$, there is not sufficient evidence to support the claim that the mean cost of repair is different among the car brands at the $\alpha = 0.05$ level of significance.

(c) Since the null hypothesis was not rejected, there is no need to do a post hoc analysis.

17. (a) The sample standard deviations for the provided data are $s_{\text{lift-off}-1} \approx 5.65$, $s_{\text{return}+1} \approx 9.97$, and $s_{+1\text{ month}} \approx 9.00$. Since the largest standard deviation is less than twice the smallest, $9.97 < 2(5.65)$, the requirement for equal population variances is satisfied.

(b) Using MINITAB, we obtain the following output:

Two-way ANOVA: Water Consumption versus Rat, Day

```
Source  DF     SS       MS       F       P
Rat      5   861.78   172.356   8.62   0.002
Day      2   635.44   317.722  15.89   0.001
Error   10   199.89    19.989
Total   17  1697.11
```

Since the treatment (day) P-value $= 0.001$, there is sufficient evidence that the mean water consumption of mice is different among the experiment levels at the $\alpha = 0.05$ level of significance.

(c) Using MINITAB with Treatment 1 representing Lift-off Minus 1, Treatment 2 representing Return Plus 1, and Treatment 3 representing Return Plus 1 Month, we obtain the following output:

```
Tukey 95.0% Simultaneous Confidence Intervals
Response Variable Water Consumption
All Pairwise Comparisons among Levels of Day

Day = 1   subtracted from:

Day    Lower   Center   Upper    -+---------+---------+---------+-----
2     -0.9152  6.167   13.25    (---------*---------)
3      7.4181  14.500  21.58                   (---------*---------)
                                -+---------+---------+---------+-----
                               0.0       7.0      14.0      21.0


Day = 2   subtracted from:

Day  Lower  Center  Upper      -+---------+---------+---------+-----
3    1.251  8.333   15.42          (---------*---------)
                                -+---------+---------+---------+-----
                               0.0       7.0      14.0      21.0


Tukey Simultaneous Tests
Response Variable Water Consumption
All Pairwise Comparisons among Levels of Day

Day = 1   subtracted from:

        Difference      SE of              Adjusted
Day     of Means     Difference  T-Value   P-Value
2          6.167        2.581     2.389    0.0885
3         14.500        2.581     5.617    0.0006

Day = 2   subtracted from:

        Difference      SE of              Adjusted
Day     of Means     Difference  T-Value   P-Value
3          8.333        2.581     3.228    0.0225
```

The interval for Return Plus 1 minus Lift-off minus 1 includes 0 and the P-value $= 0.0885$ for this comparison, which is not small, so we do not reject the null hypothesis that $\mu_{\text{lift-off}-1} = \mu_{\text{return}+1}$. The interval for Return Plus 1 Month minus Lift-off minus 1 does not include 0 and the P-value $= 0.0006$, which is small, so we reject the null hypothesis that $\mu_{\text{lift-off}-1} = \mu_{\text{return}+1\ \text{month}}$. Finally, the interval for Return Plus 1 Month minus Return Plus 1 does not include 0 and the P-value $= 0.0225$, which is small, so we reject the null hypothesis that $\mu_{\text{return}+1} = \mu_{\text{return}+1\ \text{month}}$. Thus, we conclude that

$$\mu_{\text{lift-off}-1} = \mu_{\text{return}+1} \neq \mu_{\text{return}+1\ \text{month}} \text{ or } \underline{\mu_{\text{lift-off}-1}} \quad \underline{\mu_{\text{return}+1}} \quad \underline{\mu_{\text{return}+1\ \text{month}}}.$$

19. (a) Using MINITAB, we obtain the following output:

Two-way ANOVA: Wait Time versus Day, Procedure

```
Source       DF      SS       MS       F       P
Day           6  6538.75  1089.79   249.50   0.000
Procedure     1     3.02     3.02     0.69   0.438
Error         6    26.21     4.37
Total        13  6567.97
```

Since the treatment (procedure) P-value $= 0.438$, there is not sufficient evidence to support the claim that the mean cost of repair is different among the car brands at the $\alpha = 0.05$ level of significance.

(b)

Observation	1	2	3	4	5	6	7
Wait time before new procedure	11.6	25.9	20.0	38.2	57.3	32.1	81.8
Wait time after new procedure	10.7	28.3	19.2	35.9	59.2	31.8	75.3
d_i = after − before	−0.9	2.4	−0.8	−2.3	1.9	−0.3	−6.5

Using technology, $\overline{d} \approx -0.93$ minutes and $s_d \approx 2.96$ minutes, where we measure differences as wait time after new procedure minus wait time before new procedure. The hypotheses are $H_0 : \mu_d = 0$ versus $H_1 : \mu_d \neq 0$. The level of significance is $\alpha = 0.05$. The test statistic is $t_0 = \dfrac{\overline{d}}{s_d / \sqrt{n}} = \dfrac{-0.93}{2.96 / \sqrt{7}} \approx -0.83$.

Classical approach: Since this is a two-tailed test with 6 degrees of freedom, the critical values are $\pm t_{0.025} = \pm 2.447$. Since the test statistic $t_0 \approx -0.83$ falls between the critical values $\pm t_{0.025} = \pm 2.447$ (i.e., since the test statistic does not fall within the critical region), we do not reject H_0.

P-value approach: The P-value for this two-tailed test is the area under the t-distribution with 6 degrees of freedom to the left of the test statistic $t_0 = -0.83$ plus the area to the right of $t_0 = 0.83$. From the t-distribution table in the row corresponding to 6 degrees of freedom, 0.83 falls between 0.718 and 0.906 whose right-tail areas are 0.25 and 0.20, respectively. We must double these values in order to get the total area in both tails: 0.50 and 0.40. So, $0.40 < P$-value < 0.50. (Using technology, we find P-value ≈ 0.438.) Because the P-value is greater than the level of significance $\alpha = 0.05$, we do not reject H_0.

Conclusion: There is not sufficient evidence at the $\alpha = 0.05$ level of significance to support the quality control manager's claim that the new loading procedure changes the wait time.

(c) The P-values for the two approaches are both 0.438. Yes, it appears that the method presented in this section is a generalization of the matched-pair t-test.

13.4   Two-Way Analysis of Variance

1. In a completely randomized design, the researcher examines a single factor fixed at k levels and randomly distributes the experimental units among the levels. In a randomized complete block design, there is a factor whose level cannot be fixed. So the researcher partitions the experimental units according to this factor, forming blocks. The experimental units are then randomly assigned to the blocks, being sure each block has each treatment. In a factorial design, the researcher has two variables A and B, called factor A and factor B. The factors are fixed, so factor A has a levels and factor B has b levels. The experimental units are then uniformly distributed among the cells formed by the factors, and the response variable is measured at each of the ab cells.

339

3. An interaction plot is a graph that illustrates the role of interaction in a factorial design.

5. The plots are relatively parallel, so there is no significant interaction among the factors.

7. The plots cross, so there is significant interaction among the factors.

9. **(a)** Main effect of factor $A = \dfrac{20+14+1+3}{4} - \dfrac{12+8+6+7}{4} = 1.25$;

Main effect of factor $B = \dfrac{6+7+1+3}{4} - \dfrac{12+8+20+14}{4} = -9.25$.

Interaction effects: If factor B is fixed at low and factor A changes from low to high, the response variable increases by $\dfrac{20+14}{2} - \dfrac{12+8}{2} = 7$ units. On the other hand, if factor B is fixed at high and factor A changes from low to high, the response variable increases by $\dfrac{1+3}{2} - \dfrac{6+7}{2} = -4.5$ (decreases by 4.5) units. So the change in the response variable for factor A depends on the level of factor B, meaning there is an interaction effect between factors A and B. If factor A is fixed at low and factor B changes from low to high, the response variable increases by $\dfrac{6+7}{2} - \dfrac{12+8}{2} = -3.5$ (decreases by 3.5) units. On the other hand, if factor A is fixed at high and factor B changes from low to high, the response variable increases by $\dfrac{3+1}{2} - \dfrac{20+14}{2} = -15$ (decreases by 15) units. So the change in the response variable for factor B depends on the level of factor A, meaning there is an interaction effect between factors A and B.

(b)

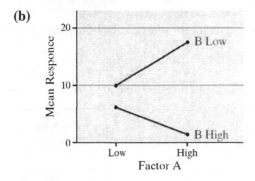

11. **(a)** Since the interaction P-value is 0.836, which is large, there is no evidence of an interaction effect.

(b) Since the P-value for factor A is 0.003, which is small, there is evidence of difference in means from factor A. Since the P-value for factor B is 0.000, which is small, there is also evidence of a difference in means from factor B.

(c) MSE = 45.3

13. **(a)** Since the interaction P-value is 0.000, which is small, there is evidence of an interaction effect

(b) In part (a), we found evidence of an interaction effect. Therefore, we do not consider main effects because they could be misleading.

(c) MSE = 31.9

15. Using MINITAB with the provided data, we obtain the following output:

Two-way ANOVA: Response versus Factor A, Factor B

Source	DF	SS	MS	F	P
Factor A	1	30.15	30.150	0.32	0.579
Factor B	2	912.90	456.452	4.84	0.021
Interaction	2	6.80	3.402	0.04	0.965
Error	18	1699.27	94.404		
Total	23	2649.13			

(a) Since the interaction P-value is 0.965, which is large, there is no evidence of an interaction effect.

(b) Since the P-value for factor A is 0.579, which is large, there is no evidence of difference in the means from factor A. Since the P-value for factor B is 0.021, which is small, there is evidence of a difference in the means from factor B.

(c) The lines in the interaction plot are close to parallel, supporting the conclusion that there is no interaction effect.

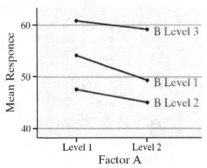

(d) The Tukey's test for factor A is unnecessary since there is no evidence for difference in means. For factor B, we use MINITAB to perform Tukey's test. The results are:

```
Tukey 95.0% Simultaneous Confidence Intervals
Response Variable Response
All Pairwise Comparisons among Levels of Factor B

Factor B = 1  subtracted from:

Factor B   Lower   Center   Upper   --+---------+---------+---------+----
2         -18.55   -6.150   6.251   (-------*-------)
3          -3.53    8.875  21.276                (-------*-------)
                                    --+---------+---------+---------+----
                                    -15        0        15        30

Factor B = 2  subtracted from:

Factor B   Lower   Center   Upper   --+---------+---------+---------+----
3          2.624   15.03   27.43                       (-------*-------)
                                    --+---------+---------+---------+----
                                    -15        0        15        30


Tukey Simultaneous Tests
Response Variable Response
All Pairwise Comparisons among Levels of Factor B

Factor B = 1  subtracted from:

           Difference    SE of            Adjusted
Factor B   of Means   Difference  T-Value  P-Value
2           -6.150      4.858     -1.266    0.4317
3            8.875      4.858      1.827    0.1893
```

```
Factor B = 2  subtracted from:

           Difference    SE of              Adjusted
Factor B   of Means    Difference  T-Value  P-Value
3             15.03       4.858     3.093    0.0165
```

The interval for $B_2 - B_1$ includes 0 and the P-value = 0.4317 for this comparison, which is large, so we do not reject the null hypothesis that $B_1 = B_2$. Likewise, the interval for $B_3 - B_1$ includes 0 and the P-value = 0.1893, which is large, so we do not reject the null hypothesis that $B_1 = B_3$. Finally, the interval for $B_3 - B_2$ does not include 0 and the P-value = 0.0165, which is small, so we reject the null hypothesis that $B_2 = B_3$. Thus, the Tukey's test for factor B is ambiguous. It shows $B_1 = B_2$ and $B_1 = B_3$ but $B_2 \neq B_3$. That is, $\underline{B_1 \;\; B_2} \;\; \underline{B_3}$.

17. (a) This is a 2×3 factorial design with 2 replications within each cell.

(b) Using MINITAB with the provided data, we obtain the following output:

Two-way ANOVA: Cholesterol versus Gender, Age

```
Source       DF     SS       MS      F     P
Gender        1   310.08   310.08   2.51  0.164
Age           2  2177.17  1088.58   8.81  0.016
Interaction   2   628.17   314.08   2.54  0.159
Error         6   741.50   123.58
Total        11  3856.92
```

Since the interaction P-value is 0.159, which is large, there is no evidence of an interaction effect.

(c) Since the P-value for gender is 0.164, which is large, there is no evidence of difference in the means for the two genders. Since the P-value for age is 0.016, which is small, there is evidence of a difference in the means for the three age groups.

(d) The plots are not parallel, so there is significant interaction among the factors. This result contradicts the result found in part (b).

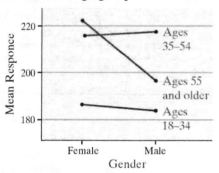

(e) The Tukey's test for gender is unnecessary since there is no evidence for difference in means for the two genders. For age, we use MINITAB to perform Tukey's test:

```
Tukey 95.0% Simultaneous Confidence Intervals
Response Variable Cholesterol
All Pairwise Comparisons among Levels of Age
Age = 1  subtracted from:

Age  Lower   Center  Upper   ---+---------+---------+---------+---
2    7.3765  31.50   55.62                (---------*--------)
3    0.1265  24.25   48.37             (---------*--------)
                             ---+---------+---------+---------+---
                             -25        0        25        50
```

```
Age = 2   subtracted from:
Age   Lower   Center   Upper   ---+---------+---------+---------+---
3     -31.37  -7.250   16.87   (---------*---------)
                               ---+---------+---------+---------+---
                               -25        0        25        50
```

Tukey Simultaneous Tests
Response Variable Cholesterol
All Pairwise Comparisons among Levels of Age

Age = 1   subtracted from:

Age	Difference of Means	SE of Difference	T-Value	Adjusted P-Value
2	31.50	7.861	4.007	0.0166
3	24.25	7.861	3.085	0.0490

Age = 2   subtracted from:

Age	Difference of Means	SE of Difference	T-Value	Adjusted P-Value
3	-7.250	7.861	-0.9223	0.6473

The interval for $\mu_{35-54} - \mu_{18-34}$ does not include 0 and the P-value = 0.0166 for this comparison, which is small, so we reject the null hypothesis that $\mu_{18-34} = \mu_{35-54}$. Likewise, the interval for $\mu_{55+} - \mu_{18-34}$ does not include 0 and the P-value = 0.0490, which is small, so we reject the null hypothesis that $\mu_{18-34} = \mu_{55+}$. Finally, the interval for $\mu_{55+} - \mu_{35-54}$ includes 0 and the P-value = 0.6473, which is large, so we do not reject the null hypothesis that $\mu_{35-54} = \mu_{55+}$. Thus, the Tukey's test for age shows $\mu_{18-34} \neq \mu_{35-54} = \mu_{55+}$. That is, $\underline{\mu_{18-34}} \quad \underline{\mu_{35-54} \quad \mu_{55+}}$.

19. **(a)** Using technology, we find the sample standard deviation the data within each cell: $s_{3.75/301} \approx 311$, $s_{3.75/400} \approx 320$, $s_{3.75/353} \approx 257$, $s_{4/301} \approx 298$, $s_{4/400} \approx 250$, $s_{4/353} \approx 168$, $s_{5/301} \approx 236$, $s_{5/400} \approx 222$, and $s_{5/353} \approx 267$. The largest standard deviation (320) is less than twice the smallest standard deviation (168), so the requirement of equal population variances is satisfied. [320 < 2(168).]

   (b) Using MINITAB with the provided data, we obtain the following output:

   Two-way ANOVA: Strength versus Slump, Mixture

Source	DF	SS	MS	F	P
Slump	2	1234813	617406	8.95	0.002
Mixture	2	1824169	912084	13.23	0.000
Interaction	4	256415	64104	0.93	0.469
Error	18	1241100	68950		
Total	26	4556496			

   Since the interaction P-value is 0.469, which is large, there is no evidence of an interaction effect.

   (c) Since the P-value for slump is 0.002, which is small, there is sufficient evidence of difference in the means for the three types of slump. Since the P-value for mixture is 0.000, which is small, there is evidence of a difference in the means for the three mixtures.

(d)

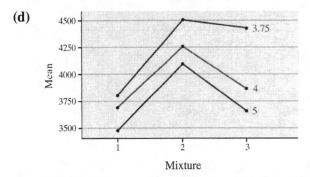

(e) We use MINITAB to perform Tukey's test. The results are:

```
Tukey 95.0% Simultaneous Confidence Intervals
Response Variable Strength
All Pairwise Comparisons among Levels of Slump

Slump = 1   subtracted from:

Slump   Lower   Center   Upper   --------+---------+---------+--------
2       -634.3  -318.3   -2.4              (---------*----------)
3       -835.4  -519.4   -203.5  (----------*---------)
                                 --------+---------+---------+--------
                                    -600       -300       0

Slump = 2   subtracted from:

Slump   Lower   Center   Upper   --------+---------+---------+--------
3       -517.1  -201.1   114.9            (---------*----------)
                                 --------+---------+---------+--------
                                    -600       -300       0

Tukey Simultaneous Tests
Response Variable Strength
All Pairwise Comparisons among Levels of Slump

Slump = 1   subtracted from:

        Difference   SE of                Adjusted
Slump   of Means     Difference  T-Value  P-Value
2       -318.3       123.8       -2.572   0.0481
3       -519.4       123.8       -4.196   0.0015

Slump = 2   subtracted from:

        Difference   SE of                Adjusted
Slump   of Means     Difference  T-Value  P-Value
3       -201.1       123.8       -1.625   0.2612

Tukey 95.0% Simultaneous Confidence Intervals
Response Variable Strength
All Pairwise Comparisons among Levels of Mixture

Mixture = 1   subtracted from:

Mixture   Lower    Center   Upper   ---+---------+---------+---------+---
2         320.691  636.7    952.6                   (------*-----)
3         -2.086   313.9    629.9            (-----*------)
                                    ---+---------+---------+---------+---
                                      -500       0        500       1000

Mixture = 2   subtracted from:

Mixture   Lower    Center   Upper   ---+---------+---------+---------+---
3         -638.8   -322.8   -6.803  (------*-----)
                                    ---+---------+---------+---------+---
                                      -500       0        500       1000
```

```
Tukey Simultaneous Tests
Response Variable Strength
All Pairwise Comparisons among Levels of Mixture
Mixture = 1  subtracted from:
          Difference      SE of                Adjusted
Mixture   of Means    Difference   T-Value    P-Value
2            636.7        123.8      5.143      0.0002
3            313.9        123.8      2.536      0.0517

Mixture = 2  subtracted from:
          Difference      SE of                Adjusted
Mixture   of Means    Difference   T-Value    P-Value
3           -322.8        123.8     -2.608      0.0448
```

Tukey's test for Slump: The interval for $\mu_4 - \mu_{3.75}$ does not include 0 and the *P*-value = 0.0481 for this comparison, which is small, so we reject the null hypothesis that $\mu_{3.75} = \mu_4$. Next, the interval for $\mu_5 - \mu_{3.75}$ does not include 0 and the *P*-value = 0.0015, which is small, so we reject the null hypothesis that $\mu_{3.75} = \mu_5$. Finally, the interval for $\mu_5 - \mu_4$ includes 0 and the *P*-value = 0.2612, which is large, so we do not reject the null hypothesis that $\mu_4 = \mu_5$. Thus, we have $\mu_{3.75} \neq \mu_4 = \mu_5$ or $\underline{\mu_{3.75}} \quad \underline{\mu_4 \quad \mu_5}$. That is, the Tukey's test indicates that the mean 28-day strength for slump 3.75 is significantly different from the mean 28-day strength for slump 4 and slump 5.

Tukey's test for Mixture: The interval for $\mu_{400} - \mu_{301}$ does not include 0 and the *P*-value = 0.0002, which is small, so we reject the null hypothesis that $\mu_{301} = \mu_{400}$. Next, the interval for $\mu_{353} - \mu_{301}$ includes 0 and the *P*-value = 0.0517, which is not small, so we do not reject the null hypothesis that $\mu_{301} = \mu_{353}$. Finally, the interval for $\mu_{353} - \mu_{400}$ includes 0 and the *P*-value = 0.0448, which is small, so we reject the null hypothesis that $\mu_{400} = \mu_{353}$. Thus, we have $\mu_{301} = \mu_{353} \neq \mu_{400}$ or $\underline{\mu_{301} \quad \mu_{353}} \quad \underline{\mu_{400}}$. That is, the Tukey's test indicates that the mean 28-day strength of mixture 67-0-400 is significantly different from the mean 28-day strength of the other two mixtures.

21. **(a)** Using technology, we find the sample standard deviation the data within each cell:

$s_{\text{specialty / Chicago}} \approx 4.00$, $s_{\text{specialty / Bolingbrook}} \approx 3.20$, $s_{\text{specialty / Peoria}} \approx 3.63$, $s_{\text{general / Chicago}} \approx 2.50$,

$s_{\text{general / Bolingbrook}} \approx 3.91$, , and $s_{\text{general / Peoria}} \approx 2.52$. The largest standard deviation (4.00) is less than twice the smallest standard deviation (2.50), so the requirement of equal population variances is satisfied. [4.00 < 2(2.50).]

(b) Using MINITAB with the provided data, we obtain the following output:

Two-way ANOVA: Cost versus Type, Location

```
Source          DF        SS         MS       F      P
Type             1     0.720     0.7200    0.06   0.804
Location         2    31.126    15.5630    1.39   0.287
Interaction      2     3.573     1.7867    0.16   0.854
Error           12   134.560    11.2134
Total           17   169.980
```

Since the interaction *P*-value is 0.854, which is large, there is no evidence of an interaction effect.

(c) Since the *P*-value for type is 0.804, which is large, there is no evidence of difference in the means for the type of service center. Since the *P*-value for location is 0.287, which is large, there is no evidence of a difference in the means for the locations.

(d)

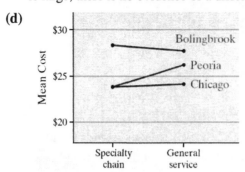

(e) Since there were no significant main effects, there is no need to do Tukey's tests.

Chapter 13 Review Exercises

1. (a) We look in the table of critical values for Tukey's Test with $\alpha = 0.05$ and where the row corresponding to $v = 16$ intersects with the column corresponding to $k = 7$ to find the critical value $q_{0.05,16,7} = 4.741$.

(b) We look in the table of critical values for Tukey's Test with $\alpha = 0.05$ and where the row corresponding to $v = 30$ intersects with the column corresponding to $k = 6$ to find the critical value $q_{0.05,30,6} = 4.302$.

(c) We look in the table of critical values for Tukey's Test with $\alpha = 0.01$ and where the row corresponding to $v = 40$ (since there is no row in the table for $v = 42$) intersects with the column corresponding to $k = 4$ to find the critical value $q_{0.01,42,4} \approx q_{0.01,40,4} = 4.696$.

(d) For this test, $k = 6$ and $v = n - k = 46 - 6 = 40$, so we look in the table with $\alpha = 0.05$ and where the row corresponding to $v = 40$ intersects with the column corresponding to $k = 6$ to find the critical value $q_{0.05,40,6} = 4.232$.

3. (a) The hypotheses are: $H_0 : \mu_{organic} = \mu_{mineral} = \mu_{surface}$ versus H_1 : At least one of the mean is different from the others.

(b) (1) Each sample must be a simple random sample.
(2) The three samples must be independent of each other.
(3) The samples must come from normally distributed populations.
(4) The populations must have equal variances.

(c) Since *P*-value $= 0.000$ is smaller than the $\alpha = 0.01$ level of significance, the researcher will reject the null hypothesis and conclude that the mean concentration of dissolved carbon is different in at least one of the collection areas.

(d) Answers will vary. One possibility follows: Yes, the boxplots support the results obtained in part (c). The boxplots indicate a lower concentration of dissolved carbon in ground water obtained in mineral soil than from surface water and ground water obtained from organic soil.

(e) The needed summary statistics are: $\overline{x}_{\text{organic}} \approx 14.867$, $\overline{x}_{\text{mineral}} \approx 10.027$, $\overline{x}_{\text{surface}} \approx 13.045$,

$\overline{x} \approx 12.345$, $s_{\text{organic}}^2 \approx 39.015$, $s_{\text{mineral}}^2 = 24.789$, $s_{\text{surface}}^2 \approx 15.419$, $n_{\text{organic}} = 31$, $n_{\text{mineral}} = 47$,

and $n_{\text{surface}} = 44$, and $n = 122$, and $k = 3$. Thus,

$$\text{MST} = \frac{31(14.867 - 12.345)^2 + 47(10.027 - 12.345)^2 + 44(13.045 - 12.345)^2}{3-1} \approx 235.636,$$

$$\text{MSE} = \frac{(31-1) \cdot 39.015 + (47-1) \cdot 24.789 + (44-1) \cdot 15.419}{122 - 3} \approx 24.990, \text{ and}$$

$$F = \frac{\text{MST}}{\text{MSE}} = \frac{235.636}{24.990} \approx 9.429$$

(f) From the MINITAB output we have: $-7.571 < \mu_{\text{mineral}} - \mu_{\text{organic}} < -1.999$;

$-4.589 < \mu_{\text{surface}} - \mu_{\text{organic}} < 1.056$; and $0.518 < \mu_{\text{surface}} - \mu_{\text{mineral}} < 5.520$.

The first interval does not contain 0, so we reject $H_0 : \mu_{\text{organic}} = \mu_{\text{mineral}}$.. The second

interval contains 0, so we do not reject $H_0 : \mu_{\text{organic}} = \mu_{\text{surface}}$. The third interval does not

contain 0, so we reject $H_0 : \mu_{\text{mineral}} = \mu_{\text{surface}}$. Thus, we have $\mu_{\text{organic}} = \mu_{\text{surface}} \neq \mu_{\text{mineral}}$ or

$\underline{\mu_{\text{organic}} \quad \mu_{\text{surface}}} \quad \mu_{\text{mineral}}$. Thus, the Tukey's test indicates that the mean dissolved

carbon is equal in the surface water and in the ground water taken from organic soil, but it differs from the mean dissolved carbon concentration in ground water taken from mineral soil.

5. From the MINITAB output we have: $-6.914 < \mu_{\text{select structural}} - \mu_{\text{no. 1}} < 13.064$;

$1.936 < \mu_{\text{select structural}} - \mu_{\text{no. 2}} < 21.914$; $-2.989 < \mu_{\text{select structural}} - \mu_{\text{below grade}} < 16.989$;

$-1.139 < \mu_{\text{no. 1}} - \mu_{\text{no. 2}} < 18.839$; $-6.064 < \mu_{\text{no. 1}} - \mu_{\text{below grade}} < 13.914$; and

$-14.914 < \mu_{\text{no. 2}} - \mu_{\text{below grade}} < 5.064$. The first interval contains 0, so we do not reject

$H_0 : \mu_1 = \mu_2$.. The second interval does not contain 0, so we do not reject $H_0 : \mu_1 = \mu_3$.

The third interval contains 0, so we do not reject $H_0 : \mu_1 = \mu_4$. The fourth interval contains

0, so we do not reject $H_0 : \mu_2 = \mu_3$. The fifth interval contains 0, so we do not reject

$H_0 : \mu_2 = \mu_4$. The sixth interval contains 0, so we do not reject $H_0 : \mu_3 = \mu_4$. Thus,

Tukey's test is ambiguous. It indicates that $\mu_{\text{select structural}} \neq \mu_{\text{no. 2}}$, but that

$\mu_{\text{select structural}} = \mu_{\text{no. 1}} = \mu_{\text{no. 2}} = \mu_{\text{below grade}}$ or $\underline{\mu_{\text{select structural}} \quad \mu_{\text{no. 1}} \quad \mu_{\text{below grade}}} \quad \mu_{\text{no. 2}}$.

7. (a) Using MINITAB, we obtain the following output:

Two-way ANOVA: Distance versus Person, Catapult

```
Source    DF      SS       MS       F      P
Person     3   45.688  15.2292  16.01  0.001
Catapult   3  105.688  35.2292  37.03  0.000
Error      9    8.563   0.9514
Total     15  159.938
```

Since the treatment P-value $= 0.000$, we reject the null hypothesis that the population means are equal. Thus, we conclude that at least one mean is different from the others.

(b) Using MINITAB , we obtain the following output:

```
Tukey 95.0% Simultaneous Confidence Intervals
Response Variable Distance
All Pairwise Comparisons among Levels of Catapult

Catapult = 1  subtracted from:

Catapult   Lower   Center   Upper   ------+---------+---------+---------+
2         -1.656   0.5000   2.656   (-------*------)
3          1.844   4.0000   6.156              (------*-------)
4          4.094   6.2500   8.406                        (------*------)
                                    ------+---------+---------+---------+
                                       0.0       3.0       6.0       9.0

Catapult = 2  subtracted from:

Catapult  Lower   Center   Upper   ------+---------+---------+---------+
3         1.344   3.500    5.656            (-------*------)
4         3.594   5.750    7.906                    (------*------)
                                   ------+---------+---------+---------+
                                      0.0       3.0       6.0       9.0

Catapult = 3  subtracted from:

Catapult   Lower   Center   Upper   ------+---------+---------+---------+
4         0.09438  2.250    4.406           (------*-------)
                                    ------+---------+---------+---------+
                                       0.0       3.0       6.0       9.0


Tukey Simultaneous Tests
Response Variable Distance
All Pairwise Comparisons among Levels of Catapult

Catapult = 1  subtracted from:

           Difference       SE of              Adjusted
Catapult   of Means      Difference   T-Value   P-Value
2            0.5000        0.6897      0.7249    0.8847
3            4.0000        0.6897      5.7996    0.0012
4            6.2500        0.6897      9.0618    0.0000

Catapult = 2  subtracted from:

           Difference       SE of              Adjusted
Catapult   of Means      Difference   T-Value   P-Value
3            3.500         0.6897      5.075     0.0031
4            5.750         0.6897      8.337     0.0001

Catapult = 3  subtracted from:

           Difference       SE of              Adjusted
Catapult   of Means      Difference   T-Value   P-Value
4            2.250         0.6897      3.262     0.0405
```

The interval for $\mu_2 - \mu_1$ includes 0 and the P-value = 0.8847 for this comparison, which is large, so we do not reject the null hypothesis that $\mu_1 = \mu_2$. The interval for $\mu_3 - \mu_1$ does not include 0 and the P-value = 0.0012, which is small, so we reject the null hypothesis that $\mu_1 = \mu_3$. The interval for $\mu_4 - \mu_1$ does not include 0 and the P-value = 0.0000, which is small, so we reject the null hypothesis that $\mu_4 = \mu_1$. The interval for $\mu_3 - \mu_2$ does not include 0 and the P-value = 0.0031, which is small, so we reject the null hypothesis that $\mu_2 = \mu_3$. The interval for $\mu_4 - \mu_2$ does not include 0 and the P-value = 0.0001, which is small, so we reject the null hypothesis that $\mu_2 = \mu_4$. Finally, the interval for $\mu_4 - \mu_3$ does not include 0 and the P-value = 0.0405, which is

348

small, so we reject the null hypothesis that $\mu_3 = \mu_4$. Thus, the Tukey's tests indicate that the means of Mark IV V2 and Balloon Ballista are equal, but the means of Hydrolaunch and Waterworks II are different. That is, we conclude: $\mu_1 = \mu_2 \neq \mu_3 \neq \mu_4$

or $\underline{\mu_1 \ \mu_2} \ \ \underline{\mu_3} \ \ \underline{\mu_4}$.

(c) The boxplots shown to the right support the results found in parts (a) and (b).

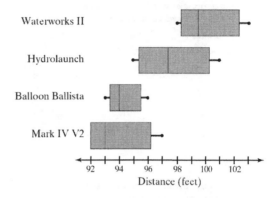

9. (a) Using technology, we find the sample standard deviation the data within each cell:
$s_{M/\text{one 8 hr}} \approx 3.42$, $s_{M/\text{two 4 hr}} \approx 2.92$, $s_{M/\text{two 2 hr}} \approx 2.39$, $s_{F/\text{one 8 hr}} \approx 4.72$, $s_{F/\text{two 4 hr}} \approx 2.70$, and $s_{F/\text{two 2 hr}} \approx 3.87$. The largest standard deviation (4.72) is less than twice the smallest standard deviation (2.39), so the requirement of equal population variances is satisfied. [$4.72 < 2(2.39)$.]

(b) Using MINITAB with the provided data, we obtain the following output:

Two-way ANOVA: Score versus Gender, Program

```
Source        DF     SS       MS       F      P
Gender         1    20.83    20.833   1.77   0.196
Program        2   890.60   445.300  37.90   0.000
Interaction    2    24.07    12.033   1.02   0.374
Error         24   282.00    11.750
Total         29  1217.50
```

Since the interaction P-value is 0.374, which is large, there is no evidence of an interaction effect.

(c) Since the P-value for gender is 0.196, which is large, there is no evidence of a difference in the means for gender. Since the P-value for program is 0.000, which is small, there is evidence of a difference in the means for type of driving program.

(d) The lines in the interaction plot shown to the right are close to parallel, supporting the conclusion that there is no interaction effect.

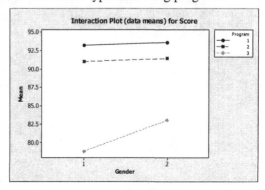

(e) The Tukey's test for gender is unnecessary since there is no evidence of a difference in means. For type of program, with Program 1 = One 8-hour session, Program 2 = Two 4-hour session, and Program 3 = Two 2-hour sessions, we use MINITAB to perform Tukey's test. The results are:

```
Tukey 95.0% Simultaneous Confidence Intervals
Response Variable Score
All Pairwise Comparisons among Levels of Program

Program = 1  subtracted from:

Program   Lower   Center   Upper    ---+---------+---------+---------+---
2         -6.03   -2.20    1.626                        (-------*------)
3        -16.33  -12.50   -8.674    (-------*-------)
                                    ---+---------+---------+---------+---
                                    -15.0     -10.0      -5.0       0.0

Program = 2  subtracted from:

Program   Lower   Center   Upper    ---+---------+---------+---------+---
3        -14.13  -10.30   -6.474          (------*-------)
                                    ---+---------+---------+---------+---
                                    -15.0     -10.0      -5.0       0.0


Tukey Simultaneous Tests
Response Variable Score
All Pairwise Comparisons among Levels of Program

Program = 1  subtracted from:

          Difference      SE of               Adjusted
Program   of Means     Difference   T-Value   P-Value
2           -2.20         1.533      -1.435    0.3394
3          -12.50         1.533      -8.154    0.0000

Program = 2  subtracted from:

          Difference      SE of               Adjusted
Program   of Means     Difference   T-Value   P-Value
3          -10.30         1.533      -6.719    0.0000
```

The interval for $\mu_{\text{two 4 hr}} - \mu_{\text{one 8 hr}}$ includes 0 and the P-value = 0.3394 for this comparison, which is large, so we do not reject the null hypothesis that $\mu_{\text{one 8 hr}} = \mu_{\text{two 4 hr}}$. The interval for $\mu_{\text{two 2 hr}} - \mu_{\text{one 8 hr}}$ does not include 0 and the P-value = 0.0000, which is small, so we reject the null hypothesis that $\mu_{\text{one 8 hr}} = \mu_{\text{two 2 hr}}$. Finally, the interval for $\mu_{\text{two 2 hr}} - \mu_{\text{two 4 hr}}$ does not include 0 and the P-value = 0.0000, which is small, so we reject the null hypothesis that $\mu_{\text{two 4 hr}} = \mu_{\text{two 2 hr}}$. Thus, we have $\mu_{\text{one 8 hr}} = \mu_{\text{two 4 hr}} \neq \mu_{\text{two 2 hr}}$ or $\underline{\mu_{\text{one 8 hr}} \quad \mu_{\text{two 4 hr}}} \quad \mu_{\text{two 2 hr}}$. That is, the Tukey's test indicates that the mean score after taking one 8-hour defensive driving class is equal to the mean score after taking two 4-hour classes, but that the mean score after taking two 2-hour classes is different.

Chapter 14

Inference on the Least-squares Regression Model and Multiple Regression

14.1 Testing the Significance of the Least-squares Regression Model

1. There are two requirements for conducting inference on the least-squares regression model. First, for each particular value of the explanatory variable x, the corresponding responses in the population have a mean that depends linearly on x. Second, the response variables are normally distributed with mean $\mu_{y|x} = \beta_0 + \beta_1 x$ and standard deviation σ The first requirement is tested by examining a plot of the residuals against the explanatory variable. If the plot shows any discernible pattern, then the linear model is inappropriate. The normality requirement is checked by examining a normal probability plot of the residuals.

3. The y-coordinates on the regression line represent the predicted mean value of the response variable for any given value of the explanatory variable.

5. If we do not reject $H_0 : \beta_1 = 0$ then the best point estimate of y is just $\overline{y}$.

7. **(a)** Using technology, we get: $b_0 = -2.3256$ as the estimate of β_0 and $b_1 = 2.0233$ as the estimate of β_1.

   (b) We calculate $\hat{y} = 2.0233x - 2.3256$ to generate the following table:

x	y	$\hat{y}$	$y - \hat{y}$	$(y - \hat{y})^2$	$(x - \overline{x})^2$
3	4	3.74	0.26	0.0654	5.76
4	6	5.77	0.23	0.0541	1.96
5	7	7.79	-0.79	0.6252	0.16
7	12	11.84	0.16	0.0265	2.56
8	14	13.86	0.14	0.0195	6.76
			Sum:	0.7907	17.20

   $$s_e = \sqrt{\frac{\sum(y - \hat{y})^2}{n-2}} = \sqrt{\frac{0.7907}{5-2}} \approx 0.5134 \text{ is the point estimate for } \sigma.$$

   (c) $s_{b_1} = \dfrac{s_e}{\sqrt{\sum(x - \overline{x})^2}} = \dfrac{0.5134}{\sqrt{17.20}} \approx 0.1238$

   (d) The hypotheses are $H_0 : \beta_1 = 0$, $H_1 : \beta_1 \neq 0$; df $= n - 2 = 5 - 2 = 3$ so the critical values are $\pm t_{0.025} = \pm 3.182$. The test statistic is $t_0 = \dfrac{b_1}{s_{b_1}} = \dfrac{2.0233}{0.1238} = 16.345$, which is in the critical region so we reject H_0 (P-value $< 0.001 < \alpha = 0.05$). There is sufficient evidence to indicate that there is a linear relationship between x and y.

9. (a) Using technology, we get: $\beta_0 \approx b_0 = 1.2$ and $\beta_1 \approx b_1 = 2.2$.

(b) We calculate $\hat{y} = 2.2x + 1.2$ to generate the following table:

x	y	$\hat{y}$	$y - \hat{y}$	$(y - \hat{y})^2$	$(x - \bar{x})^2$
-2	-4	-3.20	-0.80	0.6400	4
-1	0	-1.00	1.00	1.0000	1
0	1	1.20	-0.20	0.0400	0
1	4	3.40	0.60	0.3600	1
2	5	5.60	-0.60	0.3600	4
			Sum	2.4000	10

$$s_e = \sqrt{\frac{\sum(y - \hat{y})^2}{n - 2}} = \sqrt{\frac{2.4}{5 - 2}} = 0.8944 \text{ is the point estimate for } \sigma.$$

(c) $s_{b_1} = \dfrac{s_e}{\sqrt{\sum(x - \bar{x})^2}} = \dfrac{0.8944}{\sqrt{10}} = 0.2828$

(d) The hypotheses are $H_0 : \beta_1 = 0$, $H_1 : \beta_1 \neq 0$. df $= n - 2 = 5 - 2 = 3$ so the critical values are $\pm t_{0.025} = \pm 3.182$. The test statistic is $t_0 = \dfrac{b_1}{s_{b_1}} = \dfrac{2.2}{0.2828} = 7.778$, which is in the critical region so we reject H_0 (P-value $= 0.004 < \alpha = 0.05$). There is sufficient evidence to indicate that there is a linear relationship between x and y.

11. (a) Using technology, we get: $\beta_0 \approx b_0 = 116.6$ and $\beta_1 \approx b_1 = -0.72$.

(b) We calculate $\hat{y} = -0.72x + 116.6$ to generate the following table:

x	y	$\hat{y}$	$y - \hat{y}$	$(y - \hat{y})^2$	$(x - \bar{x})^2$
20	100	102.20	-2.20	4.8400	400
30	95	95.00	0.00	0.0000	100
40	91	87.80	3.20	10.2400	0
50	83	80.60	2.40	5.7600	100
60	70	73.40	-3.40	11.5600	400
			Sum	32.4000	1000

$$s_e = \sqrt{\frac{\sum(y - \hat{y})^2}{n - 2}} = \sqrt{\frac{32.4}{5 - 2}} = 3.2863 \text{ is the point estimate for } \sigma.$$

(c) $s_{b_1} = \dfrac{s_e}{\sqrt{\sum(x - \bar{x})^2}} = \dfrac{3.2863}{\sqrt{1000}} = 0.1039$

(d) The hypotheses are $H_0 : \beta_1 = 0$, $H_1 : \beta_1 \neq 0$. df $= n - 2 = 5 - 2 = 3$ so the critical values are $\pm t_{0.025} = \pm 3.182$. The test statistic is $t_0 = \dfrac{b_1}{s_{b_1}} = \dfrac{-0.72}{0.1039} = -6.928$, which is in the critical region so we reject H_0 (P-value $= 0.006 < \alpha = 0.05$). There is sufficient evidence to indicate that there is a linear relationship between x and y.

13. (a) Using technology, we get: $\beta_0 \approx b_0 = 12.4932$ and $\beta_1 \approx b_1 = 0.1827$.

(b) Using technology, we calculate $\hat{y} = 0.1827x + 12.4932$ to generate the table:

x	y	$\hat{y}$	$y - \hat{y}$	$(y - \hat{y})^2$	$(x - \bar{x})^2$
27.75	17.5	17.5640	-0.0640	0.0041	1.6782
24.50	17.1	16.9701	0.1299	0.0169	3.8202
25.50	17.1	17.1528	-0.0528	0.0028	0.9112
26.00	17.3	17.2442	0.0558	0.0031	0.2066
25.00	16.9	17.0615	-0.1615	0.0261	2.1157
27.75	17.6	17.5640	0.0360	0.0013	1.6782
26.50	17.3	17.3356	-0.0356	0.0013	0.0021
27.00	17.5	17.4269	0.0731	0.0053	0.2975
26.75	17.3	17.3813	-0.0813	0.0066	0.0873
26.75	17.5	17.3813	0.1187	0.0141	0.0873
27.50	17.5	17.5183	-0.0183	0.0003	1.0930
			Sum	0.0819	11.9773

$$s_e = \sqrt{\dfrac{\sum (y - \hat{y})^2}{n - 2}} = \sqrt{\dfrac{0.0819}{11 - 2}} = 0.0954$$

(c) A normal probability plot shows that the residuals are approximately normally distributed.

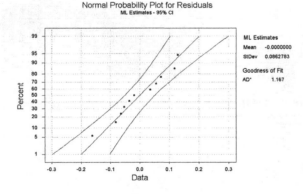

Normal Probability Plot for Residuals
ML Estimates - 95% CI

(d) $s_{b_1} = \dfrac{s_e}{\sqrt{\sum (x - \bar{x})^2}} = \dfrac{0.0954}{\sqrt{11.9773}} = 0.0276$

(e) The hypotheses are $H_0 : \beta_1 = 0$, $H_1 : \beta_1 \neq 0$. df $= n - 2 = 11 - 2 = 9$ and so the critical values are $\pm t_{0.005} = \pm 3.250$. The test statistic is $t_0 = \dfrac{b_1}{s_{b_1}} = \dfrac{0.1827}{0.0276} = 6.630$, which is in the critical region and so we reject H_0 (P-value $< 0.001 < \alpha = 0.01$). There is enough evidence to support the claim of a linear relationship between height and head circumference.

(f) For a 95% confidence interval we use $t_{\alpha/2} = t_{0.025} = 2.262$:

Lower bound: $b_1 - t_{\alpha/2} \cdot s_{b_1} = 0.1827 - 2.262 \cdot 0.0276 = 0.1203$

Upper bound: $b_1 + t_{\alpha/2} \cdot s_{b_1} = 0.1827 + 2.262 \cdot 0.0276 = 0.2451$

(g) We can use the regression equation to give the best guess of:
$$\hat{y} = 0.1827x + 12.4932 = 0.1827 \cdot 26.5 + 12.4932 = 17.34 \text{ inches.}$$

15. (a) Using technology, we get: $\beta_0 \approx b_0 = 2675.6$ and $\beta_1 \approx b_1 = 0.6764$

(b) Using technology, we calculate $\hat{y} = 0.6764x + 2675.6$ to generate the table:

x	y	$\hat{y}$	$y - \hat{y}$	$(y - \hat{y})^2$	$(x - \overline{x})^2$
2300	4070	4231.32	-161.32	26025.6	338724
3390	5220	4968.62	251.38	63191.6	258064
2430	4640	4319.26	320.74	102874.9	204304
2890	4620	4630.41	-10.41	108.4	64
3330	4850	4928.04	-78.04	6089.5	200704
2480	4120	4353.08	-233.08	54326.2	161604
3380	5020	4961.86	58.14	3380.7	248004
2660	4890	4474.84	415.16	172361.9	49284
2620	4190	4447.78	-257.78	66449.7	68644
3340	4630	4934.80	-304.80	92902.8	209764
			Sum	587711.3	1739160

$$s_e = \sqrt{\frac{\sum (y - \hat{y})^2}{n - 2}} = \sqrt{\frac{587711.3}{10 - 2}} = 271.04$$

(c) A normal probability plot shows that the residuals are normally distributed.

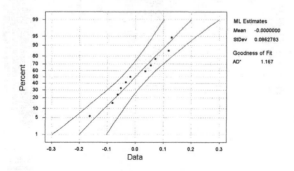

Normal Probability Plot for Residuals
ML Estimates - 95% CI

ML Estimates
Mean   -0.0000000
StDev   0.0862783

Goodness of Fit
AD*   1.167

(d) $s_{b_1} = \dfrac{s_e}{\sqrt{\sum(x-\bar{x})^2}} = \dfrac{271.04}{\sqrt{1,739,160}} = 0.2055$

(e) The hypotheses are $H_0 : \beta_1 = 0$, $H_1 : \beta_1 \neq 0$. df $= n - 2 = 10 - 2 = 8$ and so the critical values are $\pm t_{0.025} = \pm 2.306$. The test statistic is $t_0 = \dfrac{b_1}{s_{b_1}} = \dfrac{0.6764}{0.2055} = 3.291$, which is in the critical region and so we reject H_0 (P-value $= 0.011 < \alpha = 0.05$). There is enough evidence to support the claim of a linear relationship between 7-day strength and 28-day strength of this type of concrete.

(f) For a 95% confidence interval we use $t_{\alpha/2} = t_{0.025} = 2.306$:
Lower bound: $b_1 - t_{\alpha/2} \cdot s_{b_1} = 0.6764 - 2.306 \cdot 0.2055 = 0.2025$
Upper bound: $b_1 + t_{\alpha/2} \cdot s_{b_1} = 0.6764 + 2.306 \cdot 0.2055 = 1.1503$

(g) We can use the regression equation to calculate the mean 28-day strength:
$\hat{y} = 0.6764x + 2675.6 = 0.6764 \cdot 3000 + 2675.6 = 4704.8$ psi.

17. (a) Using technology, we get: $\beta_0 \approx b_0 = 0.5975$ and $\beta_1 \approx b_1 = 0.9764$.

(b) Using technology, we calculate $\hat{y} = 0.9764x + 0.5975$ to generate the table:

x	y	$\hat{y}$	$y - \hat{y}$	$(y - \hat{y})^2$	$(x - \bar{x})^2$
0.23	1.21	0.8221	0.3879	0.1505	0.3481
0.94	-0.57	1.5153	-2.0853	4.3485	0.0144
1.40	-0.59	1.9645	-2.5545	6.5253	0.3364
3.86	5.89	4.3664	1.5236	2.3213	9.2416
3.25	5.90	3.7708	2.1292	4.5335	5.9049
-2.53	-2.58	-1.8728	-0.7072	0.5001	11.2225
1.89	0.06	2.4429	-2.3829	5.6782	1.1449
-1.91	1.78	-1.2674	3.0474	9.2868	7.4529
-2.01	0.06	-1.3651	1.4251	2.0308	8.0089
3.00	5.79	3.5267	2.2633	5.1225	4.7524
0.90	-1.57	1.4763	-3.0463	9.2797	0.0064
			Sum	49.7772	48.4334

$s_e = \sqrt{\dfrac{\sum(y - \hat{y})^2}{n - 2}} = \sqrt{\dfrac{49.7772}{11 - 2}} = 2.3518$

(c) A normal probability plot shows that the residuals are approximately normally distributed.

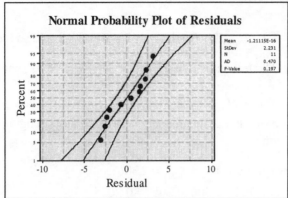

(d) $s_{b_1} = \dfrac{s_e}{\sqrt{\sum (x-\bar{x})^2}} = \dfrac{2.3518}{\sqrt{48.4334}} = 0.3379$

(e) The hypotheses are $H_0 : \beta_1 = 0$, $H_1 : \beta_1 \neq 0$. df $= n - 2 = 11 - 2 = 9$ and so the critical values are $\pm t_{0.005} = \pm 1.833$. The test statistic is $t_0 = \dfrac{b_1}{s_{b_1}} = \dfrac{0.9764}{0.3379} = 2.890$, which is in the critical region so we reject H_0 $\left(P\text{-value} = 0.018 < \alpha = 0.1 \right)$. There is enough evidence to support the claim of a linear relationship between the monthly rate of return on the S&P 500 and the monthly rate of return of UTX.

(f) For a 90% confidence interval we use $t_{\alpha/2} = t_{0.005} = 1.833$:
Lower bound: $b_1 - t_{\alpha/2} \cdot s_{b_1} = 0.9764 - 1.833 \cdot 0.3379 = 0.3570$
Upper bound: $b_1 + t_{\alpha/2} \cdot s_{b_1} = 0.9764 + 1.833 \cdot 0.3379 = 1.5958$

(g) We can use the regression equation to calculate the mean rate of return:
$\hat{y} = 0.9764(4.2) + 0.5975 = 4.698\%$

19. (a) There does not appear to be much of a relationship between calories and sugar:

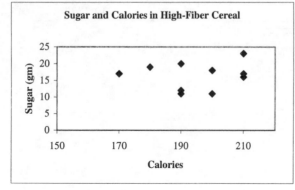

(b) Using technology, we get $\hat{y} = 0.0821x + 0.93$.

(c)

x	y	$\hat{y}$	$y - \hat{y}$	$(y - \hat{y})^2$	$(x - \bar{x})^2$
200	18	17.3571	0.6429	0.4133	11
210	23	18.1786	4.8214	23.2462	178
170	17	14.8929	2.1071	4.4401	711
190	20	16.5357	3.4643	12.0013	44
200	18	17.3571	0.6429	0.4133	11
180	19	15.7143	3.2857	10.7959	278
210	23	18.1786	4.8214	23.2462	178
210	16	18.1786	-2.1786	4.7462	178
210	17	18.1786	-1.1786	1.3890	178
190	12	16.5357	-4.5357	20.5727	44
190	11	16.5357	-5.5357	30.6441	44
200	11	17.3571	-6.3571	40.4133	11
			Sum	172.3214	1867

$$s_e = \sqrt{\frac{\sum (y - \hat{y})^2}{n - 2}} = \sqrt{\frac{172.3214}{12 - 2}} = 4.1512$$

(d) A normal probability plot shows that the residuals are approximately normally distributed.

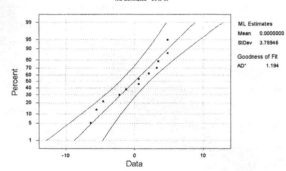

(e) $s_{b_1} = \dfrac{s_e}{\sqrt{\sum (x - \bar{x})^2}} = \dfrac{4.1512}{\sqrt{1867}} = 0.0961$

(f) The hypotheses are $H_0 : \beta_1 = 0$, $H_1 : \beta_1 \neq 0$. df $= n - 2 = 12 - 2 = 10$ and so the critical values are $\pm t_{0.005} = \pm 3.169$. The test statistic is $t_0 = \dfrac{b_1}{s_{b_1}} = \dfrac{0.0821}{0.0961} = 0.854$, which is not in the critical region and so we do not reject H_0 $(P\text{-value} = 0.413 > \alpha = 0.01)$. There is not enough evidence to support the claim of a linear relationship between calories and sugar content in high-fiber cereals.

(g) For a 95% confidence interval we use $t_{\alpha/2} = t_{0.025} = 2.228$:

Lower bound: $b_1 - t_{\alpha/2} \cdot s_{b_1} = 0.0821 - 2.228 \cdot 0.0961 = -0.1320$

Upper bound: $b_1 + t_{\alpha/2} \cdot s_{b_1} = 0.0821 + 2.228 \cdot 0.0961 = 0.2962$

(h) The scatter plot and hypothesis test show that there is not a sufficiently strong linear relationship to warrant using the regression equation and so we should just use $\bar{y} = 17.1$ gm as our best estimate of the sugar content.

21. (a) Using technology, we get $\hat{y} = 2,018,994\, x - 3,771,542,830$.

(b) The hypotheses are $H_0 : \beta_1 = 0$, $H_1 : \beta_1 \neq 0$. df $= n - 2 = 11 - 2 = 9$. For a test at the 1% level of significance, the critical values are $\pm t_{0.005} = \pm 3.250$. Using technology we get that the test statistic is $t_0 = 21.812$, which is in the critical region and so we reject H_0 $\left(P\text{-value} < 0.001 < \alpha = 0.01\right)$. There is enough evidence to support the claim of a linear relationship between year and population of the U.S.

(c)

U.S. Population

(d)

Residuals vs Year

(e) The scatter plot seems to show some curvature so a linear model does not seem appropriate. This is verified by the pattern of the residuals in the residual plot.

(f) The moral is that the results of the hypothesis test taken alone are unreliable—the hypothesis test by itself may indicate a linear relationship exists when there is none, and it should always be used in conjunction with a scatter diagram of the data and an examination of the residuals.

23. (a)

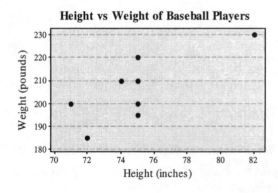

Height vs Weight of Baseball Players

358

(b) Using technology, we get $\hat{y} = 3.361x - 45$. The hypotheses are $H_0 : \beta_1 = 0$, $H_1 : \beta_1 \neq 0$. df $= n - 2 = 9 - 2 = 7$ so for a test at the 5% level of significance, the critical values are $\pm t_{0.025} = \pm 2.365$. Using technology we find that the test statistic is $t_0 = 3.13$, which is in the critical region so we reject H_0 $(P\text{-value} = 0.017 < \alpha = 0.05)$. There is enough evidence to support the claim of a linear relationship between height and weight of baseball players.

(c) With Randy Johnson removed, we get $\hat{y} = 3.611x - 63.472$. The hypotheses are $H_0 : \beta_1 = 0$, $H_1 : \beta_1 \neq 0$. df $= n - 2 = 8 - 2 = 6$ and so for a test at the 5% level of significance, the critical values are $\pm t_{0.025} = \pm 2.447$. Using technology we find that the test statistic is $t_0 = 1.53$, which is not in the critical region so we do not reject H_0. Since Randy Johnson has sufficient effect on the relationship to change the outcome of the hypothesis test, he is an influential observation.

14.2 Confidence and Prediction Intervals

1. A confidence interval is an interval constructed about the predicted value of y, at a given level of x, and is used to measure the accuracy of the mean response of all the individuals in the population at that level. A prediction interval is an interval constructed about the predicted value of y and is used to measure the accuracy of a single individual's predicted value at a given level for x. Since there is more variability in individuals than in means, for the same level of confidence, the prediction interval will always be wider than the confidence interval.

3. (a) From 14.1.7, the regression equation is $\hat{y} = 2.0233x - 2.3256$ and so the predicted mean value of y when $x = 7$ is $\hat{y} = 2.0233(7) - 2.3256 \approx 11.8$.

(b) From 14.1.7 we have that $n = 5$, $s_e = 0.5134$, $\overline{x} = 5.4$ and $\sum(x - \overline{x})^2 = 17.20$. For a 95% confidence interval with df $= n - 2 = 3$, we use $t_{0.025} = 3.182$.

$$\hat{y} \pm t_{\alpha/2} \cdot s_e \sqrt{\frac{1}{n} + \frac{(x^* - \overline{x})^2}{\sum(x - \overline{x})^2}} = 11.8 \pm 3.182 \cdot 0.5134 \cdot \sqrt{\frac{1}{5} + \frac{(7 - 5.4)^2}{17.20}}$$

$$= 11.8 \pm 1.0 = (10.8, 12.8)$$

(c) The predicted value of y is also $\hat{y} = 11.8$.

(d) $$\hat{y} \pm t_{\alpha/2} \cdot s_e \sqrt{1 + \frac{1}{n} + \frac{(x^* - \overline{x})^2}{\sum(x - \overline{x})^2}} = 11.8 \pm 3.182 \cdot 0.5134 \cdot \sqrt{1 + \frac{1}{5} + \frac{(7 - 5.4)^2}{17.20}}.$$

$$= 11.8 \pm 1.9 = (9.9, 13.7)$$

359

(e) In (a) and (b) we are predicting the mean response (a point estimate and an interval estimate) for the population of individuals with $x = 7$. In (c) and (d) we are predicting the response (a point estimate and an interval estimate) for a single individual with $x = 7$.

5. (a) From 14.1.9, the regression equation is $\hat{y} = 2.2x + 1.2$ and so the predicted mean value of y when $x = 1.4$ is $\hat{y} = 2.2(1.4) + 1.2 = 4.3$.

(b) From 14.1.9 we have that $n = 5$, $s_e = 0.8944$, $\bar{x} = 0$ and $\sum (x - \bar{x})^2 = 10$. For a 95% confidence interval with df $= n - 2 = 3$, we use $t_{0.025} = 3.182$. The bounds are:

$$\hat{y} \pm t_{\alpha/2} \cdot s_e \sqrt{\frac{1}{n} + \frac{(x^* - \bar{x})^2}{\sum (x - \bar{x})^2}} = 4.3 \pm 3.182 \cdot 0.8944 \cdot \sqrt{\frac{1}{5} + \frac{(1.4 - 0)^2}{10}}.$$

$$= 4.3 \pm 1.8 = (2.5, 6.1)$$

(c) The predicted value of y is also $\hat{y} = 4.3$.

(d) The bounds are:

$$\hat{y} \pm t_{\alpha/2} \cdot s_e \sqrt{1 + \frac{1}{n} + \frac{(x^* - \bar{x})^2}{\sum (x - \bar{x})^2}} = 4.3 \pm 3.182 \cdot 0.8944 \cdot \sqrt{1 + \frac{1}{5} + \frac{(1.4 - 0)^2}{10}}.$$

$$= 4.3 \pm 3.4 = (0.9, 7.7)$$

7. (a) From 14.1.13, the regression equation is $\hat{y} = 0.1827x + 12.4932$ and so the predicted mean value of y when $x = 25.75$ is $\hat{y} = 0.1827(25.75) + 12.4932 = 17.20$ inches.

(b) Using technology we get a 95% confidence interval of $(17.12, 17.28)$ inches.

(c) The predicted value of y is also $\hat{y} = 17.20$ inches.

(d) Using technology we get a 95% prediction interval of $(16.97, 17.43)$ inches.

(e) In (a) and (b) we are predicting the mean head circumference (a point estimate and an interval estimate) for the population of children who are 25.75 inches tall. In (c) and (d) we are predicting the head circumference (a point estimate and an interval estimate) for a single child with a height of 25.75 inches.

9. (a) From 14.1.15, the regression equation is $\hat{y} = 0.6764x + 2675.6$ and so the predicted mean value of y when $x = 2550$ is $\hat{y} = 0.6764 \cdot 2550 + 2675.6 = 4400.4$ psi.

(b) Using technology we get a 95% confidence interval of $(4147.8, 4653.1)$ psi.

(c) The predicted value of y is also $\hat{y} = 4400.4$ psi.

(d) Using technology we get a 95% prediction interval of $(3726.3, 5074.6)$ inches.

(e) In (a) and (b) we are predicting the mean 28-day strength (a point estimate and an interval estimate) for the population of all concrete that has a 7-day strength of 2550 psi. In (c) and (d) we are predicting the 28-day strength (a point estimate and an interval estimate) for a single batch of concrete with 7-day strength of 2550 psi.

11. (a) From 14.1.17, the predicted mean value of y when $x = 4.2$ is given by
$\hat{y} = 0.9764 x + 0.5975 = 0.9764 \cdot 4.2 + 0.5975 = 4.698\%$ return.

(b) Using technology we get a 90% confidence interval of $(2.234\%, 7.163\%)$ return.

(c) The predicted value of y is also $\hat{y} = 4.698\%$.

(d) Using technology we get a 90% prediction interval of $(-0.267\%, 9.664\%)$ return.

(e) The best point estimate for the return on United Technologies stock in an individual month when the return on the S&P 500 is 4.2% is the population mean (of all months when the return on the S&P 500 is 4.2%). However the interval estimates will differ because the variability of individuals will be greater than the variability of sample means.

13. (a) We showed in 14.1.19 there was not a significant linear relationship between sugar content and calories in high-fiber cereals. Therefore, it does not make sense to construct either a confidence interval or prediction interval based on the least squares regression equation.

(b) For a 95% confidence interval for the mean sugar content we just use the y-values in our sample. The summary statistics are $n = 12$, $\bar{y} = 17.08$ and $s_y = 4.100$. For 95% confidence with df $= n - 1 = 11$, we use $t_{.025} = 2.201$ and get:

$$\bar{y} \pm t_{0.025} \cdot \frac{s_y}{\sqrt{n}} = 17.08 \pm 2.201 \cdot \frac{4.100}{\sqrt{12}} = 17.08 \pm 2.61 = (14.5, 19.7) \text{ grams.}$$

14.3 Multiple Regression

1. A correlation matrix is a matrix that shows the linear correlation among all variables under consideration in a multiple linear regression model.

3. If the null hypothesis is rejected, we conclude that at least one of the explanatory variables is linearly related to the response variable. It is possible that one or more of the $\beta_i = 0$ even though the null hypothesis is rejected.

5. The difference between R^2 and adjusted R^2 is that R^2 becomes larger as more explanatory variables are added to the regression model regardless of their contribution to the explanation of the response variable. Adjusted R^2 compensates for this ability to artificially increase R^2 by simply adding more explanatory variables. It modifies R^2 based on the sample size, n, and the number of explanatory variables, k. Adjusted R^2 actually decreases if the additional variable does little to explain the variation in the response variable. So the adjusted R^2 is better for determining whether an additional explanatory variable should be added to the model.

7. (a) The slope coefficient of x_1 is 3.This indicates that $\hat{y}$ will increase 3 units, on average, for every one unit increase in x_1 provided x_2 remains constant. The slope coefficient of x_2 is -4. This indicates that $\hat{y}$ will decrease 4 units, on average, for every one unit increase in x_2, provided x_1 remains constant.

(b) $\hat{y} = 5 + 3x_1 - 4x_2$
$\hat{y} = 5 + 3(10) - 4x_2$
$\hat{y} = 35 - 4x_2$

(c) $\hat{y} = 5 + 3x_1 - 4x_2$
$\hat{y} = 5 + 3(15) - 4x_2$
$\hat{y} = 50 - 4x_2$

(d) $\hat{y} = 5 + 3x_1 - 4x_2$
$\hat{y} = 5 + 3(20) - 4x_2$
$\hat{y} = 65 - 4x_2$

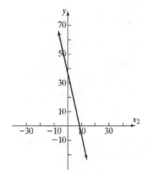
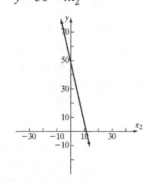
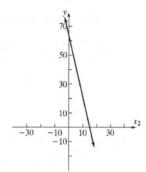

(e) Changing the value of x_1 has the effect of changing the y-intercept of the graph of the regression line.

9. (a) $R^2_{adj} = 1 - \left(\dfrac{n-1}{n-k-1}\right)\left(1-R^2\right) = 1 - \left(\dfrac{25-1}{25-3-1}\right)\left(1-0.653\right) = 0.603$

(b) $F = \dfrac{R^2}{1-R^2} \cdot \dfrac{n-(k+1)}{k} = \dfrac{0.653}{1-0.653} \cdot \dfrac{25-(3+1)}{3} = 13.173$

(c) $R^2_{adj} = 1 - \left(\dfrac{25-1}{25-4-1}\right)\left(1-0.655\right) = 0.586$

Do not add the new variable. Its addition reduces the proportion of variance explained by the model.

11. (a) Correlations: x1, x2, x3, y

```
          x1         x2        x3
x2   -0.460
x3    0.183    -0.012
y    -0.748     0.788     0.258
```

Because the correlations among the explanatory variables are all between -0.7 and 0.7, multicollinearity does not appear to be a problem.

(b) Regression Analysis: y versus x1, x2, x3

```
The regression equation is
y = 7.96 - 0.104 x1 + 0.936 x2 + 0.115 x3


Predictor        Coef   SE Coef       T       P
Constant       7.9647    0.5407   14.73   0.000
x1           -0.10354   0.02080   -4.98   0.003
x2            0.9359     0.1999    4.68   0.003
x3            0.11524    0.03188   3.61   0.011


S = 0.245127    R-Sq = 94.0%    R-Sq(adj) = 91.0%

Analysis of Variance

Source           DF       SS      MS       F       P
Regression        3   5.6485  1.8828   31.33   0.000
Residual Error    6   0.3605  0.0601
Total             9   6.0090
```

The regression equation is $\hat{y} = 7.9647 - 0.1035x_1 + 0.9359x_2 + 0.1152x_3$.

(c) From the output in part (b), our test statistic is $F_0 = 31.33$. Since P-value < 0.001, we reject the null hypothesis and conclude that at least one of the explanatory variables is linearly related to the response variable.

(d) From the output in part (b), conclude the following:

Reject $H_0 : \beta_1 = 0$ since $t_{\beta 1} = -4.98$ and P-value $= 0.003 < \alpha = 0.05$.

Reject $H_0 : \beta_2 = 0$ since $t_{\beta 2} = 4.68$ and P-value $= 0.003 < \alpha = 0.05$

Reject $H_0 : \beta_3 = 0$ since $t_{\beta 3} = 3.61$ and P-value $= 0.011 < \alpha = 0.05$

13. (a) Correlations: x1, x2, x3, x4, y

```
           x1       x2       x3       x4
x2     -0.184
x3      0.182   -0.106
x4     -0.166   -0.558    0.291
y      -0.046    0.932   -0.063   -0.750
```

Because the correlations among the explanatory variables are all between −0.7 and 0.7, multicollinearity does not appear to be a problem.

(b) Regression Analysis: y versus x1, x2, x3, x4

```
The regression equation is
y = 279 + 0.07 x1 + 1.15 x2 + 0.390 x3 - 2.94 x4

Predictor        Coef   SE Coef       T       P
Constant       279.02     61.34    4.55   0.003
x1              0.068     1.159    0.06   0.955
x2             1.1460    0.1546    7.41   0.000
x3             0.3897    0.2639    1.48   0.183
x4            -2.9378    0.8235   -3.57   0.009


S = 13.1177    R-Sq = 95.9%    R-Sq(adj) = 93.6%
```

```
Analysis of Variance
Source          DF       SS       MS      F       P
Regression       4   28152.4   7038.1   40.90   0.000
Residual Error   7    1204.5    172.1
Total           11   29356.9
```

The regression equation is $\hat{y} = 279.02 + 0.068x_1 + 1.1460x_2 + 0.3897x_3 - 2.9378x_4$.

$F_0 = 40.90$ and P-value < 0.001 so we reject the null hypothesis and conclude that at least one of the explanatory variables is linearly related to the response variable.

Based on the regression output, we see that x_1 and x_3 have slope coefficients that are not significantly different from zero (P-value > 0.05).

(c) The variable x_1 has the highest P-value. After removing this variable, the regression equation becomes:
$\hat{y} = 282.33 + 1.1426x_2 + 0.3941x_3 - 2.9570x_4$
The new test statistic is $F_0 = 62.29$ and P-value < 0.001 so the model is still significant.

The variable x_3 has a slope coefficient that is not significantly different from zero. Removing this variable gives
$\hat{y} = 281.62 + 1.1584x_2 - 2.6267x_4$
The new test statistic is $F_0 = 76.89$ and P-value < 0.001 so the model is still significant. Both of the explanatory variables have slope coefficients that are significantly different from zero.
Reject $H_0 : \beta_2 = 0$ since $t_{\beta_2} = 7.89$ and P-value $< 0.001 < \alpha = 0.05$
Reject $H_0 : \beta_4 = 0$ since $t_{\beta_4} = -3.54$ and P-value $= 0.006 < \alpha = 0.05$

(d)

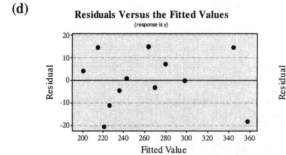

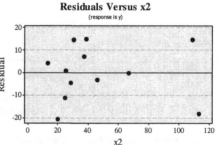

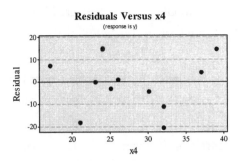

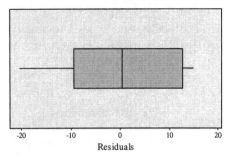

None of the residual plots show any discernible pattern, and the boxplot does not show any outliers. Therefore, the linear model is appropriate.

(e) $\hat{y} = 281.62 + 1.1584x_2 - 2.6267x_4$
$= 281.62 + 1.1584(35.6) - 2.6267(29)$
$= 246.68$

(f)

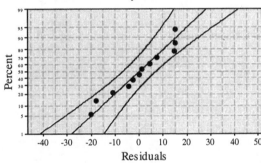

Because the points are roughly linear (i.e. lie within the confidence bounds), it is reasonable to conclude that the residuals are normally distributed. Therefore, it is reasonable to construct confidence and prediction intervals.

(g) 95% Confidence Interval: $(237.45, 255.91)$

95% Prediction Interval: $(214.93, 278.43)$

15. (a) Yes, the P-value is very small so we would reject the null hypothesis and conclude that at least one of the explanatory variables is linearly related to the response variable.

(b) $b_1 = -0.87$: A one point increase in the computer confidence variable reduces the computer anxiety measurement by 0.87 point, on average, provided all other explanatory variables remain constant.

$b_2 = -0.51$: A one point increase in the computer knowledge variable reduces the computer anxiety measurement by 0.51 point, on average, provided all other explanatory variables remain constant.

$b_3 = -0.45$: A one point increase in the computer liking variable reduces the computer anxiety measurement by 0.45 point, on average, provided all other explanatory variables remain constant.

$b_4 = 0.33$: A one point increase in the trait anxiety variable increases the computer anxiety measurement by 0.33 point, on average, provided all other explanatory variables remain constant.

(c) $\hat{y} = 84.04 - 0.87(25) - 0.51(19) - 0.45(20) + 0.33(43) = 57.79$

(d) $R^2 = 0.69$ indicates that 69% of the variance in computer anxiety is explained by the regression model.

(e) This statement means that the requirements of a multiple linear regression model were checked and were met.

17. (a) Regression Analysis: Wind Chill versus Air Temp, Wind Speed

```
The regression equation is
Wind Chill = - 12.5 + 1.33 Air Temp - 0.414 Wind Speed

Predictor        Coef  SE Coef       T      P
Constant     -12.5091   0.9194  -13.61  0.000
Air Temp      1.33408  0.04024   33.16  0.000
Wind Speed   -0.41430  0.03365  -12.31  0.000

S = 1.62942    R-Sq = 99.3%    R-Sq(adj) = 99.1%
```

The regression equation is $\hat{y} = -12.509 + 1.334x_1 - 0.414x_2$.

(b)

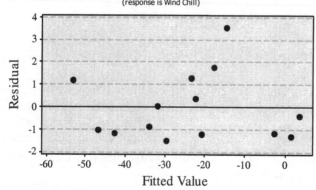

Residuals Versus the Fitted Values
(response is Wind Chill)

Residuals Versus Air Temp
(response is Wind Chill)

Residuals Versus Wind Speed
(response is Wind Chill)

Normal Probability Plot of the Residuals
(response is Wind Chill)

There is a pattern in the residual plot so we would conclude that the linear model is not appropriate.

19. (a) Correlations: Slump, 7-day psi, 28-day psi

```
                Slump    7-day psi
7-day psi      -0.460
28-day psi     -0.753      0.737
```

Because the correlation between Slump and 7-day strength is between −0.7 and 0.7, multicollinearity does not appear to be a problem.

(b) Regression Analysis: 28-day psi versus Slump, 7-day psi

```
The regression equation is
28-day psi = 3891 - 296 Slump + 0.552 7-day psi

Predictor     Coef   SE Coef      T      P
Constant    3890.5     828.8   4.69  0.002
Slump       -295.9     109.9  -2.69  0.027
7-day psi   0.5523    0.2171   2.54  0.034

S = 276.505   R-Sq = 76.0%   R-Sq(adj) = 70.1%

Analysis of Variance
Source           DF        SS       MS      F      P
Regression        2   1942115   971058  12.70  0.003
Residual Error    8    611639    76455
Total            10   2553755
```

The regression equation is $\hat{y} = 3890.5 - 295.9x_1 + 0.552x_2$.

(c)

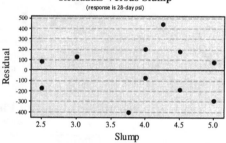

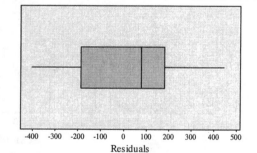

Normal Probability Plot of the Residuals
(response is 28-day psi)

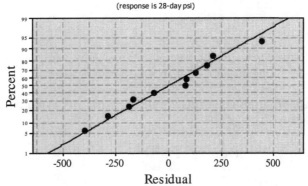

Residual

None of the residual plots show any discernible pattern, and the boxplot does not show any outliers. Therefore, the linear model is appropriate.

(d) $b_1 = -295.9$: A one unit increase in slump of the concrete decreases the 28-day strength by 295.9 pounds per square inch, on average, provided the other variable (7-day strength) remains constant.

$b_2 = 0.552$: A one pound per inch increase in the 7-day strength increases the 28-day strength by 0.552 pounds per square inch, on average, provided the other variable (slump) remains constant.

(e) $R^2 = 0.760$ means that 76.0% of the variance in 28-day strength is explained by the model. $R^2_{adj} = 0.701$ (or 70.1%) modifies the value of R^2 taking the sample size and number of explanatory variables into account.

(f) From part (b), we have $F_0 = 12.70$ and P-value $= 0.003 < \alpha = 0.05$. Therefore, we reject the null hypothesis and conclude that at least one of the explanatory variables is linearly related to the 28-day strength of the concrete.

(g) From part (b), we have the following:
Reject $H_0 : \beta_1 = 0$ since $t_{\beta 1} = -2.69$ and P-value $= 0.027 < \alpha = 0.05$
Reject $H_0 : \beta_2 = 0$ since $t_{\beta 2} = 2.54$ and P-value $= 0.034 < \alpha = 0.05$

(h) $\hat{y} = 3890.5 - 295.9(3.5) + 0.552(2450) = 4207.3$ psi

(i) $\hat{y} = 4207.3$ psi (the prediction is the same for an individual as it is for the mean response, given particular values for the explanatory variables).

(j) 95% Confidence Interval: $(3988.6$ psi, 4427.2 psi$)$
95% Prediction Interval: $(3533.6$ psi, 4882.2 psi$)$

369

21. (a) Correlations: Engine, HP, Weight, MPG

```
               Engine        HP  Weight
HP             0.323
Weight         0.092    0.370
MPG           -0.812   -0.230  -0.477
```

Because the correlation between the explanatory variables are all between -0.7 and 0.7, multicollinearity does not appear to be a problem.

(b) Regression Analysis: MPG versus Engine, HP, Weight

```
The regression equation is
MPG = 35.2 - 0.00257 Engine + 0.0154 HP - 0.00184 Weight

Predictor        Coef      SE Coef      T       P
Constant       35.181        3.112   11.31   0.000
Engine     -0.0025675    0.0004576   -5.61   0.001
HP            0.01539      0.01127    1.37   0.214
Weight     -0.0018431    0.0005841   -3.16   0.016

S = 0.902302    R-Sq = 86.0%    R-Sq(adj) = 80.0%


Analysis of Variance

Source           DF      SS      MS       F       P
Regression        3  35.028  11.676   14.34   0.002
Residual Error    7   5.699   0.814
Total            10  40.727
```

The regression equation is $\hat{y} = 35.181 - 0.00257x_1 + 0.0154x_2 - 0.00184x_3$.

(c) From the output in (b), we get $F_0 = 14.34$ and P-value $= 0.002 < \alpha = 0.05$. We reject the null hypothesis and conclude that at least one of the explanatory variables is linearly associated with gasoline mileage.

(d) From part (b), we have the following:

Engine: Reject $H_0 : \beta_1 = 0$ since $t_0 = -5.61$ and P-value $= 0.001 < \alpha = 0.05$

Horsepower: Do not reject $H_0 : \beta_2 = 0$ since $t_0 = 1.37$ and P-value $= 0.214 > \alpha = 0.05$

Weight: Reject $H_0 : \beta_3 = 0$ since $t_0 = -3.16$ and P-value $= 0.016 < \alpha = 0.05$

We conclude that engine size and weight are linearly associated with gas mileage, but not horsepower. Horsepower, x_2, should be removed from the model.

(e) Removing the variable x_2, horsepower, we get:

$\hat{y} = 36.904 - 0.00237x_1 - 0.00156x_3$

$F_0 = 18.57$ and P-value $= 0.001 < \alpha = 0.05$. The remaining slope coefficients are significantly different from zero.

Reject $H_0 : \beta_1 = 0$ since $t_0 = -5.19$ and P-value $= 0.001 < \alpha = 0.05$

Reject $H_0 : \beta_3 = 0$ since $t_0 = -2.71$ and P-value $= 0.027 < \alpha = 0.05$

(f)

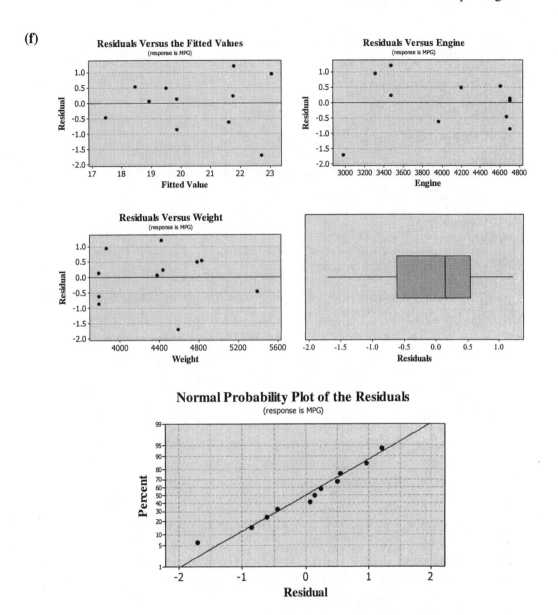

None of the residual plots show any discernible pattern, the boxplot does not show any outliers, and the normal probability plot looks roughly linear. Therefore, the linear model is appropriate.

(g) $b_1 = -0.00237$: A one cubic centimeter increase in engine size decreases the gas mileage by 0.00237 mile per gallon, on average, assuming that vehicle weight remains constant.

$b_3 = -0.00156$: A one pound increase in vehicle weight decreases the gas mileage by 0.00156 mile per gallon, on average, assuming that engine size remains constant.

371

(h) $R^2 = 0.823$; 82.3% of the variance in gas mileage is explained by the regression model. $R^2_{adj} = 0.779$ modifies the value of R^2 taking the sample size and number of explanatory variables into account.

(i) 95% Confidence Interval: $(19.822, 21.601)$

95% Prediction Interval: $(18.348, 23.075)$

23. (a) **Correlations: Square Footage, Bedroom, Baths, Asking Price**

```
              Square Foota      Bedroom        Baths
Bedroom          0.791
Baths            0.731          0.759
Asking Price     0.749          0.738         0.669
```

Yes; because the correlations among the explanatory variables are larger than 0.7, multicollinearity may be a problem.

(b) **Regression Analysis: Asking Price versus Square Footage, Bedroom, Baths**

```
The regression equation is
Asking Price = 161 + 0.0268 Square Footage + 16.8 Bedroom + 8.7 Baths

Predictor           Coef  SE Coef      T      P
Constant          161.17    45.50   3.54  0.006
Square Footage   0.02682  0.02394   1.12  0.292
Bedroom            16.76    19.29   0.87  0.407
Baths               8.70    21.40   0.41  0.694

S = 38.1912    R-Sq = 62.5%    R-Sq(adj) = 50.0%

Analysis of Variance
Source          DF     SS     MS     F      P
Regression       3  21855   7285  4.99  0.026
Residual Error   9  13127   1459
Total           12  34982
```

The regression equation is $\hat{y} = 161 + 0.0268x_1 + 16.76x_2 + 8.70x_3$.

(c) From the output in (b), we get $F_0 = 4.99$ and $P\text{-value} = 0.026 < \alpha = 0.05$. We reject the null hypothesis and conclude that at least one of the explanatory variables is linearly associated with asking price.

(d) From part (b), we have the following:
Square Footage: Do not reject $H_0 : \beta_1 = 0$ since $t_0 = 1.12$ and $P\text{-value} = 0.292 > \alpha = 0.05$
Bedrooms: Do not reject $H_0 : \beta_2 = 0$ since $t_0 = 0..87$ and $P\text{-value} = 0.407 > \alpha = 0.05$
Baths: Do not reject $H_0 : \beta_3 = 0$ since $t_0 = 0.41$ and $P\text{-value} = 0.694 > \alpha = 0.05$
We conclude that none of the slope coefficients are significantly different from 0. This directly contradicts the result we obtained from part (c).

(e) The variable x_3, baths, has the highest P-value. Removing this variable, we get:

Regression Analysis: Asking Price versus Square Footage, Bedroom

```
The regression equation is
Asking Price = 164 + 0.0300 Square Footage + 20.2 Bedroom

Predictor            Coef  SE Coef     T      P
Constant           163.79    43.12  3.80  0.003
Square Footage    0.03000  0.02166  1.39  0.196
Bedroom             20.16    16.64  1.21  0.253

S = 36.5624    R-Sq = 61.8%    R-Sq(adj) = 54.1%


Analysis of Variance

Source            DF     SS     MS     F      P
Regression         2  21614  10807  8.08  0.008
Residual Error    10  13368   1337
Total             12  34982
```

The new regression equation is
$$\hat{y} = 163.79 + 0.03x_1 + 20.16x_2$$

Do not reject $H_0 : \beta_1 = 0$ since $t_0 = 1.39$ and P-value $= 0.196 > \alpha = 0.05$

Do not reject $H_0 : \beta_2 = 0$ since $t_0 = 1.21$ and P-value $= 0.253 > \alpha = 0.05$

Neither of the slope coefficients are significantly different from 0.

The variable x_2, bedrooms, has the next highest P-value. Removing this variable, we get:

Regression Analysis: Asking Price versus Square Footage

```
The regression equation is
Asking Price = 181 + 0.0508 Square Footage

Predictor            Coef  SE Coef     T      P
Constant           181.07    41.55  4.36  0.001
Square Footage    0.05077  0.01352  3.75  0.003

S = 37.3326    R-Sq = 56.2%    R-Sq(adj) = 52.2%

Analysis of Variance
Source            DF     SS     MS      F      P
Regression         1  19651  19651  14.10  0.003
Residual Error    11  15331   1394
Total             12  34982
```

The new regression equation is
$$\hat{y} = 181.07 + 0.0508x_1$$

Reject $H_0 : \beta_1 = 0$ since $t_0 = 3.75$ and P-value $= 0.003 < \alpha = 0.05$

The slope coefficient for x_1, square footage, is significantly different from 0.

(f)

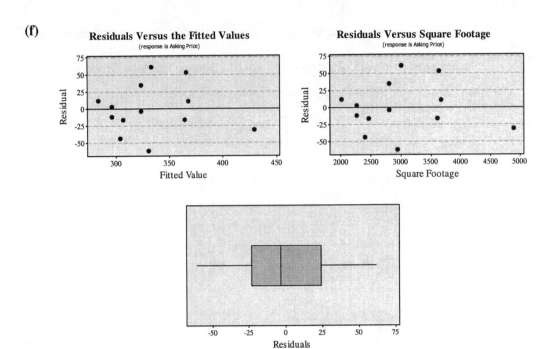

Residuals Versus the Fitted Values
(response is Asking Price)

Residuals Versus Square Footage
(response is Asking Price)

Normal Probability Plot of the Residuals
(response is Asking Price)

None of the residual plots show any discernible pattern, the boxplot does not show any outliers, and the normal probability plot looks fairly linear. Therefore, the linear model is appropriate.

(g) $b_1 = 0.0508$: This indicates that if the house increases by 1 square foot, then the asking price will increase by $50.80, on average.

(h) 95% Confidence Interval: $(305.4, 351.2)$

We are 95% confident that the mean asking price of all 2900-square foot houses is between $305,400 and $351,200.

95% Prediction Interval: $(243.0, 413.6)$

We are 95% confident that the asking price of a randomly selected 2900-square foot house is between $243,000 and $413,600.

25. (a)

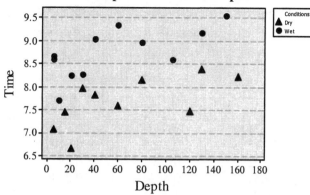

Scatterplot of Time vs Depth

(b) Regression Analysis: Time versus Depth, Conditions

```
The regression equation is
Time = 8.35 + 0.00682 Depth - 1.14 Conditions

Predictor        Coef    SE Coef       T      P
Constant       8.3511     0.1597   52.30  0.000
Depth        0.006816   0.001766    3.86  0.001
Conditions    -1.1359     0.1787   -6.36  0.000

S = 0.407631   R-Sq = 74.2%   R-Sq(adj) = 71.3%

Analysis of Variance
Source           DF       SS       MS       F      P
Regression        2   8.5814   4.2907   25.82  0.000
Residual Error   18   2.9909   0.1662
Total            20  11.5723
```

The regression equation is $\hat{y} = 8.351 + 0.00682x_1 - 1.136x_2$.

(c) For the explanatory variable x_1, depth, $t_0 = 3.86$ and the P-value = 0.001. So, we reject the null hypothesis and conclude that there is a significant linear relation between depth and time needed to drill another 5 feet.

For the explanatory variable x_2, condition, $t_0 = -6.36$ and the P-value < 0.001. So, we reject the null hypothesis and conclude that there is a significant linear relation between condition and time needed to drill another 5 feet.

(d) 95% Confidence Interval: $(7.598, 8.196)$

We are 95% confident that the mean time it takes to drill an additional 5 feet is between 7.598 minutes and 8.196 minutes.

95% Prediction Interval: $(6.990, 8.804)$

We are 95% confident that for a randomly chosen drilling, it will take between 6.990 minutes and 8.804 minutes to drill an additional 5 feet.

Chapter 14 Review Exercises

1. (a) Using the results from Chapter 4 we have: $\beta_0 \approx b_0 = 30.3848$ and $\beta_1 \approx b_1 = -2.7977$. We use the regression equation to calculate the mean mpg for cars with 3.8-liter engines: $\hat{y} = -2.7977(3.8) + 30.3848 \approx 19.8$ mpg.

(b) Using technology, we calculate $\hat{y} = -3.5339x + 32.12$ to generate the table:

x	y	$\hat{y}$	$y - \hat{y}$	$(y - \hat{y})^2$	$(x - \bar{x})^2$
3.1	20	21.7119	-1.7119	2.9307	0.0016
3.8	20	19.7535	0.2465	0.0607	0.4356
2.2	25	24.2299	0.7701	0.5931	0.8836
4.6	18	17.5154	0.4846	0.2349	2.1316
3.8	21	19.7535	1.2465	1.5537	0.4356
2.2	24	24.2299	-0.2299	0.0528	0.8836
2.7	22	22.8310	-0.8310	0.6906	0.1936
3.5	21	20.5929	0.4072	0.1658	0.1296
4.6	18	17.5154	0.4846	0.2349	2.1316
2.0	26	24.7894	1.2106	1.4656	1.2996
3.8	20	19.7535	0.2465	0.0607	0.4356
3.0	19	21.9917	-2.9917	8.9503	0.0196
3.4	20	20.8726	-0.8726	0.7615	0.0676
2.2	24	24.2299	-0.2299	0.0528	0.8836
2.2	26	24.2299	1.7701	3.1334	0.8836
			Sum	20.9414	10.8160

$$s_e = \sqrt{\frac{\sum(y - \hat{y})^2}{n - 2}} = \sqrt{\frac{20.9414}{15 - 2}} \approx 1.2692$$

(c) A normal probability plot shows that the residuals are normally distributed.

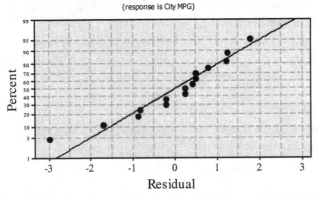

Normal Probability Plot of the Residuals
(response is City MPG)

(d) $s_{b_1} = \dfrac{s_e}{\sqrt{\sum(x - \bar{x})^2}} = \dfrac{1.2692}{\sqrt{10.8160}} = 0.3859$

(e) The hypotheses are $H_0 : \beta_1 = 0$, $H_1 : \beta_1 \neq 0$. df $= n - 2 = 15 - 2 = 13$ so the critical values are $\pm t_{0.025} = \pm 2.160$. The test statistic is $t_0 = \dfrac{b_1}{s_{b_1}} = \dfrac{-2.7977}{0.3859} = -7.250$, which is in the critical region so we reject H_0. There is enough evidence to support the claim of a linear relationship between engine displacement and mpg. (*P*-value < 0.001)

(f) For a 95% confidence interval we use $t_{0.025} = 2.160$ and get bounds:

$$b_1 \pm t_{\alpha/2} \cdot s_{b_1} = -2.7977 \pm 2.160 \cdot (0.3859) = -2.7977 \pm 0.8335 = (-3.6312, -1.9642).$$

(g) We have $n = 15$, $s_e = 1.2692$, $\overline{x} = 3.14$ and $\sum (x - \overline{x})^2 = 10.8160$. For a 90% confidence interval with df $= n - 2 = 13$, we use $t_{0.05} = 1.771$. The bounds are:

$$\hat{y} \pm t_{\alpha/2} \cdot s_e \sqrt{\frac{1}{n} + \frac{(x^* - \overline{x})^2}{\sum (x - \overline{x})^2}} = 19.8 \pm 1.771 \cdot (1.2692) \cdot \sqrt{\frac{1}{15} + \frac{(3.8 - 3.14)^2}{10.816}}$$

$$= 19.8 \pm 0.735 = (19.065, 20.535)$$

Using Minitab, the interval is $(19.018, 20.489)$.

(h) The predicted value of y is also $\hat{y} = 19.8$ mpg.

(i) The bounds are:

$$\hat{y} \pm t_{\alpha/2} \cdot s_e \sqrt{1 + \frac{1}{n} + \frac{(x^* - \overline{x})^2}{\sum (x - \overline{x})^2}} = 19.8 \pm 1.771 (1.2692) \sqrt{1 + \frac{1}{15} + \frac{(3.8 - 3.14)^2}{10.816}}.$$

$$= 19.8 \pm 2.248 = (17.552, 22.048)$$

Using Minitab, the interval is $(17.389, 22.118)$.

(j) The best point estimate for the mpg of an individual car with engine displacement of 3.8 liters is the population mean (of all cars with 3.8-liter engine displacement). However the interval estimates will differ because the variability of individuals will be greater than the variability of sample means.

3. (a) Using technology, we get $\beta_0 \approx b_0 = -399.2$ and $\beta_1 \approx b_1 = 2.5315$. We use the regression equation to calculate the mean rent of a 900-square-foot apartment in Queens: $\hat{y} = -399.2 + 2.5315 (900) = 1879.15$

So, the mean rent of a 900-square-foot apartment in Queens is $1879.15.

(b) Using technology, we calculate $\hat{y} = -399.2 + 2.5315x$ to generate the table:

x	y	$\hat{y}$	$y - \hat{y}$	$(y - \hat{y})^2$	$(x - \bar{x})^2$
500	650	866.55	-216.55	46,893.9	160,000
588	1215	1089.32	125.678	15,795	97,344
1000	2000	2132.3	-132.3	17,503.3	10,000
688	1655	1342.47	312.528	97,673.8	44,944
825	1250	1689.29	-439.29	19,2974	5625
1259	2700	2787.96	-87.959	7736.7	128,881
650	1200	1246.28	-46.275	2141.38	62,500
560	1250	1018.44	231.56	53620	115,600
1073	2350	2317.1	32.9005	1082.44	29,929
1452	3300	3276.54	23.462	550.465	304,704
1305	3100	2904.41	195.593	38,256.4	164,025
				474,227	1,123,552

$$s_e = \sqrt{\frac{\sum (y - \hat{y})^2}{n - 2}} = \sqrt{\frac{474,227}{11 - 2}} \approx 229.547$$

(c) A normal probability plot shows that the residuals are normally distributed.

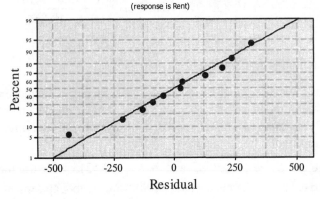

Normal Probability Plot of the Residuals
(response is Rent)

(d) $s_{b_1} = \dfrac{s_e}{\sqrt{\sum (x - \bar{x})^2}} = \dfrac{229.547}{\sqrt{1,123,552}} = 0.2166$

(e) The hypotheses are $H_0 : \beta_1 = 0$, $H_1 : \beta_1 \neq 0$. df $= n - 2 = 11 - 2 = 9$ so the critical values are $\pm t_{0.025} = \pm 2.262$. The test statistic is $t_0 = \dfrac{b_1}{s_{b_1}} = \dfrac{2.5315}{0.2166} = 11.687$, which is in the critical region so we reject H_0. There is enough evidence to support the claim of a linear relationship between square footage and rent.

(f) For a 95% confidence interval we use $t_{0.025} = 2.262$ and get bounds:

$$b_1 \pm t_{\alpha/2} \cdot s_{b_1} = 2.5315 \pm 2.262(0.2166) = 2.5315 \pm 0.4899 = (2.0416, 3.0214).$$

(g) We have $n = 11$, $s_e = 229.547$, $\bar{x} = 900$ and $\sum(x-\bar{x})^2 = 1,123,552$. For a 90% confidence interval with df $= n - 2 = 9$, we use $t_{0.05} = 1.796$. The bounds are:

$$\hat{y} \pm t_{\alpha/2} \cdot s_e \sqrt{\frac{1}{n} + \frac{(x^* - \bar{x})^2}{\sum(x-\bar{x})^2}} = 1879.15 \pm 1.796(229.547)\sqrt{\frac{1}{11} + \frac{(900-900)^2}{1,123,552}}$$

$$= 1879.15 \pm 124.30 = (\$1754.85, \$2003.45)$$

Using Minitab, the interval is $(\$1752.20, \$2006.00)$.

(h) The predicted value of y is also $\hat{y} = \$1879.15$.

(i) The bounds are:

$$\hat{y} \pm t_{\alpha/2} \cdot s_e \sqrt{1 + \frac{1}{n} + \frac{(x^* - \bar{x})^2}{\sum(x-\bar{x})^2}} = 1879.15 \pm 1.796(229.547)\sqrt{1 + \frac{1}{11} + \frac{(900-900)^2}{1,123,552}}$$

$$= 1879.15 \pm 430.60 = (\$1448.55, \$2309.75)$$

Using Minitab, the interval is $(\$1439.60, \$2318.60)$.

(j) Although the predicted rents in parts (a) and (h) are the same, the intervals are different because the distribution of the means, in part (a), has less variability than the distribution of the individuals, in part (b).

5. (a) Using technology we get: $\beta_0 \approx b_0 = 67.388$ and $\beta_1 \approx b_1 = -0.2632$.

(b) Using technology, we calculate $\hat{y} = -0.2632x + 67.388$ to generate the table:

x	y	$\hat{y}$	$y - \hat{y}$	$(y - \hat{y})^2$	$(x - \bar{x})^2$
15	65	63.440	1.560	2.433	598.81
16	60	63.177	-3.177	10.093	550.87
28	58	60.019	-2.019	4.076	131.57
61	60	51.334	8.666	75.101	463.52
53	46	53.439	-7.439	55.344	183.04
43	66	56.071	9.929	98.582	12.46
16	56	63.177	-7.177	51.509	550.87
25	75	60.808	14.192	201.403	209.40
28	46	60.019	-14.019	196.527	131.57
34	45	58.440	-13.440	180.627	29.93
37	58	57.650	0.350	0.122	6.10
41	70	56.597	13.403	179.627	2.34
43	73	56.071	16.929	286.587	12.46
49	45	54.492	-9.492	90.099	90.81
53	60	53.439	6.561	43.042	183.04

61	56	51.334	4.666	21.772	463.52
68	30	49.492	-19.492	379.924	813.93
			Sum	1876.869	4434.24

$$s_e = \sqrt{\frac{\sum(y-\hat{y})^2}{n-2}} = \sqrt{\frac{1876.869}{17-2}} = 11.1859$$

(c) A normal probability plot shows that the residuals are normally distributed.

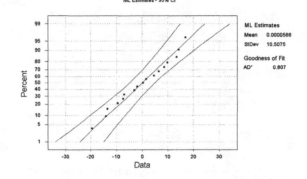

Normal Probability Plot for Residuals
ML Estimates - 95% CI

(d) $s_{b_1} = \dfrac{s_e}{\sqrt{\sum(x-\bar{x})^2}} = \dfrac{11.1859}{\sqrt{4434.24}} = 0.1680$

(e) The hypotheses are $H_0 : \beta_1 = 0$, $H_1 : \beta_1 \neq 0$. df $= n - 2 = 17 - 2 = 15$ so the critical values are $\pm t_{0.025} = \pm 2.131$. The test statistic is $t_0 = \dfrac{b_1}{s_{b_1}} = \dfrac{-0.2632}{0.1680} = -1.567$, which is not in the critical region so we do not reject H_0. There is not enough evidence to support the claim of a linear relationship between age and grip strength.

(f) Since there is no significant linear relationship, the best estimate is the sample mean grip strength, which is 57 psi.

7. (a) **Correlations: Midterm, Project, Course Grade**

	Midterm	Project
Project	-0.076	
Course Grade	0.704	0.526

No; the correlation between midterm and project is between −0.7 and 0.7, multicollinearity does not appear to be a problem.

(b) **Regression Analysis: Course Grade versus Midterm, Project**
```
The regression equation is
Course Grade = - 91.3 + 1.52 Midterm + 0.441 Project

Predictor    Coef  SE Coef      T      P
Constant   -91.29    30.77  -2.97  0.021
```

380

```
Midterm    1.5211   0.3148   4.83  0.002
Project    0.4407   0.1170   3.77  0.007

S = 3.99690   R-Sq = 83.3%   R-Sq(adj) = 78.5%

Analysis of Variance
Source          DF      SS      MS      F      P
Regression       2  558.27  279.14  17.47  0.002
Residual Error   7  111.83   15.98
Total            9  670.10
```

The regression equation is $\hat{y} = -91.29 + 1.5211x_1 + 0.4407x_2$.

(c)

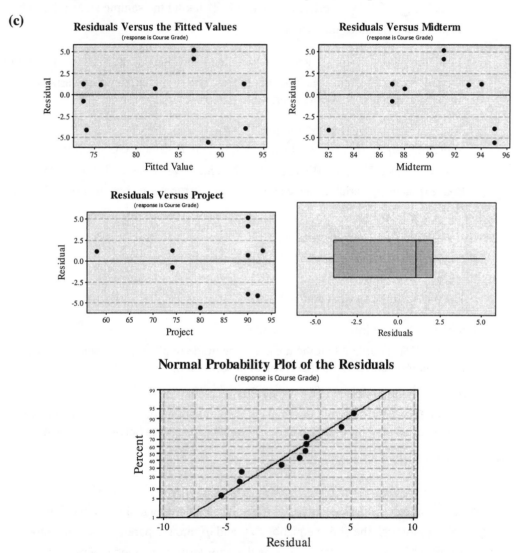

None of the residual plots show any discernible pattern, the boxplot does not show any outliers, and the normal probability plot looks fairly linear. Therefore, the linear model is appropriate.

(d) $b_1 = 1.5211$: This indicates that when midterm grade increases by 1 point, the course grade increases by 1.5211 points, on average, assuming the project grade remains constant.

$b_2 = 0.4407$: This indicates that when the project grade increases by 1 point, the course grade increases by 0.4407 point, on average, assuming the midterm grade remains constant.

(e) $R^2 = 0.833$; 83.3% of the variance in course grade is explained by the regression model. $R^2_{adj} = 0.785$ modifies the value of R^2 taking the sample size and number of explanatory variables into account.

(f) From the output in (b), we get $F_0 = 17.47$ and P-value $= 0.002 < \alpha = 0.05$. We reject the null hypothesis and conclude that at least one of the explanatory variables is linearly associated with course grade.

(g) From part (b), we get the following:
Midterm: Reject $H_0 : \beta_1 = 0$ since $t_0 = 4.83$ and P-value $= 0.002 < \alpha = 0.05$
Project: Reject $H_0 : \beta_2 = 0$ since $t_0 = 3.77$ and P-value $= 0.007 < \alpha = 0.05$
Both explanatory variables have slope coefficients that are significantly different than zero.

(h) $\hat{y} = -91.29 + 1.5211x_1 + 0.4407x_2$
$= -91.29 + 1.5211(85) + 0.4407(75)$
≈ 71
The predicted mean final course grade is 71.

(i) 95% Confidence Interval: $(69.00, 82.04)$

We are 95% confident that the mean course grade of all students who score an 83 on their midterm and a 92 on their project is between 69 and 82.

95% Prediction Interval: $(64.04, 87.00)$

We are 95% confident that the final course grade of a randomly selected student who scored an 83 on their midterm and a 92 on their project is between 64 and 87.

9. The least squares regression model is given by:

$$y = \beta_0 + \beta_1 x + \varepsilon$$

where y is the dependent variable, taking values that are related to the independent variable, x, through the above equation, β_0 and β_1 are the parameters of the model which are estimated from sample data, and ε is the error term in the model, a random variable which is normally distributed with mean 0 and variance σ^2. To perform inference on the least-squares regression line we need to verify that the sample is obtained by simple random sampling and that the residuals are normally distributed with constant error variance.

Chapter 15

Nonparametric Statistics

15.1 An Overview of Nonparametric Statistics

1. Parametric procedures are based on some assumptions about the distribution of the population that is being examined, and typically involve the estimation of a population parameter, such as the mean or variance of the population. Nonparametric methods, perhaps better called distribution-free methods, make no assumptions about the underlying population distributions and usually do not involve estimating any population parameters, although they may be used to perform inference about population parameters such as the population median.

3. The power of a test is the probability of making a Type II error, i.e. the error of not rejecting the null hypothesis when the alternative hypothesis is in fact correct.

5. Nonparametric tests are typically less powerful and less efficient than parametric tests. Nonparametric tests are often misused; that is, they are often used when a more powerful parametric method is appropriate.

15.2 Runs Test for Randomness

1. A phenomenon is random if individual outcomes are unpredictable, although there may be an overall pattern, in terms of frequencies, to large numbers of outcomes. A run is an unbroken sequence of occurrences of the same type.

3. (a) $n = 14$, $n_1 = 6$, $n_2 = 8$ and $r = 6$.

   (b) Since $n_1 \leq 20$ and $n_2 \leq 20$, the critical values are 3 and 12, from Table IX.

   (c) The test statistic is $r = 6$, which is not in the critical region and so we do not reject H_0. There is not enough evidence to support the claim that the sequence is not random.

5. (a) $n = 19$, $n_1 = 9$, $n_2 = 10$ and $r = 5$.

   (b) Since $n_1 \leq 20$ and $n_2 \leq 20$, the critical values are 5 and 16, from Table IX.

   (c) The test statistic is $r = 5$, which is in the critical region and so we reject H_0. There is enough evidence to support the claim that the sequence is not random.

7. $n = 18$, $n_1 = 11$ (fastballs), $n_2 = 7$ and $r = 8$. Since $n_1 \leq 20$ and $n_2 \leq 20$, the critical values are 5 and 14, from Table IX. The test statistic is $r = 8$, which is not in the critical region and so we do not reject H_0. There is not enough evidence to support the claim that the sequence of pitches is not random.

383

9. $n = 14$, $n_1 = 8$ (on-time flights), $n_2 = 6$ and $r = 8$. Since $n_1 \leq 20$ and $n_2 \leq 20$, the critical values are 3 and 12, from Table IX. The test statistic is $r = 8$, which is not in the critical region and so we do not reject H_0. There is not enough evidence to support the claim that the arrival status of a flight is not random.

11. $n = 20$, $n_1 = 14$ (accepted bottles), $n_2 = 6$ and $r = 4$. Since $n_1 \leq 20$ and $n_2 \leq 20$, the critical values are 5 and 14, from Table IX. The test statistic is $r = 4$, which is in the critical region and so we reject H_0. There is enough evidence to support the claim that the filling machine is not random in the way that it over- or under-fills bottles.

13. $n = 45$, $n_1 = 24$ (positive changes), $n_2 = 21$ and $r = 28$. Since $n_1 > 20$ the critical values are $\pm z_{0.025} = \pm 1.96$. To compute the test statistic, we calculate

$$\mu_r = \frac{2n_1 n_2}{n} + 1 = \frac{2 \cdot 24 \cdot 21}{45} + 1 = 23.4,$$

$$\sigma_r = \sqrt{\frac{2n_1 n_2(2n_1 n_2 - n)}{n^2(n-1)}} = \sqrt{\frac{2 \cdot 24 \cdot 21(2 \cdot 24 \cdot 21 - 45)}{45^2(45-1)}} = 3.301, \text{ and}$$

$$z_0 = \frac{r - \mu_r}{\sigma_r} = \frac{28 - 23.4}{3.301} = 1.39, \text{ which is not in the critical region so we do not reject } H_0.$$

There is not enough evidence to support the claim that stock price fluctuations are not random.

15. (a) A A A B B B B A A B A B

(b) $n = 12$, $n_1 = 6$ (A's), $n_2 = 6$ and $r = 6$. Since $n_1 \leq 20$ and $n_2 \leq 20$, the critical values are 3 and 11, from Table IX. The test statistic is $r = 6$, which is not in the critical region so we do not reject H_0. There is not enough evidence to support the claim that the sequence of residuals is not random.

17. Answers will vary.

15.3 Inferences about Measures of Central Tendency

1. If the null hypothesis is true, then we would expect that about half of the observations will be greater than M_0 and about half smaller. Thus the mean value of k (the number of observations either greater than or less than the median) should be $\frac{1}{2}n$.

3. Answers will vary. If the true median $M > M_0$ then we would expect the majority of observations to be greater than M_0 (giving plus signs) and few observations to be less than M_0 (giving minus signs). In this case k is the number of minus signs, and it will be relatively small. So a small value of k is evidence against the null hypothesis and in support of the alternative hypothesis, $H_1 : M > M_0$.

5. Since $H_1 : M < 8$, this is a left-tailed test and k = the number of plus signs = 8. We have $n = 13 + 8 = 21 \le 25$ and so the critical value, from Table X, is 6. Since $k > 6$ we do not reject H_0. There is not enough evidence to support the claim that the median is less than 8.

7. Since $H_1 : M \ne 100$, this is a two-tailed test and k = the smaller of the number of minus signs and the number of plus signs = 21. We have $n = 21 + 28 = 49 > 25$ and so the critical value, from the normal tables, is $-z_{\alpha/2} = -z_{0.025} = -1.96$. The test statistic is

$$z_0 = \frac{(k+0.5) - \dfrac{n}{2}}{\sqrt{n}/2} = \frac{(21+0.5) - \dfrac{49}{2}}{\sqrt{49}/2} = -0.86 > -1.96 \text{ so we do not reject } H_0. \text{ There is not}$$

enough evidence to support the claim that the median differs from 100.

9. We first convert the data to plus and minus signs (and zeros) by comparing the data values to $M_0 = 12$. This gives: $+ + + + - + + - + + - + + + 0$. There are 11 plus signs and 3 minus signs. Since $H_1 : M > 12$, this is a right-tailed test and k = the number of minus signs = 3. We have $n = 11 + 3 = 14 \le 25$ and so the critical value, from Table X, is 3. Since $k \le 3$ we reject H_0. There is enough evidence to support the claim that the median is greater than 12.

11. We record plus signs for values > 4.90 and minus signs for values < 4.90 and count 6 plus signs and 13 minus signs. Since $H_1 : M < 4.90$, this is a left-tailed test and k = the number of plus signs = 6. We have $n = 6 + 13 = 19 \le 25$ and so the critical value, from Table X, is 5. Since $k > 5$ we do not reject H_0. There is not enough evidence to support the claim that the median pH is less than 4.90.

13. We record plus signs for values > \$62,000 and minus signs for values < \$62,000 and count 9 plus signs and 2 minus signs (and one 0). Since $H_1 : M > \$62,000$, this is a right-tailed test and k = the number of minus signs = 2. We have $n = 9 + 2 = 11 \le 25$ and so the critical value, from Table X, is 2. Since $k \le 2$ we reject H_0. There is enough evidence to support the claim that the median income of lawyers who recently graduated from law school is greater than \$62,000.

15. We record plus signs for values > \$800 thousand and minus signs for values < \$800 thousand and count 7 plus signs and 7 minus signs. Since $H_1 : M > 800$, this is a right-tailed test and k = the number of minus signs = 7. We have $n = 7 + 7 = 14 \le 25$ and so the critical value, from Table X, is 3. Since $k > 3$ we do not reject H_0. There is not enough evidence to support the claim that the median baseball salary is greater than \$800,000.

17. P-value = $P(X \le k) = P(X \le 5)$ calculated from the binomial formula with $n = 19$ and $p = 0.5$. Using technology we get P-value = 0.0835.

19. P-value = $P(X \le k) = P(X \le 2)$ calculated from the binomial formula with $n = 11$ and $p = 0.5$. Using technology we get P-value = 0.0327.

15.4 Inferences about the Difference between Two Medians: Dependent Samples

1. If we compute the differences as Population 2 – Population 1, then the researcher's claim is that $M_D > 0$, where M_D is the median of the differences between the observations in the matched pairs data.

3. Since $H_1 : M_D > 0$, this is a right-tailed test and the test statistic is $T = |T_-| = 16$. The critical value for $n = 12$ and $\alpha = 0.05$ is 17 (from Table XI). Since $T < 17$ we reject H_0. There is enough evidence to support the claim that $M_D > 0$.

5. Since $H_1 : M_D < 0$, this is a left-tailed test and the test statistic is $T = T_+ = 33$. The critical value for $n = 15$ and $\alpha = 0.05$ is 30 (from Table XI). Since $T \geq 30$ we do not reject H_0. There is not enough evidence to support the claim that $M_D < 0$.

7. Since $H_1 : M_D \neq 0$, this is a two-tailed test and the test statistic is $T = \min\left(T_+, |T_-|\right)$ $= \min(50, 121) = 50$. The critical value for $n = 18$ and $\alpha/2 = 0.025$ is 40 (from Table XI). Since $T \geq 40$ we do not reject H_0. There is not enough evidence to support the claim that $M_D \neq 0$.

9. Since $H_1 : M_D > 0$, this is a right-tailed test and $T = |T_-| = 300$. The critical value for $n = 40$ and $\alpha = 0.05$ is $-z_\alpha = -z_{0.05} = -1.645$ (since $n > 30$). The test statistic is

$$z_0 = \frac{T - \dfrac{n(n+1)}{4}}{\sqrt{\dfrac{n(n+1)(2n+1)}{24}}} = \frac{300 - \dfrac{40(40+1)}{4}}{\sqrt{\dfrac{40(40+1)(2 \cdot 40+1)}{24}}} = -1.48 > -1.645 \text{ so we do not reject } H_0.$$

There is not enough evidence to support the claim that $M_D > 0$.

11. From the computations in the table below we get $T_+ = 12$, $|T_-| = |-33| = 33$ and $n = 9$.

Before	After	After – Before	Absolute Value	Signed Rank
23.5	19.75	-3.75	3.75	-9
18.5	19.25	0.75	0.75	4.5
21.5	21.75	0.25	0.25	1.5
24	22.5	-1.5	1.5	-7.5
25	25	0	0	0
19.75	19.5	-0.25	0.25	-1.5
35	34.25	-0.75	0.75	-4.5
36.5	35	-1.5	1.5	-7.5
52	51.5	-0.5	0.5	-3
30	31	1	1	6

Since $H_1 : M_D < 0$, this is a left-tailed test and the test statistic is $T = T_+ = 12$. The critical value for $n = 9$ and $\alpha = 0.05$ is 8 (from Table XI). Since $T \geq 8$ we do not reject H_0. There is not enough evidence to support the claim that the median waistline has decreased.

13. From the computations in the table below we get $T_+ = 5$, $|T_-| = |-16| = 16$ and $n = 6$.

Blue	Red	Red – Blue	Absolute Value	Signed Rank
0.582	0.408	-0.174	0.174	-4
0.481	0.407	-0.074	0.074	-1
0.841	0.542	-0.299	0.299	-6
0.267	0.402	0.135	0.135	3
0.685	0.456	-0.229	0.229	-5
0.45	0.533	0.083	0.083	2

Since $H_1 : M_D \neq 0$, this is a two-tailed test and the test statistic is $T = \min\left(T_+, |T_-|\right)$
$= \min(5,16) = 5$. The critical value for $n = 6$ and $\alpha = 0.05$ is 2 (from Table XI). Since $T \geq 2$ we do not reject H_0. There is not enough evidence to support the claim that the median reaction times are different.

15. From the computations in the table below we get $T_+ = 31$, $|T_-| = |-5| = 5$ and $n = 8$.

Initial	5 Years	5 Yrs – Initial	Absolute Value	Signed Rank
38	52	14	14	8
58	60	2	2	2.5
65	72	7	7	5
74	72	-2	2	-2.5
56	54	-2	2	-2.5
36	48	12	12	7
56	58	2	2	2.5
52	60	8	8	6

Since $H_1 : M_D > 0$, this is a right-tailed test and the test statistic is $T = |T_-| = 5$. The critical value for $n = 8$ and $\alpha = 0.05$ is 5 (from Table XI). Since $T \geq 5$ we do not reject H_0. There is not enough evidence to support the claim that the median clarity of the lake has increased.

17. From the computations in the table below we get $T_+ = 26$, $|T_-| = |-29| = 29$ and $n = 10$.

Thrifty	Hertz	Hertz – Thrifty	Absolute Value	Signed Rank
21.81	18.99	-2.82	2.82	-5
29.89	48.99	19.1	19.1	10
17.9	19.99	2.09	2.09	4
27.98	35.99	8.01	8.01	7
24.61	25.6	0.99	0.99	2
21.96	22.99	1.03	1.03	3
20.9	19.99	-0.91	0.91	-1
47.75	36.99	-10.76	10.76	-8
33.81	26.99	-6.82	6.82	-6
33.49	20.99	-12.5	12.5	-9

Since $H_1 : M_D > 0$, this is a right-tailed test and the test statistic is $T = |T_-| = 29$. The critical value for $n = 10$ and $\alpha = 0.05$ is 10 (from Table XI). Since $T \geq 10$ we do not reject H_0. There is not enough evidence to support the claim that the median car rental for Thrifty is less than that for Hertz.

19. (a) $H_0 : M_D = 0$ and $H_1 : M_D \neq 0$.

(b) Since P-value $< 0.001 < 0.05 = \alpha$ we should reject H_0 and conclude that space flight affects the red blood cell count of rats.

15.5 Inferences about the Difference between Two Medians: Independent Samples

1. If the two medians are the same, then the sum of the ranks of the observations from population X should be close to the sum of the ranks of the observations from population Y. The test statistic essentially measures the size of the sum of ranks for the sample from population X. If this sum is unusually small, then that is evidence that $M_x < M_y$ and if this sum is unusually large then that is evidence that $M_x > M_y$.

3. Since $H_1 : M_x \neq M_y$, this is a two-tailed test. As $n_1 = 12$, $n_2 = 15$ and $\alpha = 0.05$, the critical values are $w_{0.025} = 50$ (from Table XII) and $w_{0.975} = n_1 n_2 - w_{0.025} = 12 \cdot 15 - 50 = 130$. The test statistic is $T = S - \dfrac{n_1(n_1 + 1)}{2} = 170 - \dfrac{12 \cdot 13}{2} = 92$ which is not in the critical region and so we do not reject H_0. There is not enough evidence to support the claim that $M_x \neq M_y$.

5. Since $H_1 : M_x < M_y$, this is a left-tailed test. As $n_1 = 18$, $n_2 = 16$ and $\alpha = 0.05$, the critical value is $w_{0.05} = 96$ (from Table XII). The test statistic is

$$T = S - \frac{n_1(n_1 + 1)}{2} = 210 - \frac{18 \cdot 19}{2} = 39 \text{ which is less than } w_{0.05} = 96 \text{ and so we reject } H_0.$$

There is enough evidence to support the claim that $M_x < M_y$.

7. Since $H_1 : M_x > M_y$, this is a right-tailed test. As $n_1 = 15$, $n_2 = 15$ and $\alpha = 0.05$, we first look up $w_{0.05} = 73$ (from Table XII).

Then the critical value is $w_{0.95} = n_1 n_2 - w_{0.05} = 15 \cdot 15 - 73 = 152$. The test statistic is

$$T = S - \frac{n_1(n_1 + 1)}{2} = 250 - \frac{15 \cdot 16}{2} = 130 \text{ which is not greater than } w_{0.95} = 152 \text{ and so we do}$$

not reject H_0. There is not enough evidence to support the claim that $M_x > M_y$.

9. Since $H_1 : M_x \neq M_y$, this is a two-tailed test. As $n_1 = 22 > 20$, $n_2 = 25 > 20$ and $\alpha = 0.05$, the critical values are $\pm z_{\alpha/2} = \pm z_{0.025} = \pm 1.96$. We first calculate

$$T = S - \frac{n_1(n_1 + 1)}{2} = 590 - \frac{22 \cdot 23}{2} = 337 \text{ and then the test statistic is given by}$$

$$z_0 = \frac{T - \dfrac{n_1 n_2}{2}}{\sqrt{\dfrac{n_1 n_2 (n_1 + n_2 + 1)}{12}}} = \frac{337 - \dfrac{22 \cdot 25}{2}}{\sqrt{\dfrac{22 \cdot 25 \cdot (22 + 25 + 1)}{12}}} = 1.32 \text{ which is not in the critical region so}$$

we do not reject H_0. There is not enough evidence to support the claim that $M_x \neq M_y$.

11. From the computations in the table below we have $n_1 = 17$, $n_2 = 14$ and $S = 300$.

Denver	Chicago	Denver Ranks	Chicago Ranks
99,000	198,000	4	19
161,900	183,000	13	17
209,900	38,500	21	1
429,700	172,000	28	15
122,900	150,000	8	11
170,000	53,500	14	2
227,000	680,000	22	30
865,000	116,500	31	6
135,900	107,000	9	5
180,000	592,000	16	29
245,000	74,500	23	3
137,000	283,500	10	25
189,900	285,000	18	26

267,500	120,000	24	7
154,200		12	
202,900		20	
305,700		27	
	Sum =	300	

Since $H_1 : M_x \neq M_y$, this is a two-tailed test. The critical values are $w_{0.025} = 70$ (from Table XII) and $w_{0.975} = n_1 n_2 - w_{0.025} = 17 \cdot 14 - 70 = 168$. The test statistic is

$$T = S - \frac{n_1(n_1 + 1)}{2} = 300 - \frac{17 \cdot 18}{2} = 147$$ which is not in the critical region and so we do not

reject H_0. There is not enough evidence to support the claim that the median house price in Denver differs from that in Chicago.

13. From the computations in the table below we have $n_1 = 8$, $n_2 = 8$ and $S = 74.5$.

Carpeted	Uncarpeted	Carpeted Ranks	Uncarpeted Ranks
11.8	12.1	10	12
8.2	8.3	4	5
7.1	3.8	2	1
13	7.2	13	3
10.8	12	8	11
10.1	11.1	6.5	9
14.6	10.1	16	6.5
14	13.7	15	14
	Sum =	74.5	

Since $H_1 : M_x > M_y$, this is a right-tailed test. From Table XII $w_{0.05} = 16$, and so the

critical value is $w_{0.95} = n_1 n_2 - w_{0.05} = 8 \cdot 8 - 16 = 48$. The test statistic is $T = S - \dfrac{n_1(n_1 + 1)}{2}$

$$= 74.5 - \frac{8 \cdot 9}{2} = 38.5$$ which is not greater than $w_{0.95} = 48$ and so we do not reject H_0. There

is not enough evidence to support the claim that the median amount of bacteria in carpeted rooms is greater than that in uncarpeted rooms.

15. From the computations in the table below we have $n_1 = 22$, $n_2 = 20$ and $S = 609$.

Lincoln	Clarendon	Lincoln Ranks	Clarendon Ranks
0.11	0.06	12	2
0.09	0.09	7.5	7.5
0.21	0.14	26.5	18
0.09	0.16	7.5	20.5

390

0.07	0.03	3	1
0.30	0.12	31.5	14
0.41	0.29	36.5	30
0.33	0.10	33.5	10.5
0.20	0.41	24.5	36.5
0.22	0.08	28	4.5
0.34	0.14	35	18
0.46	0.14	39	18
0.19	0.12	22.5	14
0.67	0.08	41	4.5
0.75	0.09	42	7.5
0.19	0.10	22.5	10.5
0.30	0.21	31.5	26.5
0.33	0.16	33.5	20.5
0.20	0.13	24.5	16
0.42	0.12	38	14
0.25		29	
0.47		40	
	Sum =	609	

Since $H_1 : M_x \neq M_y$, this is a two-tailed test. As $n_1 = 22 > 20$ and $\alpha = 0.05$, the critical

values are $\pm z_{\alpha/2} = \pm z_{0.025} = \pm 1.96$. We first find $T = S - \dfrac{n_1(n_1 + 1)}{2} = 609 - \dfrac{22 \cdot 23}{2} = 356$

and then the test statistic is given by $z_0 = \dfrac{T - \dfrac{n_1 n_2}{2}}{\sqrt{\dfrac{n_1 n_2 (n_1 + n_2 + 1)}{12}}} = \dfrac{356 - \dfrac{22 \cdot 20}{2}}{\sqrt{\dfrac{22 \cdot 20 \cdot (22 + 20 + 1)}{12}}} = 3.43$

which is in the critical region so we reject H_0. There is enough evidence to support the claim that the median calcium level in rainwater in Lincoln County, Nebraska, differs from the median level in Clarendon County, South Carolina.

17. From the computations in the table below we have $n_1 = 15$, $n_2 = 15$ and $S = 262$.

Prof. A	Prof. B	Prof. A's Ranks	Prof. B's Ranks
A	A	3	3
A	A	3	3
B	A	10	3
B	B	10	10
B	B	10	10

C	B	19.5	10
C	B	19.5	10
C	B	19.5	10
C	B	19.5	10
C	C	19.5	19.5
C	C	19.5	19.5
D	C	26.5	19.5
D	C	26.5	19.5
D	D	26.5	26.5
F	F	29.5	29.5
	Sum =	262	

Since $H_1 : M_x \neq M_y$, this is a two-tailed test. Assuming that $\alpha = 0.05$, the critical values are $w_{0.025} = 65$ (from Table XII) and $w_{0.975} = n_1 n_2 - w_{0.025} = 15 \cdot 15 - 65 = 160$. The test statistic is $T = S - \dfrac{n_1(n_1 + 1)}{2} = 262 - \dfrac{15 \cdot 16}{2} = 142$ which is not in the critical region and so we do not reject H_0. There is not enough evidence to support the claim that the median grade differs in the two classes.

15.6 Spearman's Rank-Correlation Test

1. Since Spearman's rank correlation test depends only on the ranks of the data values, as long as the data is ordinal, and so can be ranked, we can perform this test to determine if there is an association between the variables.

3. (a) The scatterplot appears to show a positive linear association.

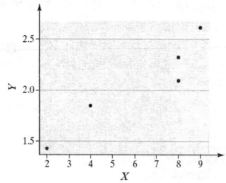

(b) The table shows the data and their ranks:

X	Y	Rank of X	Rank of Y
2	1.4	1	1
4	1.8	2	2
8	2.1	3.5	3
8	2.3	3.5	4
9	2.6	5	5

We use technology to calculate the correlation coefficient of the ranks and get $r_s = 0.975$.

(c) With $n = 5$ and $\alpha = 0.05$ (two tails), the critical values are ± 1.000 and since the test statistic is not greater than 1.000, we do not reject H_0. Note that when $n = 5$, this test is too insensitive to detect an association at the $\alpha = 0.05$ level. However at the $\alpha = 0.10$ level of significance, the critical values are ± 0.900 and since $r_s = 0.975 > 0.900$ we would reject H_0 and conclude that there is an association between X and Y.

5. (a) The scatterplot appears to show a negative linear association.

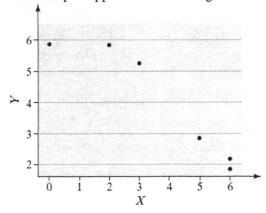

(b) The table shows the data and their ranks:

X	Y	Rank of X	Rank of Y
0	5.8	1	6
2	5.7	2	5
3	5.2	3	4
5	2.8	4	3
6	1.9	5.5	1
6	2.2	5.5	2

$r_s = -0.968$, the correlation coefficient of the ranks (found using technology). Note: the formula in the text gives $r_s \approx -0.957$. The two values are not identical when there are ties among the ranks and the formula is only approximate.

(c) With $n = 6$ and $\alpha = 0.05$ (two tails), the critical values are ± 0.886 and since the test statistic is less than -0.886, we reject H_0 and conclude that there is an association between X and Y.

7. (a) The table shows the data and their ranks:

% with Bachelor's	Per Capita Income ($)	Rank of X	Rank of Y
17.4	24,289	1	1
29.8	33,749	9	9
24.6	29,043	4	4
22.3	26,100	2	2
23.7	28,831	3	3
26.8	30,758	8	8
25.0	29,944	6	7
26.4	29,340	7	5
24.7	29,372	5	6

$r_s = 0.950$, the correlation coefficient of the ranks (found using technology). Note: $r_s = 0.95$, using the approximation formula. As we are testing for a positive association, this is a right-tailed test and with $n = 9$ and $\alpha = 0.05$ (one tail), the critical value is 0.600. Since the test statistic is greater than 0.600, we reject H_0. There is enough evidence to support the claim that per capita personal income and percentage of the population with at least a bachelor's degree are positively associated.

(b) The scatterplot appears to show a positive linear association.

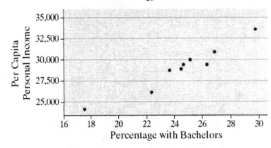

Scatterplot of
Per Capita Personal Income
vs Percentage with Bachelors

9. (a) The table shows the data and their ranks:

Per Capita Income ($)	Birth Rate	Rank of X	Rank of Y
28,960	13.7	7	6.5
32,637	13.4	8	5
42,345	13.1	9	3
29,683	13.7	6	6.5
22,252	11.5	1	1

394

25,307	14.1	3	8
23,753	13.3	2	4
26,356	15.6	4	9
27,610	12.3	5	2

$r_s = 0.092$, the correlation coefficient of the ranks (found using technology). Note: $r_s \approx 0.096$ using the approximation formula. As we are testing for a negative association, this is a left-tailed test and with $n = 9$ and $\alpha = 0.05$ (one tail), the critical value is -0.600. Our test statistic is positive and so we do not reject H_0. There is no evidence to support the claim that per capita personal income and birth rate are negatively associated.

(b) The scatterplot appears to show little association.

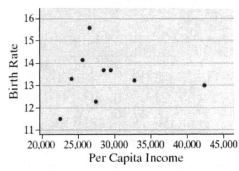

Scatterplot of Birth Rate vs Per Capita Income

11. (a) The table shows the data and their ranks:

Housing Cost ($)	Commute Time (min)	Rank of X	Rank of Y
165,700	20.7	5	5
128,900	19.5	2	2.5
170,200	28.0	6	6
164,600	20.0	4	4
138,700	19.5	3	2.5
126,100	18.4	1	1

$r_s = 0.986$, the correlation coefficient of the ranks (found using technology). As we are testing for a positive association, this is a right-tailed test and with $n = 6$ and $\alpha = 0.05$ (one tail), the critical value is 0.829. Since the test statistic is greater than 0.829, we reject H_0. There is enough evidence to support the claim that housing cost and commute time are positively associated.

(b) The scatterplot perhaps shows a positive association, but it is difficult to judge.

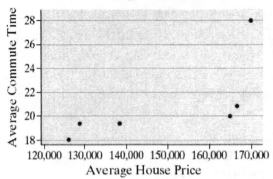

Scatterplot of
Average Commute Time
vs Average House Price

13. The table shows the data and their ranks:

X	Y	**Rank of** X	**Rank of** Y	$d = Y - X$	d^2
2	5	1	1	0	0
3	8	2	2	0	0
4	11	3	3	0	0
5	14	4	4	0	0
6	17	5	5	0	0
				$\sum d^2 =$	0

$r_s = 1.000$, the correlation coefficient of the ranks (found using technology). X and Y are perfectly positively associated as we can see from the scatterplot:

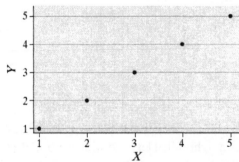

Scatterplot of Y vs X

15.7 Kruskal-Wallis Test

1. The sum of ranks for the combined samples will have the value $N(N+1)/2$. If each of the samples comes from the same distribution, then the sum of ranks for sample i should be approximately equal to the fraction n_i/N of the total sum of ranks. Thus the expected value for the sum of ranks of sample i is $n_i(N+1)/2$. The test statistic effectively sums the squared deviations of the ranks in sample i from their expected values. If one of the samples comes from a distribution that differs from that of the others, then its ranks will be unusually small or unusually large and result in a large value for H.

3. **(a)**   The tables shows the ranks and the computations based on those ranks:

	X Ranks	Y Ranks	Z Ranks
	6.5	10	4.5
	1.5	12	8
	11	3	1.5
	4.5	6.5	9
R_i	23.5	31.5	23
R_i^2	552.25	992.25	529
n_i	4	4	4
R_i^2/n_i	138.063	248.063	132.250

The test statistic is calculated as:

$$H = \frac{12}{N(N+1)}\left[\frac{R_1^2}{n_1}+\cdots+\frac{R_k^2}{n_k}\right]-3(N+1)$$

$$= \frac{12}{12(12+1)}\left[\frac{138.063}{4}+\cdots+\frac{132.25}{4}\right]-3(12+1)=0.875$$

(b)   Since there are three populations and each sample size is ≤ 5 we use Table XIV and get a critical value of 5.6923 (corresponding to $\alpha=0.049$).

(c)   The test statistic is not greater than the critical value and so we do not reject H_0. There is not enough evidence to support the claim that the distributions are different.

5. **(a)** H_0: the distributions of the populations are the same.

   H_1: at least one population distribution differs from the others.

(b)   The calculations are summarized in the table:

	Monday	Tuesday	Wednesday	Thursday	Friday
n_i	8	8	8	8	8
R_i	48	226	144	194.5	207.5
R_i^2	2,304	51,076	20,736	37,830	43,056
R_i^2 / n_i	288	6,385	2,592	4,729	5,382

$$H = \frac{12}{N(N+1)}\left[\frac{R_1^2}{n_1} + \cdots + \frac{R_k^2}{n_k}\right] - 3(N+1)$$

$$= \frac{12}{40(40+1)}\left[\frac{2,304}{8} + \cdots + \frac{43,056}{8}\right] - 3(40+1) = 18.771$$

(c)   We get the critical value from the χ^2 tables. With df = $k-1 = 5-1 = 4$ we find $\chi_{0.05}^2 = 9.488$.

(d)   Since the test statistic is greater than the critical value, we reject H_0. There is enough evidence to support the conclusion that the distribution of births varies by day of the week.

(e)   Monday births clearly differ from births on other days of the week.

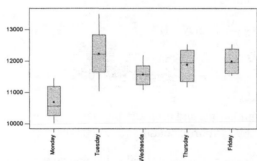

Boxplots of Monday - Friday
(means are indicated by solid circles)

7. The table shows the ranks for the data and the calculations based on those ranks:

Sludge plot	Spring disk	No till	Spring chisel	Great Lakes bt
1.5	23.5	18	18	10
6.5	18	3.5	23.5	23.5
26.5	26.5	13.5	3.5	6.5
18	30	23.5	10	18
10	28.5	1.5	21	13.5
6.5	28.5	13.5	13.5	6.5

R_i	69	155	73.5	89.5	78
R_i^2	4761	24025	5402.25	8010.25	6084
n_i	6	6	6	6	6
R_i^2/n_i	793.50	4004.17	900.38	1335.04	1014.00

$$H = \frac{12}{N(N+1)}\left[\frac{R_1^2}{n_1} + \cdots + \frac{R_k^2}{n_k}\right] - 3(N+1)$$

$$= \frac{12}{30(30+1)}\left[\frac{4761}{6} + \cdots + \frac{6084}{6}\right] - 3(30+1) = 10.833$$

We get the critical value from the χ^2 tables. With df $= k-1 = 5-1 = 4$ we find $\chi_{0.05}^2 = 9.488$. Since the test statistic is greater than the critical value, we reject H_0. There is enough evidence to support the conclusion that the distribution of corn plant yield varies by plot type.

9. The table shows the ranks for the data and the calculations based on those ranks:

	Simple	**Go/No Go**	**Choice**
	7	16	15
	11.5	3	11.5
	9	6	13
	4	17	14
	5	10	8
	1	2	18
R_i	37.5	54	79.5
R_i^2	1406.25	2916	6320.25
n_i	6	6	6
R_i^2/n_i	234.375	486.000	1053.375

$$H = \frac{12}{N(N+1)}\left[\frac{R_1^2}{n_1} + \cdots + \frac{R_k^2}{n_k}\right] - 3(N+1)$$

$$= \frac{12}{18(18+1)}\left[\frac{1406.25}{6} + \cdots + \frac{6320.25}{6}\right] - 3(18+1) = 5.237$$

We get the critical value from the χ^2 tables. With df $= k-1 = 3-1 = 2$ we find $\chi_{0.01}^2 = 9.210$. Since the test statistic is not greater than the critical value, we do not reject H_0. There is not enough evidence to support the conclusion that the distribution of reaction time varies by stimulus.

11. The table shows the ranks for the data and the calculations based on those ranks:

	Large Family	Passenger Vans	Midsize Utility
	15.5	9.5	13.5
	6	6	20.5
	6	4	19
	2.5	12	9.5
	17.5	2.5	9.5
	17.5	15.5	20.5
	13.5	1	9.5
R_i	78.5	102	50.5
R_i^2	6162.25	10,404	2550.25
n_i	7	7	7
R_i^2 / n_i	880.321	1486.286	364.321

$$H = \frac{12}{N(N+1)}\left[\frac{R_1^2}{n_1} + \cdots + \frac{R_k^2}{n_k}\right] - 3(N+1)$$

$$= \frac{12}{21(21+1)}\left[\frac{6162.25}{7} + \frac{10,404}{7} + \frac{2550.25}{7}\right] - 3(21+1) = 4.933$$

We get the critical value from the χ^2 tables. With df $= k - 1 = 3 - 1 = 2$ we find $\chi_{0.01}^2 = 9.210$. Since the test statistic is not greater than the critical value, we do not reject H_0. There is not enough evidence to support the conclusion that the distribution of chest compression varies by vehicle category.

Chapter 15 Review Exercises

1. For the given data, $n = 25$, $n_1 = 14$ (number of E's), $n_2 = 11$ (number of W's) and $r = 9$. Since $n_1 \le 20$ and $n_2 \le 20$, the critical values are 8 and 19, from Table IX. The test statistic is $r = 9$, which is not in the critical region and so we do not reject H_0. There is not enough evidence to support the claim that the sequence is not random.

3. We first convert the data to plus and minus signs (and zeros) by comparing the data values to $M_0 = 15$. This gives: $+ + + + + - + + + + + - + - + - + - - -$. There are 13 plus signs and 7 minus signs. Since $H_1 : M > 15$, this is a right-tailed test and $k =$ the number of minus signs $= 7$. We have $n = 20 \le 25$ and so the critical value, from Table X, is 5. Since $k > 5$ we do not reject H_0. There is not enough evidence to support the claim that the median number of hours students talk on the phone per week is greater than 15.

5. From the computations in the table below we get $T_+ = 12$, $|T_-| = |-33| = 33$ and $n = 9$.

Height (inches)	Arm Span (inches)	Arm Span – Height	Absolute Value	Signed Rank
59.5	62	2.5	2.5	6
69	65.5	-3.5	3.5	-9.5
77	76	-1	1	-3
59.5	63	3.5	3.5	9.5
74.5	74	-0.5	0.5	-1.5
63	66	3	3	7.5
61.5	61	-0.5	0.5	-1.5
67.5	69	1.5	1.5	4
73	70	-3	3	-7.5
69	71	2	2	5

$T_+ = 32$ and $T_- = -23$. Since $H_1 : M_D \neq 0$, this is a two-tailed test with test statistic $T = |T_-| = |-23| = 23$. The critical value for $n = 10$ and $\alpha = 0.05$ is 8 (from Table XI). Since $T > 8$ we do not reject H_0. There is not enough evidence to support the claim that an individual's height and arm span are different.

7. From the computations in the table below we have $n_1 = 16$, $n_2 = 12$ and $S = 216$.

Female	Male	Female Ranks	Male Ranks
0.474	0.541	6	10
0.743	0.659	21	17
0.538	1.05	9	28
0.436	0.88	4	25
0.48	0.577	7	13
0.531	0.752	8	22
0.398	0.849	3	24
0.561	0.544	12	11
0.633	0.464	16	5
0.596	0.675	14	18
0.831	0.626	23	15
0.725	0.393	20	2
0.887		26	
0.905		27	
0.711		19	
0.338		1	
	Sum =	216	

Since $H_1 : M_x \neq M_y$, this is a two-tailed test. The critical values are $w_{0.005} = 42$ (from Table XII) and $w_{0.995} = n_1 n_2 - w_{0.005} = 16 \cdot 12 - 42 = 150$. The test statistic is

$T = S - \dfrac{n_1(n_1+1)}{2} = 216 - \dfrac{16 \cdot 17}{2} = 80$ which is not in the critical region and so we do not

reject H_0. There is not enough evidence to support the claim that the median reaction time of males differs from that of females.

9. The table shows the data and their ranks:

Engine Displacement	City mpg	Rank of X	Rank of Y
3.1	20	7.5	5.5
3.8	20	12	5.5
4.6	18	14.5	1.5
2.2	25	3	13
3.8	21	12	8.5
3.1	23	7.5	11
2.7	22	5	10
3.5	21	10	8.5
4.6	18	14.5	1.5
2.0	26	1	14.5
3.8	20	12	5.5
3.0	19	6	3
3.4	20	9	5.5
2.2	24	3	12
2.2	26	3	14.5

Using technology to calculate the correlation coefficient of the ranks we get $r_s = -0.814$.
Note: $r_s = -0.777$, using the approximation formula. As we are testing for a negative association, this is a left-tailed test and with $n = 15$ and $\alpha = 0.05$ (one tail), the critical value is -0.446. Since the test statistic is less than -0.446, we reject H_0. There is enough evidence to support the claim that engine displacement and fuel economy are negatively associated.

11. (a) H_0: the distributions of the populations are the same.

   H_1: at least one population distribution differs from the others.

(b) The calculations are summarized in the table:

	Organic	Mineral	Surface
n_i	31	47	44
R_i	2,355.5	2,119.5	3,028.0
R_i^2	5,548,380	4,492,280	9,168,784
R_i^2 / n_i	178,980	95,580	208,381

$$H = \frac{12}{N(N+1)}\left[\frac{R_1^2}{n_1} + \cdots + \frac{R_k^2}{n_k}\right] - 3(N+1)$$

$$= \frac{12}{122(122+1)}\left[\frac{5,548,380}{31} + \cdots + \frac{9,168,784}{44}\right] - 3(122+1) = 17.199$$

(c) We get the critical value from the χ^2 tables. With df $= k - 1 = 3 - 1 = 2$ we find $\chi^2_{0.05} = 5.991$.

(d) Since the test statistic is greater than the critical value, we reject H_0. There is enough evidence to support the conclusion that the distribution of concentration of dissolved organic carbon varies by collection area.

(e) The distributions do appear to differ.

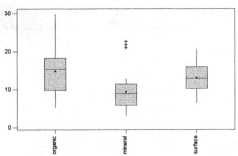

Boxplots of organic - surface
(means are indicated by solid circles)

13. In general, parametric procedures are based on some assumptions about the distribution of the population that is being examined, and typically involve the estimation of a population parameter, such as the mean or variance of the population. Nonparametric methods, perhaps better called distribution-free methods, make no assumptions about the underlying population distributions and usually do not involve estimating any population parameters, although they may be used to perform inference about population parameters such as the population median. Nonparametric tests generally have fewer assumptions, some have simple computations and some can be applied to qualitative data such as rankings. However, they are typically also less powerful and less efficient than parametric tests. The tests are tabulated below with some of the differences.

Nonparametric Test	Parametric Test	Differences
Runs test for randomness	None	
One-sample sign test	z-Test or t-Test	The nonparametric test is a test of the median and the parametric test is of the mean. The parametric test requires that data come from a normal distribution or the sample size be large.

403

Wilcoxon Matched-Pairs Signed-Ranks Test	Paired t-Test for Dependent Samples	The nonparametric test is a test of the medians and the parametric test is of the means. The parametric test requires that the differences be normally distributed or the sample size be large. The nonparametric test requires that the differences have a symmetric distribution.
Mann-Whitney Test	Welch's t-Test for Independent Samples	The nonparametric test is a test of the medians and the parametric test is of the means. The parametric test requires that the differences be normally distributed or the sample sizes be large. The nonparametric test requires that the distributions of the two populations be the same, except possibly for the medians.
Spearman's Rank-Correlation Test	Hypothesis Test of the Significance of β_1	The nonparametric test is only for an association and so can also be used on ordinal data whereas the parametric test is only applicable to quantitative data. The parametric test requires that the residuals be normally distributed with constant error variance.
Kruskal-Wallis Test for One-Way ANOVA	F-test for One-Way ANOVA	The parametric test requires that the data come from populations that are normally distributed with the same variance and tests if the means are all the same. The nonparametric test requires only that the data can be ranked and tests if the distributions are all the same.

Appendix B

Lines

1. (a) Slope $= \dfrac{1-0}{2-0} = \dfrac{1}{2}$

    (b) If x increases by 2 units, y will increase by 1 unit.

3. (a) Slope $= \dfrac{1-2}{1-(-2)} = -\dfrac{1}{3}$

    (b) If x increases by 3 units, y will decrease by 1 unit.

5. Slope $= \dfrac{y_2 - y_1}{x_2 - x_1} = \dfrac{0-3}{4-2} = \dfrac{-3}{2}$

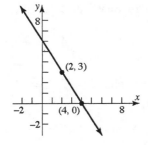

7. Slope $= \dfrac{y_2 - y_1}{x_2 - x_1} = \dfrac{1-3}{2-(-2)} = \dfrac{-2}{4} = -\dfrac{1}{2}$

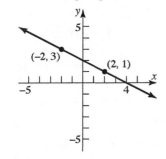

9. Slope $= \dfrac{y_2 - y_1}{x_2 - x_1} = \dfrac{-1-(-1)}{2-(-3)} = \dfrac{0}{5} = 0$

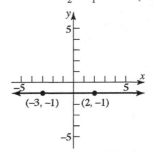

11. Slope $= \dfrac{y_2 - y_1}{x_2 - x_1} = \dfrac{-2-2}{-1-(-1)}$

       $= \dfrac{-4}{0}$ undefined.

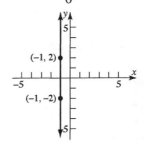

13. $P = (1, 2); m = 3$

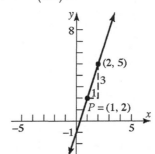

405

15. $P = (2,4); m = -\dfrac{3}{4}$

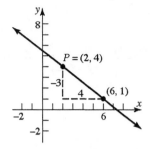

17. $P = (-1,3); m = 0$

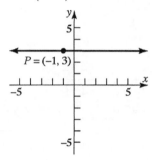

19. $P = (0,3)$; slope undefined

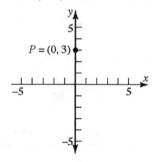

21. Slope $= 4 = \dfrac{4}{1}$

If x increases by 1 unit, then y increases by 4 units.
Answers will vary. Three possible points are:
$x = 1+1 = 2$ and $y = 2+4 = 6$
$(2,6)$
$x = 2+1 = 3$ and $y = 6+4 = 10$
$(3,10)$
$x = 3+1 = 4$ and $y = 10+4 = 14$
$(4,14)$

23. Slope $= -\dfrac{3}{2} = \dfrac{-3}{2}$

If x increases by 2 units, then y decreases by 3 units.
Answers will vary. Three possible points are:
$x = 2+2 = 4$ and $y = -4-3 = -7$
$(4,-7)$
$x = 4+2 = 6$ and $y = -7-3 = -10$
$(6,-10)$
$x = 6+2 = 8$ and $y = -10-3 = -13$
$(8,-13)$

25. Slope $= -2 = \dfrac{-2}{1}$

If x increases by 1 unit, then y decreases by 2 units.
Answers will vary. Three possible points are:
$x = -2+1 = -1$ and $y = -3-2 = -5$
$(-1,-5)$
$x = -1+1 = 0$ and $y = -5-2 = -7$
$(0,-7)$
$x = 0+1 = 1$ and $y = -7-2 = -9$
$(1,-9)$

27. $(0, 0)$ and $(2, 1)$ are points on the line.

Slope $= \dfrac{1-0}{2-0} = \dfrac{1}{2}$

y-intercept is 0; using $y = mx + b$:

$$y = \dfrac{1}{2}x + 0$$
$$2y = x$$
$$0 = x - 2y$$
$$x - 2y = 0 \text{ or } y = \dfrac{1}{2}x$$

29. $(-1, 3)$ and $(1, 1)$ are points on the line.

Slope $= \dfrac{1-3}{1-(-1)} = \dfrac{-2}{2} = -1$

Using $y - y_1 = m(x - x_1)$

$$y - 1 = -1(x - 1)$$
$$y - 1 = -x + 1$$
$$y = -x + 2$$
$$x + y = 2 \text{ or } y = -x + 2$$

31. $y = 2x + 3$; Slope = 2; y-intercept = 3

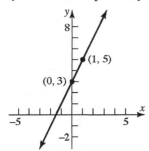

33. $\dfrac{1}{2}y = x - 1$; $y = 2x - 2$

Slope = 2; y-intercept = -2

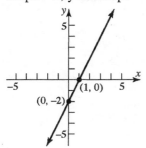

35. $y = \dfrac{1}{2}x + 2$; Slope $= \dfrac{1}{2}$; y-intercept = 2

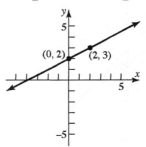

37. $x + 2y = 4$;

$$2y = -x + 4 \rightarrow y = -\dfrac{1}{2}x + 2$$

Slope $= -\dfrac{1}{2}$; y-intercept = 2

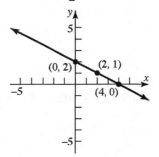

39. $2x - 3y = 6$;

$$-3y = -2x + 6 \rightarrow y = \dfrac{2}{3}x - 2$$

Slope $= \dfrac{2}{3}$; y-intercept = -2

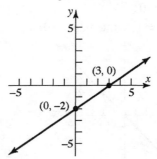

41. $x + y = 1$; $y = -x + 1$

Slope = -1; y-intercept = 1

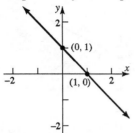

43. $x = -4$; Slope is undefined

y-intercept - none

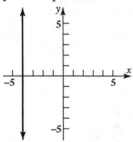

45. $y = 5$; Slope = 0; y-intercept = 5

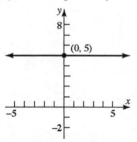

47. $y - x = 0$; $y = x$

Slope = 1; y-intercept = 0

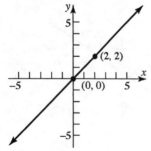

49. $2y - 3x = 0$; $2y = 3x \rightarrow y = \dfrac{3}{2}x$

Slope = $\dfrac{3}{2}$; y-intercept = 0

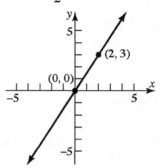

408